DESIGN-TECH: BUILDING SCIENCE FOR ARCHITECTS

2ND EDITION

JASON ALREAD, THOMAS LESLIE, and ROB WHITEHEAD

Routledge
Taylor & Francis Group

NEW YORK AND LONDON

First edition published by Architectural Press 2007

Second edition published 2014
by Routledge
711 Third Avenue, New York, NY 10017

and by Routledge
2 Park Square, Milton Park, Abingdon, Oxon OX14 4RN

Routledge is an imprint of the Taylor & Francis Group, an informa business

© 2014 Taylor & Francis

British Library Cataloguing in Publication Data
A catalogue record for this book is available from the British Library

Library of Congress Cataloging in Publication Data
Alread, Jason.
Design-tech : building science for architects / Jason Alread, Thomas Leslie and Rob Whitehead. – Second edition.
pages cm
Includes index.
1. Architectural design. 2. Engineering design. I. Leslie, Thomas, 1967– II. Whitehead, Rob. III. Title.
NA2750.A5585 2014
720–dc23
2013032291

ISBN: 978-0-415-81784-4 (hbk)
ISBN: 978-0-415-81785-1 (pbk)
ISBN: 978-1-315-81705-7 (ebk)

Acquisition Editor: Wendy Fuller
Editorial Assistant: Emma Gadsden
Production Editor: Alanna Donaldson

Typeset in Univers Light by
Servis Filmsetting Ltd, Stockport, Cheshire

Printed and bound in the United States of America by Sheridan Books, Inc. (a Sheridan Group Company).

CONTENTS

LIST OF FIGURE CREDITS

INTRODUCTION AND ACKNOWLEDGEMENTS

The second edition of *Design-Tech* reflects changes in both the profession and in our teaching since the first edition was published in 2007.

Developments in design and construction have moved very quickly in the last seven years, and we have seen the effects of new digital tools, newly urgent emphasis on efficiency and performance, and the popularization of digital fabrication techniques change both building realization and studio teaching since the first edition. More difficult financial times have forced a leaner approach to design and construction, and technology has played an even greater role in how architects, engineers, and contractors conceive and execute buildings. At the same time, the worsening effects of global climate change have produced a greater—though, in our minds, still not great enough—urgency in developing strategies for buildings that use less energy, that work with flows of wind, solar energy, and water on their sites, and that take Buckminster Fuller's prescient charge to "do more with less" seriously. These seemingly dire influences are matched, however, by brilliant developments in programs such as Ecotect, Revit, and even Sketchup, all of which give designers the ability to think about the multiple forces acting on their designs—ecological, economic, structural, etc.—in integrative, fluent ways. If the problems designers face have grown over the last seven years, so have the tools to solve them that we have at our disposal. We have tried to cover these developments in expanded or new chapters that reflect the way young designers, in particular, will need to think and the skills we think they will need in the next few years.

We have also taken the opportunity to rewrite substantial portions of the book to reflect developments in our own teaching. SCI-TECH, the graduate technologies sequence at Iowa State from which this book grew, has evolved as we have taught these subjects again and again. Teachers learn too, and since the first edition came out we have kept dog-eared copies of the first edition of *Design-Tech*, making notes where we felt things could work better, correcting minor errors, and finding gaps that needed addressing. We have added new chapters on digital fabrication, high-rise structures, and zoning, along with a new chapter on specifications.

This edition also features a substantially rewritten section on structures written by our longtime colleague Rob Whitehead, whose research on structures teaching has transformed the way we teach the subject in our graduate and undergraduate programs. These sections offer an even more intuitive approach, one that we've seen at work in Rob's classes, and one that should prove valuable to students encountering structures for the first time as well as for professionals who need a reminder or two about some basic principles. While making this chapter more logical and understandable, we have kept the data tables and basic mathematical background that give valuable backup to the more conceptual elements of this section.

In spirit, however, *Design-Tech* retains substantially the same approach as it did in the first edition. We have still tried to channel the voice of the grizzled veteran in the back of the office, quietly dispensing advice and mentoring young architects, and while we can still only aspire to the breadth and depth of knowledge that these figures seemed to have in our experience, a few additional years have brought us a bit closer to that level. We still believe the time is right for a reassessment of what "tech" means in architectural curricula. This discussion has been led recently by an upstart group of young faculty, the Building Technology Educators' Society, and it has enjoyed the quiet and patient sponsorship of Ed Allen, whose inspiration permeates these pages. Some of these programs have adopted *Design-Tech* as a standard text, and more than anything we're pleased to see the book's ethic springing up throughout the field—namely that understanding how things are built, and how they perform, gives designers a fundamental grammar that can work with other important socio-cultural vectors in creating humane, appropriate, and efficient buildings.

We remain deeply indebted to a generation of technology educators who have gone before us, and whose books have inspired and been constantly used by us. *Design-Tech* is, we think, best seen as an addition to important, vital books such as Ed Allen's *Fundamentals of Building Construction* and (with Joseph Iano) his *Architect's Studio Companion*, Francis D. K. Ching's *Building Construction Illustrated*, Mario Salvadori's *Structures for Architects*, Rowland Mainstone's *Developments in Structural Form*, Harry Parker's *Simplified Engineering for Architects and Builders* (improved and expanded by James Ambrose), Victor Olgyay's *Design With Climate*, Charlie Brown and Mark DeKay's *Sun, Wind, and Light*, Ernst Neufert's *Architect's Data* and the perennial *Architectural Graphic Standards*. We have referenced these books, among many others, throughout our work, and have noted at the end of each section where one might turn for further information or elucidation.

Likewise, our careers have been informed by important mentors and teachers. Professor Leslie owes much of his technical background to teachers at Illinois and Columbia, especially Mir Ali, Tony Webster and Robert Silman; colleagues at Foster and Partners and Ove Arups, in particular David Nelson, Nigel Dancey, Peter Lassetter, Kevin Dong, Eric Ko, and (fondly remembered and greatly missed) Jon Markowitz; and a raft of collaborators on the Stanford University Center for Clinical Sciences Research project. Finally, Professor Leslie would like to particularly acknowledge the teaching and guidance of the late Don Bergeson at Illinois. It is, sadly, too late to propose this book as extra credit for Prof. Bergeson's Environmental Systems class, but Leslie wishes (for many reasons) that this was still possible.

Professor Alread thanks his good fortune for having started his education under the guidance of Martin Gundersen and Bernard Voichysank at the

University of Florida, and later to have the mentorship of Thomas Beeby at Yale. Mentors in practice have continued that education with firm and patient guidance, in particular Rick Rados, John Locke and Mark Schmidt. Professor Alread must also thank his longtime collaborators, Paul Mankins, Tim Hickman and Todd Garner, who keep him ever mindful of the need to be humble and relentless in the pursuit of good work.

Many of Professor Whitehead's most influential teachers from Iowa State and University of Texas at Austin have also become colleagues in practice, in teaching, or in many cases, both. Andy Vernooy is remembered for instilling the importance of always connecting technical information with its cultural significance; Mark Engelbrecht for his insistence on seeing what's possible, not just what's difficult; Kate Schwennsen for her inspirational professionalism and infectious laugh; Rod Kruse for his tireless pursuit of refined designs at all scales; Cal Lewis for demonstrating that design excellence comes from a comprehensive clarity of thoughts and diagrams; and Gregory Palermo for showing how an encyclopedic knowledge of design and a nurturing soul can produce a passion for work and life.

Our teaching at Iowa State has been influenced and supported by colleagues who have welcomed our attempts at innovation, offered commentary and suggestions for our coursework, and reviewed elements of this book. Clare Cardinal-Pett deserves the distinct credit for giving us the chance to re-write the tech curriculum within the friendly confines of our Master's program, and for constantly pushing us toward experimentation and innovation. Jamie Horwitz, Marwan Ghandour, Karen Bermann, Kimberly Zarecor, Ulrike Passe, Nadia Anderson, and Mikesch Muecke have welcomed the development of our coursework as the Graduate Faculty, and the graduate students who have gone along for this ride deserve special mention for their willingness to serve as guinea pigs, and for their constructive feedback and productive energy. The Technology Faculty in the Department have also been valuable resources and have supported this project, and we're grateful for the support of David Block, Bruce Bassler, Matthew Fisher, Gregory Palermo, Ulrike Passe, and Jim Bolluyt. Cal Lewis and Gregory Palermo, the Chairs of the Architecture Department over the last 12 years, have given us the academic space and resources to turn our scrappy class notes into this book. A sincere thanks to Deans Mark Engelbrecht and Luis Rico-Guittierez who have made sure that the College of Design remains an energetic environment in which teaching and technology are taken as seriously as research and design.

A generous Subvention Grant from Iowa State's Vice Provost for Research's office provided funding for many illustrations and graphics. These clear, interesting, and occasionally humorous graphics were developed by Anna Aversing, Sade Reed, and Isabelle Leysens from several napkin sketches and post-it notes. We are quite grateful for their dedicated work. Finally, a special thanks goes out to Heidi Hohmann and Ann Sobiech-Munson for contributing incredibly instructive chapters in their respective fields of expertise—landscape architecture and specification writing.

Technology, for all the hype, is essentially an explanation of *how* things work. Design is a much higher calling, since it builds and expands upon how we do things to consider *why* we do certain things—often resulting in bigger statements that involve the experiential, societal, and cultural issues alongside basic spatial and volumetric considerations. We hope this book helps everyone (students, educators, practitioners, etc.) understand more about the critical relationship between how and why buildings are built by seeing the connections between design and technology.

A NOTE ON MEASUREMENT

Throughout this book, we've used both metric and imperial (American) units in parallel. Our hope is that it can be used equally well for both systems.

To do this, we've gone beyond standard conversions and instead tried to translate meaningful units of measure back and forth. In our view, it's not been enough to say—accurately—that a 12-foot span is equivalent to a 3.6576-meter span. That may be true, but no metric designer would start with a number like this. Both systems have their "idioms," or standard basic dimensions. So, in situations like this, we've gone for easy comprehensibility over dead accuracy, and called 12-foot spans 3.5 meters. Occasionally this gets us into a slightly awkward situation in examples, where translation errors pile up, and we've been forthright about where this happens and about the minor adjustments needed to get things back on track.

That principle applies generally to the mathematical examples throughout the book. This isn't intended as an authoritative reference, and where we have faced the choice between absolute precision or general understanding we've opted for the latter. One of the great joys of architecture is working with expert consultants, gaining a bit of insight into their field, and assimilating their advice and work. We've intended this book to be an introduction to the various specialties included, and a general reference. In part because of its global scope, the information here is necessarily subject to a wide range of local conditions, and professional consultants should be engaged for any project of reasonable size.

To all our kids at home,
Olivia & Calvin, Adrian & Finnegan, Theo & Sophia
And to all our kids at school

PART 1

DATA

1

HUMAN FACTORS: ANTHROPOMORPHICS

The body	Range of motion
	Human scale
	The 95th percentile
Ergonomic/ anthropometric design	How we fit into a built environment
	Human productivity
	Hazards to well-being

DESIGN FOR PEOPLE

One of the main issues designers face when approaching a building project is, "How big should it be?" This is determined by the intended use, number of users, circulation needs, furniture, and equipment requirements. Once these are accounted for the question becomes, "How much individual space do the people need?"

There are resources that can assist in determining the typical size and arrangements of people, furniture, and spaces. The human body has been measured and statistically averaged to provide information that can accommodate most of the population. This does not mean you shouldn't measure your own surrounding environment and decide whether or not you think it's adequate, but these resources can help with understanding how others have solved these same problems.

Another primary issue that designers face is when it's appropriate to "redesign the wheel". There are arguments for re-examining problems without knowing the standard approach, because that allows for new ideas to emerge. Many times, however, these are problems that have been considered many thousands of times and those solutions are available for your review. Always starting from scratch is impractical; always using the standard approach limits creativity and progress. Be aware of what information is available, and then decide what to use and what to discard.

THE BODY

The laws of physics and the mechanics of the body govern human movements within buildings. We balance in certain ways, walk within a small range of speed, sit comfortably based on our pressure points, and can reach things based on predictable sets of movements. Designing within the tolerances of most people requires an understanding of two issues:

The *95th percentile* is the range of human sizes that are accommodated within typical structures. A 2.1m (7') tall person falls outside of this range, as does a 180kg (400lb) person. A 0.9m (3') tall person may or may not, depending on whether you are expected to accommodate children. Sometimes it is necessary to duplicate functions at different heights or spacing in order to serve all users. The sizes also evolve as the averages change over time and cultural differences are taken into account (Figure 1.1).

Range of motion covers how a body can maneuver from a position in space. Reach, rotation, sight lines, standing and sitting positions all factor into the range of motion.

REFERENCES/MEASUREMENT CHARTS

Building guides such as *Timesaver Standards, Architectural Graphic Standards, and Neufert's Architects Data* give you building and furniture configurations with the average sizes of the occupants already factored in. References like Diffrient's (1982) *Humanscale* and Dreyfus' (2001) *The Measure of Man and Woman: Human Factors in Design* allow you to see the detailed dimensions of the body, which provides the opportunity to decide for yourself which layouts work. Typically, the general planning information is adequate unless you're designing furniture or equipment that requires customizing how a person interacts with it. Codes also have requirements for minimum sizes, in the case of

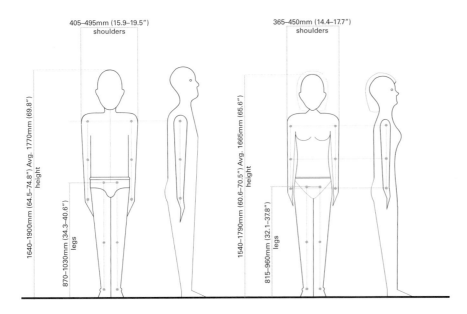

1.1
Typical body measurements.

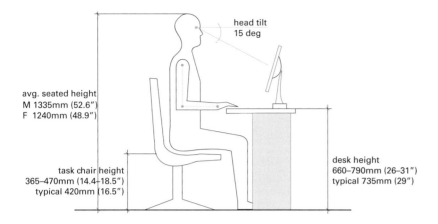

avg. seated height
M 1335mm (52.6")
F 1240mm (48.9")

head tilt
15 deg

task chair height
365–470mm (14.4–18.5")
typical 420mm (16.5")

desk height
660–790mm (26–31")
typical 735mm (29")

1.2
The body's relationship to individual equipment.

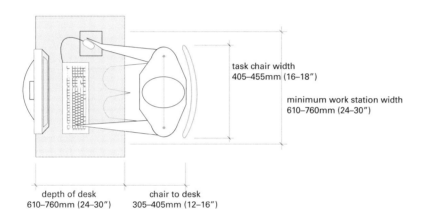

task chair width
405–455mm (16–18")

minimum work station width
610–760mm (24–30")

depth of desk
610–760mm (24–30")

chair to desk
305–405mm (12–16")

fire exit pathways (Chapter 9, Life safety), or ranges of heights and reach for people with disabilities (Chapter 10, Accessibility).

There are two different methods for figuring out the amount of space people need, but both are based on the same basic idea, that humans take up a certain amount of space and move in similar ways when going about their daily activities. The first method is to look at an individual body and the activity they are undertaking, such as working at a computer station (Figure 1.2). Starting from this point you can add up all of the intended users, their activities, required circulation, add in service areas and every other individual area required to get the size of a building. This method is impractical for most buildings due to the immense complexity of having to account for every person and their movements. The second method uses guides based on average overall sizes of room types, such as a conference room (Figure 1.3). These planning guides, like DeChiara's *Time Saver Standards*, have already taken into account the area for individuals, their circulation and other typical needs. The individual method for designing spaces works for situations that require customization, but the guides to typical building and room size are often more effective because they have used the experience of many previous successful projects to test their validity.

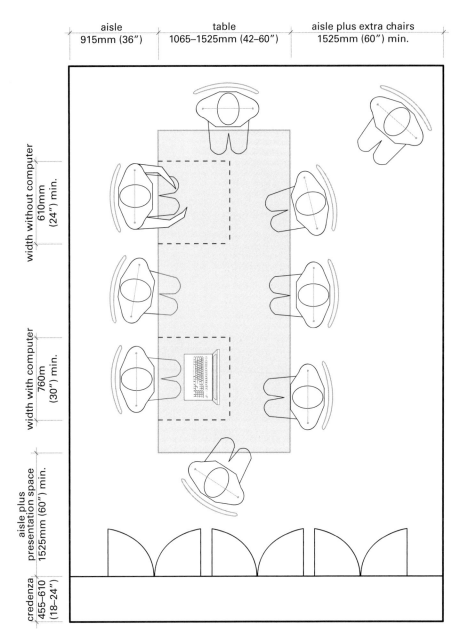

aisle
915mm (36")

table
1065–1525mm (42–60")

aisle plus extra chairs
1525mm (60") min.

width without computer
610mm
(24") min.

width with computer
760m
(30") min.

aisle plus
presentation space
1525mm (60") min.

credenza
455–610
(18–24")

1.3
The body's relationship to specific use room.

ERGONOMIC/ANTHROPOMETRIC DESIGN

Ergonomics are design factors intended to maximize productivity or efficiency by minimizing fatigue and discomfort.

Anthropometrics are the measurements of the human body for use in comparison or design.

Most building projects accommodate people and therefore have a relationship to ergonomics. Taking into account how people interact with a project requires a detailed look at the sizes and heights of everything we see and touch. This is done by considering the design from the perspective of a person inside the space. Plan drawings are only one tool for understanding this, and usually not the most descriptive as no one actually experiences a building in plan. Sections, interior elevations, perspectives and detail drawings offer a greater opportunity to see the design from a human point of view. Human eye level for standing adults varies between 1.2m and 1.8m (4' and 6') and seated heights average between 0.9m and 1.4m (3' and 4.5'). These are the points of view that must be considered along with the parameters of how a body moves through and interacts with a space.

The issue of productivity has been carefully studied, thoroughly dissected, extensively tested and widely published. Still it is a difficult and often moving target. Even the most efficient layout can create overly repetitive actions, become tiresome to the user and begin to hurt efficiency. Adequate light is needed, but efficiency improves when the light levels vary. Consistent environmental comfort can be maintained, but variations in climate seem to improve productivity. In the 1960s and '70s many elementary and secondary schools were built without windows. This was seen to have many positive impacts, such as higher energy efficiencies and fewer distractions for students. The logic of this was supported by research studies such as C. T. Larson's 1965 compilation, *The effect of windowless classrooms on elementary school children*, which suggested that there should be no adverse effect in schools without windows. Student performance in these schools briefly increased, and then steadily dropped over time. The children needed mental breaks to improve concentration, and natural light provides desirable variations in the environment. This has been supported in many recent studies such as the Heschong Mahone Group's report "Daylighting in Schools", which shows long term increases of 5 to 25 percent in student performance in daylit environments.

The positive effects of some variety in human environments cannot be overstated. Studies on the ideal workplace have consistently shown that people respond well to variations in environment. Rather than find the ideal fixed workplace, researchers realized this basic human tendency: *we like change and we get bored easily*. Add to this that no two people react to changes the same way. So don't get too consumed with determining the perfect consistent solution. Flexibility, variability, individual preference and the ability to change can be just as important as basic efficiency.

The following are some standard heights and rules of thumb that are helpful to know in order to accomplish many projects dealing with human inhabitation. Be sure to check local building codes for compliance:

Desk/conference/dining table height	710–760mm (28–30")
Desk depth	610–915mm (24–36")
Dining table for four depth (square or round)	760–1220mm (30–48")
Kitchen counter height	865–915mm (34–36")
Kitchen counter depth	535–610mm (21–24")
Bar/low bank transaction standing counter height	1065mm (42")
High bank/ticket transaction counter height	1400mm (55")
Bath sink height	760–915mm (30–36")
Guardrail height	1065mm (42")
Handrail height	840–915mm (33–36")
Door width	710–915mm (28–36")
Door handle height	915–1065mm (36–42")
Light switch height	1065–1220mm (36–48")

Window mullion height to avoid	1525mm (60")
Side chair/bench height	405–455mm (16–18")
Side chair/bench depth	455mm (18")
Stair riser maximum	175mm (7")
Stair run minimum	280mm (11")
Corridor width	900–2440mm (36–96")
Ceiling height minimums	2.1m (7') garage, 2.4m (8') house, 2.75m (9')+ office

CONCLUSION

Anthropometrics and ergonomics give designers an idea of how to start a project. No building can be properly conceived without a basic idea of how people will be using it, and we typically use a variety of precedents and references in the initial stages of design. While the reference materials give an idea of the most efficient sizes or layouts, building design involves more factors than pure efficiency or the ability to be flexible. Keep in mind the larger goals of each project. The most efficient church design, laid out by using dimensional diagrams, would look like a low budget classroom, not at all matching the expectations or aspirations of the user group. A designer should be able to deal equally with pragmatics and intangibles when conceiving a project. Use the references to avoid mistakes and understand common standards but also consider your everyday environment carefully. Catalogue the things you see that work well and the things that work poorly. The ability to design great environments is a synthetic process that requires the consideration of many factors at one time. The decision making process must be able to flow naturally from a vast collection of both outside references and personal knowledge.

FREQUENTLY ASKED QUESTIONS

Why are rooms in the standard reference books generally square or rectangular?
The reference guides typically demonstrate minimum and common sizes for efficient arrangement of spaces. Because most building components and furniture come in right angles, this tends to be the most efficient way to fabricate and inhabit buildings. Deviations from rectangular volumes generally create less efficient space, but can offer design advantages when applied skillfully. Don't, however, assume that spaces that are square in plan must be boring and spaces that are shaped are interesting. The quality of a space has more to do with light, materials, texture, acoustics, articulation and detailing than it does shape.

How do you decide how big to make a conference or dining table?
This is determined by two primary factors, first is the shape of the table and second is the amount of space each person needs. The shape can vary from round to long and rectangular. Round tables tend to democratize participation in

discussions and can be laid out without concern to orientation. However, when tables get large people can be sitting too far away from the person opposite. Rectangular shapes have ends that favor privileged seating, can fit into narrow rooms, and allow for users to sit fairly close to the person opposite. If presentations need to be made in smaller rooms, rectangular tables are typically used, while in large meeting halls round tables are typically used. Individual space determines the size of table. This ranges from about 610–760mm (24–30") per person, with the smaller size for seating only and the larger sizes for full dining or laptop use. Up to 915mm (36") can be provided, but this begins to distance individuals from interaction with one another.

GLOSSARY

Anthropometrics: The measurements of the human body for use in comparison or design.

Ergonomics: Design factors intended to maximize productivity or efficiency by minimizing fatigue and discomfort.

Range of motion: How a body can maneuver from a fixed position.

The 95th percentile: The range of human sizes that are accommodated within typical structures. The number takes into account the sizes of the middle 95 percent of the population, without the top and bottom 2.5 percent.

FURTHER READING

DeChiara, J. (1990). *Timesaver Standards for Building Types*. New York: McGraw-Hill.

DeChiara, J. (2001). *Timesaver Standards for Interior Design and Space Planning*. New York: McGraw-Hill.

Diffrient, N. (1982). *Humanscale 1,2,3–4,5,6–7,8,9*. Cambridge, MA: MIT Press.

Dreyfus, H. (2001). *The Measure of Man and Woman: Human Factors in Design*. New York: John Wiley & Sons.

Heschong, L. (2003) *Windows and Classrooms: A Study of Student Performance and the Indoor Environment*. Heschong Mahone Group. For the California Energy Commission.

Larson, C. T. (1965). *The Effect of Windowless Classrooms on Elementary School Children*. Architectural Research Laboratory, Dept. of Architecture, Univ. of Michigan, Ann Arbor.

Neufert, E. and Neufert, P. (2002). *Architects Data*. London: Blackwell Science; pp. 15–19 and sections on building types.

Panero, J. and Zelnik, M. (1979). *Human Dimensions & Interior Space*. New York: Whitney Library of Design.

Ramsey, C. G. and Sleeper, H. R. (2007). *Architectural Graphic Standards*, 11th edition. New York: John Wiley & Sons; Chapter 1, Human Dimensions.

2

HUMAN FACTORS: BASIC HUMAN COMFORT

Human body	Reaction to climate changes
	The basic issues of warming and cooling the body
	The comfort zone
Climate control	History
	Active systems
	Passive systems

THE PRIMARY ISSUES OF HUMAN COMFORT

The human body is capable of life within a fairly wide range of the earth's environmental conditions. Outside of the poles, people inhabit virtually every part of the earth. Within the range of overall climatic conditions is a tighter range of coziness that promotes human productivity called the "comfort zone". People construct shelters in order to modify the natural environment in ways that create more livable spaces. In this section we will study the factors of comfort we're trying to control.

The main issue for comfort, or even survival, is temperature. Radiation, air movement, humidity and precipitation all factor into comfort to lesser degrees and ultimately affect the way the body feels air temperature.

THE HUMAN BODY

The human body reacts to hot or cold environments with an attempt to maintain a constant core body temperature. Our natural reactions can accommodate a range of temperatures and still feel comfortable. There are two sets of reactions the body has to extreme conditions (Figure 2.1):

Reaction to hot, humid environments
The body gains more heat than it can use and tries to shed the excess. This heat must be moved from the body core to the skin and lungs to dissipate to the environment. The heart rate increases to move blood flow to the periph-

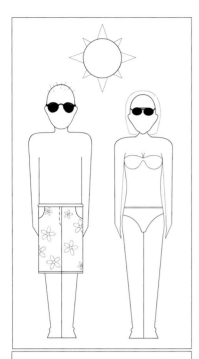

HOT-HUMID ENVIRONMENT

increased blood flow to periphery
dilation of blood vessels at skin
perspiration

EXTREME COLD ENVIRONMENT

goose pimples (increases heat prod. 1–2x)
involuntary shivering (increases heat prod. 6x)
prioritized blood flow to core, eventual frostbite

2.1
The body's reaction to extreme
ends of the environment.

ery and blood vessels at the skin dilate to move heat to outer layers of the body. Breathing rates increase to move heat from the lungs faster. Perspiration occurs to cool the skin, however in humid environments it does not evaporate quickly, limiting its effectiveness. Heat exhaustion followed by heat stroke are extreme cases of thermal stress.

Reaction to extreme cold

The body loses heat faster than it can produce it and tries to generate heat by involuntary movement. "Goose pimples" (small muscle contractions at the skin) occur, increasing total body heat production by 1–2 times resting levels. Involuntary shivering can also occur (muscle contractions of whole parts of the body) which increases heat production by 6 times resting levels. In an attempt to keep vital organs functioning, the body prioritizes blood flow. Under extreme stress the body eventually allows limbs to succumb to frostbite while protecting the core and brain functions.

While the body maintains a constant core temperature for efficient functioning, this does not mean that buildings should maintain a constant temperature and humidity all day or all year long.

The human body and its thermal control systems are designed to allow for constant environmental changes. Fluctuations in temperature, air movement and light are beneficial and stimulating. Human senses respond well to some change and our range of daily activities typically changes, making variable environments both necessary and desirable.

2.2
The main factors affecting human comfort.

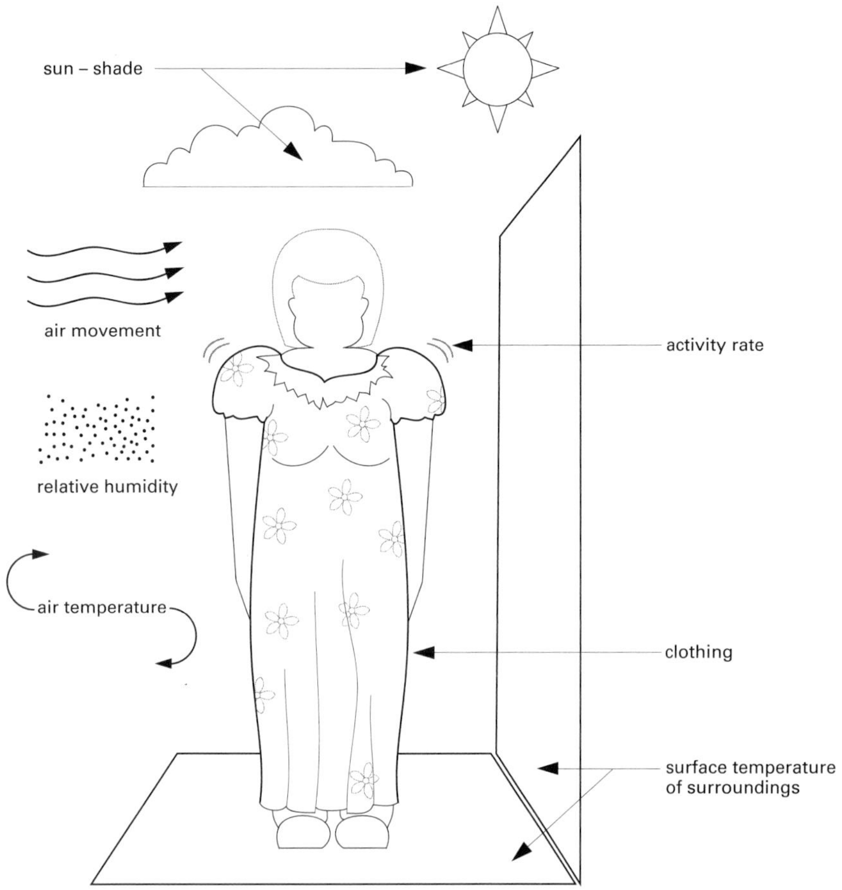

The major factors affecting thermal comfort are as follows (Figure 2.2):

1 *Activity* increases your metabolic rate, which raises body temperature.
2 *Clothing* acts as an insulator, allowing your body to retain more heat rather than losing it to the environment.
3 *Air movement* increases the skin's ability to remove heat by evaporation of perspiration.
4 *Air temperature* is what your exposed skin feels; if it's above your skin temperature it feels warm, if it's below it feels cool.
5 *Surface temperatures of surroundings* radiate heat and cold into the fluid medium of air, and conduct heat and cold directly from the body in contact with a surface.
6 *Relative humidity* is the amount of moisture in the air. This affects how well perspiration can cause evaporative cooling; very dry air can create dehydration and discomfort.
7 *Sun and Shade* affect the way your body is warmed by radiant heat from the sun. Air temperature may be the same in sun and shade, but your body surface will heat when directly exposed to the sun's radiation.

The sensation of thermal comfort occurs when the body is in equilibrium with its physical environment. The seven factors listed above all interact to produce relative degrees of thermal comfort in various situations.

For example, if the outside temperature were 72F (22C) with a relative humidity of 50 percent most people would feel quite comfortable at rest. The body, lightly insulated by clothing, is in equilibrium with the surrounding air temperature and air moisture. Going for a run would make you feel hot and sweaty due to the increase in body temperature and the resulting perspiration in an effort to create cooling. If you stop and a breeze is blowing you would feel slightly cold, due to evaporative heat loss without the increased body temperature of running. Now put on a black business suit while the breeze stops and stand on the street in the sun. This will make you feel uncomfortably warm because the suit both over-insulates and absorbs the radiant heat from the sun, raising your skin temperature above 88F (31C).

The next day, if it's a windless 62F (16.7C) with the same 50 percent humidity and you sit outside with a swimsuit on, in direct sunlight, you would likely feel comfortable again. The radiant heat from the sun will increase the skin temperature above the air temperature to a comfortable level; however, any wind will quickly overcome this effect and cause too much cooling.

The body also reacts to radiant heat from surfaces like walls. Skin is approximately 88 degrees F; if the walls in a room are over that temperature the body will be warmed, otherwise you will lose heat to the room. Stand next to a cold window in the winter and you will get uncomfortably cold quickly, but even a 65F (18C) wall will draw heat from inhabitants. Conduction, or direct contact with cold or warm materials, quickens the reaction. Stand on a cold, marble floor in a 70F (21C) house in the winter and your entire body will feel cold quickly.

This illustrates the fact that thermal comfort is affected by all of the seven major factors listed above. No single temperature or humidity is comfortable to everyone in every condition. Frequently, building environments are designed with a target median comfort level of the air temperature only, and that may or may not be appropriate for the use of the project. Different cultures and regions also tend to react to temperature shifts in various ways; while Americans turn up the heat, the British often put on a sensible sweater. People from colder environments tend to react to hot weather with greater discomfort than those from warm environments and the reverse is also true. The popular belief that your blood is "thinner" and less resistant to cold if you're from a warm environment is not supported by fact, but nonetheless people grow accustomed to their typical discomforts in environmental conditions and are less tolerant of opposite extremes.

The "comfort zone" is a defined and charted combination of factors—air movement, air temperature, relative humidity and radiation where a human body with average clothing at rest in the shade will be comfortable (Figure 2.3).

Looking at the Bioclimatic Chart, the comfort zone is an oval area that exists between 70 and 82 degrees F (21 and 28C) and 20 to 80 percent relative humidity (RH). At higher humidity levels the temperature lowers, due to the inability of the body to use evaporative cooling.

The comfort zone can be extended in any direction by using radiant heat, air moisture, wind, or a combination of these factors. For example, 63F (17C) dry bulb and 40 percent RH is below the comfort zone temperature shown on the chart, but within the humidity comfort. A person could be made comfortable by extending the comfort zone down through adding 100 BTU/hr of radiant heat, shown in the horizontal lines below the comfort zone oval.

85 degrees F with 30 percent RH is above the comfort zone temperature,

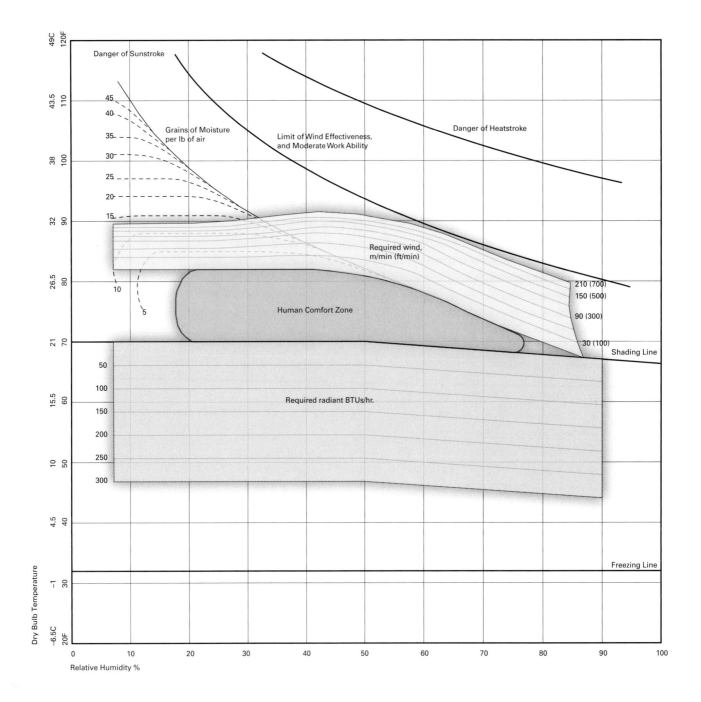

but within the lower part of the humidity comfort zone. A person could be made comfortable by three different methods or a combination of them. Adding a wind speed of 60m/min (200ft/min) would raise the comfort zone, as shown in the curved wind lines above the comfort zone oval. Adding 8 grains of moisture per pound of dry air to the atmosphere would also raise the comfort zone, as shown in the dashed lines in the upper left hand side of the chart. Reducing the Mean Radiant Temperature (MRT) of the surrounding surfaces to 80F (26.7C) would again raise the comfort zone. Depending on the conditions, it may be preferable to use one method over the others, or a combination of factors. In this example, 30 percent relative humidity is acceptable, but on the lower end

2.3
The Bioclimatic Chart for temperate zone climates.

of comfort so adding moisture might add most to the comfort of the inhabitants. Adding this much moisture may prove to be difficult, however, so it is possible to add 5 grains of moisture and a lower wind speed such as 30m/min (100f/min). Once you combine factors it is necessary to interpolate more on the chart, but the primary benefit of using this diagram is to determine appropriate passive strategies for environmental control rather than specific calculations of system design.

The chart also assumes that a person is in normal clothing and at rest in the shade. Active environments like a gymnasium would require lower temperatures, lower humidity, lower MRT, or a combination of all three. Different areas within a building may also require different conditions. The locker room in a gymnasium would not benefit from being colder, but the humidity level may typically be raised due to the use of showers. A grocery store desires colder temperatures and lower humidity to keep food fresher. People in a grocery are normally wearing the coat they had on outside in cold weather and are not at rest while walking up and down the aisles, so it is acceptable to lower temperature and humidity. In the summer, the cool interior of a grocery is usually a relief from the exterior heat. Keep in mind the specific needs of the inhabitants you are designing for and deviate from the charts as necessary to achieve appropriate comfort.

CLIMATE CONTROL

Buildings offer many services to the inhabitants, but one of the automatically assumed functions is modifying climate. While we will cover traditional building types by region later, it should be noted that there are many different ways to achieve the comfort zone. The systems humans use to modify climate are typically broken into two types: "Active" and "Passive" systems. Most modern buildings use a combination of the two systems, but the introduction of new technologies has drastically changed the way we approach comfort, frequently for the worse.

Active Systems are mechanically driven heating and cooling systems. These can range from simple fans or hot water radiators to fully air-conditioned and furnace heated systems. The "Active" part of these systems is the energy required to drive the heating and cooling. None of the active systems could run without a source of power driving them. Even a traditional fireplace has an active component because the wood it burns is an outside fuel consumed to run the system.

Passive Systems heat and cool with no outside energy or power required to run the system. An operable window is part of a passive system (apart from the fact that you are the power that operates it). Windmills, evaporative water–cooling, fixed sun shading, windbreaks, thermal mass walls, and strategically placed vegetation are all components of a passive system. Not usually considered in the passive definition is the energy used to produce the building components. This is called "embodied energy" and can sometimes make a passive system more costly or environmentally damaging than an active system, so don't automatically assume that all passive is good and all active is bad. These decisions require designers to research which systems are the most appropriate.

Historically, heating has been the easiest modification to handle. Wood or

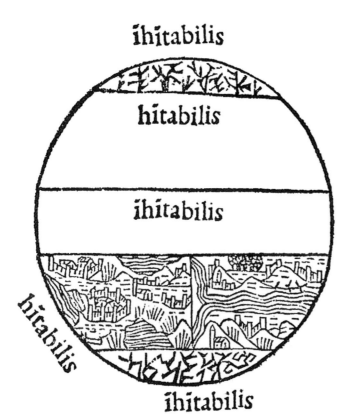

coal burning stoves have been around for ages, whereas cooling has been much more difficult to achieve. This generally drove larger populations to temperate zones, where it never got overly hot and heating to comfort was possible (Figure 2.4). Temperate zones tend to have brief warm summers, longer moderate fall and spring weather, and colder winters. Hybrid building types developed in these areas that allowed for summer breeze cooling, minimal fall and spring environmental needs, and efficient winter wood and coal heating.

More recently, systems have been developed that make tropical zone cooling possible, and therefore we've seen large population shifts to regions where previously inhabitation had been limited by heat and humidity. One hundred years ago, the notion of moving to a climate like Miami, Florida or Kuala Lumpur was extreme, while residing in Buffalo, New York or Helsinki was considered reasonable—now the opposite might be seen as true. Cultural and political reasons aside, people have decided that with adequate cooling it is more pleasant to live in warmer environments. Buildings in general can be built initially more economically where there is no freeze/thaw cycle. Also, when air conditioning is included in homes, vehicles and workplaces, being in the outdoor environment becomes a matter of choice rather than necessity. However, the long-term energy used to enable this transformation has been enormous and increasingly costly. In an effort to lose as little cooling or heat as possible, buildings have been sealed tight—creating unhealthy air quality. Generating power to run mechanical systems is also costly and has a negative environmental impact. Because buildings are one of the primary consumers of energy, intelligent design decisions can have a large effect on long-term costs and environment impacts, while still maintaining reasonable human comfort.

CONCLUSION

The reason for understanding the science of human comfort is to create comfortable shelter. During the development of a design project many of the tasks related to attaining comfort are handled by consulting engineers. Their primary job is to take what the architect has designed and make it comfortable with active environmental control systems, without modifying the building design. Frequently they will not make suggestions for changing the building design to make it more efficient, not out of ignorance but because that is how their role has been defined. Most of the decisions about a building's environmental efficiency and ability to use passive systems will have been made by the time schematic design is done, before consulting engineers have even begun work. The goal is to understand what makes people environmentally comfortable and how to most effectively design the building to take advantage of passive systems during early planning. Understanding comfort requires consideration of the specific use and purpose of the proposed building, along with the factors that create a comfortable environment.

FREQUENTLY ASKED QUESTIONS

Why doesn't everyone use passive control systems in the design of new buildings?
While this is the traditional way of creating buildings from the time before modern HVAC (Heating, Ventilation, and Air Conditioning) systems, concerns about the cost of energy in the 1970s caused most designers to seal buildings tight in an effort to limit heating and cooling losses. Controlled, active, mechanical systems are very predictable in terms of managing human comfort, while passive systems can be less certain. These two factors over time caused a loss of the basic knowledge required to create passive structures. With the re-emergence of concerns about the environment and the cost of energy, designers are again engaged in trying to make buildings more passive, but it takes time to educate the profession, consultants, and clients.

If skin temperature is 31C (88F), why does that air temperature feel hot?
Because we normally wear clothes that allow us to insulate against cooler temperatures. Most shower or bath water is at or above this 31C (88F) temperature, because this is what feels comfortable to naked skin. Activity rates also generate heat, making this temperature uncomfortable. At rest, in the shade, unclothed, with some air movement, 31C (88F) air temperature would feel neutral.

GLOSSARY

Air: a mixture of the following gases:

Nitrogen: 78%
Oxygen: 21%
Carbon dioxide: 0.03%
Water vapor
Trace elements such as helium and krypton in small amounts.

BTU (British Thermal Unit): the quantity of heat required to raise 1 pound of water 1 degree Fahrenheit in temperature.

Celsius: Metric temperature scale that measures the freezing point of water at 0 degrees and the boiling point at 100 degrees (at normal atmospheric pressure).

$$C = (F - 32) / 1.8$$

Condensation: The process by which a gas or vapor changes to a liquid.

Dew point: the temperature at which air becomes 100 percent saturated with moisture and changes state from gas to liquid.

Dry bulb temperature: a measure of the heat intensity at a point in degrees (F, C or K).

Enthalpy: The total heat (both latent and sensible) of a substance.

Fahrenheit: U.S. temperature scale that measures the freezing point of water at 32 degrees and the boiling point at 212 degrees (at normal atmospheric pressure).

$$F = (C \times 1.8) + 32$$

Kelvin: Scientific temperature scale where absolute zero is measured as 273 degrees below the freezing point of water. Each Kelvin degree equals one Celsius degree.

$$K = C - 273$$

Latent heat: Heat transfer involved in the change of state of a substance (usually the evaporation or condensation of water, perspiration or, refrigerant).

Metabolism: Burning of fuel (food) to maintain a constant body temperature.

Rate of metabolism: how much food is burned in a given amount of time is generally proportional to body weight. It is dependent on:

Activity—rate increases at higher activity levels.

Gender—male rates are typically 15 percent higher than female rates for the same activity level.

Health and age—older or ill people have lower rates.

Amount and weight of clothing.

Surrounding atmosphere—temperature, humidity, wind and radiant heat.

Relative humidity: the ratio of the amount of water vapor in the air at a specific temperature to the maximum amount that the air could hold at that temperature, expressed as a percentage.

Sensible heat: a change in the heat content of a substance that causes the substance to change temperature (measured in BTUs).

Wet bulb temperature: a temperature taken with a thermometer whose bulb is surrounded by a layer of wet gauze. The difference between wet and dry bulb temperatures, measured with a sling psychrometer, shows the dew point temperature or the temperature at which water condenses (typically on a surface).

FURTHER READING

Neufert, E. and Neufert, P. (2000). *Architect's Data*, 3rd ed. London: Blackwell Science; pp. 19–23.

Olgyay, V. (1963). *Design with Climate: Bioclimatic Approach to Architectural Regionalism*. Princeton, NJ: Princeton University Press.

3
ENVIRONMENT: BASIC CLIMATOLOGY

Climate zones	Cool, temperate, hot-arid, hot-humid
	Regional climate evaluation methods
	Thermal, solar, wind, humidity, and precipitation factors
Climate strategies	Traditional regional building types
	Economical, physical, and psychological needs
	Determining the correct approach
Microclimates	Site selection factors
	Working with rather than against your environment

INTRODUCTION

Climatology is the science that deals with prevailing weather conditions. It's important to understand the climatic conditions when designing a structure, in order to create a desirable environment for the inhabitants and to deal most efficiently with the weather's impact on the building.

Systems for mechanically modifying building environments can allow virtually any structure to maintain human comfort, but the efficiency/cost of the system and quality of the interior air are drastically affected by the decisions made during building design.

Regional differences in climate create vastly different requirements for the design of buildings. This may not seem apparent, based on the similar "look" of buildings in varying places, but each region places a different set of forces on a structure. These differences can be clearly seen by studying traditional regional building types that were built without mechanical heating or cooling. Designers are often faced with the issue of borrowing building styles from other regions, regardless of their climatic efficiency. It becomes the responsibility of designers to not only create technically efficient structures, but also to determine what the regionally appropriate character of a building is.

CLIMATE ZONES

Depending on the source, the earth is usually categorized into four, five, or more climate zones. We'll use the four zone descriptions for simplicity. The descriptions cover the zones in the U.S. and Europe, and the chart shows worldwide areas (Figure 3.1). The U.K. is mostly in the temperate zone, with northern areas into the cool climates; the U.S. has all four zones represented. While most of the variances are a factor of latitude (measurement lines circling the globe *parallel* to the equator and at intervals north and south), there are many variances based on other factors such as altitude, proximity to large bodies of water, prevailing winds, ground surface conditions and vegetation.

Hot–humid climates
   Gulf Coast U.S., Central Africa, Southern Europe, and Southeast Asia
   Summer sun very high in the sky
   Winter days relatively long and warm
   Long summer
   High humidity

Hot–arid climates
   Southwestern U.S. and inland Central America, North Africa, Middle East,
      and Central Australia
   Summer sun very high in the sky
   Short sunny winter
   Minimum precipitation

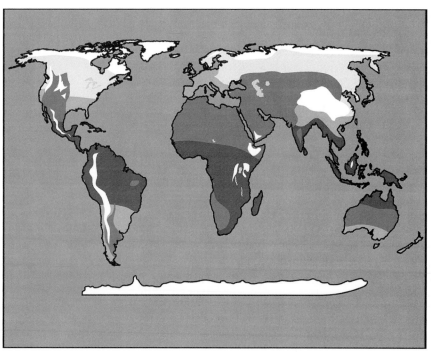

| ■ HOT/HUMID | ■ DRY | ■ TEMPERATE | □ COLD | □ POLAR/HIGHLANDS |

3.1
World Climate Zone Map.

Large daily temperature swings
Low humidity

Temperate climates
Middle U.S. latitudes, most of Europe, Southern Russia, and Northern China
Four distinct seasons: cold winter, hot/humid summer, intermediate spring
and fall
Moderate length days
The sun changes height in the sky more than in hot climates
Typically it snows and a frost layer forms in winter

Cool climates
45 degree north latitude, Northern U.S. and Canada, Northern Europe and
Russia, all areas near the poles
Very long, cool summer days
Very short winter days—sun very low in the sky
Heavy snow and deep frost layers

Regional climactic analyses can be obtained through local meteorological socie-
ties or in resource texts (a good example is in *Sun, Wind and Light* by Brown
and DeKay). The information is extremely helpful in determining how to design
for the local climate. The following factors are most important and are shown
in many charts:

- *Thermal analysis* shows the range and distribution of temperatures throughout the year. The dew point (the point at which airborne moisture condenses
to liquid) and the diurnal cycle (24-hour cycle of day to night) of temperatures
are also shown and give a good picture of just how comfortable the outside
temperatures are.
- *Solar analysis* shows the hours of sunshine broken up quantitatively for clear
and cloudy days. Simply put, knowing how sunny it is provides an essential tool for design. A building in a very sunny place should both utilize and
protect from the sun's heat while using the direct light without glare. A building in a cloudy environment will not have as much radiant heat and will need
to have more open window area to capture daylight.
- *Wind analysis* shows wind direction and velocity. Keep in mind that these
may be measured in an open field or on top of a building; small site differences like a hill or trees can completely alter this data. Wind can also be
blocked or channeled into different directions from the prevailing conditions.
- *Humidity analysis* shows an average percentage of relative humidity during
the day for each month. Humidity affects both comfort and building durability.
Condensation, corrosion, mold and discoloration can be caused by moisture
collecting on or inside of building assemblies. Still air, heat, and moisture
provide perfect growing conditions for bacteria, mold, and other undesirable
problems. Comfort also is largely a factor of dew point; 70 percent humidity
at 70F (20C) is comfortable but at 90F (32C) is unbearable. This is because
at higher temperatures the high relative humidity prevents the body from
cooling through evaporation of perspiration.
- *Precipitation analysis* shows average monthly totals of rain and snow. High

and low extreme amounts of precipitation are often shown and help determine if the rain/snow comes steadily or in short bursts. Very wet or dry places also require special attention in building assembly. Wet environments need to shed excess water very quickly and the conventional means for accomplishing this, such as gutters and downspouts, are not always adequate. Foundation problems can also occur in wet locations due the increased hydrostatic pressure of underground water against walls and basement floor slabs. Dry environments can desiccate materials (absorbing moisture out of a material) causing them to shrink and split or crack. Soils in dry environments can also shift unpredictably, causing foundation problems.

CLIMATE STRATEGIES

Studying the building types of indigenous people in different climate zones gives a clear picture of what the most important factors are in dealing with the local climate. There is a simple logic that develops, without the use of mechanical means of comfort or the benefit of scientific calculations, which gets right to the heart of the problem. With thousands of years to work on the problem of shelter and the incentive of basic survival, the most efficient solutions were developed and continually refined to high degrees. All of the basic principles of these building types apply to modern designs and most can be adapted without needing to copy the style or look of the original building.

Hot–humid climates

In these climatic conditions it's most important to use natural breezes for cooling, while shading from the hot sun. These climates also tend to have heavy rainfall, so large roof overhangs help shed water and keep the sun from penetrating far into the space. Open, operable walls and raised floors promote cooling of the air and the structure. Buildings benefit from being spread apart from one another to maximize breezes, and narrow buildings with tall windows promote cross ventilation. The heaviest heat gains are on the west side, from the late afternoon sun in the summer, so narrow orientations east to west are preferred (Figure 3.2).

Traditional buildings of this type are open raised huts with large roof overhangs. Single large rooms with few intervening walls allow for breezes. Tall ceilings allow heat to rise and be carried away with cross ventilation.

Hot–arid climates

Desert type climates have high heat gains from the sun in the daytime and frequent cool weather at night. Less ventilation is needed than in humid climates due to the low humidity, which makes evaporative cooling much more effective. Massive walls can be used to absorb heat during the day and emit it back at night. Minimal overall surface exposure to the sun is preferable; joined structures assist in keeping exterior wall surface reduced. Narrow ends are oriented east to west, which minimizes heat gains from low east and west sun while maximizing low winter sun on the south side. Evaporative pools of water near the structure assist in promoting cooling (Figure 3.3).

Desert pueblo and other adobe structures are typical traditional structures

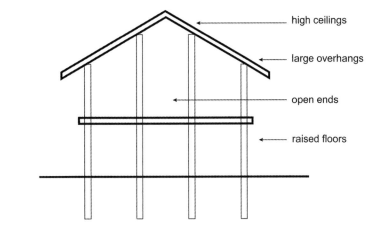

high ceilings

large overhangs

open ends

raised floors

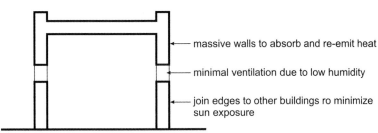

massive walls to absorb and re-emit heat

minimal ventilation due to low humidity

join edges to other buildings ro minimize sun exposure

in these environments. The massive clay brick walls transfer heat and cooling through thermal shift and are less vulnerable to water disintegration because of the small rain amounts. Small windows allow for some cooling without letting in much heat and the structures tend to be clustered together, minimizing exterior exposure.

Temperate climates

Temperate climates tend to have large shifts between summer and winter temperatures, which favor hybrid building types that can transform themselves. Protection from north winter winds is important with open glazed areas to the low winter sun on the south. Large overhangs on the east and west sides protect from summer sun while shaded outdoor living areas take advantage of temperatures during warm parts of the year. Deciduous trees allow for shading in the summer when leaves are full and warming in the winter when the leaves fall. The windows should be operable to promote summer cooling breezes with good protection from winter cold (Figure 3.4).

Wigwams and tipis are typical Native American examples of these building types as they were very transformable to more open or closed exterior shells. Bungalow style homes are also hybrid buildings, with projecting sleeping porches that could open on three sides for cooling, and compact central areas that could be heated efficiently.

Cool climates

Colder climates require buildings that will lose as little heat as possible and can protect against large amounts of snow. Protection from the northern wind is important in building orientation and entry location. Snow loads can be very

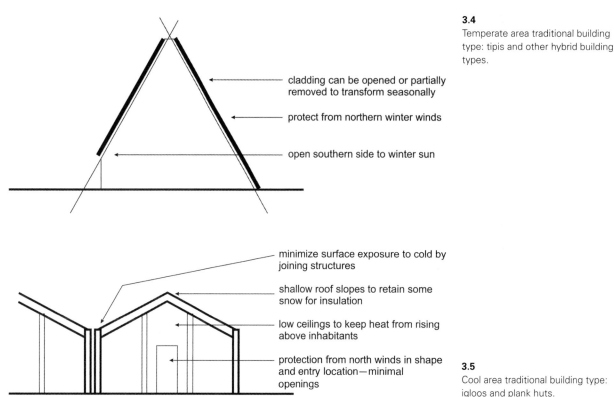

cladding can be opened or partially removed to transform seasonally

protect from northern winter winds

open southern side to winter sun

3.4
Temperate area traditional building type: tipis and other hybrid building types.

minimize surface exposure to cold by joining structures

shallow roof slopes to retain some snow for insulation

low ceilings to keep heat from rising above inhabitants

protection from north winds in shape and entry location—minimal openings

3.5
Cool area traditional building type: igloos and plank huts.

heavy, but retaining some snow on roofs is desirable for insulation value. Low winter sun from the south should be used to heat larger southern exposures. Minimum surface areas should be exposed to cold; joined structures are used to retain heat rather than avoid sun. Openings should be well insulated and located for maximum solar heat gain (Figure 3.5).

Igloos and timber huts are common examples of traditional building types. These structures are heavily insulated and often joined together to protect against wind and cold exposure. Roof slopes are designed to shed some snow and retain the rest for insulation.

Apart from the fundamental issues of climate control are both economical and emotional needs. The best solutions to buildings balance these appropriately for the inhabitants. Stone may provide the best material to accomplish a task, but may not be affordable or locally available. Minimal windows may improve the thermal efficiency of a structure, but access to view and sunlight are physically and emotionally very desirable.

Determining the correct approach to a project requires a synthesis of information. The limitations of the site or the desired arrangement of the program frequently will not allow the building to take maximum advantage of passive climatic strategies. The idea is to keep in mind the environmental factors while dealing with the myriad other requirements of designing a project. Choose the primary goals of the building and design to those while mitigating the problems.

MICROCLIMATES

Studying weather data and looking at traditional buildings gives us an idea of regional conditions; however, variations of terrain, vegetation, altitude and relationships to bodies of water create different localized conditions. These microclimates may vary significantly from the prevailing regional environment.

Topography affects comfort by a general lowering of temperature at altitude. In tropical parts of the world it is quite common to build in mountainous regions to find cooler temperatures. In a smaller-scale example, cool air is heavier than warm and settles in low areas or valleys. Finding the correct location on a slope depends on the region (Figure 3.6).

Hot–humid regions use the top of the hill. Air movement is most important in these zones, as shading can be accomplished through other means.

Hot–arid regions use the lower slopes to maximize heat loss. Wind cooling is relatively unimportant and south exposure is desirable to trap heat during the day. The southeast side of the hill protects from the hot western afternoon sun.

Temperate regions can move down the slope toward the cooler air but need more consideration of summer cooling breezes. Careful study of the specific wind vs. cold pool conditions, and which is more beneficial, needs to be considered.

Cool regions tend to use the upper slope, out of the cold lower level, facing south to catch the winter sun and to be protected from the north wind.

Vegetation provides a number of microclimatic effects. Dense coniferous (evergreen) trees or shrubs can provide wind barriers in the winter. Deciduous trees provide summer shade and allow sun through in the winter to promote solar heating. Plant and grassy covers reduce temperatures by absorbing the heat and not reflecting it onto other surfaces; conversely, urban paved areas are typically warmer than their surroundings.

Water, being dense and having a large surface area touching the ground, is usually cooler in the summer and warmer in the winter than the surrounding terrain. Close proximity to bodies of water tends to moderate temperature extremes. During the day, when the land is warmer than the water, cool air flows from over the water onto the land. This cycle reverses itself at night due to convective loops of warm air rising and being replaced by cooler air from over the water (this opposes the effect of the second law of thermodynamics that would normally have warm flow to cool). The moderating effect depends on the size of the body of water and is most effective when the temperature variation between water and land is the greatest.

CONCLUSION

The goal of studying micro- and macroclimatic conditions is to work with, rather than against, your local environment. There are always conflicting issues during project development and the designer's responsibility is to conscientiously create a hierarchy of what's most important. These issues must ultimately support one another as a cohesive whole. Basic site orientation, building proportion, consideration of microclimatic conditions, local vegetation, relationship to the sun and wind are all part of the earliest stages of the design process and have the most dramatic effect on the environmental efficiency and comfort of the project.

Building at top of hill to maximize breeze.

HOT–HUMID CLIMATES

- open, raised huts are common
- need large roofs with overhangs to avoid sun and shed rain
- open walls and raised floors to encourage evaporation of moisture by breezes
- structures spread out to maximize breezes
- narrow buildings with tall windows to promote cross ventilation
- heavy heat gains on east side and higher gains on west side

Building at bottom east to maximize heat loss. Hill protects from west afternoon sun.

HOT–ARID CLIMATES

- desert pueblos and other adobe structures are common
- less ventilation needed due to low humidity
- massive walls used to absorb heat during the day and emit it back during evenings
- minimal surface exposure to sun—joined homes together to minimize surface area exposed to sun
- buildings oriented with narrow ends to east and west maximize overhead summer sun on end walls and maximize low winter sun on south
- near evaporative pools for cooling

Low western sun

Building in middle of hill to balance cool lower air and upper breezes.

Top of hill

TEMPERATE CLIMATES

- wigwams and tipis are typical Native American examples
- protection from north winter winds
- open to winter sun on south
- shaded open areas with east and west shade overhangs in summer
- deciduous trees nearby shade in summer and allow winter sun
- open for summer breezes
- need to seasonally transfrom from warm to cold conditions

Building on upper slope out of cold lower air. Set to southeast to protect from northwest winter wind.

Bottom of hill

COOL CLIMATES

- igloos and plank and timber huts are common examples
- protection from north winds in shape and entry location
- use low south winter sun to heat walls
- protect from heavy snow, but retain some for insulating value
- minimum surface exposure to cold—often joined homes together to minimize exterior area and to retain heat rather than avoid sun
- minimal un-insulated openings

3.6
Climate zone building responses.

FREQUENTLY ASKED QUESTIONS

How do I determine what the weather conditions are at my site?
Most cities have information on weather history for a number of previous years. You need to check conditions in the general location for at least five to ten years previously in order to get an accurate picture of the prevailing conditions. Keep in mind that often these readings are from the local airport or on top of a building, which is normally not the same as the conditions you are designing for. Look at the immediate surroundings to get an idea of how winds, sunlight, water flow, cold air pooling, and snow will be affected. The NOAA (National Oceanographic and Atmospheric Administration) in the U.S. and the Met Office in the U.K. provide national weather forecasting and meteorological history for most regions.

What if I'm in between climate zones, or the charts don't match my local conditions?
The charts are only intended to provide strategies for dealing with climatic conditions. It's more important to be aware of local conditions than to follow an abstract guideline. Generally you use strategies that minimize the mechanical load on a building, so if it's more warm than cold, breezes are most important; if it's more cold than warm, conserving heat and borrowing solar gains are most important. Every different site, even in the same town, should be dealt with first generally from local historical data and then very specifically for it's individual microclimatic conditions.

GLOSSARY

Conduction: Heat flow through a homogeneous material (solid, liquid or gas) or between two objects in direct contact.

Convection: Heat transfer by the moving parts of a liquid or gas. This occurs where a river eddies or air diffuses into a room. Natural convection occurs due to heat's natural tendency to move from an area of higher temperature to an area of lower temperature. Forced convection moves the heat by a fan or pump.

Desiccate: Absorbing moisture out of a material, which can cause them to shrink and split or crack.

Micro climate: A climatic condition that varies from the surrounding areas due to variation in terrain, vegetation, altitude, and relationships to bodies of water.

Precipitation: Rain and snow. Fog can count as well but is typically part of humidity. Usually measured in inches using a rain gauge.

Radiation: Transmission of heat energy by electromagnetic waves from a warm substance to a cool one.

Wind: Measured by direction and velocity. Critical to note are the prevailing winds by season.

FURTHER READING

Brown, G. Z. and DeKay, M. (2001). *Sun, Wind and Light: Architectural Design Strategies*, 2nd edition. New York: John Wiley & Sons.

Olgyay, V. (1963). *Design with Climate: Bioclimatic Approach to Architectural Regionalism*. Princeton, NJ: Princeton University Press; Chapter 1, Part 1, pp. 1–13, 44–52.

4

ENVIRONMENT: SOLAR GEOMETRY

The Earth's rotation	The changing angle and position of the sun
	Solar path diagrams
Sun control strategies	Solar gains
	Daylighting

INTRODUCTION

Solar geometry follows the study of climatology as a particular area of interest to designers. While the wind, rain, temperature, and humidity all affect the design of buildings, the sun typically has the greatest impact on the aesthetics and performance of a project. None of the other climactic forces typically offer as much opportunity to harness its power, or create as many issues to deal with.

The sun provides two distinct issues to confront. The first issue is thermal; the sun is the primary source of all natural heating. This heat can be beneficial or problematic depending on the situation, and in most cases it is both. The second issue is light; the sun provides the most desirable lighting quality in most cases. These two factors determine a large part of the shape, site placement, and exterior skin of buildings. While artificial lighting and heating systems can replace or offset solar light and heat, the effects of the sun are always too powerful to ignore when designing a project.

There are a number of terms that are important to know in order to understand the way the sun strikes the earth. The first are "latitude" and "longitude" lines, which are abstract measurement lines inscribed around the earth. Latitude is the angular distance north or south of the earth's equator, measured in degrees along a meridian, as on a map or globe. Longitude is the angular distance on the earth's surface, measured east or west from the prime meridian at Greenwich, England (Figure 4.1), to the meridian passing through a position, expressed in degrees (or hours), minutes and seconds.

The other important terms to know are sun "altitude," "azimuth," and "solstice." These are the terms used to discuss the measurements of sun position as calculated in Figure 4.4. Sun azimuth is the horizontal angular distance of the

4.1
The prime meridian of the world,
located in Greenwich, England.

sun from a reference direction (typically north or south), measured in degrees in a radial pattern (where the sun is east to west). Sun altitude is the vertical angle of the sun, measured in degrees from a horizontal plane (how high the sun is in the sky). The solstice is either of the two times a year when the sun is at its zenith (directly overhead) over the Tropic of Cancer or the Tropic of Capricorn. In the northern hemisphere the summer solstice occurs about June 21, when the sun is over the Tropic of Cancer; the winter solstice occurs about December 21, when the sun is over the Tropic of Capricorn. This reverses itself in the southern hemisphere. The summer solstice has the longest daylight of the year and the winter solstice has the shortest (Figure 4.2).

rotational axis

latitude

Tropic of Cancer

equator

Tropic of Capricorn

longitude

solstice
June 21st,
approx.

equinox
Sept/Mar
21st, approx.

solstice
Dec 21st,
approx.

Because of the angle of the earth to the sun, the particular latitude of a location will have a different solar orientation. These differences in the angles of the sun throughout the year determine the strategies used to alternatively bring the light and heat in or keep it out. Often these two desires, light and heat, are in direct conflict with one another and difficult decisions need to be made about which is more important. Understanding the way the sun lights and heats a space is essential to making the right decisions.

4.2
Relationship of the sun to the earth at the solstices and equinoxes.

THE EARTH'S ROTATION

The arc of the sun changes throughout the year due to the fact that the earth's rotational axis is at an angle to the orbit of the earth around the sun (Figure 4.3). This change in angle determines the amount of solar radiation any point on the earth will receive during a day. The amount of radiation is determined in two ways: the first is the number of hours the sun will strike a point on the surface. The lower the sun angle, the less time it will be visible from a point on the earth; the higher the angle, the more time it will be visible. The second way the amount of solar radiation is determined is at what angle it strikes the surface of the earth. The more direct the angle, the more heat is absorbed.

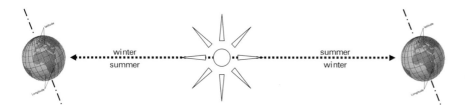

winter
summer

summer
winter

4.3
Relationship of the sun to the earth during a revolution in orbit.

As any casual observer notes, the warmest part of the year is typically not the summer solstice and the coldest is not the winter solstice. The cold or warm weather typically persists and intensifies past the longest or shortest day of the year by a couple of months. This is primarily due to the ability of mass to retain and transmit heat or cold, commonly called "thermal shift." We see this phenomenon in many small ways; sunglasses left on the dashboard in summer stay hot after being removed from the sun for a brief period of time while a stone bench remains cold well into a warm day. The larger the heated or cooled mass, the longer it takes to return to ambient air temperature. The mass of the land and water on the earth tends to retain the heat or cold from entire seasons and "shift" that temperature load past the point of solar heating or lack thereof. This same strategy is used in thermal mass elements on buildings to combat temperature shifts from day to night; the earth simply does this at a much larger scale.

The location of the sun in the sky can be easily calculated for any hour of day throughout the year by using a sun path diagram. Because the height of the sun is dependent on the angle of the earth to the sun, charts are projected by latitude. The higher the degree of latitude, the farther you are from the equator. The equator is 0 degrees and the north and south poles are 90 degrees. All angles between are split between north and south, so a chart labeled 60 degrees latitude can be used for north or south simply by rotating it top to bottom. Some charts are labeled this way and have a set of information both right-side-up and upside-down, to be read for whichever hemisphere (north or south) you are calculating. Typically charts show latitude increments of 4 degrees apart; therefore if you are looking for information at the latitude between two charts it is necessary to interpolate the information.

Don't let the initially confusing layout of these charts be intimidating; with some practice they become easy to use. When looking at the chart imagine you are lying on your back looking at the sky, so east is to your left. An example follows of how to determine the position of the sun using the chart shown (Figure 4.4).

Naples, Italy is at 40 degrees north latitude, so the 40 degree north latitude sun path diagram chart is appropriate. As noted above, the charts can be used for latitudes north and south of the equator simply by flipping them upside down. The dark curved month lines should bow downwards in the northern hemisphere and upwards in the southern hemisphere. To determine the position of the sun in the sky at 4pm on August 21 first find the curved August 21/April 21 line on the chart—it should be listed on both sides. Trace this line across the chart until you reach the vertical line that reads 4pm—afternoon times are right of center, morning times are left, which corresponds to the position of the sun in the east in the morning and west in the afternoon. The intersection of the August 21 line and the 4 pm line lands on a radial circle that reads 30 degrees, which is the altitude angle of the sun above the horizon. Lastly find the radial line that runs from the intersection to the outside circle and read the azimuth as 260 degrees, or 10 degrees shy of due west—this is the horizontal angle of the sun from the reference point of 0 directly to the north. You can also measure the angle as 80 degrees west of due south.

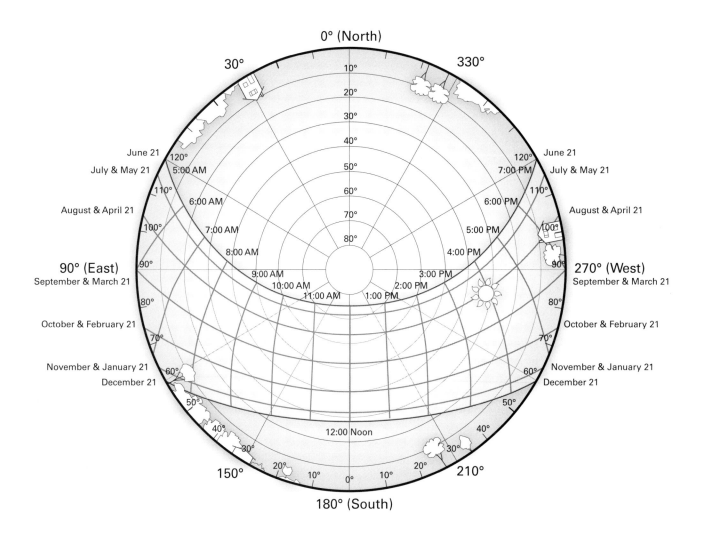

4.4
40 degree north latitude sun path diagram.

SUN CONTROL STRATEGIES

Solar gains

The angles of the sun are the primary determining factor in heat gain for buildings. Depending on the climate or time of year, this heat gain may be desirable or not. A basic rule of thumb is that in cold climates you want to maximize winter solar gains, while in hot climates you try to minimize solar gains year round.

The variables to be dealt with were covered mainly in the climatology section; however, let's summarize the solar conditions (Figure 4.5):

Hot–humid climates
   Need large roofs with overhangs to avoid sun and shed rain
   Heavy heat gains on east side and higher gains on west side

Hot–arid climates
   Massive walls used to absorb heat during the day and emit it back during evenings
   Minimal surface exposure to sun

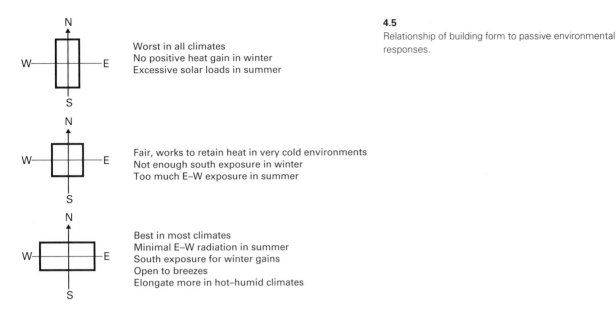

Worst in all climates
No positive heat gain in winter
Excessive solar loads in summer

Fair, works to retain heat in very cold environments
Not enough south exposure in winter
Too much E–W exposure in summer

Best in most climates
Minimal E–W radiation in summer
South exposure for winter gains
Open to breezes
Elongate more in hot–humid climates

4.5
Relationship of building form to passive environmental responses.

Buildings oriented with narrow ends to east and west—minimizing overhead summer sun on end walls and maximizing low winter sun on south

Temperate climates
Open to winter sun on south
Shaded open areas with east and west shade overhangs in summer
Deciduous trees nearby shade in summer and allow winter sun

Cool climates
Use low south winter sun to heat walls
Minimal un-insulated openings

Where solar gain heat is collected, it can be radiated directly into the space by use of passive thermal mass walls, or more actively moved with ventilation systems to distribute the heat. Most of the time a hybrid of passive and active systems can maximize the use of naturally collected radiant solar heat.

Daylighting

Up to 50 percent of the energy use of many modern buildings comes from artificial illumination, and frequently spaces are over-lit, causing unnecessary additional expense. While the efficiency of the systems used to maintain building comfort, including lighting, have improved over the last 40 years, the amount of energy used has stayed roughly the same. We're using the energy more efficiently, but we're continually using more of it.

The use of daylighting has often been avoided due to concerns over solar radiation gains, or a desire to keep lighting more consistent. There are, however, strategies that can be used to mitigate both of these concerns.

There are three components of daylighting systems:

1 *Exterior environment:* The sky, sun, land and adjacent structures change the intensity of the light. The brightness of the sun changes due to vegetation

and clouds, while the direction shifts throughout the year. The ground around the building (i.e. grass or concrete) reflects different amounts of light into the space.

2 *Interface medium:* The glazing and building fenestration, or aperture through which the daylight enters the space. Openings act as filters for different conditions, often different openings should be used for heat gain versus daylight.

3 *Interior environment:* The shape and reflectance of the space will distribute light in different ways. Deeper, lower spaces get less sunlight, and lighter colored floors tend to reflect light deeper into a space.

The depth of a space affects how well it can be lit. Depths of twice the floor to ceiling height can potentially be daylit. Light shelves and reflectors can allow the light to penetrate deeper into the space without direct radiant solar gain. There are two basic rules to remember—the higher the window the farther the light penetrates, and if you cannot see the sky through the opening, the light level will drop off quickly when it's overcast. A common strategy for minimizing artificial light, but maintaining light levels, is to separate light circuits and put the lights close to the windows on photocell sensors. This allows these lights to be off when the daylight level is high enough and to come on if its overcast or the sun is not in the right position to adequately light the space.

Light travels into openings in a number of ways and slight shifts in exterior openings can have large effects on the amount of light and solar radiation that enters a space (Figure 4.6). Unrestricted openings allow light deep into a space but can promote heat gain during warm months, when it's undesirable. Small overhangs can limit summer exposure, while allowing winter solar radiation. The amount of overhang can be determined by using the sun path chart to chart the location of the sun for different times of year. Light shelves can solve the problem of limiting summer sun radiation, while reflecting light deeper into a space than a simple overhang can accomplish. Diffusers spread the light evenly throughout a space with patterned glazing. This typically limits vision through the glass, but can produce even and softer daylighting. Light scoops can solve the problem of heat gain versus light by putting light deeper into a space without large heat gaining window openings at the exterior wall of a building. All methods of building openings offer both design and environmental opportunities. Elegant solutions make these two demands work together.

CONCLUSION

The goal of thinking about solar geometry is not only about passive environmental control. The natural environment presents concerns that buildings are forced to respond to, and these environmental factors are the basis on which all shelters are constructed. The environment offers a means of understanding how to create and express the appearance of a structure. From the factors of the environmental forces placed on a building, a language of form can be created that communicates with the natural world in a very fundamental way.

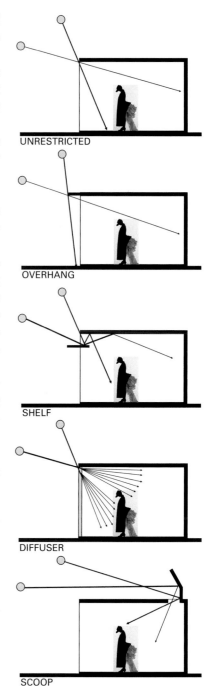

UNRESTRICTED

OVERHANG

SHELF

DIFFUSER

SCOOP

4.6
Types of exterior openings for solar radiation and light.

FREQUENTLY ASKED QUESTIONS

How do I find the longitude and latitude of a site?
Basic information can be found on a typical map or globe that will have longitude and latitude lines indicated at 10-degree intervals. Local maps often show a greater level of detail. Most cities will have an indication of longitude and latitude easily found in the index of an atlas or online.

How do I determine if the sun will directly enter a space?
Find the sun path diagram for the latitude of your site, select the chart closest and interpolate if the exact latitude chart is not available. Calculate the position of the sun for morning, noon, and late afternoon hours for the summer, winter, and fall/spring. Using the angles and azimuths you've gathered, draw a plan and section of the space with window locations and exterior roof overhangs shown. Graphically draw the horizontal and vertical angles of the suns location for each of the times and seasons as they pass through the window openings, using separate plans and sections for each. The representative sets of drawings will give you a good overview of the amount of sun that enters the space throughout the year, and will allow you to make modifications to achieve the results you desire. Most computer modeling systems also have the ability to calculate sun path projections if the model is built accurately, but keep in mind ground conditions, vegetation and surface colors, which are often not part of a computer model.

GLOSSARY

Latitude: The angular distance north or south of the earth's equator, measured in degrees along a meridian, as on a map or globe.
Longitude: Angular distance on the earth's surface, measured east or west from the prime meridian at Greenwich, England, to the meridian passing through a position, expressed in degrees (or hours), minutes and seconds.
Sun azimuth: The horizontal angular distance of the sun from a reference direction (typically north or south), measured in degrees in a radial pattern.
Sun altitude: The vertical angle of the sun, measured in degrees from a horizontal plane.
Sky zenith: The point at which the sun is directly overhead the observer on the earth's sphere.
Solstice: Either of the two times a year when the sun is at its zenith over the Tropic of Cancer or the Tropic of Capricorn. In the northern hemisphere the summer solstice occurs about June 21, when the sun is over the Tropic of Cancer, the winter solstice occurs about December 21, when the sun is over the Tropic of Capricorn. This reverses itself in the southern hemisphere. The summer solstice has the longest daylight of the year and the winter solstice has the shortest.
Thermal shift: The ability of mass to retain heat or cold and transmit it at a later time.

FURTHER READING

Brown, G. Z. and DeKay, M. (2001). *Sun, Wind and Light: Architectural Design Strategies*, 2nd edition. New York: John Wiley & Sons.

Hawkes, D., McDonald, J., and Steemers, K. (2002). *The Selective Environment*. New York: Spon Press; Chapter 8, Environmental Design Checklist, pp. 122–151.

Kwok, A and Grondzik, W. (2011). *The Green Studio Handbook*, 2nd edition. Oxford: Elsevier.

Neufert, E. and Neufert, P. (2000). *Architect's Data*, 3rd edition. London: Blackwell Science; pp. 151–165.

Ramsey, C. G. and Sleeper, H. R. (2007). *Architectural Graphic Standards*, 11th edition. New York: John Wiley & Sons; pp. 61–62.

PART 2

PRE-DESIGN

5
PROGRAMMING AND PROGRAM/BRIEF ANALYSIS

Programming	Asking the right questions
	Information gathering
	Developing a program/brief
Analysis	Areas schedules
	Bubble diagrams
	Adjacencies and affinities
	Stratification
Solving towards design	"Building the diagram" versus "finding the fit"
	Building grain

PROGRAMMING

Programming is the art and science of determining the functional requirements of a designed object. We often assume that this is a simple task, and for well-known building types (single family residences, speculative office buildings, etc.) this may be the case. However, discerning the requirements for more complex or less deterministic building types—hospitals or retail shops, for example—may be more difficult. What, for example, is the exact function of an art museum? Certainly we could list a set of rooms with suggested areas, but it is unlikely that this process would set the problem up correctly. The "function" of an art museum according to Louis Kahn was "a set of spaces that are good for the viewing of art." Even this usefully vague description, however, doesn't address the civic, commercial, and educational requirements that today's art museum might face. The building housing such an institution would include functions—branding, public spaces, a civic image—that couldn't be included in a traditional areas schedule.

Programming is therefore both an objective and a subjective process. Discerning what our clients need (or want) will involve discussions about square footage/meterage and relationships between spaces. However, it is the architect's task to also figure out the larger issues that underlie our clients' needs, and to see whether those can be addressed architecturally. Typically, developing a program/brief is an additional service for architects in the U.S.

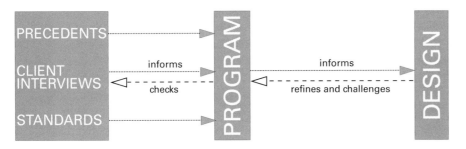

5.1
The programming and program analysis process

and U.K., but it does happen frequently. As often as not, we will be confronted on a new job with a program/brief written by a client or a space planner. Even if this is the case, good practice suggests that this document be thoroughly questioned.

When architects are asked to prepare a program/brief or brief, we rely on several sources of information regarding what elements are necessary, how much space each of these may take up (either in absolute or relative terms), what services or qualities these spaces require, and what relationships each space should have to one another. This is a process of "problem seeking," not "problem solving" in the words of the Texas architectural firm Caudill Rowlett Scott, who pioneered systematic approaches to programming in the 1960s and 1970s. To gain reliable information, architects will often interview clients and users, often using existing facilities as a benchmark. Are the spaces being used now large enough? Are there services that should be provided? What does or does not work with the current arrangements, and what suggestions might the day-to-day users have for improving their environment? We may also study other installations of the type, either through a literature search or site visits, to glean information about current space and functional standards. In some cases (health care, for instance) there will be well-published standards that will list much of this information. However, it is almost always beneficial to see these standards in action and to decide whether inherent problems or shortcomings in standard design need to be addressed (Figure 5.1).

Information from this exercise will typically be tabulated in the form of an areas schedule (or program/brief) that lists the space requirements for the proposed design. Usually this will break down required uses into individual rooms, grouped according to how the client sees their functional relationships. The schedule will list room titles or uses, area in square feet/meters or square meters, and may include further information about required proportions, qualities (daylight, for example), or services. Areas schedules are usually drawn up using spreadsheet software (e.g. Microsoft Excel), which allows users to enter data cells for room names, areas, and qualities, as well as programmed cells that can manipulate, compare, or sort this information (Table 5.1). Using spreadsheets we can easily subtotal building areas, compare sizes, or later in the process estimate how close to the original program/brief our developing design may be.

Several rules of thumb for estimating space requirements are shown in Table 5.2. These are drawn from daily experience and are not universally applicable, but they give a good idea of where a programming exercise might start. All of these assumptions deserve to be tested with any client—for example,

Table 5.1 A typical areas schedule, with space names, required areas, and a matrix of requirements.

	Net assignable square feet	Net non-assignable square feet	Gross square feet	Level	Daylight	Public/private	Plumbing
Living room	300			1	1	1	0
Kitchen	150			1	1	2	1
Dining room	150			1	1	1	0
Bedrooms							
Master bedroom	250			*2*	*2*	*4*	*0*
Child's bedroom	120			*2*	*2*	*4*	*0*
Child's bedroom	120			*2*	*2*	*4*	*0*
Office	100			1	1	3	0
Bathrooms							
Downstairs bathroom		60		*1*	*2*	*3*	*1*
Upstairs bathroom		60		*2*	*2*	*4*	*1*
Playroom	300			0	3	4	0
Furnace room		120		0	4	5	1
Storage							
First floor closet		20		*1*	*4*	*5*	*0*
Second floor closet		10		*2*	*4*	*5*	*0*
Basement storage		110		*0*	*4*	*5*	*0*
Circulation							
Stairs basement/first		50					
Stairs first/second		50					
Corridors (est.)		100					
SUBTOTAL NSF	1490	580					
TOTAL NSF	2070						
TOTAL GSF			2484				

a common exercise in an early programming meeting is to tape out on the floor an assumed office size, allowing users or clients to get a sense for what a 10-square-meter office actually looks like. Also of interest at this stage are typical "net to gross" ratios. "Net" space in a building includes all rentable, or assignable areas, such as offices or apartments, clerical spaces or meeting rooms. "Gross" space includes all "house" or non-assignable spaces such as hallways, bathrooms, lobbies, and service rooms. Generally the rule of thumb is that any space in a building that could be rented is "net", while any space that cannot be rented is "gross." Net-to-gross ratios are taken perhaps too seriously by developers, especially considering the qualities that "gross" spaces such as atriums, cafes, or lounges can add to a building's function. Nonetheless, they are so universally used as benchmarks of efficiency that they are worthy of study. A third type of area that includes walls, shafts, and columns is termed "construction area" and is calculated to arrive at a total figure for the "footprint area" of a building.

Table 5.2 Rules of thumb for estimating space requirements during preliminary design phases.

	Allowance per person, square meters	Allowance per person, square feet
Standard office	12	125
Clerical office	5	50
Manager's office	14	150
Conference room	1	15
Dining rooms—banquet	1	13
Dining rooms—cafeteria	1	12
Dining rooms—table service	1	16
Retail—ground floor	3	30
Retail—department store	4	40
Library—reading rooms	3	35
Overall	5	50
Museums	1	15
Theaters—fixed seats	1	8
Theaters—movable seats	1	15
Lobby	0.5	3
Backstage is typically as large as seating area		
Elementary classroom	2	20
Secondary classroom	2	25
Large secondary classroom	1	15
Gymnasium	12	125
University classroom	1	15
University seminar room	2	20
University lecture hall	1	12
Apartments	23	250
Hospital	93	1000

PROGRAM/BRIEF ANALYSIS

No matter who creates the program/brief, the first step in our design process is almost always to analyze its implications. Here we are looking for ways to translate a list of requirements into a strategy for form (architectural, landscape, engineering, etc.). As such, architects rely on several graphic conventions to help "spatialize" a program/brief. While these may give the appearance of objective problem solving, they should be approached with great caution. Ideally, these exercises should be seen as ways of questioning and understanding the data in the program/brief. It is very rare that a satisfactory form will emerge solely out of a diagramming process—more often this process will help

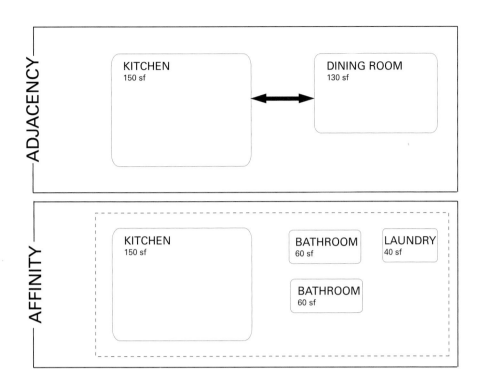

5.2
Adjacencies versus affinities.

us understand the problem in spatial terms, and our concepts will emerge from this understanding. It is important to remember, too, that program/brief analysis is an "inside out" method of strategizing. More often than not, we will *also* be analyzing our site (see Chapter 6) during this phase, and any solutions that emerge will need to be holistic, balancing what we discover from the internal organization and from external forces.

Traditionally, architects begin with "bubble diagrams," or very loose representations of areas drawn to scale from the program/brief with relationships between these areas noted by lines indicating connectivity. The areas themselves are often color-coded, labeled with names and areas, and typically drawn as ovals or rectangles with curved corners. These shapes allegedly remind us that we are not yet designating "rooms"—we are rather interested in the area that a given activity is likely to take up.

Connectivity is often indicated in one of two categories—*adjacencies* and *affinities* (Figure 5.2). Adjacencies represent relationships between activities that require direct circulatory access. A typical example in residential design is the relationship between a kitchen and a dining room. Here, there are good reasons to locate areas adjacent to one another to enable quick, efficient movement of people or goods from one to another. Affinities, on the other hand, indicate activities that share something besides circulatory convenience and thus may tend toward one another in a building for reasons of performance or constructability. Here, a good residential example is kitchens and bathrooms. While there is no pressing need for circulation between these two spaces, they share a requirement for plumbing. To save the costs involved with excessive piping, "wet" activities are often grouped near one another, sharing plumbing stacks and drains (see Chapter 41). Other affinities may include the need for daylighting, security, visibility, privacy, fresh air, or sound attenuation.

ADJACENCY REQUIREMENTS

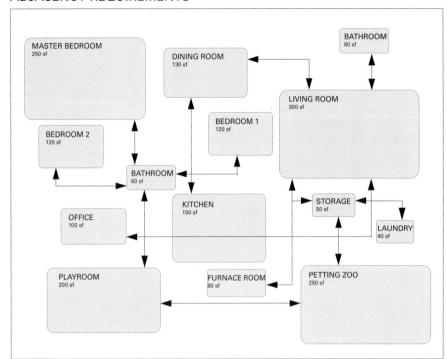

5.3
A first layout of adjacency requirements for the areas schedule in Table 5.1.

AFFINITIES REQUIREMENTS

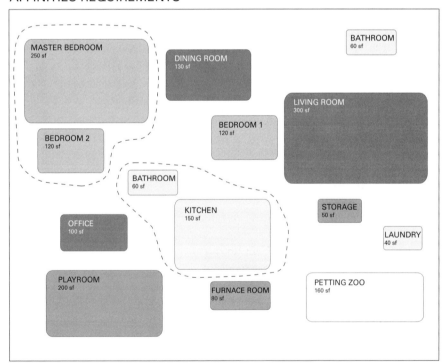

5.4
A first layout of affinity requirements for the areas schedule in Table 5.1.

A useful bubble diagram will often show adjacencies as solid lines connecting one program/brief element to another, while showing affinities as an outline surrounding like elements. Note how spaces relate in terms of circulation (adjacency) and servicing (affinity) (Figures 5.3 and 5.4). In the former, the kitchen

PROGRAMMATIC LAYOUT ATTEMPT

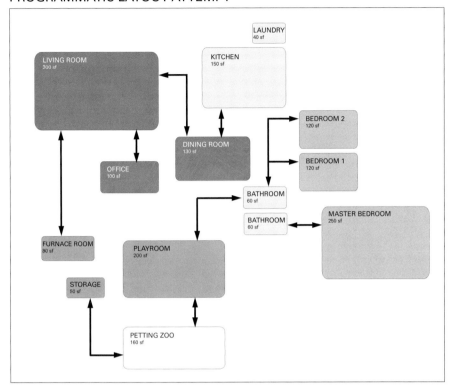

5.5
Initial layout based on the findings
of the first adjacency and affinity
diagrams.

and dining room are connected by a solid line, while in the latter the kitchen and bathrooms are circled by a dashed line. These indicate the need for physical proximity due to circulatory and functional reasons, respectively. Through an iterative process, bubble diagrams will be re-drawn and re-drawn until efficient strategies emerge for deploying spaces and program/brief elements relative to one another. Here, one might think of the connecting and encircling lines as rubber bands, the goal being to tighten these up as much as possible. Figures 5.5 and 5.6 show several iterations for a small residence. Note that a balance is gradually struck between the ideal circulation scheme and the goal of collecting all wet areas around a single plumbing stack. Note, too, that the "final" scheme is only an efficient organization—it is hardly "architectural" and will benefit from a more forceful sculpting of these elements into real spatial proposals.

An additional tool for program/brief analysis is the spreadsheet (e.g. Microsoft Excel). A building program/brief that is entered as a spreadsheet can be manipulated to discover patterns, repetitive elements, or shared requirements in important ways. The areas schedule in Table 5.1 contains additional entries representing the spaces' requirements for daylighting, privacy, and plumbing. In each case, the architect has entered a "1" if the requirement is absolute, "2" if the requirement is desirable, and "3" if the element does not require the attribute in question. The Data Sort tool in a typical spreadsheet program can then be used to show patterns in use, performance, or servicing. By sorting this data by these requirements, patterns emerge that suggest how these spaces might be deployed. The sort shown, for example, indicates what elements require access to plumbing (Table 5.1). Note that none of these

PROGRAMMATIC LAYOUT ATTEMPT

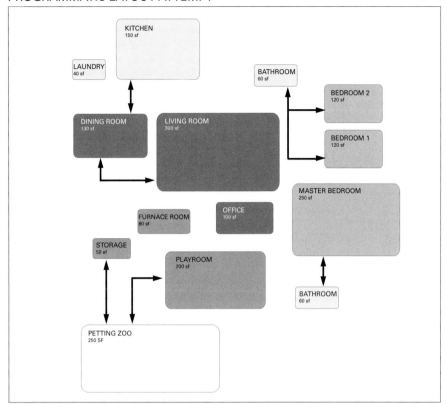

5.6
Further refinement as the programmatic elements begin to find their place in the overall hierarchy.

spaces require daylight. This suggests that these elements might be grouped into a single core in the center of a floor plate, where they will not take up potentially precious perimeter, naturally illuminated space. While the examples shown are simple, this process can be a powerful organizational tool for larger buildings.

Another useful tool during program/brief analysis is a *stratification diagram* (Figure 5.7). This sorts out spaces based on where they "want" to be in a building's section. In many cases, this will be very simple: an office building, for example, has a set of lobby functions on the ground floor, perhaps parking in the basement, and then a long run of office floors for its remainder. However in many complex program/briefs, such as libraries, museums, sports facilities, etc., it is useful to sort out adjacency requirements to ground level: what elements, for example, must be immediately accessible to an entry level lobby, what elements can be one or two floors above and below, what elements can be reached by elevator and have no need to be near an entry level, and what elements can be underground. On a tight urban site where street level space may be at a premium, this exercise can provide valuable opportunities to prioritize space on floor plates, and may give some clues about how the building may be ordered sectionally.

Table 5.3 A data sort of the areas schedule in Table 5.1 based on plumbing.

	Net assignable square feet	Net non-assignable square feet	Gross square feet	Level	Daylight	Public/private	Plumbing
Kitchen	150			1	1	2	1
Bathrooms							
Downstairs Bathroom		60		1	2	3	1
Upstairs bathroom		60		2	2	4	1
Furnace room		120		0	4	5	1
Living room	300			1	1	1	0
Dining room	150			1	1	1	0
Office	100			1	1	3	0
Bedrooms							
Master bedroom	250			2	2	4	0
Child's bedroom	120			2	2	4	0
Child's bedroom	120			2	2	4	0
Playroom	300			0	3	4	0
Storage							
First floor closet		20		1	4	5	0
Second floor closet		10		2	4	5	0
Basement storage		110		0	4	5	0

Note that other important aspects of the spaces (public/private in particular) align with the sort. This may be the start of a possible design strategy.

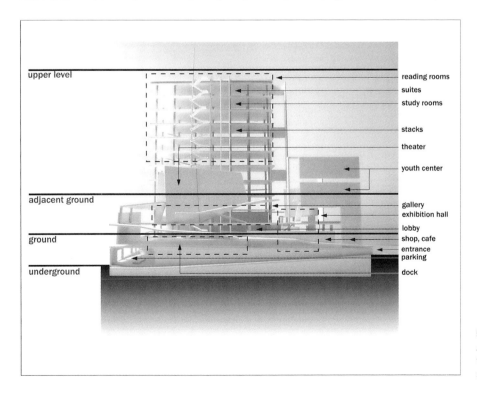

5.7
A stratification diagram showing the organization of a program in section.

MOVING INTO DESIGN

Bubble diagrams, and other graphic strategies designed to generate architectural form from objective program/brief data, have developed a bad reputation over the past generation. In our opinion, this is largely due to the late modernist myth that simply figuring out the most efficient solution to a programmed problem, and then "building the diagram," could produce architecture on its own. This is a very reductivist view. However bubble diagrams and spreadsheets can be powerful methods for discovering the patterns of use and function on which a clever architectural scheme may be based. Very often, initial programmatic assumptions will be altered or questioned as the initial schematic strategies are produced—how close, for example, one is required to meet targets for office sizes or lobby spaces may change dramatically as architectural ideas are explored. Invariably, we'll try experiments from both ends, attempting to find architecturally significant patterns in how the program fits together and looking at how architectural ideas can be fulfilled or matched by the program (Figure 5.8).

An important aspect of turning the corner from data analysis to design synthesis is to recognize just how the spaces required by various activities may be woven together, or how they may "fit" in three dimensions. Three-dimensional models—whether physical or virtual—may play a key role in understanding the architectural implications of a diagram produced by analysis. At this stage, volumetric models (boxes) are often less useful than floor plate models, which can show possible plan arrangements on multiple floors while giving a rudimentary glimpse of what the resulting spaces and building masses might suggest. The digital model in Figure 5.9 shows a provocative first step that may well inform the building shape, its major spaces, and its basic organization.

One aspect to look for at this point is clues to the building's *grain*; that is, overlaps of dimensions, bay sizes, floor heights, etc., that may suggest a pattern or order to the building's spaces and massing. This will become imperative as the design process moves toward structural layout and bay sizes but may be evident at this early stage. A classic example here is the fortunate coincidence between office dimensions (often $10' \times 10'$) and parking stalls (often $10' \times 30'$). Noticing potential alignments through a building's structure at this point will make subsequent stages of structural design much more efficient.

FREQUENTLY ASKED QUESTIONS

What's the difference between a program, an areas schedule, and a brief?
These are all different names for the same thing. "Program" is the American term for what British architects call a "brief." To confuse things further, the "brief" is also often referred to as a "schedule" in the U.K., which in the U.S. refers to the project's calendar.

LINEAR

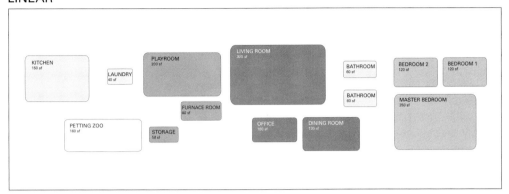

CENTRALIZED

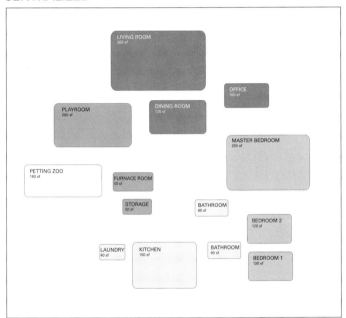

5.8
Two architectural strategies imposed on the program.

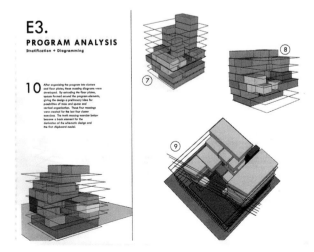

5.9
A step toward massing, with a complex program laid out in three dimensions, within the confines of a tight site.

GLOSSARY

Adjacencies: Relationships between program elements that suggest physical proximity based on shared qualities or requirements.

Affinities: Relationships between program elements that suggest physical proximity based on circulatory requirements.

Bubble diagrams: Drawings showing the relative areas of programmed spaces and their desired relationship. These can provide a useful first step toward understanding the spatial consequences of programmatic imperatives.

Construction area: A measure of the floor area taken up by walls, columns, shafts, etc.

Grain: A pattern or order that emerges based on an understanding of typical sizes of elements of the program/brief. Often the primary goal in analyzing an architectural program.

Gross area: A measure of building area that includes all spaces—'assignable' and otherwise (i.e. circulation, toilets, elevators, etc.).

Net area: A measure of building area that includes only 'assignable' spaces such as offices or apartments.

Net to gross: A percentage derived by dividing the assignable area of a building (net) by the total area (gross). Often seen as a measure of efficiency, but not always accurate in its assessment of how well a building may work.

Program (or brief): A written document that lists the required performance aspects of a designed object. In architectural situations, this often takes the form of a list of spaces with areas and qualities ascribed to them, but this is not necessarily a complete description.

Programming: Determining the fundamental functional requirements of a designed object.

Stratification diagram: A drawing (or model) showing the desired distribution of a given program/brief in a multistory situation.

FURTHER READING

Peña, W., Parshall, S., and Kelly, K. (1987). *Problem Seeking: An Architectural Programming Primer*. Washington: AIA Press.

6

SITE ANALYSIS

Outside in	The fundamentals of site analysis
	Data gathering and analysis
Process	Where to find data
Documentation	Strategies for pattern finding
	Presenting information
	Using spatial analysis to inform design

FORM FINDING FROM THE OUTSIDE IN

In program analysis, architects seek patterns and ordering strategies based on the inherent structures of a building's functions and requirements. This is essentially an "inside out" process. Meanwhile, we are often examining a building's context to see how a project can best fit into its site—an "outside in" process. In the best cases, the final form, rhythm, massing, and spatial sequences of a project will be a dialogue between what we find out from the project's internal and external requirements. Usually, this is a case of balancing, of finding convenient overlaps between competing requirements, and of assessing the relative values and merits of solving both sets of challenges and opportunities.

While getting the functional disposition of a project correct is a major goal in satisfying clients and users, architects have a responsibility to cities, neighborhoods, and surrounding residents, owners and the public to assess how such functional solutions can most appropriately and sensitively nestle in to existing contexts. Site analysis is thus not only concerned with our clients and users, but with the larger community. Much of our work in this area will be concerned with negotiating our clients' needs with the welfare and quality of life of their surroundings. Site analysis is thus a delicate process, and the need for a thorough understanding of a project's physical, social, and cultural contexts in addition to its circulatory patterns, aesthetic traditions, and public uses is part of our responsibility beyond simply pleasing a client.

We are also under distinct regulatory pressure in this phase. Many localities have zoning regulations, historic preservation requirements, traffic or pedestrian laws, and review processes to ensure that development takes place within the boundaries of community standards and functions. While the power of development money may occasionally override responsible growth, architects have the power—and the responsibility—to ensure that our work creates buildings that are "good neighbors," and that do not simply exploit community resources or environments for corporate or personal gain. While local zoning or aesthetic regulations may seem onerous, they represent encoded values that we are duty-bound to recognize. Challenges that adhere to the spirit of such regulations may be welcomed, however this is usually the result of patient, respectful consideration on the part of designers and clients to understand the underlying reasons for what may seem like petty requirements.

PROCESS

Like program analysis, we suggest a diagrammatic approach that emphasizes clear documentation, graphic analysis, and the development of a holistic understanding, rather than an attempt at high-speed form finding. The successful resolution of site conditions and requirements is more likely to come from a design idea inspired by our integration of this data, rather than directly from the data itself. A typical site analysis package will be documentary in nature, often showing many pages of graphic or tabular information, followed by some very preliminary design diagrams that show strategies likely to best resolve the site's particular issues.

The first steps of site analysis involve gathering data. Often architectural teams will get a detailed survey map as a base for recording and presenting our findings, as well as for studying the physical context of our site. Google Earth and other web-based mapping resources are valuable in this regard but need to be supplemented by accurate and more detailed information. Direct observation is imperative—architects need extensive access to the site, often recording activity on and around it for an entire day or more. Topographic surveys that show the shape of the land in plan form are likewise required for sites with significant changes in elevation, and extensive photography is necessary to record the scale of the surroundings, as well as the massing, materials, and styles of surrounding buildings. There are also significant intangible elements to any site analysis that can only be gained by careful observation, by walking not only the site but also its surroundings, and by immersion in the daily activities of its neighbors. What is the pace of life around the site like? Do we sense nearby activities through sound or smell? Are there amenities (restaurants, coffee shops, post offices, cinemas) that might benefit our program or be reinforced by the sudden infusion of our client's staff? Are there local building traditions that we can respond to, challenge, or simply acknowledge?

Likewise, we need to document the regulatory and legal aspects of the site. Using public records and documents, the site's legal dimensions need to be confirmed, and a full exploration of its allowable uses, building size and type, and required amenities or concessions must be fully documented (see Chapter 8, Zoning and Building Codes). Typically, this will come in the form of a zoning designation, which is determined by municipal authorities. A full understanding of this information is vital prior to commencing design work, as obtaining variances may be difficult.

Finally, our responsibility to design efficient buildings requires us to study and document the climatological properties of our site. Of particular interest will be the site's relationship to the sun. Ideally, buildings will take advantage of winter sun and summer shade, requiring studies of the sun's position throughout the year. How surrounding buildings, planting, or topography modify the sun's effects on the site are of particular interest, as are the effects our intervention will have on neighboring properties. To do an accurate solar study, the approximate latitude of the site is needed. From this, solar angles for any day of the year can be calculated using published solar charts that show the position of solar paths on a flattened "sky chart." While this data is particularly useful in designing facades and shading devices, a more holistic overview of the sun's effects on a site can be gleaned by running a solar path study using digital modeling. Running typical days for each of the four seasons will give a good idea of the site's exposure during key times of the year, suggesting massing and planting strategies that can take advantage of climate-appropriate techniques to add shade or exposure. This study can also identify likely open areas that will provide direct sunlight, and may indicate areas of the site where glare might be a problem. In addition to solar studies, documentation of daily temperature, precipitation, and cloud cover averages is required to assess insulation, facade porosity, and the importance of outdoor exposure. Finally, it is important to study wind patterns on the site, to see if we might be able to take advantage of summer breezes, or to easily block winter winds. Climate data can be found on the website of the National Oceanic and Atmospheric Administration (www.noaa.gov), or the "Met Office."

DOCUMENTATION

No client will tolerate being confronted with a massive list of traffic, zoning, climate, and historical data. Architects have the responsibility of not only documenting these issues, but also of teasing out patterns and overlaps amongst these areas. Just like programming, the "analysis" in site analysis demands that we also make some tentative suggestions about what all these findings suggest.

One way to begin this process is to document our findings in a consistent, graphic method. Architects will often use a set of aerial photographs as underlays for diagrams—or "vignettes" that summarize the data that we've found in visual ways (Figure 6.1). A traffic diagram, for instance, might layer a set of arrows over an aerial photograph indicating where automobile traffic flows, using arrowheads to show direction, line weight to show relative intensities, and color to show types of traffic (truck, vehicular, bike, etc.). The same aerial might underlay diagrams showing pedestrian connections, zoning information, locations of amenities in the neighborhood, etc. (Figures 6.2 to 6.8). A larger-scale aerial photograph might show regional traffic connections, population concentrations, or larger amenities such as airports, train stations, or shopping centers. Meanwhile, a more detailed view might be used to show more detailed information such as planting locations, data on neighboring structures, or likely entries and exits into the site.

In constructing these diagrams, it is important to be both accurate and clear.

Location N

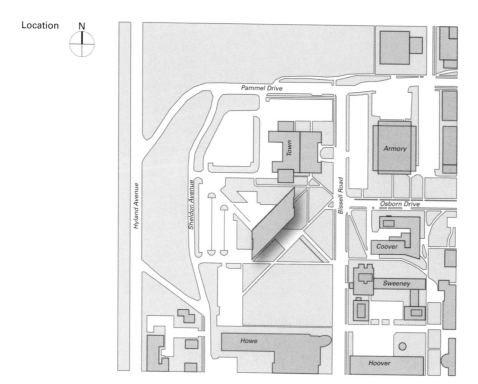

6.1

A basic map of a project's site, using an aerial photo as an underlay.

Site Boundaries N

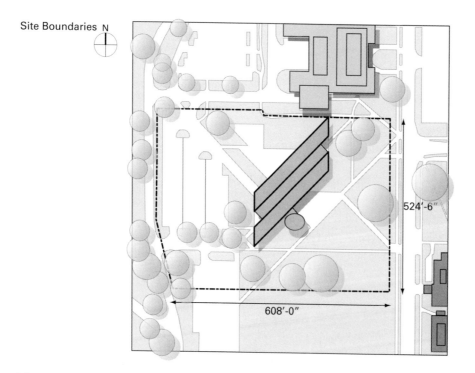

6.2

Further information on location will include legal boundaries and site dimensions.

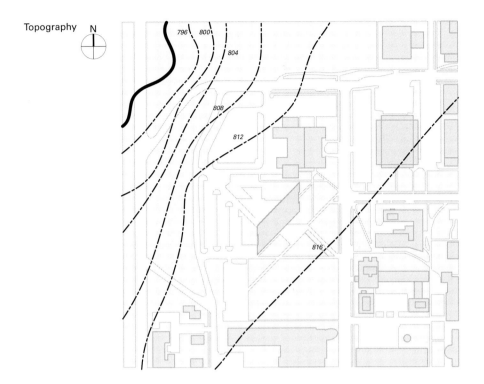

6.3
Understanding the geography of the site includes a full topographical survey.

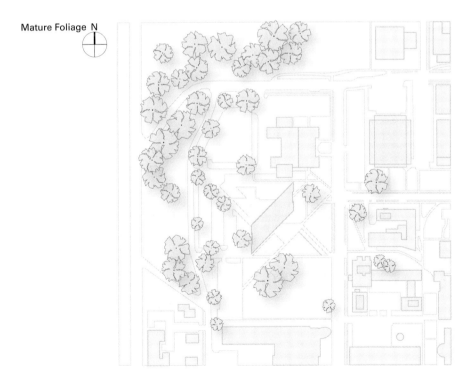

6.4
Site analysis may include information from landscape architects or arborists on plant types and locations.

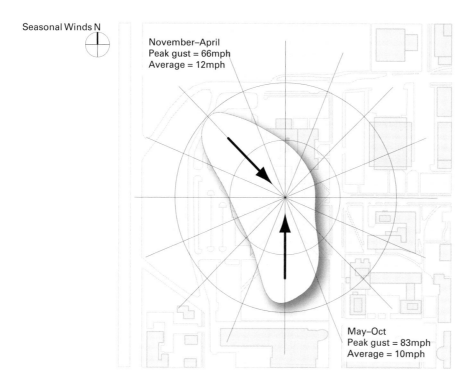

Seasonal Winds N

November–April
Peak gust = 66mph
Average = 12mph

May–Oct
Peak gust = 83mph
Average = 10mph

6.5
Understanding the local climate and microclimate is critical to producing an efficient building.

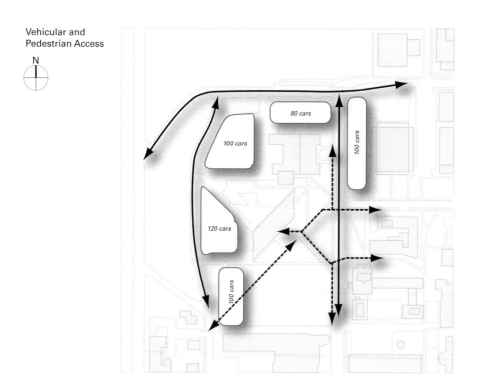

Vehicular and
Pedestrian Access

N

80 cars

100 cars

100 cars

120 cars

100 cars

6.6
Circulatory patterns on a site may provide important clues.

Service Access N

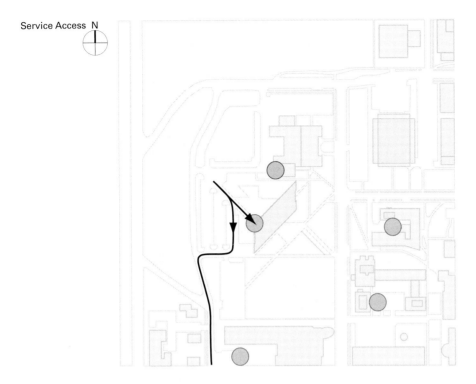

6.7
Service access is an important aspect of siting and program layout.

Solar Path N

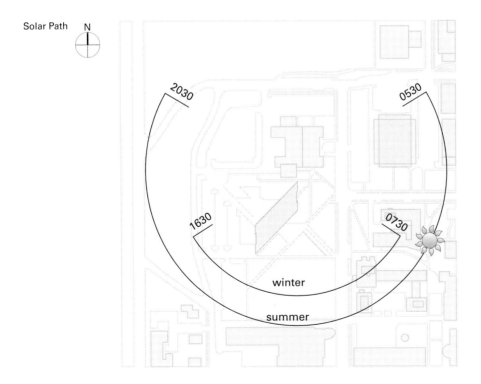

6.8
The sun's path around and over a site.

A good site analysis package will strive to convey the overall themes inherent in the site. (Is it automobile-intensive or pedestrian-intensive? Is there a consistent set of materials or styles in its neighbors? Are there portions of the site that offer greater civic presence? Are there opportunities to take advantage of the climatic patterns we've discovered?) It will do this by highlighting the most important information and by presenting an easily graspable graphics package. Consistency in the form of a regularly used set of underlays, a repetition of colors for like types of data, and visual cues that link information with graphic gestures can be helpful in establishing comparative methods—it can be easy to see parallels between various sets of data this way. By far the best models for good explanatory diagrams can be found in Edward Tufte's *Envisioning Information* (1990), which offers strategies for presenting data graphically in ways that are rigorously accurate and yet begin to tell the stories that we might otherwise leave for an accompanying narrative.

As this data is assembled, certain patterns may become evident—the site's solar orientation, for example, may suggest a major exterior space that happens to coincide with a good connection to local pedestrian networks. As often as not, of course, we will find sets of information that offer contradictory suggestions—there may be good pedestrian access in the same area that offers the best truck access, for example. In any event, it is now our responsibility to read potential design strategies from the developing large picture of site information. Often the best test of our analysis comes from preliminary schemes—massing, circulatory, or climatic—that will dredge up the inherent contradictions and overlaps in what the site tells us.

A typical site analysis package will include both graphic vignettes and an accompanying narrative. It will often parallel a similar package of program analysis. Both studies will present to the client a study of the forces at work on a design—from the inside out (program analysis) and from the outside in (site analysis). Both may suggest initial formal, massing, or circulatory strategies. Often, what we find from one may contradict the other. But these provide the clay from which the final design will be sculpted, and the contradictions we discover will invariably form the challenges of schematic design. Both sets of analysis are concerned with stating the problems of the project clearly; both speak to what the building will be made up from, and what it is designed to achieve. Because these studies are painstaking, they may well seem like they are taking precious time away from the bold gestures and forms that architects may want to jump into early in the process. But, properly executed, they offer the firmest footing for moving ahead. Understanding the external forces at work on a site early in the process is the surest step toward eliminating awkward or insensitive relationships with a project's neighbors.

TYPICAL INFORMATION CONTAINED IN A SITE ANALYSIS PACKAGE

Location: Information from client on-site's situation, its legal definition, its size and orientation, and understood jurisdictions.

Context: Photographs, drawings, and studies of surrounding buildings and spaces.

Geography: Documentation of land formations, bodies of water, soil composition (typically done by the client's consultants).

Flora: Information on plants on and around site.

Climate: Information on recorded weather patterns. May include temperature averages, rainfall data, wind speeds, and susceptibility to climatic extremes (hurricanes, tornadoes, etc.).

Circulation: Documentation of traffic patterns that affect the site. May include diagrams of automobile traffic, parking inventory, adjacency of arterial streets, rail lines, airports, etc. May also include detailed observations of pedestrian patterns around and across site.

Orientation: Position of site relative to solar path, prevailing winds, and views from and toward itself. Solar orientation is particularly important, as significant energy savings may be realized by a careful development of a design with daylighting and heating patterns in mind.

FURTHER READING

Tufte, E. (1990). *Envisioning Information*. Cheshire, CT: Graphics Press.

White, E. T. (1983). *Site Analysis: Diagramming Information for Architectural Design*. Tucson, AZ: Architectural Media.

7

SITE AND BUILDING ECOLOGY

Site analysis	Slope (building, planting, paving)
	Soil patterns
	Vegetation
	Wildlife
	Geology
	Surface and subsurface water
	Climate (based on topography)
Soils	Mechanics
	Types and properties
	Geotechnical engineering
	Drainage
	Contour drawings
	Cut and fill
	Wetlands
	Erosion/stabilization
	Topography and building form
Water movement	Precipitation
	Percolation
	Berms and swales (open systems)
	Pipe, inlet, catch basin, manhole (closed systems)
	Grade slopes for hard and soft surfaces

INTRODUCTION

All buildings have very specific natural relationships to their site. The most basic of these relationships are with the ground and the climate. The physical properties of a site not only affect what can or cannot be built there, but also what is appropriate to construct. As architects, we must know how to thoroughly assess a site—often very quickly. We also need to be able to judge the probable future conditions of a site—because we think in this way when designing a structure that does not exist yet, but will operate 20, 50 or 100 years forward in time.

From a purely functional point of view the ground plane of the site must do two things at a minimum; be capable of supporting the load of a building and keep water flowing away from the structure. Soil conditions and water movement have a tremendous impact on every design solution, and these factors frequently determine many of the design possibilities or limits of a project.

The notion that we, as humans, exist not just on the ground but also between the space of the earth and sky is made very apparent by the process of building. To place a building on the ground means that you must typically dig into the earth for support. The act of digging moves soil from one place to another—and it must be placed in a stable fashion or it will wash away. You are also replacing open permeable ground with something typically hard and impermeable (a building and site paving). This disrupts the flow of water into the ground and creates an imbalance that requires mitigation. Water must find its path from the sky into the ground in ways that allow environmental systems to function properly. In a sustainable natural system: rain falls onto the earth—nourishes plants, which cleanse the air—percolates into the ground, cleansing and filtering the water—establishes a consistent water table height and ground moisture/humidity level—travels to open water, replenishing streams and lakes—and re-evaporates starting the cycle again. You can see how interrupting this flow with roads, parking, and buildings could be detrimental to the overall environment (and your drinking water). To fully understand a site, a myriad of environmental conditions along with social and aesthetic concerns must be taken into account to make appropriate design decisions.

ENVIRONMENTAL SITE ANALYSIS

The first factor of site assessment is slope. Grade is rarely flat, even when it appears to be, and the amount plus the direction of the site slope often determines both the location and form of a project. In order to judge grade slope, a survey is done of the site, resulting in a scaled contour map that can be used to understand the shape of the land. This map becomes the basis for most site assessments, as it allows the three-dimensional forms to be collapsed into an easy-to-read plan format. The contour map needs to be augmented with photographs in order to judge the slope perceptually—often a difference of 15cm (6") in height can block a view or run water a different direction, and most contour maps use intervals from 0.3m (1') to 1.5m (5') in height. Also, it is very easy to over-abstract your perception of a site with plan drawings and be surprised when you see it in person.

Soil patterns are judged by type and depth. Soil types will be covered later but typically range from course rock to fine clays. Soils accommodate two different functions between surface and subsurface material. Soils on the surface determine plant growth possibilities, drainage capability, and erosion potential. Most surface soils can be roughly judged visually but may also need to be analyzed by a geotechnical engineer or horticulturalist. The soils below grade are judged by their ability to support building load (compressibility), further drainage capacity, plasticity (more plastic soils swell and heave with moisture or frost), underground pollution, and amount of organic vs. inert material. Organic materials cannot support load, due to their decomposition over time.

The existing vegetation on the site is included in most surveys. Soil patterns determine what is possible in the future. Existing plants are judged by size, condition, aesthetics, ability to tolerate construction or modifications to the site, and their compatibility with new or planned vegetation. It's also important to understand how the existing plants may stabilize or hold soil in position and promote drainage. Site plantings also tell you about the condition of the soil and what types of success future vegetation may have; often it's wise to maintain growth patterns and plant types that have been shown to be successful previously.

Existing wildlife is judged in terms of the importance of the site to their movement patterns, and whether the site is critical to their survival. This is not a common issue on many sites but is always important to note, particularly on rural sites or big planning projects.

Geology in site analysis deals with underground rock and soil layers. These can provide support for building foundations and limit the location of underground construction. Geotechnical engineers, who conduct soil borings and provide an analysis of the soils, rock and load-bearing capacity, do studies of subgrade conditions. They will also typically make recommendations on the type of suitable foundation systems for the proposed building.

Surface and subsurface water concerns deal with natural drainage and underground water table levels. Surface drainage can be judged in part through the contour drawings, but viewing the site in person shows the erosion potential of the water movement. Subsurface water is typically understood through the test borings done by the geotechnical engineer. Boring logs show the depth of the water table at various points on the site, and this typically indicates the maximum depth of building spaces without significant subsurface water mitigation.

Climate in relation to siting has been covered previously, but site slope, direction, shading, and ground cover are all parts of the physical properties of climatic site analysis.

SOILS

Soil mechanics describe the characteristics and performance of different types of soils under varying circumstances. In extreme situation soil conditions can make building impossible or cost prohibitive on a site. This is largely due to problems supporting a building, moving water away from foundations/basements, or site pollution.

Soil types and properties dictate the bearing capacity, frost action, and drainage of the site. The range of soil types runs from gravel to clay—the primary differences between the types are the size of particles making up the soil. The coarser and harder the particles, the better it is to build on. Larger particles (like gravel) have higher bearing capacity, little to no frost action, and excellent drainage. Smaller particles (such as clay or silt) shift and move under bearing loads, heave when frozen, and drain poorly. Poor soils often require foundation systems that go to the depth of the rock layer to obtain enough support (Table 7.1).

Determination of the properties of ground conditions for construction often requires the assistance of a geotechnical engineer. Geotechnical engineers offer both structural and groundwater advice by studying the surface and subsurface

Table 7.1 Soil types chart, showing the United Soil Classification System (USCS).

Type	Letter	Symbol	Description	Value as a foundation material	Frost Action	Drainage
Gravel and gravely soils	GW		Well-graded gravel, or gravel-sand mixture, little or no lines	Excellent	None	Excellent
	GP		Poorly graded gravel, or gravel-sand mixture, little or no lines	Good	None	Excellent
	GM		Silty gravels, gravel-sand-silt mixtures	Good	Slight	Poor
	GC		Clay-gravels, gravel-clay-sand mixtures	Good	Slight	Poor
Sand and sandy soils	SW		Well-graded sands, or gravelly sands, little or no fines	Good	None	Excellent
	SP		Poorly graded sands, or gravelly sands, little or no fines	Fair	None	Excellent
	SM		Silty sands, sand-silt mixtures	Fair	Slight	Fair
	SC		Clay-sands, sand-clay mixtures	Fair	Medium	Poor
Silts and clays	ML		Inorganic silts, rock flour, silty or clay-fine sands, or clay-silts with slight plasticity	Fair	Very high	Poor
	CL		Inorganic clays of low to medium plasticity, gravelly clays, silty clays, or lean clays	Fair	Medium	Impervious
	OL		Organic silt clays of low plasticity	Poor	High	Impervious
	MH		Inorganic silts, micaceous or diatomaceous fine sandy or silty soils, elastic silts	Poor	Very high	Poor
	CH		Inorganic clays of high plasticity, fat clays	Very Poor	Medium	Impervious
	OH		Organic clays of medium to high plasticity, organic silts	Very Poor	Medium	Impervious
Highly organic soils	Pt		Peat and other highly organic soils	Not suitable	Slight	Poor

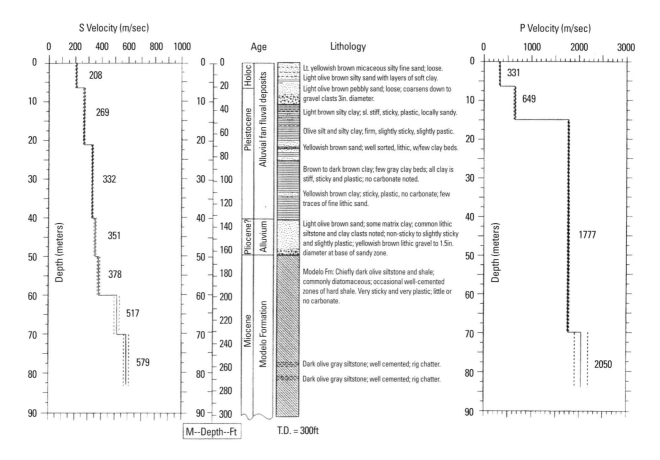

soils along with the rock layers below a site. They use a boring rig to drill, or drive a piling tube to pull soil cores out of the ground for study (Figure 7.1). These cores are examined and recorded in a boring log, which shows the type, depth, and condition of the soils below grade. The study of subgrade soils also determines whether the soils are *undisturbed*, meaning they are well-compacted load-bearing material and not recently deposited fill—"recently" in this case is in geological time and can mean anything less than a million years or so. Multiple borings are typically done in various places on the site to get a complete picture of the range of conditions. These borings go to various total depths depending on the type of building planned, often with big projects the borings are requested to go until they hit rock. Borings to rock depth make multiple attempts to run the bit to refusal. This assures that they are not hitting a thin plate of rock, but a large area of stone capable of bearing load.

Drainage through soils is dependent on the coarseness of the material. Gravels and sands drain well, and clays trap the moisture. This potential for moisture freeze and heave is most critical under the foundations of buildings, and is the reason foundations are always below the frost line. Fine soils that don't drain well also tend to shift and move, which can cause problems in areas close to buildings and under paved areas. In areas where clay is present you would normally specify a deeper layer of gravel and sand under slabs and foundations, and possibly additional drainage tiles as well.

Contour drawings are the tool used to study the surface shape of the site. Contour maps and plans are done by survey teams using transepts to mark the

7.1

Typical soil boring log, showing soil types and pressure required to drive the core to the specified depth.

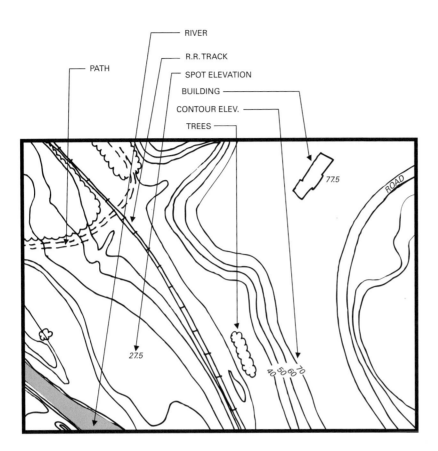

PATH

RIVER

R.R. TRACK

SPOT ELEVATION

BUILDING

CONTOUR ELEV.

TREES

77.5

ROAD

27.5

40 50 60 70

7.2
Contour drawing showing typical
range of site conditions.

variations in height across a site. These point heights are recorded relative to a relative datum height—some cities have standard datum points, other times sea level is used, sometimes the height of a fixed object on the site like a fire hydrant cap is used. The points are then joined into continuous lines that mark a level height across the site. The lines curve to follow the specified height, which is normally in 0.3m to 1.5m (1′ to 5′) increments (Figure 7.2). The more contours desired for precision, the greater the number of points that need to be surveyed. There are common databases available for site survey information, but conditions change so information should be verified as recent and accurate.

Cut and fill refers to the amount of soil removed from site areas and added to others during construction. Ideally the amount of soil removed or *cut* equals the amount added or *filled*. It makes little sense and creates unnecessary expense to truck dirt in or out of a site if it can be avoided. This supposes that the fill on the site is *clean*, or without contaminates, and is well compacted. Determining the amount of cut and fill is done by studying the original and proposed contours on a site plan and adjusting the location of the contours to equalize dirt movement amounts (Figure 7.3). Keep in mind that building foundations and basements can displace large amounts of earth depending on how deep they go.

Wetlands are designated low-lying areas where water collects and percolates into the ground. These areas need to be protected when developing a site because they are often the primary watershed destination for a large area

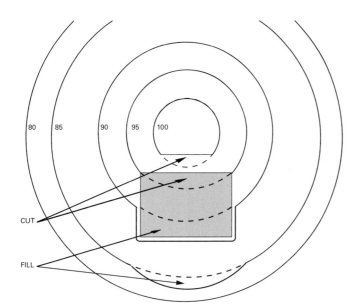

DETERMINING APPROXIMATE CUT AND FILL VOLUME

– using contour plan of before and after, calculate
   area between new and original contours
– multiply area by contour interval
– if cut or fill stops on a contour level, divide area
   in half

CONT.	CUT	FILL
85		200
90		400
95	300/2 = 150	
100	200	
	350(5') = 1750 cu.ft	600(5') = 3000 cu.ft

of land, and a problem is created when the water has no place to go. Wetlands are difficult to replace or move as their ecosystem and soil types have been naturally developed to manage water flow. Code requirements vary, but typically require no modification of wetlands or replacement with an area larger than the size of the original—this is because the new area is likely to be much less efficient at managing water flow. Flow patterns to wetlands also need to be maintained, so the water movement can reach the appropriate low-lying area.

Erosion of grade can occur very easily with even slight modifications to the existing conditions. The natural conditions of a site have usually achieved a balance with the slope, water movement, and vegetation holding the soil in place. When forming new slopes the *angle of repose* is the maximum slope that will not shift over time with water and soil pressure to a lower angle. The rule of thumb on this angle is 45 degrees, but that does not take into account erosion by water or wind, soil type, vegetation root systems or foot traffic (Table 7.2). Moisture in small amounts will percolate into the soil, but in larger amounts it will run down the slope taking small particles of dirt and vegetation along. This eventually creates rivulets and trenches that destabilize ground conditions and become progressively worse. The best way to combat erosion is to keep the slopes low and to prevent the water from channeling into a narrow run. Vegetation with substantial root systems, works most effectively in maintaining stable ground conditions, both holding soil in place and promoting water dispersion and percolation.

Topography and soil conditions can have a tremendous affect on building form. Steep slopes require the building to either float above the ground, dig into the ground, or a combination of the two (Figure 7.4). Even moderate and low slopes create opportunities for formal responses as the floors of buildings are almost always completely flat. Building entries and exits must all meet exterior grade as well. The flow of water across a site requires modifying the shape of the ground because all water must flow away from the building and this can be very difficult to accomplish. Subgrade soil conditions can affect form due to

7.3
Cut and fill calculations.

Table 7.2 Site slope recommendations.

Material	Minimum slope	Maximum slope	Recommended slope
Grass			
Lawn	1–100	1–4	1.5 to 10–100
Athletic	1–200	1–50	1–100
Walkways			
Direction of travel	1–200	1–8	less than 1:20
Cross slope	1–100	1–25	1 to 2–100
Accessible route max		1–12	
Accessible route, not a ramp		1–20	
Street			
Direction of travel	1–200	1–5	1 to 10–100
Parking	1–100	1–20	2 to 3–100

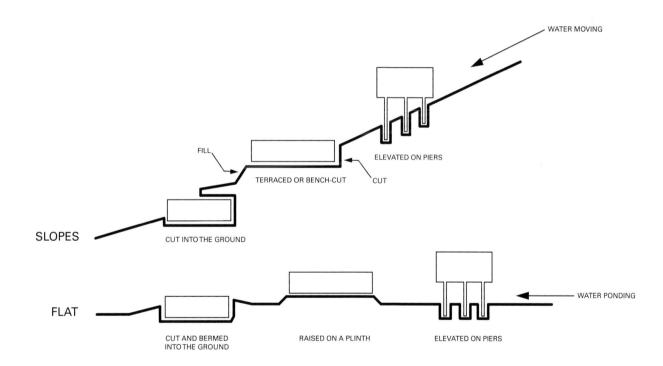

7.4
Building relationship to ground slope.

the type of foundation system required to support the building. Avoiding certain areas of the site because of wetland or water flow patterns also affects architectural responses to the site, and this is often an early part of the fundamental design process that begins with site analysis.

WATER MOVEMENT

Precipitation is the primary source of all water movement across a site (unless you're dealing with river or tidal conditions). The amount can vary, but the situations that cause buildings the most problems are the extreme ends of the spectrum—drought and storms. No rain for prolonged periods lowers the water table and can allow soil to shift and crumble. Storm waters are the bigger problem and move large amounts of water over the ground rapidly. This water can wash away the soil or, more significantly, run directly into buildings if not considered fully.

Percolation is water moving through the soil surface into the underground aquifer. When a new building is built, most site planning ordinances request that the project move water into the ground at the same rate as an undisturbed site. This means a variety of things, but mostly it requires the building keep its water on the site and not run it into the street or adjacent properties. Building roofs and paved areas cause immediate problems because they no longer allow for water percolation. This water must be sent to an area of the site where it can be collected and allowed to percolate into the site or run into the city storm sewers. Ground percolation and storm sewer systems can only handle a certain amount of load at one time, so retention ponds are often created on-site to hold the water—let it percolate over time—or run into the sewer through a restricted opening that has an allowable flow determined by code. In urban areas the retention areas can sometimes be bypassed, but storm sewers have a limited capacity. The other concern is that water moved to open water through pipes has lost its ability to naturally filter and clean itself through the ground, plus it has picked up pollutants from the paved areas. This begins a cycle of progressively worsening water quality, reinforcing the desire to keep as much water as possible percolating through the ground.

Berms and swales are open system methods of shaping the ground to move water into the ground. Swales are lower ground that focuses the water into an area to percolate into the ground. Channels can be cut to run water to retention areas, but bio-swale systems are typically preferred. Bio-swales distribute water to spread out areas that remove soil and pollution from groundwater runoff. Berms are raised ground that keeps the water away from a particular location, such as a building wall. Berms typically don't focus the water; rather, they simply discourage a direction of flow.

The pipe, inlet, catch basin, and manhole are components of a closed system method of moving water underground to a storm sewer. The inlet captures the water, sending it into an underground pipe. The pipe slopes to feed the water to the base of a manhole. This water then moves into the storm sewer system that intersects the manhole location. Catch basins typically sit at the curb line of a street and collect water from the open system gutter (Figure 7.5). Pipes can also be used to run water under a structure then bring the water back to an above-grade spreader that allows for site percolation.

Grade slope minimums are the least allowable angles that surfaces must maintain to keep water moving and to prevent ponding. This slope is a minimum of 2 percent for planted areas, with 3 percent minimum recommended. The minimum slope for paved areas is 0.5 percent, with 1 percent minimum recommended.

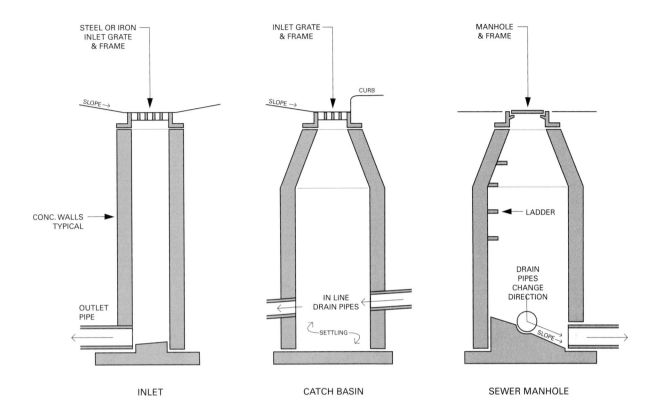

STEEL OR IRON
INLET GRATE
& FRAME

SLOPE →

CONC. WALLS
TYPICAL

OUTLET
PIPE

INLET

INLET GRATE
& FRAME

CURB

SLOPE →

IN LINE
DRAIN PIPES

SETTLING

CATCH BASIN

MANHOLE
& FRAME

LADDER

DRAIN
PIPES
CHANGE
DIRECTION

SLOPE →

SEWER MANHOLE

CONCLUSION

7.5
Inlet, catch basin, and manhole configurations.

Site ecology is the component of site analysis that deals with the physical condition of the ground you're building on. Most of these analysis skills need to become part of your integrated ability to see potential opportunities and liabilities quickly when looking at a site. Often architects are asked to look at a number of sites to assist the owners in making a decision of where to build. The factors covered here are the basics of what you are expected to know, and this does not include cultural and aesthetic issues regarding the site. Observe the physical conditions of sites you look at every day and begin to develop a mental reference of how to deal with a large variety of conditions. This skill, like most of the others you've learned about building technologies, must become part of a holistic integrated method of design that can weigh many factors at one time. You should be able to look at drawings of a site, visit the actual location, and then have an initial feel for how appropriate the site is for construction and where might be likely locations on the site to explore and avoid developing.

FREQUENTLY ASKED QUESTIONS

What makes a site unacceptable to build on?
Common site problems are poor or unstable soil conditions, contaminated soils, wetland areas that are too large to be avoided, slopes too steep, or difficulty of supplying basic services such as power, water, and electricity. Most of these conditions can be mitigated, but frequently the expense makes it more logical to find another place to build.

How can you tell how deep a building can go for underground spaces?
The primary concerns for the depth of underground spaces are the height of the water table and the depth of bedrock. In projects of any significant size (larger than a house) it is common to have a geotechnical engineer drill cores to judge site soil conditions. These borings show the height of the water table and depth of bedrock. The lowest floor normally wants to be above the highest level of the water table otherwise flooding is likely. This can be mitigated with sump pumps and waterproofing, but eventually every pump fails. The depth of bedrock is an indication of how difficult it is to excavate the site. While it is possible to dig out rock, the cost is normally prohibitive if another solution is available.

GLOSSARY

Berms and swales: Open system methods of shaping the ground to move water in a desired direction.

Cut and fill: Refers to the amount of soil removed from site areas and added to others during construction.

Geology: For construction this analysis deals with underground soil and rock layers used to support building loads.

Grade: The level of the ground surface of a site.

Grade slope minimums: 2 percent for planted areas, with 3 percent minimum recommended. The minimum slope for paved areas is 0.5 percent, with 1 percent minimum recommended.

Percolation: Water moving through the soil surface into the underground aquifer.

Pipe, inlet, catch basin, and manhole: Closed system methods of moving water under ground to a storm sewer.

Precipitation: Rain, fog, snow—the primary source of all water movement onto and across a site.

Soil types and properties: Dictate the bearing capacity, frost action, and drainage of the site.

Wetlands: Designated and often protected low-lying areas where water collects and percolates into the ground.

FURTHER READING

Hawkes, D., McDonald, J., and Steemers, K. (2002). *The Selective Environment*. New York: Spon Press; Chapter 8, Environmental Design Checklist, pp. 122–151.

Neufert, E. and Neufert, P. (2000). *Architect's Data*, 3rd edition. London: Blackwell Science; pp. 51–58.

Ramsey, C. G. and Sleeper, H. R. (2000). *Architectural Graphic Standards*, 10th edition. New York: John Wiley & Sons; Chapter 2, Sitework.

8

ZONING AND BUILDING CODES

Zoning codes	Uses and types
	Floor area ratios
	Massing and setbacks
	Connections—access and parking
Building codes	Fire codes
	Mechanical, plumbing, and the codes

INTRODUCTION

Building takes place in sociopolitical realms, in addition to the more obvious physical world. Government bodies are charged with ensuring that their physical environments—cities, towns, neighborhoods—are reasonably safe, and that individual developments enhance, rather than diminish, quality of life and property values nearby. Landowners' rights are not unlimited, and the legal ability to build tends to stop where it infringes on the rights or economic health of others.

Traditionally, landowners who were affected by construction or activity on an adjacent property could seek redress through nuisance laws, but the unpredictability of court rulings and the resulting patchwork of legal precedents could not keep pace with the development of complex urban development by the end of the nineteenth century. Formal regulations for construction and use began to appear in the 1880s, mostly as building heights in cities began to reach skyscraper dimensions. Property owners near tall buildings suffered from a lack of light and (it was claimed) ventilation. Tenement buildings in New York were among the first to meet municipal resistance, however; in response to deteriorating slum conditions, the city passed legislation restricting their height based on the adjacent street width. Around the same time, the first restrictions on usage appeared in San Francisco, where public laundries were banned from certain neighborhoods. The motivation for this legislation, however, had more to do with the city's burgeoning racial tension—laundries were typically owned by immigrants, and this regulation was struck down quickly. Zoning has, ever since, walked a fine line between a genuine concern for human safety and sanitation, and ulterior motives that range from the healthy desire to make a reasonable profit to barely concealed social and racial exclusion (see Amanda Erickson, "The Birth of Zoning Codes, a History," *The Atlantic*, June 19 2012).

Building height was the subject of restrictive codes in Chicago in 1894 and in New York in 1916. While Chicago adopted a strict height limit, New York's zoning code was based on a more sophisticated system of heights and *setbacks* that allowed buildings to rise higher in the center of their site than on the street edges. These setback regulations led to a recognizable New York type of sky-scraper, one that rose to a straight cornice along its edges with a higher, more or less pyramidal, massing within.

Court battles in the U.S. finally established the right of cities to legislate uses in the 1920s. The growing use of the automobile made zoning an economic priority as cities began to lose commercial and residential development to suburbs, and municipalities found themselves either competing for business and industry with more permissive codes, or for residential and small-scale commercial development that depended more on the quality of life factors that came with more restrictive zoning.

Europe has a stronger tradition of governmental control over building use and construction, and the adoption of modern zoning, more commonly referred to as Development Control, occurred in the post-World War II construction boom, during which urban rebuilding had to be coordinated to ensure efficient placement of amenities and commercial areas. Transportation infrastructure also played a major role in how new urban areas were planned and developed.

Municipalities also have an interest in ensuring that construction within their jurisdictions are neither fire nor safety risks. As firefighting is almost always a public service, cities and towns can require building owners to comply with standards of fire resistance that limit the risk to firefighters, and there is a com-pelling public interest in making sure that building fires cannot easily spread through crowded districts. Building codes, therefore, focus largely on issues of fire resistance, suppression, and escape (see Chapter 9). Additionally, the public interest is served by making sure that people can access amenities and busi-nesses regardless of their ability to walk, see, hear, climb stairs, etc. Building codes therefore also cover minimal standards for circulation that enable wheel-chair users and others with limited navigational or movement abilities to use buildings.

ZONING CODES

Most American zoning codes follow a "building block" model in which a municipality is divided into residential, commercial, and industrial districts (Figure 8.1). Each of these is subdivided according to density or particular usage. For example, most residential districts will be labeled "single-family" or "multi-family" depending on whether individual homes or apartments are being encouraged there. Zoning districts will exclude most other uses, so that a factory cannot be located in a residential zone, for instance (though it may also be in the municipality's interest to prevent lower-tax-paying residential uses from occupying a potentially more lucrative industrial area). Additional formulas

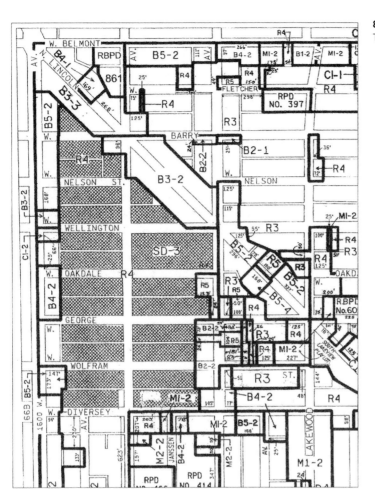

8.1
Typical zoning map for a large city.

for density and occupancy can create a fine-grained list of allowable occupancies, and the addition of "accessory uses" to districts can allow small variations to strictly allowable uses. To ensure that new construction is compatible with existing, most building block codes base important massing restrictions on the use and density allowed. These take the form of setback requirements from lot lines, streets, adjacent buildings, and/or sidewalks; height is also regulated based on zoning designation, as are lot sizes and the amount of lot covered by construction. A zoning designation will also require—and may limit—the amount of parking based on use and size.

Building block codes promote and ensure orderly development; they usually seek to push undesirable activities such as industry or roadside commercial, "strip" development away from more pleasant residential or commercial districts. In this sense, they have been remarkably successful in preserving the character, density, and quality of life in countless neighborhoods and downtowns. However, there are inherent problems with such a model. By pushing less desirable functions toward city edges, such codes encourage "sprawl," or the tendency for cities to grow uncontrollably at their perimeters. Segregation of residential and "working" zones also inherently separates workers from workplaces. These two tendencies have created cities that are more and more dependent on automobiles to move people from function to function. While

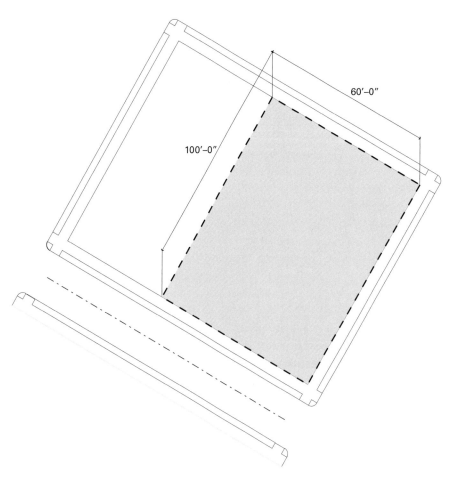

8.2
Lot lines will be designated in
municipalities' zoning or assessor
maps.

few would argue for mixing high-intensity industry with residential neighbor-hoods, the strict division of cities into such zones does tend to eliminate the liveliness and economic synergy that come with mixing mid-scale commercial and residential uses as happened naturally in pre-zoning era cities.

As a result, new experiments in zoning offer alternatives to such strict divisions. Some allow or encourage compatible uses to occur in proximity to one another in mixed-use developments, while others look to developers to propose mixtures of uses that will create this blended environment within a single, planned development.

While the use of a project will usually be determined before we're involved, designers must be aware of the limitations imposed by zoning codes on building massing. Most importantly, the zoning code may require us to set the building back from existing property lines, street centerlines, or neighboring structures (Figure 8.2). In residential districts, these setbacks may be considerable to ensure privacy and a sense of spaciousness along streets. In denser neighborhoods the setbacks will be more concerned with keeping the physical continuity of a streetscape, but fire safety will play a role as well; buildings that are constructed of combustible material, or walls with windows that are not fire protected (see Chapter 9) must be set back far enough from their neighbors that a fire in one building cannot easily spread to another. Additional requirements may include planting, parking, pedestrian walks, and limitations on signage size or configuration (Figure 8.3).

NO SETBACK REQUIRED
AT INTERNAL LOT LINE –
SEE BUILDING CODE FOR
FENESTRATION LIMITS

10'–0" SETBACK FROM
LOT LINE ON OAK ST.

55'–0"

80'–0"

5'–0" SETBACK FROM
LOT LINE ON 1ST AVE.

30'–0" SETBACK FROM
CENTRELINE OF MAIN ST.

8.3
Zoning will often require setback
or "build-to" lines that may
significantly alter the allowable
footprint of a building site.

A building's massing will be determined by a combination of these setbacks along with height limits and, particularly in dense urban areas, limits on floor area ratios. Height limits can be straightforward dimensions or numbers of stories, or they may involve more complicated formulas that are based on setbacks from a lot line or street centerline. In the latter case, zoning codes may give a "cornice height" limit at the edge of the site, while permitting taller construction within, as long as that construction stays within a setback angle from the cornice line. These restrictions are designed to maintain a humane scale along a street while allowing developers to maximize lettable area.

Floor area ratio (FAR) allows more flexibility in massing. These limits specify a total permissible area based on the size of the lot itself, and permit the developer to build to any height, as long as the total allowable area is not exceeded (Figure 8.4). So, for example, a site with an FAR of 16 would allow a 16-story building covering the entire site—or a 32-story building covering only half of it. Even though that would be a significantly taller structure, the open space on the remainder of the lot and the more slender proportions that resulted would effectively open up the streetscape and could offer an important civic amenity in the form of a park or plaza.

Floor area ratios also offer municipalities a way to provide incentives through multipliers. These allow developers to trade amenities such as public plazas, internal public circulation, or (in mixed-use developments) affordable housing for increased FARs. A typical incentive might be an addition of four or five to a designated FAR for street-level retail, for example. This would raise the FAR in the above scenario from 16 to 20, allowing a developer to build a 20-story building over the whole site, or a 40-story building over half of it. The city would benefit from a more lively streetscape, while the developer would gain additional rent from the increase in stories and, therefore, lettable space. Municipalities can

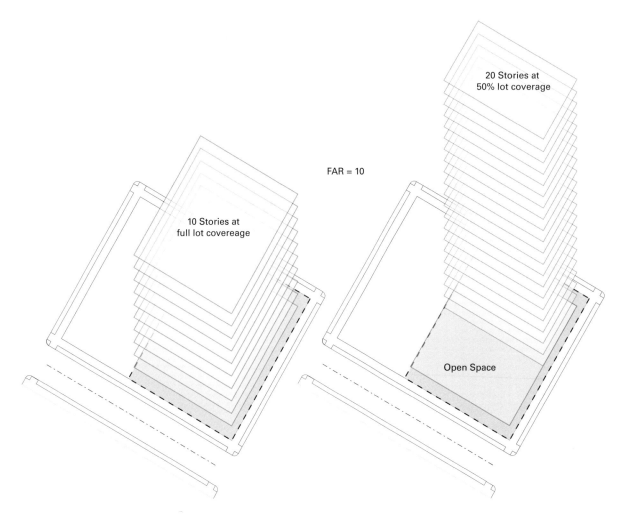

FAR = 10

20 Stories at
50% lot coverage

10 Stories at
full lot covereage

Open Space

8.4
Floor Area Ratio (or "FAR").

use these multipliers as leverage for other desirable outcomes such as historic preservation, increased energy efficiency, or architectural features that are consistent with the district's character (Figures 8.5 and 8.6).

Such tradeoffs can also allow developers to buy and sell air rights between sites. A church, for example, that has no intention of exploiting the allowable FAR above it might be able to sell the rights to that area to an adjacent development. In this scenario, the new development essentially uses the open space above an adjacent lot as the open space allowing it to grow taller. These tradeoffs can be quite lucrative for institutions located in dense commercial areas, allowing them to remain a part of the district's fabric while permitting developers to profit.

While these are all examples of "win-win" zoning, the reliance on FARs and incentives can have unintended consequences. An amenity that is "priced" too low can become overused. Plazas, for example, that might provide some necessary breathing space as an occasional break in the urban fabric, can quickly become empty, underused spaces that break up the continuity of a city street if they occur one after the other. Park Avenue in New York City is a good example of this. And if such incentives are universally underpriced, they can become irresistible enticements to overbuild, which can have dire consequences if supply of lettable space outstrips a district's demand.

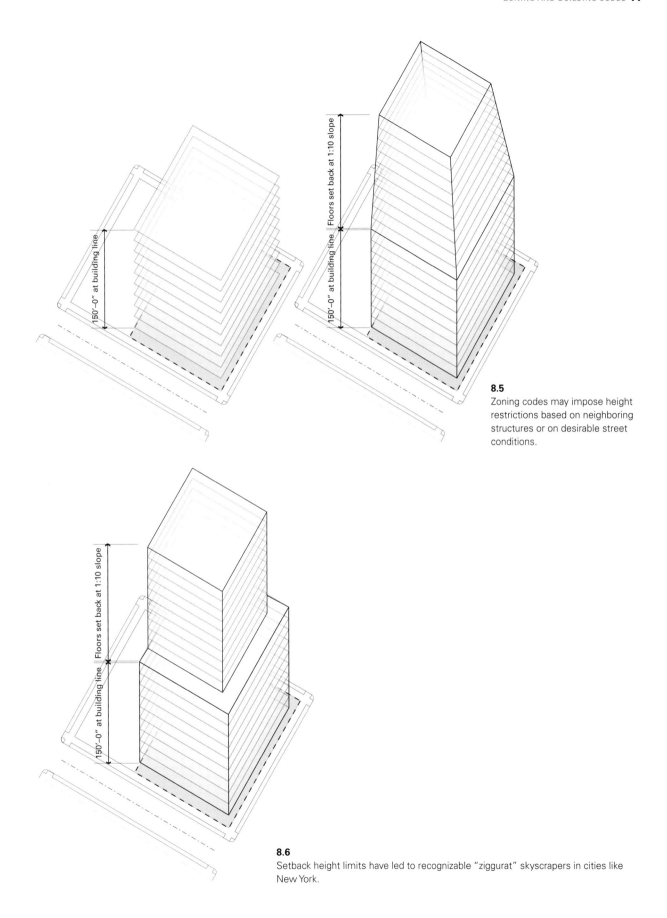

8.5
Zoning codes may impose height restrictions based on neighboring structures or on desirable street conditions.

8.6
Setback height limits have led to recognizable "ziggurat" skyscrapers in cities like New York.

More strategic approaches to zoning include performance-based codes, which demand a certain mix of populations and uses for large development areas, leaving it up to the developers to meet these targets however they see fit. So-called "Smart Codes" are really "form-based" codes, which allow a wide range of uses provided that the development conforms to certain massing and architectural restrictions. These are designed to create more aesthetically consistent neighborhoods while allowing a diverse mix of activities. Free market advocates, however, will often point to cities such as Houston, which has never had a zoning code, as evidence that real estate markets are to some extent self–regulating, though the results can lead to sprawl and to detrimental use adjacencies such as single-family houses backing up to tall commercial developments.

BUILDING CODES

Most of these issues are covered by local building codes. These are ordinances adopted into law by municipalities, counties, states, or nations that typically prescribe various parameters of building performance. Public authorities have an interest in making sure that buildings don't present undue hazards, both to their citizens and to their emergency response entities. Europe tends to operate by national codes, while America has long had a tradition of local authorities making their own code (Chicago and New York, for example), or adopting one of a number of commercially available building codes, often with some modifications to take into account local conditions.

Building codes are primarily concerned with fire (see Chapter 9), but municipalities also have interests in making sure that any building served by its fire and police departments meet minimum standards for electrical and structural work as well. Municipal water supplies and sewer systems also mean that towns and cities can regulate how plumbing systems use water and discharge waste, and their charge to ensure health, safety, and welfare means that they can also require minimum sanitation standards. Thus, in addition to regulating issues of construction and circulation relating to fire, municipal codes will almost always include electrical, plumbing, ventilation, and structural standards. Municipalities have the right to inspect new construction, and they may condemn buildings that do not meet code standards for issues of life safety.

This panoply of code information can be daunting. However, a design that understands the fundamental performance requirements of buildings in emergency situations will often meet the code just by adopting a logical approach. Indeed, there is a movement in some countries away from *prescriptive* codes, which require buildings to be designed to a rigid set of dimensional and material criteria, and toward *performance-based* code compliance, which requires designers to assert that their designs will perform correctly. While this adds liability to the design team, it allows for great flexibility in approaching life safety issues and is likely to lead to better solutions through evolution. Codes typically change in response to disasters, while performance-based solutions often evolve during design.

In addition to government-based building codes, there will often be a number of codes, both written and unwritten, to which building designs must comply.

Worker safety may be mandated by unions or by government labor departments. Buildings for a particular purpose—laboratories, for example—may be subject to design guidelines from public or institutional entities. Finally, insurance companies may require policy holders to design to standards beyond those of building codes. In fact, insurance companies have often been at the forefront of code development.

CONCLUSIONS

The legal framework in which architects design can be challenging, both in terms of keeping up to date on what codes will impact a building project, and in achieving the designs we and our clients desire while conforming to massing, construction, circulation, and services regulations offered by municipal codes. While it is possible to request and to receive variances from municipal officials, these are never guaranteed and the outcomes are not predictable. Few things impact on a design more than a previously unknown code provision that doesn't permit something we've planned on or worked with for months. Therefore, it is always worth the time and energy to make sure we are thoroughly familiar with the legal and regulatory environment that our projects occur within. If a project is slated for a new or unfamiliar municipality, it may be worth investing in a local code consultant to make sure that the project complies with all of the zoning and building code nuances there. In general, understanding the principles behind zoning and building code legislation at least lets us know what to look for: in a project's initial stages, we will want to make sure that we understand setback, massing, parking, and aesthetic criteria from the local zoning ordinance, and as a project progresses we will want to consult the local building code constantly as we consider construction types and circulation strategies.

FREQUENTLY ASKED QUESTIONS

Why are there limits on how much parking I can put on a site? Shouldn't there be as much as possible?
While adequate parking is a necessity for commercial and residential programs, cities have to balance the effects of parking lots on the fabric of downtown areas. Excessive parking means larger open spaces and less continuity in the urban fabric. Very dense cities may also want to intentionally limit the convenience associated with driving in order to encourage public transport use.

Can't I make alterations to my own house without the city getting involved?
Cities have an interest in maintaining minimum fire and life safety standards for three reasons. Most importantly, first responders are placed at risk when entering a private house that may not meet code. However, municipalities are also concerned with fire spread, meaning they can mandate separation and construction for any type of building to prevent large conflagrations. Finally, resale value is severely compromised by code shortcomings, and municipalities also have an interest in keeping average property values as high as possible.

GLOSSARY

Accessory use: An allowable use permitted only when attached to a larger, conforming use. A residential building, for instance, is usually allowed to have a home office as an "accessory use."

Building block zoning: Typical American zoning that divides municipalities into Residential, Commercial, and Industrial uses (among others). These will be subdivided further into density or finer grained allowable use districts. Also called *Euclidean* zoning after the town of Euclid, OH, whose zoning law was first upheld by the Supreme Court in 1926.

Floor area ratio: A measure of allowable development on a site based on a multiplier (FAR) of the site's footprint. A site, for example, with a total area of 50,000 square feet (5000 square meters) and an FAR of 6 could permit a building of 30,000 square feet in total.

Planned unit development: A large development with multiple uses, subject to overall performance-based zoning.

Setbacks: Mandatory minimum distances between any construction and a lot line, a street center-line, or an adjacent building. Can also refer to massing requirements that require construction above a given height to taper away from streets or public ways.

Smart codes: A zoning approach that focuses on massing, aesthetics, and walkability instead of usage.

FURTHER READING

Erickson, Amanda (2012). "The Birth of Zoning Codes, a History," *The Atlantic*, June 19.

PART 3

CIRCULATION

9

LIFE SAFETY

Basic building safety	Building integrity
	Fire containment
	Occupant notification
	Escape
Emergency egress	Occupancy load
	Exiting
	Distance
	Elements

MAKING BUILDINGS SAFE

A prime responsibility of architects is that of designing out dangerous conditions. Overwhelmingly, we're concerned with what happens in the event of fire, but life safety also covers a variety of daily issues such as falls, collisions, and air quality.

LIFE SAFETY—THE BASICS

Our overwhelming life safety concern as architects is fire. Over 3000 Americans typically die in house fires each year, and fire can kill or injure by both burning and (more commonly) asphyxiation. Unfortunately, many of the same qualities that make our buildings work—partitioning, enclosure, and security, for example—make them more dangerous in a building fire (Figure 9.1).

We generally have four strategies for ensuring that occupants in our buildings face minimal danger from fire (Figure 9.2). First, we concentrate on *building integrity*; that is, making sure that the building's structure and fabric remain intact for as long as possible during a fire. Second, we lay out buildings to provide *containment*, preventing the fire from spreading uncontrollably. Third, our buildings must *notify* occupants of the dangerous situation, and fourth, the layout must enable occupants to *escape* the danger quickly and safely.

9.1
Building fires—especially in multistory buildings—are usually the gravest danger facing occupants.

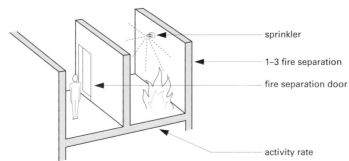

sprinkler

1–3 fire separation

fire separation door

activity rate

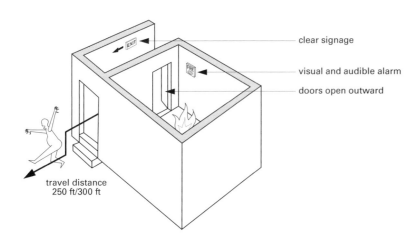

clear signage

visual and audible alarm

doors open outward

travel distance
250 ft/300 ft

9.2
Basic strategies to minimize the danger of fire in buildings.

Building integrity involves the selection of materials and systems that maintain their protective and functional characteristics even in the event of a major fire. Generally, larger-scale buildings must be built of more robust materials, while smaller buildings permit more flammable construction. Typically, codes require certain types of construction based on the anticipated use of the building—often referred to as the *occupancy type*—as well as the building's size and/or height. The more dangerous the building type, or the larger or taller the building, the more conservative the code is likely to be. This is based on scale and economics—houses, for example, would be prohibitively expensive to construct in only noncombustible (i.e. not wood) materials. Codes allow that, since a smaller number of people would be put in danger from a single-family house fire, requirements need not be as stringent as for, say, a skyscraper.

The level of integrity for a given type of construction is measured in hours. This suggests the amount of time that a particular structure or component will survive a typical building fire. However, in practice, this may not arise directly from testing. Materials and their typical performance rating are given in Table 9.1. In addition to rating components by hours, some codes will further distinguish between "noncombustible" and "combustible" construction, essentially dividing types into those that provide fuel for fire (wood) and those that don't (steel and concrete).

Steel, however, presents particular issues of building integrity (Figure 9.3). While it will generally not ignite in building fires, it is susceptible to softening

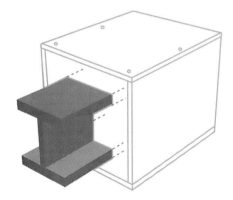

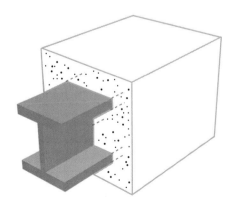

9.3
Building integrity mandates protective coverings for vulnerable structural materials.

and eventually melting if the surrounding fire is hot enough. Large building fires can produce temperatures as high as 1000C (1800F). Steel loses half of its strength at around 650C (1200F) and begins actually *melting* at 1370C (2500F). Particularly in tall buildings, therefore, steel must be somehow protected and insulated from the heat of a fire. This can be achieved by wrapping it in another material such as gypsum board, spray-on fireproofing, or terra cotta.

Once a fire has begun, our primary concern becomes *containment*—minimizing the danger area and preventing the fire from spreading. This can be accomplished in two ways: *passive containment* relies on the integrity of the building's partitioning system to keep the fire compartmentalized, while *active containment* seeks to actually suppress the fire and to put it out.

Compartmentalization relies on robust floor, wall, and ceiling assemblies that will prevent a fire from spreading from one space to another. Keeping compartments relatively small ensures that the fire will have a limited fuel supply, thus controlling its temperature. At the same time, a properly assembled fire container will give occupants in adjacent areas time to evacuate the building and firefighters time to begin their operations. As with building integrity, fire containment relies on building elements that are fire rated, usually in hours. Depending on the danger inherent in one building program (storage of flammable liquids, for example), a room or space may trigger a containment requirement. Materials and assemblies range in their performance widely, with concrete providing the best inherent fire separation, followed by masonry, drywall and timber.

Multistory spaces in buildings—for example, atria—present particular concerns for fire safety, as they can serve as a conduit for rapid fire spread and can be easily mistaken for safe fire exiting by occupants (Figure 9.4). Nevertheless, they are often architecturally important elements for orientation, daylighting, etc. To ensure their safety, spaces opening into atria must generally be fully sprinklered, reducing the risk of fire and smoke getting into the space in the first place. Fully fire-resistant walls must separate occupied areas from the atrium itself, and exiting must typically take evacuees *away* from the atrium rather than toward it. Finally, most codes require active smoke evacuation from large atrium spaces (note that this will usually cause extreme air balancing problems and may suck lobby doors shut).

Active suppression usually involves a piped supply of water at high pressure and sprinkler heads located at regular intervals throughout a building area (Figure 9.5). Sprinkler heads rely on heat-sensitive connections to hold a valve closed. If this melts, the valve springs open and water from the piped supply drenches the affected area. Various designs for sprinkler heads can create different patterns of water diffusion, but in most cases sprinklers must be located at approximately 15' (5m) intervals to be truly effective. Additional care must be taken to ensure coverage in corners and where built-in furniture or level changes in ceilings may "shade" floor areas from a sprinkler's pattern. While sprinklers are effective (the industry claims that there has never been a fatality due to fire in a building with operable sprinklers), they present a constant threat of accidental discharge, which can damage finishes and contents beyond salvage. In programs with valuable or water-sensitive holdings (e.g. computer server rooms or art galleries), so-called

ATRIA

PROBLEMS

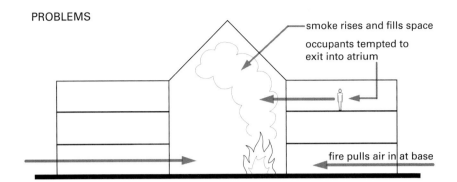

smoke rises and fills space

occupants tempted to exit into atrium

fire pulls air in at base

SOLUTIONS

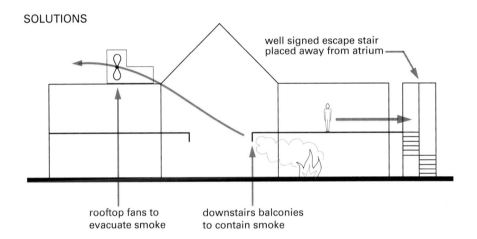

well signed escape stair placed away from atrium

rooftop fans to evacuate smoke

downstairs balconies to contain smoke

9.4
Buildings with atria present particularly serious fire and escape issues.

"dry" sprinkler systems may be installed. These may connect to an empty pipe system that is charged by arriving firefighting crews, or to a supply of suppressive gas, usually Halon, that replaces the oxygen in the affected area and thus starves the fire. Note that this last option creates a life-threatening condition itself, and thus must be accompanied by an alarm and an adequate time delay to ensure that occupants can safely leave the area before it discharges.

Notification lets building occupants know there is a dangerous situation (Figure 9.6). This can be as simple as a battery-powered smoke alarm, which senses abnormal densities of particulates in the air and sets off an attention signal. The most sophisticated notification devices, however, can analyze information from different areas of the building and can inform occupants of the best course of action using public address or signals.

Finally, *escape* is the aspect of life safety that most affects our designs. All buildings must have a circulation system that foresees a threatening situation that requires rapid exiting. In some cases this will be coincident with the main functional circulation, but in larger buildings we often have to provide dedicated emergency exiting that allows occupants to efficiently and safely evacuate. Here, we must be concerned with the safety of the route itself, and whether

ACTIVE SUPPRESSION

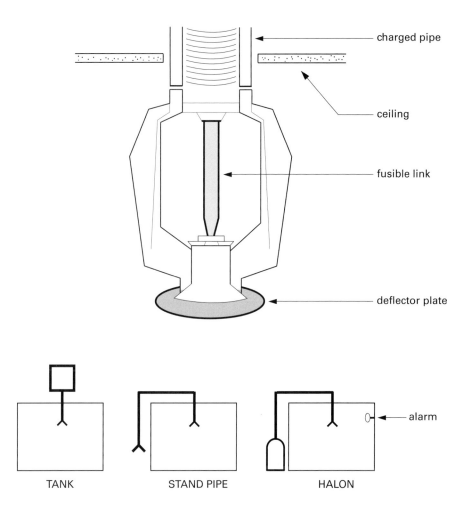

charged pipe

ceiling

fusible link

deflector plate

TANK   STAND PIPE   HALON

alarm

it can be protected adequately from an unpredictable fire that may be burning near or around it, in addition to the speed at which people can move through it and the capacity of the area into which it leads. We must also think ahead and ensure that there is never even the possibility that this route could be accidentally blocked, closed off, constricted, or otherwise encumbered. Escape routes from buildings typically involve elements that we recognize instantly—fire stairs and fire exits, for example. However, as designers we must always consider the entire occupiable building as a potential exiting path.

Fire safety is one of the great success stories of western building construction. It is exceptionally rare for a large building fire in Europe or America to cause fatalities, and these usually result from failures to adhere to the local building codes in design, construction, or usage. This has not always been the case, but such recent examples as the Torre Windsor building fire in Madrid (2005), the MINFRA tower fire in Caracas, Venezuela, and the Field Building fire in Chicago (both 2004), all of which damaged large areas of building while

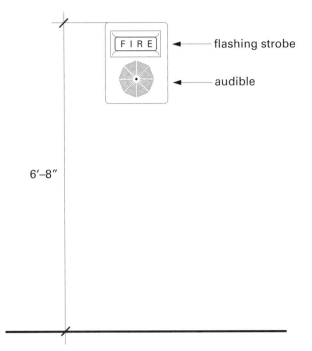

6'–8"

flashing strobe

audible

9.6
Notification must typically take two forms in public buildings—visible and audible.

causing no deaths or serious injuries, point to the great success of fire codes in the twentieth century.

BUILDING EVACUATION

Because of its direct relationship to architectural design, it is worth focusing in some detail on the mechanics and operations of a building's circulation system in a fire. Successful evacuation relies on the above life safety requirements (building integrity, fire containment, and adequate notification) *and* an awareness of the particular circumstances likely to occur in the event of an emergency. Specifically, human nature often results in irrational behavior during a life-threatening event, and buildings that moments before were simply going through their day-to-day operations must suddenly be adequate to safely accommodate large crowds of frightened, often panicking, occupants moving at high speeds. When deaths due to fire occur, they are often attributable to exit routes that are either unclear or inadequately sized for the number of evacuees involved.

Most prevalent amongst building codes is a concern for the *number* of exits for a given space or building. For a room of any size, it is good practice to provide at least two distinct exits spaced well apart from one another. If a fire blocks one exit, the other should be immediately available, visible, and accessible from all parts of the space. A good rule of thumb is that any two exits should be spaced so that the linear distance between them is more than half of the space's largest diagonal dimension (Figure 9.7). For spaces with higher populations, codes may require more than two exits; generally a third exit is required

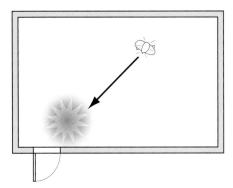

A single exit from a room is a potentially hazardous condition, as the exit may be blocked by fire.

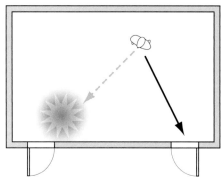

A second exit from a room, if properly placed, offers an alternative exit. This is usually required for occupancies over 50 persons, but is good practice in all circumstances. Larger occupancies may require a third exit.

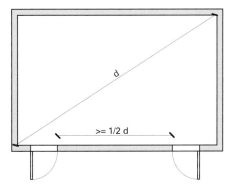

A good rule of thumb (often required by code) is to separate fire exits by at least half the largest diagonal dimension of the space being served. This ensures that no single fire can immediately block all exits.

once the anticipated population reaches 500, while a fourth exit will typically be required once 1000 persons are expected in a space. In addition to number, safe exiting must take into account the exit width. Many early fires (especially the Iroquois Theater Fire in downtown Chicago in 1903) resulted in fatalities despite having numerous exits. When ordered, crowds can move relatively quickly through well-designed spaces. However when panicked, crowds will compress, making movement difficult and often blocking otherwise adequate doorways in particular. A safe width for exiting must take into account the "tributary" effect of evacuation, as more and more people join a flow toward stairs or doorways.

Generally, life safety codes will again require buildings to be classified by use, and will offer floor area ratios to determine the likely population, or *occupancy* of a given room or area. Note that these are often quite conservative estimates as they assume that a fire will occur at a time of maximum occupancy (this is, in fact, often the case). Frequently, codes will also give a cutoff point at which two exits must be provided, often 50 persons. However, it should be kept in mind that good practice suggests leaving two exits for any significant space; while a single office is small enough to allow rapid exit through one door, even a small meeting room for ten persons could merit a more robust exiting strategy.

9.7
The need for two exits in heavily occupied spaces.

Once the occupancy is determined, minimum widths are generally assigned based on a linear measure per occupant. A typical figure given is 0.5cm (0.2") per person. An exit for a room holding 300 occupants in this scenario would require a width of:

$$300 \text{ persons} \times 0.5\text{cm} (0.2") \text{ per person} = 150\text{cm} (60")$$

Note that this requires that a *clear width* to serve the calculated population for the entire exiting process. Thus all doors, corridors, ramps, etc. along the exit path would need to be 150cm clear. There is occasionally an exception made for door jambs or handrails, which may be allowed to impede the required width by a small amount. For areas of relatively low occupancy, an absolute minimum width is usually required, often 1110cm (44") in the United States. This figure will govern if the occupancy is small, say only 20 persons:

$$20 \text{ persons} \times 0.5\text{cm} (0.2") \text{ per person} = 10\text{m} (4")$$

Here, one can immediately see that the width calculation won't give a realistic figure, and the absolute minimum width must be used. Some circulation elements, particularly stairs, may require a slightly wider width multiplier and/or absolute minimum width. This takes into account the slower pace occupants are likely to take while negotiating stairs and typically boosts the multiplier to 0.75cm (0.3") per person.

For reasons of both fatigue and panic behavior, travel distance to a point of safety must be minimized. Generally, no exiting path may exceed 75m (250') of travel distance in an unsprinklered building, or 90m (300') in one that is sprinklered (Figure 9.8). Note that this precludes the use of unprotected ramps and stairs as part of an exiting route, as the distances they add to traverse a vertical story will often push the total over the allowed limit.

There are common circumstances, however, in which stairs in particular can be excluded from the travel route, essentially forming an "exit" that can serve as the end of a 75m (250') escape path. If the stair is protected by a robust, fireproof enclosure (usually concrete), if it maintains an acceptable

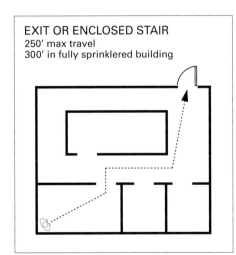

EXIT OR ENCLOSED STAIR
250' max travel
300' in fully sprinklered building

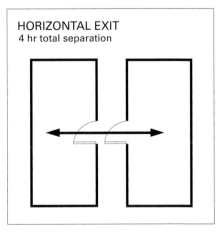

HORIZONTAL EXIT
4 hr total separation

9.8
Code-mandated travel distances must assume actual routes through rooms and corridors.

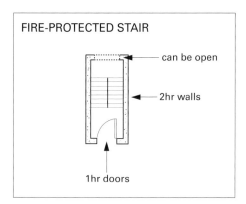

width throughout its travel, if it provides adequate landings, and if it discharges directly to an exterior space, a stair may be termed a *fire stair*, and most codes assume that the travel distance ends once occupants are protected by this construction (Figure 9.9). This is critical for high-rise construction, as very tall buildings may require up to half a mile of travel back and forth along flights of stairs to exit from top floors (see Chapters 10 and 11, Accessibility, and Stairs and Ramps for further information).

Exits must have adequate *discharge space* once they leave the building. Usually codes require exits to open onto outdoor, public space, although some exceptions permit exiting into yards or courts, provided these again have a clear connection to public walkways, streets, etc. Some high-rise codes permit stairs to exit into a fireproof corridor on the ground floor that leads to a street, thus permitting stairs to be contained within a central core. On rare occasions, some exiting from stairs may be permitted into a building lobby; while convenient, this is not good practice as conditions in the lobby will not be knowable from upper floors, where occupants make their decision about escape routes.

Some considerations when designing for exiting include the following:

Exit travel must be intuitive and unimpeded; therefore any doors (in corridors, to staircases, etc.) must open in the anticipated direction of escape. To prevent crushing, these doors must have *panic hardware* installed that will automatically unlock and open if hit or pressed. Panic hardware must extend across the full width of the door, and is best located at waist level, between 36" and 42" above the floor so that the body's center of mass will contact it. Arms and hands may well be trapped against other parts of the door (Figure 9.10).

Stairs leading to basements must have clear indications at the ground floor that evacuees should not continue down further, but should exit the stair there. Many codes require a physical gate to prevent panicked occupants from running into the basement, but in practice these are often left open to avoid inconvenience. No matter what the code, signage at the exiting level is good practice.

Common sense suggests that occupants not be forced to exit through areas
of danger (storage, kitchens, machine rooms, factory floors). While codes will
often prohibit individual instances of this, good practice again requires architects to consider likely evacuee behavior and to guard against accidental circulation into these areas.

Despite our best efforts, occupants will often evacuate a building through
the same route that brought them in—whether or not there is a more convenient or safer path. Codes often require that a building's "main" entrance thus be
sized to allow half of the building's population to escape through it.

Elevators are notoriously prone to failure during building fires. Worse, they are
likely to get stuck at floors that are fully ablaze. Therefore, elevators may never
count as code exits and usually must be disabled when a building alarm goes

off, returning immediately to the ground floor and waiting there. Firefighters may then use a special key to unlock the cabs' mechanisms in order to gain access to the affected areas.

CONCLUSIONS

A building's circulatory design is an important aspect of its architectural impact. Very often we want to use these spaces to celebrate the building's functions or connections. Yet fire codes are rigorous in how these spaces may be used or configured; codes often prohibit furniture or storage in any designated exit route. It is worth considering a second circulatory system in large buildings dedicated to fire escape. This may consist of stairs with dedicated uses, or networks of corridors that are not accessed during typical daily operation. While this may seem wasteful of space and resources, the inherent safety of a properly designed exiting system may allow other, purely architectural circulatory elements to be arranged and developed according to different requirements.

At the same time, the requirements of life safety systems may align with architectural desires. Fire stairs, for example, may be worthy elements of expression in an overall architectural massing strategy as they provide both vertical emphasis and (if expressed or clad on the outside in glass) natural human scale. Renzo Piano's headquarters building for Debis in Berlin, Germany, for example, uses a main fire stair as a metaphorical "prow", offering a distinctive finish to the building mass (Figure 9.11). Life safety systems, while notoriously onerous in their requirements are, like so many other aspects of building design, best considered early in the process, when their particularities may be absorbed into an overall architectural strategy.

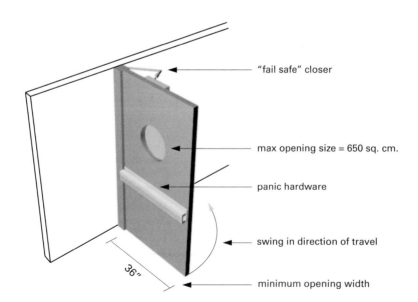

"fail safe" closer

max opening size = 650 sq. cm.

panic hardware

swing in direction of travel

36"

minimum opening width

9.11
Exit doors have particular requirements to ensure their proper operation during a fire.

FREQUENTLY ASKED QUESTIONS

Are codes absolute? Or if my design falls just outside of the code's parameters, will it be rejected by code officials?
Compliance with codes is interpreted by government and/or institutional officials. Often, municipalities will permit these officials to issue variances that permit single instances of non-compliance. However, this does not necessarily come with a waiver of responsibility for the designers, and in the event of a fatality or injury due to fire the design's non-compliance may expose the design team to significant legal risk.

Can fire walls include glass?
For low fire ratings (1 hour, in particular) walls and doors may have limited amounts of glass. However this must typically be wire glass, which provides additional structural integrity in a fire. Glass products that use chemical interlayers for additional fire resistance are also available and may provide significant protection for larger areas. However this comes at additional expense, which may limit its acceptability.

How do wheelchair users evacuate a multistory building in a fire?
Most codes assume that wheelchair users can be assisted or carried down short runs of stairs. However, for buildings above three stories, there are code requirements for additional space within fire stair enclosures large enough for one or two wheelchair parking spaces. These provisions assume that rescue will come within the rated time for these enclosures and that these occupants can be carried by firefighters.

Why do most elevators in newer buildings have fire doors in front of them? Is this to keep people from using them in a fire?
Recent codes recognize the potential for elevator shafts to act as very efficient fire chimneys, particularly given their lightweight doors and tall, narrow spaces. Large buildings will often have fail-safe closer doors that will activate and seal off elevator lobbies from occupied or potentially combustible areas to prevent fire infiltration into vulnerable elevator shafts.

Why shouldn't I use fire sprinklers in hotel rooms to hang clothes? Is this a safety issue?
Not so much. Most sprinklers contain a small, fragile vial of liquid that, when heated, expands rapidly, breaking the vial and eliminating the only barrier to a fully pressurized pipe system behind. Hangars are notorious for breaking this vial and deluging hotel rooms.

GLOSSARY

Active containment: Fire control strategy relying on mechanical systems (usually piped water) to suppress fire.

Building codes: Regulatory documents that restrict construction to established, safe practices. May be *prescriptive*, giving detailed dimensional and/or material criteria, or *performance-based*, requiring design teams to assert acceptable levels of building performance.

Building integrity: The element of life safety design that emphasizes the reliability of the building's structure and fabric during a fire or other hazardous situation.

Clear width: A measure of an escape component's capacity. Often determined by multiplying the worst-case anticipated occupancy by a code-specified width (typically 2″ or 5cm per person), but generally no less than 44″ (112cm) for corridors and stairs.

Containment: The element of life safety design that discourages fire from spreading.

Discharge space: A public or open area that is sized to accommodate the escaping population of a building.

Escape: The element of life safety design that enables occupants to physically remove themselves from hazardous situations.

Fire resistance: The ability of a component or material to withstand fire without burning or transmitting dangerous amounts of heat. Usually determined in laboratory settings.

Fire stair: A staircase that meets all code requirements for access and is separated from any occupied or potentially hazardous area by a significant fire-resistive wall (usually 2 hours or more).

Notification: The element of life safety design that alerts occupants of a hazardous situation

Occupancy type: Classification of a building or building space based on its perceived use. Specified by most building codes as a means of assessing integrity and escape requirements.

Panic hardware: Bars and latches on doors that enable operation by pressure instead of turning. Usually required by codes on doors in fire exits or corridors to prevent panicking crowds from piling up against them.

Passive containment: Fire control strategy relying on the fire-resistive nature of construction materials to contain fire.

Travel distance: The length of a path drawn from a room to the first place of fire refuge— usually an exterior exit or fire-protected staircase. Typically limited by codes to no more than 250′ or 75 meters, occasionally more if the building is fully provided with sprinklers.

FURTHER READING

Allen, E. and Iano, J. (2002). *The Architect's Studio Companion: Rules of Thumb for Preliminary Design*, 3rd edition. New York: Wiley; Chapter 1, Designing with Building Codes, pp. 3–14.

10

ACCESSIBILITY

Accessibility	Definitions
	Legal history
Anthropometric data	Basic parameters of wheelchair dimensions
	Fine grained data—grips, etc.
Accessible design	Principles
	Requirements
Stairs	Rise and run
	Code and ADA requirements
	Detail design—treads, handrails, landings, and guardrails
Ramps	Code and ADA requirements
	Detail design—surfaces, handrails, and landings

INTRODUCTION

In designing for the "general public," the profession has had a history of leaving a significant percentage of that public out, either providing routes that are inaccessible to some or making circulation and function within a building difficult for others.

Nearly one in five Americans and Europeans are unable to fully negotiate or use architectural configurations designed for the average occupant. Disabilities come in a variety of forms, and increasingly our profession is charged with creating inclusive environments that restrict fewer individuals from the spaces we design.

There is a long legal history behind the current standard of "universal" or "accessible" design. Prior to World War II, there was no federal legislation making discrimination against persons with disabilities illegal. As veterans who had been wounded or disabled returned, and as medical care increased both quality and quantity of life for those with disabilities, a movement grew seeking protection against discrimination in hiring. However it was not until 1964 that the federal government took up the problem of environmental discrimination. Employers could still prevent people with disabilities from working, however unintentionally, by providing inaccessible environments and workplaces.

Legislation through the 1960s and 1970s required federally funded buildings to comply with a short list of architectural standards designed to remove barriers to users of wheelchairs. An ANSI standard was developed to provide reliable standards of design. However, the federal government's efforts did not apply to the private sector, and civil rights advocates continued to press for comprehensive accessibility legislation.

THE AMERICANS WITH DISABILITIES ACT—THE LEGAL CLIMATE IN AMERICA

In 1990, the ADA was signed into law, extending civil rights protection to roughly 43 million Americans with disabilities. It covered broad areas of employment, public services and accommodations and housing.

While the ADA has provided a much needed change in opening up jobs, activities, and environments for people with disabilities, it has had numerous critics—not for its intent, but rather for its mechanism. Because the ADA is civil rights legislation, it is enforced by civil courts. Every place of employment or public accommodation must comply directly with the quantitative information of the ADA, under threat of lawsuit from potentially injured parties.

In the United States, compliance is mandatory for all employers, government agencies, and "privately operated establishments in which the public are served." These entities must make "reasonable accommodations" for any person with a disability. Case law has generally required *any* new construction for these entities to comply with ADA and for *existing* construction to be modified on an as-needed basis. Renovation of an existing building is a tricky situation. These projects will generally be required to provide "reasonable" accommodation.

Note that virtually the only completely exempt building type is single-family residential housing. Even this, however, has become the subject of code requirements. "Visitability" is an important idea in residential design, encouraging at least one accessible entry and a suite of rooms (including a toilet room) that can be easily negotiated by wheelchair users.

Other building types pose different challenges. Sports arenas and theaters, for example, present particularly tricky design problems because of their sloped seats. It is generally not practical to allow accessible routes to every seat in a theater, but it is also discriminatory to cluster all accessible seating at the front or at the rear. Strategies that offer some variety in locations, views, access to ancillary spaces, and ticket pricing have all been successfully employed in these types of project.

Society has demanded an increased awareness and response to accessibility issues. Thus, like life safety codes, we propose to offer basic strategies that can be incorporated early in the design process, eliminating "retrofit" solutions and inevitable frustration later on.

UNIVERSAL DESIGN—GOOD PRACTICE

"Accessible Design," "Disabled Design," and "Handicapped-Accessible" are all problematic terms as they imply a special effort being made for users of wheelchairs and other disability-specific equipment or components. Recently the term "Universal Design" has been used as a way of pointing out that our buildings should incorporate accessibility principles as a matter of course. "Clip-on" solutions are not only aesthetically problematic; they stigmatize and separate occupants with disabilities. The "stair lift" is a prime example of this. Users of wheelchairs must operate loud machinery to travel a short distance, while their companions who can walk must wait for them to be lifted into place. (Often these require a key or assistance from a security guard, thereby heightening the problem.) A better solution would be to find ways to take up—or eliminate—small changes in level, making the experience of the building the same for all users.

With that in mind, recall some basic anthropomorphic dimensions (see Figure 10.1). Allowing for wheelchair passage in corridors, for example, is relatively simple—910mm (36") provides enough clearance for operators to comfortably maneuver. Obstructions that limit this distance to 810mm (32") for brief periods are also acceptable. However, most corridors must accommodate people traveling in both directions. Life safety code minimums of 110mm (44") do not allow someone to move sideways past a wheelchair; this is obviously an awkward situation. Even allowing enough room for someone to comfortably walk past a wheelchair—1220mm (48")—does not allow for the obvious case of two wheelchair users passing at the same time. 1500mm (60") allows this to occur comfortably and therefore, from a Universal Design standpoint, this should be a working minimum dimension.

Note that the 1500mm (60") dimension is also the required space for a wheelchair user to turn completely around, based on the width of a typical

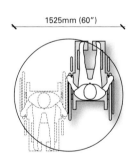

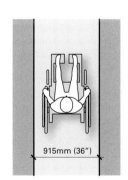

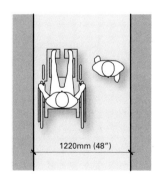

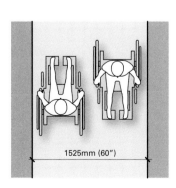

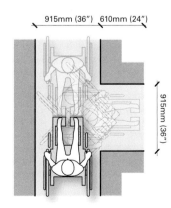

10.1
Basic planning dimensions for wheelchair accessibility in circulation areas.

device. While it is possible to turn a wheelchair in the "T" shape as shown, allowing room for a full 180-degree turn allows users to maneuver comfortably. The 1500mm (60") minimum corridors obviate any tricky or uncomfortable maneuvering. This is also important for elevator cabs; while a "T" turn will allow a wheelchair user to maneuver in and out, it may require difficult maneuvering to turn around inside the cab. Rather than backing in, frustrated wheelchair users may simply face the back wall and reverse out of a cab in this situation— an awkward and potentially dangerous situation if there is traffic in front of the cab door. If room for a full 1500mm turn is allowed inside the cab, the user can access the elevator without special effort.

Perhaps the most pressing needs occur in toilet rooms. While some advocates prefer separate toilet rooms that provide full 1500mm (60") maneuvering clearances, the "separate but equal" provisions in ADA require some percentage of multi-stall toilet rooms to meet minimum anthropomorphic requirements. Toilet rooms with the minimum dimensions required for an ADA-acceptable stall require the user to make a difficult transfer, using grab bars and turning around between the wheelchair and the toilet fixture. (Note, too, that because of planning efficiencies, the dedicated "accessible" stall is often at the far end of a series of stalls. The user must therefore *back out* down the row of stalls to exit if the stall is in use—hardly a desirable result.) A much better (though more spatially intensive) stall design would allow the user to maneuver a wheelchair parallel to the fixture, and simply transfer laterally, and would include a 1500mm turning circle as well (see Figure 10.1).

UNIVERSAL DESIGN—FINE GRAIN

In addition to these relatively simple planning standards, we need to pay attention to the smaller-scale anthropomorphic requirements of a variety of occupants. Most pressing is the need to provide accommodations for persons who need to reach services—shelves, sinks, telephones, door handles, and elevator buttons—from a sitting position (Figure 10.2). While the geometry of the occupant's reach allows greater high and low reach from a "side approach,"—that is, where the occupant can pull alongside the required service—a comfortable height for both front and side approaches limits any critical elements to around 1090mm (43"). In general, avoid placing any service—in particular electric outlets—lower than 455mm (18") from floor height. Note that there is a narrow overlap between the reach of wheelchair users and persons who are much taller than average, between 910mm (36") and 1090mm (43") above floor height.

Here, again, bathrooms present a unique set of challenges (Figure 10.3). Hand washing requires a front approach, yet this is the least efficient geometry. Countertops must therefore be configured so that a person in a wheelchair can maneuver their legs *under* the countertop, yet comfortably move their hands *above* it. This generally restricts lavatory rims and adjacent counter surfaces to 760–865mm (30–34") above floor height (also an acceptable range for countertops, desks, and tables) (Figure 10.3). A particular problem here is that persons with limited sensation in their legs can be bruised, cut, or even burned by water pipes under the sink. Care must be taken to either insulate these or to

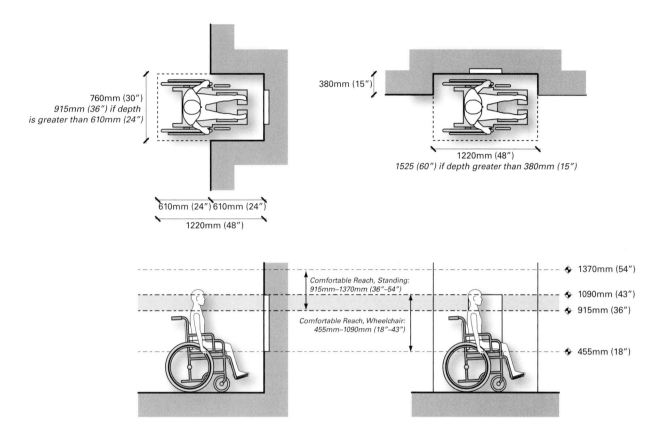

760mm (30")
915mm (36") if depth
is greater than 610mm (24")

380mm (15")

1220mm (48")
1525 (60") if depth greater than 380mm (15")

610mm (24") 610mm (24")

1220mm (48")

1370mm (54")

Comfortable Reach, Standing:
915mm–1370mm (36"–54")

1090mm (43")

915mm (36")

Comfortable Reach, Wheelchair:
455mm–1090mm (18"–43")

455mm (18")

10.2
Planning dimensions for front and side reach based on wheelchair anthropometric data.

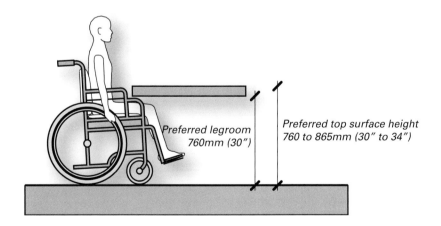

Preferred legroom
760mm (30")

Preferred top surface height
760 to 865mm (30" to 34")

10.3
Countertop and lavatory
requirements for wheelchair use.

configure them in a way that is unlikely to cause injury. Lavatories and counters must also be a more than a minimum distance away from the wall—430mm (17")—to enable comfortable reach.

Similar principles apply to drinking fountains and telephone booths. In these cases, however, positions that are comfortable for persons using wheelchairs will not be accessible to tall, ambulant users. Therefore, almost inevitably, at least one phone or drinking fountain must be provided at an alternate height.

A final consideration is for occupants who are visually or hearing impaired. Persons who have visual impairments navigate using a cane, which detects changes in floor texture, edges of walls, etc. ADA quite sensibly reminds us not to design corridors with protrusions (such as telephones) that project from the wall without some indication at floor level. Likewise, overhead hazards, such as open-stringer staircases, are notoriously dangerous to persons using canes as their first indication that an obstacle is in their way is often by bumping their head.

UNIVERSAL DESIGN — VERTICAL CIRCULATION

Perhaps the most pressing requirement of accessibility legislation is the common sense idea that all major areas of a building (public and the majority of work locations) must be accessible by a common route. This means that persons in wheelchairs must, for the majority of the design, be able to access rooms and spaces in the same manner as ambulatory occupants.

At a site planning level, this means that certain percentages of parking lots must be designed to accommodate users who must transfer from their vehicle to a wheelchair. Generally, a space 96" wide meets this requirement, although drivers requiring transfer from a custom van generally need a 1500mm (60") space parallel to their vehicle to operate a lift. Designated accessible spaces must be signed, must be immediately adjacent to an accessible curb cut, and must be located conveniently to building entries and amenities.

An "accessible route" may contain no vertical discontinuity of more than 13mm (0.5"). Any change in level greater than this must be traversed by a ramp, or (second best) a mechanical lift. Ramps are divided in to two categories—those whose slope is less than 1:20 (one meter of rise for every 20 meters of run) and those whose slope is between 1:12 and 1:20 (Figure 10.4). No ramps steeper than 1:12 are considered accessible. Ramps shallower than 1:20 have no limits on their length or height. Steeper ramps are limited to 740mm (30") of rise before they must offer a landing of at least 1500mm (60") in length. This allows users to rest and it will break the fall of a person who loses control coming down, a more serious issue (Figure 10.4).

Ramps with a rise greater than 15mm (6") must also be provided with handrails that prevent users from falling off the edge and that permit users to grip and pull themselves along. Handrails must be designed for side approach, i.e. between 860mm and 970mm (34" and 38") from floor level, and must have a gripping surface that is equivalent to a 38mm (1.5") diameter cylinder. Adequate clearance between the handrail and any wall is, of course, required. Handrails must also extend beyond the top and bottom of ramps, parallel with the ground surface, to allow unsteady walkers to grip the rail prior to stepping on to the ramp. To prevent clothing from catching on the end of a handrail, it must typically be returned, either to a post or to a wall, or it must have a connection immediately adjacent to its end. Likewise, guardrails at a slightly higher level must be provided at landings where a fall of more than 460mm (18") presents itself.

Stairs present a more complex set of issues (see Chapter 11 for a full discussion). Even though wheelchair users typically cannot use them, stairs

Slopes of 1:20 (5%) or shallower are not limited in length, but may be tiring.

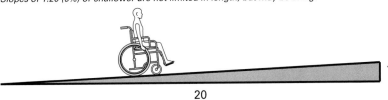

20

1

10.4
Ramp slopes rated by accessibility.

Slopes of 1:16 (6.25%) to 1:20 (5%) require landings every 40 horizontal feet.

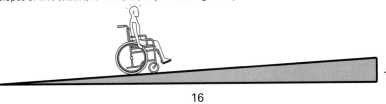

16

1

Slopes of 1:12 (8.33%) to 1:16 (6.25%) require landings every 30 horizontal feet.

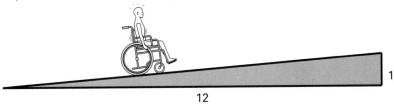

12

1

Slopes steeper than 1:12 (8.33%) are not considered accessible.
Slopes greater than 1:8 (12.5%) are difficult for ambulatory users.

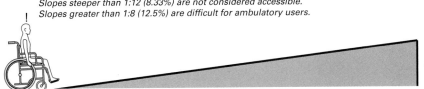

1

are covered by ADA since a significant percentage of otherwise ambulatory people are nonetheless limited in their range of motion, balance, or visual abilities. In addition, stairs are often the most dangerous public element of a building—the Center for Disease Control estimates that 1300 Americans die every year from falls on residential stairs—and thus the ADA provides standards that account for the difficulty otherwise ambulatory users have on these elements.

The most important attributes of stair design for safety and comfort are the design of the tread and the design of the handrail. Some codes allow riser heights of 200mm (8") in residential situations, however this figure is quite tall for people with limited range of motion; anthropometric data suggests that 180–190mm (7"–7.5") should be the maximum riser height. Adequate space for a human foot must be provided on each horizontal tread, usually no less than 280mm (11") for interior stairs. Additionally, adequate toe space must be provided at each riser, yet the stairs must not present a tripping hazard. Therefore, ADA specifies that nosings should extend no more than 40mm (1.5") from the riser face. Open risers are no longer permitted due to the tripping hazard they pose. To catch falling occupants, it is advisable to have no more than 16 total risers in one run of stairs—most codes will required a landing for every 12" of height. Finally, it is critical that the treads and risers in a continuous stair be uniform—changes in riser height in particular can cause serious falls. For exterior stairs, particularly those that might become wet or ice-encrusted, tread and riser dimensions must be adjusted, usually to 380mm (15") minimum for treads and 5" maximum for risers.

Because doors must be pulled into the occupant's space, they present particular difficulties for wheelchair users. In confined spaces, users may actually become trapped by doors that do not have adequate clearance to allow wheelchairs to travel around the edge of the opening door. Likewise, adequate space should be maintained to the side of any door to allow easy access from either direction (Figures 10.5 and 10.6).

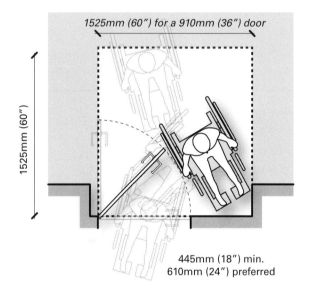

10.5
Space requirements for wheelchairs at doors.

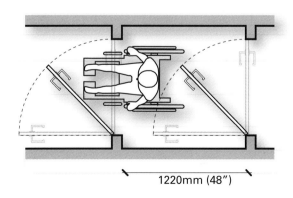

10.6
Space requirements for wheelchairs in sequential doors.

OTHER POINTS TO CONSIDER

There are typically serious accessibility concerns for a number of other building components, in particular elevator size and layout, configuration and required force for door openers and handles, shower stalls, vending machines, floor grates, and signage. Again, these are often readily achievable if they are considered near the outset of a design but can cause problems if they are only examined as the design is detailed.

As with codes, a strategic approach is almost always better than a checklist done as the design is in progress. Designs that do the following will invariably stand a better chance of meeting the intent of accessibility legislation in the U.S. or Europe:

- Avoid level changes where possible. For multistory buildings, assume each floor needs to be dead level over its whole area.
- Where level changes are required, understand that space will be required for ramps or lifts. Assume that any level change will have 20 times its height in ramp run (though, in a pinch, this can be reduced to 12 times height, plus landings).
- Allow adequate space in the planning stages for generous toilet rooms, incorporating 1500mm (60") turning circles for people using wheelchairs. A 3350mm (11') wide bay will (barely) allow a plumbing chase, stall depth and adequate clearance.
- Allow adequate space in the planning stages for generous stairs, incorporating runs as shallow as reasonably possible. As a rule of thumb, allow at least a 3350mm by 6100mm (11' by 20') plan area for a scissor stair serving a 4600mm (15') floor to floor height.
- No public corridor should be less than 1500mm (60") wide.
- On the pull side of doors, allow a minimum clear maneuvering space of 1525mm square for a 910mm (36") door, while on the push side this can be reduced to a 1220mm (48") square (see Figure 10.5). Doors in sequence must be designed to allow adequate maneuvering room for opening (see Figure 10.6). Doors arranged in sequence should open in the same direction to prevent wheelchair users from becoming trapped between them.

Unfortunately, common sense is not always insurance against a technical accessibility issue. Case law at the moment suggests that the letter of the law, in addition to its intent, must be followed. However, also keep in mind that lawsuits are more likely to arise in cases where people are inconvenienced, frustrated, or insulted by a building's design. Sensitivity to different levels of motion, vision, etc., is something society demands of us. Like life safety (see Chapter 9), it is not technically difficult to produce an environment that allows access to all, but this does take patience and attention to detail to ensure an integrated solution.

FREQUENTLY ASKED QUESTIONS

My design has multiple entrances/levels that will require extensive ramps and elevators to make them work. Do all of these have to be accessible to meet American codes?
The Americans with Disabilities Act requires only that 60 percent of all building entries be accessible, but that these be the entries most commonly used by building occupants or users. Level changes are a different story. Any part of a building that serves an occupational, commercial, or public purpose should be fully accessible by wheelchair users. While some case law has suggested that offices, in particular, can provide a certain percentage of accessible work areas (a so-called "program-based solution"), designers should keep in mind that meetings, conversations, or work groups could meet anywhere in a building, and that this could be exclusionary if all areas aren't accessible.

Do I need an elevator? My design has multiple levels but is very small.
Perhaps not. Most buildings of less than three stories, or less than 300m² (3000ft²) are exempted under ADA (exceptions are shopping centers and health-care providers). Accessibility regulations generally exempt residential uses, although multi-unit facilities will typically be required to provide a percentage of accessible units. This, however, excludes wheelchair users from amenities or occupied spaces on floors above ground, which is not a desirable situation. Adequate accommodation on the ground level must be provided.

Does every seat in a stadium or theater need to be accessible?
No. The ADA in particular makes very clear that only a small percentage of seats—about 1 percent for large facilities—must be accessible, in addition to a certain number of aisle seats with removable arms. However, recent case law has pointed out the need to distribute these seats throughout an arena or theater. Placing all accessible seating at the back of a theater, for instance, has been seen as discriminatory, as wheelchair users have no opportunity to occupy any but the least desirable seats.

My project involves an historic structure. Does the existing fabric need to be totally altered to provide full accessibility?
Most accessibility legislation recognizes the impossibility of retrofitting full access into existing, pre-legislation structures. The ADA makes specific exceptions for existing structures, in which any alteration must itself be accessible, and historic structures, in which accessibility requirements are limited to site, entry, and major spaces. Even these, however, are to be balanced with the perceived impact on the building's historic fabric and may be negotiated with local or state Historic Preservation authorities.

GLOSSARY

Accessible: Generally, building spaces or elements that allow full use by those with impaired mobility.

Clear: Unobstructed. Usually refers to floor space in which a user can maneuver a wheelchair.

Guardrail: A railing intended to prevent a user from falling at a level change. Must be located at or above the average human center of gravity (about 1060mm (42") above a walking surface) where there is a significant drop beyond.

Handrail: A grippable surface intended to offer additional stability to a stair or ramp user. Must be located at a comfortable gripping height, usually 860mm (34") above either stair nosings or ramp surfaces.

Ramp: A slanted surface that enables ambulatory and wheelchair-using occupants access between levels. Slopes less than 1:20 aren't considered ramps, while slopes greater than 1:12 restrict access by wheelchair users.

Universal Design: A design philosophy that eschews "accommodation" in favor of circulation and accessibility principles that integrate, rather than segregate, users of varying mobility.

FURTHER READING

Evan Terry Associates, P. C. (2002). *Pocket Guide to the ADA*, revised edition. New York: Wiley.

Henry Dreyfuss Associates (2002). *The Measure of Man and Woman: Human Factors in Design*. New York: Wiley; especially Differently Abled People, pp. 35–43, and A Universal Work Chair, p. 44.

Osterberg, A. E. and Kain, D. J. (2002). *Access for everyone: A Guide to Accessibility with References to ADAAG*. Ames, IA: Iowa State University Facilities Planning & Management. *Note: This title is available for purchase through Iowa State University: www.fpm.iastate.edu/accessforeverone*

11
STAIRS AND RAMPS

Principles	Human movement
Stairs—treads and risers	Proportions
	Details
Configuration	Flights
	Landings
	Width
	Special stairs
Fall protection	Handrails
	Guardrails

VERTICAL MOVEMENT

Invariably buildings require people to move through them vertically, and even those of one story will often have minute level changes that require careful design. Thousands are injured every year on stairs in particular. While codes and accessibility legislation have prescribed basic dimensional data for both stairs and ramps, it is important to think about these elements from anthropometric principles, which will often suggest more generous provision than typical codes allow.

The average European or American person can lift their foot about 400mm (16") while standing but will quickly tire if forced to do this repeatedly (Figure 11. 1). For about 90 percent of the population, raising the foot 150mm to 200mm (6" to 8") is relatively easy. However for the remaining 10 percent (children under 5, the elderly or those with a mobility impairment) this motion is difficult or excessively tiring. The average human foot is about 265mm (10.4") long with the majority of the body's weight concentrated at its rear.

Stairs can thus easily be too steep or too short. Steep stairs are dangerous both because they can cause fatigue (a contributor to slips and falls), and because they present a difficult descent (Figure 11. 2). Short stairs are dangerous because a climber can easily misplace their step, centering their weight beyond the edge of the stair tread, potentially causing a fall as well.

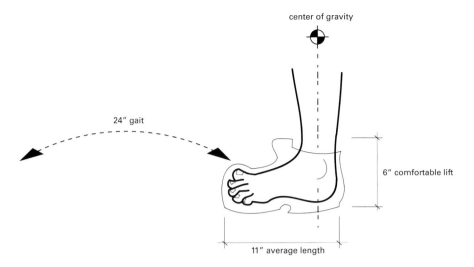

center of gravity

24" gait

6" comfortable lift

11" average length

11.1
The basics of stair design start with the human foot and gait.

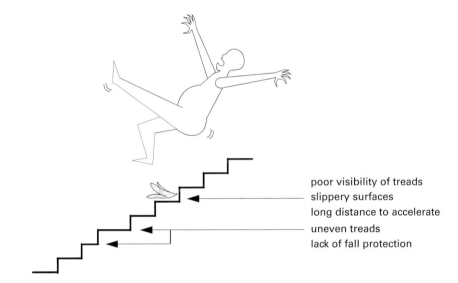

poor visibility of treads
slippery surfaces
long distance to accelerate
uneven treads
lack of fall protection

11.2
Stairs present some of the most prevalent dangers in buildings.

STAIRS—TREADS AND RISERS

The key to designing a safe stair is the careful proportioning of *treads*, the flat pieces of the stair, and *risers*, the vertical pieces. In addition to leg lift and foot size, these two dimensions should be coordinated to match a typical human gait for comfort and ease of use (Figure 11. 3).

Treads should be made of a non-slip surface to ensure good traction between foot and stair. While wood is often acceptable, commercial installations should be made of something with greater traction—carpet, vinyl or concrete, for instance. Smooth surfaces such as glass should be roughened by sandblasting or a similar process. Exterior stairs should also provide for drainage, to keep the treads as dry and ice-free as possible.

Minimum tread dimensions vary according to use; however, they should generally be no less than 280mm (11") to ensure full contact between foot and stair. Exterior stairs should be slightly longer, reflecting both the quicker pace during outside walking and the possibility of water or snow during inclement

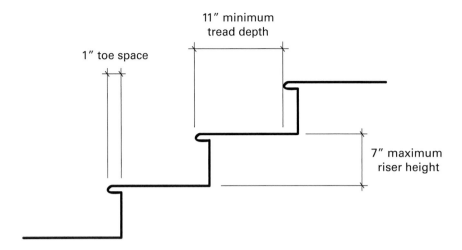

1" toe space

11" minimum
tread depth

7" maximum
riser height

11.3
Stair dimensions must be based on
comfortable walking gaits and foot
lengths.

weather. Generally, exterior stairs have treads 360mm (14") or longer, though care should be taken that treads occur at a natural rhythm to the human gait— about 610mm (24"). Some codes make exceptions for stairs connected directly to a building entrance and allow exterior stairs in these cases to have treads 300mm (12") or larger. Residential construction is generally held to less stringent standards and may have treads as short as 230mm (9"); however, this can be a contributing factor to dangerous falls.

Riser heights are usually limited to 180mm (7"). Some codes will make exceptions up to 210mm (8.25") for residential applications. This is seen by many professionals as a dangerous exception and does not represent good practice. Exterior stairs should have risers no higher than 130mm (5").

The geometry of the human foot means that a slight overlap between the back of the heel of the climbing foot and the toe of the resting foot must be provided. This is usually done by setting the face of the riser back 25mm (1") from the *nosing*, or front edge, of the tread above. To prevent catching the toe, nosings are typically rounded, or have a sloped underside. Nosings greater than 25mm (1") present a tripping hazard and must be avoided.

Because of the natural walking stride's length, the relation between tread and riser is crucial. The typical rule of thumb for sizing treads and risers in relation to one another is that the sum of the tread length (measured from nosing to nosing) plus twice the riser height should be as close to 635mm (25") as possible:

$$2R + T = 635mm \ (25")$$

Other rules of thumb include adding the tread length to the riser height to get as close to 460mm (18") as possible:

$$R + T = 460mm \ (18")$$

And multiplying tread length by riser height to get as near to 1850mm (73") as possible:

$$R \times T = 1850mm \ (73")$$

All of these are shortcuts for a brief bit of trigonometry describing the fact that stairs, to be safe, must occur within a relatively narrow range of pitch angles—between about 18 degrees and 35 degrees.

STAIRS—CONFIGURATION

While proper tread and riser sizing can create a generally safe, comfortable stair, additional considerations involving the stair's length, landings, and fall protection must also be taken.

First, stairs are limited in height to prevent acute fatigue while climbing and to arrest any falls that occur while descending. Building codes will often limit the total height of a stair flight to 3600mm (12'), though this height can still cause a potentially fatal fall. Better practice is to limit stairs to 16 risers in a straight run, which will translate to just over a 2740mm (9') height if the above formulae are employed.

To reach floor heights greater than 9', therefore, an intermediate landing will be necessary (Figure 11. 4). Landings must be of sufficient length in the direction of travel to fully arrest a falling person—usually 1220mm (48"). In

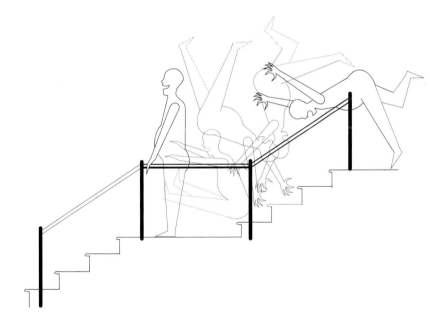

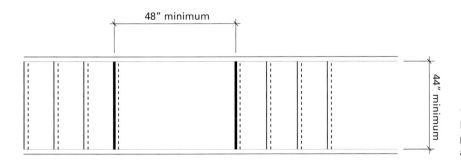

11.4
Landings provide important fall protection and must be sized to arrest a tumbling user.

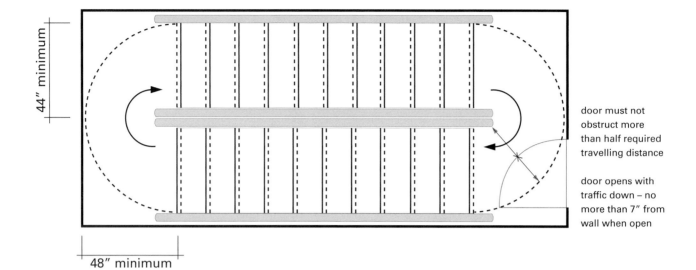

44" minimum

48" minimum

door must not
obstruct more
than half required
travelling distance

door opens with
traffic down – no
more than 7" from
wall when open

multistory construction, stairs will typically double back at intermediate landings to arrive back at the stair entrance in plan—this is called a *scissor stair*.

Occupants using stairs quickly establish a walking rhythm that must not be
disrupted by variations in tread or riser size. Any variation greater than 3mm
(⅛") in either dimension will be noticeable, and may cause stumbling, 'flatfoot-
ing' or tripping.

Stair width is often determined by life safety codes based on emergency
evacuation conditions. However at minimum stairs should allow the comfortable passage of two users going in opposite directions—1120mm (44")—in
commercial or public installations. For residences, stairs may be as narrow
as 920mm (36"), which allows passage for only one person at a time safely.
Stairs that serve as fire exits must additionally be sized for the occupancy
they serve, usually 8mm (0.3") per assumed evacuee. Where "scissor stairs"
are used, landings must be sized to maintain this width throughout the stair
(Figure 11. 5). This is often shown on plans by drawing an arc from the outside
edge of one flight to the other. Any doors entering in to the fire stair must be
configured so that they do not open in to the path of travel, and they cannot
reduce the required travel width by more than 50 percent at any point in their
swing. Where stairs are used for evacuating people with motion impairments,
their width must be at least 1220mm (48") to permit carrying.

Curved or winding stairs present special hazards (Figure 11. 6). Where stairs
are curved, they present varying tread widths, which can disrupt climbing
rhythm if users move from one side to the other. At the tighter radius, care
must be taken to ensure adequate tread depth, while the outer radius must
be checked to ensure the treads are not too wide. Usually curved stairs are
designed by taking the likely centerline of travel, about 355mm (14") from
the handrail, and using that line to determine tread/riser sizes. Winding stairs,
which 'turn' through a square 90 degrees, present similar issues with tread
depth at their short ends. Spiral stairs are usually not permitted in commercial
or public buildings, as their extremely tight radii rarely offer adequate foot room.
In general they should be a last resort, even in residential or industrial applications, because of their serious fall potential.

11.5
Most high-rise buildings will use
a scissor stair to provide landings
at each floor level in a compact
package.

measure stair treads at 18″ from handrail

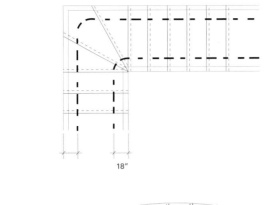

18″

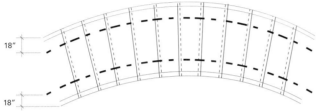

18″

18″

11.6
Curved and winding stairs present particular hazards and must be designed to allow a comfortable gait at the correct distance from handrails.

HANDRAILS AND GUARDRAILS

Stairways and ramps require two types of fall protection: *handrails* that provide grips for users, and *guardrails* that prevent users from falling off (Figure 11. 7). Handrails must present an easily graspable bar. On stairs, these are required whenever there are more than two risers present, while on ramps handrails are only required for ramps steeper than 1:20 slope. For stairs greater than 1220mm (48″) wide, handrails must be provided on both sides of a stair. For stairs greater than 2240mm (88″) wide, an additional handrail must be provided in the center of the stair.

Handrails are generally placed from 760–860mm (30–34″) above the tip of the nosing. The ADA does not acknowledge the geometrical difference between a stair and ramp and requires the handrails to be placed between 860mm and 960mm (34″ and 38″) above the walking surface—thus 860mm (34″) is a good default height for both. Handrails must have an equivalent gripping surface to a 38mm (1.5″) diameter cylinder, they must be uninterrupted by posts or brackets, and they must be located a good distance away from side walls—usually 38mm (1.5″) (Figure 11. 8). Handrails that are not continuous must extend beyond the top and bottom stair tread to signal the change in direction and to provide for falls from the last stair. At the topmost stair, handrails must extend an additional 300mm (12″) beyond the last nosing, while at the bottom they must extend 300mm (12″) plus one tread width. Handrails must be returned to a post or wall or must have some way of shedding clothing that might otherwise become caught, and the space between the rail and the nosings must either be solid or have a tight enough mesh (<4″) that neither a limb nor a small child's head could become caught in a fall.

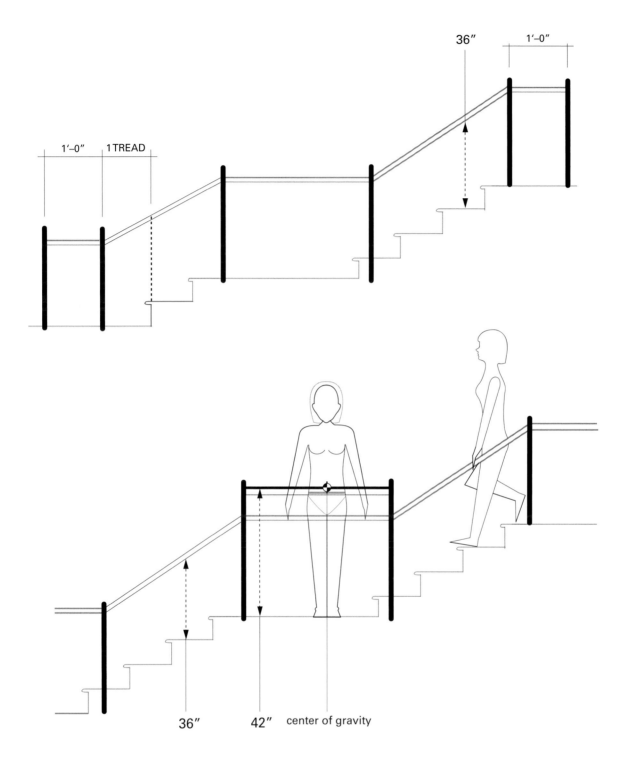

11.7
Configuration of handrails, which provide gripping surfaces for stair users, and guardrails, which provide fall protection.

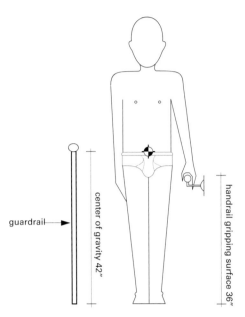

11.8
Configuration of handrails in
particular must allow for a
comfortable, obstacle-free grip.

guardrail ▸

center of gravity 42"

handrail gripping surface 36"

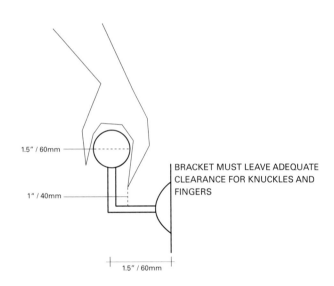

1.5" / 60mm

1" / 40mm

BRACKET MUST LEAVE ADEQUATE
CLEARANCE FOR KNUCKLES AND
FINGERS

1.5" / 60mm

Most codes require open landings to have a different configuration if it presents a falling hazard over 450mm (18″) high. Guardrails in these instances must be 1060mm (42″) high, with the same requirements for solidity as handrails. While this initially seems like a contradiction given the lower required handrail height, guardrails perform a very different function from handrails. The latter must provide a gripping surface for a hand that naturally rests 860–960mm (34–38″) above foot height. Guardrails, however, prevent falls, and must therefore be placed above the average center of gravity of a typical human body. This is about 960mm (38″) above floor height in an average male, 1060mm (41.8″) above floor height in the 99th percentile male. Detailing the connection between hand and guard rails thus presents particular problems.

Two fine points of handrail and guardrail design are worth noting. When laying handrails out on a stair, it is often advisable to stagger adjacent flights of scissor stairs to ensure that their respective handrails hit a common point at the landings. This prevents a vertical discontinuity between flights that is usually unsightly and can create an uncomfortable transition between flights. Usually the upper flight is set back by one tread, so that its handrail "lands" at the same point in section as the end of the handrail on the lower flight. These two points are then connected by a horizontal rail segment, providing a clean detail. Careful thought about the three-dimensional nature of the handrail and guardrail at landings is required to achieve a detail that looks clean while functioning well (Figure 11. 9).

11.9
A carefully thought out arrangement of handrail and guardrail.

A second design consideration involves the difference in height between handrails and guardrails. When designing stairs with landings requiring guardrails, there will be an offset between the required height of the handrail and that of the guardrail. To integrate both elements, systems are often designed that cantilever a steel handrail off of a glass or metal plate designed to guardrail height. This combined element satisfies both requirements in a single assembly. Note, too, that if properly designed, the handrail extension at the bottom of a stair may be faired in to a descending guardrail plate, again providing a neat aesthetic fix to a difficult arrangement.

FREQUENTLY ASKED QUESTIONS

Why are stairs covered by accessibility codes? Surely they can't be traversed by wheelchair users?
Mobility is a continuum, not an either/or state. While much accessibility legislation covers wheelchair usage, much of the American-European population is mobile but requires some accommodation for difficult actions such as climbing or descending stairs. Stairs are particularly difficult for many elderly, or those with chronic joint pain, and thus the design of these elements should account for a range of potential usage.

Why aren't open stair treads allowed? And why do stair treads require nosings? I know I've seen open treads somewhere before.
Open treads present a serious tripping hazard. Without a riser for the user to sense where treads start and stop, it is much more likely that someone will move their foot too far forward while climbing, and catch the edge of the next riser up with their toe. Unfortunately, a stair presents a series of relatively acute edges to the falling occupant on the ascent, often resulting in facial injuries. This is a relatively recent addition to American codes so many buildings may still have this dangerous condition. Nosings prevent the opposite occurrence. A natural human stride up a normal staircase does not completely offset one foot from another. A nosing allows a bit of an overlap between toe and heel, the most comfortable (and most balanced) stance.

GLOSSARY

Landing: A flat, level portion of a staircase that provides one or more steps of rest ascending, and can arrest falls while descending. Usually a minimum of 1120mm long (44″).

Nosing: The lip of a stair tread, designed to allow toes enough room underneath while the other foot negotiates the tread. Usually 25mm (1″) deep.

Rise: The vertical distance between stair tread surfaces. Generally no more than 200mm (8″).

Rise-to-run: A measure of a staircase's ease of use. Not all slopes are easy for human legs to negotiate. While minimum runs and maximum rises help, additional formula are often used to ensure a comfortable stride or gait. In particular, the formula:

$$2R + T = 635mm\ (25")$$

is useful for designing traversable stairs.

Other rules of thumb include:

$$R + T = 460mm\ (18")$$
$$R \times T = 1850mm\ (73")$$

Run: The horizontal distance between stair nosings or risers. Generally no less than 280mm (11").

Scissor stair: A stair that doubles back on itself, usually with landings at floor levels on only one side. Most commonly used in high-rise buildings as they are efficient.

FURTHER READING

Templer, J. (1992). *The Staircase: Studies of Hazards, Falls, and Safer Design*. Cambridge, MA: MIT Press.

12

ELEVATORS AND ESCALATORS

Elevators	History
	Types—hydraulic, traction and self-contained
	Safety features
	Convenience—number, speed, and capacity
	High-rise systems
Escalators	Configuration
	Arrangements

INTRODUCTION

Until the 1870s, building owners and users were limited to muscle power to move freight and people up and down in buildings. This was often cleverly achieved, for instance by using pulleys and ropes to haul merchandise into attic storehouses in Amsterdam, or yoking animal power to winches that moved materials to the top of gravity feed systems in typical agricultural buildings. But the need for human power to move up and down buildings limited most structures to five stories, the extent of human comfort. Note that until the completion of the Washington Monument in 1884 (169m), the tallest man-made structures were all uninhabitable spires.

Platforms for moving freight and people vertically were nothing new in the nineteenth century; the innovations that made the elevator popular were electric and hydraulic motive power, and devices to keep elevator platforms from falling. Safety, rather than actual lifting power, was the key innovation in the development of workable elevators for populated high-rise buildings. Teagle elevators were employed in multistory mills in Britain in the 1840s, using overhead cables, pulleys, and side rails to move workers and material. These were relatively sophisticated, using counterweights to offset the weight of the cab itself. However, the rope was the only vertical support for the cab, and, if it broke, there was nothing to prevent the cab from falling and crushing whatever was inside.

The first working safety device on a passenger elevator was demonstrated in 1853 by Elisha Graves Otis, involving toothed metal grips attached to the elevator car's main cable or rope by long pawls. If the rope were cut, the pawls would release the grips, which would then grab on to the side rails, stopping the cab. Still driven by steam power, the first Otis Safety Elevator was installed in the five-story Haughwout Store at Broadway and Broome Street in New York in 1857. Innovations after Otis' death in 1861 included the use of hydraulic pressure, rather than steam, to raise elevator platforms. Comfort remained a serious issue as stops were sudden and the ride could be disturbingly noisy.

ELEVATORS—PRINCIPLES

Contemporary elevators come in three types (Figure 12.1). Hydraulic (piston) elevators rely on a piston located beneath the cab and require a basement machine room to provide hydraulic power. Traction elevators use a rooftop machine room to house a system of cables, pulleys (or sheaves) and counterweights. Motive power elevators use traveling systems (such as rack and pinion) to drive the cab itself. In each case, the cab is must be supported by

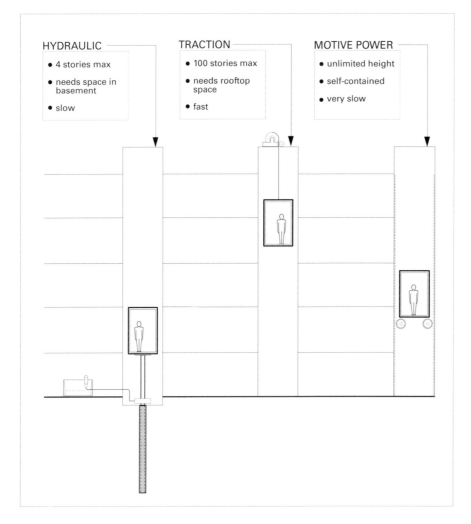

HYDRAULIC
- 4 stories max
- needs space in basement
- slow

TRACTION
- 100 stories max
- needs rooftop space
- fast

MOTIVE POWER
- unlimited height
- self-contained
- very slow

12.1
Elevator types.

ELEVATOR ANATOMY

12.2
Elevators are complex mechanical
systems, but their basic parts are
straightforward.

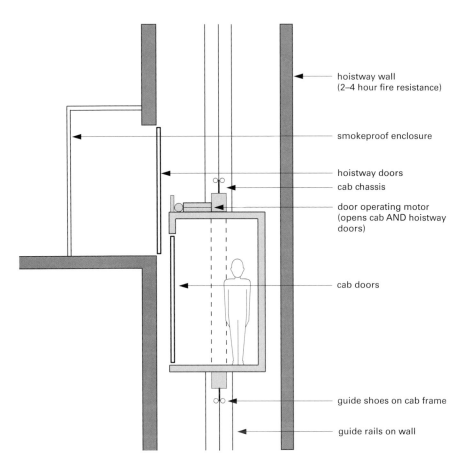

hoistway wall
(2–4 hour fire resistance)

smokeproof enclosure

hoistway doors
cab chassis
door operating motor
(opens cab AND hoistway
doors)

cab doors

guide shoes on cab frame

guide rails on wall

guide rails to ensure a smooth, reliable motion. The cab will typically be housed within a steel box that is connected to the driving element, and that contains biaxial rollers that keep the cab true relative to the guide rails.

Some equipment is common to all three types. A hoistway that provides space for travel will run the full height of the building plus overruns at the top and bottom (Figure 12.2). This shaft poses inherent dangers, in that the tall vertical space makes an ideal fire chimney, and its height presents a fall hazard. The fire danger is typically addressed by providing a one hour fire separation between the shaft and any occupied area, often by means of self-closing fire doors. The fall danger is more complex. Most codes require that elevators have two sets of doors; one mounted on the cab, and the other at each floor level attached to the hoistway wall. Interlocking mechanisms ensure that the two doors only open when the elevator cab is level with a floor. Power to open the doors is typically attached to the cab itself, by means of a motor and rail attached either above or below the cab doors. The hoistway requires solid walls on at least three sides, to prevent crushing as the cab runs past floors and to provide adequate support (Figure 12.3). Within the cabs themselves, control and signal mechanisms must be accessible to both able-bodied and wheelchair users.

ELECTRIC PASSENGER ELEVATORS

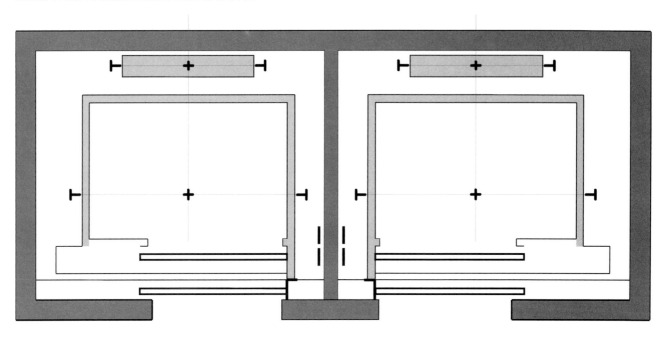

Hydraulic elevators

The simplest elevators are hydraulic and use oil-filled pistons to push the cabs up through a shaft. When ascending, a pump fills the piston with oil, which can then be slowly released to bring the cab back down. Hydraulic systems require a large machine room at the lowest level of the hoistway to accommodate the pump and oil reservoir. They also typically require a drilled hole in the ground to hold the piston when the cab is at its lowest point. Their main advantage is that they do not require any significant space at the top of the hoistway for mechanical equipment. Hydraulic elevators are relatively slow, with a maximum speed of about 60 meters per minute (200 feet per minute), and their travel is limited to four or five stories due to the pressure required in the plunger.

Traction elevators

Most large-scale installations use an overhead machine room and a system of cables and pulleys to move elevator cabs. Known as traction systems, these use motors at the top of the shaft to turn grooved traction sheaves. Cables sit in these grooves and are attached to the top of the cab's frame below at one end, and a counterweight at the other. The counterweight is sized to balance the weight of the cab, plus a percentage of the anticipated passenger or freight load, and a set of slack cables is usually attached to the base of the elevator cab to balance the changing weight of the cables above as the elevator travels up and down. While a single steel cable would ordinarily be sufficient to hold the load of a typical elevator cab, they are usually ganged into groups of five or six to allow sufficient traction on the sheaves—this also provides a very high safety factor should one of the cables fray. Various roping arrangements can be implemented to both increase traction and to gain mechanical advantage through pulleys. Additionally, a three-sheave system can allow the mechanical room

12.3
Elevators in plan.

to occupy a basement position. However, all of these come at the expense of extra cable, which must be constantly maintained.

Traction machines are expensive due to their roping requirements. Likewise, the placement of heavy motors at the top of a tall shaft necessitates major structure to both hold their dead load and to absorb the constant reactions of cabs starting and stopping. Access is often more difficult and machine rooms generally require a story and a half above the top of the shaft to hold the motors and allow proper access. Despite the high maintenance required on cables, traction elevators tend to be inexpensive in terms of life cycle cost, in part because they can re-generate electricity when descending—often up to 40 percent of the power required to hoist them. Likewise, they are much faster than hydraulic elevators, as typical speeds range from 75 to 150 meters per minute (250 to 500 feet per minute). In extreme circumstances, high-rise elevators may travel as fast as 600 meters per minute (2000 feet per minute), and their rise is limited only be the deflection of steel cables.

Self-contained motive power

In unusual circumstances, elevators may be required in situations that do not permit a machine room at the top or bottom of the shaft. Several products exist that place the motive power within the cab or counterweight itself, relying on a rack and pinion to raise and lower the cab. This is a particularly good system for observation cabs, as it eliminates the bulky counterweight. Likewise, new products include hydraulic elevators with integral pistons placed within the hoistway to avoid the excavation required for a large plunger hole. These latter systems are limited in height, usually to three stories.

ELEVATORS—SAFETY

Most systems rely on at least two systems to stop the cab in an emergency. The cab's speed is monitored by a *governor*, a wheel connected to a dedicated set of cables that contains a centrifugal switch. As the cab exceeds allowable speeds, the governor trips, setting into motion friction brakes that rub against the guide rails, slowing the cab's travel. At a catastrophic speed, the governor will trip a second set of switches, releasing spring-loaded steel jaws that will clamp on to the guide rails, stopping the cab quickly. Because of the redundancy of cables and the ability of the motor to brake the cab's travel, this is extremely rare.

More common are accidents involving tripping hazards and crushing. Elevators are required to have floor leveling devices that will nudge an arriving cab to within 6mm (0.25") of the landing's level, and interlocks that will prevent doors from opening in any misaligned position. Likewise, at the base of the shaft, a significant overrun is required, with buffering springs to absorb any substantial overrun (note that these springs are *not* there to stop a falling cab). All cabs must fully enclose passengers so that limbs are not endangered by passing structure, and all hoistways must be fully enclosed for the same reason. Finally, doors must be equipped with mechanical sensors that will trigger an instant reversal when an object prevents their closure, and they must be limited in the amount of force they can produce. Higher end installations will typically include an infrared sensor that will detect anything in the doors' paths, causing them to open before hitting a late passenger.

Because they are electronically controlled, elevator cabs have the unfortunate tendency in a fire of stopping at a burning floor because of the intense heat involved. Therefore, elevators are quite dangerous means of "escape" and must be sent automatically to the ground floor with no intermediate stops if the building fire alarm is triggered. This safely discharges passengers who might have been aboard during the emergency, prevents new passengers from using the cabs, and provides convenient transport to arriving fire fighters, who can override the emergency instructions by means of a special key and then take the elevator to a floor just below the suspected fire.

In the event of a power outage, some occupancies (hospitals in particular) must provide emergency power to elevators, allowing them to move to the nearest floor to discharge passengers. However, in commercial and most residential occupancies there is often no such requirement. Occupants must be able to access an emergency phone, usually wired directly to building security or a police operator. Cabs will typically be fitted with an emergency hatch on their roof to allow rescue crews to remove stranded passengers, who can then exit through the closest hoistway door, above. Passenger discomfort can be lessened in these situations by providing a confirmation light indicating that assistance is on the way. Observation cabs that include views out can also make this rare occurrence less stressful. To prevent panicked passengers from attempting to escape into the hoistway, which would become dangerous if the system was suddenly re-energized, hatches must usually be locked from the outside, and hoistway doors must have a mechanical interlock that prevents their being opened by normal human efforts. In the unlikely event that these doors are opened, hoistway shafts must be designed to prevent limbs from being crushed if the cab does begin to move suddenly. In all cases—even a fire—the cab is a much safer environment than the hoistway.

ELEVATORS—CONVENIENCE

While a variety of codes will require various safety features as described above, elevators must be designed to comfortably and conveniently move passengers, and this is a more difficult task than might at first be assumed. Building occupants, in general, have unrealistic expectations about waiting and travel times—studies have shown that frustration is apparent after only 25 seconds of wait. Particularly in high-rises, which may discharge more than half of their population within 15 minutes at the end of a work day, the capacities required of elevators are formidable.

Three factors determine the total waiting and travel time for elevators—speed, capacity, and number. While speed in feet per minute seems an obvious component, this is tempered by the elevators' performance while *on station*; that is, while passengers are loading and unloading. Here, the size of the door and the speed at which it opens and closes has a significant effect, particularly in buildings of considerable height. Doors that open in the center will halve the time that the elevator cab is stopped with no passenger movement, while *two-*

speed doors will further decrease this inherent inefficiency by opening more quickly. Likewise, while capacity has a positive effect on efficiency, it is limited by the fact that more passengers will typically require more stops, leading to longer round trip times. Generally, the single greatest variable in determining system convenience is number—that is, a larger number of smaller elevators will always be preferable in a multistory system. This, of course, is more expensive, as more hoistways, motors, etc., must be purchased, and all elevator companies will provide extensive design services to assist in the realization of an economical balance between cost and performance. The ultimate measure of a system is its *handling capacity* (HC), which is the percentage of a building's population that can be accommodated within a five-minute period and is equal to:

$$HC = 300p/I$$

where p is the number of passengers per car and I is the required interval, or waiting time. (Note that 300 seconds gives us the five-minute capacity). A good rule of thumb in planning, however, is to provide one elevator for every 3000 square meters (30,000 square feet) of occupied space, with a minimum of two for any multistory commercial or institutional building.

In large high-rises, control of an elevator system can greatly increase efficiency. The earliest controls involved a single "call" button that could only be operated while the elevator was idle—each trip was made independently of any other. Control systems have become more sophisticated, first with electro-mechanical systems able to "log" all requests and collect them as the cab travels up and down the hoistway, and later with electronic systems that assign calls to the nearest (or least full) cab. Contemporary control systems are micro-processor based, with sophisticated programs that can quickly determine strategies for minimizing overall waiting time, assign cabs for passengers who have been waiting the longest, and gradually learn from traffic patterns.

Another major convenience factor is layout, particularly the arrangement of cab entrances in a lobby. Where there are more than one or two cabs, visibility is a necessity and passengers should be able to see clearly which elevators are arriving. Long runs of single openings present problems in that passengers must hurry to catch arriving cabs, while double-loaded lobbies require passengers to look in two directions at once. While space-intensive, radial layouts provide the best grasp of the elevator bank's status. Another strategy is to provide screens showing the location, direction of travel, and even likely arrival time for each cab in the system, allowing users to move to the arriving cab's position well before its arrival.

Floor space in front of elevator entrances must be adequately sized to permit entering and exiting traffic to flow freely in the worst (most loaded) situation. Efficiency is dramatically impaired when doors must be held open to await passengers who are held up by congestion. In general, 0.5 square meters (5 square feet) should be allowed for each anticipated passenger in an elevator lobby, although 0.7 square meters (7 square feet) per person is the general threshold of comfort. In no case should opposing banks of elevators be closer than 2500mm (8'), and good practice suggests that a minimum of 3000–3660mm (10–12') is required to allow for constant flow.

HIGH-RISE ELEVATOR SYSTEMS

The development of the skyscraper has continued to spur development in elevator systems. As structural techniques improved in the 1950s, several major advances in elevator design followed, permitting the jumbo high-rises of the 1960s and 1970s.

The two primary problems with high-rise elevator design relate to travel time and floor plate footprint. As buildings pass about 20 stories, travel times become so long that even high speed elevators will not be able to handle the populations such buildings house. To overcome this, more elevators can be provided; however, at some point the number of shafts required will take up too much floor area to be economical. Several strategies can increase the passenger capacity of each shaft (Figure 12.4). *Zoned systems* provide banks of low, mid and high-rise elevators that travel directly between the lobby and the appropriate zone. This system uses more floor space, but it provides very efficient service to high-rise floors. *Double deck* cabs feature two passenger compartments stacked atop one another, with a two-story entry lobby that segregate passengers according to even and odd floors. While this doubles the capacity of each shaft, it also doubles the number of stops and leads to disconcerting moments in each cab as the other stops for passengers. For buildings over about 250 meters, the most efficient system is a *sky lobby* arrangement, where express elevators run to a set of transfer floors at roughly even intervals throughout the building. From these transfer floors, local elevators then run to individual floors. Because the local shafts can 'stack' (with appropriate structural separation), this multiplies the capacity of each shaft by the number of transfer floors.

In addition to passenger elevators, any building requiring the movement of goods or equipment will be outfitted with a dedicated *freight elevator*, typically

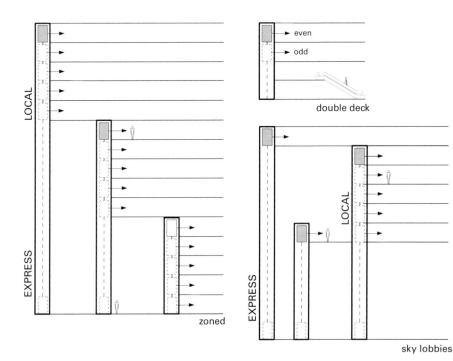

double deck

zoned

sky lobbies

12.4
Banking strategies for high-rise elevator systems

one for every 30,000 square meters (300,000 square feet) of commercial or industrial space. Such elevators should connect as directly as possible to a loading dock, if provided, and to a "back of house" circulatory system. Freight elevators will generally be sized according to the largest anticipated piece of equipment in the building, and will be outfitted with interior finishes designed to absorb constant cart or dolly traffic. In some situations, a passenger elevator will include hooks to hang blankets that can protect higher end finishes, allowing the cab to be used for freight. In all cases, buildings with elevators must have at least one that will allow a full-sized stretcher to comfortably move in and out.

ESCALATORS AND CONVEYORS

For applications involving only a few stories and high pedestrian capacities, escalators may present a better solution to vertical transport than elevators. Because their start and finish points are usually visible, they provide a more intuitive wayfinding strategy, and their capacities are much higher than comparably priced elevators. Their expense, however (often US$100,000–$300,000 per installation), may be prohibitive in many situations.

Escalators operate by a running a continuous chain attached to self-leveling treads around a drive motor, usually at the top of the run. In the United States, escalators' slopes have been standardized at 30 degrees. Flat runs at the top and bottom allow the treads to level out, and provide a kinesthetic cue to passengers that the landing is approaching. To prevent catching feet or clothing, the treads must be ridged, and must enter a "combplate" at both ends. Moving handrails are geared to the drive chain as well, and must return at floor level, again to prevent ingesting hands (Figure 12.6).

The arrangement of escalators in a multistory building may be based on efficiency, in which case a scissor arrangement may be most appropriate, or on exposure to key elements on a floor (i.e. retail), in which case parallel stacks

12.5
Elevator cabs are often showpieces for detailing and mechanical expression.

12.6
Typical escalator dimensions.

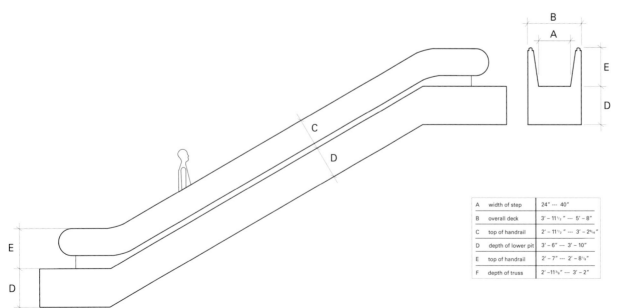

A	width of step	24" --- 40"
B	overall deck	3' – 11½" --- 5' – 8"
C	top of handrail	2' – 11½" --- 3' – 2⁹⁄₁₆"
D	depth of lower pit	3' – 6" --- 3' – 10"
E	top of handrail	2' – 7" --- 2' – 8⅛"
F	depth of truss	2' –11⅜" --- 3' – 2"

may work best. The former is essentially a double helix, with up and down traffic separated into distinct paths, while the latter pairs up and down escalators, enforcing a walkaround to go from one floor to the next. In cases where massive efficiency is required (train stations, stadiums), multiple parallel escalators may be set to run predominantly in one direction, depending on the flow of traffic.

The layout of escalators involves figuring both the horizontal run required to achieve a given height, and allowing for the truss that enables them to be self-supporting for rises up to 7.3m (24') (Figure 12.5). The truss is hollow, allowing space for the return path of treads. For larger installations, intermediate support may be required. While generally limited to 12.2m (40') of rise, installations involving continuous support and intermediate drive motors have enabled rises of up to 48m (160') in unusual situations such as the Washington Metro. An exterior escalator in Hong Kong uses several sequential escalators to move commuters up and down a 400m height.

Moving passenger conveyors are continuous tread surfaces that operate horizontally, moving occupants over large distances with minimal vertical change (no more than 12°). These are most typically used in airports, where distances to gates are often extreme for passengers with luggage. To allow user choice, conveyors are usually limited to 90m (300'). Conveyors must operate at a slow enough speed to allow safe embarking and disembarking. As a result, they generally move at a pace slower than typical walking speeds. While most users will walk on them, doubling their speed, others often see conveyors as a chance to rest. This can block traffic, and therefore good practice is to ensure that faster users can easily pass standing passengers, a minimum clear width of 1000mm (40") is recommended. Dimensions for handrail heights and thicknesses are typically similar to those of escalators.

FREQUENTLY ASKED QUESTIONS

Why aren't elevators allowed as exits in a fire situation?
Elevators present an extreme fire danger in that they are located in vertical shafts, which can act as chimneys, and offer no alternative exit if the hoistway shaft is broached by flame or smoke. Worse, fire and heat can damage elevator doors, guiderails, or fascia panels, causing cabs to stop at floors that are aflame. Occupants then have no escape. Typically, detailed signage is required at all elevator landings that shows the location of nearby emergency exits or fire stairs.

Are there special rules for glass elevators? Exterior elevators?
Glass (or "observation") elevators may be exempt from hoistway requirements as they typically occur in atria. Often a solid wall (or a carefully designed glass wall) will still be required at each landing, and this wall must be continuous to avoid crushing hazards for maintenance personnel or a foot or hand trapped in a door. At the base, a wall or a physical separation is required to avoid occupants reaching in to the path of a traveling car. Guide rails must be provided to keep cabs aligned within the hoistway. If the hoistway walls are substantially built—out of concrete, for instance—the rails may

be mounted directly to them. They are usually placed in line with the cab's center of gravity, and thus aligned with the cab's plunger (for hydraulic) or cable connection (for traction). Exterior cabs must be outfitted with extensive (and expensive) waterproofing, as door operating motors must still be mounted on top of the cab itself.

GLOSSARY

Car or cab: The enclosure, structure, and mechanics associated with the traveling, occupied portion of an elevator system. Typically this includes guides, structure (usually steel), walls, roof, and floor, control panel, and doors with motor and chain drive. It must meet accessibility standards for wheelchair users (especially turnaround and control panel access), and safety standards to prevent walls, roof, or floor from being breached by panicked occupants in an emergency.

Counterweight: In a traction system, a large weight attached to a cab's cables which balances the anticipated typical traveling weight of the cab.

Dumbwaiter: A small elevator system designed for freight only. Often not subject to as many of the safety regulations as a passenger elevator, but limited in size and height.

Governor: A safety device that senses excess cab speed and triggers brakes.

Guide rails: Precision elements (usually steel), that are typically attached to hoistway walls, on which the cab's guide wheels roll to ensure straight travel.

Hoistway: The 'tube' through which an elevator cab moves. Typically includes a fire-resistive group of surrounding walls and door assemblies at each landing. Often subject to very stringent fire and safety codes, as they provide ideal chimneys for the spread of smoke and flame, and numerous crushing hazards for anyone within.

Hydraulic elevator: A vertical transportation system composed of an enclosed cab, a hoistway, and a hydraulically activated plunger system that is usually bored into the ground and filled from a reservoir and pump at basement level.

Landing: An area of floor that is designed to accommodate access in and out of elevator cabs. Subject to building code legislation for fire separation, and accessibility codes for call buttons, alerts, and door configuration.

Motive power: A system in which an elevator's motors are part of the cab assembly. While rare, this arrangement offers savings in space.

Overrun: A designed space at the top of an elevator hoistway that provides additional travel distance for cabs and for anyone (typically maintenance personnel) who may be on the cab's roof.

Platform lift: An unenclosed elevator cab, usually traversing a short distance and often used only for wheelchair access. Must typically have a full set of guard and handrails, and must meet additional safety standards to prevent crushing of fingers, etc. that may be extended through rails.

Traction elevator: A vertical transportation system composed of an enclosed cab, a hoistway, and a motor, cables, and sheaves that are typically located at the top of the hoistway.

Two-speed doors: On an elevator cab and hoistway, an opening system that moves door leaves at two different speeds, saving space and reducing opening time.

FURTHER READING

Gray, L. E. (2002). *From Ascending Rooms to Express Elevators: A History of the Passenger Elevator in the 19th Century.* New York: Elevator World, Inc.

Strakosch, G. R. ed. (1998). *The Vertical Transportation Handbook.* New York: Wiley.

PART 4

MATERIALS

13

WOOD

Trees	Types: deciduous and coniferous
	Hard vs. soft woods
	Dimensional lumber
	Sustainability
Species	Examples
	Framing/structural
	Finish/cabinetry
History	Laugier's primitive hut
	Framing types
	Traditions
Wood construction	The carpentry trade
	Framing carpentry
	Light framing
	Heavy timber
	Finish carpentry
	Cabinetry
	Doors, windows, trim
	Paneling
	Floors

INTRODUCTION

Wood is one of the most prevalent building materials in the world. Approximately 90 percent of buildings constructed in the United States each year are framed with wood, while that percentage is only 15–20 percent in the U.K. Timber is one of the only 100 percent renewable building materials and it doesn't naturally produce any toxic by-products in its conversion from tree to product. Trees have one of the longest life spans of all living things—the oldest living trees are 5000 years old. Timber has obvious advantages over other materials: it can regenerate (if properly harvested) and provide a continuous low-energy supply for our use; wood is recyclable, waste efficient, biodegradable and nontoxic. It has proven to be very energy efficient, and trees play a major role in soaking up carbon dioxide, reducing the effects of climate warming.

There are an immense number of species and types of wood products.

Each type has its own character and appropriate use. Many woods are most commonly used for structural purposes, while others are best suited for finish work. The properties, availability, and cost of the many types of wood vary considerably. Some types of timber are also inappropriate to use under any circumstances due to their rarity or the forestry practices used to harvest them. Making the responsible decision can be a difficult and moving target, which requires some research and careful specifying.

While many technological advances have been made in the development of new materials, few can rival the strength, durability, beauty, workability, and versatility of wood. New technologies in wood production have also modified the ways we can use this material, and it continues to be one of the primary structural and finish materials architects use on projects. Chances are good that you will never work on a project that does not involve wood in one way or another, and in many cases you will need to know what species to select and how it will work in the environment you've created.

TREES

Commercial lumber is classified into "hardwoods" and "softwoods". Hardwoods come from broad leaf or deciduous trees and softwoods come from evergreen or coniferous trees. While most commercial hardwoods are physically harder or denser than most commercial softwoods, the classification refers to the type of tree only and does not always describe the hardness of the wood.

Wood is cellular material and due to the microstructure of longitudinal cells wood has different structural properties parallel to the grain vs. perpendicular to the grain. Parallel to the grain wood is strong and stiff; perpendicular it is weaker and deformable (Figure 13.1). On the basis of performance by unit weight, most seasoned construction timber is as least as stiff and as strong as structural steel.

Commercially marketed lumber includes dozens of tree species. When trees

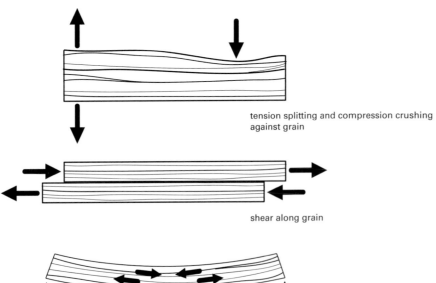

tension splitting and compression crushing against grain

shear along grain

shear along grain in bending

13.1
Timber resistance to vertical and horizontal pressure.

Table 13.1 Lumber nominal and actual surfaced dimensions.

Nominal dimensions mm (")		Actual seasoned and surfaced dimensions mm (")	
25	(1)	19	(¾)
50	(2)	38	(1½)
75	(3)	64	(2½)
100	(4)	89	(3½)
125	(5)	114	(4½)
150	(6)	140	(5½)
200	(8)	185	(7¼)
250	(10)	235	(9¼)
300	(12)	285	(11¼)
350	(14)	335	(13¼)
400	(16)	385	(15¼)

are commercially cut or "harvested" the cellular hollows are filled with moisture, commonly called "sap". Trees are sawn into rough lumber while in a saturated or "green" condition. Construction timber must be "seasoned" before use, which dries most of the sap. This seasoning is accomplished through stacking the wood in the open air for a period of months or more commonly by heating it in a kiln for a period of days. The process of seasoning causes the lumber to shrink considerably, and it continues to shrink (or in some cases expand) until it is in equilibrium with the moisture content of the surrounding air. Wood expansion is due much more to moisture than thermal factors, and the changing moisture content needs to be taken into account to allow expansion/contraction in any final assembly.

Most lumber is surfaced after seasoning, which reduces it to its final dimensions and gives the wood smooth faces. The edges are rounded or "eased" to reduce splinters and make the wood easier to handle.

All of this rough cutting, seasoning, shrinking, and surfacing explains why there is such a difference between "nominal" and "actual" sizes of timber in the U.S. However, in the U.K. metric sizes are close to the actual size of timber you purchase (Table 13.1). If lumber is "sawn" in the U.K. it is not planed so it is actual size, while planed lumber is 3 to 5mm smaller than listed (so a planed 100×50mm in the U.K. is about 95×47mm). The most common of construction timbers is nominally called a 2×4 (100×50) – which implies a piece of wood 2" deep, by 4" wide (100mm wide, by 50mm deep), by the length, which is normally called out in board feet or meters. Note that when calling out the size of lumber, the thickness is called out first in the U.S. (feet and inches) but the opposite is true in the metric system. For example a metric 100×50mm equals an imperial 2×4". A brief size verification of U.S. lumber will show that the depth is actually 1.5", the width is 3.5" and the length is very close to what is listed. The boards are rough-cut at the actual size, except for the length that is cut at the end of the process. The shrinking and surfacing reduces the nominal size dramatically. The final surfacing process creates boards that follow a standard amount of size decrease: 1" nominal = ¾" actual, 2" to 6" nominal reduce

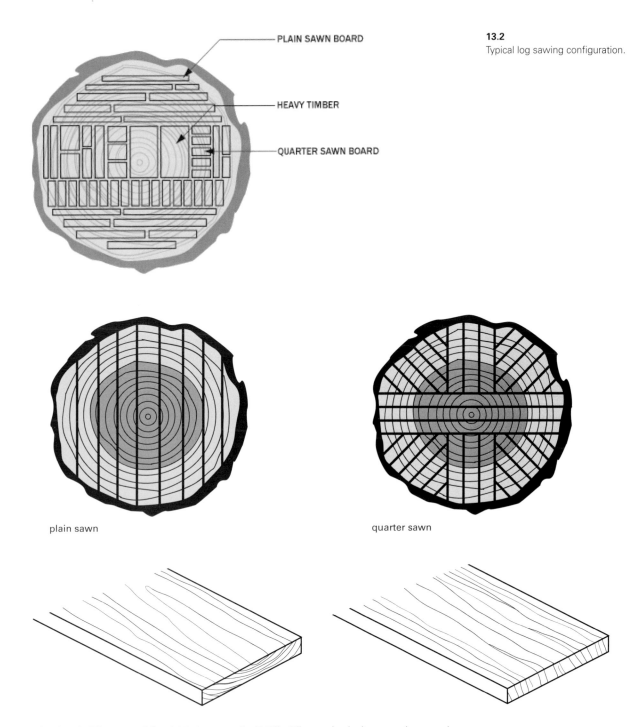

PLAIN SAWN BOARD

HEAVY TIMBER

QUARTER SAWN BOARD

plain sawn

quarter sawn

size by 0.5"—so a 6" width is actually 5.5"; 8" nominal sizes and up reduce size by 0.75"—so a 14" width is actually 13.25". 16" (400mm) is the typical maximum nominal board width and board lengths run from 6 feet (1.8m) to 24 feet (7.3m) in 2-foot (0.6m) increments.

How the boards are cut from a log affects the strength and appearance (Figure 13.2). Plain sawn lumber has a variety of noticeable grain patterns and tends to twist, cup, and wear unevenly. It can also have grain patterns on the surface that peel apart and separate. It is typically less expensive to produce and purchase (Figure 13.3).

13.3
Plain and quarter sawn boards.

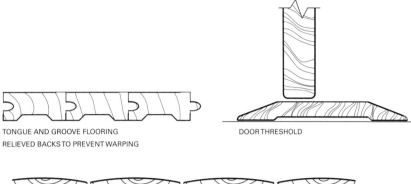

13.4
Board warp.

TONGUE AND GROOVE FLOORING
RELIEVED BACKS TO PREVENT WARPING

DOOR THRESHOLD

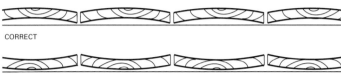

CORRECT

INCORRECT

NOTE: THE BOARDS WILL CURL
TOWARD THE BARK SIDE OF WHERE
THEY CAME FROM THE LOG.

Quarter sawn lumber has more even grain patterns than plain sawn, wears better, warps less, and is less affected by surface splitting. It is typically more expensive due to the additional difficulty and waste materials from the cutting pattern.

Lumber is also milled in ways that resist warping. Tongue and groove floors, door thresholds, and wood sills frequently have *relieved* backs, meaning the side facing down has a notch cut to promote curling down rather than up (Figure 13.4). These notches assist in keeping wood from curling, but the most reliable way to prevent problems like this is to use a better cut of wood (like quarter sawn) and also relieve the back of the piece.

Lumber is graded on both structural and visual scales; each scale is based on the species of wood. Typically hardwoods are rated visually (because they are used for finish purposes) and softwoods are graded structurally (because they are used for framing and construction).

A major issue facing all timber harvesting is sustainability. Entire species of trees have been eliminated due to overcutting, and the environmental impact of clear cutting forests has proven devastating. The general quality of timber has at times decreased over the last century and we are more recently beginning to understand how to manage this issue on a global scale. The complexity of these issues makes a simple unchanging list of what trees to use and not use worthless. Wood is the main cooking fuel for nearly half the world's population—so banning species has at times reduced the worth of that tree to the point that it is no longer valued and therefore used as firewood or cleared for agriculture more quickly than if it was exported for construction. The goal is to stay aware of what timber is being responsibly harvested. What "responsible" means can be debated, but the goal is to reach zero loss forestry—the cutting and growing need to take place equally. Also, forests need to retain a diverse population of vegetation, rather than becoming single species farms. Some locales have banned the use of certain woods in publicly funded projects, but the ultimate responsibility for using appropriate species lies with the designer and builder—only the people designing and constructing a building can determine what goes in and what stays out. The decision requires research, and sources like the U.S. Forest Service, the Forest Stewardship Council (www.fsc.org), CITES (Convention on International Trade in Endangered Species (www.cites.org), and The Nature Conservancy (www.nature.org) can assist.

SPECIES

Most people are familiar with the common species of wood—Douglas Fir and Southern Pine for construction, and Oak, Maple, Cherry, Teak, etc. for finishes. To list all of the types is too cumbersome, but some species descriptions will be helpful.

Certain types of woods are naturally resistant to problems without preservatives or special treatment. Wood in general is decay-resistant when its moisture content is below 20 percent. This can be hard to control in many situations, and all applied treatments eventually fail—so decay resistant woods are often used for exterior applications. Redwood, Cedar, Bald Cypress, Black Locust, Teak, and Black Walnut are the most common decay-resistant species. Termite-resistant species include Redwood, Eastern Red Cedar, and Bald Cypress. The properties and uses of different wood species are described in Table 13.2.

Table 13.2 Common wood species, their properties, and typical uses.

Name	Uses	Notes
Western Red Cedar	cladding	weathers to grey, closet linings, resists rot
Douglas Fir	construction to furniture	grows fast and straight
Southern Pine	construction to furniture	grows fast and straight
Spruce	construction and scrap	lower quality and not durable
Yew	furniture and finishes	limited availability
Yellow Poplar	construction and moldings	little grain, paints well
Ash	finishes and veneer	decorative, similar to oak
Bubinga	veneer	African exotic, dark red
Cherry	finishes, veneer, furniture	medium to light red color
Elm	finishes and furniture	slowly returning after Dutch Elm Disease
Mahogany	finishes and furniture	dark color, medium grain, resists rot
Maple	veneer, flooring, furniture	light grain, can take stain poorly
Red Oak	veneer, finishes, furniture	red to brown, coarse, strong grain
White Oak	veneer, finishes, floors	lighter brown, hard, stains well, can resist rot
Padauk	finishes and furniture	strong red color, exotic
Teak	finishes and furniture	warm brown, resists rot
Redwood	cladding, furniture	warm red, resists rot, avoid old growth trees (in general)

HISTORY

Wood is traditionally known as the first building material. Abbé Laugier proposed in 1753 that the first human impulse to construct shelter resulted in the "Primitive Hut"—the first act of (western) architecture (Figure 13.5). This is a wooden four-post structure with a simple roof, fulfilling the most basic need

13.5
Abbé Laugier's primitive hut, from 1753.

of shelter—but one created by humans rather than found in nature. There are many other traditions of wood design, and its ease of use and prevalence throughout the world gives it a special quality in the realm of design. Stone and masonry were certainly used early on to create monumental works—some of which are our oldest remaining artifacts of early culture, but wood was certainly used for most construction in places that had timber available.

The nature of construction before engineering was trial and error. Each generation learned from the previous and transmitted that knowledge forward—refining it to the particular circumstances and cultural heritage of the builders' society. This pattern has been repeated thousands of times—until we are faced with similar problems that have been addressed by our earliest ancestors. This is a knowledge base too powerful to ignore, yet we frequently do, and often times neglect to study our own traditions when we're deciding how to create assemblies. Don't make this mistake—as Bruce Mao says, "Stand on someone's shoulders. You can travel farther carried on the accomplishments of those who came before you. And the view is so much better." Learn the difference between looking back in nostalgia and using tradition to move forward.

Barn construction is a good example to see how this refinement and tradition can work. Entire communities would come together to raise a barn and the lessons were shared throughout the community. These structures have an almost inevitable quality of appearance, each detail has been thought out to maximize the use of local materials, available technology, and need for durability (Figure 13.6).

13.6
Barn heavy timber joint, from the late 1800s.

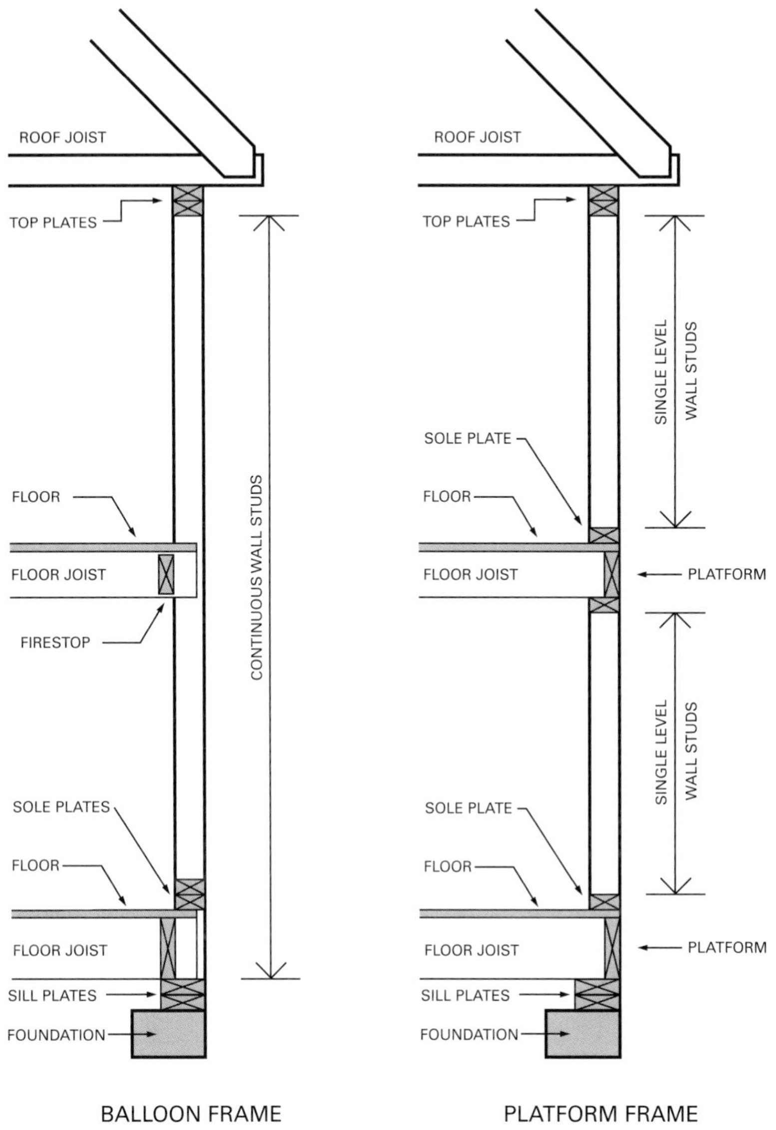

BALLOON FRAME

PLATFORM FRAME

The method of assembling building frames has responded to the need for fast construction as well. After the Chicago fire of 1871 there was a need to reconstruct buildings quickly. Out of this need was developed the *balloon type wood framing system*. This framing system raises an exterior wood frame the entire height of the building; the floors are then inserted inside this exterior frame and it can be sheathed and enclosed quickly. The system only works for two-story structures (due to the available lengths of wooden studs), but it allows for full height wall assembly on the ground, which can then be simply propped up and joined together easily (Figure 13.7).

The more common method currently used is *platform wood frame construction*, where each story of wall framing is constructed and propped into place. Then the upper floor joists and floor sheathing are constructed, and the next level can commence building wall frames on the new floor. This allows for more than two floors to be constructed and uses smaller wooden wall studs. There are, however, still limits to the overall height based on building fire safety codes.

WOOD CONSTRUCTION

A carpenter is the classification of the tradesperson who will be dealing with the woodwork at a building site or millwork shop. This person has been trained to deal with wood as an apprentice and knows more than most architects about wood construction. Many project field superintendents were carpenters by trade before they took on more senior roles. Learn from construction professionals—ask them how they would do something—study how they put things together. Many younger architects are immediately discredited on job sites because they draw things that are shown incorrectly or inefficiently. Be flexible on assembly and firm on durability and aesthetics. Think about how someone would assemble what you're drawing—mentally go through the steps; if you can't put it together in your head it will be difficult or impossible in the field.

One of the roles of a carpenter is assembling the framing. Wood framing is of two primary types: *heavy timber* and *light frame* (Figure 13.8). Heavy timber construction consists of exposed columns, girders, beams and decking large enough to be slow to catch fire. This type of construction is used in a large

13.8
Heavy and light wood framing.

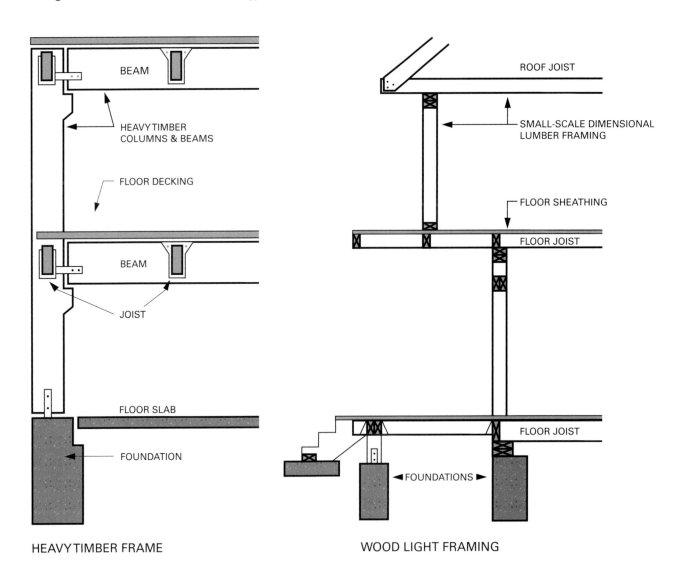

HEAVY TIMBER FRAME

WOOD LIGHT FRAMING

range of building sizes and types. The large size of timbers used in this type of construction makes it appropriate for regular, repetitive bays and simple building shapes. Light frame construction, such as the balloon and platform types, is usually made up of nominal 50mm (2") framing members spaced closely together and concealed. Light frame construction, with its small member sizes, adapts easily to more intricate building forms than heavy frame construction. Often metal studs are used in place of wood in light frame construction, which can be less expensive, easier to assemble, and more fire resistant, but they are typically much less rigid. Wood is better suited to making stiffer assemblies, but is not the typical choice for large-scale or commercial building types.

Another role of carpenters is in cladding and sheathing the building. This is often done in wood as paneling, siding, shingles, or shakes. Base sheathing is often plywood or other fiber based sheet products, and it can be applied to the exterior walls and roof, along with the interior floors. Waterproofing is placed over this sheathing and then the finish material is applied. Careful attention needs to be shown to the ways sheathing can shift and expand; so appropriate gaps should be built into the assembly to avoid buckling. Fasteners also should be selected and placed so not to stain the wood or cause leaks into the area behind the sheathing (see Chapter 30, Building Envelopes).

Finish carpentry involves all of the finished or exposed woodworking on the interior and sometimes exterior of the building. Examples of finish work are cabinets, wall paneling, wood floors, stair railings, floor and crown trim, interior doors and frames, and finish window framing (windows are typically pre-manufactured and installed as part of the exterior sheathing). Much of the finish wood is prepared in a millwork shop and fitted in place at the job site. The more work that can be done at the shop the better the result will typically be. Quality control is much higher in the shop and therefore the level of precision and quality of finish is superior. Certain things need to be done in the field in order to custom fit the space, and a good field carpenter will consistently determine whether a project is acceptable or great. Again, don't underestimate the building trades; learn as much as possible from them. Combative relationships with construction teams always negatively impact your project.

The assembly of wood is much more involved than simply deciding whether to use screws or nails to put pieces together. Wood joinery has a long history of developing different types of joints for different purposes (Figure 13.9). Within the decision of how to join any two pieces of a building assembly together is an attitude about the overall structure. Some joints try to hide the fact that they are two separate pieces, while others accentuate and celebrate the joints. Considering the juncture of any two pieces or materials should be a design decision and treated as such. Consistency and intention in detailing tends to hold the overall feel of a building together.

CONCLUSION

Wood is one of the easiest materials to work with and one of the most difficult to master. It can do almost every building function well and is remarkably versatile and beautiful. As designers it is our responsibility to use it responsibly—and there is some resistance to doing this. Information is not always easy to gather

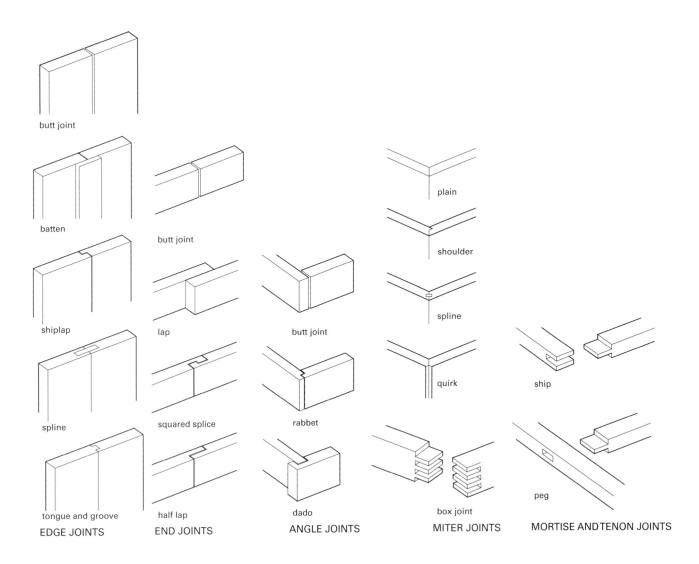

butt joint

batten

butt joint

plain

shoulder

shiplap

lap

butt joint

spline

spline

squared splice

rabbet

quirk

ship

tongue and groove

EDGE JOINTS

half lap

END JOINTS

dado

ANGLE JOINTS

box joint

MITER JOINTS

peg

MORTISE AND TENON JOINTS

13.9
Wood joint types

on the best sustainable practices, and architects/builders have been doing things the same way for so long that it's hard to change. Specifying certified woods can add expense but is the easiest way to source wood responsibly. The use of wood offers endless design opportunities and the better you understand the options the more design potential is available.

FREQUENTLY ASKED QUESTIONS

How do you decide between using plain or quarter sawn lumber?
Plain sawn lumber is usually less expensive than quarter sawn, but of a lower finish quality. The decision tends to rest on whether the lumber will be exposed or in a condition where some abrasion or warping will negatively affect performance or aesthetics. Concealed structural wood is typically plain sawn, as it is not exposed to view and is normally part of an assembly that will not be affected by small amounts of warping or cupping. Exposed wood, such as decking or finish cabinetry, is preferably quarter sawn because there are less potential impacts of warping and a desire for a higher finish quality.

Is there a list available for what types of lumber are sustainable?
The short answer is no. A major issue facing all timber harvesting is sustainability. While there are lists available that recommend what woods to use or avoid, the issue is too complex to be stable over a long period of time, meaning the lists go out of date quickly. This is an area where designers must stay abreast of the latest research and information on lumber acceptability and one of the reasons why practicing sustainably requires constant re-education.

GLOSSARY

Balloon framing: system that raises exterior studs the full wall height with floors inserted into the frame.

Carpenter: The classification of the tradesperson who will be dealing with the woodwork at a building site or millwork shop.

Easing: Rounding the edges of lumber to limit splintering at the corners.

Plain sawn: Lumber cut straight across the log in the most efficient pattern.

Platform framing: System that constructs single floor height studs with platform floors at each level before proceeding.

Quarter sawn: Lumber cut toward the centerline of the log in fourths, resulting in more even grain patterns.

Sap: The moisture that fills the cellular hollows of wood.

Seasoning: Drying the sap from recently cut trees until it is at a specified moisture content.

Softwoods: Lumber from evergreen or coniferous trees.

Veneer: Thin wood sheet glued to the face of a core material, or to other veneers to form plywood.

FURTHER READING

Levin, E. (1972). *The International Guide to Wood Selection*. New York: Drake Publishers; pp. 12–27.

Lefteri, C. (2003). *Wood: Materials for Inspirational Design*. Mies, Switzerland: RotoVision SA; Chapter on How to Buy Wood, pp. 12–13.

14

MASONRY

Masonry basics	Masonry types
	Production and quarrying
	Properties
	Common uses
History	Early uses of masonry
	Technology developments
	Modern use
Masonry construction	Assembly methods
	Patterns
	The arch and lintel
	Colors, finishes, textures
	Problem issues
	The masonry trade

INTRODUCTION

Masonry is based on the need to build semi-permanent structures from durable individual units that can be stacked and adhered together. We consider masonry to be: clay brick, clay tile, concrete masonry units (CMUs), glass block, terra cotta, adobe, and stonework. Masonry construction has been found that is over 16,000 years old, and it has been continually refined from that time for durability, aesthetics, and versatility.

Masonry is long lasting, weather resistant, and can provide building structure and cladding or both. Masonry is also fire resistant, provides thermal comfort, resists abuse, and reduces sound penetration. Systems may be designed as walls, columns, piers, pilasters, lintels, and arches, but they always work most efficiently in compression. Masonry is used in virtually every type of building application, and the colors and finishes of masonry are almost limitless.

Typical masonry construction is made up of small building units, which create maximum versatility of building form. Manufactured masonry units are made of clay, concrete, or glass and may be solid or hollow. Solid units have less than 25 percent open voids and are usually cored or have indentations that reduce weight and provide a better surface for mechanical bonding of the mortar.

Hollow masonry units are more than 25 percent open and the voids, or cells, are large enough to contain reinforcing bars and grout.

Manufactured clay masonry units are molded or extruded and then heated at over 870C (1600F). Adobe units are cured at low temperatures, sometimes by sun drying, and gain strength from emulsifiers or other binders. CMUs are molded from low water mixture concrete and gain strength through the chemical hydration of the cement.

Mortar and grout are the bonding materials used to adhere masonry units together. Mortar is spread, or "buttered", between units by the mason during stacking. Grout is poured or spread into cells and cavities in walls or between tiling units to fill gaps. Mortar and grout are made of a cement, aggregate, and water mixture similar to concrete—but with less aggregate and sometimes more water content to remain workable, spreadable, and pourable. Once the mortar or grout is placed between masonry units it sets quickly, due to the drying absorption of the porous masonry.

Masonry construction is often initially more expensive than other types of construction, but has an excellent life cycle cost. The construction is very durable, long lasting, low maintenance, and energy efficient. It is also has a low environmental impact and is inert when downcycled as fill material.

Please note that while you may frequently see and hear the term "masonary", there is only one "a" in the word.

MASONRY BASICS

The most common type of masonry is the clay brick. *Bricks* are made in modular and non-modular sizes with specific nominal and actual dimensions (Table 14.1). The nominal dimensions in brick sizing are based on a completed assembly—meaning the final size in the wall with mortar joints included. The most common brick size is the "modular" brick that is nominally 8" deep, 4" wide, and 2.6" high in the U. S., and $225 \times 112.5 \times 75$mm for the British Standard coordinating brick size. The height/width/depth dimensions are for common reference only, as units may be placed into the wall system in any orientation. The actual size of this unit is 7⅝" D, 3⅝" W, and 2¼" H, with a ⅜" mortar bed in the U.S. and $215 \times 102.5 \times 65$mm (or 73mm), with 10mm mortar joints in the U.K. This makes vertical coursing 8 inches high for every 3 rows of standard running bond in the U.S. and 225mm high for 3 rows in the U.K., with 4 to 8" increments of wall length in the U.S. and 112.5 to 225mm increments in the U.K. Working with these dimensions when designing is called "using brick module"—understanding that height/openings/corners can only occur at increments of these dimensions. Re-dimensioning an entire project (and the attendant ridicule) due to not considering "brick module" is almost a comical right of passage for young architectural interns. Other brick sizes and mortar bed thicknesses are possible and can be found in Figure 14.1. Keep in mind when using any material like brick, that labor costs far outweigh material costs—therefore using larger, more expensive individual units is cheaper overall due to the fact that fewer of them need to be placed to make a wall (this only works up to a reasonable size of unit, i.e. small enough for one person to easily carry). The rough dimensions of the basic modular brick have been in use

Table 14.1 Standard brick sizes and vertical coursing.

	Unit designation	Nominal dimensions (inches)			Joint thickness (inches)	Actual dimensions (inches)			Vertical coursing
		W	H	D		W	H	D	
U.S.	Modular	4	2⅔	8	⅜	3⅝	2¼	7⅝	3 Courses = 8"
					½	3½	2¼	7½	
	Engineer modular	4	3⅕	8	⅜	3⅝	2¾	7⅝	5 C = 16"
					½	3½	2¹³⁄₁₆	7½	
	Closure modular	4	4	8	⅜	3⅝	3⅝	7⅝	1 C = 4"
					½	3½	3½	7½	
	Roman	4	2	12	⅜	3⅝	1⅝	11⅝	2 C = 4"
					½	3½	1½	11½	
	Norman	4	2⅔	12	⅜	3⅝	2¼	11⅝	3 C = 8"
					½	3½	2¼	11½	
	Engineer Norman	4	3⅕	12	⅜	3⅝	2¾	11⅝	5 C = 16"
					½	3½	2¹³⁄₁₆	11½	
	Utility	4	4	12	⅜	3⅝	3⅝	11⅝	1 C = 4"
					½	3½	3½	11½	

	Unit designation	Joint thickness (mm)	Actual dimensions (mm)			Vertical coursing
			W	H	D	
U.K.	Standard coordinated	10	215	65	102.5	3 C = 210mm
	Imperial	10	215	73	102.5	3 C = 234mm
	Thin format	10	240	52	115	4 C = 238mm
	Standard format	10	240	71	115	3 C = 238mm
	1½ Standard format	10	240	113	115	2 C = 238mm
	3½ Standard Format	10	240	113	175	2 C = 238mm

Note: U.K. nominal and actual dimensions are equivalent. Check with masonry manufacturer to verify specifications.

for over 2500 years because of its size it is easy to handle and place with one hand for an entire work day.

Clay tiles are far less commonly used since the large-scale production of CMUs became widespread. Clay tiles were largely used for structural applications, as they were often larger open cell units that could be easily placed and grouted full if needed. They are also used as interior wall backup with brick veneers placed over top. CMU construction has taken the place of clay tiles in the U.S. because the expense is less and the durability/strength of the concrete units are higher. Tiles are, however, still used in applications such as fireplace flues (where they are more heat resistant than concrete) and underground drainage systems (where they resist leakage better than concrete). They are also used when the glazed tile look is desired or in situations where vandalism is a concern because they can be cleaned of paint and stains easier than unglazed CMUs.

CMUs are molded from zero-slump concrete and cured with hot water ranging from 38C (100F) mist to 175C (350F) steam. This makes the units very strong and resistant to cracking and chipping. Most CMUs have hollow cores to reduce

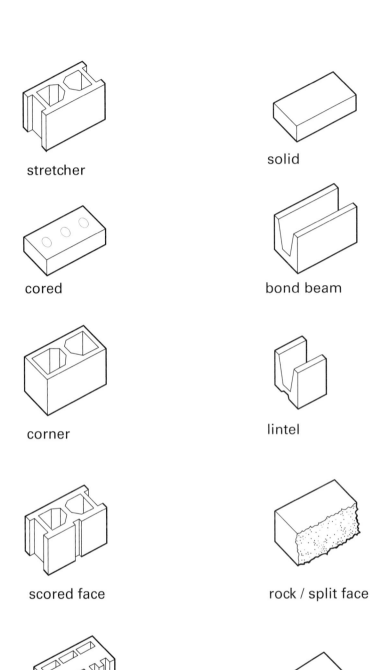

stretcher

solid

cored

bond beam

corner

lintel

scored face

rock / split face

fluted

sill / coping

14.1
Basic concrete masonry unit shapes.

weight and allow for grout and reinforcing bars. The most common nominal size for a CMU in the U.S. is 8″ W, 8″ H and 16″ L, the actual size being 7⅝″ × 15⅝″; in the U.K. this is 24cm W, 23.8cm H and 49.5cm L. This makes each block row height the same as 3 "modular" bricks and allows the two systems to be tied together easily in composite wall construction. Again, using the standard nominal block dimensions is referred to as designing in "block module", and many times this module controls the overall dimensions and all other openings of the building you're designing. CMUs come in many shapes and sizes to accomplish various tasks and produce different finishes (Figure 14.1). The versatility and compressive strength of these units, paired with the fact that they are easily combined with steel reinforcing bars for tension capacity, make them nearly ubiquitous in most construction. They are resistant to corrosion, termites, winds, weather and can be colored or textured easily.

Terra cotta is used as a part of, or over masonry wall systems. Terra cotta moldings were used extensively around the turn of the twentieth century to produce colors and shapes not possible in other materials and much less expensively than stone carvings. This type of construction is no longer common but may be encountered as part of building restoration, and more modern ceramic glazing systems can reproduce the look of original hand-cast terra cotta moldings. Modern large-scale glazed ceramic tile and terra cotta cladding systems are becoming more common, and provide a durable, attractive exterior finish that is hung in curtain wall fashion rather than grouted onto the surface of a wall.

Glass blocks act as a hybrid type of masonry, using what was traditionally a thin glazing and making it into a compact translucent/transparent modular wall unit. While not used for load-bearing walls, the versatility of the material creates many types of applications from entire facades, window openings, interior partitions, floors, skylights, and stairways. The glass blocks allow for light to pass, can self support without framing, manage thermal transmission, control sound transmission, and can be made vandal and even bullet resistant. Typical blocks are made from two halves bonded together, although solid block are also available. Common square sizes are from (115mm to 300mm) 4.5" to 12". Rectangular, 45-degree corner, bullnose, and radius blocks shapes are also available by various manufacturers. The surface finishes of blocks range from clear to translucent to various wave and molded grid patterns. Cement-based mortar is normally used to assemble wall systems, however, silicone-based mortars can be used to reduce sound transmission or increase earthquake resistance (Figure 14.2).

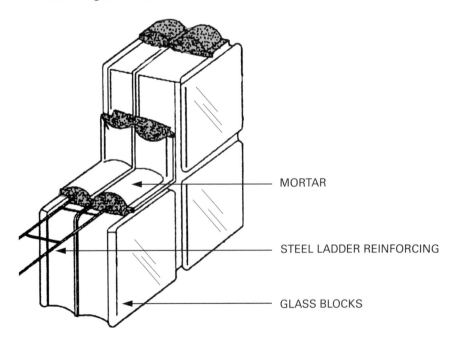

MORTAR

STEEL LADDER REINFORCING

GLASS BLOCKS

14.2
Typical glass block assembly.

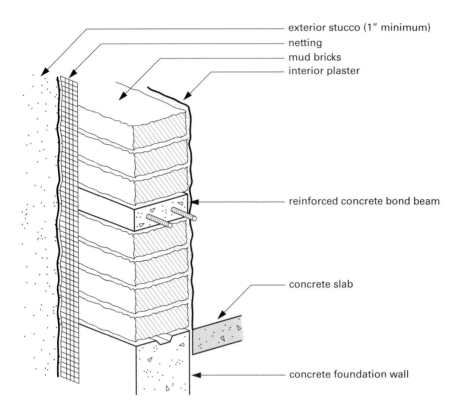

exterior stucco (1″ minimum)
netting
mud bricks
interior plaster

reinforced concrete bond beam

concrete slab

concrete foundation wall

14.3
Adobe wall assembly.

Adobe walls are made from mud for both the masonry unit and the mortar. This type of construction uses sun-dried mud bricks layered in a roughly 1:10 ratio of width to height. Actual thicknesses vary from location to location based on the traditional methods of local construction and intentional "tuning" of the thickness of the wall for thermal load shifting. The most important consideration with adobe is the control of water, as the sun-dried bricks will dissolve under moisture. Well-built structures dissolve at a rate of 25mm (1″) in 20 years in areas of 254–635mm (10–25″) of rainfall per annum. This type of building system makes sense in dry areas that can effectively use thermal mass walls. Earth-walled buildings are very ecologically friendly—taking a minimum of energy to construct, using limitless supplies of natural building material, and recycling themselves back into the earth with no adverse biological impact (Figure 14.3).

Stone masonry was historically used as a structural material; however, in modern buildings its use is primarily restricted to veneers, facing, flooring, cabinetry, and decorative detailing. This is due to the extreme cost and difficulty of working with large-scale stone pieces—under almost any circumstances construction can take place vastly cheaper and with more consistent results by using the stone as surface rather than structure. Stone is quarried from particular locations worldwide that can produce consistent color, pattern, and texture for production. These qualities are both dependent on the stone type and the methods of fabrication and finishing. Harder stones, like granite, keep their finish and color longer than softer stones, like limestone, that change over time due to exposure. The three rock classes are igneous, sedimentary, and metamorphic, although classifications are made by stone type and name rather than by class (Table 14.2). The class of stone determines not only how it was formed, but its durability and properties as well—and you should be able to

Table 14.2 Stone properties.

	Igneous rock	Sedimentary rock		Metamorphic rock	
	Granite	Limestone	Sandstone	Marble	Slate
Physical properties					
Compressive strength (psi)	15,000–30,000	4000–20,000	3000–20,000	10,000–23,000	10,000–15,000
Shear stress (psi)	1800–2700	1000–2000	1200–2500	900–1700	
Weight (psf)	156–170	147–170	135–155	165–178	170–180
Absorption of water (percent by weight)	0.13	2.63	4.16	0.33	0.23
Texture	Typical coarse to fine crystals, often with various colors	Fine crystalline to granular	Granular with sand grain visible	Smooth granular to course crystalline, typically showing veining	Fine crystalline flat layers can show cleft surface

Note: Properties vary considerably, check with quarry or supplier for actual appearance

note the type and class of most stones on sight. Unlike brick, common sizes of stones vary greatly depending on the type and fabrication. Most stone installations of any scale will be custom fabricated, and the details will be worked out with the fabricator or manufacturer.

HISTORY

The first uses of masonry date to prehistoric times and the first molded bricks have been found in Egypt dating to 16,000 years ago. The first fired bricks date from 5000 BC, which is the same time frame as the first quarried and cut stones were used in construction. By 3000 BC brick glazing and coloring was taking place, and with the discovery of bronze around 2500 BC adequate tools were available to cut stone with precision. Masonry is the longest lasting of building materials (in stone form) and represents the oldest intact buildings from antiquity forward.

Sumerian and Babylonian cultures began the more sophisticated uses of masonry around 3500 BC, developing not only baked and glazed bricks, but also early forms of vaulting—setting the stage for the ability to span distances with small modular units, a triumph of intellect and form making. This skill was built upon for thousands of years, being further advanced by the Greeks who manipulated structures with subtle variances in the dimensions of building elements to create an "animation" most evident in the "entasis" (slight curvature from top to bottom) of the Greek column. The Romans furthered the skill of masonry construction not only in engineering feats, but also in the large-scale production of masonry building materials. Fired brick was an industrially produced product in Roman times and the widespread use of masonry pushed forward ever more ambitious projects. One of the most impressive of Roman technical feats is the Pantheon, a concrete cupola spanning 40 meters with a masonry drum support resisting horizontal load. Later, in the Eastern Roman Empire, the Hagia Sophia cupola was constructed, spanning 35 meters in a lighter expression than the Pantheon and forming the height of ancient masonry and concrete expression. This knowledge was subsequently lost for a thousand years.

14.4
Romanesque church tower, from
the late 1300s. Rome, Italy.

In the middle ages, roughly 1000 AD, Romanesque churches begin to re–
discover the use of spanning arches and vaults to create large-scale structures.
These buildings, however, were still largely dependent on very thick load-
bearing walls for support (Figure 14.4). The discoveries made at this time also
centered on the ability to speed up the construction process. Stone and brick
fabrications were streamlined and made more precise, and it was this precision
that made possible the increased sophistication of the later Gothic churches.

By the fourteenth century the skill of the builders was such and the material
properties of masonry were understood well enough to begin to lighten the
wall and roof structures significantly. This makes very evident the nature of
minimizing the amount of material by maximizing the understanding and effort
put into assembling it. The Gothic cathedrals explode the exterior walls into

14.5
Duomo di Siena, twelfth to
fifteenth centuries. The lower
section of the church was begun
in the Romanesque style, with the
vaulting done later in the Gothic
style.

gigantic openings and use stone traceries to form the roof vaults as lightweight
spider webs of structure that seem to float in the air (Figure 14.5). Further
sophistication leads architecture into the Renaissance era, where the material
properties of construction become less the generator of form, and the ideas of
the designer begin to generate formal properties of buildings. This is where we
depart from the historical discussion of masonry as a technical development,
until the modern era.

With the invention of the iron, and later steel, frame as the primary structural support for larger buildings, the role of masonry changed. The Monadnock
Building in Chicago, from 1891, represents one of the last load-bearing masonry
skyscrapers in the U.S. (Figure 14.6). Standing 16 stories tall, its walls at the
base are over 8 feet thick, narrowing progressively as the height increases.

14.6
Monadnock building, 1889–1891, Chicago, Illinois by Burnham and Root.

16. MONADNOCK BUILDING, 1889-91   BURNHAM AND ROOT

Most structures after this time would either use masonry as a structural material for low-height buildings or as a surface cladding only. We are currently in the ideologically uncertain position of deciding how to use this material; that has fundamentally changed its purpose from 16,000 years of building structure to the last 100 years of being cladding.

MASONRY CONSTRUCTION

Basic assembly methods of masonry are based on the vast history of the material. The standard steps in the industrial production of clay bricks are shown in the chart (Figure 14.7), while quarries typically drill and blast large chunks of stone to be then sawn into sizes suitable for transport to manufacturing facilities or local stone fabricators.

Brick wall types begin with the structural, or solid, masonry wall, which is made up of multiple rows of bricks locked together to achieve greater strength. All joints are filled with mortar to create a unified load-bearing wall that can withstand heavy vertical and horizontal forces. The brick can be bonded or mixed with CMU units to create a stronger wall, particularly if the block is reinforced with grout and rebar (Figure 14.8).

Brick or brick/block cavity walls use two "wythes" (a wythe is a single row) of brick with an air space typically 50mm (2") wide. The air space creates additional insulation value for the wall and acts as a barrier against moisture

14.7
Clay brick production.

penetration. Moisture that gets through or around the first layer of brick runs down the air gap—and metal flashing combined with weep holes at the base of the wall release the moisture back to the outside. The two wythes are linked together with metal wall ties embedded in the mortar joints (Figure 14.9).

Reinforced brick walls are constructed with the gap from a cavity wall, but the gap is filled with grout and reinforcing steel. This creates a structurally stronger wall, and is typically used for vertical piers, columns and in horizontal lintels and bond beams (Figure 14.10).

Brick veneer walls use a backup system of wood or metal structure and act as the vertical cladding system. The backup structure assumes the entire vertical load and the brick, or other masonry, provides the weather barrier (Figure 14.11).

The look of any wall surface is determined by both the selection of masonry material and the mortar joints applied by the mason. Different joints provide various looks and weathering capabilities—the primary purpose of the mortar joint shape at the exterior face of the wall is to prevent moisture from entering the assembly. Figure 14.12 shows the types of joints and their relative quality of moisture shedding capacity. Architects tend to like mortar joints that are deeper and cast shadows; Frank Lloyd Wright would rake the horizontal joints on his homes and leave the vertical joints flush to accentuate this effect. These types of joints are usually not as durable, but a weathered joint can often have the same effect with better long-term performance.

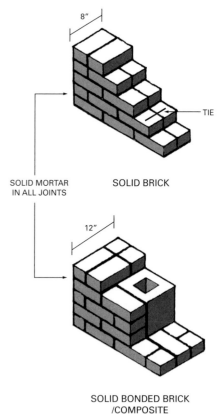

14.8
Solid masonry.

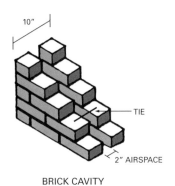

10"

— TIE

2" AIRSPACE

BRICK CAVITY

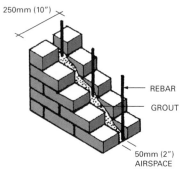

250mm (10")

— REBAR

— GROUT

50mm (2")
AIRSPACE

14.10
Reinforced masonry.

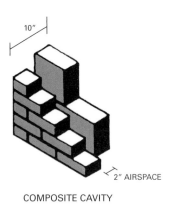

10"

2" AIRSPACE

COMPOSITE CAVITY

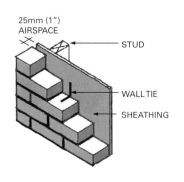

25mm (1")
AIRSPACE

— STUD

— WALL TIE

— SHEATHING

14.11
Veneer masonry.

14.9
Cavity masonry.

The pattern in which masonry is laid out has both structural and historical significance. While the running bond is typically thought of as standard in brick layout, it simply provides the most efficient way to slather brick onto a horizontal surface, while still making it look somewhat structural. The traditional structural bonds always had some bricks turned with their short face or 'header' to the outside, which locked the multiple rows of bricks together (see Figure 14.13 for brick terminology). The various patterns emerged out of historical traditions and the artful skill of the mason in designing various wall patterns that were both attractive and served the technical purpose required. There are many patterns and variations; a few of the most common in stone and brick are shown in Figure 14.14.

Along with the various wall patterns are the types of openings made in masonry walls. The most basic opening is made with a "lintel" or beam that spans the top of the opening, allowing the load from above to be transferred to either side and down the load-bearing structure. This strategy is limited by the strength of the material used to span and the potential deflection that can occur over time. In older brick structures the lintel was often stone or wood, these being the only longer structural materials available. Wood had an obvious problem—in a fire the lintel failed and the entire wall fell, which is why even current code requirements do not allow any masonry to be carried on wood support structure. Modern lintels can be made from concrete, steel, or even grouted into the brick with rebar, giving the appearance of no structure at all carrying the brick.

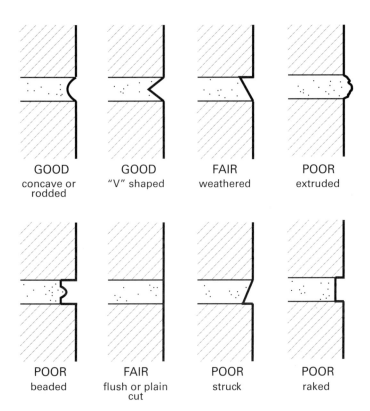

14.12
Mortar joint types and weathering quality.

GOOD
concave or rodded

GOOD
"V" shaped

FAIR
weathered

POOR
extruded

POOR
beaded

FAIR
flush or plain cut

POOR
struck

POOR
raked

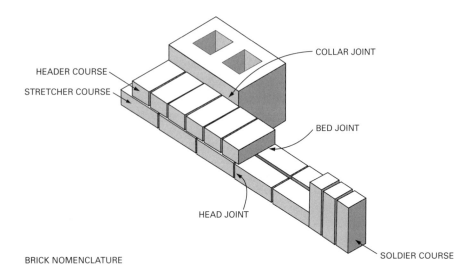

HEADER COURSE

STRETCHER COURSE

COLLAR JOINT

BED JOINT

HEAD JOINT

SOLDIER COURSE

BRICK NOMENCLATURE

14.13
Brick nomenclature.

The development of the arch was instrumental in creating large openings that did not rely on the limited length of solid stone lintels. Arches can be made from brick or stone masonry units (Figure 14.15), and range from completely flat "jack" arches to tall Gothic arches. The arch creates longer spans by the compressive nature of the masonry material and must follow certain rules and formal relationships to function properly. Not only is the opening spanned, but also horizontal sideways load is being placed into the wall below, requiring some mass or other strategy to counteract this force. The frequency with which arches are misused, malformed and distorted is not only a fundamental

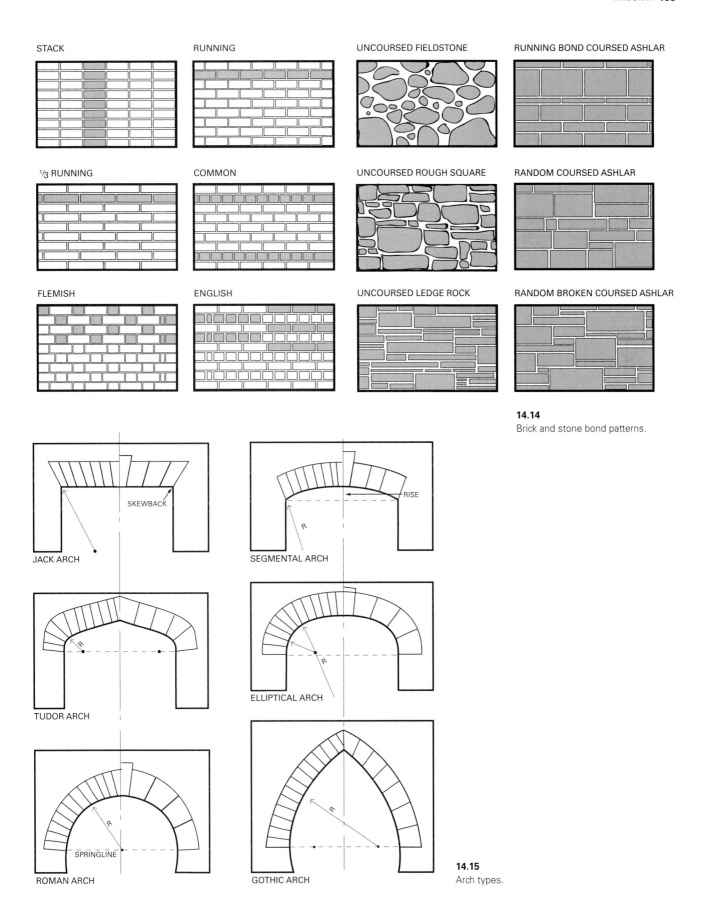

STACK

RUNNING

UNCOURSED FIELDSTONE

RUNNING BOND COURSED ASHLAR

¹/₃ RUNNING

COMMON

UNCOURSED ROUGH SQUARE

RANDOM COURSED ASHLAR

FLEMISH

ENGLISH

UNCOURSED LEDGE ROCK

RANDOM BROKEN COURSED ASHLAR

14.14
Brick and stone bond patterns.

JACK ARCH

SKEWBACK

SEGMENTAL ARCH

RISE

R

TUDOR ARCH

R

ELLIPTICAL ARCH

R

ROMAN ARCH

SPRINGLINE

R

GOTHIC ARCH

R

14.15
Arch types.

structural misunderstanding, but also the loss of a formal language of architecture based on 3500 years of accumulated knowledge.

Colors, finishes and textures are virtually limitless in both brick, concrete and stone masonry. Bricks can be glazed in matte or gloss finishes to create extremely uniform or varied appearances. The surfaces of bricks are often patterned with tools, such as brushes or wires, to create different textures and adhesion of the glazing materials. Concrete can be integrally colored and different surfaces are available, from natural to glazed. Concrete surfaces can also be textured or split, to form very rough finishes. Stone types come in almost every color, and the finishes can intensify and modify the natural color. Standard stone finishes are polished (glossy—best to show color), honed (smooth but matte—and often dull), flame finished (granite mainly, rough but close to flat), sawn (showing the circular fabrication marks), or split faced (roughly split and unfinished). Each texture has different qualities depending on the type of stone, and certain materials are better suited to some finishing methods than others.

Lastly, all materials pose particular problems that can only be effectively dealt with if the designer knows what to expect. Masonry offers a few common problems, some of which are controlled by careful assembly; some are controlled by good design detailing. All involve water penetration.

The first problem is efflorescence, commonly seen as a white staining on the exterior surface of a masonry wall. Efflorescence is a leaching of salt minerals out of the mortar, caused when water gets into the brick assembly and has no path to get out. Eventually the water infiltrates the mortar from the inside, causing the mortar to slowly dissolve. This also commonly happens in basement foundation walls that are painted, the moisture cannot evaporate through the wall and eventually destroys the mortar—ironically this is typically accelerated by homeowners who don't like the slightly stained mortar in basement walls and decide to "fix" them with latex paint. Efflorescence is controlled by properly flashing the base of cavity walls and keeping the weep holes unclogged. Often, the weep holes are "wicked" by placing a piece of rope into the hole to prevent it from getting clogged with mortar during construction and exterior soil or debris after construction. Careless masons can sometimes clog the air gap with excess mortar, keeping the water from reaching the weeps and causing water buildup. The effluent salt deposits can sometimes be difficult or impossible to clean if they bond to the masonry surface—or the water can go through to the interior surface of the wall, creating lingering mold and internal water damage. Be sure to make your intentions clear on the drawings and watch for this condition during field visits.

The other issue for masonry in temperate climates is the freeze/thaw cycle. Water penetrates everywhere it can and expands when it freezes, blowing things apart. Typical reasons for water to enter masonry structures are: bad decisions on mortar profiles which pull standing water into joints by capillary action, insufficient expansion joints that cause cracking of the mortar, foundation movement that causes cracking of mortar and masonry, bad window or door flashing that allows water into the system, and roof leaks that pour water into the system. Minor problems have a tendency to amplify themselves over time; a small crack gets progressively bigger as more water is allowed in—eventually causing failure. Another related problem with water penetration is the internal rusting of steel lintels—which occasionally fail with spectacular results, potentially removing entire walls or segments of buildings.

CONCLUSION

Brick is one of the simplest building products, yet one of the more difficult materials to deal with. Its history spans to the earliest structures built by humans and it has remained essentially the same for millennia. The variations of application and form are nearly endless, yet it has definite rules for how it can be effectively used. The best way to learn to deal with masonry is from the masons on job sites. Along with carpenters, masons are some of the most skilled craftspeople at a construction site. The time it takes to develop skill as a mason is lengthy and they go through an apprenticeship process as part of their training. The craft of building with masonry requires not only knowledge of the material's capabilities but also the ways it can fail. This requires the experience of people like masons, who have seen it perform over time. The other issue with masonry is its fundamental change in the past century from a structural material to cladding. This makes the appropriate use of brick challenging at times. It is certainly a durable building skin, but how should it be represented as a skin rather than structure? These are the types of decisions designers must struggle with while determining the appropriate expression of a material.

> *The brick is a different master. How ingenious: a small, handy, usable format for every purpose. What logic there is in the bonding. What spiritedness in the joints. What wealth there is in even the simplest wall surface. But what discipline this material demands.*
>
> *Ludwig Mies van der Rohe*

FREQUENTLY ASKED QUESTIONS

What does designing in brick/block module mean?
Because bricks and blocks are typically modular materials they form wall lengths based on the dimensions of the units selected for construction. Therefore a standard brick wall will normally fall on 8" or 225mm increments of length. It is more expensive and less aesthetically pleasing to cut the units to make other sizes work, so most buildings constructed of brick or block have wall lengths and openings placed on these increments of size.

Why do we now normally only use brick masonry as a veneer rather than a structural material?
The obvious answer is expense, but that doesn't mean that bricks themselves are costly. The material itself is not prohibitively expensive; brick is rather economical as a raw material. The expense primarily comes from the labor involved to assemble a wall, and, as in most building assemblies, the labor

cost far outweighs the material cost. The other issue with cost is that work on other parts of a building cannot begin until the shell is completed. If the shell has an open frame or block wall exterior it can be assembled and closed in quickly, which allows inside work to occur while the outside brick cladding is applied. Finally, load-bearing masonry needs to be thicker to accommodate structural concerns. This thickness can be come problematic for light entering a space in taller buildings, where window openings can get quite deep at the base.

GLOSSARY

Adobe: Unfired mud brick masonry units.

Brick: Clay fired modular masonry unit.

Clay tile: Open cell clay fired modular masonry units.

CMU: Concrete masonry unit. A low water to cement ratio modular masonry unit.

Efflorescence: A leaching of salt minerals out of mortar, causing staining.

Glass block: Glass masonry units, typically with open cell interior spaces for insulation.

Grout: High water small aggregate concrete mixture poured into block assemblies or used to finish gaps in tile.

Lintel: Beam that spans the top of a wall opening.

Mortar: Low water and no aggregate concrete mixture used to bind masonry units together.

Rebar: Reinforcing steel bars used in hybrid concrete and masonry assemblies for tensile strength.

Stone Masonry: Stone units quarried to be used primarily as veneer or sitework masonry.

Wythe: A single row of bricks in a wall assembly.

FURTHER READING

Neufert, E. and Neufert, P. (2002). *Architects Data*. London: Blackwell Science; pp. 62–67, 171.

Pfiefer, G., Ramcke, R., Achtziger, J., and Zilch, K. (2001). *Masonry Construction Manual*. Basel; Boston; Berlin: Birkhauser; pp. 9–29.

Ramsey, C. G. and Sleeper, H. R. (2000). *Architectural Graphic Standards*, 10th edition. New York: John Wiley & Sons; Chapter 4, Masonry.

15

STEEL

Raw material	Iron ore/carbon
	Alloys
	Strength/stiffness
	Fire/corrosion
History and production	Discovery to artisan production
	Bessemer—technology
	Carnegie—mass production
	Modern steel mills
Steel fabrication	Structural elements/shapes
	Structural framing types
	Joining methods
	Finishing

INTRODUCTION

The discussion of steel in architecture is fundamentally linked to iron. This, simply put, is because steel *is* a form of iron. Cast iron becomes steel when carbon is removed, making the material stronger. Humans have used iron for 5000 years, but its substantial use in architecture spans only about 200 years. The first architectural uses were as fasteners and reinforcement, with larger pieces becoming available as production skill increased.

The most significant leap in the use of iron occurred when it began to become a structural material, replacing wood and masonry as a building's means of support. Like most other new materials, the expression of iron originally took the form of the materials it replaced, with early detailing looking like masonry or wood elements—but eventually designers created forms that were unique to the material properties of iron and steel. Steel is the material we still use to create most of our large-scale structures, whether it is in the form of rolled structural members or reinforcement in concrete frames. Understanding the material properties of steel is essential to not only the structural design of buildings, but to a formal and sustainable approach to making architecture.

Steel is extremely valuable as a building material because it is so strong in both tension and compression. It is much more time-consuming and energy intensive to produce than construction timber and architects must understand what shapes it comes in and how shops typically work with it in order to design effectively. The decisions of when to use steel, what type, shape, size, thickness, finish, and fabrication method are difficult and can greatly affect performance, cost, durability, and aesthetics. As with most materials there are complex issues with the appropriate or best use of the material and the rather severe environmental impact of a material that requires vast energy to produce.

RAW MATERIAL

Common carbon steel is over 98 percent iron (Fe) with the remainder being primarily carbon (C) and trace elements of silica (Si), manganese (Mn), chromium (Cr), and nickel (Ni). The character of steel differs from iron in its increased strength yet still malleable quality.

The raw material used to form iron comes from mined rock referred to as iron ore. This high iron content rock is placed in a blast furnace for the process of *smelting*, which refines or purifies the iron ore into *pig iron*. As the iron ore reaches melting point and becomes fluid, lime is added to the mixture and combines with the rock portion of the ore forming *slag*. This slag is lighter than the iron so the furnace is tapped from the bottom releasing the smelted or refined pig iron (Figure 15.1).

Pig iron contains up to 10 percent impurities, much of it carbon. The pig iron is relatively easy to produce with sufficient heat and is the material we commonly see as cast iron. It is very hard, but also brittle, with about 4 percent carbon content. Producing steel requires another refining process to remove some

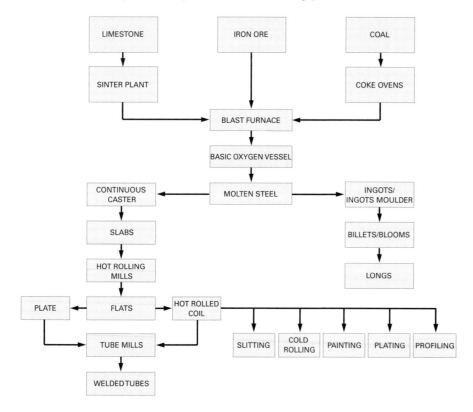

15.1
Steel production flow chart.

Table 15.1 Steel/iron types and properties

	Yield strength (MPa)	Tensile strength (MPa)	Melting temperature (K)
Iron	50	200	1809
Mild steel	220	430	1765
High-carbon steel	350–1600	650–2000	1570
Low-alloy steel	290–1600	420–2000	1750
High-alloy steel	170–1600	460–2000	1680
Cast iron	50–400	10–800	1403

	Typical Uses
Low-carbon ("mild") steel	Low-stress uses. General constructional steel, suitable for welding.
Medium-carbon steel	Medium-stress uses; machinery parts–nuts and bolts, shafts, gears.
High-carbon steel	High-stress uses; springs, cutting tools, dies.
Low-alloy steel	High-stress uses; pressure vessels, aircraft parts.
High-alloy ("stainless") steel	High-temperature or anticorrosion uses; chemical or steam plants.
Cast iron	Low-stress uses; cylinder blocks, drain pipes.

carbon and other undesired elements, and until the mid-nineteenth century was extremely difficult, time-consuming, and expensive to make. Most construction steel is "mild steel" and has about 0.25 percent of carbon content.

Steel is classified into non-alloy, low-alloy, and alloy steel. Non-alloy steel is common carbon steel. This is the material used for most construction, as it is strong, malleable, structurally predictable, and relatively inexpensive (Table 15.1).

Alloy steel has other metals added into it in sufficient quantity to create unique properties of the resultant metal. The most common steel alloy used in construction is stainless steel, which has up to 20 percent chromium and nickel added to resist corrosion and improve appearance. All stainless steel is not alike, as there are variations of alloys that change depending on the intended use of the product. Keep in mind that under certain circumstances stainless steel can rust, particularly in seacoast or chemical environments. It is also much harder and more brittle than carbon steel, making it significantly more difficult to cut, drill, weld, and bend. Lastly, stainless steel is much more expensive than carbon steel.

Low-alloy steels are very similar to carbon steel, with small amounts of metals added to increase strength, hardness, and corrosion resistance. One of the most common in architecture is "weathering" or COR-TEN steel, which is corrosion resistant. COR-TEN is carbon steel alloyed with copper, which oxidizes and forms a thin rust layer on the surface of the metal—preventing further corrosion. The effect is self-renewing, as any new penetrations or abrasions of the surface will form a new patina and reseal the material. The visual result is a red rusted surface, so care needs to be taken on the appropriate situations for use. It also tends to continually shed some of the oxidation, causing staining of areas below the rain drip line of the metal.

Carbon steel is sometimes referred to as a "soft steel" because it is a highly ductile material. It has a high *elastic limit* (or modulus of elasticity), meaning it will return to its original shape after deformation under a high load. After the elastic limit is reached it will not return to its original shape but also does not immediately fail. These properties of reliable stiffness, high elastic limit, and ductility allow for predictable calculations of required structural needs. This means that steel can be used economically in buildings because you can precisely size structural members.

Corrosion occurs because steel is exposed to a thin layer of water and oxygen. Humidity levels below 60 percent do not promote rust, unless the steel is frequently exposed to water. Salt water and chemicals also create corrosion difficulties; therefore rural desert steel buildings are far less prone to rust than industrial seacoast steel buildings.

Fire affects steel in an entirely different way than it does wood. While steel is essentially fire resistant in terms of burning, it loses strength at temperatures that can easily be reached by building fires. At 650C (1200F) steel loses 50 percent of its strength, therefore most structural steel needs to be protected by fire-resistant insulation. Ultimately the goal of any building fire code is not to prevent damage but to provide a reasonable amount of time for escape before failure occurs.

HISTORY AND PRODUCTION

Iron has been found in human settlements 5000 years old. It is believed the first iron pieces came from meteorite fragments, which had smelted the material through high heat. The remains of Egyptian King Tutankhamen from 3000 BC had large amounts of gold fabricated into objects, but small amounts of iron sewn into the burial garments of the king. In the thirteenth century the first primitive steels were produced through very crude and imprecise methods. The first method is to heat the iron to over 1350C (2500F), which was very difficult to achieve. The other method is through pounding the carbon out of the iron while constantly heating the metal. This was the method used to make high-quality armaments, with the blades of swords being heated and pounded to achieve higher strength from the iron.

In the 1700s, England had perfected the basic smelting method for making iron and crude steel, but the raw material costs were astoundingly high. To run the kilns for production of one ton of iron required ten acres of forest. England was running out of trees and looked to the Colonies for production capacity.

During the first part of the industrial revolution iron was in huge demand, but not strong enough for many applications. The railroads in particular found iron rails too unreliable for long-term heavy train loads, with many derailments caused by tracks shattering or breaking. Steel at the time was seen as strong enough, but still an artisan produced material—extremely time-consuming and in small-scale production. Henry Bessemer solved this problem by inventing the Bessemer Converter, which increased the temperature of kilns and removed carbon by introducing cold air into the furnace. The cold air combined with the carbon in iron, ignited and drove up the temperature, then blew free of the furnace removing almost all of the carbon content. Carbon could then be reintroduced in exacting amounts, which made quality control very high.

Andrew Carnegie perfected the mass production of steel at Bethlehem

Steel by buying all of the components of steel manufacture—from mining ore to furnace fuel. He then proceeded to increase profits by controlling labor costs. This created some of the most contentious and disastrous early union labor disputes in the U.S.

The beginnings of steel buildings completely changed the form of modern cities. Between the ability to build much higher than was previously possible with masonry construction, and the invention of the elevator by the Otis Company, building heights soared. This was a building type that had no historical precedent, and the skyscraper became something uniquely identified with architecture in the U.S.

By the early 1950s, 85 percent of all manufactured products contained some steel; 50 million steel food cans were used every single day. The raw energy and limited life cycle of these products in a time before any recycling is troubling to imagine. Unfortunately we are not better off now, which is why the life cycle of all products—from pop cans to buildings—is a cause for not just concern, but active resource management.

Modern steel mills are virtually completely automated compared to those of the first part of the twentieth century. This creates not only healthier work environments, but also greater efficiency. Nonetheless, steel production requires a vast amount of energy. This can be offset in life cycle costs due to the extreme strength benefit and durability of steel compared to other materials, but both need to be considered to make responsible decisions. Strength means less material can be used to achieve the same goal as a weaker but lower impact material, and durability means the material will not require recycling, or downcycling, for a long period of time.

FABRICATION

Raw steel in the mill is poured into forms to make ingots. These ingots are then milled into rough shapes in preparation for rolling into specific shapes. Large-scale rolling operations often take multiple passes to reach final dimensions. The rolling process also increases the strength of the material through compression and alignment of the metal's grain structure (Figure 15.2). Rolled products are divided into two types—sections and plates. Sections or shapes are heat rolled while in a red-hot state. Plates can be hot rolled or cold rolled. Cold rolling allows for thinner and more even surfaces than hot rolling. The typical shapes available are: bars, plates, W shapes, M shapes, S shapes, and HP shapes (which are all "I" shaped sections), channels, angles, tees (which are normally cut from "I" shapes), pipes, square tubes, and rectangular tubes (Figure 15.3). Steel can also be cast into customized forms, but the expense is very high; casting is more frequently done from easier materials to work with such as iron or aluminum. When nonstandard shapes are needed, built-up shapes are created, which are welded from plates or portions of standard sections.

The shapes of steel sections are standardized for both size and strength. Dimensions and properties of commercially available steel sections are available in the *Manual of Steel Construction*, published by the American Institute of Steel Construction and *The Steel Designer's* and *Steel Detailer's Manuals*, published by Blackwell Science in the U.K. These books are indispensable for

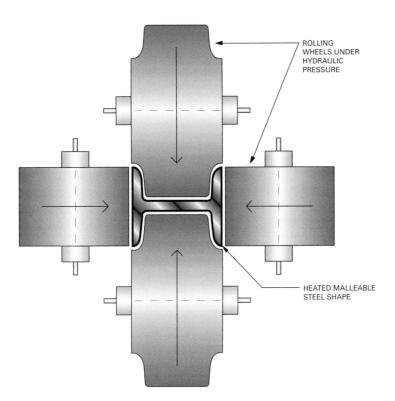

ROLLING
WHEELS UNDER
HYDRAULIC
PRESSURE

HEATED MALLEABLE
STEEL SHAPE

15.2
Modern rolling mill diagram.

	W SHAPE (Wide Flange) The most common shape with greatest variety of size options. It has parallel flange surfaces, with typically unequal web and flange thicknesses.
	HP SHAPE (H -Shaped Pilings) It has parallel flange surfaces with equal web and flange thicknesses.
	S SHAPE (American Standard) American Standard beams have sloped flange surfaces of approximately 17% with both equal and unequal average web and flange thicknesses.
	M SHAPE (Miscellaneous) Shapes that connot be classified as W, HP, or S types. Limited shape sizes and production. Flange slopes vary.
	C SHAPE American Standard channels have sloped flange surfaces equal to S shapes with both equal and unequal average web and flange thicknesses.
	MC SHAPE Shapes that connot be classified as C type. Limited shape sizes and production. Flange slopes vary.
	L SHAPE Angles with both equal and unequal leg lengths.

	WT SHAPE Structural tee cut from W shapes.
	MT SHAPE Structural tee cut from M shapes.
	ST SHAPE Structural tee cut from S shapes.
	PIPE Open tubing of various diameters and thicknesses. Sizes typically refer to inside diameter.
	SQUARE AND RECTANGULAR TUBING Various dimensions and thicknesses. Sizes typically refer to outside dimension of flat surfaces. Outside corner radius may be up to 3 times the wall thickness.
	MC SHAPE Shapes that connot be classified as C type. Limited shape sizes and production. Flange slopes vary.
	SQUARE AND ROUND BARS Solid sections of various weights and thicknesses.

15.3
Standard rolled
structural steel shapes.

detailing projects as they cover not only the standard sizes of steel shapes, but also the methods for joining steel elements together.

Structural framing types in steel are more varied than in wood but fall into several categories. The simplest framing type is post and beam, which is virtually the same as a wood system. Multi-bay truss systems function similarly, with the simple beams being replaced by open trusses. Multistory or high-rise construction works on a post and beam system, but lateral loads due to wind forces create the need for horizontal bracing which can be higher than the gravity loads. Long-span construction creates large areas of free space uninterrupted by intervening walls or columns. Steel is particularly well suited to long-span construction due to its high strength to weight ratio and ability to form strong construction joints in trusses. Hybrids of all of these systems allow for virtually any building form to be created with steel. No other material offers steel's strength—combined with high performance in tension, bending, and compression.

Steel can be joined in two ways—welding and bolting. This decision is based on a number of factors. The basic rule of thumb is "weld in the shop—bolt in the field". Welding can be done much more effectively in a controlled environment, whereas bolting is easily accomplished on-site. Aesthetic and structural considerations can also dictate the method of assembly; however, most often it can be done either way. Welding has a number of choices in finished appearance. Often the structural requirements of a weld will not match the desire for a clean or consistent finish. Understanding basic weld marks on a shop drawing can save the trouble of having pieces arrive on-site in an unsatisfactory manner (Figure 15.4). Basic weld marks to look for are field assembly flags, flush or convex weld finishes, and continuous or stitch welds.

One of the factors to consider when designing large steel elements is the size of individual pieces; remember if it can't fit on a truck, it shouldn't be finished in the shop. Often large portions of an assembly can be made in the shop, with the final form finished by a few simple bolts on-site. Keep in mind when detailing bolting that room must be left for the fabrication to take place, meaning there needs to be space for a wrench to fit and for hands or equipment to operate tools (Figure 15.5). Another factor to consider is the steel finish. Painted or galvanized pieces will have the finish destroyed by welding on-site, and then the original finish will be "matched" with a can of spray paint. This tends to be completely unsatisfactory in appearance. Think through the assembly and finishes carefully to decide how to join steel elements together.

All exterior carbon steel must be finished to avoid corrosion. This goes for most interior carbon steel as well, but not to the same degree. We have previously discussed stainless and weathering steel, which have corrosion resistance capabilities, but exterior carbon steel has particular problems with finishes. The primary problem is the durability of the finish; steel is very dimensionally active so it tends to move throughout the year. Most paint cannot always stretch to accommodate this movement and eventually cracks—and then the degradation cycle begins. Water penetrating the cracks separates the paint quickly and in freeze-thaw environments it gets progressively worse. Hidden conditions also cause problems, such as the joint between two steel sections thermally shifting, removing the protective coating, trapping the moisture, and

WELD SYMBOLS

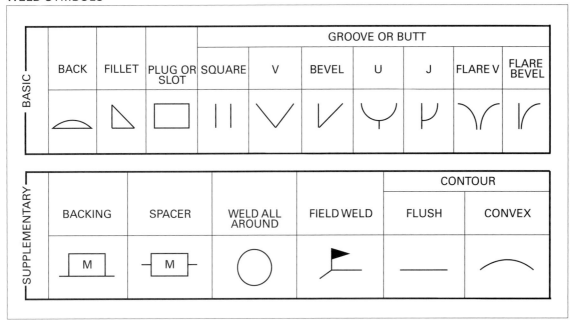

STANDARD LOCATION OF ELEMENTS OF A WELDING SYMBOL

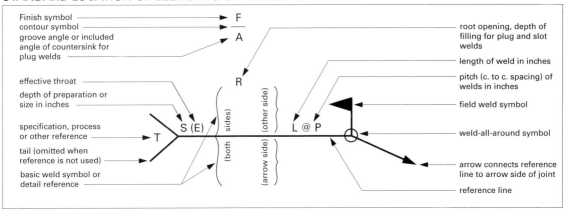

15.4
Weld symbols.

typically leave at least 1/4" clearance for assembly tools, more if rotation or other operation is required

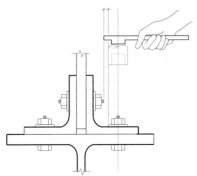

15.5
Fabrication clearance.

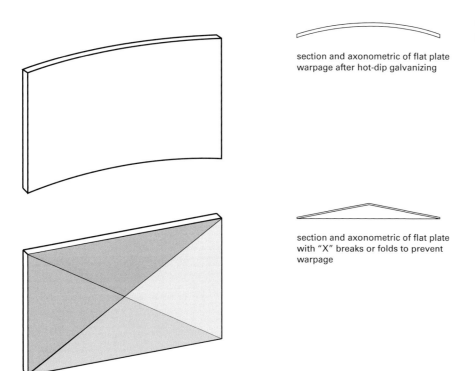

section and axonometric of flat plate warpage after hot-dip galvanizing

section and axonometric of flat plate with "X" breaks or folds to prevent warpage

15.6
Break pattern to prevent warp.

rusting from within. Galvanizing can help protect steel, as the zinc forms a corrosion-resistant coating. Keep in mind that there are two types of galvanizing: electroplating and hot-dip galvanizing. Electroplating is an electrically applied micro-thin coating that flakes off quickly. Hot-dip galvanizing requires the entire piece to be dipped in a zinc bath, making a much thicker, more reliable, and more expensive coating. There is no choice to be made here; long-term durability requires hot dipping. Electroplating is typically ineffective for exterior building components; you are better off using higher quality paint rather than spending resources on the electroplating. Keep in mind that galvanizing tanks are limited in size and will require thoughtful consideration of the size of individual steel pieces you use. Hot-dip galvanizing can also warp thin steel plates due to the temperatures of the molten zinc. Breaking plates with a minimal cross or "v" shaped seam can prevent warping (Figure 15.6). Like many situations in buildings, you must judge the maintenance capabilities of the owner and the life cycle of the project. For high abuse projects, like parking garages or coastal buildings, it is common to use hot-dip galvanized *and then* epoxy coated exterior steel pieces, because stainless steel is cost prohibitive.

CONCLUSION

The basic benefits of steel are very high strength in tension and compression, precise shapes, shop or field assembly, a limitless variety of formal possibilities, infinite finish options, and a straightforward honesty of structural expression. This is countered by high embodied energy, difficulty of fabrication, corrosion problems, thermal movement, high thermal conductivity (condensation issues), and fire resistance difficulties. You must understand these factors to use steel effectively, but it is unavoidable in most construction as a structural, cladding, fastening, and finish material. Pay particular attention to steel assemblies that are exposed or vulnerable to corrosion. Rust is a constant issue with steel and must be handled carefully while detailing the material. Exposed fabrications also are an area where detailing skill is important, as there are many options for how to bolt or weld the material together. Steel is very strong and very heavy, so use it in areas where the need for strength is more critical than low weight and keep in mind that energy-intensive materials should be used sparingly and appropriately.

FREQUENTLY ASKED QUESTIONS

What is an alloy metal?
Metal alloys are basic materials, like steel, that have other elements added to modify the properties of the original material. This is normally done to either improve the strength or corrosion durability of the metal. COR-TEN and stainless steel are examples of alloys designed to resist the natural oxidation of standard steel. COR-TEN has copper added to allow for limited surface oxidation and stainless has chromium and nickel added to resist any oxidation. Chromium molybdenum steel is an alloy designed to improve the strength of standard steel for particular high strength applications.

If steel doesn't burn, why does it need to be covered with a fireproof coating?
While steel is essentially fire resistant in terms of burning, it loses strength at temperatures that can easily be reached by building fires. At 650C (1200F) steel loses 50 percent of its strength, therefore most structural steel is protected by fire-resistant insulation that will keep the steel from heating up for long enough to evacuate building inhabitants.

GLOSSARY

Alloy: Metal with added elements to modify its properties.
COR-TEN steel: A corrosion-resistant weathering steel. Carbon steel is alloyed with copper, which oxidizes and forms a patina on the surface of the metal, preventing further corrosion.
Elastic limit: The point at which a material will no longer return to its original shape after being bent or deformed. Steel has a high elastic limit.
Electroplating: Is an electrically applied micro-thin coating. For steel this is usually a zinc coating. Electroplating is typically not durable enough for most exterior building applications.
Galvanizing: Zinc coating to prevent corrosion.
Hot-dip galvanizing: A corrosion resistance method that requires the entire piece to be dipped in a zinc bath, making a much thicker, more reliable, and more expensive coating.
Iron: Basic metal material created from iron ore.
Iron ore: High iron content mined rock.

Pig iron: Metal material that comes from the blast furnace after smelting, it contains up to 10 percent impurities, much of it carbon. This is the material we normally see manufactured into cast iron.

Powder coating: A process of durably bonding a colored powder to metal. The metal is heated and an electrically charged powder coats the steel, melting and bonding to the surface of the material.

Slag: Lime that has combined with rock in iron processing to purify the metal mixture.

Smelting: Blast furnace process for purifying iron ore into pig iron.

Stainless steel: An alloy of steel which has up to 20 percent chromium and nickel added to resist corrosion and improve appearance.

Steel: Iron modified to have a low carbon content to increase strength.

FURTHER READING

Davison, B. and Owens, G. (2003). *Steel Designer's Manual.* Oxford: Blackwell Science Ltd.

Eggen, A. P. and Sandaker, B. N. (1995). *Steel, Structure, and Architecture.* New York: Watson Guptil Publications; pp. 10–28.

Hayward, A., Weare, F., and Oakhill, A. (2002). *Steel Detailers' Manual.* Oxford: Blackwell Science Ltd.

American Institute of Steel Construction (1994). *Manual of Steel Construction: Allowable Stress Design.* AISC.

16

GLASS

Glass basics	Glass composition
	Glass fabrication
	Transparency
History	The discovery of glass
	Technological developments
Properties and technology	Strength—heat/laminations
	Color
	Thermal transmission
	Light transmission/coatings
Applications	Windows
	Storefronts
	Curtain walls
	Skylights
	Roofs/canopies
	Other structures

INTRODUCTION

Glass is a remarkable material; it is transparent, rock hard, and chemically inert enough to resist the most corrosive acids. Humans first discovered how to make glass about 4000 years ago from the earth's most abundant raw material, sand. Through a lengthy process of trial, error, and perseverance it became possible to make objects of what is essentially transparent rock. Its use was restricted to jewelry and pots until some 2000 years later, when the technology emerged to create flat glass for windows. This solved the basic conundrum of the need for shelter as protection and the need for light as illumination. Glass provided the perfect solution as a strong, durable, and cheap building material.

To be able to successfully use any material you need to understand its properties. Glass has two characteristics, beyond its transparency, that make it particularly useful in architecture. The first is that it resists weathering extremely well; it doesn't scratch, haze, or degrade under ultraviolet radiation. The second is its radiation transmission; air temperature moves relatively slowly through glass while solar radiation moves quickly. This offers the designer many possibilities for working with the material. As the technology of glass production improves, we have been able to manipulate both its light transmission quality and its thermally resistive properties. By combining glass with other materials the possibilities for its use have continually increased. The glass we typically use now in buildings is one component of a composite material designed to solve multiple issues, while still retaining the fundamental material properties of simple glass.

GLASS BASICS

Glass is most commonly referred to as a "super-cooled liquid", meaning it is molecularly amorphous, like a liquid, but is in a solid state. The secret to glass transparency is in this molecularly amorphous composition. Most materials form crystalline microstructures between heating and cooling. These crystals are what make materials opaque. Silicon is a material that does not automatically form dense microcrystalline structures (Figure 16.1). Fortunately, silicon in oxide form is silica, which is most commonly referred to as ordinary sand. Sand is not pure in its composition, but some of the other oxides commonly found mixed with the silica make the production of glass easier.

The basic means of producing glass involves melting the silica, then cooling it in very controlled ways. Certain temperature ranges favor the formation of crystals, so the glass is brought through those temperatures quickly and slowed through the rest of the process. Other oxides besides silica are added to the mixture to lower the melting temperature; pure silica melts at over 1700C. Iron oxide, normally found in sand, reduces this temperature because it absorbs heat more easily. The addition of other materials also assists in melting temperatures, workability, reduced crystal formation, durability, and color. The reason most glass is green is due to the iron oxide in the sand; removing it would be far too expensive so it has become a natural part of the material. The most common mixture of materials is referred to as soda-lime glass, and has been produced with minor variations since the mixture was developed in ancient Rome. The soda reduces the melting temperature to below 800C and the lime vastly increases durability.

16.1
Glass molecular crystalline structure.

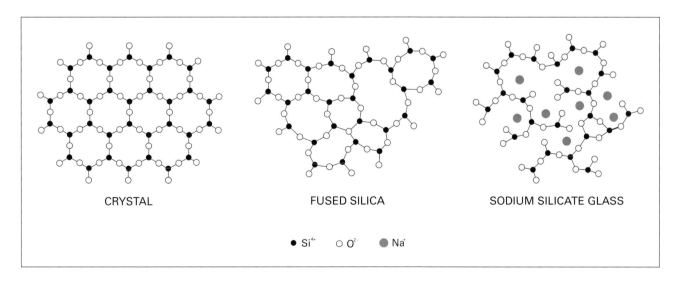

CRYSTAL   FUSED SILICA   SODIUM SILICATE GLASS

● Si^{4+} ○ O^{2-} ● Na^+

The process of glass making involves more than just chemical properties. The skill of the glassmaker must be precise and originally required both technical prowess and harsh work conditions. The temperatures, gases, and effects of breaking the material proved extremely dangerous at times. Lessons such as never inhaling air from the blowing tube are life threatening. The three parts of the glass making process are melting, forming and controlled cooling. Melting occurs at super high temperatures, where the various components are mixed. Forming takes place as temperatures fall into the zone where glass is hot enough to work and still viscous. The final cooling process is typically referred to as "annealing", or controlled heating and cooling to achieve a solid state without crystal formation.

For a thousand years, up until about 100 years ago, glass was formed for windows in two primary ways. The first is by "crowning" or blowing a cylinder of glass, cutting it down the side and flattening it. The second way is called "spinning", which is done by blowing a bulb and spinning the glass until it forms a disk (Figure 16.2). In the 1700s early plate casting took place, but the surface quality was very uneven. In the late 1800s the first presses were developed to make glass bricks and, shortly after, drawing and rolling were developed. All of these methods create difficulties with the quality of the surface of the glass. Anything the molten glass touches creates unevenness and imperfections

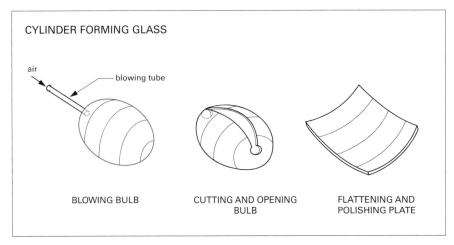

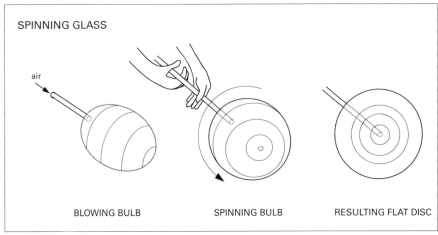

16.2
Forming and spinning glass.

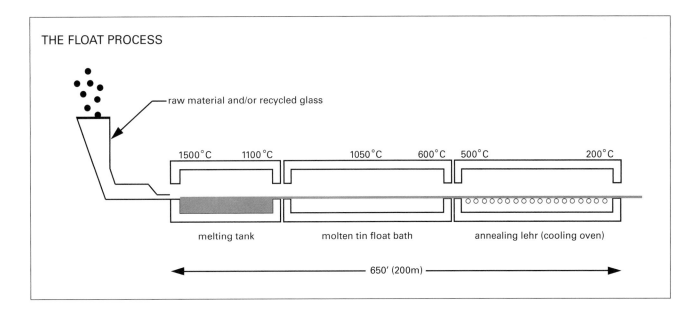

THE FLOAT PROCESS

raw material and/or recycled glass

1500 °C   1100 °C   1050 °C   600 °C   500 °C   200 °C

melting tank   molten tin float bath   annealing lehr (cooling oven)

650' (200m)

which required additional grinding and polishing to remove. In the 1950s "float glass" was developed by Pilkington, which forms the plate by pouring the glass onto molten tin. The tin melts at a lower temperature than the glass and has a higher density; this makes both sides of the glass pane perfectly flat (Figure 16.3). Most of the glass now produced for building components is created this way. During the 1970s tinting was added to glass in an attempt to improve performance, but the dark glass often reduced visible light too much and didn't reduce solar gains enough. The newer technologies involve laminating and suspending thin films into the glass assemblies to improve performance.

16.3
Float process.

HISTORY

The discovery of glass took place roughly 4000 years ago, the first examples being found in the eastern Mediterranean. It was most likely an accident; silica from pottery kilns melting and mixing with ash from the hearth and forming a crystallized glass. By 3500 years ago, pressed and molded glass vessels were being made in Egypt. Two thousand years ago, glass blowing was discovered, which made possible thin transparent sheets durable enough for windows. The Mediterranean climate, however, didn't need glazing to control the interior environment. Vitruvius speaks at length about building materials in his *Ten Books on Architecture*, but glass is absent from the discussion. Its use was more novelty than function; cold weather was not severe and was mitigated by fireplaces, which benefited from openings to clear the smoke. The northward push of the Roman Empire into temperate climate zones sees the first substantial use of glass in architecture, and the development of glass production as an industry in Venice, the Middle East, and Germany.

The most impressive early versions of architectural glass were created during the Gothic age by the primary agency for construction in northern Europe—the Church. Romanesque churches, which preceded the Gothic, had

16.4
Medieval stained glass window.

small openings made necessary by the heavy construction and frequent need for defense. Gothic churches shifted to a search for lighter structures and more illumination. The lighter structural frames increased the need for larger panes of glass, and the technology was pushed to meet the demands. Most of the cathedral glass is "stained glass"—or smaller colored pieces of glass set into larger frames with lead strips connecting them. The glass was tinted with metal oxides during melting and painted with a black pigment to produce the detailed imagery (Figure 16.4).

A shift in patronage during the sixteenth century made large glass panes more typical in residences of the wealthy ruling class, and during the seventeenth century the "conservatory" or greenhouse became an important building type (Figure 16.5). This movement from religious structure to secular and then to public/farm building propelled the technology of glass continually forward, eventually making it reasonable and affordable for most structures. The conservatory also created some of the inspiration for the new age of modern architecture, with lightweight iron structures and entirely glass skins. The early modernists envisioned the future world of buildings as transparent, light-filled boxes. As Paul Scheerbart writes in 1914 in his influential work, *Glasarchitektur*:

> *we live for the most part in closed rooms. These form the environment from which our culture grows. Our culture is to a certain extent the product of our architecture. If we want our culture to rise to a higher level,*

16.5
Glass conservatory, Palm House,
Kew Gardens, London, 1848.
Decimus Burton and Richard Turner.

we are obliged, for better or worse, to change our architecture. And this only becomes possible if we take away the closed character from the rooms in which we live. We can only do that by introducing glass architecture, which lets in the light of the sun, the moon, and the stars, not merely through a few windows, but through every possible wall, which will be made entirely of glass – of coloured glass. The new environment, which we thus create, must bring us a new culture.

The force that has driven much of contemporary architecture comes from technology and its relationship to culture. Two of the most influential technological advancements have been lightweight metal frame structure and large-scale glass fabrication.

PROPERTIES AND TECHNOLOGY

The glass we use today in buildings has been highly refined to achieve a few main goals; strength, safety, clarity, size, high light transmission, and low thermal transmission. We are also developing technologies that can embed electronic capabilities into glass, making it act intelligently.

Strength and safety are related properties because the reason for strength is in part due to basic durability and also to concerns about injury if glass breaks. While glass is hard, it is also brittle and tends to fail suddenly. The results of a break, with standard annealed float glass, are sharp, heavy shards of broken material—not what you want to put your hand through or, worse, have fall from stories above onto the street below. The property of strength is dealt with in a number of ways, such as heat-treating, wire embedding, and laminating.

Heat-treating is accomplished through heating and quenching annealed glass (Figure 16.6). This rapid cooling of the surface of the glass hardens it, while the interior is still fluid. During the cooling of the glass the interior shrinks less than the outside, putting the surface into tension. The surface tension and interior compression makes the glass stronger and alters its breaking characteristics. Full heat-treating is referred to as "tempering" and causes the glass to break into small pieces with no sharp edges. While this glass is much stronger than standard annealed, it is vulnerable to small cracks or chips that can explode the entire pane. The side and rear windows in cars are made of this type of material, along with the glass in most buildings' doors and some windows.

Wire embedded or "wire glass" is made by pressing wire mesh into the glass during forming. It holds the glass together when broken, creating greater fire resistance, security, and safety. It allowed for glass to be used in some situations where transparency was previously not possible. Wire glass use is frequently discouraged as more advanced laminations replace it and due to safety problems with jagged metal edges protruding from broken panes.

Laminated glass is made by sandwiching a plastic sheet between glass layers (Figure 16.7). This plastic material is typically polyvinyl butyral (PVB), pressed

16.6
Glass tempering process.

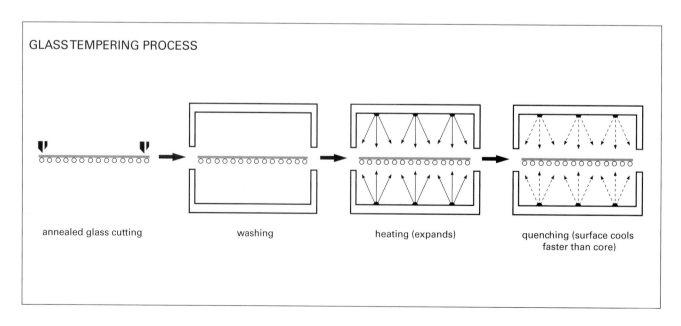

GLASS TEMPERING PROCESS

annealed glass cutting   washing   heating (expands)   quenching (surface cools faster than core)

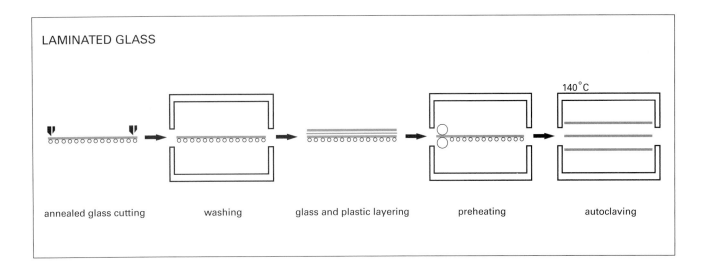

LAMINATED GLASS

annealed glass cutting   washing   glass and plastic layering   preheating   autoclaving

and autoclaved for about 4 hours at 140C at 827kPa (120psi). Laminated glass combines the hard, durable, but brittle glass with the elastic PVB. Laminated glass that breaks will adhere to the PVB, making it safer. Automobile front windows are made this way, where breaking tempered glass at high speed would still be dangerous. It also dampens sound transmission and can resist attack and explosion; bullet proof glass is laminated with high strength plastics. Another appealing aspect of laminated glass is that it can be cut after manufacture; tempered glass cannot be cut after fabrication. In more extreme situations tempered glass can be laminated to increase safety.

Clarity has to do with both the finish and color of the glass. The development of float glass has created perfectly flat and consistent surfaces. This, combined with precision annealing and oxide admixtures, inhibits any visible crystalline formations, making common annealed float glass virtually invisible when clean. Color is more difficult to control as naturally occurring iron oxides in sand give the glass a green tint. While some other oxides reduce the green tint, the complete removal requires separation of the iron from the silica sand. This is a difficult process and raises the temperature at which the silica melts, making the "water white" glasses very expensive. Another strategy used to make glass less green is by making it stronger, and therefore thinner, so the tint is less dense. This system of thinner stronger glass is seen in cavity glazing, commonly referred to as double glazing or "thermopane", however the primary purpose of this type of glass is for thermal resistance. At times clarity is not the desired goal, and glass surfaces are intentionally rolled with patterns to create different effects, laminated with patterned films or other materials, or have ceramic fritting screened to surfaces.

Size is dependent on the manufacturing process. Float glass production is expensive and requires equipment to maintain large pools of molten tin. The size of the tank determines the maximum width of the glass. Production runs are continuous and can create virtually any length. The problem becomes how big an individual piece can get and still be safely moved. Glass is heavy, difficult to lift, and if the aspect ratio becomes more than about 4 to 1 it becomes much more fragile. Common float beds are at most about 3.6m (12") wide, because glass panes much wider are difficult to move and not in high demand. Where

16.7
Glass laminating process.

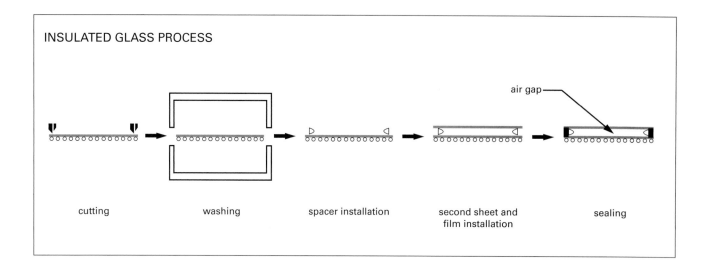

INSULATED GLASS PROCESS

cutting   washing   spacer installation   second sheet and film installation   sealing

air gap

double glazing is used there is also the size limitations of the machinery that vacuum seals and binds the edges of the glass. Maximum sizes of double glazing units are typically about 3m by 3.6m (10' by 12').

High light transmission and low thermal transmission are also related properties. Any clear glass provides high light transmission; the problem is how to limit thermal transmission and ultraviolet color degradation while bringing in daylight. This was originally done with curtains and shades, but these limited view and provided a fire hazard in commercial applications. Dark tinted and reflective glass was the next solution, but this proved to limit light too much and produced the undesirable "fishbowl effect" of not being able to see out at night while those outside could see in. The most effective solution has been through the use of multiple glazing (Figure 16.8). By trapping dry air between panes of glass, the thermal transmission of heat and cold can be significantly reduced. To function properly the air must be dry, clean, and still—to act as an insulator and not start a thermodynamic loop of air inside the assembly. This is achieved by introducing a molecular sieve or desiccant material into the glass cavity to promote dryness. The glass is vacuum-sealed and often high-performance gases, such as argon, replace the air left in the cavity. Into this cavity can also be introduced coated films that reduce and reflect heat transmission and UV rays. This film can be placed onto the inside surfaces of the glass or suspended in the middle of the panes—further reducing air movement. The films are completely invisible, and the total performance of sophisticated multiple-glazed systems can be similar to the thermal transmittance (U-value) of a cavity brick wall.

Smart walls use the basic technology of lamination and expand upon the films used inside the glass to create walls that can transform based on environmental changes and even generate energy. In the most basic form the interior film can be tinted, colored, or patterned to create different qualities of light transmission. In a smart wall application, the film can also be charged electrically, creating an electrochromic material that changes from transparent to opaque when a charge is applied. The field of laminated materials is where most of the newest technology is being applied. Thin film photovoltaics can generate energy by sandwiching photoelectric generator cells into glass panels, turning unwanted heat gain into power. Other electrical thin films can

16.8
Insulated glass process.

make skins that have "intelligent" behavior, sensing the exterior and interior environment and making changes to the window opacity and the building's environmental systems to maintain comfort. Glass is also becoming part of information transfer, as liquid crystal and heads-up displays can be integrated directly into the skin of a building. The need for this technology has not yet been demonstrated to the degree that makes it cost effective, but we will continually see developments in this area of glass production.

APPLICATIONS

Windows are the most commonly thought of glass application (Figure 16.9). This is simply a glass pane held into a frame that is supported by the wall

16.9
Basic glazing type applications.

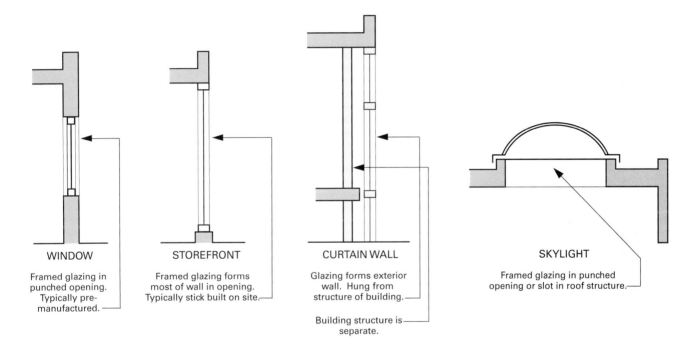

WINDOW
Framed glazing in punched opening. Typically pre-manufactured.

STOREFRONT
Framed glazing forms most of wall in opening. Typically stick built on site.

CURTAIN WALL
Glazing forms exterior wall. Hung from structure of building.

Building structure is separate.

SKYLIGHT
Framed glazing in punched opening or slot in roof structure.

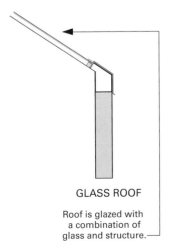

GLASS ROOF
Roof is glazed with a combination of glass and structure.

structure. All horizontal building glass can be considered windows, but architects usually refer to windows as punched openings in a solid wall plane. This separates them from storefront and curtain wall applications.

Storefronts are multiple window units forming a large or total portion of the wall. They are pieced together in a pre-manufactured frame that supports its own load but is still framed into a wall structure. Storefront frames are lightweight and usually span no more than two stories, so wind load requirements are low.

Curtain walls are entire walls made of glass panes, or a combination of glass and other materials in a frame or frameless system of support. The curtain wall acts independently from the structure of the building, supporting itself and essentially acting as a cladding clipped onto the surface of the building. Most modern high-rise buildings are of this type as the structural system has been separated from the exterior wall.

Skylights are basically windows that face the sky. They are punched or linear strips of glazing in an otherwise solid roof structure. The demands of weather on skylights can be significantly higher than on windows, and the effects of water and minerals standing on glass can etch or stain it permanently.

Glass roofs make the entire top surface glazed with a combination of structure and glass. This is commonly seen in greenhouses and atriums, but elsewhere it is difficult to mitigate the direct solar radiation enough for everyday use. This type of system is also prone to leaking as it thermally moves in response to variations in temperature from above and below. Lastly, horizontal glass has a tendency to always be dirty and very difficult to clean.

Other Structures can be made from glass for architectural applications. We have focused on glass as an exterior cladding material, but its use in other ways is nearly limitless. Glass is commonly used in furniture, as guardrails, partitions, doors, floors, stairs, in tiles, sinks, mirrors, and other places too numerous to mention. It can be made into almost any shape, color, opacity, and has structural capabilities when used properly. It is one of the most versatile materials we use, and the technology of its fabrication is continually expanding.

CONCLUSION

Glass is as unavoidable as wood in architecture, and possibly more so as no reasonable alternatives to architectural glass are available. It is a very straightforward material that is being constantly modified and improved with new technology. The majority of glass production causes relatively minimal environmental impact compared to many other building materials, and it has no rivals in performance. Effectively, using both active and passive glass technology is essential to sustainable design, and a thorough knowledge of applications and assembly is a necessity for every building designer.

FREQUENTLY ASKED QUESTIONS

Why is glass clear and green?
The secret to glass transparency is in its molecularly amorphous composition. While most materials form crystalline structures, the basic building material of

glass, silica, does not form crystalline structures when heated and cooled in a precise fashion. The green color comes from iron oxides that occur naturally in the silica sand that is melted to form glass.

What is safety glass?

Safety glass refers to glass that has been modified in one of two ways to protect it from injuring people if it breaks. One type of safety glass is tempered, a process of heat strengthening that causes the surface of the glass to be in tension. When broken, tempered glass shatters into small rounded pieces rather than the larger sharp plates that standard, annealed glass can become. The other method for making safety glass is laminating, which adheres a layer of plastic in-between sheets of glass. When broken, the plastic clings to the glass preventing it from flying free.

GLOSSARY

Crowning glass: Traditional method for making windows by blowing a cylinder and cutting it open to form a flat plate.

Curtain Wall: Entire walls made of glass panes, or a combination of glass and other materials in a frame or frameless system of support.

Double glazing or "thermopane": Glass outer layers with a vacuum-sealed inner air gap for thermal resistance.

Float glass: Modern method for forming flat glass sheets by cooling them on a bed of molten tin.

Glass: A molecularly amorphous material made from melting and cooling silica sand.

Heat-treating: A method for strengthening accomplished through heating and quenching annealed glass.

Laminated glass: A type of pane made by sandwiching a plastic sheet between glass layers.

Photovoltaic glass: A method for generating solar energy by laminating thin film photoelectric generator cells into glass panels.

PVB: Polyvinyl Butyral, a plastic material typically used as the inner layer in laminated glass.

Smart walls: Uses the basic technology of lamination and expands upon the films used inside the glass to create walls that can transform based on environmental changes and even generate energy.

Spinning glass: Traditional method for making windows by blowing a cylinder and spinning it until it flattens into a thin plate.

Storefront: Multiple, stick-built window units forming a large or total portion of the wall.

FURTHER READING

Neufert, E. and Neufert, P. (2002). *Architects Data.* London: Blackwell Science; pp. 166–173.

Ramsey, C. G. and Sleeper, H. R. (2000). *Architectural Graphic Standards*, 10th edition. New York: John Wiley & Sons; pp. 512–514.

Wiggington, M. (1996). *Glass in Architecture.* London: Phaidon.

17

CONCRETE

Raw material	Cement and Portland Cement
	Aggregate
	Water
	Hydration
	Cement production
	Concrete production
History	Discovery
	Modern rediscovery
Concrete construction	Reinforced concrete
	Precast vs. cast in place
	Prestressed
	Post-tensioned
	Control joints
	Cold joints
	Formwork
	Placement
	Slump/strength
	Colors

INTRODUCTION

Concrete is a very hard, durable, monolithic building material defined as a mixture of cement, aggregate, and water. It is common to hear the terms cement and concrete used interchangeably; however, cement is only the powder that binds the aggregate together when mixed with water to form concrete. Concrete is a "plastic" material, as it can be molded into almost any shape—because it starts as a liquid and hardens into solid form. It is remarkably strong in compression and when combined with the tensile properties of steel creates the most versatile of structural building materials. This is a material that we consider commonplace, yet the fact that it is possible to pour a liquid material that dries in hours to the consistency of stone is amazing to consider.

Concrete is relatively inexpensive as a base material, but the difficulty of working with it can make the labor costs high. It is also a very energy intensive material to create, requiring over 80 separate and continuous operations for production. In 1990 cement production was the sixth most energy-intensive industry in the U.S., necessitating 18,700,000 tons of coal burning and 1,398,400,000 kW (worth $700,000,000/400,000,000 GBP) of power usage.

RAW MATERIAL

While cement is the key component of concrete it makes up only about 11 percent of the total mix. The remainder of the mixture is (approximately) 16 percent water, 6 percent air, 26 percent sand (fine aggregate), and 41 percent gravel or crushed stone (course aggregate). This is the mixture that arrives on a construction site inside the cement mixing truck.

The type of cement that is used in modern construction is called Portland Cement. Portland Cement binds the other materials in concrete together through the process of hydration. Concrete hydration is a chemical reaction that occurs when the cement powder is mixed with water, resulting in heat and a crystallized bond forming between the wet cement and the aggregate. This bond becomes stronger as the water evaporates from the mixture, and concrete never loses this strength, in fact it continues to become stronger over time.

Portland Cement is made by combining ground limestone and shale/clay in a furnace heated to over 1480C (2700F). The resulting material is called clinker, which is pulverized and mixed with powdered gypsum to form Portland Cement (Figure 17.1). The basic chemical components of Portland Cement are Calcium (Ca), Silicon (Si), Aluminum (Al) and Iron (Fe). The first rotary kilns allowed for economical cement production starting in 1895, with the first large U.S. kilns constructed in 1895. Thomas Edison is credited with developing the first long kilns, which doubled production by lengthening the kiln from 24m (80') to 46m (150'). The kilns are long tubes that continuously rotate to mix and process the raw materials into clinker. This is a massive machine, a 46 to 185m (150 to 600')

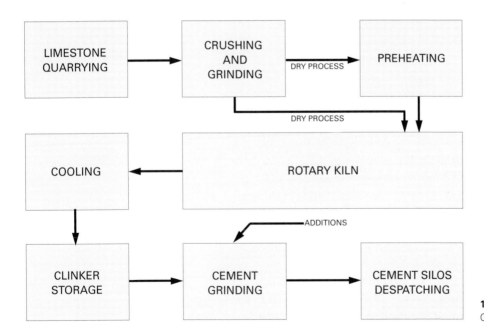

17.1
Cement production process.

17.2
Rotary cement kiln.

long, 3.6m (12″) diameter, 3500C (6300F) furnace that is constantly spinning—an impressive engineering feat (Figure 17.2).

Cement powder is extremely fine; one pound contains approximately 150 billion grains. This is mixed with the aggregate, which can be fine sand or larger pieces of stone. The majority of concrete is this rock, which provides the strength of the material. The size of the aggregate is dependent on the application—small jobs can use sand only, but any substantial structure will use larger pieces of stone. The water is added to the mixture shortly before placement because the hydration begins immediately. The water needs to be clean for the hydration to proceed properly; contaminated water can inhibit or prevent the chemical reaction from taking place. The rule with water is that it needs to be of potable (or drinking) quality. The quality of the stone aggregate also matters, as the aggregate color affects the concrete color—after hydration occurs and the water evaporates nearly 80 percent of concrete is the aggregate. Aggregate should not contain high contents of iron or other corrosive metals, because they will oxidize and eventually stain the surface. This mixture comes to the site from the concrete plant in trucks that rotate the mixture to keep it consistent and delay hydration, but if the truck is not emptied within a certain amount of time (typically about 90 minutes or 300 revolutions of the truck cylinder) the driver is forced to dump the mix before it hardens in the cylinder. Most plants have a dump area that collect unused concrete that is brought back, and, while this averages about 2–3 percent, it can be recycled into gravel, aggregate, and retaining wall materials.

HISTORY

The basic form of cement is a naturally occurring compound of limestone and shale; however its development as a building material was by chance at first

17.3
Pantheon dome, 118–126 AD,
Rome, Italy.

and later by the development of manufactured cement as a reliable and predictable building material. The Egyptians used gypsum mortars from 3000 BC and the Greeks used lime mortars before the Romans developed concrete as an independent construction material. Romans used naturally occurring cement powder from Pozzuoli, Italy near Mt. Vesuvius to build parts of many ancient buildings from concrete, the most remarkable example being the 40m dome of the Pantheon (Figure 17.3). Pliny reported a common mortar mixture of one part lime to four parts sand, while Vitruvius reported two parts pozzolana to one part lime.

During the Middle Ages concrete technology had deteriorated, but in the 1700s the first hydraulic cements were developed for the use of stucco finishes. In 1824 a bricklayer named Joseph Aspdin invented Portland Cement by burning ground chalk with clay in a kiln until CO_2 was removed. The resulting material was finely ground and named after the stones it resembled, quarried on the isle of Portland, England.

CONSTRUCTION

Concrete has advantages over many other construction materials because it can single-handedly solve the primary problems of structure; it works well in compression, bonds with steel to handle tension, can be formed into almost any shape with many surface textures and finishes, and provides fireproof construction.

The development of reinforced concrete is tied to the production of steel. Concrete is inherently strong in compression but lacks strength in tension. Combining reinforcing steel (rebar) with concrete works effectively because the cement bonds with the steel to form a monolithic material; the concrete also acts as a fireproofing insulator for the steel (Figure 17.4). Reinforced concrete can be made into post and beam systems as well as shell structures; the durability of concrete allows it to act as both structure and enclosure for a building. The most common limitation on this type of structure (beyond the expense) is the inadequate insulation qualities of solid reinforced concrete—it transmits too much thermal load (enough to form condensation on the interior surface in extreme conditions). Particular care needs to be taken in situations where moisture can penetrate the surface, often the steel rebar is epoxy coated and the surface of the concrete is sealed to prevent corrosion from happening due to water movement or condensation.

Concrete for construction can be handled in two common ways, *precast* and *cast in place*. Precast concrete is made in a factory under carefully controlled conditions. Because both the strength and finish of concrete is partly dependent on the temperature of hydration, field cast concrete can be unpredictable and uneven. Precast concrete solves many of these problems because the water to

17.4
Typical assembly, with reinforced steel in concrete beam.

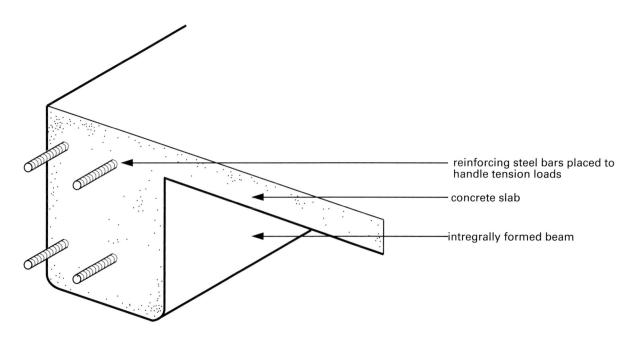

reinforcing steel bars placed to handle tension loads

concrete slab

intregrally formed beam

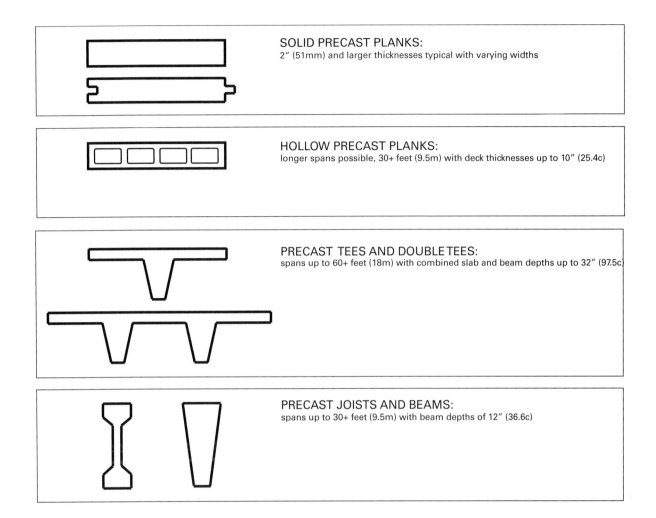

SOLID PRECAST PLANKS:
2" (51mm) and larger thicknesses typical with varying widths

HOLLOW PRECAST PLANKS:
longer spans possible, 30+ feet (9.5m) with deck thicknesses up to 10" (25.4c)

PRECAST TEES AND DOUBLE TEES:
spans up to 60+ feet (18m) with combined slab and beam depths up to 32" (97.5c)

PRECAST JOISTS AND BEAMS:
spans up to 30+ feet (9.5m) with beam depths of 12" (36.6c)

17.5
Standard precast deck and beam shapes.

cement ratio is exacting and the temperature of hydration is constant. Factory casting also allows for precise corners, accurate opening locations, and predictable cast-in plates or other desired elements cast into the concrete (Figure 17.5)—as there is no problem of shifting field formwork. Precast structures can also be constructed at any time of the year and in any weather, whereas rain and extreme cold can delay field cast construction. Lastly, if there is a problem you can see it before construction occurs—often it is impossible to correct a problem once concrete has been cast in place. The liability of precast is the need to assemble the components on-site, which can lose the elegant quality of monolithic construction. The joints are often joined by welding together steel plates cast into the concrete at the joint location, making for cumbersome connection points. This is only an issue in conditions where the structure can be seen; if it is hidden behind cladding there is no problem—however the finish improvement over cast in place no longer matters if the concrete is hidden. Pier Luigi Nervi was able to consider precast concrete frames in elegant and impressive structures that integrated cast in place elements and the necessary joints in the structure (Figure 17.6).

Cast in place construction occurs on-site with the concrete poured into forms. This type of construction requires a larger safety factor than precast due to the aforementioned unpredictability of site conditions. The skill of the

contractor along with good detailing and specifying are critical if the concrete is intended to be exposed. While it is possible to reject a concrete pour, it almost never happens unless there is a serious structural problem. Removing concrete pours is very difficult and delays the entire job schedule—both contractors and owners will expect the designer to figure out a way to "deal" with finish or opening placement problems that occur during casting. In many cases the formwork for one floor has not come off before the next is being cast—meaning two floors would need to be taken down in order to fix a problem. Cast in place concrete has a rougher quality than precast which is part of the aesthetic; this is generally presented to a client in the same fashion as a blue jeans disclaimer, "some imperfections and variations in the material are to be expected and give it a unique and desirable quality". Much of the unique quality of cast in place structures also comes from the completely monolithic characteristics of the material; it can flow together without interruption at assembly joints. This creates entirely new formal possibilities not available in any other material, as seen in the work of designers like Eero Saarinen and Felix Candela (Figure 17.7).

The method of reinforcement in the concrete has a big effect on its structural performance. While most reinforcement is simply placed into the concrete form before casting, the steel can be manipulated in two common ways to improve performance. Prestressed concrete works by stretching the steel reinforcement and holding it in tension while the concrete is poured. Once the concrete begins to dry the steel is released, which pulls the concrete into tension. The tension both strengthens the concrete element and limits cracking. This method is most commonly used in precasting factories, where proper quality control can be maintained (Figure 17.8). Post-tensioned concrete works

17.7
Thin shell concrete structure,
restaurant, Xochimilco, 1958, Felix
Candela.

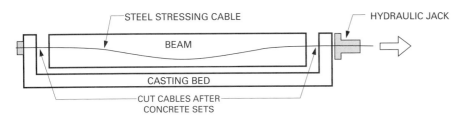

STEEL STRESSING CABLE — HYDRAULIC JACK

BEAM

CASTING BED

CUT CABLES AFTER
CONCRETE SETS

PRESTRESSED CONCRETE BEAM

17.8
Pre- and post-tensioned beam
diagrams.

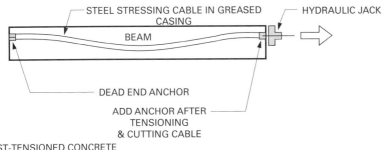

STEEL STRESSING CABLE IN GREASED
CASING — HYDRAULIC JACK

BEAM

DEAD END ANCHOR

ADD ANCHOR AFTER
TENSIONING
& CUTTING CABLE

POST-TENSIONED CONCRETE
BEAM

in a similar fashion; however, the tension is added by stretching reinforcing cable through the concrete after it has begun to set. This is the method used in most cast in place situations; large hydraulic jacks pull the cable to over 9000kg (20,000lb) tension before wedges are placed to hold the cable taught and the ends of the cable are cut off. Both methods place the reinforcing in pre-determined curves that pull the bottom of the slab in the center and the tops on the ends, following the lines of force placed on the structural element. Tensioning methods are used almost exclusively for beams and slabs, shapes that work both in tension and compression. Tensioning would have less effect on columns or other primarily compressive structural elements.

Remember that all concrete cracks. Concrete normally hydrates and dries unequally; creating uneven surface tensions which, along with natural thermal and foundation movements in buildings, works against concrete's lack of strength in tension. Steel reinforcement assists in limiting the cracking but cannot fully prevent it. The idea is to keep the cracks from pulling the concrete apart (which is handled by reinforcement) and to maintain an acceptable aesthetic finish. The finish cracking of small concrete pieces or structural elements is minimal, but large wall planes and particularly large floor slabs can be problematic. The method of dealing with this is through control joints. Control joints are grooves cut, troweled, or cast into the concrete that gather the cracks into a "controlled" location (Figure 17.9). We're all familiar with these joints in sidewalks and driveways, but they follow three particular rules for effective use.

17.9
Control joint diagrams.

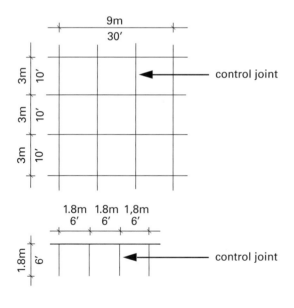

Typical concrete slab with control joints at approximately 3m (10') on center. Keep aspect ratios close to equal in order to minimize cracking outside of joints.

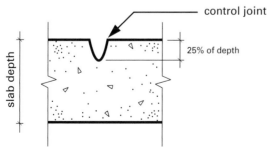

Typical 1.8m (6') wide sidewalk uses 1.8m (6') control joints to maintain 1:1 aspect ratio.

Control joints must be 25% of slab depth to control cracking. Joints can be grooved with a tool before hydration or saw cut after.

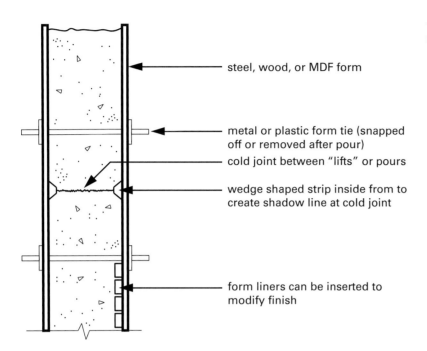

steel, wood, or MDF form

metal or plastic form tie (snapped off or removed after pour)

cold joint between "lifts" or pours

wedge shaped strip inside from to create shadow line at cold joint

form liners can be inserted to modify finish

First, they need to be cut or cast 25 percent of the depth of the slab—more lessens strength too much, less doesn't force all cracks to occur there. Second, 3 meters (10') is the maximum distance of slab distance without a control joint. This can be longer in some circumstances, but the 10-foot rule works in most circumstances. Last, an even aspect ratio of one to one should be maintained if possible. This means that the control areas need to be almost square, which is why 2 meter (6' 6") wide sidewalks have joints about every 2 meters (6' 6"); 3 meter (10') joints would make rectangles that would tend to crack in the middle rather than in the control joint. The joints in a grid pattern should also line up—shifting joints into an offset brick pattern may look good at first but will eventually crack outside of the control joints.

Another type of concrete joint is the cold joint. Cold joints are the juncture between two concrete pours. Because concrete can only be transported and placed in limited quantities, there are inevitably breaks between pours. These joints often exhibit different colors of concrete touching one another and overlap of concrete from one pour seeping onto the next. Cold joints are often concealed in vertical formwork by casting a reveal or groove in the surface to hide the joint (Figure 17.10). In thin ground slabs, these joints are often separated from one another with a felt or neoprene material that prevents one pour from bonding with the next. This separation is called an expansion joint. Expansion joints are intended to allow for movement between two areas that are expected to shift or settle unevenly, like an on grade slab meeting a building entrance. The slab will float with the ground expansion, while the building should remain fixed on its foundations. The joint prevents the movement of one system from damaging the other. Expansion joints are also built into separate segments of a building that has an irregular or elongated form. The movement of a building's shape should be considered in a similar fashion to a ground slab—aspect ratios of one to one are best. Large-scale expansion joints can sometimes allow for over 300mm (12") of movement, and more extreme cases can be seen in very long, thin structures like bridges that may need to allow for meters of total movement.

Concrete formwork is the means of shaping all concrete structures. Formwork determines not only the shape but also the finish of the concrete. Concrete buildings are essentially built twice—first the formwork is constructed in the shape of the building, then the concrete is poured, then the formwork is removed. Custom formwork is often constructed by carpenters and must be precisely built because it needs to be almost waterproof and incredibly strong. Concrete is very fluid when first poured and will leak out of any openings in the form; it is also very heavy (over 135lb per cubic foot/659kg per cubic meter) and can destroy a weak form. There are no second chances with most pours, so a thorough knowledge of how forms are made is essential for designers to work with design possibilities. Forms can be made of wood or metal, lined with various types of materials, and are both pre-manufactured and custom built (Figure 17.11). The material and texture of the form transmits itself onto the surface of the concrete, so even the wood grain from plywood is visible after the form is removed. All forms come in limited sizes, with the standard 1.2 × 2.4m (4 × 8") sheet of plywood creating the most common wood module. Metal forms can be made in many other sizes and often have fewer form ties. The form ties are metal or plastic rods that pass through the formwork, holding the two sides together, and making a pattern of indentations in

17.11
Kimball Museum of Art, concrete construction, 1967–1972, Fort Worth, Texas, Louis Kahn.

the surface of the concrete. Wooden or metal strips, textured form liners, and chemical sprays can be added into the form before pours to change the surface appearance. All of these formwork issues need to be taken into account, along with the color of the aggregate and cement, to get the desired finish.

Concrete comes from the cement plant in trucks that can pour the material directly into place or into another means of moving the concrete across the site. Given the limited time between water mixture and hydration, the placement must occur relatively quickly. In order to move concrete up onto taller building structures, vessels that can lift and pour with cranes are filled, or pumping systems are used. Pumping trucks can take multiple loads from cement trucks and pump the material through hoses and pipes into tall structures. A pumping truck will normally run almost continually throughout the day in a large pour, because it needs to be thoroughly cleaned if not in use. The placed concrete is then sometimes vibrated into place in formwork, or surface finished by screeding (flattening with a long bar or plank), and troweling smooth. Final finishes can be added by brooming, raking, rotary troweling, or sandblasting. All finishing needs to occur at a time when the concrete is soft enough to take the finish, yet hard enough to retain it—it also helps if it's not raining. Only a limited area can be done at one time, as too large an area cannot be completed before the concrete hydrates beyond workability.

The workability and strength of concrete are at direct odds with one another. The lower the water to cement ratio, the stronger the concrete; however, the more water, the easier it is to work. Concrete develops its strength quickly, up to 75 percent of total strength in 7 days and full strength in 28 days. Testing of strength is done in two ways. First is a slump test, which consists of filling a plastic cone with the concrete mixture, placing it on the ground and pulling the cone. The amount of collapse, or slump, is used as an indication of water to cement ratio before the concrete is determined acceptable to be placed. The other test is a cylinder break. Small diameter cylinders are poured from each cement truck that arrives on-site; these are numbered and sent to a testing lab where they are crushed after 7 days. If the acceptable strength is reached there is no problem, if not the contractor has the option of deferring to a 28-day break, which typically is much stronger. If the concrete does not meet strength specifications it may need to be removed and replaced, difficult to do 7 to 28 days after the building has been built on top of it. The typical range of concrete strength is 1150–1800kg (2500–4000lb) of compressive force per square inch, with higher-strength concrete available.

To deal with the desire for higher-strength concrete, which is much harder to work with, admixtures have been developed that allow for more workability without adding water. Admixtures can also assist when pouring in very cold or hot temperatures. Superplasticizers and mid range water reducers are the most common admixtures; they allow the concrete to be manipulated longer without affecting water-cement ratios. Admixtures are expensive and can make structural engineers nervous due to frequent abuses on job sites of adding water above the specified ratios to keep concrete fluid. They are often necessary, but keep in mind that they can also affect the finish and color of the concrete.

Concrete can be colored through the use of various pigments, stains, and etchings. Integrally colored concrete has the pigment mixed into the cement powder, which has a limited effect due to the high percentage of aggregate in concrete. When concrete cures it tends to send the water and finer cement particles to the edges of the form, making the surface smooth and composed of mostly the cement powder and fine aggregate, so mostly you see the color of these materials, but it is rather inexact and unpredictable. The surfaces of concrete can be sandblasted or acid etched, which removes this layer of cement and fine aggregate, exposing the larger aggregate and dramatically changing the appearance of the surface. Surface pigments can be painted or blown on after curing, which stain the top layer a color, but the inconsistency of the concrete tends to make this a mottled effect. Lastly paints and sealers can color the surface but wear off and fade over time.

CONCLUSION

Concrete is a material that fundamentally changes the rules of construction and form making. It can do things no other material can and has little formal historical precedent. Newer technologies are making the material stronger, which again modifies what was previously thought possible. Like all materials there is an ethical component to the use of concrete; it can do many things but its energy use and environmental impact are large. Cement manufacturing plants often burn vast quantities of coal and have begun the use of burning waste materials for fuel, some of which is nontoxic; however, the use of fuel materials like used automobile tires can have negative environmental impacts. Unsound environmental practices can only be confronted with sound research by designers and subsequent education of the user groups. That may mean specifying only certain cement producers and convincing the client of this—or avoiding the use of a material altogether. The threshold has been raised on what it means to responsibly assemble a project—and this is an integral part of an architect's task.

FREQUENTLY ASKED QUESTIONS

How do you determine if a concrete pour is strong enough to handle the design load?
Concrete is specified in various strengths, which determine the mix ratios at the cement plant. Once it arrives on-site the contractor must approve that the mix is correct as specified by the structural engineer. There are frequently slump tests, which show an indication of the amount of water in the mix before pouring, and cylinder breaks, which are small pours of concrete from the mix that are brought to a lab and tested for strength by compressing them to failure. Concrete reaches 75 percent of its strength after 7 days, so after a week they run the test and you typically know if a problem exists.

How do you know when to use control or expansion joints?
Control joints are intended to prevent cracking in a random pattern in concrete slabs. The joints focus the normal slab movement onto the weaker joints, causing a "controlled" crack pattern. Expansion joints are intended to allow for movement between two areas that are expected to shift or settle unevenly, like an on-grade slab meeting a building entrance. The slab will float with the ground

expansion, while the building should remain still. The joint prevents the movement of one system from damaging the other.

GLOSSARY

Aggregate: Stones and gravel added to the concrete mixture to create volume, strength and durability.

Cast in place concrete: Construction that occurs on-site with the concrete poured into forms assembled in their final location. This type of construction requires a larger safety factor than precast due to the unpredictability of site conditions, and it results in a more varied finish.

Cement: A powder that binds the other materials in concrete together through the process of hydration. Concrete hydration is a chemical reaction that occurs when the cement powder is mixed with water, resulting in heat and a crystallized bond forming between the wet cement and the aggregate.

Cold joint: The juncture between two concrete pours.

Concrete: A mixture of cement, water, and aggregate that hydrates to form a solid building material.

Control joint: Grooves cut or cast into the concrete that gather the cracks into a "controlled" location.

Expansion joint: Joint intended to allow for movement between two areas that are expected to shift or settle unevenly.

Precast concrete: Concrete building components made in a factory under carefully controlled conditions. The water to cement ratio is exacting and the temperature of hydration is constant making it more predictable and precise than cast in place concrete.

Portland cement: A commercially manufactured cement made by combining ground limestone and shale/clay in a furnace heated to over 1480C (2700F).

Rebar: Reinforcing bars of steel used to provide tension strength in hybrid concrete/steel pours.

FURTHER READING

Nervi, P. L. (1965). *Aesthetics and Technology in Building*. Cambridge, MA: Harvard University Press; pp. 1–21.

Ramsey, C. G. and Sleeper, H. R. (2000). *Architectural Graphic Standards*, 10th edition. New York: John Wiley & Sons; Chapter 3, Concrete.

18

ALUMINUM

Raw material and production	Bauxite—alumina
	Smelting
	Alloys
	Recycling
	Strength/stiffness
	Fire/corrosion
History	Discovery to small-scale production
	Electrolysis—technology
Aluminum fabrication	Methods of producing shapes
	Joining methods
	Galvanic action
	Finishing

INTRODUCTION

Aluminum, in relative terms, is a very recently discovered metal. Copper has been used for over 7500 years, bronze for 4000, iron and steel for over 3000 years. Aluminum was only discovered about 200 years ago, in 1808. Its properties, compared to other metals, are what have made it so ubiquitous in such a short time. It's a third the weight of steel for the same quantity, highly resistant to corrosion, conducts electricity twice as efficiently as the same weight of copper, forms more easily than other metals and is easier to cut, can be alloyed to rigid or ductile states, finishes very smoothly, can be electrically dyed (anodized), and is easily recyclable. All of this, however, comes at a cost.

Aluminum contains the most embodied energy of any commonly used building material. In fact, it has over five times the embodied energy of the same weight of steel, and is over three times as energy intensive as its closest metal, copper (Table 18.1). The process used to extract the material from the mined ore uses vast amounts of electricity and produces significant amounts of waste and toxicity. This is balanced by the performance of the resulting product. Simply put, no other material can do everything that aluminum does. The use of the material becomes an exercise in appropriateness—deciding when and where the performance outweighs the impact.

Table 18.1 Approximate embodied energy of common building materials.

	Energy content	
	joules/gram	**BTU/lb**
Sand	42	18
Wood	430	185
Lightweight concrete	2186	940
Gypsum board	4255	1830
Brickwork	5115	2200
Cement	9533	4100
Glass	25,808	11,100
Porcelain	26,273	11,300
Plastic	43,013	18,500
Steel	44,640	19,200
Lead	60,218	25,900
Zinc	64,635	27,800
Copper	68,820	29,600
Aluminum	240,638	103,500

18.1
Miss Britain III, one time fastest boat in the world, clad in aluminum.

Aluminum is typically not used as a primary structural material. This is because it lacks the strength of materials like steel. It requires large sizes to approach the strength of steel, which is impractical, and is not resilient when alloyed to increase strength—making it unable to absorb impact and deflection before failing (low modulus of elasticity). For smaller, less demanding, support tasks it works very well, and adds less load into the overall structure because of its light weight (Figure 18.1).

RAW MATERIAL

Aluminum is the most plentiful metal in the earth's crust (8 percent), but must be mined from bauxite ore. The process begins much like steel with large-scale mining operations, but the process used to extract and refine the metal is much different and more energy intensive. The following is the process as described courtesy of Alcoa, the largest producer of aluminum in the world (Figure 18.2).

1 *Mining:* Bauxite is an ore rich in aluminum oxide, formed over millions of years by chemical weathering of rocks containing aluminum silicates. It was first mined in France and has since been found in many locations around the world. Today, most bauxite mining is in the Caribbean, Australia, and Africa.
2 *Refining:* To turn bauxite into alumina, the ore is ground and mixed with lime and caustic soda, pumped into high-pressure containers, and heated. The aluminum oxide is dissolved by the caustic soda, then precipitated out of this solution, washed, and heated to drive off water. What's left is the sugar-like white powder called alumina, or aluminum oxide (Al_2O_3).
3 *Alumina:* Alumina chemicals are used to purify water and to make refractory bricks, ceramics, adhesives, catalysts, and fire-retardant fillers for fabrics and plastics.
4 *Smelting:* Alumina becomes aluminum in an electrolytic reduction process known as smelting. Alumina is dissolved in a cryolite bath inside large, carbon-lined cells called pots. When a powerful electric current is passed

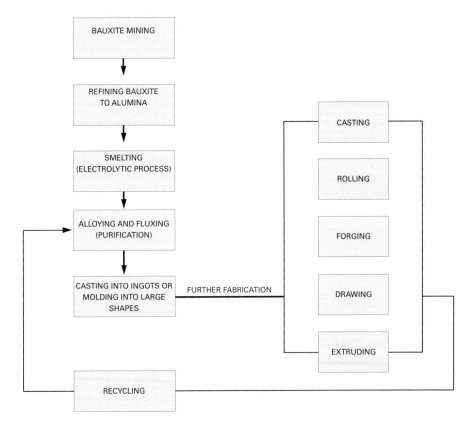

18.2
Aluminum manufacturing process.

through the bath, aluminum metal separates from the chemical solution and is siphoned off.

5 *Fabricating:* Aluminum from the smelting pots goes into furnaces for precise mixing with other metals to form various alloys with specific properties designed for particular uses. The metal is purified in a process called fluxing, then poured into molds or cast directly into ingots. Further fabrication may include casting, rolling, forging, drawing, or extruding—some of the ways manufacturers make thousands of different finished products, from beverage cans to cars to jet aircraft.

6 *Recycling:* Of the 100 billion or so beverage cans produced annually in the U.S., roughly two-thirds are returned for recycling (a bit over one-third are returned in Britain). So is 85–90 percent of the aluminum in cars. Recycling saves 95 percent of the energy it would take to make new metal from ore, and it lessens the need for solid waste disposal.

Aluminum secondary smelting, *scrap recycling*, accounts for approximately 33 percent of all primary aluminum produced in the U.S. There are approximately 68 major secondary processing plants in the U.S. and 22 in the U.K. These processing plants are typically located near urban areas where large supplies of scrap aluminum are available. Aluminum recycling and secondary smelting requires preprocessing of the scrap aluminum to remove impurities, followed by re-melting of the aluminum. To maintain sufficient purity, the re-melted aluminum is mixed with pure aluminum produced in a primary smelting plant (typically a 50–50 mix). Prior to melting various mechanical, thermal, chemical, and magnetic techniques are used to separate contaminants and non-aluminum materials from the scrap. In contrast to the electricity intensive process of primary aluminum smelting, melting of scrap to yield secondary aluminum involves primarily natural gas usage. The argument that it is more expensive to process recycling than it saves is not true of aluminum; to save 95 percent of the energy-intensive raw material process is significant in dollars and environmental impact.

Aluminum corrodes very slowly; it quickly forms a protective oxide skin on exposed surfaces. This can eventually break down, but is typically stable for long periods of time even in marine conditions. Painting or anodizing can extend the corrosion resistance.

Fire affects aluminum earlier than materials like steel. It melts completely at 660C (1220F) and loses strength far before that. This makes it impractical as a primary structural material, beyond problems of its low modulus of elasticity.

HISTORY

The earliest known uses for alumina date to 7000 years ago, when Persian potters made vessels from a clay containing the oxide to increase strength. Ancient Egyptians used aluminum oxides in dyes, make-up, and medicine. There was no use of aluminum as a metal, however, until much later. While it is abundant in the earth's crust, it doesn't occur naturally as a metal and is hard to transform from raw material to metallic form.

In 1808, Sir Humphry Davy discovered the existence of aluminum. Danish physicist, Hans Christian Oersted, managed to produce a few droplets of the metal shortly thereafter. Through the course of improving production about 1.8 metric tons (2 tons) were produced by 1869. This brought the cost down dramatically, from £425 per kilogram ($550 per lb) to £13 per kilogram ($17 per lb). In the early 1880s, aluminum was considered a semi-precious material, more rare than silver.

Charles Martin Hall was a student at Oberlin College when he saw aluminum for the first time as a rare metal. After graduation, he experimented with ways to make the material commercially viable. He learned how to make aluminum oxide—alumina—and he fashioned his own carbon crucible. In February 1886, he filled the crucible with a cryolite bath containing alumina and passed an electric current through it. The result was a congealed mass that he allowed to cool then shattered with a hammer. Inside were several small pellets of pure aluminum. This process, electrolysis, is how aluminum is processed today at a much larger scale.

FABRICATION

Foundries produce complex metal shapes by melting aluminum or aluminum alloys and pouring the molten metal into a mold to solidify into the desired shape. Aluminum casting accounts for 32 percent of all metal castings in the U.S. and 8 percent in the U.K., with the majority of these castings being done for the automotive industry. There are four main methods used for casting metals: sand casting, investment casting, permanent mold casting, and die-casting.

Die casting and permanent mold casting together account for over 80 percent of all aluminum casting. Due to aluminum's low melting temperature, inexpensive steel and iron can be used for forming the dies and molds. The molten aluminum feeding the casting line is derived from three different sources: ingots from a primary aluminum producer, molten aluminum directing from a smelting plant, or partially processed recycled aluminum scrap.

Casting consists of pouring molten aluminum into molds. Once in the mold, the aluminum solidifies into the defined shape. Three different casting methods are used: sand casting, permanent mold casting, and die-casting.

Sand casting is the most versatile method and the most economical for producing small quantities. Over 70 percent of all metal casting uses this process. Almost any shape mold can be produced from fine sand and binder mixture (usually clay). After casting, the sand molds must either be hauled to landfills or reconditioned. Thermal sand reclamation processes are available that remove the binder material from the sand and allow the sand to be reused.

Investment casting uses a ceramic mold that was created around a plastic or wax replica of the desired metal shape. Prior to casting, the ceramic mold is fired which increases the mold strength and burns away the plastic or wax replica, removing it from the mold. Investment casting is capable of creating higher precision casts than sand casting.

Permanent mold casting uses steel or other metal molds to shape the molten aluminum. Molten aluminum is forced into the mold under gravity or with the aid of a vacuum. Permanent mold castings are stronger than sand castings and less expensive for large production quantities.

Die casting is used for producing accurate components that require little

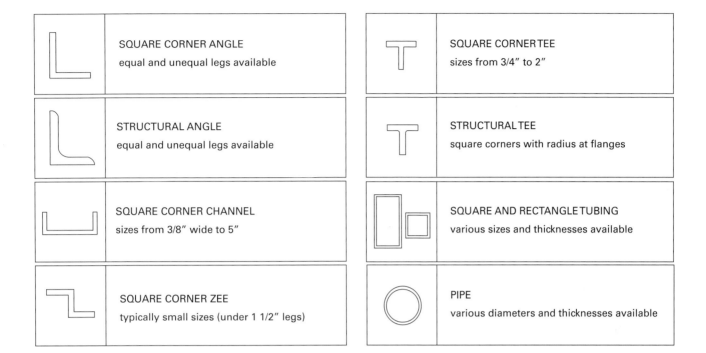

	SQUARE CORNER ANGLE equal and unequal legs available		SQUARE CORNER TEE sizes from 3/4" to 2"
	STRUCTURAL ANGLE equal and unequal legs available		STRUCTURAL TEE square corners with radius at flanges
	SQUARE CORNER CHANNEL sizes from 3/8" wide to 5"		SQUARE AND RECTANGLE TUBING various sizes and thicknesses available
	SQUARE CORNER ZEE typically small sizes (under 1 1/2" legs)		PIPE various diameters and thicknesses available

18.3
Standard aluminum shapes.

subsequent matching. The molten aluminum is forced under high pressure into steel molds or dies that shape and cool the molten aluminum.

Extrusion is the process of pressing heated aluminum through a die under extreme force to produce the desired shape. Extrusions can be made in literally thousands of complex shapes, but the most commonly used shapes are readily available (Figures 18.3 and 18.4). Billets are preheated and forced by a ram through one or more dies to achieve the desired cross section. The product is long in relation to its cross-sectional dimensions and has a section other than that of a rod, bar, pipe, or tube.

Rolling is the process of forming thin aluminum sheets from slab ingots that are up to 660mm (26") thick, 6m (20') long, and weigh up to 18 metric tons (20 tons). The slab is heated in a furnace and rolled between powered rollers until the plate is approximately 25mm (1") thick. The plates are further reduced in finishing mills where they are hot rolled to a thickness of 6–10mm (0.25–0.4").

Forging is the process of forming aluminum by impacting and/or squeezing a preheated aluminum blank between two halves of a die. A succession of dies may be needed to achieve the final shape. Forging provides advantages over casting in that internal microstructure can be oriented to improve strength, and internal defects or porosity are minimized. The aluminum blank is typically heated to 315–480C (600–900F), but some cold forging is also performed in the industry. Cold forging is performed on billets at room temperature. This process involves high die costs and is typically limited to high production volumes but results in very strong materials.

Aluminum comes in different classifications from 1000 to 7000 series, to be used for varying purposes (Table 18.2). Each series of aluminum is alloyed with other agents to modify the properties of the material. 1000 series is almost pure aluminum and 7000 series is the strongest, but the numbers do not indicate a progressive strengthening of the material (2000 and 7000 series

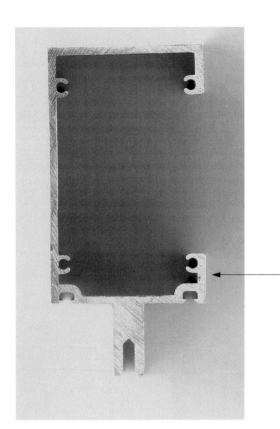

18.4
Aluminum extrusion.

detailed shapes made possible
by extusion die

Table 18.2 Aluminum classification series

Aluminum classification	Primary alloying agent	Characteristics	Uses	Common types
1000	None	Soft, weldable, corrosion resistant	Food/Chemical resistance	1050, 1200
2000	Copper	Heat treatable, non-weldable, high strength, poor corrosive resistance	Aircraft construction	2014
3000	Manganese	Non-heat treatable, medium strength, weldable, corrosive resistant	Marine environments	3103, 3003
4000	Silicon		Used as welding rod	
5000	Magnesium	Non-heat treatable, weldable, and very corrosive resistant	Pressurized applications, marine environments, including shipbuilding	5454, 5083
6000	Magnesium and Silicon	Heat treatable, medium strength, weldable, corrosive resistant	Architectural extrusions, intricate shapes, structural members	6063, 6061, 6082
7000	Zinc	Heat treatable, age hardens, some weldable, some unweldable, very high strength, poor corrosion resistance	Aircraft construction, motorcycle and bicycle frames, armored vehicles	7020 weldable 7075 non-weldable

are the highest strength series). Common types of each series have individual numbers, such as 7075 aluminum, which is the strongest. Many of the highest-strength aluminum alloys (such as 7075) are not weldable. Aluminum welds are not as strong as the parent material, therefore additional material is needed to maintain strength, while steel welds can be made as strong as the material being joined, limiting weakness at the joints.

Aluminum can be joined in two ways—welding and bolting. This decision is based on a number of factors. The basic rule of thumb is the same as steel, "weld in the shop—bolt in the field". Welding can be done much more effectively in a controlled environment, whereas bolting is easily accomplished on-site. Aluminum welding is significantly more difficult than steel and cannot be easily done on-site. As noted above, not all aluminum series are even weldable, so often bolting is the only choice. Aesthetic and structural considerations can also dictate the method of assembly because often it can be done either way, but one method can have significant strength or visual impact. One of the factors to consider is the size of a metal assembly—remember, if it can't fit on a truck, it shouldn't be finished in the shop. Many times large portions of an assembly can be made in the shop, with the final form finished by a few simple bolts on-site. Another factor to consider is the metal finish. Painted or anodized pieces will have the finish destroyed by welding on-site, and then the original finish will be "matched" with a typically inferior method, such as spray paint. This normally results in a finish less durable and aesthetically compromised. Think through the assembly and finishes carefully to decide how to join metal elements together.

A common problem with all metals in assemblies is galvanic action. This is corrosion caused by dissimilar materials touching one another in a wet environment. An electrical current flows between different metals as one "sacrifices" itself to the other (Table 18.3). The galvanic series runs from the more stable or "most noble" metals to the most corrosive or "least noble" metals. The least noble metal corrodes when in direct contact with the more noble metal—the farther apart they are in the scale the more corrosion occurs (Table 18.4). This can cause catastrophic failures, such as stainless steel panels eating carbon steel fasteners,

Table 18.3 Galvanic series

(Least Noble)		Magnesium
+		Zinc
		Aluminum 1000
		Cadmium
		Aluminum 2024-T4
		Steel or Iron, Cast iron
		Chromium iron (active)
		Stainless Steel Type 304, 316 (active)
	Current Flow	Lead, Tin
		Nickel (active)
		Brasses, Copper, Bronzes, Copper-Nickel alloys, Monel
		Silver Solder
		Nickel (passive)
		Chromium iron (passive)
		Stainless Steel Type 304, 316 (passive)
		Silver
−		Titanium
(Most Noble)		Graphite, Gold, Platinum

Table 18.4 Galvanic action between materials.

	Aluminum	Copper	Galvanized Steel	Lead	Stainless Steel	Zinc	Brass	Bronze	Iron/Steel	Monel
Aluminum	●		○	◐	○	○	●	●	◐	○
Copper			◐	◐	●	●	◐	◐	●	◐
Galvanized Steel				○		○	◐	◐	◐	◐
Lead							◐	◐	○	◐
Stainless Steel			◐	◐		●	●	●	◐	●
Zinc Alloy				○			●	●	●	●

Key: ● Galvanic action likely

○ Galvanic action possible over time

◐ Galvanic action negligible

resulting in wall panels dropping off of buildings. Chemically active materials can also create galvanic action—the most common being concrete eating aluminum when in direct contact in moisture. The method of limiting this is intelligent selection of systems and isolation of materials. Isolation generally takes place with inert washers or spacers, such as nylon and plastic. Keeping direct contact in check is very important to avoid major problems with corrosion. Aluminum is one of the least noble metals and always needs to be handled carefully.

Aluminum does not always need to be finished when used in building applications, but it normally is. The finish types most commonly used are painting and anodizing. Painting aluminum is similar to most other materials; however, because aluminum has a very high thermal expansion rate, the paint can crack over time. Aluminum can also be anodized, which is an oxide coating applied as a dye with an electric current (Figure 18.5). The finish is then chemically bonded to the surface and cannot be flaked off or cracked. It can however be scratched, because it is a thin coating, and this cannot be repaired in the field. Anodizing leaves the finish of the aluminum exactly the texture of the surface of the pre-prepared metal, but tends to be matte. Any color can be obtained and the color stability has improved over the classic fading of red to pink or black to brown that was common 20 years ago. Most aluminum windows and other pre-manufactured building components are anodized.

CONCLUSION

The basic benefits of aluminum are strength to weight ratio, more precise shapes than steel, easy shop or field assembly, a limitless variety of formal possibilities, infinite finish options, and a lightweight corrosion-resistant material. This is countered by the highest embodied energy of any common building material, difficulty of fabrication, potential for surface abrasion, thermal instability, high thermal conductivity (condensation issues), and fire resistance difficulties. Some people would argue that we should simply stop using aluminum, and it is likely overused, but its economy combined with its unique properties make it difficult to avoid. This is another example of a material that has its appropriate applications, but should be considered carefully before automatically selecting it.

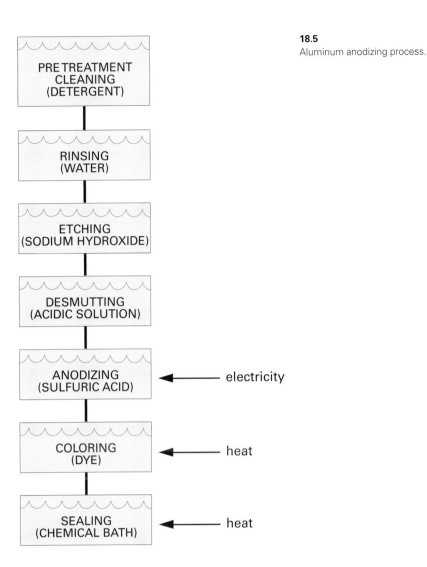

18.5
Aluminum anodizing process.

FREQUENTLY ASKED QUESTIONS

How do you decide when it's appropriate to use aluminum?
Aluminum has a high cost of embodied energy, but it can do many things no other material can. It has a very high strength to weight ratio and can lighten assemblies that require weight reduction. It also has corrosion resistance, and it can be used more economically than stainless steel in many corrosion-resistant applications. It is recyclable, but often difficult to separate from hybrid assemblies in building systems in order to recycle.

How do you know whether to use rolled, forged, or cast aluminum?
Casting allows for very specific shapes due to the molding process, but it typically is not as strong as rolled or forged aluminum. Rolling makes a limited number of shapes (such as angles and bars) because it is a linear fabrication process. Forging presses shapes using dies and can be very expensive but produces very strong pieces. Typically you're looking for the most economical way to achieve your desired result.

GLOSSARY

Alloy: A metal mixed with added elements or other metals to modify its properties.

Alumina: Aluminum oxide produced from bauxite by an intricate chemical process. It is a white, powdery material that looks like granulated sugar. Alumina is an intermediate step in the production of aluminum from bauxite and is also a valuable chemical on its own.

Anodizing: An electrochemical process for applying a protective or decorative coating to metal surfaces.

Bauxite: An ore from which alumina is extracted and from which aluminum is eventually smelted. It takes four parts bauxite to make one part aluminum.

Brazing: Joining metals by flowing a thin layer of molten, non-ferrous filler metal into the space between them.

Casting: The process of forming molten metal into a particular shape by pouring it into a mold and letting it harden.

Cold mill: The equipment on which aluminum is rolled into sheet or foil by passing it through pairs of rollers under pressure. In cold rolling, the incoming metal is normally at room temperature.

Extrusion: The process of shaping material by forcing it to flow through a shaped opening in a die.

Fabricate: To work a material into a finished state by machining, forming, or joining.

Flat-rolled products: Aluminum plate, sheet, or foil products made by passing ingot through pairs of rolls, successively reducing its thickness and increasing its length.

Forging: A metal part worked to predetermined shape by one or more processes such as hammering, pressing, or rolling.

Ingot: A cast form suitable for re-melting or fabricating. An ingot may take many forms: some may be 9m (30') long and weigh 13.6 metric tons (15 tons); others are notched or specially shaped for stacking and handling.

London Metal Exchange (LME): The international trading body that facilitates the worldwide open market buying and selling of metals.

Magnesium: A light, silvery, moderately hard, metallic element used in processing metals and chemicals, and in alloying aluminum to give it desired metallurgical properties.

Mill products: Metal that has been fabricated into an intermediate form before being made into a finished product. The most common fabricating processes for aluminum are rolling, extruding, forging, and casting. For example, aluminum sheet, a mill product, is used to make beverage cans, a finished product.

Pot: In aluminum production: the electrolytic reduction cell in which alumina dissolved in molten cryolite is reduced to metallic aluminum. A series of cells connected electrically is called a potline.

Smelt: To fuse or melt ore in order to extract or refine the metal it contains.

FURTHER READING

Ching, F. D. K. (2001). *Building Construction Illustrated*. New York: John Wiley & Sons; section 12.09.

Ramsey, C. G. and Sleeper, H. R. (2000). *Architectural Graphic Standards*, 10th edition. New York: John Wiley & Sons; pp. 260–263.

19

COMPOSITE MATERIALS

Introduction	Synergetic performance in materials
	Early types of composites
Principles	Binders
	Reinforcements
	Isotropic and anisotropic behavior
	Lamination and strength-building
Materials	Plywood
	Fiberglass
	Carbon fiber
	Metal sandwich panels

INTRODUCTION

A good deal of our work as architects deals with fairly straightforward materials—wood, steel, concrete, glass, and aluminum form the bulk of our material "palette." We take for granted that these materials' properties are more or less fixed—we may use stronger or weaker woods, steel may be alloyed for greater durability or strength, and so forth, but most of these still have a fairly narrow range of strength and workability.

What if, however, we could fine-tune the materials we used to maximize performance where we needed it? If, for example, we could take a high-strength material and combine it with a high-workability material, we could put the stronger stuff only where it was absolutely necessary, making a component that might be generally easier to work with, and strong where it mattered. This is the principle behind composites—materials that are made of more than one substance that retain their own individual properties, but that combine to produce greater functionality than either material on its own. While the architectural use of composites has been limited so far by cost and production, these represent one of the most promising developments in construction for the next 25 or so years.

The idea behind composites is not really new, nor is it entirely man-made. Papier mâché, for example, is a good example of two "constituent" materials (paper and glue) being combined to take advantage of their individual properties. Neither the paper nor the glue could hold a three-dimensional form on its own, but as the glue dries it "locks" the paper fibers into position, and the resulting composite becomes dimensionally stable, and quite strong. Medieval wattle-and-daub construction used similar principles to take advantage of straw fibers' inherent strength, and mud's ability to hold them in place. All forms of concrete are really composites of aggregate and mortar, but reinforced concrete is a particularly successful application of two materials with complementary strengths—steel in tension, and concrete in compression. Again, the cured concrete holds the otherwise flexible steel reinforcing in place, guaranteeing its structural performance.

Modern composites date back to the invention of Bakelite in 1907, a combination of paper or cloth with an early phenolic resin. At high temperatures, the resin softened and the material could be formed or molded. As it cooled, the material retained its shape while it hardened, resulting in objects with complex shapes and inherent surface strength. At around the same time, an ancient technique of layering thin sheets of wood with thinly spread adhesive was revived by the American timber industry. Originally used for door panels and automotive components, plywood became useful to the building industry with the application of waterproof adhesives in the 1930s. Because it could be laid up quickly and formed into complex curved shapes while the adhesive cured, plywood saw extraordinary development and usage during World War II, in applications ranging from boats and airplanes to temporary shelters and mass-produced leg splints designed by Charles and Ray Eames. The Eames took what they learned from this commission and began to design influential mass-produced office and home furniture using the material in the late 1940s. World War II also saw the first production use of fiberglass, which embedded cloth woven from glass fibers in resin to create strong, moldable shapes that were useful in aircraft and naval applications.

PRINCIPLES

By definition, all composite materials are made of two or more *constituents*. In most architectural applications, one of these constituents is a *matrix* and one is *reinforcement*. Usually, the matrix is a material that can be softened or hardened, either by temperature or chemical curing. When solid, this material is often strong in compression but weak in tension, like concrete. Typical matrices include resins or epoxies, natural adhesives, and cements. The matrix is impregnated with reinforcement that is usually fibrous and flexible, such as cloth, paper, woven glass fabric, or even loose glass fibers. Note that either of these material groups on their own would be either too weak or flexible to perform in any structural situation. Glass, for example, is brittle on its own, but when protected by a resin matrix it can be "encouraged" to be strong—the glass in this case adds its strength, while the matrix shares potentially fracturing stresses among thousands of individual glass fibers.

Matrices and reinforcement are either mixed or *laid up*. The former can involve simply combining the two elements and stirring, while the latter requires careful setting out of reinforcement sheets and brushing or saturating them with the desired matrix. These sheets may have a *grain*, or a direction in

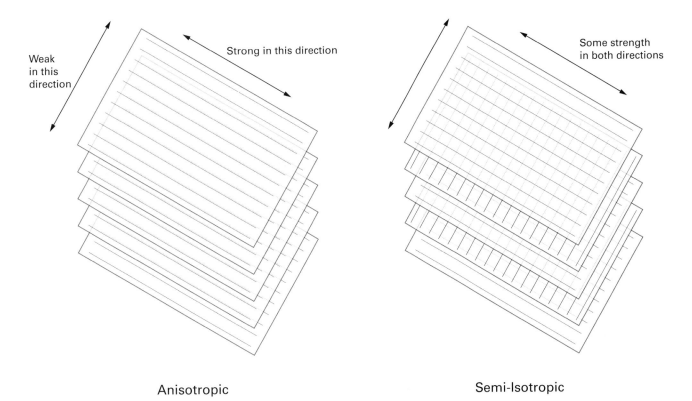

Anisotropic

Semi-Isotropic

which they are stronger or weaker (wood sheets are a good example of this). If the component needs to be strong only in one direction, the sheets can be laid up so that these grains align. If, however, the component is likely to experience stress in several different directions, the sheets can be laid up so that layers alternate direction, ensuring that the finished product will be strong along multiple axes. Components or materials with a strong grain are called *anisotropic*, while those with equal strength (or weakness) in all directions are called *isotropic* (Figure 19.1).

As the composite is laid up, its component sheets may be laid over or into a mold that gives them their final shape; this can also occur after sheets are adhered to one another but before the matrix has been set. Usually, a mechanical force is applied to press the material into the mold, guaranteeing a tight adherence to the desired geometry. This is sometimes done by pressure, either on the mold side (vacuum bag) or the material side (pressure bag). The composite may also be pressed between two molds to ensure details and configurations on both sides of the resulting element. Composites that use liquid and loose reinforcement may also be simply poured into a three-dimensional mold (see Chapter 35, Custom Fabrication).

Simple adhesives may then just be allowed to cure over time, while some polymers and resins will either be heated or cooled until they are set (known as *thermosetting*). This process usually requires an oven, called an *autoclave*, that can deliver precise temperatures. The dimensions of these ovens often limit the size of composite components. Following curing, the component may be finished with protective or decorative finishes, and it may be drilled, cut, or otherwise fabricated with finer operations to add connections or details.

While these components are often fairly simple in their form—typically a thin

19.1

Laying up sheets of material with a very defined grain allows us to fine-tune the strength of a composite to match predicted loads.

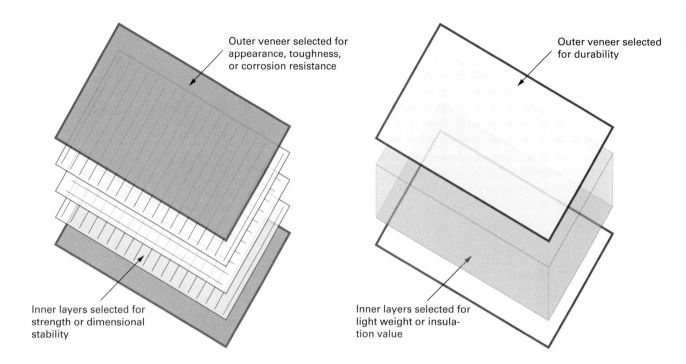

Outer veneer selected for appearance, toughness, or corrosion resistance

Inner layers selected for strength or dimensional stability

Outer veneer selected for durability

Inner layers selected for light weight or insulation value

shell wrapped around a mold or cast in a thin, flat sheet—the laying-up process permits a very clever process of specific placement to add strength in discrete locations. By adding additional layers of reinforcement and matrix in areas of high stress, the component can be very finely tuned to meet specific loading requirements (Figure 19.2). Imagine, for instance, a fiberglass boat deck where one area is likely to have high cargo traffic. This area might be given additional layers of reinforcement and matrix to provide a deeper (and therefore stronger— see Chapters 24 and 25) structural depth. These layers could even be shaped to create downstand beams instead of a thick slab, saving weight—critical in boat design—while providing an area of greater strength. Unlike steel beams, which must be rolled, or concrete slabs, which require extensive carpentry work to add special structural elements like downstand beams, the laying-up process permits extensive customization and carefully placement of material.

19.2
The composite principle also lets us consider other functional parameters.

TYPICAL COMPOSITE MATERIALS

Plywood (Figure 19.3) is the simplest composite architects will use. It is made by peeling a log on a rotating saw into sheets of wood veneer, which are then glued together using glues that are typically made from formaldehyde and can be tuned to dry or wet conditions. Finish plywood has outer veneers that are selected for their appearance, while marine plywood has outer veneers selected for durability and water resistance. The variety of woods available for both core and outer layers means that these can be selected precisely for the application needed, and the ease with which it can be cut, nailed, or drilled makes it an important material for a variety of light applications, in particular residential construction. Plywood's strength comes from laying up veneers in several different directions, removing the weakness inherent across a single

19.3
Plywood is the most widely used composite material, here used in a classic chair.

19.4
Fiberglass is a versatile composite.

sheet of the lumber's grain—because it is isotropic, it is a good material for light floors and for residential-scale shear walls. Recent concerns about toxicity of plywood glues, especially in indoor applications, have made low-emissions plywood a popular range of products.

Fiberglass (Figure 19.4) is typically used in cladding and interior or furniture applications. As described above, it usually consists of a woven fabric of blown glass fibers within a plastic matrix—usual epoxy or polyester. Because the glass is produced in fibers instead of sheets, it tends to be free of structural flaws, making each fiber reliably strong. In addition to laying up sheets of glass fibers by hand, these may be rolled or laid mechanically, and the matrix can be applied by a robotic sprayer, making the process more efficient. Additionally, a process called *pultrusion* can introduce the matrix to a linear, rolled sheet. The resulting ribbon can then be folded or molded as it is drawn through a curing oven, creating a long, sectionally consistent component similar to aluminum extrusion. Fiberglass is often used in wet locations—for bathtubs or sinks, for instance—where its resistance to water is beneficial. Glass fibers are also sometimes introduced into a light cement matrix to create cladding panels made of *GFRC*, or *glass-reinforced cement*. The glass here acts as a distributed reinforcement, making the panels more resistant to impact. Like plywood, fiberglass uses toxic substances for its matrices, though these are generally more stable and resistant to off-gassing. Glass fibers, however, can cause irritation if touched and are considered a possible carcinogen if inhaled.

Carbon Fiber (Figure 19.5) is essentially similar to fiberglass, in that it embeds thin filaments of a strong tensile material in a matrix of resin. Instead of glass, however, CF uses fibers composed entirely of carbon atoms, which because of their crystalline structure are incredibly strong. Filaments are woven into threads, which can be used directly or woven into flexible sheets, just like glass. The process of refining carbon fibers remains costly, and CF's applications in construction so far are limited to extreme engineering situations, in particular reinforcement of high-performance concrete slabs and columns in the forms of tendons and column "wraps." But there is potential for CF wher-

19.5
Carbon fiber relies on the same laying-up principle as fiberglass or plywood.

19.6
Composites can also employ
a single material in different
configurations.

ever fiberglass is now used, especially in cladding and in lightweight structures where super-efficiency is desired. As of this writing, however, the material is more economically justified where weight and strength are more critical, such as automotive and aerospace engineering.

Metal sandwich panels are unique composites in that they segregate two different materials—or two forms of the same material—according to the need for structural performance or light weight. *Honeycomb* panels (Figure 19.6) glue thin sheets of metal (usually aluminum) to an expanded matrix, often of the same material but sometimes of foam, creating two stressed skins. Because they are tied together but separated, the two skins act together as a two-way slab, distributing loads as efficiently as a thick metal panel while eliminating most of the panel's internal weight. Another version of this applies thin aluminum sheets to both sides of a rubber or plastic interlayer, making a strong but very flexible panel that is durable and that resists warping or "oil-canning."

CONCLUSION

While advanced composites offer great promise in terms of structural performance, many of the more advanced materials have not yet proven economical in architectural applications, and for our purposes the composites most likely to be encountered in everyday practice remain plywood and fiberglass. Still, historic examples such as aluminum and plate glass show that most new technologies with possible applications do, over time, become more and more affordable through market pressures. It is very likely that carbon fiber will see more widespread use in cladding and structural applications, in particular.

If we look further afield, the burgeoning technology of *functionally gradient materials* offers even greater promise. These materials are manipulated on a molecular level to change the chemical formula of a given component according to the location of unique functional requirements or loading. A steel beam, for example, could be manufactured with stronger alloys in areas of the cross section likely to experience greatest stress, with lighter or less expensive alloys occurring in less critical areas. Such molecular-level manipulation remains prohibitively difficult and expensive but has seen useful experimentation and application in biomedical fields. While these may not see use in construction over the next generation, the promise of greater and greater 'fine tuning' of materials beyond their shape alone should spur any designer to consider how the stuff of their designs can be best conceived and formed.

FREQUENTLY ASKED QUESTIONS

What is delamination?
One of the weaknesses of composites is that they are laid up with resins or adhesives, all of which can fail by losing adhesion with their surrounding layers of matrix. If this happens, the composite behavior of the material is lost, and the layers will perform as thin, relatively weak sheets instead of the composite. This, obviously, will fail under loading. To prevent this, composite pieces are usually subject to scrupulous quality control to look for telltale bubbling after setting.

Is reinforced concrete a composite?
Absolutely, even if we tend not to think of it as a high-tech material. Concrete is strong in compression, and it is reasonably impervious to water if finished correctly. It thus serves as a good adjunct to steel, which is strong in tension but prone to corrosion. We use the concrete in a reinforced slab for compression and shear resistance, but also to protect the tension resistance in the steel rebar.

GLOSSARY

Fiber or filament: A thin, linear piece of material that possesses great tensile strength and sufficient flexibility to be incorporated into a thread or woven fabric.

Functionally gradient materials: Materials whose chemical structure changes according to the strength or functional requirements. Highly experimental technology, but with great promise for future structural applications.

Laying up: The process of assembling a composite material by interlaying sheets of reinforcement with a liquid (or at least flexible) binder.

Matrix: One component of a typical composite material that serves as a binder. The matrix (often a resin or polymer) protects the reinforcement and "locks" it into useful position.

Reinforcement: The other component of a typical composite material that provides much of the strength. Reinforcement is usually fibrous, strong in tension and/or compression, but flexible so that it can be shaped.

Thermosetting: A temperature-based process of hardening or curing. Epoxies and polymers can be "set," or permanently solidified, by high temperature baking in an autoclave, while other binders can be softened and made more flexible by heat, after which they can be cooled to achieve a final, solid configuration.

FURTHER READING

Fernandez, J. (2006). *Material Architecture*. Oxford: Architectural Press.

Kaw, A. K. (1997). *Mechanics of Composite Materials*, 2nd edition. Boca Raton: CRC Press.

STRUCTURES

FORCES, LOADS, AND EQUILIBRIUM

Structural design	Historical overview and professional responsibilities
Forces	Definitions and representations
Free body diagrams	Vector geometry: representations and calculation methods
Loads	Classifications and representations Types—concentrated, distributed, gravity, and lateral Live vs. dead, and environmental
Load transfer	Tributary area Element analysis
Equilibrium	Definitions Rotational vs. translational equilibrium Equilibrium in support conditions

INTRODUCTION

Structural design involves the artful integration of load-resisting materials, forms, and components in the creation of a strong, stable, stiff, and serviceable buildings. Somewhat uniquely, structural design must synthesize a broad range of quantitative *and* qualitative aspects of design and construction. The process of selecting, developing, and integrating a structural system and its components into a design project has a profound influence on the building's form, behavior, budget, and overall design aesthetic.

The sciences behind structural design principles are all relatively recent, as is the structural engineering profession itself. For centuries, structural design was considered part of the tasks assigned to the architect/master builder. Rules of thumb, intuitive solutions, and "collected wisdom" became the unofficial—and not always successful—approach taken by these designers. The *Ecole Polytechnique* in Paris in the mid-eighteenth century established structural design engineering as its own discipline. Over the last few centuries, the profession has benefited by integrating a myriad of new information into designs, including the reliable standards for the capabilities of materials, an ever evolving set of advanced modeling and analysis tools, and new construction and manufacturing techniques. These advancements have greatly expanded the range of possible building forms and increased the ability to better predict certain structural behaviors.

Because structures have a complexity of behavior that demand a professional's knowledge and care to ensure the health, safety, and welfare of building occupants are protected, structural designers are key members of any project design team. Many options are seemingly possible for potential building forms and materials, and a structural designer plays a critical role in assessing a full range of potential consequences of these decisions. At the beginning stages of a design process, structural engineers have the capacity to help architects select potential structural systems and construction techniques which meet the big picture performance goals of the projects design and budget (structures typically account for 15–25 percent of an overall project budget). Because engineers understand the complexities of structural behavior and the rigorous design standards necessary to ensure structural integrity, engineers will apply rigorous design standards to the design and documentation of the structural system and its components in construction documentation. Finally, structural engineers often bring a rich understanding of construction techniques to the construction administrative phase of design to assist in the review of testing information, shop drawing analysis and critical field observations. While architects are allowed to provide structural design documentation for small structures in certain municipalities, structural engineers are required for all medium-to-large size buildings.

The following descriptions and summaries of structural design aren't intended to be used in the preparation for code compliant structures. The complexities of codes, calculations, and complex structural behaviors are best addressed by practicing professionals. Instead, this information is primarily intended to demonstrate how an understanding of the concepts of structural behavior can facilitate the selection and configuration of systems and their discrete components in the creation of responsive (and responsible) designs. Hopefully, seeing how and why certain structures work will allow designers to improve their ability to cooperatively create efficient, effective, and beautiful architectural solutions that are responsive to the demands of the structural conditions (Figure 20.1).

Developing a better understanding of structural design principles need not be overly complex or exclusively mathematical. Humans instinctively recognize some forms as structurally sound (Figure 20.2), and have developed a life-time of experiences understanding structural behavior by lifting, moving, and balancing items. In the following chapters we will look how these basic intuitively understood concepts of structural behavior can be confirmed and enhanced through integration of more conventional structural design tools (engineering–based terminology, graphic representations of behavior, and methods of mathematical analysis).

FORCES

The basis for understanding all structural behavior begins by considering that structures are subjected to a variety of *forces*, which attempt to cause a

20.1
Renzo Piano's California Academy
of Sciences in San Francisco.

20.2
At its highest levels, structural
design is a complex, highly
technical field, and yet many of its
foundational concepts are quite
basic and intuitive.

change in the motion or the geometric configuration of a physical body, such
as a building. However, because most structures in architecture are intended
to remain *static* (in a state of rest), we are concerned about not only the forces
that are exerted upon a system, but the types of forces working within the
system that are resisting the potential changes in motion or geometry.

The behavior of forces can be described and visualized using basic terminology and graphic representational techniques. When combined, these basic representations of behavior help designers imagine and quantify structural behavior
in overall systems or particular components. As an example, in Figure 20.3, the
combined weight of the person and the weights are forces that are attempting

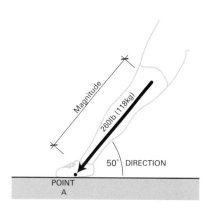

20.3
The weight of the strongman and the barbells combine to become the force that runs through the system to the ground.

to produce a change in his motion (from standing to falling) or a change in the configuration of his body (e.g., sagging under the weight). Forces can be represented by arrows and labels to better describe the specific condition (in this case, only the accumulated value of all of the weight at the legs is represented in the diagram). All forces consist of three separate, quantifiable variables:

- *Magnitude*, or the amount of force: This is measured in units of mass, i.e. kilograms (kg), pounds (lb), or kips (a "kilo-pound," or 1000 pounds). This magnitude represents the amount of push or pull imparted to an object.
- *Direction*, or the orientation of the force: This is usually measured by an angle from a reference axis, labeled in degrees.
- *Sense*, or direction of action: This describes whether the force is acting positively along its orientation, or negatively—essentially, whether the force is "pushing" or "pulling" the object.

These variables may all be graphically represented by an arrow, known as a *vector*. The arrow's length is keyed to the magnitude (a greater force is depicted as a longer arrow), and the arrow head location and angle of orientation are keyed to the direction and sense of the force in question. As an example, in the figure, the man is dividing and channeling the total force in the system (his weight and the barbell weight) through his legs into the ground below. If each leg holds the same amount of weight, let us assume that the magnitude of this force is 260lb (118kg). The angle of the legs in relationship to the ground plane tells us that the direction of the force is 50 degrees. The stance looks a bit un--natural, perhaps because we understand that a wider stance means the legs (particularly the knees) will have to resist against a certain degree of outward (or horizontal) pressure. This can be confirmed through trigonometry and basic strategies of graphic representation of a *free body diagram*.

THE FREE BODY DIAGRAM

A free body diagram, or a force diagram, is a device used to graphically represent and mathematically analyze forces acting on a body. It can be used to help determine the value and direction of unknown forces within a system. In order to abstract forces into a geometrically solvable diagram, we can use the

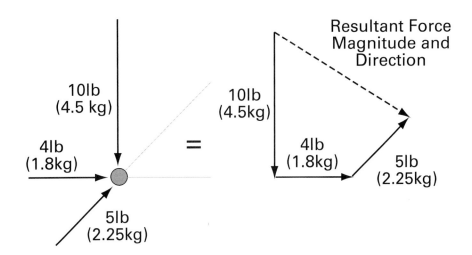

20.4
Because they are acting concurrently, these three different forces will combine together to produce one resultant force upon the point.

Principle of Transmissibility, which states that forces in a free body diagram can be rearranged spatially, provided that their directions and quantities of all vectors remain the same.

The two diagrams shown in Figure 20.4 represent the same static situation, except the forces involved can be arrayed in a geometrically convenient fashion that allows for unknowns to be more easily solved. The forces can only be rearranged if they originally were all acting *concurrently*, or put another way, acting upon the same point in space.

Returning to the weight lifter's legs again, we can see that the diagonal downward force can also be represented as the geometric result of both horizontal and vertical force components (Figure 20.5). The ability to represent loading conditions with different components allows us to easily evaluate the implications of changing certain aspects of the structure. For instance, if the weight lifter stood with a narrower stance, the vertical component of the force would remain unchanged (it represents the pure gravitational load of the man and the weights, 200lb (90kg) per leg), but the diagonal and horizontal forces reduce dramatically. It becomes a more efficient structural orientation.

While simple math can be used to solve these equations, unknown forces can also be easily solved graphically using any vector-based drawing software that allows accurate line lengths and orientations (this is the benefit of accurately representing force magnitude with the arrow's length). By simply drawing the system to scale, the force lines can simply be measured.

These types of calculations are helpful with structural systems that need to have both vertical and horizontal components at their supports, such as funicular structures (cables and arches). For instance, if a portion of a bridge was hung from cables held between two supports, intuition (and free body diagramming) tells us that the supports must hold up the vertical weight of the bridge and it must resist a horizontal force caused by the natural tendency of the bridge weight to pull the system inward. If a designer wanted to change the geometry of the form (to have less sag perhaps), the vertical force would remain the same but the horizontal force would increase—this would then increase the magnitude of the resultant force (the force in the cable). In other words, manipulating the geometry of a form directly affects the magnitude of forces within a system.

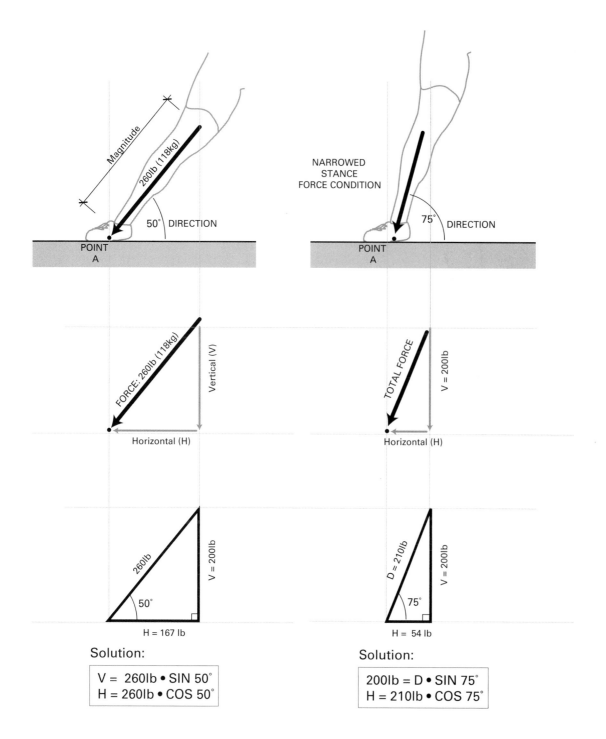

Solution:

$$V = 260lb \bullet SIN\ 50°$$
$$H = 260lb \bullet COS\ 50°$$

Solution:

$$200lb = D \bullet SIN\ 75°$$
$$H = 210lb \bullet COS\ 75°$$

We can use vector geometry to figure out how forces will affect structural elements and what effect different modifications in the geometry and orientation of structural components will have in the distribution of forces. This ability to simultaneously quantify forces as mathematical entities and visualize their actions allows us to simulate structural behavior. Finding an architectural response to a loading condition, matching the physics with a form, is one of the most basic fundamental skills in structural design.

20.5
The diagonal force can also be represented by vertical and horizontal components. Note that the vertical force component from the first scenario (left side) becomes the mathematical basis to solve for the revised resultant force "D" in the second scenario (right side).

But before we can trace how forces move through a building, we must understand the full extent of forces acting upon a structure, including the causes, locations, and collective magnitudes of its *loads*.

LOADS

Loads are forces acting upon, or within, a structure. Loads cause internal stress within a structure, *deform* or change the shape of the structure—in the worst case, they will cause the structure to fail, or break. Graphically these loads can be abstracted into force vectors, as described above. According to Newton's third law of motion, in order to remain in a static state, these actions must be resisted by equal and opposite forces within the system, typically known as *reactions*. In order to develop a design that has the capacity to resist these loads, structural designers must summarize and analyze the type, and magnitude, of loading anticipated to occur. Structures are subject to three basic types of loads:

- *Dead loads* (Figure 20.6) include the weight of the structure itself, and any elements carried by the structure that are intended to remain in place permanently. These can also be referred to as *static loads*.
- *Live loads* (Figure 20.7) include all elements supported by a structure that can move, or will move during the life of the structure. Also referred to as *dynamic loads*, this category includes *repeated loads* (loads which occur again and again, often with regular rhythm) and *impact loads* (in which concentrated loads occur on a structure during a brief period of time).
- *Environmental loads* (Figure 20.7) are loads are a subset of *live loads*, but the causes of these loads are natural phenomena. Also known as *lateral loads*, these loads tend to push or deform the structure sideways. These include: wind loads, seismic/earthquake loads, thermally induced movement, snow/rain/ice loads, and lateral pressure from soil and/or groundwater loading. These loads are often quite irregular and unpredictable in terms of magnitude, direction, and duration.

20.6
Dead loads arise from the structure itself and permanently fixed building elements.

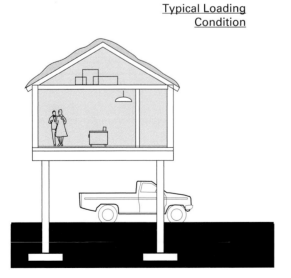

Typical Loading
Condition

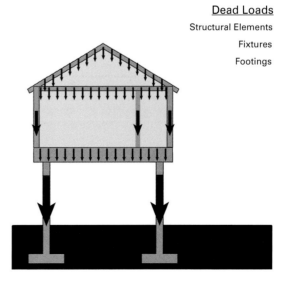

Dead Loads
Structural Elements
Fixtures
Footings

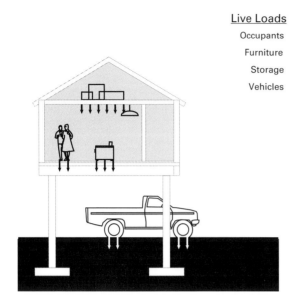

Live Loads
Occupants
Furniture
Storage
Vehicles

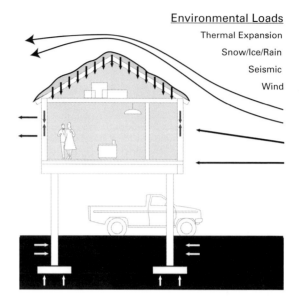

Environmental Loads
Thermal Expansion
Snow/Ice/Rain
Seismic
Wind

Dead and live loads may be either *concentrated*, or applied essentially at a point, or *distributed* over a continuous area of the structure; they are typically *gravity loads* that act in a downwards manner. Concentrated loads, or point loads, are represented by a single force vector which acts upon a specific point in space. Distributed loads are represented as a continuous line of vectors spread along a line, or across a plane. Figure 20.8 shows three loads—one concentrated and two distributed—all three have similar effects on how the structural system is supported. In the first two cases, the structure will have to carry a load of 300kg—concentrated in the first case, distributed in the second—to its supports on either end. Because concentrated loads and distributed loads will have similar macro-effects on a system's state of equilibrium, a *distributed* load can be graphically represented as a single concentrated load, acting at the center of the length of the distributed load, having the same magnitude as the

20.7
Live loads (including environmental loads) arise from moveable or temporary elements.

20.8
Dead and live loads can be further classified into concentrated (point) loads and distributed loads.

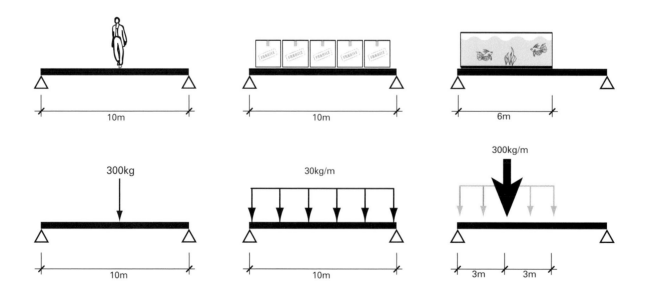

entire distributed load, as shown in the third example. The structure's *supports* won't "know" whether the load is concentrated or distributed; but, as we'll see in later chapters, these two loads will be handled differently within the structural *element* itself.

All structures are subject to a variety of these load combinations, and determining the worst-case scenario for these load factors helps ensure the structure is designed to safely resist all expected scenarios. There are typically specified loading factors in design codes for dead loads based on the type of construction, live load factors determined by the type of occupancy, and environmental load factors based on geographical location. Tables 20.1–20.3 show some common assumptions for typical building dead loads and live loads. However,

Table 20.1 Typical assumptions for live loads.

Usage	Live load	
	kg/m²	lb/ft²
Assembly areas, fixed seats	300	60
Assembly areas, lobbies	500	100
Assembly areas, movable seats	500	100
Stages and platforms	750	150
Balconies	500	100
Balconies, single family residence, smaller than 10m²	300	60
Offices	250	50
Lobbies, meeting rooms	500	100
Offices where filing is intensive	600	125
Habitable attics	150	30
Bedrooms	150	30
Residential other than sleeping	200	40
Apartments and hotel rooms	200	40
Apartment and hotel buildings, public areas	500	100
Catwalks	125	25
Corridors, main floor	500	100
Storage, light	600	125
Storage, heavy	1200	250
Dance halls, dining rooms, bars	500	100
Library stacks	750	150
Library reading rooms	300	60
Garages, cars only	250	50
Garages, trucks	750	150
Light manufacturing	600	125
Heavy manufacturing	1200	250

(continued overleaf)

Table 20.1 (continued)

Usage	Live load	
	kg/m²	lb/ft²
Rest rooms	300	60
Classrooms	200	40
Stadium seating	500	100
Retail, main floor	500	100
Retail, upper floors	400	75

Table 20.2 Typical weights of architectural materials.

Material	Weight	
	kg/m³	lb/ft³
Snow	128	8
Cedar	361	22.5
Soft Maple	529	33
Douglas Fir	545	34
Southern Pine (shortleaf)	561	35
Southern Pine (longleaf)	657	41
Teak	689	43
Hard Maple	705	44
Particleboard	721	45
White Oak	753	47
Ice	913	57
Water	1000	62.4
Earth, loose	1218	76
Earth, packed	1538	96
Sand, dry	1603	100
Damp clay	1763	110
Limestone	2308	144
Concrete	2404	150
Glass	2564	160
Aluminum	2644	165
Marble	2692	168
Slate	2756	172
Granite	2804	175
Wrought iron	7692	480
Steel	7853	490

Table 20.3 Typical weights of architectural assemblies.

Material	Weight	
	kg/m²	lb/ft²
100mm brick	195	40
200mm brick	390	80
100mm concrete masonry wall	97.5	20
150mm concrete masonry wall	136.5	28
200mm concrete masonry wall	170.625	35
300mm concrete masonry wall	268.125	55
2 × 4 stud wall with one layer gypsum board each side, insulation	263.25	54
2 × 6 stud wall with one layer gypsum board each side, insulation	287.625	59
Glass curtain wall	316.875	65
25mm layer of reinforced concrete	282.75	58
25mm layer of unreinforced concrete	268.125	55
Steel deck	58.5	12
2 × 6 joist floor with plywood deck	121.875	25
2 × 8 joist floor with plywood deck	131.625	27
2 × 10 joist floor with plywood deck	141.375	29
2 × 12 joist floor with plywood deck	165.75	34
Tile in ½" mortar bed	380.25	78
Granite flooring (⅜")	146.25	30
Hardwood floor	58.5	12
Shingle roof	48.75	10
Built-up roof	141.375	29
Clay tile roof	365.625	75
Acoustic ceiling	29.25	6
Gypsum board ceiling	73.125	15

simply adding up these loads based on anticipated use and materiality is insufficient to determine the necessary loading for a structure. Because buildings need to have the capacity to allow for a change in use, design codes include *load factors or factors of safety* which are essentially multipliers to be applied to the anticipated loads. For example, a mezzanine may require the structural design to support a dead load factor of 1.2 times the calculated weight and a 1.6 live load multiplier factor—both factors help establish a degree of structural redundancy and help account for any permanent changes to the building load or even short-term changes in occupancy. These factors of safety are applied throughout the building to determine the required strength for structural components and they are typically determined by local codes.

FORCE TRANSFER AND DISTRIBUTION

These methods of representing structural loading, support conditions, and force vectors may seem somewhat abstract, perhaps due to their strictly two–dimensional qualities, but they represent important three-dimensional behaviors for how forces flow through a structural system. The manner is which forces work their way through a system is inextricably linked with its manner of construction and arrangement of components. Even though structures are interconnected, engineers often divide up the design of the system into a series of smaller elements that can be solved in relation to each other. This *finite element analysis* approach allows engineers to design each component in the system based upon the anticipated loads.

In order to achieve this analysis, loading conditions throughout the structure need to be established and quantified. Next, one has to know the length of each component's span and its frequency of spacing in order to find the *tributary area* for what is being supported by each component. This information is then represented two-dimensionally (using the types of loading examples shown above) to solve for support conditions and internal forces within each component to create a state of equilibrium.

Even though buildings are supported from the ground up, analyzing the way forces move through the system starts at the top and works its way downward. Typically loads are transferred from the smallest members that are spanning modest distances, such as the roof/floor decking that spans between joists, to the progressively larger, stronger, set of components, such as the beams that carry the joists and span between columns.

Forces are transferred, consolidated and accumulated throughout the structure until their eventual transfer into the foundation. Note that in the Figure 20.9, examples of both distributed and concentrated loads are shown. Interestingly, even though the joists that hold up the roof are acting as concentrated loads upon the beam below, they essentially are imparting an equally distributed load along the length of the beam. Also note that there are typically two sets of arrows represented at connection points; these arrows are reminders that the forces in the system must be in equilibrium.

EQUILIBRIUM

Fundamentally, structural design is concerned with establishing a state of *static equilibrium*. While all buildings move to some degree, the desired state for most structures and structural elements is one of limited or no movement—a state of being at rest.

We are generally interested in finding ways to counteract external forces on a structure to produce equilibrium. This means developing systems and techniques that will react against forces or cancel them out with internal forces. An example is shown in Figure 20.10. In the scenario on the left, a person pulling with 67.5kg (150lb) of force on a rope with no resistance will not be in equilibrium. The person and the rope will *translate*, or move, in a predictable way. On the other hand, a person pulling with 67.5kg (150lb) of force on a rope, against another person pulling with 67.5kg (150lb)

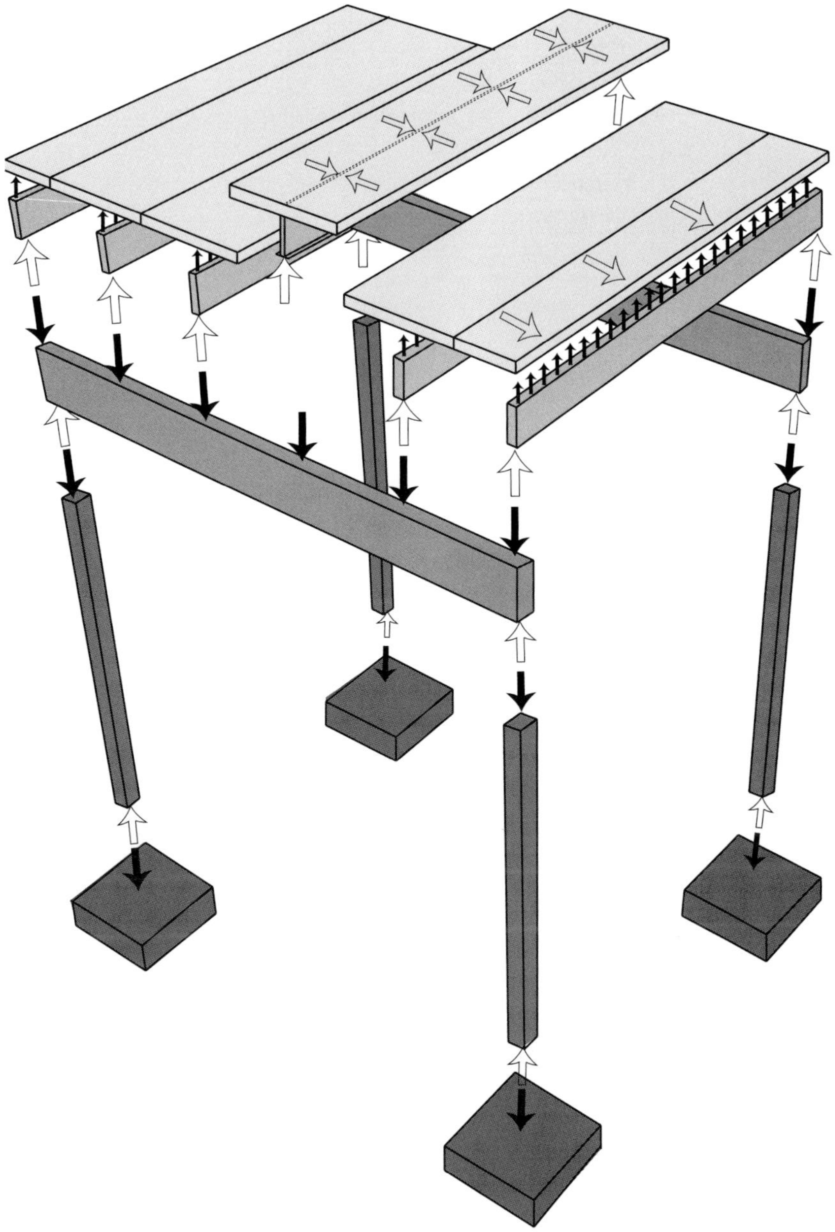

20.9
Forces transfer through a structural
frame from the roof down to the
foundations.

20.10
Applying a force can result in
translation or the development of
a reaction in a structural system to
create a state of equilibrium.

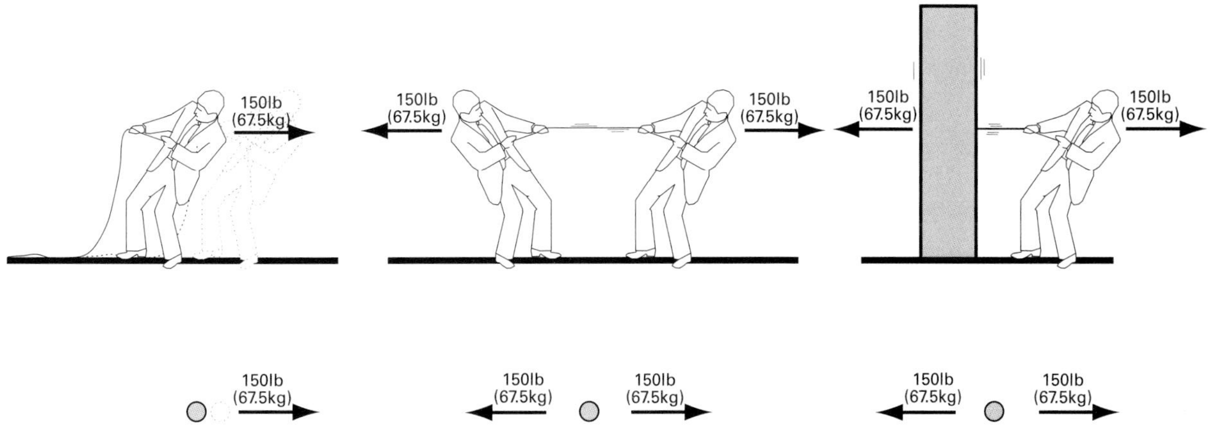

150lb
(67.5kg)

150lb
(67.5kg)

150lb
(67.5kg)

150lb
(67.5kg)

150lb
(67.5kg)

150lb
(67.5kg)

150lb
(67.5kg)

150lb
(67.5kg)

150lb
(67.5kg)

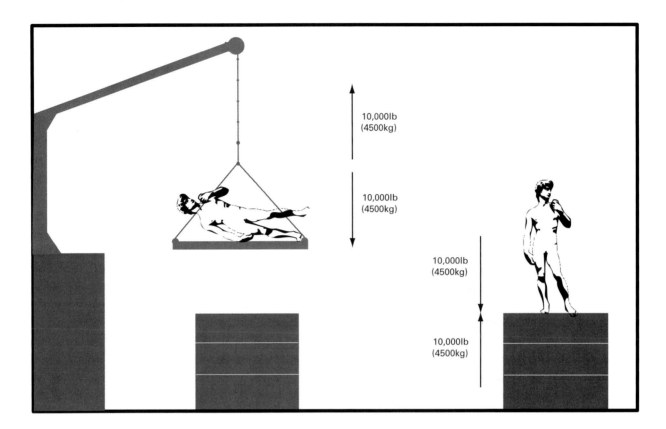

20.11
Two systems in translational equilibrium.

of force will produce *equilibrium*. That is, the two forces will resist one another equally, and no translation, or motion, will occur. While the rope (and the people pulling) will experience internal *stresses* (see Chapter 21), the outside observer will not notice any movement; the system will be in equilibrium.

Likewise, a person pulling with 150lb (67.5kg) of force on a rope that is anchored, or fixed, to a structure may also experience equilibrium. In this case, *reactions* develop within the structure, and between the structure and the ground. In the case shown, the person's pull is resisted by the solid mass of the wall, and the friction developed between the wall and the ground. Again, both the wall and the person pulling will "feel" internal stresses and pressures, but there will be no visible movement to an outside observer.

These two cases can be represented by vector diagrams. In the first instance, the pull is not resisted, and motion would occur. In the second instance, the pull is resisted by a simultaneous, equal and opposite pull. No motion occurs, and we say that the system is in equilibrium. In the third instance, the pull is passively resisted by the mass and friction of the wall, and again the system is in equilibrium. Note that the resisting forces created by both the person and the wall in the former examples are both represented in the same manner, with a vector arrow pointed in the opposite direction as the force.

A more architectural example is shown in Figure 20.11. Here, a sculpture weighing 10,000lb (4533kg) is being hung from a cable and then placed upon a pedestal. A gravitational force equal to the weight of the sculpture pulls it down toward the earth's center. This pull is resisted by an internal force, a *reaction*, that develops within the cable and the pedestal's material, equal to the weight of the sculpture but opposite in direction. In both scenarios, forces must also develop in the earth itself to support the floors, the pedestals, and the sculptures. Each of these situations describes *translational equilibrium*, that is, a balanced system in which the sculptures remain in one location. If the cable or pedestal can only develop resisting force less than the load applied, the sculpture will accelerate toward the ground.

The direction of arrows in the diagrams indicates the type of stresses that are occurring within the system. The vector arrows pointing towards each other indicate that the pedestal is in compression. When the arrows point away from each other, it indicates that the cable is in tension. The nature of these stresses will be discussed in Chapter 21.

Translational equilibrium is important; buildings need to stay in the same place, and need to resist collapsing. Equally important in structural design, however, is *rotational equilibrium*, the stability of a system around any given point. The example of a seesaw shown in Figure 20.12 demonstrates how the system maintains in both translational and rotational equilibrium. Here, the combined weights of the riders are resisted by a reaction in the central pylon equal to the sum of their weights (100lb + 200lb = 300lb, or 45kg + 90kg = 135kg), to keep the system in translational equilibrium.

But note that the rider's weights are also balanced around the pivot. This requires that the sum of each weight multiplied by its distance from the pivot is equivalent to the other weight multiplied by its distance from the pivot. The distance from each weight to the pivot is called a *lever arm*. The force acting on the pivot—the product of the weight times the lever arm—is called a *moment* and it is measured in foot-pounds (ft-lb) or kilogram-meters (kg-m).

The force implied by each rider *around* the pylon is equal to their weight multiplied by their respective lever arms:

45kg × 3m = 135kg-m	100lb × 10ft = 1000ft-lb
90kg × 1.5m = 135kg-m	200lb × 5ft = 1000ft-lb

Since the two moments are equal and opposite, the net moment on the pylon is 0 kilogram-meters or foot-pounds, and the system is in rotational equilibrium.

If one of the riders moved position relative to the pylon, the seesaw would remain in translational equilibrium but it would create an unbalanced moment around the pivot point and the seesaw would rotate. Likewise, if the riders maintained their position, but we added weight to one of the riders, we would again have an unbalanced moment. Developing strategies to resist against rotation certainly happens within structural elements, like the seesaw, but it also can be looked at from the macro-scale of how a building tries not to rotate when subjected to horizontally acting forces, such as wind or seismic conditions, occur.

These horizontal forces try to push their way through the building, unless they are resisted somehow within the building structure. The Principle of Transmissibility tells us that these horizontal forces don't have to be resisted at the exact point where they act upon the building, but they do have to be resisted somewhere along the line of action/plane. Structural designers use this fact to conveniently locate and design elements engineered to provide

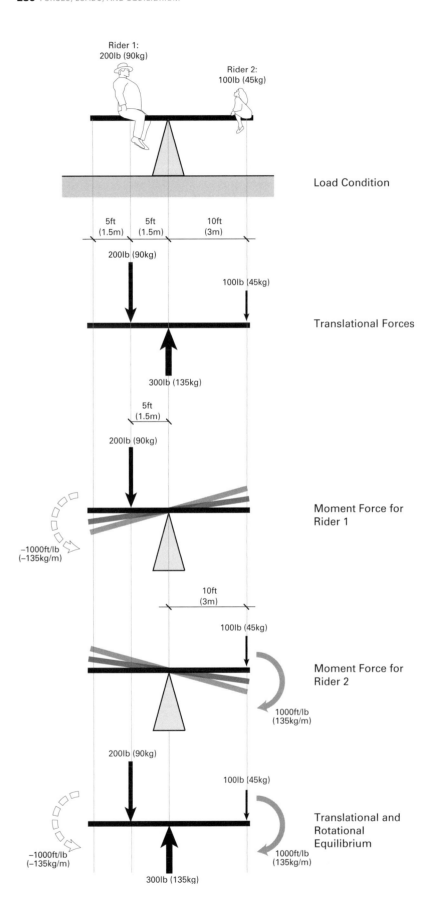

Rider 1:
200lb (90kg)

Rider 2:
100lb (45kg)

Load Condition

5ft
(1.5m) 5ft
(1.5m) 10ft
(3m)

200lb (90kg)

100lb (45kg)

Translational Forces

300lb (135kg)

5ft
(1.5m)

200lb (90kg)

Moment Force for
Rider 1

−1000ft/lb
(−135kg/m)

10ft
(3m)

100lb (45kg)

Moment Force for
Rider 2

1000ft/lb
(135kg/m)

200lb (90kg)

100lb (45kg)

Translational and
Rotational
Equilibrium

−1000ft/lb
(−135kg/m)

1000ft/lb
(135kg/m)

300lb (135kg)

20.12
A system in translational and
rotational equilibrium.

Frame without force applied.

The force will transmit all the way through the frame if it isn't met with resistance.

Forces can be transmitted through the frame and into the ground.

20.13
Example of the Principle of Transmissibility. Note that pinned connections between members and at supports are shown to better illustrate force translation.

stability against geometric rotation (Figure 20.13). In order to maintain equilibrium, structural systems must account for the effects caused by all kinds of loading conditions, including lateral loads, and often times structural components will be integrated into a system's design for the sole purpose of maintaining rotational stability. These strategies, such as the inclusion of shear walls, braced frames, and moment connections will be discussed in Chapter 27, Frames and Connections.

EQUILIBRIUM IN SUPPORT CONDITIONS

Rarely, of course, do we find many structural support conditions that resemble seesaws, however, the same concepts and mathematical strategies can be applied solve these more common support scenarios. Similar to the way in which the seesaw found balance by calculating the moment forces caused by the two loads around one support, we can flip the diagram over and use the same strategy to solve a loading condition that has a single load and two means of support.

Example: *As shown in Figure 20.14, a large vehicle, weighing 4000lb (1814.4kg) breaks down and stops three-fourths of the way across an 80ft (24m) bridge span. What reactions are required at each of the supports to maintain the bridge's equilibrium?*

Answer: The weight of the vehicle is the load on the system (we are ignoring the weight of the bridge itself or other cars for the sake of clarity). The weight of the vehicle would be spread out across its length as a distributed load, but as we saw earlier in Figure 20.8, we can depict this as a concentrated load acting at the center of the load's length. The load must be resisted by the supports, R1 and R2, but we don't know how much load each support will need to take. But we know that, like the seesaw, there is an internal balance between the loads and their lever arm distance. In other words, in order for the bridge to remain at rest,

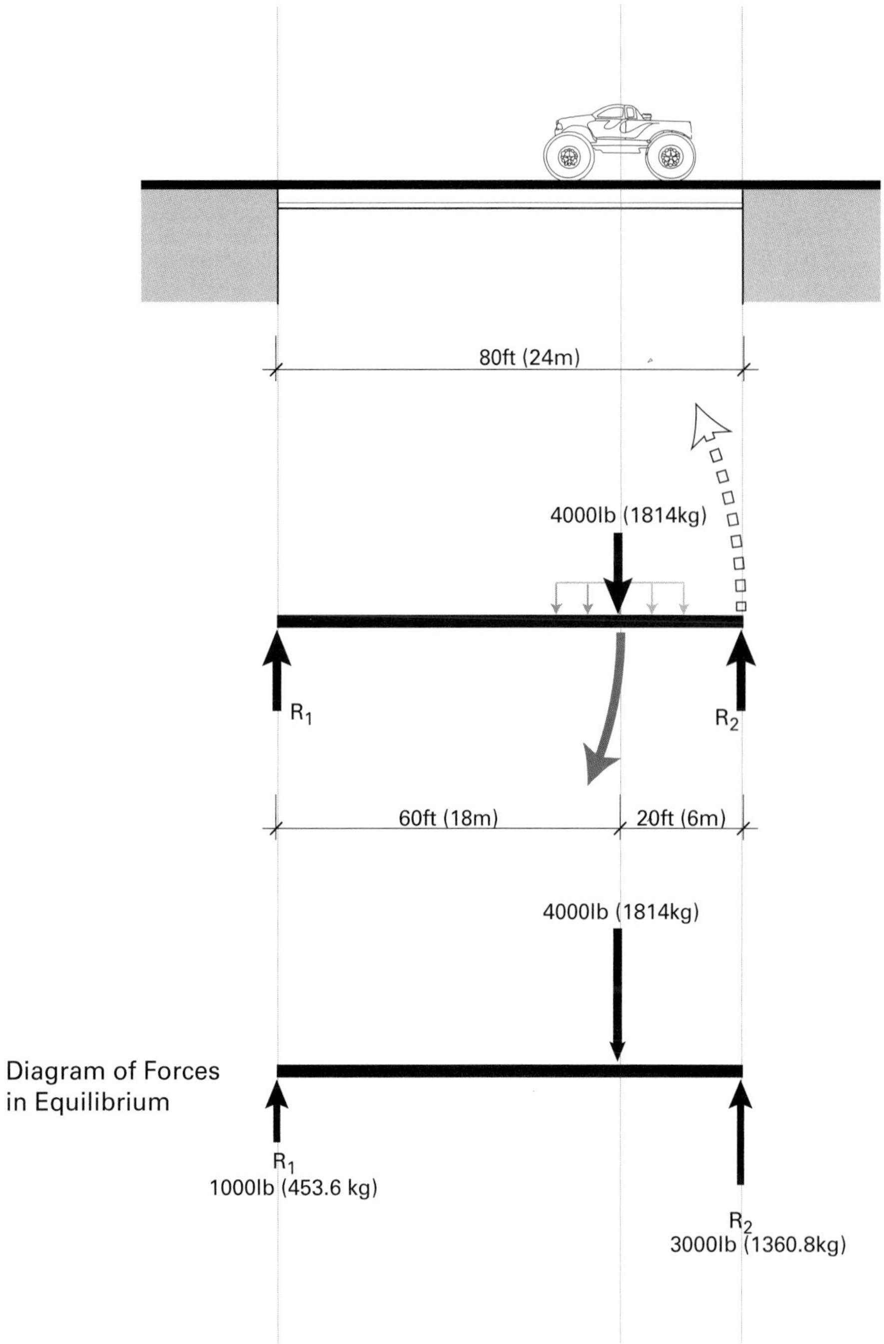

20.14
Use of rotational equilibrium to
deduce reactions in a system.

80ft (24m)

4000lb (1814kg)

R₁

R₂

60ft (18m)   20ft (6m)

4000lb (1814kg)

**Diagram of Forces
in Equilibrium**

R₁
1000lb (453.6 kg)

R₂
3000lb (1360.8kg)

i.e. to not rotate about either of its supports, the moment induced by the vehicle must be met by an equal and opposite moment induced by the reactions of the two supports. For purposes of designating direction of rotation, loads and reactions that rotate clockwise around a point create *positive* moments and counter-clockwise rotations are designated as *negative* moments (this designation alone doesn't indicate the magnitude of the moment). To achieve equilibrium, the sum of all the moments acting upon the structure around any particular point must be zero—a fact that allows us to set up equations to solve for unknown factors.

Let's first summarize the moments in the system acting about the support on the left, R1. By summing the moments around one of the supports, we eliminate R1 from the equation, allowing us to more easily solve for the value of the other support R2. We start with the assumption that the sum of all the moments around one support is equal to zero—an assumption we can make based on the fact that the type of connections used in this bridge design (pinned) do not have the structured capacity to resist bending moments. We can then figure out the moment that the locomotive imparts around this support because we know its vertical magnitude and length from the support as well as its direction of rotation.

The force represented by the vehicle would rotate in a clockwise manner around R1, so it imparts a positive value moment, M1, that is equal to its weight times its lever arm (distance to R1), or:

$$M1 = 1814.4\text{kg} \times 18\text{m} = 32,659\text{kg-m} \qquad M1 = 4000\text{lb} \times 60\text{ft} = 240,000\text{ft-lb}$$

The reaction R2 would want to rotate around R1 in a counter-clockwise direction, so we will designate this as a negative value moment, M2. Again, it imparts its force (value of which is unknown) times its lever arm (distance to R1), or:

$$M2 = -R2 \times 24\text{m} \qquad M2 = -R2 \times 80\text{ft}$$

The sum of all the moments acting around support R1 must be equal to zero, therefore M1 and M2 are equal to each other:

$\Sigma\,M$ $\qquad\qquad\qquad\qquad\qquad$ $\Sigma\,M$
$R1 = 0 = 32,659\text{kg-m} - R2 \times 24\text{m}$ $\qquad$ $R1 = 0 = 240,000\text{ft-lb} - R2 \times 80\text{ft}$
$R2 = 32,659\text{kg-m}/24\text{m} = 1360.8\text{kg}$ $\qquad$ $R2 = 240,000\text{ft-lb}/80\text{ft} = 3000\text{lb}$

Having solved for the reaction on the right, R2, we have two options for solving for R1. We could perform a similar calculation by summing the moments about R2, and solving for R1, or we could solve for R1 using what we have learned about translational equilibrium. We know that the vertical forces in the system, v, will cancel each other out as long as we designate loads and reactions as opposite values (one positive and the other negative). We can solve for R1 using:

$\Sigma\,v = 0 = 1814.4\text{kg} - 1360.8\text{kg} - R1$ $\qquad$ $R1 = 453.6\text{kg}$
$\Sigma\,v = 0 = 4000\text{lb} - 3000\text{lb} - R1$ $\qquad\quad$ $R1 = 1000\text{lb}$

It is helpful to do one last check of the equation to see if it passes the intuition test—we see that the reaction closest to the vehicle would be carrying more weight (which is correct) and that all of the forces are equal and opposite. For simple structural situations, it is often enough to remember that the desired outcome is equilibrium—that we don't want the system to either move or rotate. With a limited number of external forces, we can calculate what combination it would take to hold the system in both translational and rotational equilibrium. This is a powerful tool—one that will be used regularly to establish the reactions on different loading situations.

The limitation to this process involves the connections at either end. We have assumed—and will continue to assume—that the connections at the bridge's ends cannot themselves help resist the bending of the bridge at the ends (it will rotate freely). This type of connection is known as a *pin connection*, one that consists of an axle and bearing to hold a structural element in place, but that lets the spanning member turn or rotate. Other connection types do exist and will be discussed in Chapter 27. Throughout the next sections, we'll always assume that the structural members under consideration are pinned rather than fixed. This will help us get through some basic structural theory and allow us to more easily calculate equilibrium in systems using this method.

CONCLUSION

Understanding the basic relationship between loading conditions and the resulting forces in a structural system is a fundamental prerequisite for structural design and analysis. In order for structures to stand, they must achieve a state of equilibrium—the loads must be resisted. Designers must develop an ability to quantify loads and visualize the distribution of forces in both magnitude and direction throughout the systems in order to craft a responsive structural form. Structures achieve a state of equilibrium through the arrangement of external means of support and by understanding how to internally resist the forces and resulting stresses within a particular component.

FREQUENTLY ASKED QUESTIONS

I don't understand how a reaction can form in a structure—how does the structure know how much to "push back"?
It doesn't, of course. What happens is that the material within the structure becomes *stressed* at a molecular level and is limited by the capacity of its inherent material qualities—this will be discussed in the next chapter. The reaction is mostly a way to visualize how much work the structure has to do. What it really consists of is a state of stress, or pressure, which prevents the load we're imparting from moving the structure. When we draw an arrow as a reaction, we're describing that state of internal pressure in a convenient form, and labeling it in a way that makes sense graphically.

What is the benefit of learning methods of elemental analysis techniques like free body diagrams? Don't structural engineers simply calculate everything using advanced computer modeling systems?
Computers are often used to make final calculations based on completed digital models, but the majority of a structural engineer's design work is still based on essential concepts of structural behavior. Sometimes it is simpler to draw a free body diagram to see the forces at connections, or to calculate the magnitude of stresses within individual members. Simply put, if you do not have a good feeling about the relationship between forces, stresses, and responsive forms, you won't develop a good intuition about structural behavior and may not be able to determine the accuracy of final computer calculations.

How do we know if the seesaw or bridge will break?
With what we know so far, we don't. The next step is to figure out what's going on inside the structure itself. Everything we've dealt with so far has had to do with external loading—the real essence of structural design is to now think about how best to deploy material in a structural element to resist that loading,

to transmit those loads to the earth, and to do both in a way that gives us equilibrium and doesn't break the structure.

GLOSSARY

Concentrated load: A load that is applied at a discrete point.

Concurrent forces: The condition when three or more lines of force acting within the same plane intersect at a single point.

Dead load: Loads that will not change over the course of a structure's life.

Distributed load: A load that is spread out over a line or surface.

Environmental load: Loading caused by environmental factors (snow, rain, wind, etc.). The loads change direction and magnitude frequently. The loads can be either gravitational or lateral loads.

Equilibrium: The condition of being at rest. Any forces acting on the object must be balanced by forces adding up to equal and opposite reactions. There are two major states of equilibrium: translational and rotational.

Fixed (or moment) connection: A connection that does not permit a structural member to rotate or translate.

Force: That which tends to produce a change in the motion of a physical body. Measured in units of weight (e.g. 100 pounds).

Free body diagram: A mathematical abstraction of the forces at work on a single, monolithic structure in which the object in question is reduced to a single point.

Gravity load: Loads acting on a structure along a line between the structure and the earth's center.

Lateral load: Loads acting on a structure along lines other than those between the object and the earth's center (e.g. wind, earthquakes, etc.).

Lever arm: The distance between the action of a force and its pivot point.

Live load: Loads that may change over the course of a structure's life.

Load: Any external force acting on a structure.

Moment: The resultant force about a point, measured by multiplying the quantity of the force by its lever arm. Expressed in kilogram-meters, pound-feet, or similar units.

Reaction: A force that develops in resistance to an applied force. Can be active (e.g. pulling on a cable), or passive (e.g. a pedestal bearing the weight of something).

Statics: The physics of things at rest.

FURTHER READING

Macdonald, A. J. (1994). *Structure and Architecture*. Oxford: Butterworth-Heinemann Ltd.

Mainstone, R. J. (2001). *Developments in Structural Form*, 2nd edition. Oxford: Architectural Press; especially Chapter 2, Structural Actions.

Salvadori, M. (1963). *Structure in Architecture: The Building of Buildings*. Englewood Cliffs, NJ: Prentice-Hall; especially Chapter 1, Structure in Architecture and Chapter 2, Loads on Structures.

21

STRESS AND STRAIN

Concepts of structural behavior	Strength, stiffness, stability, serviceability, and shape
Basic states of stress	Tension, compression, torsion, and bending Element design: stress (strength)
Stress and strain	Hooke's Law: elastic and plastic behavior Modulus of elasticity Allowable stress and ultimate strength Element design: strain (stiffness)
Material behaviors	Thermal stress and strain Unique material limits Design of basic tension and compression members

BASIC CONCEPTS OF STRUCTURAL BEHAVIOR

There are five basic concepts of structural behavior that must be considered in each design: strength, stiffness, stability, serviceability, and shape. Four of these "S words" can be broken into two main categories: those that measure the internal, materially based structural capacities (*strength* and *stiffness*), and those that describe the structural behavior of the overall system and its components (*stability and serviceability*). The final word, *shape*, encompasses the other terms because the selection and orientation of certain shapes can allow components to carry more weight (strength), deflect less (stiffness), maintain geometric rigidity (stability), and enhance functional goals (serviceability). These terms will be useful in the following sections to help explore structural behaviors in more specific terms.

In the previous chapter we looked at conditions of forces and loading, and found ways to resist these externally—with forces *outside* of the structural member—to achieve a degree of *stability* through translational and rotational equilibrium. In doing so, we assumed certain structural members had enough *strength* to carry the loads we were imposing without breaking or otherwise adversely affecting the larger goals of functional *serviceability*. In this chapter, we will look more closely at the internal qualities of structural material behavior to understand the qualities of materials that make them *strong* and *stiff*.

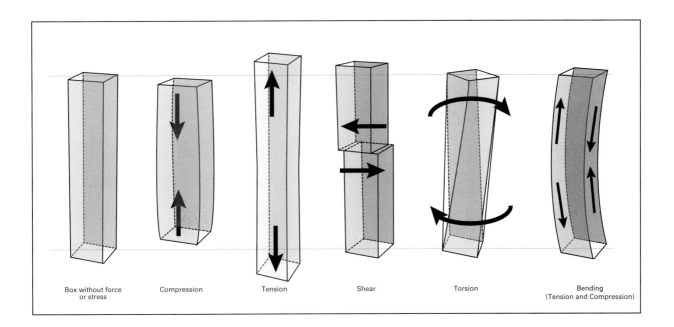

| Box without force or stress | Compression | Tension | Shear | Torsion | Bending (Tension and Compression) |

Designing structural elements to withstand or transfer these loads and forces *internally* is a central concern in structural design. Once we have established the basic performance of the system in terms of *stability* and *serviceability*, we must design the elements of that system to safely carry these loads to their resolution. In a typical architectural situation, this may involve designing floors, beams, columns, and foundations, as well as doing calculations to ensure that the soil we are building on can transmit and disperse the weight of our building throughout the ground.

All structural elements are made of materials whose resistance to loading we can confidently predict. In order to accurately analyze of the internal structural behaviors of different materials, we rely upon reliable data gleaned from centuries of empirical testing and development to enable us to predict how structural elements of various shapes and compositions will perform under loading.

There are five basic things that can happen to materials under loading: they could be pulled in tension, pushed into compression, twisted by torsion, split by shear, or curved under bending (Figure 21.1). In this chapter we will deal with the simplest two conditions—pushing and pulling. We will see how these types of stresses affect the behavior of building materials, we will size components to respond to considerations of strength and stiffness, and finally, we will look at *form-resistant systems* to see how a particular classification of structural forms can efficiently respond to states of tension and compression with basic formal and material design strategies.

BASIC STATES OF STRESS AND ELEMENT DESIGN

Stress (f) is a reflection of how materials will behave when subjected to a force. There are different types of stresses that occur in materials, depending on the type of loading to which they are subjected. Objects that are pushed and pulled

21.1
The five states of stress.

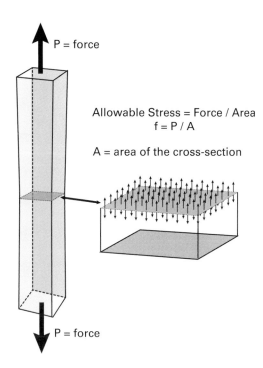

P = force

Allowable Stress = Force / Area
f = P / A

A = area of the cross-section

P = force

21.2
Representation of resistance to axial loading across entire cross sectional area.

by loads parallel to their axes are in *compression* and *tension*. *Shear* stress causes adjacent planes to try to slide past each other, distorting an object's shape instead of length. If an object is subjected to torsion, it is twisted or rotated across its section. Finally, when a material is subjected to loads perpendicular to the axis of the member, it is in *bending*.

This chapter will focus on the more easily understandable behaviors found in objects subjected to the *axial stresses* of tension and compression. Because these forces are either pushing or pulling, and not bending or twisting, the object under stress employs the entire area of its cross section to resist the loading (quite unlike objects under torsion or bending in which cross sectional *shape* matters) (Figure 21.2). This factor allows for a straightforward mathematical relationship in which stress, (f), is equal to the product of force acting upon the object, (P), divided by the cross sectional area, (A), as described in the equation:

$$f = P/A$$

Stress, then is a measurement for how much load a particular material can carry over a cross sectional area, typically denoted as either pounds per square inch (or psi) or kilograms per square centimeter (kg/cm^2). The principle of transmissibility tells us that if the size of the cross section doesn't vary along the length of an element, the magnitude of the axial stress will be the same at all locations within the element. If the area changes the stress will change.

For axially stressed components, the design of structural elements can be quite simple. Since allowable loading is given in amount of force over area, our concern is providing enough cross sectional area to adequately distribute the force we intend to apply, or selecting a material with a high enough allowable

Table 21.1 Basic strength properties for typical building materials

Material	Weight		Elastic limit		Ultimate strength			
					Tension		Compression	
	kg/cm³	lb/in³	kg/cm²	psi	kg/cm²	psi	kg/cm²	psi
Concrete	0.0023	0.083					176	2500
Brick masonry	0.0021	0.075					141	2000
Cast iron	0.0072	0.26			1757.75	25,000	5273	75,000
Wrought iron	0.0078	0.281	1757.75	25,000	3374.88	48,000	3375	48,000
A36 structural steel	0.0078	0.283	2531.16	36,000	4921.7	70,000	4922	70,000
Aluminum (6061-T6)	0.0027	0.098	2460.85	35,000	2671.78	38,000		
Douglas Fir, structural	0.0006	0.023			1054.65	15,000	274	3900
Southern Pine, dense structural	0.0006	0.023					281	4000
Oak, 1450 grade	0.0006	0.023			984.34	14,000	246	3500
Structural glass	0.0026	0.093						
Carbon fiber	0.0018	0.064			38,740.81	551,000		

Material	Allowable working stress						Modulus of elasticity	
	Tension		Compression*		Shear			
	kg/cm²	psi	kg/cm²	psi	kg/cm²	psi	kg/cm²	psi
Concrete			43.94	625			210,930	3,000,000
Brick masonry			12.30	175			914,030	13,000,000
Cast iron			632.79	9000	316.40	4500	1,054,650	15,000,000
Wrought iron	843.72	12,000	843.72	12,000	703.10	10,000	1,898,370	27,000,000
A36 structural steel	1546.82	22,000	1546.82	22,000	843.72	12,000	2,038,990	29,000,000
Aluminum (6061-T6)	1054.65	15,000	1054.65	15,000			632,790	9,000,000
Douglas Fir, structural			84.37	1200	7.03	100	112,496	1,600,000
Southern Pine, dense structural			84.37	1200	9.00	128	112,496	1,600,000
Oak, 1450 grade			77.34	1100	8.44	120	105,465	1,500,000
Structural glass							674,976	9,600,000
Carbon fiber							2,327,261	33,100,000

Note: These figures are averages, intended for illustration only. Depending on manufacture and processing, materials may vary significantly from these figures.

stress level based on the loading condition and desired area. To assist our work, structural materials have tested and published values for allowable working stress levels under tension and compression, as seen in Table 21.1. The variety of available structural capacities for different materials can have a dramatic effect on final size of structural elements.

For example, in the previous chapter we looked at a statue hanging from a cable and sitting on a pedestal but didn't consider either the materials or their relative sizes. Intuitively we could have guessed that the cable would need to be much bigger if it were made of hemp rope rather than aluminum cable—we can now confirm the magnitude of this difference with the assistance of the formula. Assume that you discover that hemp rope has an allowable working stress level in tension of 250psi (176kg/cm^2) compared to the 15,000psi (1054.65kg/cm^2) values for aluminum listed in Table 21.1. Therefore, under the same loading conditions, the hemp rope would need to have *60 times* the area of aluminum!

Using this equation, one can solve for any of the factors in the equation, depending on the unknowns, in order to evaluate different design choices. We can predict the physical effects of loading on a structural member in order to either select an appropriate material, size a component's area able to resist these anticipated forces, or even manipulate the location of structural elements to vary the amount of loading in the equation.

Example: *Size a steel rod supporting a running track as shown in Figure 21.3. The solid rod supports an area 25' long (7.6m) and 10' wide (3m) with a distributed load (both live and dead load) of 120lb/ft^2 (600kg/m^2).*

From the equation we see that in order to find the size of the rod (i.e. the area) we must first calculate the total load acting upon the cable (P). We do this by finding the total area of the running track supported by one rod (otherwise known as the *tributary area*) and multiplying this area times the distributed load values in order to find a value of the overall weight.

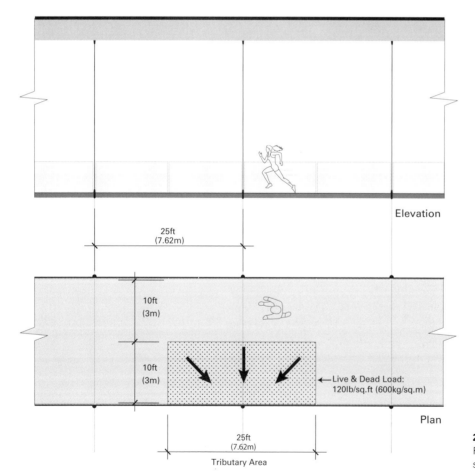

21.3
Representation of tributary area supported by tension rod.

$$P = (7.6m \times 3m) \times 600kg/m^2 = 13,680kg \qquad P = (25' \times 10') \times 120lb/ft^2 = 30,000lb$$

From Table 21.1, we see that the allowable tensile stress for steel is 22,000psi or 1540kg/cm². This means that for every square inch of cross section (perpendicular to the load) we can safely apply 22,000lb. To support the calculated load (P) of 30,000lb (13,680kg), the cable area will need to be:

$f = P/A$ or

$A = 13,680kg / 1540kg/cm^2$

$A = 8.88cm^2$

$A = P/f$

$A = 30,000lb / 22,000psi$

$A = 1.36in^2$

Note here that pounds cancel out in the equation, leaving us with a figure in square inches, so we need to find the radius of the cable that could satisfy this. Note that square centimeters and inches need to be reduced to linear measures by taking the square root of the area.

$$A = \pi r^2$$

$8.88cm^2 = \pi r^2$

$8.88cm^2/3.14 = r^2$

$2.86cm^2 = r^2$

$r = 1.68cm$

$1.36in^2/3.14 = r^2$

$1.36in^2 = \pi r^2$

$0.433in^2 = r^2$

$r = 0.658''$ or approx. ⅝"

Designers can use this information to evaluate the ramifications on the sizing and spacing of support elements if any of the design factors were to change. For instance, because the load and component size (area) are directly proportional, if the spacing of the cables were to double (thereby doubling the tributary area), the area of the cable would also have to double (although because it is a circle, doubling the area doesn't double the radius).

However, in these examples we are only evaluating an element based on its capacity to carry a load, in other words, its *strength*. Under stress, each element will also deform, and so the relative value of a material's *stiffness* also needs to be evaluated.

STRESSES AND STRAINS

Loads cause stress (tension, compression, bending or torsion) and stresses deform or *strain* supporting members. In the simplest terms, stress is what is felt, strain is what happens as a result. Different types of stress cause different types of deformations to occur. Initially we will focus on the strains caused by the axial stresses of tension and compression. If an object is pulled or pushed under loading it changes from its original shape by becoming shorter or longer—these strains are often too small to see, but the change does occur.

Simply put, strain, s, is a measure of an object's change in length (*deflection*), e, compared to its original length, L, as described in the equation:

$$s = e/L$$

In 1678, Robert Hooke, an associate of London architect Christopher Wren, discovered two key laws of structural behavior related to stress and strain.

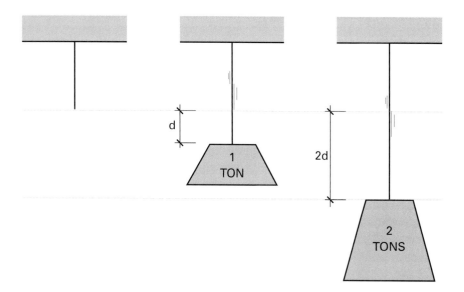

First, he found that the strain of a material is always proportional to the stress it undergoes, or in Hooke's words, "*Ut tensio, sic vis*" ("As the elongation, so is the force"). This means that doubling the force on a given structural member will double its deformation (Figure 21.4). This is a key piece of knowledge as it allows us to model large-scale structural behavior with small experiments.

Hooke's second discovery was that this relationship between force and deformation (or between "stress and strain") varies by material, and that every material will react to stress in two distinct modes. First when a material is loaded up to a certain threshold, known as the *yield point*, it will deform but then will spring back to its original shape—this is known as *elastic* behavior. Hooke found that stressing a material beyond the *yield point* will permanently deform the material—this is known as *plastic* behavior (Figure 21.5). Eventually, if the material is subjected to additional stress, it will fail entirely at the material's *ultimate strength* value. These limits must be taken into account when designing structural elements as exceeding these thresholds will cause a material to fail.

We will concentrate on elastic behavior as it describes material behavior under what we hope is ordinary loading. However, structural designers don't rely upon a material to perform reliably all the way up to its elastic limit because exceeding this limit would not only permanently deform materials, but would cause them to behave in unpredictable ways that reduce their effective strength, stiffness, and serviceability. To avoid this, factors of safety are applied to a material's ultimate strength in order to determine the acceptable value for stress that is used in designing structural members (known as the *allowable working stress*). These factor of safety ratios will vary, depending on the structural reliability of the materials. For example, from Table 21.1 we find that brick's allowable compressive stress is only 8 percent of its ultimate strength, while a more reliable material such as A36 steel has a much lower factor of safety—it is limited to 31 percent of its ultimate strength limit and 70 percent of the material's elastic limit.

Strength of a material, then, is not a single number, but a description of the magnitudes and relationships between its elastic limit and its yield stress.

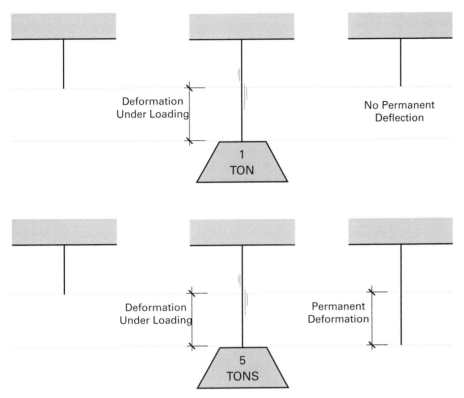

Deformation Under Loading

1 TON

No Permanent Deflection

Deformation Under Loading

5 TONS

Permanent Deformation

21.5
In elastic behavior, materials loaded within their elastic limit will spring back to their original shape after the load is removed.

Obviously, materials that are too elastic—that deform a lot in comparison to the stress they undergo—are not used structurally, but they are often useful as jointing materials or finishes. Materials that have a great deal of elastic resistance—steel in particular—make very good structural materials. However, if the elastic limit and yield stress are very close together, we refer to the material as *brittle* and tend not to employ it structurally as it will fail suddenly, rather than gradually.

Often, we will want to know how much a structural member will deflect under loading (e.g. how much a cable will stretch, or how much a beam might sag). To find this out, different materials are tested to under varying levels of stress, *f*, to determine its relative value of strain, s—for example, how many pounds it would take to stretch a material one inch. This stress/strain ratio is known as a material's *modulus of elasticity*, *E*, and is a measurement of stiffness. A material's modulus of elasticity is available in common reference books (and Table 21.1). Because it is a ratio of stress to strain, this information can be, and frequently is, graphed (Figure 21.6). Typical graphs identify the yield point (elastic range to plastic range threshold) numerically, but it is typically visually evident also by the change in slope of the stress/strain graph line—in the plastic range, materials strain at a faster rate. Different materials can be mapped on the same graph to help designers compare a range of structural behaviors when members are subjected to the same stresses.

Structural materials often times need to be selected based upon performance criteria for how relatively strong and stiff they need to be. As Figure 21.7 shows, certain materials are very strong and stiff, like steel, whereas materials

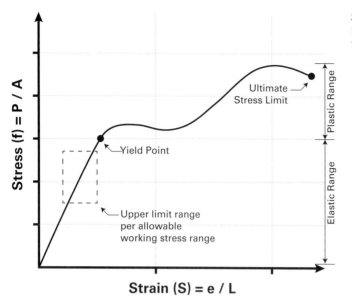

21.6
Modulus of elasticity diagram of typical material behavior thresholds and measures.

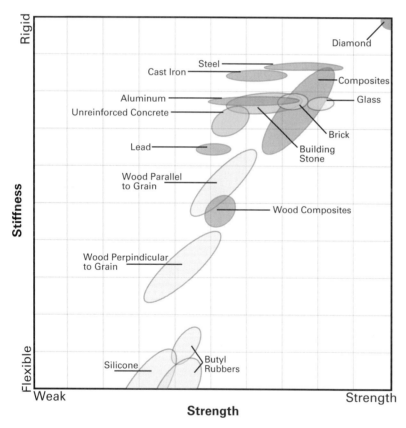

21.7
The relationship between strength and stiffness.

like silicone are predictably weak and flexible. Intuitively we might guess that if two identically sized pedestals, one made of concrete and the other of solid pine wood, were subjected to the same loading, that the concrete would probably show less deformation, simply because we understand concrete to be a stiffer material (higher E value) and this is confirmed by Table 21.1. But intuitively it isn't as easy to predict the different actual amount of deflection each would incur, or how a change in the pedestal height, area or loading conditions would also affect this result. Fortunately, as the following derivation demonstrates, the formula for verifying these factors is a simple and elegant combination of all relevant design factors. From earlier in the chapter, we know that strain, s, is a ratio of the change in dimension of a material under stress. It is a ratio of the amount of deflection, e, from its original length, L, or:

$$s = e/L$$

Because we are dealing with conditions under axial loading, we know the formula for stress, *f*, is:

$$f = P/A$$

We also know that a material's modulus of elasticity, E, is a ratio of stress, f, to strain, s:

$$E = f/s$$

So we can substitute equivalent formulas for stress and strain into this formula to get a more complete definition of a material's modulus of elasticity:

$$E = f/s$$
$$E = (P/A) \times (L/e)$$
$$E = P \times L/A \times e$$

By adjusting the formula, we can isolate the value for an object's deflection under axial loading:

$$e = (PL)/(AE)$$

This formula defines a set of proportional and inversely proportional relationships between deflection, loading, length, area and a material's stiffness. The formula shows that the total deflection of a member is proportional to its length and the force it is undergoing, and inversely proportional to its area and its modulus of elasticity. In common terms, a material will stretch more if we put more force on it, or if it is longer to begin with; and it will stretch less if we increase its cross-section or make it out of some stiffer material. In other words, the greater the cross sectional area of a member, or the greater its *E*, the more it will resist deflection. Likewise, the greater the force on a member, or the longer that member is, the greater the measured deflection will be. Given that *E* is readily available from references, this makes solving deflection equations quite simple.

Returning to the hypothetical pedestals discussed above, we find from Table 21.1 that concrete has an E value of nearly *twice* that of southern pine so we know that if the pedestals' heights, areas, and loading were identical, that the wooden pedestal would deflect (in this case compress) nearly twice as much. To make the deflections match between the two materials, we could alter the wooden pedestal by doubling its area or reducing its length by half.

Example: *Determine the expected deflections in the structural members supporting the statue shown in Figure 21.8. Assuming that buckling isn't a concern, will either of these loading conditions be likely to induce failure? How do their relative weights compare? What steps could be taken to reduce the greatest design liabilities presented in both cases?*

Solution: We begin by collecting information about the different loads, areas, lengths, and modulus of elasticity factors in the equations. Note that the deflection will ultimately be measured in either inches or centimeters, so the overall length needs to be converted to these units before inclusion in the formula. For aluminum, we take E from Table 21.1 as 9,000,000psi (632,790kg/cm²), and get:

$$e = PL/AE$$

$$e = 4500kg \times 600cm / 6.45cm^2 \times 632,790kg/cm^2$$
$$e = 10,000lb \times 240'' / 1in^2 \times 9,000,000psi$$

$$e = 0.66cm$$
$$e = 0.27''$$

The allowable working unit stress for aluminum, 15,000psi (1055kg/cm²), is far greater than the load induced, 350kg/cm² (5000psi) so it should hold the weight adequately (i.e. it is strong enough). Likewise, the load is far below the elastic limit of 35,000psi so the cable would return to its initial length once the load is removed. The amount of deflection, or relative stiffness, is worth noting as the cable only lengthens a very small amount compared to its original length. We multiply the unit weight of aluminum (0.098lb/in³ or 0.0027kg/cm³) listed in Table 21.1, times its volume (the area of cable times the length) and determine that the cable weighs only 23.52lb (10.66kg). In order to decrease the amount of

21.8
Loading conditions for sizing tension and compression supports for the statue described in text.

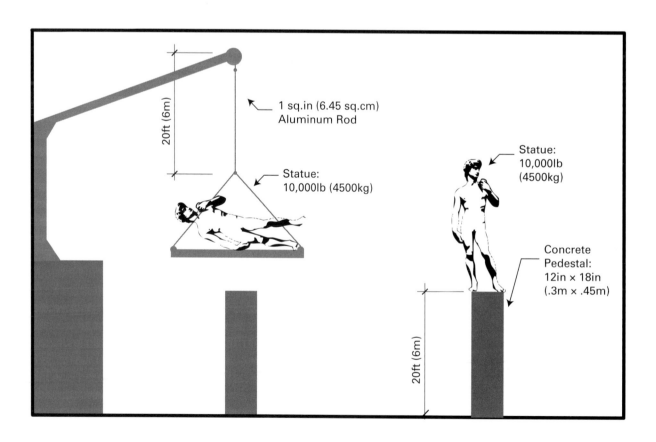

deflection, the cable could be given a larger area, A, or another material, such as A36 steel, with a higher E value could be selected.

For the concrete pedestal, we take E from Table 21.1 as 3,000,000psi (210,930kg/cm^2), and get:

$$e = PL/AE$$

$e = 4500kg \times 600cm / 1394cm^2$ $e = 10,000lb \times 40'' / 216in^2 \times 3,000,000psi$
$\qquad \times 210,930kg/cm^2$

$e = 0.009cm$ $e = 0.004''$

Here, the allowable working stress for concrete in compression is 625psi (43.94kg/cm^2), is not exceeded by the design load, which works out to 46.3psi (3.25kg/cm^2). The amount of deflection is very insignificant (and certainly not perceptible). The difference in the changing length is because the concrete has spread the load out over a much larger area. Concrete weighs nearly the same as aluminum (0.083lb/in^3 or 0.0023kg/cm^3) but because the pedestal has a larger area, the total weight of the pedestal is 4303lb (1924kg)—nearly 200 times the weight of the cable!

THERMAL STRESS AND STRAIN

Temperature changes can also induce stresses into structures under the right conditions—expanding components under heat and shrinking them upon cooling. Interestingly however, *thermal stress* only becomes an issue if *thermal strain* (the expansion or contraction of length brought about by a temperature change) is restricted. If an object is free to expand, for instance if an expansion joint is provided, then no thermal stresses will develop. Often, the size of expansion joints is determined by first calculating the anticipated amount of *thermal strain*. This can be described in the formula:

$$e = \alpha \times \Delta t \times L$$

in which thermal strain, e, (in or cm) is a product of a material's *coefficient of thermal expansion* factor, α, (in/(in/F°)) or (cm/(cm/C°)) times the change in temperature, Δt (F° or C°), and the initial length of the element, L, in inches. If this deformation is restricted, then thermal stress will develop within the component as described in the formula:

$$f = \alpha \times \Delta t \times E$$

The *thermal stress* value, f, also depends upon a material's *coefficient of thermal expansion* factor, and the change in temperature but it is also dependent on a material's modulus of elasticity, E. The value for f can be compared against the same allowable working stress level from Table 21.1 discussed earlier. Rarely will architects deal directly with these calculations, but seeing the factors involved helps us to better understand potential behavior.

For Mies van der Rohe's design of the IIT Architecture building, he chose to expose the large 120' long (36.6m) girders that support the roof structure on the outside of the building and restrict their expansion movement by using

21.9
The fixed connection between
exposed beam and column on
Crown Hall.

moment connections to the supporting columns (Figure 21.9). Because steel
has a moderate coefficient of thermal expansion and Illinois has a relatively high
yearly temperature swing (110F or 43.3C) this girder changes its length by 1″
total across its length throughout the year (0.5″ in each direction). Because of
the nature of the connections between the beams to the columns, this thermal
strain induces bending stresses to the girder and columns. Quite often in buildings, major structural components are isolated from exterior elements and temperature changes and so these sorts of calculations are done to verify expansion
joints in curtain walls or masonry veneers (aluminum curtain walls have a high
expansion values, while masonry units have a small value). Interestingly, steel
and concrete have nearly equivalent expansion factors so composite reinforced
concrete structures that are exposed to changes in temperature move at the
same rate.

MATERIAL BEHAVIOR

Many structural materials will perform nearly equally under tension and compression, but certain materials that we commonly build with do not. Brick and

stone, for example, are extraordinarily strong in compression yet fail under relatively small tension loads. Likewise, steel cables are incapable of taking any compressive force, yet they perform very well in tension. Concrete is a particularly interesting case. It is excellent in compression, yet the nature of its composition—aggregate particles held together by an adhesive matrix—means it is terrible in tension. When using concrete in anything other than pure compression, therefore, it is combined, or *reinforced* with steel to provide resistance to tension stresses.

Other materials have more complicated performance factors. Some materials are *anisotropic*, meaning that their structurally integrity is directionally dependent, like wood or fiber reinforced composites. Wood, for example, has different material properties parallel and perpendicular to the grain—it has a tendency to split along the grain well below the elastic limit. To improve structural performance in wooden composite materials, such as plywood, the grain direction of each ply is rotated perpendicularly to create a more uniform material performance in all direction. Materials that naturally have this type of multi-directional uniformity of structural integrity, such as steel, concrete, and glass, are called *isotropic*.

Correspondingly, a material's allowable stress value can be annotated with another letter adjacent to the "f" ("fc" for concrete to denote compression) or with a caveat regarding the tested direction of loading compared to the grain for wood. For the sake of clarity throughout the following sections, stress will simply be donated as "f", with the assumption that the value listed in the equation is the most restrictive allowable level of stress based upon the loading scenario.

Understanding that certain materials perform well under one type of stress, but not another, can be advantageous *if* a structural form can be configured in a manner that matches these stresses with the corresponding material. Structural forms that are designed to efficiently accommodate tension and compression stresses are called *form-resistant* systems, or *funicular shapes*.

SIMPLE TENSION AND COMPRESSION BEHAVIOR IN FUNICULAR SHAPES

One of the benefits of creating structures that deal exclusively with the axial stresses of tension and compression is that the entire cross sectional area of the component is employed in resisting the loading and deflection—quite a potential advantage if one were looking to create a highly efficient structure. But the simple cable and pedestal structures are quite limiting formally as they rely upon a pure vertical orientation of their elements without span across or enclosing any area below. Intuitively we know that elements like cables and stones can be part of a structural enclosure system, but the challenge of creating form-resistant systems is finding out how to configure the structural shape to be responsive to the loading conditions while maintaining only axial stresses within the system.

The simplest shapes to initially understand, perhaps, are tensile structures subjected to loading. Since the cable cannot take on any compression, any change in the loading conditions will only change the geometric configuration of the support and not the nature of its internal stress. For instance, a weight hanging from a tensed cable held between two hands will create the ideal structural form, in this case, two straight lines. Adding more loads in different locations will change the geometric configuration of the cable, but it will remain in tension.

For constant loading (i.e. a floor slab), the funicular geometry is mathematically complex but conceptually quite simple. A series of weights hung along a cable supported at two points will, by definition, form a funicular curve—since cables cannot perform in compression. As the distribution of weights becomes more and more consistent, the cable will tend toward a *catenary* shape (from Latin, *catena*, meaning chain). Using principles of translational and rotational equilibrium, one can quite easily calculate the reactions at the supports, and thus the force at any point along the cable. A series of funicular shapes and the corresponding internal and external forces are shown in Figure 21.10.

Funicular tensile structures are relatively recent developments—until the eighteenth century, there were virtually no materials employed in building construction that could reliably perform under tension due to the brittleness of the materials. Tensile structures have three inherent liabilities: they must be paired with compressive components at some point (the load must be transferred into the ground), they are inherently unstable when subjected to unexpected point loads or lateral loads (unless they are paired with stabilizing cables), and finally their mode of failure is inherently catastrophic because there is nothing to break their fall. Tension members are used in a variety of form-resistant systems: suspending platforms from compressed towers (like the Brooklyn Bridge, Figure 21.11), supporting roof structures with suspended cables or

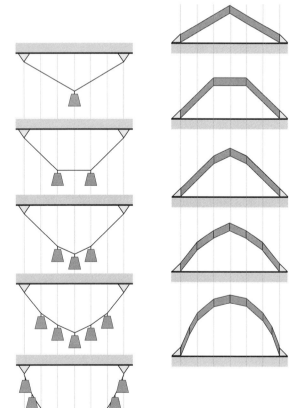

21.10
Funicular shapes in tension and their corresponding forms in compression. Additional weights create a more gradual curved catenary arc.

21.11
Structural elements designed to carry axial loads can span long distances effectively.

tensegrity systems (like Madison Square Garden), or in lightweight tension structures (such as tents, membranes, and pneumatics). A more extensive survey of tensile based long-span systems are discussed in Chapter 28.

Interestingly, these tensile funicular shapes are helpful in generating the ideal compressive shape as well. Because compressive stresses are statically opposite to tension, one can literally flip over a tensile structure to find the form of a compressive structure (a discovery famously summarized by Hooke with the phrase, "as hangs a flexible cable, so inverted, stand the touching pieces of an arch"). This principle was famously used by Antonio Gaudi, a Catalan architect/engineer to determine the structural shapes for vaults in the Sagrada Familia Church in Barcelona, Spain (Figure 21.12) and this method inspired Eero Saarinen's form for the Gateway Arch in Saint Louis (purists will note that the arch is not a true catenary shape).

Ideally, the load path suggested by the funicular shape would be followed by the compressive structure, but, historically, most haven't been geometrically accurate. Roman arches are circular instead of catenary, and therefore not purely funicular—but these shapes allowed relatively easy construction and their relative bulk allowed a wide margin of error in the calculation of load paths. In certain Gothic cathedrals however, many of the arches and vaults were developed with a more accurate funicular geometry.

One risk of creating very thin compressive structures with a geometry derived from the ideal funicular load path is the potential risk for collapse caused by unanticipated point loads or lateral loading. If the load path shifts outside of the thickness of the compressive structural element, the overall geometry of the arch can shift as the stones get out of the way of the force path (Figure 21.13). This type of failure, known as *buckling*, is a much greater concern for structural designers in compressive structures than the fear of having a member crush and fail under loading.

Buckling occurs when a relatively thin compressive member deforms or begins to bend to the side under loading. Because the wind blows, the earth shakes, and loads can change, purely vertical compressive forces within a structure can incur a slight shift horizontally, which causes bending stress (com-

21.12
Gaudi's use of funicular models was used to determine idealized form of supporting columns and vaults.

21.13
Structural elements with forms determined by specific loading conditions may be subject to deformation and eventual failure if subjected to unexpected loading.

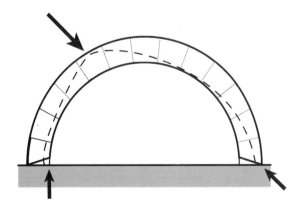

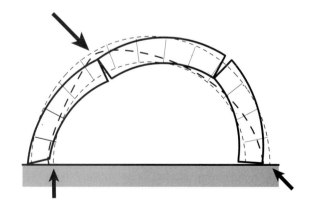

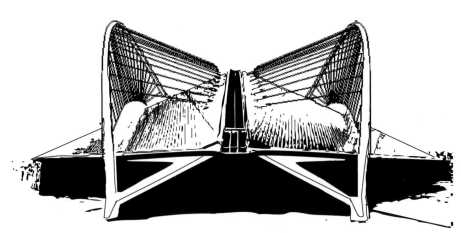

21.14
Funicular-shaped steel arches are combined with tension cables to support a long-span roof over the velodrome for the 2004 Athens Olympic stadium.

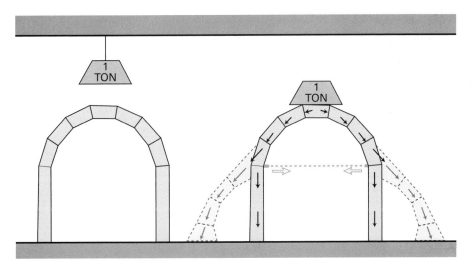

21.15
Arch structures generate an outward thrust at the base that needs to be resolved with buttresses or tie rods in order to help the structure remain stable.

pression and tension) to occur within an element—these stresses deform the shape and exacerbate the problem. Designing compressive structures to resist buckling will be covered in the chapter on columns, Chapter 25.

Compressive funicular shapes are typically different variations of the basic arch geometry. Arches can have many different configurations that work in conjunction with tension members to make a highly efficient and structurally expressive contemporary structural expression. Arches need not be made out of traditionally heavy materials either (like concrete or masonry)—many of the first iron truss frames of the nineteenth century were configured as arches, and many contemporary designers, like Santiago Calatrava, create gigantic steel arches by conjoining segmented members to make a continuous arch shape from which cable are hanged (Figure 21.14).

For all of their structural advantages, form-resistant shapes also have a unique set of potential disadvantages as well. The primary concern is the horizontal thrust generated by the form. Like the weight lifter's leg in Figure 20.3, every diagonal force has a horizontal and vertical force component and this horizontal force must be resisted somewhere within the system (perhaps at the foundation, or with a compression ring at a suspended roof or with a tension rod at an arch's thrust line as seen in Figure 21.15). Second, in order to help span long distances while minimizing thrust, funicular shapes often require very large heights to achieve their desired geometry—a strategy that isn't helpful when designing components that need to be compact in size. Additionally, both cable and arch structures also have inherent complications related to their construction, primarily because the systems are inherently unstable by themselves until construction is completed (many compressive structures need a framework for scaffolding, called centering, to be built in order to have the arch construction completed upon a stable framework). Finally, there is a risk in minimizing the size of the components or too closely matching the final form with an idealized model of loading conditions because loading conditions may unexpectedly change—designers will often apply stringent factors of safety to the size calculations of the components and integrate redundant systems for the purposes of stability.

CONCLUSION

Structural behavior can be understood more holistically by examining the degree to which it addresses strength, stiffness, stability, serviceability, and shape. These different components of structural behavior can be addressed separately or in concert with each other. Different materials will respond differently to different types of stress, and the resulting variances in material strain are a central design consideration. Additionally, there are specific fundamental relationships between a structure's loading conditions and the resulting states of stress that can be easily calculated, understood, and crafted in a way that creates a responsive structural form—specifically those that isolate the types of stress to the axial stresses of tension and compression.

FREQUENTLY ASKED QUESTIONS

On the modulus of elasticity graph, I notice that steel can continue to carry additional loading well after it has moved into the range of plastic behavior. Can't structural designers take advantage of that additional load capacity?
Once steel exceeds its elastic limit and permanently deforms, the material does become stronger as the graph indicates, mostly due to material dislocations at an atomic level. This process is called work hardening, or cold forming, and it is sometimes used to stretch or bend metal into specific shape. Even though the steel is stronger, it remains permanently deformed and is no longer *ductile*, or flexible. While metal fatigue caused by movement is a concern for some structural components, the ability of a component to return to its original shape, in other words to perform elastically, is preferred. However, if a designer needs a higher strength steel, one can simply select a higher grade steel (A50 in lieu of A36)—as the number represents the allowable elastic limit.

Visually, would there be any way of knowing if a structure was loaded past the yield point while it was under loading? Can one see plastic behavior?
There would certainly be several clues, depending on the material. One might be able to actually notice the extent of deformation happening (typically deflec-

tions are intended to remain quite small and not necessarily noticeable). For metal structures certain visible evidence of stretching occurs in tension members and thinner compressive elements may show signs of permanent buckling deformation. If the element is painted with a brittle paint or has mill scale or rust it often cracks, flakes, or peels. For concrete, it is slightly more obvious as there will be a lot of cracking.

I don't understand why funicular shapes are called form-resistant systems. Aren't all structures using their overall form as a means of accounting for the loading conditions?
In a way, yes, but other structural systems do not try to directly mimic the axial loading conditions like funicular shapes do—in fact, often times it isn't possible to do so. Structural designers always need to consider how *shape* is related to structural efficiency. In some cases, the longitudinal and cross sectional shape of a spanning member will be designed to more efficiently support a system (these are known as section-active and vector-active systems). Certain structural systems employ the entire surface area of the structure to resist loads. These surface-active systems employ similar strategies as form-resistant systems to find responsive forms.

GLOSSARY

Allowable stress: A generally accepted safe load per unit of area for a given material. Often dictated by codes or industry standards.

Anisotropic: Material with a consistent structural behavior in all directions. Steel and concrete are examples of anisotropic materials.

Compression: An internal state of stress in which a material's fibers tend to be pushed into one another.

Deflection formula: For axially loaded members (pure compression or tension), a member will change its length by a calculable amount, e:

$$e = PL/AE$$

where P is the applied load, L is the original length, A is the member's cross-sectional area, and E is the material's modulus of elasticity.

Deformation: Change in shape due to loading.

Elastic behavior: The tendency of a material to 'snap back' to its original dimensions after it is loaded within its *elastic limit*.

Elastic limit: The stress level within which a material will not permanently deform. Beyond the elastic limit, a material will change shape under loading and not return to its original form.

Factor of safety: A numerical allowance added into all structural calculations that ensures no structural material will be stressed to an unsafe limit—either to its elastic limit or to its yield stress.

Funicular: A shape that functions in pure compression or tension for a given load.

Isotropic: Material with a directional structural makeup, typically with very different abilities to resist tension and/or compression depending on whether a load is applied parallel to or perpendicular to its grain. Wood is the best known isotropic material.

Modulus of elasticity: A measure of a material's stiffness, or more technically, resistance to deformation. Measured in pounds per square inch, but not a measure of pressure or stress.

Plastic behavior: The tendency of a material to deform permanently once it is loaded past its *elastic limit*.

Strain: Deformation, measured in percentage based on the original, pre-loaded dimensions of a structural member.

Stress: A measure of internal loading on a material, defined as the total load divided by the cross-sectional area across which the load is spread.

Tension: An internal state of stress in which a material's fibers tend to pull away from one another.

Yield stress: The level of internal load per unit of area beyond which the material may fail (break, crush, or shear).

FURTHER READING

Allen, E. and Zalewski, W. (2010). *Form and Forces: Designing Efficient, Expressive Structures*. New York: John Wiley & Sons; Chapter Thirteen, Structural Materials, pp. 355–375.

Engel, H. (1997). *Structure Systems*, 4th edition. Hatje Cantz; Chapter One, Structure Systems, pp. 57–112.

Salvadori, M. (1975). *Structure in Architecture: The Building of Buildings*. Englewood Cliffs: Prentice-Hall; Chapter Three, Structural Materials, pp. 37–56, and Chapters Five and Six, Basic States of Stress and Tension and Compression Structures, pp. 79–134.

22

SHEAR AND BENDING

Introduction	Responsive structural forms
	Section resisting structures
Equilibrium in bending	Comparison to axial loading
	Effects of loading and support variations
Beam theory and bending	Internal moment resistance
	Depiction of sectional stresses
Shear stress	Horizontal and vertical shear
	Shear resistance
Shear and moment diagrams	Diagramming process
	Understanding diagrams
Responsive evolutions in form	Reducing maximum moment
	Cantilevers and continuous beams
	Moment diagram and beam profile

INTRODUCTION

In the previous chapter we looked at the relatively intuitive and mathematically elemental range of behaviors exhibited by structural components when they were subjected to only tension or compression. Structures designed specifically to resist these stresses had a demonstrated level of efficiency in their load-bearing capacity (*strength*) and their resistance to strain (*stiffness*), but in order to ensure this efficiency, their overall *shape* was somewhat restricted to a particular range of options for formal geometry and materiality, and a certain level of material efficiency needed to be sacrificed to maintain *stability*. In other words, achieving this level of relative efficiency comes with certain conditions that simply cannot be met in most structural applications.

There are obviously other options available for creating responsive structural forms and elements besides form-resistant configurations. Designers can configure structural forms to resist stress within the surface of the structure like shells and membranes (surface systems), by using a series of trusses to efficiently distribute stresses through light-weight components (vector systems), or by simply using the cross sectional qualities of the structural elements to resist a broad range of stresses (section resistant). From this group, only section-resistant systems provide structural designers with a complete range of options for formal and material configurations, including the most common structural components such as beams and slabs.

Unlike form-resistant systems which only dealt with single stress conditions, section-resistant systems must be designed to internally resist *three* different types of stresses: shear, bending, and torsion. Section-resistant systems, (or beam systems) must be responsive to the stresses they face in new ways—typically through the design, orientation, and manipulation of the cross sectional shape of its components. This chapter will focus on understanding, calculating, and graphically depicting how beams work to resist shear and bending stresses.

EQUILIBRIUM IN BENDING AND BEAM THEORY

Beams are horizontally spanning objects that carry and distribute loads across a span to supports—to remain static they must remain in translational and rotational equilibrium. This equilibrium depends upon balancing the *external* conditions (supports must be able to carry the loads) and a structure's ability to *internally* resist against the stresses and strains to which it is subjected.

Unlike axially loaded components that are only concerned with translational equilibrium between the load and support (as there is only one direction of stress applied to the systems), beams need to worry about establishing both translational and rotational equilibrium in both their external and internal conditions. Basically, even when the loading conditions are balanced, the beams will still want to rotate.

The internal behavior of objects under bending also differs significantly from what we saw in axially loaded members. When structural components are pulled or pushed axially, they are subjected to a load that runs *parallel* to the structure being loaded—these stresses are resisted by the entire cross sectional area of the object being stressed, and as long as the object maintains the same cross sectional area across its entire length, the magnitude of internal stress within the object remain the same. The value of internal stress resistance is related only to the magnitude of load and area, not the length of span.

Structures under bending stress are also concerned with the magnitude of load applied and the cross sectional area of the supporting member (although in a different manner as will be discussed in Chapter 24), but because objects under bending are subjected to loads that run *perpendicular* to the spanning object, the values of bending and shear stress that need to be resisted internally within the beam *varies across its length and is dependent upon the location of the supports*. This important concept can be verified by looking at a few basic examples.

Intuitively we know that it would be more difficult for a beam to support a lot of weight resting in the middle of its span than near the supports. Further, we know that it would be even more difficult for the beam to support the same load if we *lengthened* the span without changing the size of the beam's section (Figure 22.1). In order to allow the beam to span further, we know that we would have to either reduce the load or change the profile of the beam. Although we will do the calculations to confirm this in Chapter 24, we find that these two major considerations, the loading conditions (magnitude and place-

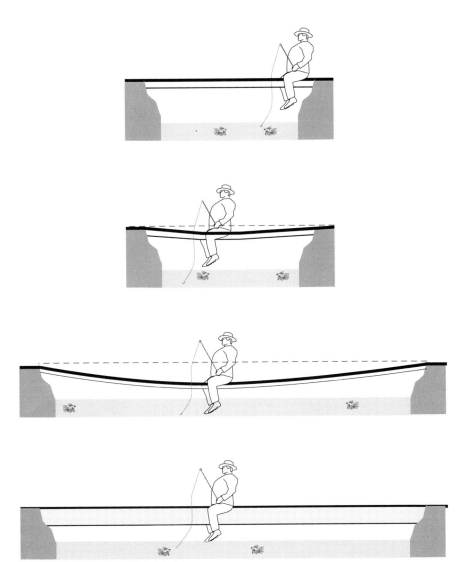

22.1
Relationship between load
placement and bending stress in
beams shown.

ment of load combined with distance between supports) and beam depth will affect the beam's behavior. However, these assumptions don't explain how the beam itself *actually works* to support the loads. For that, we have a set of concepts and calculations known as *beam theory*.

BEAM THEORY AND INTERNAL MOMENT RESISTANCE

Beam theory is an established set of information about structural behavior in beams that determines how much internal resistance to shear and bending stresses needs to provide at any point along its span—this internal resistance is greatly determined by the qualities of the component's section (thus, the section resistant classification). Essentially beam theory establishes a set of mathematical relationships between a beam's material, cross sectional area, loading, and support conditions. Using only a few calculations, designers can determine the bearing capacity of beams, the resulting magnitudes of their

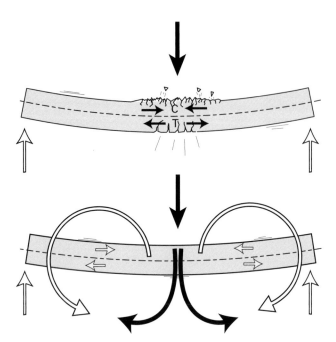

22.2
Representation of basic bending action. Beams under loading compress on the top and tense along the bottom. This force couple creates an internal bending moment that must be resisted.

deflection, and their relative resistance to internal shear stresses. The easiest introduction to the key principles of beam theory begin by coupling a few basic observations about shape and behavior with free body diagramming.

When a spanning member is loaded at a point other than its supports, it will deform into a characteristic curve shape. This curved shape tells us an important fact about beam behavior, namely, the nature of stresses acting within the beam. If a beam is loaded from above and supported on its ends, the material at the top side of the curve shortens while the bottom side elongates—in other words, the material at the top of the beam has been compacted at the same time that the material at the bottom is being stretched. These types of strains are caused by horizontally acting compressive stresses in the upper portion of the beam (pushing it together) and corresponding tension stresses acting horizontally along the bottom side of the beam (pulling it apart). From this simple observation, we can understand that quite unlike axially loaded members that resisted *either* tension or compression, beams have to resist both types of stress simultaneously (this was a challenge for historical structures that used stone for a spanning material as it has little capacity to resist tension stress).

Having two opposite stresses within the same structural component pulling and pushing in opposite ways may seem like a problem, but this internal behavior the key reason that beams are able to resist bending. Using free body diagramming we can see that these two forces are trying to rotate the beam in the *same direction*—in other words, these two stresses work together as a force couple to create an *internal* moment of resistance (Figure 22.2). We know that the value of a moment force is dependent upon the distance between a force and the point around which it rotates (a lever arm), so beams that have a deeper section create a greater distance between the stresses in the top and bottom of the beam—by extension, *deeper beams are able to provide a greater internal resisting moment, and therefore a greater resistance to bending.*

This relationship between a member's depth and its resistance to bending

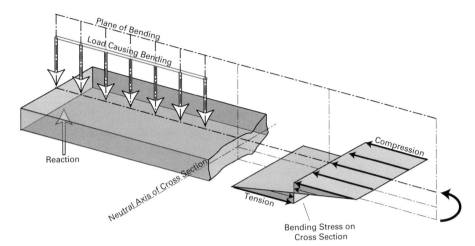

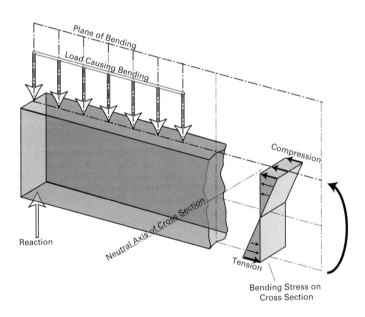

can be observed in a myriad of everyday situations, such as the way a ruler easily bends when it is flat, but becomes nearly impossible to bend when placed on its edge. In practice, the ability to simply change the depth of a beam in order to provide a greater resistance to bending is helpful as it is a relatively easy modification to make.

The reason this works is related to the magnitude of internal stresses acting in the system. For example, Figure 22.3 shows two beams with the same cross sectional area, (one is shorter and wider than the other). In the graphic, the end of the beam is cut away to show the anticipated distribution of internal stresses that would occur within each beam's cross section. It shows that the tension and compression stresses are not of a uniform magnitude across the beam depth. In fact they vary from their maximum values at the extreme fibers (top and bottom) to a region known as the *neutral axis* where no stress is occurring. This diagram clearly shows that the deeper beam has a greater level arm between the neutral axis and the outside edge of the beam, and consequentially, a smaller stress level at the outer fibers (represented by the shorter length of the vector arrows).

Note that the triangles' height and base indicate specific measures of structural capacity. The base measures maximum stress, f, while the height measures the depth of the beam. The area of each triangle can therefore be measured in kilogram-meters or foot-pounds, the same measure of *maximum moment*. The beam can resist greater moment either by accepting a greater maximum stress (increasing the triangles' areas by increasing their base) or by getting deeper (increasing the triangles' area by increasing their height). Another simple way of explaining the triangular areas shown is this: because the magnitude of forces is represented by length, longer arrows indicate higher levels of stress. The shallower beam has a shorter lever arm, so it must develop a much higher stress level (i.e. a longer arrow). This directly affects beam size as will be discussed in Chapter 24.

INTERNAL RESISTANCE TO SHEAR

Besides bending, beams must also be designed with a resistance against shear failure. Shear force deforms an object's shape by attempting to make adjacent planes within a structure slide past each other. Shear stress can be found in many different situations and scales: a bolted connection between two members sliding with respect to each other, at the conjunction of a column and slab, in the diagonal cracking of a compressive element, or even in the behavior of a simple paper punch.

There are two types of possible shear in beams, vertical shear or horizontal shear. Horizontal shear is the tendency of materials to slide in layers relative to each other—in practice, it is rarely is a concern unless the material used for the spanning member was weakly laminated longitudinally (like early glu-lam wooden structures). Horizontal shear might best be envisioned as the mechanism that ties the foreshortened compression edge of a beam to the elongated tension edge. In other words, horizontal shear is the result of the internal "force couple" that resists bending. Vertical shear is caused by the opposing vertical forces of the loads and supports trying to slice through the beam material (see Figure 22.4 of a beam with horizontal boxes and layers).

Shear failure is typically a concern for beams at, or near, its supports because the reaction force and loading are pushing in opposite directions in close proximity to each other. Interestingly, however, shear failure is rarely manifest as either a purely horizontal or vertical fracture—instead, most shear failures occur diagonally. This behavior can be attributed to the combined effect of both horizontal and vertical shear forces acting simultaneously in a beam. This behavior is best described by selecting a random square area from the side elevation of a beam and looking at how these shear forces acting in concert attempt to distort, or skew, its shape (Figure 22.5).

As we have seen earlier, beams in bending have opposing horizontal forces acting along the top and bottom (that help generate the internal resisting moments) and we know that two vertical force components must also exist

22.4
Vertical and horizontal shear failures.

Vertical Shear

Horizontal Shear

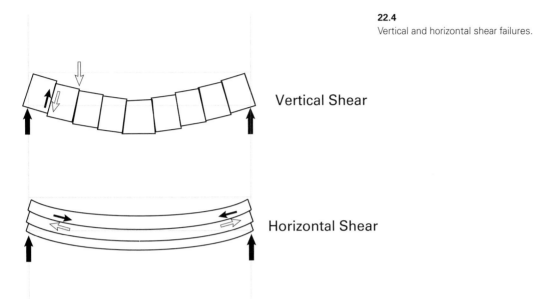

22.5
Bending causes a complex set of internal reactions, including shear.

Forces

Resisting Force

Shear Action

within the beam (as a result of the translational equilibrium between loads and reactions). As the free body diagram shows, these force components create two new diagonal resultant forces—forces that try to skew the square area by pulling two opposing corners in tension while compressing the other two corners. These equivalent tension and compression stresses basically tear at the material, and when the stress levels get high enough, it can cause diagonal tension cracks that are typically found near beam supports. There is a certain length of the beam adjacent to the edge of a support that is more or less exempt from shear, a distance more or less equal to the depth of the beam, as a result of the diagonal nature of this stress.

Shear stresses are not equally distributed across the length of the beam, or along the cross-section. In the section, shear forces are greatest at the neutral axis and shrink to zero at the top and bottom edges. Because of this, it is assumed that only the area in the middle of the beams (e.g. the web for steel beams) resists against shear.

SHEAR AND BENDING DIAGRAMS

In beams, the values of bending and shear stress can vary across the length of a beam, depending upon how and where it is loaded and supported, so the entire beam needs to be analyzed to determine the location and magnitude of its maximum stress values. One way to understand the varying magnitudes of resistance to bending and shear that a beam must generate across its length involves the a method of graphing and calculating these values in shear, V, and moment, M, diagrams—basically, these diagrams are a useful tool for sizing and understanding how beams work. Diagrams are drawn to scale, aligned with a diagram of the beam support conditions to help designers graphically see correlations between high levels of shear and moment in relation to the beam layout.

When pinned connections are used, as with the example shown, the beam isn't restrained from rotating by the connections, so the beam section itself has to do all the work to resist against the internal stresses. Shear/moment diagrams can be derived by figuratively "walking across" the beam under consideration to determine what internal loads are needed to keep the beam in translational and rotational equilibrium at every point along the beam. At any point, the sum of the translational and rotational forces acting upon the system must be zero and we use that simple fact to help us solve for unknown values in the system.

For an example, take the beam in Figure 22.6, with simple supports and two loads of 30lb (13.5kg) and 50lb (22.5kg). If we solve for the reactions R_1

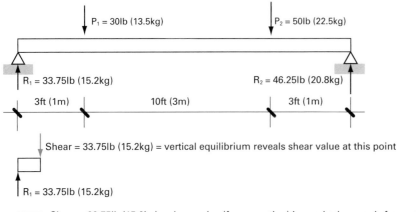

22.6
Shear diagram example, solving for shear value based on reaction and translational equilibrium.

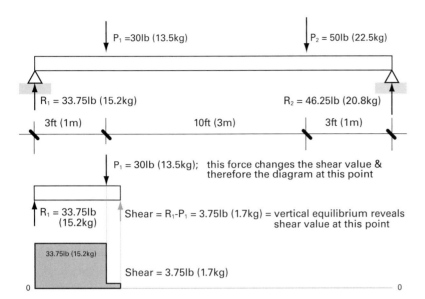

22.7
Shear diagram example, solving for shear value along beam after first load.

and R_2 we get the condition shown. If we then take a free body diagram of the left end of the beam, we find there must be an internal shear stress equal (but opposite) to R_1 to maintain translational equilibrium—without such an internal force the left end of the beam would simply move in the direction of the reaction. This is true for any free body taken of the left end of the beam, so long as the section cut occurs *before* the first load. At any point along this portion, an internal shear stress must develop to counteract the force of the reaction, and until another vertical force either pushes up or pulls down on the beam, this represents the value for the internal shear for the beam. Therefore, the shear stress in the left-most 3ft (1m) of the beam will be constant and equal to the size of the reaction, 33.75lb (15.2kg) as shown on the graph.

Looking ahead, we can see that the shear diagram can be intuitively understood by looking at the directions of the force arrows acting upon the beam. Reading from the left, the reaction "pushes" the internal shear up, the first and second forces "push" the internal shear down and the right reaction "pushes" it back up to where it starts—the profile of the diagram will follow these actions.

If we take a free body to the right of the first load (Figure 22.7), we find that the shear condition necessarily changes as a new vertical force has been added so equilibrium needs to be refigured. Summing the vertical forces, we find that there must be an internal shear stress in the beam equal to the difference between the reaction and the first load, or 3.75lb (1.7kg). The internal shear changes at the load point, as expected. Again, it follows that the shear stress will remain constant over the next 10ft (3m) of the beam at 3.75lb (1.7kg). A free body taken just to the right of the *second* load (Figure 22.8) shows that the internal shear stress must again change to keep the free body in equilibrium. In this case it will be the difference between the left-most reaction and the two forces, or 46.25lb (20.8kg). Note that this is exactly the magnitude of the reaction at the right end of the beam, and a free body taken at the right-most support will show that the shear stress drops back to 0 at the reaction.

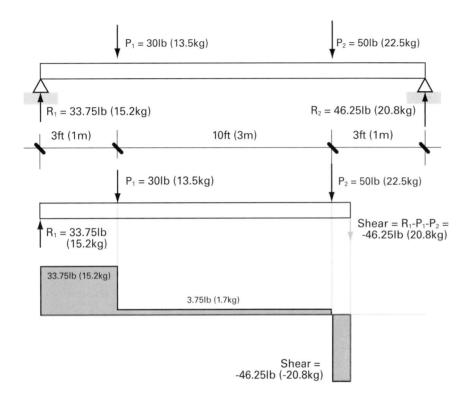

22.8
Shear diagram example, solving
for shear value along beam after
second load.

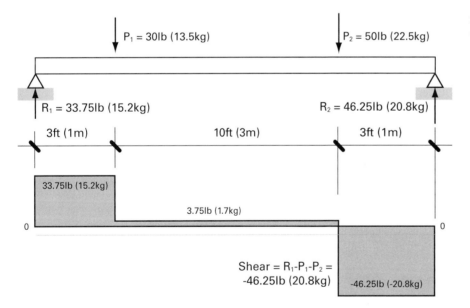

22.9
Completed shear diagram.

Interestingly, the completed shear diagram (Figure 22.9) tells us that, even though the greatest single load on the beam is 50lb (22.5kg), the maximum internal *shear* in the beam is only 46.25lb (20.8kg).

What does the shear diagram tells us about the beam's behavior? First, quite predictably as discussed earlier, the maximum shear values occur at the supports and remain at this level for a good portion of the beam's length. It is worth noting that the beam won't react any differently to a positive or negative shear value—this designation is simply a function of how the diagram was plotted (in this case, starting from the left and pushing up).

PLOTTING THE MOMENT DIAGRAM

Once we have solved for the shear forces, we can also find the moment force. What we are finding in the moment diagram is essentially how much "work" the beam has to do to resist the bending stresses applied to it—because it resists bending by generating an internal moment, we call this a moment diagram. Because we are plotting the values for a different type of stress, we will follow a different process from the shear diagram—however, the values and locations of the moment forces are directly related to the shear values.

One way of intuitively understanding what is being represented by the diagram is to visualize a person that is holding a weight which is gradually extended outward—the farther away the weight is held from the body, the greater amount of moment forces is present in the system (as moment value is the product of force load times the distance). Plotting this changing magnitude of moment force is what we are trying to diagram for the spanning members so that we can understand the worst-case scenario in the system, the maximum moment—the location at which the spanning member has to work the hardest. Akin to the arm example, we begin at the point of support and work our way outward.

Beginning, again, at the left side of the diagram, we note that there can be no internal moment at the very edge of the beam because the pinned connection allows the beam to freely rotate, so the moment value at the left end is zero. However, the reaction immediately begins to induce a moment as our 'cut' moves outward from the support (to the right in the diagram). Because moment is the product of a force times a distance, we need to know both factors—the shear diagram tells us the value of the vertical force at any distance (this is why one has to plot the shear diagram first). Therefore, just before the point of the first load, 3' (1m) in from the support, the internal moment must be 33.75lb (15.2kg) × 3' (1m), or 101.25ft-lb (15.2kg-m).

We can plot the change in value for the bending moment with a line that begins at the left support and increases upward (Figure 22.10). Moment diagrams should be drawn using some sort of vertical scale for reference (grid paper is helpful) for purposes of accuracy and legibility. Moving over further, past the point where the first load is applied to the beam, we see something important has occurred. Namely that the first load will also cause a moment force around the point that we've selected but in an *opposite* direction from that induced by the reaction. The reaction rotates clockwise around the point we're cutting, while the load rotates counter-clockwise. It is typically helpful to actually *draw* the direction of rotation around a particular point to see which moment forces are acting in which direction (Figure 22.11). Since the moments are going in opposite directions, the relative value of these two moments will begin to *cancel one another out* so the internal moment generated by the beam can be *less*. A smaller moment means less stress levels need to be generated in the outer edges of the beam as shown in the enlarged view of the beam cut away.

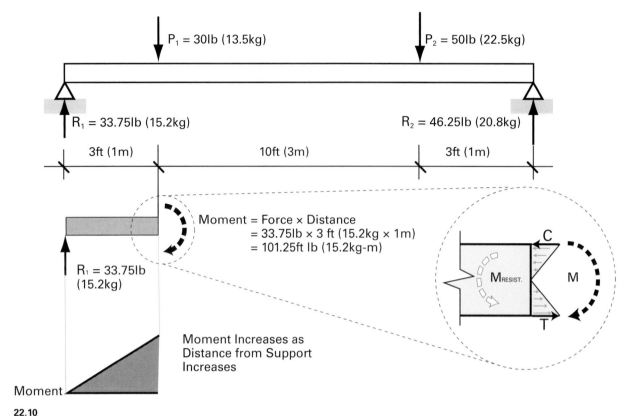

22.10
Moment diagram example.

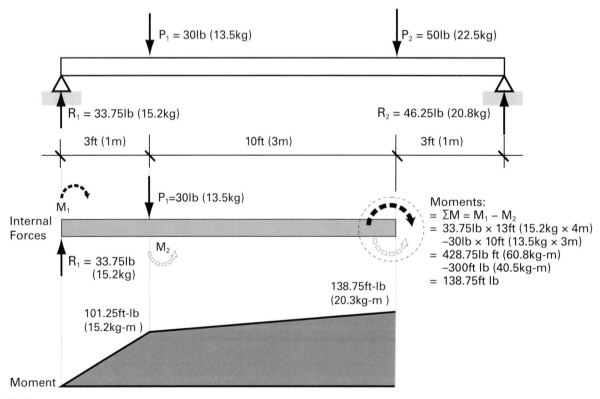

22.11
Moment diagram example.

We would anticipate that the moment would increase at a much slower rate after this point load, an assumption we can take by looking at the moment value just before the at the second load point. For conventions, if the moment is acting in the same direction as the reaction we add it to the value, if it is acting in an opposite direction, we subtract it.

$(15.2\text{kg} \times 4\text{m}) - (13.5\text{kg} \times 3\text{m})$
$= 60.8\text{kg-m} - 4.05\text{kg-m}$
$= 20.3\text{kg-m}$

$(33.75\text{lb} \times 13\text{ft}) - (30\text{lb} \times 10\text{ft})$
$= 438.75\text{ft-lb} - 300\text{ft-lb}$
$= 138.75\text{ft-lb}$

It is important to understand that this isn't telling us that the moment has increased from the previous point by this amount. Because the calculation already took into account all the moments acting on the system, this value is the new total moment, in other words, the moment has increased by 37.5ft-lb (5.1kg-m).

If we continue moving across the beam past the point where the second point load exerts a moment, we will see that it produces a moment in the same direction as the other point load (negative) and the magnitude then changes again:

$(15.2\text{kg} \times 5\text{m}) - (13.5\text{kg} \times 4\text{m}) -$
$(22.5\text{kg} \times 1\text{m})$
$= 76\text{kg-m} - 54\text{kg-m} - 22.5\text{kg-m}$
$= 0\text{kg-m}$

$(33.75\text{lb} \times 16\text{ft}) - (30\text{lb} \times 13\text{ft}) -$
$(50\text{lb} \times 3\text{ft})$
$= 540\text{ft-lb} - 390\text{ft-lb} - 150\text{ft-lb}$
$= 0\text{ft-lb}$

This is to be expected, since this occurs at a pinned connection which can't take any bending itself—this is discussed in more detail in Chapter 27. (Note that there is a 0.5kg rounding error in the metric example that we've eliminated.)

From this completed moment diagram (Figure 22.12), we can see that the greatest *moment* in the beam occurs at the second load point, 20.3kg-m

22.12
Completed moment diagram.

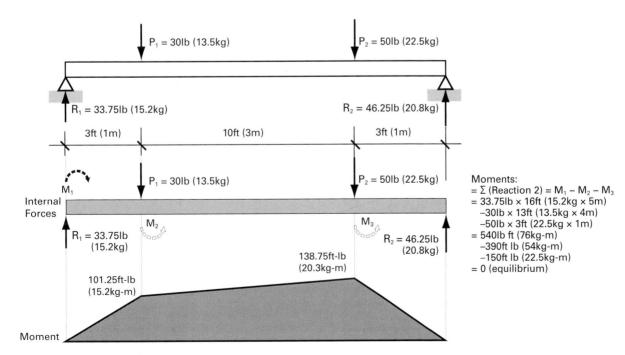

Moments:
$= \Sigma \text{ (Reaction 2)} = M_1 - M_2 - M_3$
$= 33.75\text{lb} \times 16\text{ft} \ (15.2\text{kg} \times 5\text{m})$
$\quad -30\text{lb} \times 13\text{ft} \ (13.5\text{kg} \times 4\text{m})$
$\quad -50\text{lb} \times 3\text{ft} \ (22.5\text{kg} \times 1\text{m})$
$= 540\text{lb ft} \ (76\text{kg-m})$
$\quad -390\text{ft lb} \ (54\text{kg-m})$
$\quad -150\text{ft lb} \ (22.5\text{kg-m})$
$= 0 \text{ (equilibrium)}$

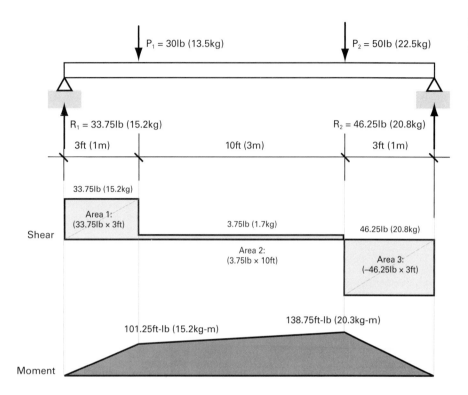

(138.75ft-lb). This is the point where the beam has to work the hardest to resist bending. This location can't be determined just by intuition; it must be graphed and calculated in this manner or using common shortcut diagrams and formulae as shown in Figure 22.13

There are numerous geometrical relationships between the shear, and moment diagram that have to do with the relationships between load, span and moment (Figure 22.14). We can use these as shortcuts to quickly draw shear-moment diagrams. First, the magnitude of a given portion of a moment diagram at any point will be equivalent to the total area to the left or right of that cut in the corresponding shear diagram. In this case, the moment at the first load point is 101.25ft-lb (15.2kg-m). This is equivalent to the area of the left-most portion of the shear diagram: 33.75lb × 3ft (15.2kg × 1m) = 101.25ft-lb (15.2kg-m).

Also, the *slope* of the moment diagram is always equivalent at a given point to the magnitude of the shear diagram at that point. For instance, the slope of the left-most portion of the moment diagram is 33.75ft-lb (15.2kg/m) which translates into a 33.75 percent slope of the line off of vertical. Note that the central part of the moment diagram has a much shallower slope, in fact 3.75ft-lb (1.7kg/m). The right-most portion of the moment diagram has, in fact, a negative slope, as suggested by the shear diagram's orientation below the base line, −46.25ft-lb (−20.8kg/m).

This last point is useful, as *the maximum moment must occur at a point of zero shear*—representing a summit or valley in the moment diagram's slope. A moment diagram must inflect, or change direction, at a zero slope/zero shear point. This allows us to very quickly determine where the highest moment stress will be. If we look at all points of zero shear along a beam's diagram, and calculate the moments at only those points, we can guarantee that because of the geometry of the graph one of these will be the maximum moment value. When designing beams in bending, therefore, we are very interested in points of zero shear, since one of those will inevitably be the point of maximum moment. Thinking this through, it becomes apparent that point loads are often locations of maximum moment, since they will often—though not always— "push" the shear diagram across the zero line.

Note, too, that for a distributed load, the complexity of line increases for each graph. Here, the *shear* value becomes a sloped line, and the *moment* value becomes a constant curve. Again, where the shear value is zero, the moment reaches its peak. There are representative examples of different relationships between loading conditions, shear diagrams, and moment diagrams shown in Figure 22.14.

MOMENT DIAGRAMS AND EFFICIENCY

Sometimes the complications inherent in the process of graphing and calculating shear and moment diagrams can obscure what is being studied. Essentially it is looking for the consequences of stress that develop in a beam based on the loading and support conditions. As shown in Figure 22.15, these diagrams

22.14
Shear/moment diagrams.

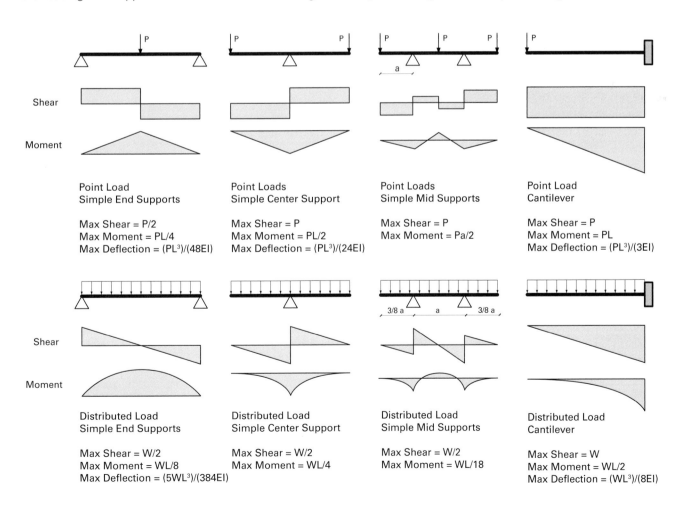

Shear

Moment

Point Load
Simple End Supports

Max Shear = P/2
Max Moment = PL/4
Max Deflection = $(PL^3)/(48EI)$

Point Loads
Simple Center Support

Max Shear = P
Max Moment = PL/2
Max Deflection = $(PL^3)/(24EI)$

Point Loads
Simple Mid Supports

Max Shear = P
Max Moment = Pa/2

Point Load
Cantilever

Max Shear = P
Max Moment = PL
Max Deflection = $(PL^3)/(3EI)$

Shear

Moment

Distributed Load
Simple End Supports

Max Shear = W/2
Max Moment = WL/8
Max Deflection = $(5WL^3)/(384EI)$

Distributed Load
Simple Center Support

Max Shear = W/2
Max Moment = WL/4

Distributed Load
Simple Mid Supports

Max Shear = W/2
Max Moment = WL/18

Distributed Load
Cantilever

Max Shear = W
Max Moment = WL/2
Max Deflection = $(WL^3)/(8EI)$

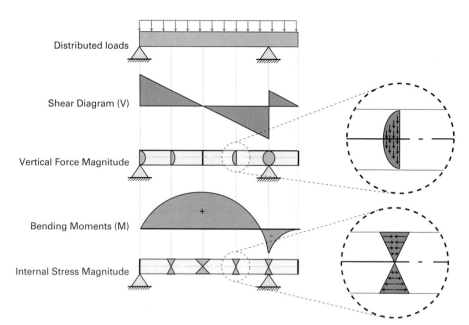

Distributed loads

Shear Diagram (V)

Vertical Force Magnitude

Bending Moments (M)

Internal Stress Magnitude

22.15
Representation of shear and
moment force values within the
beam.

can also tell us particular patterns of behavior within beams. The diagrams have a simple purpose: they provide us with the magnitude *and* location of the maximum shear and bending stresses for a particular loading and support condition. These two factors are the key pieces of information we need to know in order to properly size and shape a beam. These values will suggest a beam "section" that can accommodate these stresses. Logically then, if the loading conditions could be altered in a manner that produced lower values for maximum moment, more efficient beams (i.e. more efficient or smaller sections) could be used.

There are two common strategies that structural designers employ to help reduce maximum moment forces in beams: moving supports inward from the outer edges of a beam, and making the beam "continuous" across multiple supports. As one of the shear and moment diagrams in Figure 22.14 demonstrates, extending a beam past the supports on both sides (in this case, a double overhang) reduces the magnitude of the maximum moment dramatically by essentially reducing the span of the beam. The resulting moment value is split between the *positive* bending moment in the middle and two *negative moments* on the ends. Ideally the overhang length is extended to a point where the maximum positive and negative bending moments are equalized (approximately one third of the distance between supports) and in these cases it can reduce the overall maximum moment value by nearly *one half of the original value*. These double cantilevers have consequences related to the form and serviceability of the structure, but they also create a new set of stresses within the cantilevered portion of the beam.

Basically, along the cantilever, the shape of the beam, or its *elastic curve*, is reversed from the typical beam "sag" to more of an arch shape—the point where the curvature switches is know as the *inflection point*. As discussed earlier, the shape of the beam suggests the type of stresses that are occurring within the beam (e.g. the edge in compression is shortened). In looking at the cantilevered areas of the beam, we can see that the top edge is elongated

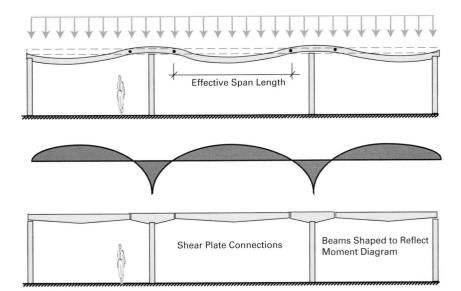

22.16
Beams spanning across multiple supports reduce effective span length.

which means that the top of the beam is now in tension while the bottom is in compression. Note that the inflection point is the location where beam's moment value is zero and is the threshold between positive and negative bending moment values. This typically isn't a problem for materials that are equally good at resisting tension and compression, like steel, but when concrete beams are using in cantilevered situations like this, the reinforcing bars will need to run along the top of the beam.

The second strategy for reducing moment involves the creation of a "continuous beam" that spans across several supports (Figure 22.16). Continuity is typically achieved by linking together several beams that are overhanging their supports (using single or double cantilevers). These beams are spliced end to end at a specific point along the span where the bending moment value is zero (this point is also the location of maximum shear, so the beams are connected with a shear plate to resist this stress). This continuity reduces the maximum moment because it essentially reduces the effective length of the beam's span thanks to the cantilever action. This approach, sometimes known as a Gerber beam system, is frequently used for long or intermediate spans for both buildings and infrastructural project. Because it spans across several supports, the beam is *indeterminate*, and cannot be analyzed by static analysis. Gerber beams are sometimes easily recognizable for another feature, their distinctly shaped profile—this is an additional strategy intended to improve the beams performance.

SHAPING ELEMENTS

Spanning members can also be made more efficient by learning from certain patterns of behavior suggested by the shear and moment diagrams. Because a moment diagram is drawn "to scale," the profile of the diagram is actually a geometrically descriptive map of the changing magnitudes of stress—the highest point on a moment diagram represents the location where the highest level of internal moment resistance needs to occur. In other words, the moment diagram is suggestive of a more idealized longitudinal shape for the beam in which the beam's depth is varied in response to the moment force. Recall that the most efficient way to resist bending is to provide a deep cross section, with enough distance to allow a significant internal moment to build up, *but* because the magnitude of moment force varies across the length of a beam, not all parts of the beam need to be as deep—so most beams that are "flat" have a certain degree of inefficiency because of this excess material.

In fact, there is an interesting correlation between the moment diagram and the funicular form of a cable—under the same loading conditions, the funicular shape and the moment diagram match. Both profiles suggest an efficient and responsive structural shape. To become more efficient, bending structures designed for efficiency do well to mimic the shape of their moment diagram, providing maximum resistance in the points of maximum bending stress. Using this information, the structural member can be sized to provide the greatest depth at the point of maximum bending stress (Figure 22.17). Arguably, statically expressive shapes such as this have an intuitively based aesthetic to them that we recognize—either through experience or instinct—as reliable, strong, and perhaps therefore as "beautiful".

22.17
Beam design can mimic the shape of the moment diagram to more efficiently distribute material where it will do the most good in resisting bending.

CONCLUSION

Certain structural elements, like beams, are subjected to more complicated types of stresses than just tension and compression. These commonly deployed structural components have to resist shear, bending, and torsional stresses and the level of these stresses varies across the length of the span and throughout the cross-sectional shape of the beam. These beams are shaped, re-orientated, and manipulated in order to be responsive to these stresses. These internal stresses can be visualized graphically and calculated mathematically using basic shear and moment diagrams. These diagrams show differing magnitudes of stresses and suggest efficient responses in the components' shaping.

FREQUENTLY ASKED QUESTIONS

It's great that there are shortcuts to drawing shear/moment diagrams, but I don't understand why these relationships work.
Shear and bending are intricately related in a beam, since both develop from the same loads and reactions. The shortcuts to drawing shear and moment diagrams are graphic ways of revealing these. Think about the relationship of moment at any given point along a beam to that of shear—if we analyze it by the free body method, the shear at one end of a beam will be just the reaction, while the moment will be that same reaction times its distance to our analytical "cut". So the *value* of the moment at any point will be the reaction (or the shear stress) times its distance, which is also the formula for the "area" of the shear diagram. Likewise, for every unit of measure we move the cut along the beam, we gain a moment equal to the amount of shear times the unit of measure— also a definition of the shear diagram's slope. Note, too, that as we increase

or move loads, both diagrams will change in ways that are necessarily related, since both rely on the magnitude and position of forces.

If it is so efficient, why don't we typically see beams with a longitudinal shape that matches the moment diagram—or double overhangs—or beams set upon multiple supports to make it continuous?

Structural design is still essentially an exercise in design, and, because of this, there is rarely one answer or solution that meets all the other needs. In all of these scenarios, there is a certain amount of structural efficiency gained which may result in the beams not having to be as big, but these modifications all have certain consequences which may tip the cost/benefit analysis away from making these changes. Structural costs are typically comprised of three relatively equal parts: weight, fabrication, and erection and so any changes to the fabrication (like customizing a beam's profile) may in fact be beneficial if it saves a significant amount of weight. Continuous beams are relatively common, especially in multistory, multi-bay buildings, but they are difficult to calculate (they are called indeterminate).

GLOSSARY

Bending: An internal state of stress in which loads are carried perpendicular to their direction. This is manifested by the development, within the structural member, of internal tension and compression.

Beam: A structural member that resists bending.

Internal moment: A force within a structural member that resists the "twist" on it imparted by an external load.

Force couple: The development of axial forces perpendicular to an external load in a beam. Usually consists of an internal compressive force on the side toward the load, and an internal tensile force on the side away from the load.

Neutral axis: A line through a beam that represents the "axle" of a force couple. This line undergoes no tension or compression while the beam is in bending.

Shear: An internal state of stress in which the particles of a material tend to slide past one another.

FURTHER READING

Ambrose, J. and Parker, H. (2000). *Simplified Engineering for Architects and Builders*. New York: Wiley; Chapter 2.2, Bending, p.43 and Chapters 4.1–4.4, Properties of Sections, pp.149–179.

Salvadori, M. (1963). *Structure in Architecture: The Building of Buildings*. New York: Prentice-Hall; Chapters 5.3 and 5.4, Simple Shear and Simple Bending, pp.86–97.

BEAMS: SHAPE AND STRENGTH

INTRODUCTION

In the last chapter, we examined the macro-behaviors of beam elements. Because these elements are loaded perpendicular to their span, they distribute and resist loads differently than axially loaded form-active elements, specifically by generating internal resistance to stresses within their respective cross-sections (thus the classification of section-active systems). We discussed how the fundamental relationship between and beam's loading and length of span determined the magnitude of stresses to be resisted (maximum bending moment and shear) and found that certain configurations of supports could reduce the amount of stress acting within the elements. We looked at ways of calculating and graphing these anticipated stresses in order to establish particular performance standards for the bending elements.

We discovered the basic correlation between a beam's depth and its capacity to resist bending (i.e. flat things are easier to bend than tall things), but we didn't determine how large the beams needed to be to resist these stress, how they might be shaped in cross section to more effectively resist these internal stresses, how a beam's effectiveness is influenced by the qualities of its materiality, or how to evaluate the beam's stiffness. This chapter, then, will explain how a beam's material qualities and distribution of cross-sectional area can be selected and configured to support the maximum anticipated bending moment and resist excessive deflection. In other words, it will explain how to size a beam that works.

EFFICIENT BEAMS

One of the concerns of using only unmodified solid rectangular spanning elements is the relative degree of structural inefficiency that results from using shapes that aren't responsive to the loading conditions—basically, there is a great deal of extra material (weight) that isn't being actively employed to resist loading. To be more responsive, therefore, requires a certain degree of modification to a beam's shape. As discussed in the previous chapter, one option is to adjust the longitudinal shape of the beam to be more in tune with the profile suggested by the moment diagram. These shapes aren't easily fabricated or mass-produced so these types of modifications are typically restricted to rare situations in which customized components were already required (such as large bridges, long-span roofs, etc.). For the average structure, we are more interested in finding ways to standardize structural shapes in the longitudinal direction.

We intuitively know that beams will need to rely upon more than just depth to efficient carry a load across a certain distance. How and why does the cross-sectional shape matter? Can beams more efficiently resist bending stresses by modifying their cross sectional shapes? In Figure 23.1, six beams are shown. Assuming the beams had the same depth, were made of the same material, and were loaded under the same conditions, how could we evaluate their relative degrees of effectiveness in resist bending?

We know that beams resist bending stress by generating an internal resisting moment and that the magnitude of this moment is dependent upon the depth

23.1
Six different profiles for potential beams.

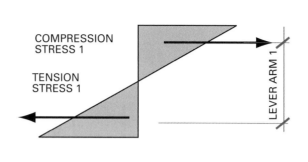

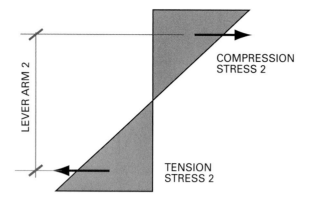

MOMENT RESISTANCE, BEAM 1   MOMENT RESISTANCE, BEAM 2

of the beam, but simply increasing a beam's depth without modifying its cross sectional profile misses an opportunity to make it more efficient. We should be able to give a beam greater cross-sectional area *where* it needs to do the most work. One way of answer the question about the relative effectiveness of the six different beams is to look at where beams need the most area to better resist bending.

To determine this, we need to take a closer look at the distribution of stresses within a beam and how bending is resisted. In a beam under loading, the internal moment is actually continuum of force that runs throughout the cross section of the beam—every portion of the beam material is either in compression or tension to varying degrees. This is represented by two separate triangles of forces with values that range from the maximum stress at the outer edge to the minimum value at the beam's neutral axis (remember that the arrows represent the level of stress acting at each point, see Figure 22.3). Within each triangle, the combined magnitude all of the force vectors stresses can be represented by a single resultant force arrow (with a value determined by the triangle's area) that runs through the triangle's centroid. When coupled with the resultant force from the opposing triangle, an internal resisting moment is produced (Figure 23.2).

A beam's capacity to generate an internal bending moment is therefore determined by the beam's ability to resist simple tension and compression in its outer fibers or regions. Therefore, a beam could be made more efficient if it placed greater cross-sectional area where it is needed the most (at the outermost fibers of the structural section) and reduced or eliminated area in locations where it is not needed (near the center of the beam's cross section).

In other words, the same quantity of material can resist internal moments more efficiently if it is placed further from the neutral axis. One way to think about this is that the distance component of the moment from the external load can be resisted by a distance component of the material's distribution throughout its section, and if we can find a way to move more material to the top and bottom edges of a beam, it should be able to do more work with less mass. An ideal beam shape, therefore, will deploy the majority of its material to the extreme top and bottom edges of its section.

23.2
Internal moment resistance is related to beam depth.

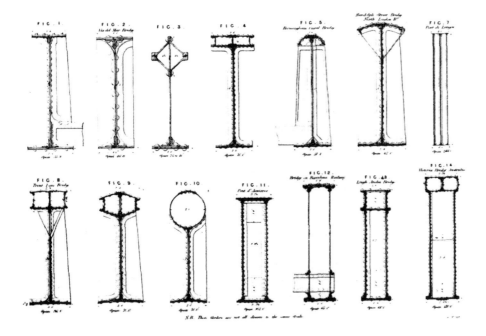

Work done by William Fairbairn in the early nineteenth century using rolled metal shapes led to the development, and eventually the standardization, of the instantly recognizable "I-beam", with thick *flanges* and the narrowest *web* possible (Figure 23.3). We'll now look at the mathematics behind Fairbairn's innovation, finding ways to measure how efficiently material is distributed throughout a beam section. This will involve some fairly abstract reasoning, but keep in mind that we're essentially looking to analyze what Fairbairn intuited—that shapes with more material at the edges can do more work, per unit of cross–sectional area.

23.3
The development of the I-shape occurred during the late eighteenth and early nineteenth century.

THREE IMPORTANT MEASUREMENTS—CENTROID, MOMENT OF INERTIA, AND SECTION MODULUS

A key element of sizing structural beams is to determine the capacity of a given shape to resist internal moments. We do this by using a number of formulae that quantify the properties of geometrical shapes, in particular the relative distance of the shape's areas in section from the neutral axis.

First among these is the *centroid*. This is a geometric property that essentially describes the center of gravity of a planar section. The centroid is an important sectional property as it determines the *neutral axis* of the section—the point at which there will be no bending-induced tension or compression, and the point at which internal tensile stresses will change to internal compressive forces in a beam under bending.

For biaxially symmetrical shapes like a solid rectangular bar, the centroid will lie at the intersection of the two axes of symmetry. As we have seen in previous examples, if the centroid is located in the middle of a cross section, then the stress at the outer limits of the beam's edge will have the same magnitude

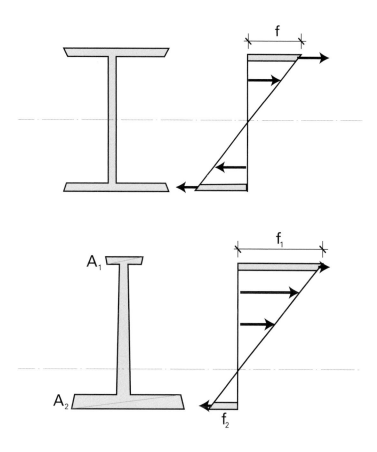

23.4
Centroid is located in center of
symmetrically shaped beam and
stress values at the top and bottom
of beam are the same as a result.

23.5
Because of concerns about
allowable stress levels for cast iron
members in tension, the lower
flange was given more area.

as the stresses in the bottom edge (the force magnitudes will follow a straight line). The value of the moment forces can be calculated by determining the length of the extreme fiber stress, f, and multiplying this by the cross sectional area of the flange, A. In simple symmetrical shapes, the amount of compression and tension stress is the same (Figure 23.4).

However, sometimes the cross-section is modified to move the centroid location either up or down vertically in order to reduce the amount of stress occurring at one outer edge of the beam in exchange for increasing it in another. This is usually done because of the inherent structural limitations of certain materials to resist certain stresses. For example, after many significant failures of cast iron "I-beam" shapes in the nineteenth century, it was determined that cast iron was quite weak in tension compared to tension. The typical cross section was cast with a much larger flange along the bottom of the beam (where the failure typically occurred), which lowered the centroid. Increasing the area along the bottom allowed the amount of tension stress, f2, to be reduced (the magnitude of f2 is represented by the length of the vector at the bottom edge). The resistance moment provided by the beam's section can be calculated as the magnitude of stresses, f1 and f2, times the area of their respective flanges, A1 and A2 remains the same. Essentially by providing more area in A2, it allowed f2 to be reduced. In other words, the beam still generates a force couple of two equal and opposite forces (Figure 23.5). Interestingly, single tee precast concrete beams take a similar approach to shape, but use the opposite form—placing most of the area at the top in compression and relying on the steel rebar (and it's very high allowable stress level) at the bottom of the beam to resist against the higher stresses.

Because there is little or no stress acting around the neutral axis area, it is a good location for a small opening to be cut through the beam web, if needed. Figure 23.6 shows the different formulas for determining the centroid for common geometric shapes. If, however, a more complex shape is proposed (like the six beams presented earlier), there is a somewhat complicated method of solving for the overall centroid location by essentially finding the average centroid of each sub-shape. However, because the location of the neutral axis is so important in understanding structural behavior, manufacturers typically publish this data for all of their components.

Once the centroid is established, one can then determine the relationship between the amount of cross-sectional area and its distance from the centroid. This value, known as the *moment of inertia, I*, is a very abstract description of cross sectional distribution of area. Its value combines the distance from the centroid and the areas of an infinite number of "fibers" to arrive at a measure of the average area $\times$ distance for every point in the beam's cross-section, and is expressed in cm^4 or in^4. Essentially it measures the amount of area that a specific shape has in relation to its distance from the neutral axis.

This is an important factor to consider in designing beams because an ideally efficient beam would have a majority of its area located at a great distance from its neutral axis. The moment of inertia value helps describe a material's stiffness against deflection and its inherent capacity to resist bending. Shapes with large amount of areas at great distances from the centroid, such as very tall I-beams with thick flanges, will have high moments of inertia, while compact shapes will have very low moments of inertia.

The moment of inertia of a shape may be calculated based on different axes depending on which direction the shape is being loaded from—this becomes a concern for columns which have to resist bending and buckling from the worst-case value for moment of inertia. Circular or square structural shapes will have the same moment of inertia value for both the x–x and the y–y axis.

Because this value is an important measurement of structural performance, it is typically included in product literature and design charts associated with particular structural elements. Rarely will designers have to calculate this value; however, Figure 23.6 includes formulae for determining the moment of inertia for common useful structural shapes.

A subtle refinement of the moment of inertia value involves dividing its value, I, by the distance between the section's centroid and its farthest edge, c, to find an object's *section modulus* value, S:

$$S = I/c$$

Like moment of inertia, section modulus is a value for the geometric properties of a particular cross-section. Section modulus is a truer representation of a shape's actual distribution of area from the neutral axis—it is measured in cm^3 or in^3, rather than cm^4 or in^4, and this difference directly reflects what we're really looking for—a measure of cross-sectional area times a length of distance. Moment of inertia is a truer representation of overall stiffness, and is used in

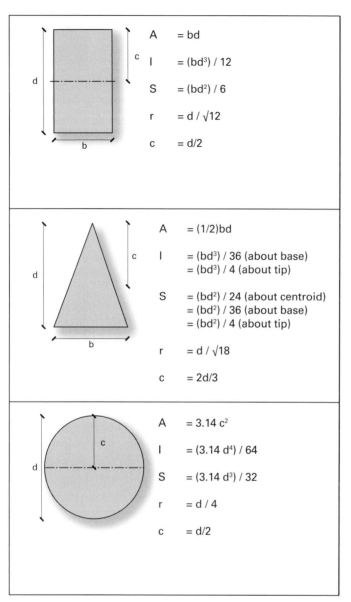

Formulae for area (A), moment of inertia (I), section modulus (S), radius of gyration (r), and centroid location (c) for typical structural shapes.

the deflection formula for beams, but the real measure of a shape's structural capacity ends up being determined by the section modulus.

One can finally begin to more closely evaluate the relative efficiencies of the six different beams from earlier. If one were to find each shape's centroid, moments of inertia, and section modulus, one would be able to mathematically verify the effectiveness (or lack thereof) of each shape's distribution of area. The higher values for "I" and "S" indicated better bending resistance.

While these calculations are critical, they really only tell us about *shape*—a beam made of soft rubber could have a high section modulus value if it were configured correctly, but that doesn't make it an effective beam. We know that materials have an inherent capacity to resist against stress and strain, but how do these principles change for members under bending? The answer is, not much. Inside the beam's cross section, both tension and compression stresses are occurring, so all we need to do is to check for a particular material's allowable stress level, f, from Table 21.1 for resistance to tension and compression stress. This means that any formula used to determine the effectiveness of a beam's resistance to bending must include factors related to the beam's material and shape.

THE FLEXURE FORMULA

The flexure formula is a surprisingly simple formula used to size beams. However, for structural designers, it is more than just a way of calculating appropriate beam sizing, it provides a clear means of understanding the interrelated nature of the three fundamental considerations used in beam design: the materiality (which is represented as the allowable stress value, f), the loading conditions (conveniently summarized as the maximum bending moment the beam must resist, M), and the effectiveness of the cross section to resist against bending (section modulus, S):

$$M = f \times S$$

The formula tells us that the maximum capacity of a beam shape to carry moment is directly related to both its maximum allowable stress and to a measure of where its material is deployed through its section. Its derivation is, admittedly, a bit complex, but it's worth understanding where this remarkably simple formula comes from; to find it, we've basically thought about how a fiber's distance from a shape's neutral axis helps determine how much resisting work it can do. Fibers that are farther away from the neutral axis can do more because they have a larger lever arm to help "twist back" against a moment load.

The flexure formula means that we need to know only three things about a beam to properly size it—the *maximum moment* it undergoes, its *section modulus*, and the material's *maximum allowable fiber stress*. Often, the loading condition (and therefore the resulting maximum moment) and beam material will have already been selected so beams can be somewhat simply sized by finding a section modulus value that is compliant with the other factors. The process of initially sizing a beam using handbooks is remarkably simple, but there is rarely only one "right answer" to allowable sizes. Skillful designers continue to look for opportunities to make sure the beam size meets a full range of priorities, including economic and aesthetic priorities—several different beams with a variety of depths and shapes may be found acceptable for different loading conditions.

Sample data on sectional shapes are shown in Table 23.1 and Table 23.2. For wood, we rely on a structural grading system that provides values for maximum "extreme fiber in bending" stress, getting around the fact that values for wood in tension are not published. Note that concrete presents an unusual situation, in that steel reinforcing takes up the tension load. Therefore, we can't simply use the flexure formula to design concrete beams and must instead find separate compressive and tensile capacities from the two materials. For the moment, we'll stick with steel and timber to cover the static principles involved.

Table 23.2 Selected timber sections sorted by s, section modulus.

Designation		Sx–x		Weight per linear foot	
metric	U.S.	cm³	in³	kg	lb
25 × 75	1 × 3	12.80	0.78	0.70	0.47
25 × 100	1 × 4	25.10	1.53	0.95	0.64
50 × 75	2 × 3	25.61	1.56	1.40	0.94
75 × 75	3 × 3	42.68	2.60	2.26	1.52
50 × 100	2 × 4	50.19	3.06	1.90	1.28
25 × 150	1 × 6	61.97	3.78	1.49	1.00
75 × 100	3 × 4	83.66	5.10	3.17	2.13
25 × 200	1 × 8	107.69	6.57	1.96	1.32
100 × 100	4 × 4	117.12	7.15	4.43	2.98
50 × 150	2 × 6	123.95	7.56	2.97	2.00
25 × 250	1 × 10	175.30	10.70	2.51	1.69
75 × 150	3 × 6	206.58	12.60	4.97	3.34
50 × 200	2 × 8	215.37	13.14	3.93	2.64
25 × 300	1 × 12	259.29	15.82	3.05	2.05
100 × 150	4 × 6	289.22	17.65	6.96	4.68
50 × 250	2 × 10	350.59	21.39	5.01	3.37
75 × 200	3 × 8	358.96	21.90	6.56	4.41
150 × 150	6 × 6	454.48	27.73	10.93	7.35
100 × 200	4 × 8	502.54	30.66	9.17	6.17
50 × 300	2 × 12	518.59	31.64	6.10	4.10
75 × 250	3 × 10	584.32	35.65	8.36	5.62
50 × 350	2 × 14	719.37	43.89	7.18	4.83
100 × 250	4 × 10	818.05	49.91	11.57	7.78
150 × 200	6 × 8	845.11	51.56	14.91	10.03
75 × 300	3 × 12	864.32	52.73	10.17	6.84
200 × 200	8 × 8	1152.42	70.31	20.33	13.67
75 × 350	3 × 14	1198.95	73.15	11.97	8.05
100 × 300	4 × 12	1210.04	73.83	14.23	9.57
150 × 250	6 × 10	1355.93	82.73	18.88	12.70
75 × 400	3 × 16	1588.21	96.90	13.78	9.27
100 × 350	4 × 14	1678.52	102.41	16.77	11.28
200 × 250	8 × 10	1849.00	112.81	25.75	17.32
250 × 250	10 × 10	1874.95	114.40	32.62	21.94
150 × 300	6 × 12	1986.95	121.23	22.86	15.37
100 × 300	4 × 16	2223.49	135.66	19.30	12.98
200 × 300	8 × 12	2709.47	165.31	31.17	20.96
150 × 350	6 × 14	2738.15	167.06	26.84	18.05
250 × 300	10 × 12	3432.00	209.40	39.48	26.55
150 × 400	6 × 16	3609.56	220.23	30.81	20.72

Table 23.2 (continued)

Designation		Sx–x		Weight per linear foot	
metric	U.S.	cm³	in³	kg	lb
200 × 350	8 × 14	3733.85	227.81	36.60	24.61
300 × 300	12 × 12	4154.52	253.48	47.79	32.14
150 × 450	6 × 18	4601.15	280.73	34.63	23.29
250 × 350	10 × 14	4729.54	288.56	46.35	31.17
200 × 400	8 × 16	4922.12	300.31	42.02	28.26
300 × 350	12 × 14	5725.23	349.31	56.10	37.73
250 × 400	10 × 16	6234.69	380.40	53.22	35.79
200 × 450	8 × 18	6274.30	382.81	47.44	31.90
300 × 400	12 × 16	7547.25	460.48	64.43	43.33
250 × 450	10 × 18	7947.44	484.90	60.09	40.41

Example: *Size an A36 steel beam to support a total distributed load of 32,000lb (14,515kg) over a span of 20ft (6.1m), as shown in Figure 23.7.*

Solution: The problem statement gives us enough information to solve for maximum moment, M, and the allowable stress, f, for steel so we can use the flexure formula to solve for the value of the section modulus, S.

There are two ways to solve for the maximum moment, M: either by solving for reactions and plotting the resulting shear and moment diagrams, or using the shortcut formulas from Figure 22.14 to solve for the maximum moment. For expedience, we will use the short cuts. In this case W is the total load (lowercase "w" would be used if the distributed load was given as a measure of weight per length). Note: the unit measure for section modulus is in inches (or cm) so we will need to convert the value of the moment into ft-in (or kg-cm).

$$M = W \times L/8$$

$$M = 14{,}515kg \times 6.1m \, (100cm/m)/8 \qquad M = 32{,}000lb \times 20' \, (12''/ft)/8$$

$$M = 1{,}106{,}768kg\text{-}cm \qquad\qquad M = 960{,}000lb\text{-}in$$

We use this value for the maximum moment and we find From Table 21.1 we can find the allowable stress, f, for steel is 22,000psi (1546.8kg/cm²). Solve for S:

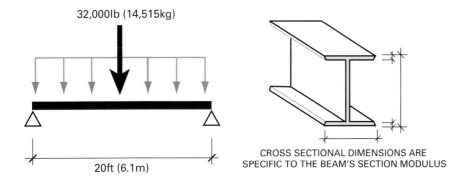

32,000lb (14,515kg)

20ft (6.1m)

CROSS SECTIONAL DIMENSIONS ARE
SPECIFIC TO THE BEAM'S SECTION MODULUS

23.7
Loading scenario representation.

$$M = f \times S \text{ or } S = M/f$$

$S = 1{,}106{,}768.8\text{kg-cm}/1546.8\text{kg/cm}^2$ $S = 960{,}000\text{lb-in}/22{,}000\text{psi}$

$S = 715.5\text{cm}^3$ $S = 43.6\text{in}^3$

Using Table 23.1 we can search for acceptable sizes for steel sections—we must find a steel section with a section modulus value *higher* than the value found in the formula. The W14 × 34 (W360 × 51) beam has a section modulus of 48.6in³ (796.55cm³).

Note that the beams designation tells us a few things: W tells us that it is a wide flange member, the 14 tells us that the beam is approximately 14″ tall and the 34 tells us that the beam weighs 34lb per linear foot (680lb total).

If for some reason this beam depth is determined to be too tall, Table 23.1 shows us that a W10 × 49 beam (W250 × 73) also has an acceptable section modulus value of 54.6in³ (894.89cm³). You may wonder how a shorter beam could have a higher section modulus—the answer can be found by looking more closely at the same table. The W10 beam not only weighs 15 pounds more per linear foot, but it has a wider *and* thicker flange. In other words, this beam has put more area to the outer edges of the beam in exchange for a shorter depth—a perfect demonstration of the properties that define section modulus.

Example: *Find the maximum allowable moment that can be supported by four 2 × 12 select structural southern pine joists (bolted together to form a single girder), Figure 23.8. How far can this beam span if it is loaded with a distributed load of 360lb per linear ft/30lb per in or 5.36kg per cm?*

Answer: In this situation, we are essentially working in reverse from the previous example. We first find the section modulus, S, for the girder by adding the actual width of each 2 × 12 together (1.5″ each) to find the equivalent member size as a 6 × 12 which has a section modulus value shown in Table 23.2 as 121.23in³ (1986.95cm³). From Table 21.1 we find the allowable stress value, f, to be 1200psi (84.37kg/cm³), so we can solve for M using the flexure formula:

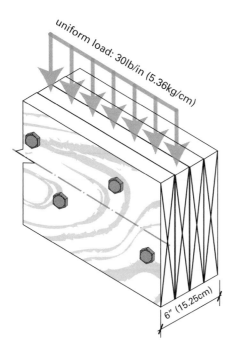

23.8
Composite wood beam shape described in problem example in text.

$$M = f\,S$$

$$M = 84.37\text{kg/cm}^3 \times 1986.95\text{cm}^3 \qquad M = 1200\text{psi} \times 121.23\text{in}^3$$
$$M = 167{,}639\text{kg-cm} \qquad\qquad M = 145{,}476\text{lb-in}$$

From the Figure 22.16 we again can use the shortcut for maximum moment for distributed loads to help us solve for. Because we don't know the length, we have to represent the total load, W, as $360\text{lb} \times L''$ ($163.3\text{kg} \times L\text{cm}$):

$$M = W \times L/8 \text{ or } L = 8 \times M/W$$
$$L = 8 \times 167{,}639\text{kg-cm}/5.36\text{kg/cm} \times L \qquad L = 8 \times 145{,}476\text{lb-in}/30\text{lb/in} \times L$$
$$L^2 = 250{,}207 \qquad\qquad\qquad\qquad L^2 = 38{,}793.6$$
$$L = 500\text{Cm} \qquad\qquad\qquad\qquad L = 197'' \text{ (or 16.4')}$$

Somewhat surprisingly for this much structural material, this span really isn't very far—perhaps only far enough to span across a large opening in a bearing wall. But again using the flexure formula as a means for evaluating the design conditions, we can see that a 6×12 doesn't have a very high S value which directly affects the allowable moment. If we had the depth available to use 6×18 member instead, we would more than double the allowable moment, allowing us to span nearly 25 percent further.

Because this is a somewhat short, heavily loaded wooden beam, we know that it is highly susceptible to horizontal shear, a condition that is potentially made worse by drilling holes in the joists in order to bolt them together (the joists would need to be staggered vertically to avoid this).

Example: *If the beam depth and loading conditions from the previous example were maintained, how much further could the beam span if it were made of A36 steel instead of wood?*

Answer: In order to find the new maximum moment, we start by finding the *highest* possible section modulus for a steel beam with approximately the same 12" depth as the wood (technically 11¼" actual depth for a 2×12) and combine this with the allowable stress for steel, 22,000psi (1546.82kg/cm^2). From the Depth column of Table 23.1, we can see that a $W10{-}77$ ($W250 \times 115$) is 10.6in (26.92cm) deep—close enough for our purposes. This beam has an S value of 85.9in^3 (1407.9cm^3).

$$M = f \times S$$
$$M = 1546.82\text{kg/cm}^2 \times 1407.9\text{cm}^3 \qquad M = 22{,}000\text{psi} \times 85.9\text{in}^3$$
$$M = 2{,}177{,}768\text{kg-cm} \qquad\qquad M = 1{,}889{,}800\text{lb-in}$$

Given this information and the same loading conditions as the previous example, we can find a new maximum length:

$$L = 8 \times M/W$$
$$L^2 = 8 \times 2{,}177{,}768\text{kg-cm}/5.36\text{kg/cm} \qquad L^2 = 8 \times 1{,}889{,}800\text{lb-in}/30\text{lb/in}$$
$$L = 1802.9\text{cm} \qquad\qquad\qquad\qquad L = 709.9'' \text{ (more than 59')}$$

Simply by changing materials we are now able to span more than four times the distance as a timber section. However, intuition and experience tells us that this situation seems nearly too good to be true.

The flexure formula tells us about strength to resist bending, but it is worth remembering that beams can also fail because they aren't stiff enough. To test this, we need to look at the amount of the beam's deflection.

DEFLECTION

Simply ensuring that a beam safely holds the load we've assumed for it doesn't necessarily mean it's the right structural member for the job—the beam may be strong enough, but it may not be stiff enough and this may affect the overall serviceability of the structure's performance. Beams must be designed to limit how much how much sagging occurs from its original position when loaded; in other words, how much a beam deflects.

As we know from previous chapters, any material under loading will change shape (axial loads will change length, beam elements will bend). Like axially loaded members, objects in bending resist deflection thanks to two major factors: the inherent stiffness of its materiality (modulus of elasticity, E) and a measure of the area resisting the deflection. Axial loads used the entire cross-section, A, to resist deformation, but in beams, it is more accurately measured by looking at a shape's inherent ability to resist bending—the moment of inertia, I.

We can find the actual deflection of a member under bending using the formulae shown in Figure 22.14 to make sure these values don't exceed our design limits. Using the previous example above for a uniformly load beam, we find that the deflection formula is $(5 \times W \times L^3)/(384 \times E \times I)$. We can see that the length of the span is the controlling criteria—doubling the span would increase the deflection by *eight times* the original value (diagrammatically shown in Figure 22.1).

In most applications, there will be a limit to how far a member can deflect before it becomes noticeable or causes problems. These problems may include relatively simple problems, like the cracking of a plaster ceiling, ranging all the way to major structural problems, such as a flat roof that becomes excessively loaded unexpectedly by water loads pooling in the roof sag. Most building codes, and good practice habits, will set limits on the maximum amount of deflection allowed for each element. Most common design standards restrict deflection to $\frac{1}{240}$th or $\frac{1}{360}$th of overall beam span/length. In practice, beams are typically sized for bending stresses first and then tested for deflection later, but past a certain length (typically spans greater than 40–50' (12–15m), deflection becomes the controlling calculation. In the previous example we just sized a steel member that spans farther than this range, so we should test it for deflection.

Example: *Find the deflection for the W10×77 steel beam sized in the previous example. Check for compliance using l/240.*

Answer: Using the formula for deflection of uniformly distributed loads found in Figure 22.14 we can see that the amount of deflection, d, is quantified by the formula from Figure 22.10 as:

$$d = 5 \times w \times L^3 / 384 \times E \times I$$

The value of w is the total load acting upon the beam per unit of length, 30lb per in × 709.9" = 21,297lb (5.36kg per cm × 1802.9cm = 9658.7kg). I was found to be 709.9" (1802.9cm), and from Table 21.1 we find E for A36 steel to be 29,000,000psi (2,038,990kg/cm²). Although typical steel construction manuals will give a value for I, we know that S = I/c in which c is the distance from the centroid and its outer edge, in this case, 5.3"

(13.46cm). We can find S from the Table 23.1 to be 85.9in^3 (1407.9cm^3) and find the I values to be 455.27in^4 (18,950cm^4). Combining all factors together we find deflection to be:

$$d = 5 \times 9658.7kg \times (1802.9cm)^3 / 384 \times 2,038,990kg/cm^2 \times 18,950cm^4 = 19cm$$
$$d = 5 \times 21,297lb \times (709.9in)^3 / 384 \times 29,000,000psi \times 455.27in^4 = 7.5''$$

These are *very high* totals for deflection. Although it might be obvious that these numbers are too high to be acceptable, we need to check it against the maximum deflection ratio given, l/240.

$$\text{Maximum deflection} = l/240 \text{ (in inches or cm)} = 197in/240 \text{ (500cm/240)}$$
$$= 0.82in \text{ (2cm) allowable.}$$

We have exceeded the amount of acceptable detention by nearly *ten times* the acceptable distance. Even though the beam works for bending, without also checking for compliance in deflection, the beam would certainly become a major problem.

There are many different strategies that the deflection formula suggests could be used to reduce this amount of actual deflection (it could be made of a stiffer material with a higher E value or use a different shape with a higher I value), but for a situation like this—in which the deflection compliance isn't even close—length matters. There is no more effective method for reducing deflection than shortening the length of span (its value is cubed in the equation).

SHEAR COMPLIANCE

Most beams that are sized to adequately resist bending and deflection are typically sufficiently large enough to also resist shear, but there are a few notable exceptions that should always be checked for compliance. Vertical shear is typically a controlling design concern in deep, slender members, with short spans that are subjected to high levels of loading. Horizontal shear can be found in short, heavily loaded, wood beams and joists as the shear force runs parallel to the wood grain and works to split the wood apart. Finally shear also becomes a concern if beams are modified with notches or holes near the end supports, so it is best to locate penetration near the center of the depth, *but* the size of these holes must be limited because of the specific nature of shear distribution in the cross section. Shear stress isn't equally distributed across the cross section—it is greatest at the neutral axis and reduces down to zero on the top and bottom edges, making an arch shape of stress lines.

Wood and steel both resist shear differently so they have different allowable shear values (see Table 21.1) and slight variances on their means for calculation. Wood is an anisotropic material with grains that run lengthwise across the beam so horizontal shear is the controlling concern—for that reason, the shear stress formula is modified to concern shear stress 1.5 times the average vertical shearing stress. Wood rectangular sections are checked for shear using the equation:

$$f = 3 \times V/2 \times bd$$

For the equation, f (typically noted as fv) is the maximum shear stress (in psi or kg/cm^2), V is the total anticipated shear load—typically found from shear diagram or shortcut calculation (in lb or kg), and bd is a representation of cross sectional area—for rectangular beams b is the breadth and d is the depth (in or cm).

Unlike wood, steel isn't susceptible to splitting along any particular orientation. Because steel is typically connected with bolted connections to other members, shear is a concern, so angles or *shear plates* are used to double ply the area where the holes are drilled. Because shear value is zero at the top/bottom edges of a steel beam, the flanges don't help to resist against shear—the area of the web does all the work. This explains why it is acceptable for steel beams to have the top and bottom edges coped to facilitate connections to other members, because the flanges don't help anyway. The formula for steel shear compliance is nearly the same as for wood:

$$f = V/A$$

But because vertical and horizontal shear stresses are the same in steel, the formula eliminates the 1.5 times modifier and simply considers the maximum shear, V, as the value to resist. Also, it is worth noting that steel webs are usually a much smaller area, A, than the cross section of a timber section. In the formula, the maximum shear is typically divided by the area of the web and checked for compliance against the allowable shearing stress unit, which is 12,000psi (843.72kg/cm^2) for steel.

Example: *Check the wood 6 × 12 girder from the previous example for compliance with shear.*

Answer: From Table 21.1 we find the allowable shear stress value to be 1200psi (84.37kg/cm^2). For the area, we have to calculate the actual area, not rely upon the nominal dimensions. 2 × 12 beams have an actual size of 1.5″ × 11.25″ (3.8cm × 28.6cm) so the combined breadth, b, of 3 members would be 4.5″ (11.43cm).

The maximum shear value, V, can be found by simply knowing that for a simply supported beam with a distributed load, the maximum shear value is half of the total vertical load (or one could see this from Figure 22.14 diagrams). In this case, the total load W is 360lb/ft × 16.4ft = 5905lb (2678.5kg) so the maximum moment, V, is half of the total load, or 2952.5lb (1340kg).

$f = 3 × V/2 × bd$
$f = 3 × 2952.5lb/2 × 4.5″ × 11.5″ = 87.48psi$, which is well below the allowable 1200psi.

SIZING BEAMS—PROCEDURE AND GUIDELINES

1 Determine loads on beam (see Chapter 20); include assumption for potential beam weight.
2 Find reactions using principles of rotational and translational equilibrium (see Chapter 20).

3   Draw shear diagram based on loads and reactions (see Chapter 22).
4   Draw moment diagram based on slopes and quantities in shear diagram (see Chapter 22).
5   Determine maximum moment from moment diagram (see Chapter 22).
6   Using maximum moment, use the flexure formula to determine required section modulus.
7   Check that selected beam weight compared to initial assumption, readjust steps if needed.
8   Repeat from step 1, now including additional weight of selected beam.
9   Check selected beam for deflection (usually $<\frac{1}{240}$ or $\frac{1}{360}$ span).
10 Check selected beam for ability to carry maximum shear based on cross–sectional area.

CONCLUSION

Horizontally spanning structural members, like beams, are commonly deployed in many structural components as primary, secondary, and even tertiary spanning components. Understanding the basic relationships between a beam's loading/support conditions, material, and cross-sectional shape is a fundamental structural design requirement. Calculating a beam's deflection under loading is also dependent on the same basic information, just simply analyzed differently. In conjunction with each other, the basic structural sizing and behavior of beams can be understood using these fundamental formulas and attributes.

FREQUENTLY ASKED QUESTIONS

If I-shaped beams are so efficient, why are other shapes ever used?
In addition to carrying loads, we often ask beams to do other things—to connect to finishes, to hang connections, etc. While W-shapes are efficient, their wide flanges restrict connections to the web—where we'd like to make any connections that involve cutting into the beam's material. (Remember that the web is closest to the neutral axis and thus least stressed). Channels and tees both offer easier access to the beam's web if we're trying to make a structural connection.

If deflection is the controlling design element in long-span beams, isn't there a way to change its cross sectional shape to resist against this deflection?
In critical situations, the beam may be *cambered*, or curved in the direction opposite to the loading, before it's installed. Once the load is applied to the structure, the beam deflects back down to a flat position (a strategy often used for the supports under flat beds of transportation vehicles). Camber can be inflected by prestressing the beam by intentionally pulling the ends together until it curves.

With so many interrelated components of loading, supports, longitudinal and cross sectional qualities that go into sizing a beam, how do designers know where to begin? Do engineers really layout and test all the possible scenarios before deciding upon one solution? If a designer changes some factor (like span layout or material) won't that potentially change a lot of things?

Most team members would rather make the best decisions possible at the earliest stage, but changes certainly will occur. At the earliest stages, structural designers are able to use certain rules of thumb about member sizing over a span to help give general ideas about depth clearances and framing strategies—it is at this point where architectural designers should also be engaged with asking a broad range of questions about what might be possible to achieve with the structure that supports the larger design ideas. One shouldn't just go "shopping" for an off-the-shelf structure system. Eventually, in the later stages of documentation, a full computer model will likely be created that assists with calculations and major changes at this stage are always time-consuming.

GLOSSARY

Centroid: A measure of a shape's "average" point in space or, more accurately, its center of gravity. This will correspond with the shape's neutral axis if it is employed as a beam, and is thus an important characteristic.

Flanges: In beam design, top and bottom elements designed to put the most possible material in the most efficient places—far from the neutral axis.

Flexure formula: A simple formula that relates allowable stress, section modulus, and maximum allowable moment: $M = fS$. The maximum allowable moment in any beam (M) is equal to the material's maximum allowable stress (f) multiplied by the section modulus of its cross-sectional shape (S).

Moment of inertia: Simply put, a weighted measure of a shape's area, accounting for both quantity of area and average distance of each point from the centroid.

Section modulus: A refinement of moment of inertia that provides a more usable number for structural calculations by counting depth one fewer times. It is found by dividing a shape's moment of inertia by the distance from its centroid to its "farthest fiber" (c): $S = I/c$

Web: In beam design, an element designed to space flanges apart from one another, and thus from the neutral axis. This may be a solid plate, as in steel W-shapes, or a much lighter element, such as the bent metal bar in open web joists.

FURTHER READING

Allen, E. and Iano, J. (2002). *The Architect's Studio Companion*, 3rd edition. New York: Wiley; Chapter 2, Designing the Structure, pp. 47–137.

Ambrose, J. and Parker, H. (2000). *Simplified Engineering for Architects and Builders*. New York: Wiley; Chapters 3.1–3.11, Investigation of Beams and Frames, pp. 60–135 and 6.1–6.5, Wood Columns, pp. 212–228.

Salvadori, M. (1963). *Structure in Architecture: The Building of Buildings*. New York: Prentice-Hall; excerpt from Chapter 7, Beams, pp. 135–169.

24

SLABS: BEHAVIOR AND ASSEMBLIES

Introduction	Section-resistant planes
How slabs work	Beams and slab analogy
	Deflection performance
Slab arrangements	One-way v. two-way slabs
	Framing proportions
	Idealized cross section
	Concrete
Floor system assemblies	Lightweight systems
	Heavy systems
Slab construction considerations	Formwork
	Design opportunities
Evolutions in efficiency	Slab orientation and manipulation
	Prestressing

INTRODUCTION

Thus far we have looked at the different ways that linear structural elements, such as cables and beams, could be designed, sized, and configured. We've seen how understanding the types of loads and stresses to which particular structural elements are subjected allows for structural designers to craft a particular response based on intentional selection of materials, form, and supports. Studying the behavior that results from pushing, pulling, and bending these objects will allow us to better understand how to design and analyze more complex, multi-directional structural systems found in horizontal planes—otherwise known as slabs and plates.

The role a slab plays in a building's structural system can vary widely, from the thinnest structural component spanning the shortest distance, to the primary means of supporting, enclosing, and articulating the spatial enclosure in the horizontal direction. As a result there are many different options for the size, arrangement, depth, and materiality of slabs.

This section will explore the various benefits and consequences of incorporating a planar structural component into the system. It will show how particular layouts and arrangements may suggest different slab layouts and/or cross sections, how these arrangements will influence the manner of bending resistance and load transfer happening within the slab, how the slab interacts with the supports elements of columns and beams, and the economic and construction consequences that result from these decisions.

HOW SLABS WORK

Even though the mathematical analysis of slabs and plates is complex, developing considerate and responsive design options for these elements need not be. Because they both resist bending and transfer perpendicularly applied loads to their supports, we can start with the basic assumption that a slab is analogous to a planar version of a beam.

There is a relative complexity of mathematics involved with slab design that is rarely necessary to perform. Slabs have been in use for long enough that an extensive body of empirical evidence makes it possible to specify, rather than engineer, slabs for most situations. Calculations are also not necessary to understand the nature of a slab's typical structural behavior—it is quite intuitive if one can start thinking of a slab as a series of tightly spaced beams.

To begin to understand slab behavior, consider a typical floor. With simple beam calculations, we could figure out a structural system composed entirely of one-dimensional beams placed side by side until the entire floor was covered (Figure 24.1). This, of course, strikes us as a very heavy solution, since we are used to seeing floor structures that have a much thinner floor thickness than the beams that carry them. However, if these beams were connected to each other to form a monolithic surface, then they no longer behave structurally as a set of individual elements. Instead of simply transferring the load along its length like a beam, slabs can transfer their loads in two directions by recruiting the structural capacity of the "slices" of slab next to it.

To understand why, we need to remind ourselves about *deflection*, the tendency of structural members to change shape under loading. A structural member under loading changes shape—a beam will curve slightly, which is another way of saying that the top edge compresses while the bottom edge elongates. The amount that a beam deflects under load is directly proportional to the load, W, and length of the beam, L, and inversely proportional to the material's modulus of elasticity, E, and the shape's moment of inertia, I (Chapter 23).

Assuming the slab shown in Figure 24.1 is loaded by a point load in the center, one "slice" of the slab will deflect a certain distance at its midpoint. Note, however, that because the slab is monolithic, its neighbors must, by necessity, deflect nearly the same amount—albeit slightly less. The amount that the adjacent slice deflects will depend on the material's stiffness—a very rigid material will tend to receive more assistance from the slice next to it than one that is spongy. This means that this adjacent slice, working backwards from the deflection, must be carrying nearly the same load as the original slice. We can work our way to the edge of the slab, and note that each individual slice carries some percentage of the original load, diminishing until we get to the (supported) edge of the slab. Thus, the single load that we've applied at the

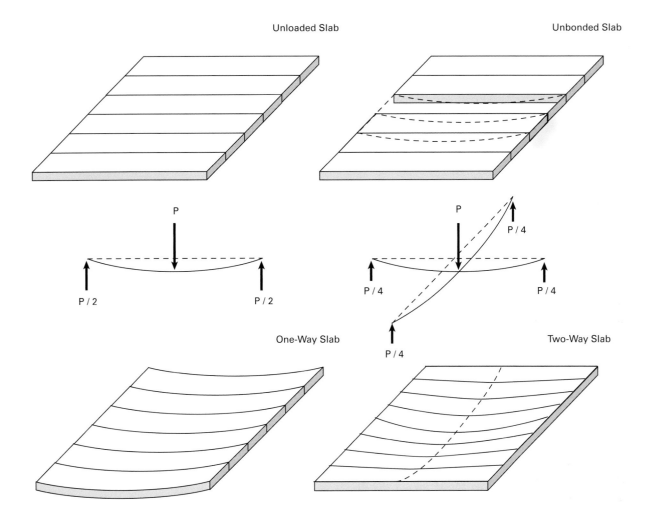

center is carried not just by the "beam" of the middle slice, but by *each slice in turn* throughout the slab.

Each "slice" helps carry the load in two ways. If we think through the mechanism that transfers the load from one slice to another, we realize that each slice will deflect as noted above, but it will also twist. This twist means that each subsequent slice deflects a bit less and thus carries a bit less of the load. In other words, quite unlike the beam, which only transmitted the load in a linear manner, the slab works multi-dimensionally to resist and distribute its load.

But questions about how much load needs to be carried by the slab (and what carries it) still need to be determined by the designer. The proportions of the structural bay and arrangement of supporting elements within the bay (beams and columns) affect structural slab behavior and may suggest potential configurations to more effectively resist the loads.

24.1
Basic slab theory of one-way and two-way support.

SLAB ARRANGEMENTS: ONE-WAY VERSUS TWO-WAY SLABS

To understand the physical consequences between different arrangements of support and the resulting slab depths and behavior, it is necessary to first

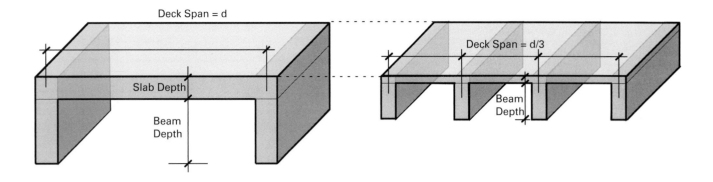

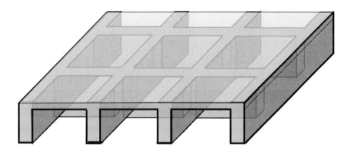

remember the primary relationship between span and depth in bending elements. Figure 24.2 imagines three different scenarios for how the slab "slices" described above might be supported. As expected, the longer slab span results in a deeper slab and supports, while the second scenario is only able to reduce the slab span at the expense of adding more supports below. Neither is taking full advantage of the capacity for slabs to transmit their load in two directions. Even though slabs have the capacity to distribute their loads in multiple directions, loads will always seek the shortest distance to a support, so in both of the scenarios with supports only running in one direction, the slab can be described as *one-way*. Finally, depending on the material, the thicker decking may become so large that it risks essentially pulling down and around the column—creating a high amount of shear called punching shear. These scenarios are still relatively efficient strategies, and under certain architectural conditions determined by serviceability, these work.

The third scenario, shows a more idealized configuration of the slab and supports—in this case, running beams in two different directions—one longitudinal and one transverse in order to form a net of support below the slab. Not only are the loads on each support reduced because of the shortening of the spans, the load itself is essentially "split" and naturally carried off in two directions. Most importantly, this scenario suggests that it isn't always necessary to have a slab *and* a beam—sometimes the slab can become an efficient network of beams. Note that these "supports" aren't intended to solely represent exposed beams running below a slab, they could also represent a typical layout of rebar in a thin elevated structural slab as well.

Whether a slab system acts as a one-way or two-way system (and to what degree of each) is ultimately determined by the proportions of the framing

24.2
Basic relationship between deck span and depth of deck and beams.

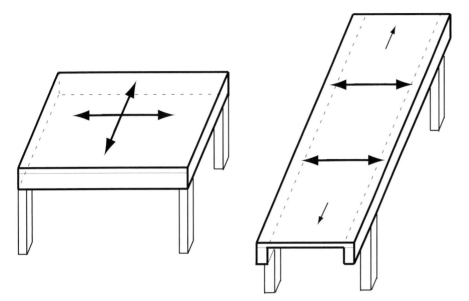

24.3
Typical one-way and two-way slab proportions based on structural bay configuration.

system (Figure 24.3). One-way slabs will have a rectangular bay shape, with the loads being primarily transferred across the slab in the short span direction, and two-way slabs ideally are equally proportioned as a square. Because both lengths of a square bay are equal it should always have the most efficient two-way performance, and thus the thinnest slab. However there are a number of reasons why we might choose column grids that are more rectangular—the shape of program spaces, the shape of the site, or the need to distribute services and in these situations. There are ways of manipulating the cross section of the one-way slabs to increase its relative efficiency. Slabs that are much longer than they are wide will tend to do most of the carrying work in one direction, mostly due to the relationship between the beam length and anticipated deflection. A slab with a bay size ratio of 2:1 will resolve nearly 90 percent of its load along its short dimension, and only 10 percent along the long direction, simply because the short dimension is stiffer. Sometimes irregularly shaped plans may be desired as well. One of the benefits of using cast-in-place concrete is that the location and size of the reinforcing can be designd to help irregularly shaped slabs perform somewhat more regularly.

If we know the slab is intended to span in one particular direction, we are tempted to find ways to increase the performance of the slab over that of a simple flat plate. To do this, we apply what we learned about the relationship between a beam's resistance to bending and its cross-sectional shape. Remember that we improved the performance of a simple rectangular beam by adding cross-sectional areas at the extreme edges, away from the neutral axes. This increased the moment of inertia (and therefore the section modulus) while often reducing the required quantity of material. We can, in fact, do the same thing with slabs, by essentially taking out material from near the slab's neutral axis. By getting rid of this unneeded extra mass, we concentrate the material where it does the most good—at the edges. Figure 24.4 shows how the idealized sectional-resistant shape of a beam can be seen in the sections of common, conventional, and highly effective slab components such as precast planks, metal decking and "T" shaped concrete components.

24.4
Idealized slab cross-section.

FLOOR SYSTEMS

The overall efficiencies of the horizontal structural system shouldn't be assessed by simply looking at the plane of the slab alone, because it is typically just one part of a larger design strategy for a floor assembly. Ultimately the choice of what type of slab and plate systems is used is based on the desired arrangement and proportion of the structural bay (one-way versus two-way), the length of the slab's span (as determined by the arrangement of the joists, beams, or trusses below), and the code for the fire resistance of the assembly. Figures 24.5 and 24.6 show a range of arrangements for different one-way and two-way common floor assemblies.

Certain project types have modest span distances and loads so they only need to use lightweight construction materials and techniques. For residential scales, wood comes conveniently in slab form, as plywood, and is combined with joists to create a one-way system. Plywood can only span modest distances between the joists as it isn't inherently very deep or strong or stiff—wood manufacturers regularly produce tables showing safe spans for various wood systems. Interestingly however, plywood is intentionally manufactured in a series of layers that alternate the grain direction to improve its performance as a slab with some degree of two-way plate action.

While steel offers a greater resistance to bending and breaking than wood, it isn't used as a flat plane, like plywood is in lightweight assemblies—it is typically bent or extruded to form a more sectional-efficient metal decking profile. The profile of steel decking again suggests that it is best used to transfer the gravity loads in a one-way system, but unlike plywood, steel decking has the capacity to span very long distances, up to 30ft (10m), depending on the depth of the deck which would allow for the elimination of intermediate

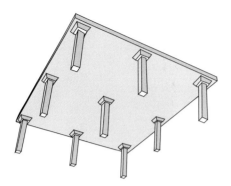

Flat Plate and Flat Slab
- Two-way structural action
- Square bays, use for light loads, spanning less than 30ft (10m)
- To span further and carry more load, switch to Flat Slab system with shear plate at columns
- Made with flat formwork, therefore relatively simple to construct
- Minimum structural depth, but heavy

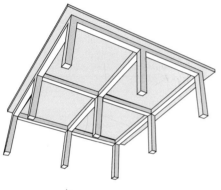

Plate and Beam
- Typically one-way structural action depending on beam layout/bay size. Two-way system shown
- Acceptable for heavy loads
- Shear between plate and columns taken up by beams
- Beams require drop-down formwork
- Slab can be substituted for other one-way systems, such as pre-cast slabs
- Deeper overall than Flat Plate, due to added depth of beams

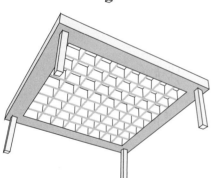

Waffle Slab
- Two-way structural action
- Square bays, with light loading, spanning more than 30ft (10m) +/-
- Shear between plate and columns taken up by nominal 'beams'
- Coffers made with domed forms secured to flat formwork may be drop downs at beams (not shown)
- Shallower total depth than One-Way Joist system, but less opportunity to integrate HVAC runs

24.5
Typical one-way slab framing assembly systems.

support members in certain arrangements. But the performance of steel deck alone doesn't provide adequate structural strength or continuous finished floor surface, so we usually pour a relatively thin layer of concrete over the decking to make a composite slab. The deck can be bolted or welded to the frame, and it provides a natural "tray" in which to pour the concrete. The finished slab is actually a composite member, and studs can be welded to the deck to ensure that the steel deck and the concrete slab work together as a one-way system.

When larger spans, heavier loads, and a greater level of fire resistance are required, reinforced concrete can be used for the entire floor assembly. If carefully considered, reinforced concrete slabs can be relatively affordable, structurally efficient, and provide vibration and sound control as well. The simplest system, and to a certain extent, least effective is the flat slab system in which a plane of a continuous depth of concrete is used across the entire bay. Although it is easy to build because it is flat, this also makes it somewhat

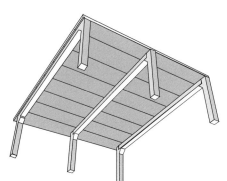

Composite Deck and Steel Joists
- Composed of steel beams (and/or joists) and corrugated metal deck, typically filled with concrete (composite deck)
- Moderate loading and spans allowable
- One-way spanning action for deck, short spans between joists
- Relatively simple and economical framing option

One-Way Pan Joists
- One-way structural action
- Non-square bays with light loads spanning more than 16' (5m) +/-
- Shear between joists and columns taken up by beams
- Made with metal pans on flat formwork, drop-down details at beams
- Greater structural depth, but slab itself can be much thinner than Flat Plate
- Limited room between joists for lighting, HVAC

Precast Planks
- Composed of precast concrete planks with steel or concrete beams (precast shown)
- One-way unsupported structural action
- Very easy to construct, with most work done off-site in factory setting
- Span vary with depth of plank, 20'–40' common
- Similar weight to poured in place concrete, but faster to erect
- Topping slab poured on top to bond planks together

24.6
Typical two-way slab framing assembly systems.

inefficient structurally because it doesn't take advantage of any cross section "lightening"—as a consequence, columns and foundations must also become larger to support this added weight. This additional weight also creates a danger of punching through around the column due to the enormous stresses. Flat plate systems add a column cap to provide more resistance to this shear (Figure 24.6).

Cast-in-place systems can obviously become progressively lighter by eliminating excess weight and increasing the depth of certain parts of the floor assembly in a manner analogous to the conventional "slab and joist" framing method. The arrangement and direction of both the slab and joist components of the system are designed to respond directly to the proportions of the structural bay. These "T" shapes were discussed in Chapter 23 as highly effective shapes to resist bending and are often used as a sectional strategy for slabs—either as one-way pan joists or two-way waffle slabs. In one-way slabs, the "T" spans the short distance, leaving a void between the deepest parts of the slab. One-way pan joists provide good-sized, accessible voids below that often allow for carefully coordinated ductwork, piping and lighting to occupy the same depth as the structure.

Knowing that two-way slabs are somewhat square in plan and are intended to distribute their forces in both direction, these same "T" shapes are poured to form a *waffle slab* arrangement. Waffle slabs are highly efficient slabs, but they offer less integrative possibilities with other building elements (Figure 24.6). Both systems offer some measure of architectural interest, as they provide a structural grain to the space below, a variety to the sectional qualities of the space, and a visual clue as to how the structural loads are moving across the space.

Often it is necessary to drill holes through the slab or otherwise locate larger openings. It is helpful to think of the way that slabs transfer loads internally as a type of two-way beam action. In two-way slabs there are two perpendicular bearing "strips" that extend between columns that are typically filled with reinforcement and should be avoided. However, there are certain areas in-between the strips that have relatively less stress and are good candidates for opening, (Figure 24.7).

Not all reinforced concrete slab systems need to be cast on-site either. In fact, two of the common strategies for making a slab more efficient that have been discussed—changing the cross sectional shape of the slab and prestressing a member—are both more effectively done in a factory setting. Different structural shapes of precast can be produced that allow for an amazing range of clear spans, but they are typically components that transfer their loads in a linear manner (better served for one-way systems). The most common precast slab is the plank system.

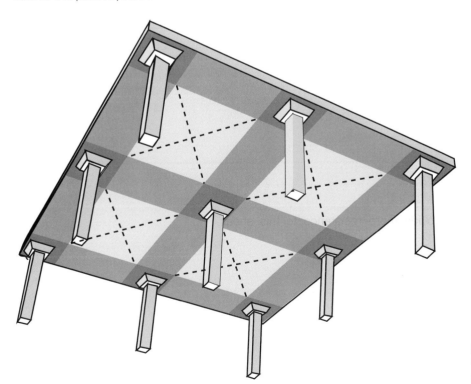

24.7
Stresses within slabs are primarily gathered and distributed in strips.

Planks are essentially wide, flat rectangles of concrete that can be trucked to a job site and laid by crane. Their proportions give them some two-way plate action, so they're reasonably efficient, but their performance can be enhanced by pouring a *topping slab*, which consists of a layer of concrete that bonds to steel cables or studs in the top of the precast planks. They can also be made more efficient by a post-tensioning process in which tendons are run through the hollow cores of the section, or they can be prestressed in the factory. They are typically connected to other structural systems either by welding embedded steel plates from the planks onto a steel support, or by pouring an integral connection beam at the ends in a concrete system.

Plates and slabs present a number of calculation problems so they are usually sized empirically, based on charts and handbooks that essentially document what sizes have safely been used in what conditions previously. The structural charts in the Appendix to Part 5 include two charts (Figures A.1 and A.2) that show relationships between span and depth for typical flooring conditions. In normal situations, standard loading and typical spans and supports will allow sizing by chart or rule of thumb.

SLAB CONSTRUCTION

Structural slabs cover such large areas within a building—floors often constitute the bulk of a building structure's weight, and thus their performance often needs to be particularly efficient. And yet buildings are frequently constructed with structural slabs that aren't particularly efficient in cross-section but are highly efficient to construct (and therefore more efficient economically). Slab design must consider the relationship between a desired structural form, material, and fabrication technique must be evaluated by the relative cost associated with its forming, erection, etc.

While plywood is the simplest way to make a concrete form, it typically isn't re-useable and it requires a great deal of conventional framing below to support the weight of the concrete during casting. There are numerous commercial products that use metal to create temporary forms for one-way and two-way slabs. These "pans" are placed on a temporary floor, "tanked" at the edges, and used to create voids in a deep concrete slab. Because of their finish, they can create architecturally acceptable surfaces, and can be re-used. These systems are thus quite economical but they still rely upon a "platform" below to support the concrete and the pans.

For building with multiple stories, it is quite labor- and resource-intensive to have to build, demount, and re-erect the formwork platform underneath the slab for each floor. There is another option, called the *lift-slab method*, in which concrete floor slabs are poured on top of another slab (using the lower floor slab as the formwork platform) and then jacking this slab up into place using hydraulic jacks on special column guides It can save a tremendous amount on formwork costs, but is somewhat risky to construct.

An intriguing refinement in two-way slab construction was carried out by Pier Luigi Nervi in a number of factory projects in the 1950s (Figure 24.8). Nervi used "ferro-cemento" pans, made by bending a wire mesh over a mold, and

24.8
An experimental concrete floor system designed by Pier Luigi Nervi for the Gotti Wool Factory in Rome (1953).

then spraying lightweight cement over the resulting shape. Because these could be—sort of—mass-produced, and because they could be made in virtually any shape, the resulting buildings have interesting ceiling patterns. In one case (the Gatti Wool Mill) the resulting "joists" conform to the lines of stress found in a typical two-way slab.

EVOLUTIONS IN SLAB EFFICIENCY

There are two basic strategies for manipulating the form of slabs to make them more efficient and or available for long-span structures: first, the slab surface can be bent and re-oriented to be more in line with the loading applied to it (to create a structural shell system), or the slab can be tilted on its edge, creating a wall/girder or a structural plate. These types of modifications essentially try to resist the stress applied to them not simply through resistance of section, but by employing the entire surface of the slab to help. In order to make a surface-resistant structure, the slab can no longer be flat—it must be tilted up, folded, or curved.

As we noticed from the previous Figure 24.1, a two-way slab under loading, the slab deflection takes on the natural funicular form of a suspended flexible plane of material, like a blanket held by its corners—this strategy tells us that the surface of the slab itself could be curved or shaped in a manner that is responsive to particular loads. A simple experiment with a piece of paper shows that by bending the paper, we can form a lightweight structure that can now hold a fairly heavy load (Figure 24.9).

This type of structural strategy is called a surface-resisting structure and includes highly expressive and efficient structural forms like domes, vaults, and thin shell systems. Flat plate sections can also be tipped up and "folded" together to create another efficient type of spatial enclosure. Simply by tilting a slab on its end it goes from being a very shallow and inefficient "beam" to a tall strong slab of concrete loaded parallel to its access-plate action. Corrugated roof decks are the smallest-scale example of this, but large-scale concrete plates have been used for aircraft hangars, sports arenas, and grand-

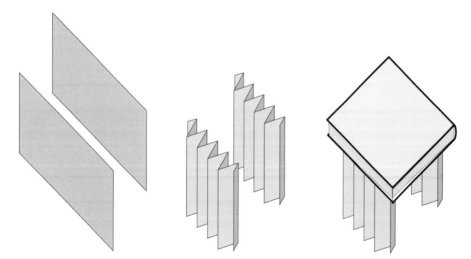

24.9
Like paper, slabs can be folded to increase bearing capacity and stability of shape.

stand roofs (See Chapter 28, Long-span Structures). All of the strategies that make slabs relatively efficient are also applicable to these systems, but as we will see in the section on long-span systems, the type of stresses within the system may vary.

When manipulating the cross-section shape isn't an option, or when a particular level of thinness is desired architecturally, slabs can still be made highly efficient through a process called post-tensioning. In this process, un-bonded reinforcing tendons are tensed with a hydraulic jack after the concrete has been poured (again creating a camber) so that when all the imposed loads are placed on the slab, it will maintain a flat shape. In effect, it is allowing the rebar to take a high amount of tensile stress. Post-tensioning can allow significantly long-spans in slabs, but long-spans are generally more economical when they consist of beams and girders. A similar process called prestressing induces an upward curve, or camber, to a structural shape before it is loaded so that its final position after loading is flat. A slightly more complex method of increasing a concrete beam's efficiency is through the introduction of additional steel members in areas undergoing tension. In *post-tensioned* beams, rubber or metal ducts are cast into the member in strategic locations. After curing, steel cables are threaded through these ducts and tightened using jacks or drills. Once tight, these cables take additional tensile load (this can also be thought of as putting the beam into artificially induced compression, taking the job of absorbing tension). In precast situations, these cables may be tightened against a formwork first, and released against the concrete after it has cured. This is known as *pre-tensioning*. The generic name for this technique is *prestressing*, denoting the fact that the concrete is assisted by the steel before it undergoes its service load (Figure 24.10).

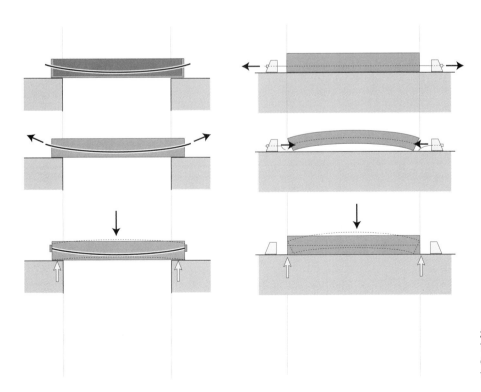

24.10
To make a slab more structurally effective it can be prestressed in two ways.

CONCLUSION

The behavior of slabs can be understood as an extension of beam theory and design. The cross-sectional profile and longitudinal strategies of beam design can be duplicated and arrayed in order to create a continuous structural slab. Slabs can array a series of horizontally spanning components ("beams") in an arrangement that is in either one-way or two-way orientation. As a result, various materials and assemblies are possible for the resulting structure. These choices affect the overall layout and placement of supports, construction considerations, and overall building behavior. The inherent inefficiencies found in particular slab arrangements can also suggest several different types of structural forms that aren't flat slabs—by curving or folding the slab, more efficient longer-span structural types become possible.

FREQUENTLY ASKED QUESTIONS

Why are the dimensions of waffle slabs limited to sizes like 2'-0" and 4'-0" square?
Because waffle slabs are poured using metal pans for formwork, we're limited to a fairly standard set of pan sizes to actually form the slab. We could custom make a whole set of pans to whatever dimensions we wanted, but this would incur a fairly substantial cost. We can tune the distance between the pans (or "domes") if wider ribs are acceptable. One way metal pans can telescope, so their length is variable.

GLOSSARY

Column cap: A conical or rectilinear element between a column and a floor plate that is designed to spread the shear force between the two over a wider cross-sectional area.

Folded plate: A thin, planar structural system that relies on "folds" or bends in its cross–section to develop bending resistance.

One-way slab (or plate): A thin, planar structural system that gains most of its structural performance from simple bending resistance along the axis of the span.

Pan joists: In concrete construction, a system of downstand concrete joists made by pouring concrete between long, linear metal pans placed upside down.

Plate: A thin slab. Slab denotes a heavy, thick material, while plate is more descriptive of metal or wood.

Slab: A structural member that gains some of its performance by two-way resistance to bending.

Two-way slab (or plate): A thin, planar structural system that gains its structural performance from a combination of bending along *and across* the axis of the span.

Waffle slab: A two-way concrete slab system made by pouring concrete between square "domes" to form a network of intersecting concrete joists.

FURTHER READING

Bill, M. (1949). *Robert Maillart*. Zurich: Verlag.

Nervi, P. L. (1958). *Structures*. New York: F.W. Dodge; pp. 98–103.

Salvadori, M. (1975). *Structure in Architecture: The Art of Building*, 2nd edition. Englewood
    Cliffs: Prentice-Hall; Chapter 10, Grids, Plates, and Folded Plates, pp. 239–292.

25

COLUMN DESIGN

Columns	Behavior and buckling
	Eccentricity in loading conditions
Buckling	Why buckling occurs in columns
	Ways to prevent columns from buckling
Column Design	Slenderness ratio
	Radius of gyration
	Effective column length and K

INTRODUCTION

At its most basic level, structural design is about creating strategies for spanning and stacking elements in an effective, affordable, and interesting manner. There is an inextricable relationship between how we span and how we stack that is related to the magnitude of loads that are developed within the system and the manner of their transmission. The previous sections have looked at the unique conditions and behaviors found in structural components that span, such as beams and slabs, including their ability to resist stress internally and effectively transfer applied loads to their supports. Spanning elements are stacked on top of each other throughout the building and eventually consolidate all of the loads to specific locations where they can be transmitted vertically through the columns and down to the foundations. Architecturally, this ability to intentionally craft a structural system that predictably transfers its loads to specific points allows the supports to be efficiently sized and accurately placed. Thinner support elements, such as columns, provide a beneficial degree of openness and flexibility of use to the space. When developed as an array of supports, the placement of columns defines architectural space, suggests potential organizational strategies within the space, and expresses the organizing logic for the structural design strategy (Figure 25.1).

Previously, we have noted that supports, or reactions, help keep a system in equilibrium and we have assumed that the vertical support element would be able to develop enough capacity to resist this compression. However, resisting compression forces is the easy part of column design—as we will see in this

25.1
Thomas Phifer's expansion of Lee
Hall at Clemson University (2012).

section, columns tend to bend before they break and as a result, they require a unique set of design responses intended to prevent this from happening.

In this section we will discuss the key elements of structural behavior in columns, including their susceptibility to a particular mode of failure, and how the material, shape, proportion, and connections of columns can be designed to help resist failure. We will demonstrate how different columns can be sized based on loading and length, and look at ways that columns can be made more efficient by changing their shape.

COLUMN BEHAVIOR AND BUCKLING

Sizing an axially loaded structural element, like a column under compression, ostensibly should simply be a matter of matching the allowable stress level of the material against the ratio of the load and cross-sectional area as was described in Chapter 21. According to the relevant equation: $f = P/A$, this element could theoretically be *any* height as long as the amount of deflection (determined by the equation $e = P \times L/A \times E$) was determined to be within an acceptable range. Even a theoretical mile-high steel column, shown in Figure 25.2, would only deflect a modest amount under relatively high levels of loading. We know, of course, that this is absurd and the column would be certain to *buckle*. So how do we explain this behavior and develop means to help prevent it?

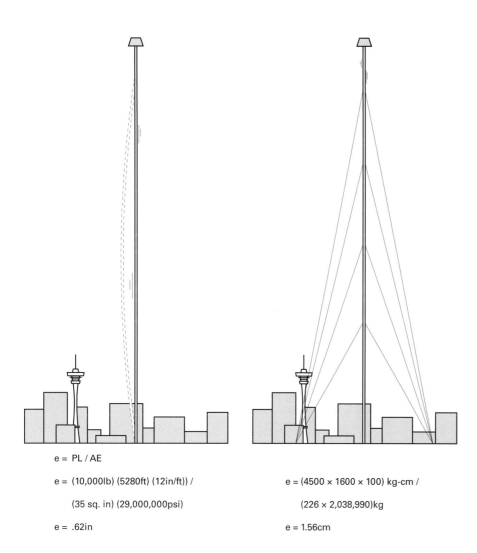

e = PL / AE

e = (10,000lb) (5280ft) (12in/ft)) /

    (35 sq. in) (29,000,000psi)

e = .62in

e = (4500 × 1600 × 100) kg-cm /

    (226 × 2,038,990)kg

e = 1.56cm

25.2
Mario Salvadori's "Mile High Column" example.

First, it is important to note that purely vertical compression loading is more theoretical than practical—columns aren't perfectly straight and vertical loads aren't applied exactly at the centroid. There can also be small imperfections of material or a shift in the orientation of the loading applied to the column that causes problems. These slight variations in the location of the load induce bending into the column and this bending can cause buckling.

In simplest terms, buckling is a state of instability that occurs within all compressive members in a structural system—it is characterized by an unexpected shift of the column's orientation as it bows out the side under loading. When this occurs, loads try to find the shortest, most direct path to resolution—for a long column, the most direct path is to bend the column out of the way rather than to compress it. This complicates the design of columns because these forces may buckle the column in any direction.

As columns begin to buckle to the side, the center of gravity of the column will move out from under the center the load so that it is no longer imparting only an axial force on the column, but bending stress as well. This shift in column position exacerbates the problem because as the column flexes from its original position, the load will actually tend to push the column further

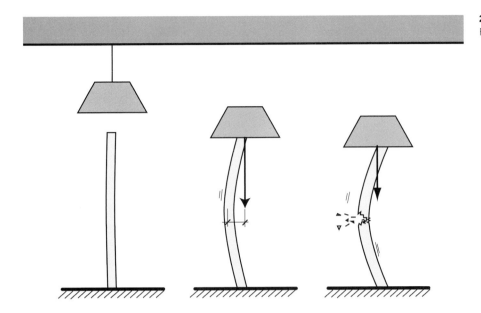

out—and as the column moves further, the moment induced by the load will increase (Figure 25.3). This creates a positive feedback loop that can cause column failure to accelerate rapidly with even just a surprisingly small load.

At this point where the column starts to bend, the column must have the capacity to resist against this bending—a capacity that depends upon the column having sectional-resistant capacities that were discussed in beam design. Quite unlike beams, which can be shaped to efficiently resist bending in a predictable orientation, columns must develop cross sectional shapes that allow for potential bending resistance in all directions as the direction a column may buckle is unpredictable.

COLUMN CONNECTIONS AND ECCENTRIC LOADS

The manner in which the load is transferred from the spanning member to the column may also induce buckling. Most of our diagrams and calculations have assumed the ideal manner of load transfer between these two elements—in other words, a direct transfer of vertical force through the centroid of the column—but quite often the physical limitations of the structural shapes and materials may necessitate a type of connection to each other that transfers the load slightly off-center, producing an *eccentric* load (Figure 25.4). Because the beam is being bent by this eccentric load, columns have to be sized and tested using a calculation similar to the flexure formula to determine if the maximum stress in the column can be accommodated. Specifically the formula looks at the column's capacity to resist compressive stresses because, under these loading conditions, the column takes a "double dose" of compression stresses from axial loading and bending. As a result, the strength of most columns will be limited by the ability to resist compressive stresses on one side.

If the column is subjected to compressive stresses that reach the material's plastic limit, a progressive failure will occur. Column failure is a particularly

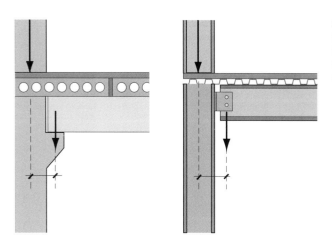

25.4
Eccentric loading can occur when the connection point of horizontal spanning members isn't rested direct on the column centroid. Columns must be sized to resist bending caused by this eccentricity.

serious problem. If beams or slabs break under loading, other elements connected to these components could help assist with the added loading resistance, but because the column is the only vertical, load-bearing structural component, there are no redundancies in the structural system. If a column fails, all of the loads that had been intentionally consolidated to this single point become unsupported, wreaking havoc on the designed state of support equilibrium throughout the system and potentially causing the collapse of the entire floor area whose loads "flow" to that column. Column failures, therefore, are usually catastrophic, and factors of safety for these elements tend to be higher than for beams.

Solving for a safe column load is mathematically complex and notoriously difficult. However, for our purposes, we can look at a handful of factors, and rely on handbooks, charts, and simple calculations to size columns with some confidence. Such calculations rely on empirical evidence more than theory—essentially documenting what's worked safely before—but the solicitation of professional expertise in column design is essential.

COLUMN DESIGN—FOUR FACTORS

The tendency of columns to buckle is regulated by four factors—the ability of the *material* to resist compression, the resistance to buckling provided by the *shape*, the ability for the column's *end* conditions to modify the structural behavior of columns, and the columns height to width ratio of *slenderness*.

A column's *material* qualities are important determinants of its relative level of strength and stiffness. In column design, engineers begin by looking at a column's stiffness to measure its potential resistance to deflection under loading. If the material is fairly stiff, like steel, it will not move much to start with, and the progressive effects of loading and deflecting will be limited.

Much like beam design, the cross sectional *shape* of a column has a major influence on its ability to carry loads. While compressive strength is measured by simply dividing the allowable load by cross sectional area, buckling resistance requires us to assess where the material is in that cross section. Area, of course, is critical, but so is location. With beams, we found the moment of inertia of various sections, which told us something about the distribution of material across a structural cross section. For columns, we use a related value, the *radius of gyration.* This value is equal to the square root of I/A, the moment of inertia divided by the area of the shape:

$$r = \sqrt{(I/A)}$$

We can see that the radius of gyration, r, is directly related to the moment of inertia, I, and inversely proportional to a shape's area, A. While not strictly correct, it may be useful to think of the radius of gyration as the *average width* of a section measured about a particular axis. Good column shapes, like good beam shapes, put the most material at the outer edges of the section. But, since we don't know in which direction bending may start, it's not enough to just put the material on two edges. Instead, it has to be deployed *around* the outside of the column's shape. The most efficient column shapes are thus hollow tubes—square or round—that dispense entirely with a web and put *all* of their material at their outer edge.

Because there is no way to predict which direction a column may begin to bend under loading, structural designers are interested in how columns will perform in multiple directions, in an attempt to determine the worst-case value for the radius of gyration (Figure 25.5). If a column's shape is anything but a hollow tube, this can be determined by looking at the shape's moment of inertia value for both the x–x and y–y directions. Any difference in the shape/distribution of area from the centroid establishes a weaker axis in the column. For example, in steel wide flange shapes, the x–x axis has a very strong resistance

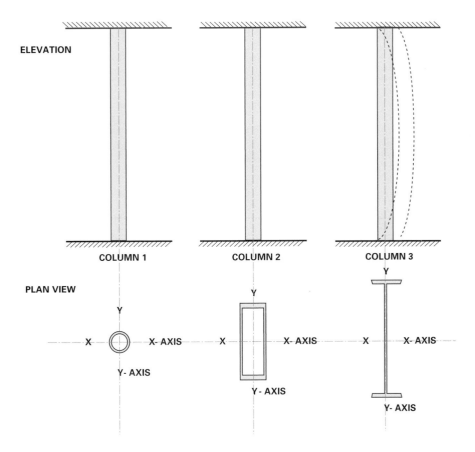

25.5
Radius of gyration comparison of three different columns.

to buckling/bending thanks to the flanges, but in the y–y axis, there is very little area distributed away from the centroid in this orientation. Therefore, the radius of gyration of this shape would assume the lower value for the moment of inertia. While W-shapes are often used instead of tubes because of their lower fabrication costs, the best choices for column shapes are so-called "compact" sections that tend to be square, with relatively deep flanges. Comparisons of related column shapes, their moment of inertia values, areas, and a reasonably accurate measure of their efficiency are given in Figure 25.6.

The third factor needed to design a column depends on the nature of a column's *end conditions*, and the degree to which these types of connections inhibit, or induce, the sort of bending that produces buckling. Although frames will be discussed in Chapter 27, it is worth noting that *how* structural elements are connected to each other is an intentional design choice intended to affect the amount, and type, of stress occurring within each element. For example, if a column wants to rotate independently from the foundation and beam above, it would have a pinned connection at both ends. Besides pinned connections (which allow rotation without translation), the end conditions of a column can be fixed with a moment connection (allowing neither rotation nor translation), and/ or they can be attached by a roller (allowing rotation and translation). All of these choices will affect the buckling tendencies of columns—fixed connections will

25.6
Comparative shapes for columns showing worst-case moment of inertia (I), area (A), and radius of gyration (r).

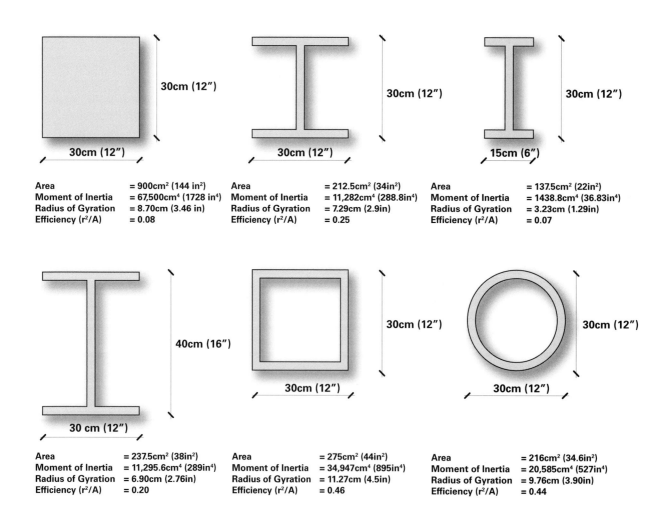

Area	= 900cm² (144 in²)
Moment of Inertia	= 67,500cm⁴ (1728 in⁴)
Radius of Gyration	= 8.70cm (3.46 in)
Efficiency (r²/A)	= 0.08

Area	= 212.5cm² (34in²)
Moment of Inertia	= 11,282cm⁴ (288.8in⁴)
Radius of Gyration	= 7.29cm (2.9in)
Efficiency (r²/A)	= 0.25

Area	= 137.5cm² (22in²)
Moment of Inertia	= 1438.8cm⁴ (36.83in⁴)
Radius of Gyration	= 3.23cm (1.29in)
Efficiency (r²/A)	= 0.07

Area	= 237.5cm² (38in²)
Moment of Inertia	= 11,295.6cm⁴ (289in⁴)
Radius of Gyration	= 6.90cm (2.76in)
Efficiency (r²/A)	= 0.20

Area	= 275cm² (44in²)
Moment of Inertia	= 34,947cm⁴ (895in⁴)
Radius of Gyration	= 11.27cm (4.5in)
Efficiency (r²/A)	= 0.46

Area	= 216cm² (34.6in²)
Moment of Inertia	= 20,585cm⁴ (527in⁴)
Radius of Gyration	= 9.76cm (3.90in)
Efficiency (r²/A)	= 0.44

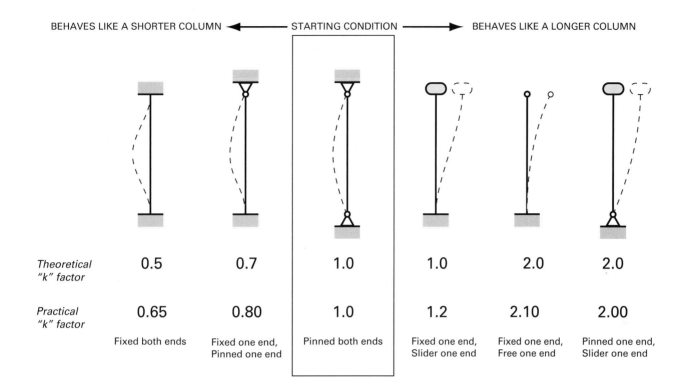

BEHAVES LIKE A SHORTER COLUMN ←		STARTING CONDITION →		BEHAVES LIKE A LONGER COLUMN	

Theoretical "k" factor   0.5   0.7   1.0   1.0   2.0   2.0

Practical "k" factor   0.65   0.80   1.0   1.2   2.10   2.00

Fixed both ends | Fixed one end, Pinned one end | Pinned both ends | Fixed one end, Slider one end | Fixed one end, Free one end | Pinned one end, Slider one end

25.7
Modifying factors for column design based upon end condition connections (k).

inhibit the sort of bending that induces buckling by 'recruiting' the stiffness of the supporting material to resist bending, while "looser" connections will allow columns to bend and thus buckle more freely. Therefore, to design columns we first assign a multiplier to the column's actual length to find the column's *effective length*.

A particular value, K, is assigned to each column depending on the end conditions. This value is multiplied times the column's actual length (K × L) to more accurately reflect the column's changing behavior (Figure 25.7). The base condition for determining the column's effective length is the pinned condition on each end—this has a theoretical K value of 1.0. A fixed connection at both ends results in a K value of 0.5, while an unfixed connection at one end results in a K value of 2.0. What this means is that a column that is fixed at both ends will theoretically deflect only half the distance as a similar column with pinned connections at both ends—in other words, it will behave as though it is a shorter column and will therefore have less of a tendency to deflect and buckle. In addition to the "theoretical" K values, tables typically give "recommended" values, indicating the complexity of actual behavior; these represent a factor of safety added to the empirically derived values and *these* should be the K-value used in designing columns.

The final factor in column design, *slenderness* is a unit-less ratio of a column's effective length to its width: K × L/r. More specifically it looks at the ratio between the column's effective length (as determined by the end conditions) and the worst-case scenario value for buckling resistance, defined as the least radius of gyration, r, (Figure 25.8). For simple rectangular sections, this is expressed as L/d, where L is the column length and d is the least dimension of the cross section. For complex sections, we replace d with r, the radius of gyration.

Depending on their slenderness ratio, columns can be classified as short,

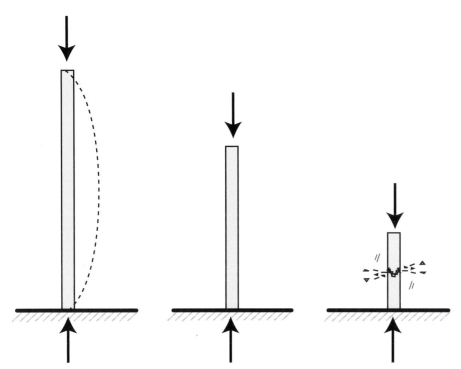

25.8
Columns with a high slenderness ratio will fail by buckling; the mode of failure for intermediate columns isn't easily predictable.

intermediate, or long. Short columns won't have a tendency to buckle (they are relatively thick compared to length) so their mode of failure would occur by crushing at the yield limit of the material. Intermediate columns can fail by either buckling or crushing and so predicting the behavior of columns within a certain range of proportions depends upon empirical testing of performance. Long columns, predictably, will always fail in buckling. The value of this ratio differs by material, for instance a long wood column has slenderness ratio between 30 and 50 whereas a steel column's may be classified as a long column if its ratio is over 150, but it should not exceed 200. Once a column has been sized, the slenderness ratio can be checked against these limits.

Certain critical mathematical relationships relevant to column design were published 1757 by the Swiss mathematician, Leonard Euler, including the key observations about the role of slenderness in columns (long before any slender columns had been built—or even conceived). Euler discovered that buckling is related to the proportions of a column (specifically its slenderness) and its relative stiffness (modulus of elasticity) and that the ultimate fiber strength (or yield stress) of a material is *irrelevant* for long slender column design because they will buckle before they break. Thus, columns of a certain length tend to be more nearly the same size than we might expect, no matter what the material. Stiffer materials may be more slender, but stronger materials may not be.

Euler developed a formula that identified the load at which a given column of a particular length could be expected to fail in buckling. This amount is known as the Euler Load and for columns it is more important than the allowable compressive stress. In the formula, P is the critical buckling load/Euler Load, E is the modulus of elasticity for the column material, I is the moment of inertia for the column's cross section, and L is the effective length (after modification from end condition):

$$P = \pi^2 \times E \times I / L^2$$

Obviously from the equation, the length of the column is the most influential variable, which is what we would expect, but a very stiff material with a high modulus of elasticity value helps considerably as well.

Even though buckling is a concern, it is worth pointing out that columns can take an enormous amount of weight. For example, using Euler's formula we can find the capacity for a modestly sized A36 steel column, such as a W16 × 40 (W410 × 60) with a moment of inertia of 273in^4 (610,837cm^4) we would find the maximum load of:

$$P = (3.14)^2 \times 29{,}000{,}000\text{psi} \times 273\text{in}^4 / (33\text{ft} \times 12\text{in/ft})^2 = 497{,}770\text{lb}$$
$$P = (3.14)^2 \times 2{,}038{,}990\text{kg/cm}^2 \times 610{,}837\text{cm}^4 / (10\text{m} \times 100\text{cm/m})^2 = 225{,}784\text{kg}$$

This means that one column this size could hold up four floors of loading with a bay size of 1000ft^2 at 124lb/ft^2. However, because of the potentially catastrophic effects of column failure, we don't want to come close to this level of loading. This equation has no factor of safety. However, in order to actually size a column we can rely upon published tables of empirically derived—and usually conservative—allowable stresses for columns of typical structural materials. Tables for steel are published by the American Institute of Steel Construction (AISC), while those for various types of timber are published by the National Lumber Manufacturers Association and the Southern Pine Association.

Because of the data published in these tables, we essentially only need to know the load acting upon the column and the effective length (K × L) to find acceptable range of column size (or if one knew a desired column size and length, an allowable load amount could be found). After a column is selected we will need to check its slenderness ratio against the maximum slenderness ratio recommendations for its material. For our purposes, a design guide of summary information for common shapes in steel and wood is shown in Tables 25.1, 25.2 and 25.3.

Example: *Design a column carrying 30,000lb (13,500kg) of floor load for a warehouse floor with story height of 20ft (6m) in Southern Pine (allowable load 105kg/cm^2 or 1500psi) and compare this column size with a steel column under the same conditions. The column is pinned at one end and fixed at the other.*

Solution: From the chart shown in Figure 25.7, we find that a column pinned at one end and fixed at the other has a recommended design value for K of 0.80. The column's *effective length*, Le, is therefore:

$$Le = K \times L$$

Le = (0.80) (6m)	Le = (0.80) (20ft)
Le = 4.8m	Le = 16ft

For Southern Pine, we begin with the top row and select the effective length, Le, for the member, in this case 16ft (4.8m). Reading down from here, we find that there are no listings for columns smaller than a 6 × 8 (150 × 200) member. The allowable loading for

Table 25.1 Allowable axial loading for selected A 36 steel column shapes.

NOMINAL SIZE— METRIC	NOMINAL SIZE— IMPERIAL	EFFECTIVE UNSUPPORTED LENGTH (KL) WITH RESPECT TO LEAST RADIUS OF GYRATION–METRES														
		1.80M (6')		2.10M (7')		2.4M (8')		2.7M (9')		3.0M (10')		3.3M (11')		3.6M (12')		3.9M (13')	
		kg (000)	lb (000)	kg (000)	lb (000)	kg (000)	lb (000)	kg (000)	lb (000)	kg (000)	lb (000)	kg (000)	lb (000)	kg (000)	lb (000)	kg (000)	lb (000)
W 100 × 19	W 4 × 13	28	62	26	57	23	51	20	45	18	39	14	32	12	27	10	23
W 130 × 24	W 5 × 16	37	83	36	79	33	74	31	69	29	64	26	58	23	52	21	46
W 150 × 24	W 6 × 16	38	85	36	81	35	78	33	74	32	70	29	65	27	60	25	55
W 130 × 28	W 5 × 19	44	97	41	92	39	87	36	81	34	75	31	69	28	62	25	55
W 150 × 30	W 6 × 20	49	109	47	105	45	101	43	96	41	91	38	85	36	80	33	74
W 150 × 37	W 6 × 25	62	137	59	132	57	126	54	120	51	114	48	107	45	100	42	93
W 200 × 46	W 8 × 31	80	178	78	174	76	169	74	164	72	159	69	154	67	148	64	142
W 250 × 49	W 10 × 33	85	189	83	184	81	179	78	173	75	167	72	161	70	155	67	149
W 200 × 52	W 8 × 35	90	201	89	197	86	191	84	186	81	180	78	174	76	168	73	162
W 250 × 58	W 10 × 39	101	224	98	218	95	212	93	206	90	199	87	193	83	185	80	178
W 200 × 59	W 8 × 40	104	230	101	225	99	219	96	213	93	206	90	200	87	193	83	185
W 200 × 71	W 8 × 48	125	277	122	270	119	264	116	257	112	249	108	241	105	233	101	224
W 250 × 73	W 10 × 49	130	289	128	284	126	279	123	273	121	268	118	262	115	256	112	249
W 310 × 79	W 12 × 53	140	312	138	307	135	301	133	295	130	288	127	282	124	275	120	267
W 250 × 80	W 10 × 54	144	319	141	313	139	308	136	302	133	296	130	289	127	282	124	275
W 200 × 86	W 8 × 58	151	335	147	327	144	319	140	311	136	302	132	293	127	283	123	273
W 310 × 86	W 12 × 58	154	342	151	336	149	330	145	323	142	316	139	309	136	302	132	294
W 250 × 89	W 10 × 60	160	355	157	349	154	343	151	336	148	329	145	322	141	314	138	307
W 360 × 91	W 14 × 61	162	359	158	352	155	345	152	338	149	331	145	323	142	315	138	306
W 200 × 100	W 8 × 67	174	387	171	379	167	370	162	360	158	350	153	339	148	328	142	316
W 310 × 97	W 12 × 65	175	389	173	384	171	379	168	373	165	367	162	361	160	355	157	348
W 360 × 101	W 14 × 68	180	400	177	393	173	385	170	377	166	369	162	360	158	351	154	342
W 250 × 101	W 10 × 68	181	402	178	395	175	388	171	381	168	373	164	365	161	357	157	348
W 310 × 107	W 12 × 72	194	431	191	425	189	420	186	413	183	407	180	400	177	393	174	386
W 360 × 110	W 14 × 74	196	436	193	429	189	421	185	412	181	403	177	394	173	384	168	373
W 250 × 115	W 10 × 77	204	454	201	447	198	439	194	431	190	422	186	413	182	404	177	394
W 250 × 115	W 10 × 77	205	456	202	448	198	440	194	432	191	424	186	414	182	405	178	395
W 310 × 117	W 12 × 79	213	473	210	467	207	461	204	454	201	447	198	439	194	432	191	424
W 360 × 122	W 14 × 82	217	482	213	474	209	465	205	456	201	446	196	435	191	425	186	413
W 250 × 131	W 10 × 88	234	521	231	513	227	504	223	495	218	485	214	475	209	464	204	453
W 310 × 129	W 12 × 87	235	522	232	515	229	508	225	501	222	493	218	485	215	477	211	468
W 360 × 134	W 14 × 90	246	547	243	541	241	536	239	530	236	524	233	517	230	511	227	504
W 310 × 143	W 12 × 96	259	575	256	568	252	560	248	552	245	544	241	535	237	526	232	516
W 310 × 158	W 12 × 106	286	636	283	628	279	620	275	611	271	602	266	592	262	582	257	572
W 360 × 162	W 14 × 109	297	661	294	654	291	647	288	640	285	633	282	626	278	618	274	609
W 310 × 179	W 12 × 120	324	721	320	712	316	702	311	692	307	682	302	671	297	660	292	648

Note: *Consult AISC Steel Handbook for full range of structural shapes*

(FEET) IN KIPS AND KG × 1000

4.2M (14')		4.5M (15')'		4.8M (16')		5.1M (17')		5.4M (18')		5.7M (19')		6.0M (20')		6.3M (21')		6.6M (22')		7.0M (23')	
kg (000)	lb (000)	kg (000)	lb (000)	kg (000)	lb (000)	kg (000)	lb (000)	kg (000)	lb (000)	kg (000)	lb (000)	kg (000)	lb (000)	kg (000)	lb (000)	kg (000)	lb (000)	kg (000)	lb (000)
9	20	8	17	7	15														
18	39	15	34	14	30	12	27	11	24	9	21	9	19	8	18				
23	50	20	45	18	39	16	35	14	31	13	28	11	25	10	23	9	21	9	19
21	47	18	41	16	36	14	32	13	29	12	26	10	23	9	21				
30	67	27	61	24	54	22	48	19	42	17	38	15	34	14	31	13	28	12	26
38	85	35	77	31	69	27	61	25	55	22	49	20	44	18	40	16	36	15	33
61	136	59	130	55	123	53	117	50	110	46	102	43	95	39	87	36	79	32	72
64	142	61	135	57	127	54	120	50	112	46	103	43	95	39	86	35	78	32	72
70	155	67	148	63	141	60	133	56	125	53	117	49	109	45	100	41	91	37	83
77	170	73	162	69	153	65	145	61	135	57	126	52	116	48	106	43	96	40	88
80	177	77	170	72	161	69	153	65	144	60	134	56	125	52	115	47	105	43	96
97	215	93	206	89	197	84	187	79	176	74	165	69	154	64	143	59	131	54	120
109	242	106	235	103	228	99	221	96	213	92	205	89	197	85	188	81	180	77	171
117	260	113	252	110	244	106	235	102	227	98	218	94	209	90	199	85	189	81	179
121	268	117	260	114	253	110	244	106	236	102	227	98	218	94	209	90	200	86	190
118	262	113	251	108	239	103	228	97	215	91	202	85	189	79	175	72	161	66	147
129	286	125	277	121	269	117	260	113	250	108	241	104	231	99	221	95	210	90	199
135	299	131	290	126	281	122	272	118	263	114	254	110	244	105	234	100	223	95	212
134	297	130	288	126	279	121	269	117	259	112	248	107	237	102	226	97	215	91	203
137	304	131	292	126	279	119	265	113	251	106	236	99	221	93	206	86	190	78	174
153	341	150	334	147	326	144	319	140	311	136	303	133	295	129	286	125	277	121	268
149	332	145	322	140	311	135	301	130	289	125	278	120	266	114	253	108	241	102	227
153	339	149	330	144	320	140	310	135	299	130	289	125	278	120	267	115	255	109	242
170	378	167	370	163	362	159	354	155	345	151	336	147	327	143	318	139	308	135	299
163	363	158	352	153	341	148	329	143	317	137	304	131	292	125	278	119	265	113	250
173	384	168	373	163	362	158	351	153	339	147	327	142	315	136	302	130	289	124	275
173	385	168	374	163	363	158	352	153	340	148	328	142	316	136	303	131	290	124	276
187	415	183	407	179	398	175	389	171	380	167	370	162	360	158	350	153	339	148	328
181	402	175	389	170	377	163	363	158	351	152	337	145	323	139	308	132	293	125	277
199	442	194	430	188	417	182	405	176	392	170	378	164	364	157	349	151	335	144	319
207	459	203	450	198	440	194	430	189	420	184	409	179	398	174	386	169	376	164	364
224	497	220	489	217	482	213	474	210	466	206	458	202	449	198	440	194	432	190	422
228	506	223	496	219	486	214	475	209	464	203	452	198	440	193	428	187	416	181	403
252	561	248	550	242	538	237	526	231	514	226	502	220	489	214	475	208	462	202	448
270	601	266	592	262	583	258	574	254	564	249	554	245	544	240	533	235	523	230	512
286	636	281	624	275	611	269	597	263	584	256	569	250	555	243	540	236	525	222	493

Table 25.2 Allowable axial loading for selected A 36 steel tube column shapes.

NOMINAL SIZE— METRIC	NOMINAL SIZE— IMPERIAL	WEIGHT		EFFECTIVE UNSUPPORTED LENGTH (KL) WITH RESPECT TO LEAST RADIUS OF GYRATION–												
				1.80M (6')		2.10M (7')		2.4M (8')		2.7M (9')		3.0M (10')		3.3M (11')		3.6M (12')	
		kg/m	lb/ft	kg (000)	lb (000)	kg (000)	lb (000)	kg (000)	lb (000)	kg (000)	lb (000)	kg (000)	lb (000)	kg (000)	lb (000)	kg (000)	lb (000)
75mm Pipe	3" Pipe	11.30	7.58	17	38	16	36	15	34	14	31	13	28	11	25	10	22
89mm Pipe	3.5" Pipe	13.58	9.11	22	48	21	46	20	44	18	41	17	38	16	35	14	32
76 × 76 × 6.4	3 × 3 × ¼	13.13	8.81	24	53	22	49	20	44	17	38	15	33	12	27	10	23
75mm Extra Strong Pipe	3" Extra Strong Pipe	15.28	10.25	23	52	22	48	20	45	18	41	17	37	15	33	13	28
102mm Pipe	4" Pipe	16.09	10.79	27	59	26	57	24	54	23	52	22	49	21	46	19	43
102 × 102 × 4.8	4 × 4 × 3/16	14.04	9.42	29	64	27	61	26	58	25	55	23	51	21	47	19	43
89mm Extra Strong Pipe	3.5" Extra Strong Pipe	18.63	12.50	30	66	28	63	27	59	25	55	23	51	21	47	19	43
102mm Extra Strong Pipe	4" Extra Strong Pipe	22.33	14.98	36	81	35	78	34	75	32	71	30	67	28	63	27	59
75mm Double Extra Strong Pipe	3" Double Extra Strong Pipe	27.70	18.58	41	91	38	84	35	77	31	69	27	60	23	51	19	43
127mm Pipe	5" Pipe	21.79	14.62	37	83	36	81	35	78	34	76	33	73	32	71	31	68
102 × 102 × 7.9	4 × 4 × 5/16	22.11	14.83	45	100	43	95	41	90	38	84	35	78	32	72	29	65
152 × 152 × 4.8	6 × 6 × 3/16	21.66	14.53	48	107	47	105	46	102	45	99	43	96	42	93	41	90
152mm Pipe	6" Pipe	28.28	18.97	50	110	49	108	48	106	46	103	45	101	44	98	43	95
127mm Extra Strong Pipe	5" Extra Strong Pipe	30.98	20.78	53	118	51	114	50	111	48	107	46	103	45	99	43	95
102mm Double Extra Strong Pipe	4" Double Extra Strong Pipe	41.06	27.54	66	147	63	140	60	133	57	126	53	118	49	109	45	100
152mm Extra Strong Pipe	6" Extra Strong Pipe	42.59	28.57	75	166	73	162	72	159	70	155	68	151	66	146	64	142
203mm Pipe	8" Pipe	42.56	28.55	77	171	76	168	75	166	73	163	72	161	71	158	70	155
203 × 203 × 6.4	8 × 8 × ¼	38.49	25.82	88	196	87	193	86	190	84	187	83	184	81	180	79	176
152 × 152 × 9.5	6 × 6 × 3/8	40.97	27.48	90	201	88	196	86	191	84	186	81	180	78	174	76	168
127mm Double Extra Strong Pipe	5" Double Extra Strong Pipe	57.47	38.55	97	216	94	209	91	202	88	195	84	187	80	178	77	170

METRES (FEET) IN KIPS AND KG × 1000

3.9M (13')		4.2M (14')		4.5M (15')'		4.8M (16')		5.1M (17')		5.4M (18')		5.7M (19')		6.0M (20')		6.3M (21')		6.6M (22')		7.0M (23')	
kg (000)	lb (000)	kg (000)	lb (000)	kg (000)	lb (000)	kg (000)	lb (000)	kg (000)	lb (000)	kg (000)	lb (000)	kg (000)	lb (000)	kg (000)	lb (000)	kg (000)	lb (000)	kg (000)	lb (000)	kg (000)	lb (000)
9	19	7	16	6	14	5	12	5	11	5	10	4	9								
13	29	11	25	10	22	9	19	8	17	7	15	6	14	5	12	5	11	5	10		
9	19	8	17	7	15	6	13	5	11	5	10										
11	24	9	21	8	18	7	16	5	12	5	11										
18	40	16	36	15	33	13	29	12	26	10	23	9	21	9	19	8	17	7	15	6	14
18	39	16	35	14	30	12	27	11	24	9	21	9	19	8	17	7	16	6	14	6	13
17	38	15	33	13	29	11	25	10	23	9	20	8	18	7	16	6	14				
24	54	22	49	20	44	18	39	16	35	14	31	13	28	11	25	10	22	9	21	9	19
17	37	14	32	13	28	11	24	10	22												
29	65	29	64	26	58	25	55	23	51	21	47	19	43	18	39	16	36	14	32	13	30
26	58	23	51	20	44	18	39	15	34	14	31	13	28	11	25	10	23	9	21	9	19
39	87	37	83	36	80	34	76	32	72	31	68	29	64	27	60	25	56	23	51	19	43
41	92	40	89	39	86	37	82	36	79	34	75	32	71	30	67	28	63	27	59	25	55
41	91	39	86	36	81	34	76	32	71	29	65	27	59	24	54	22	48	20	44	18	41
41	91	36	81	32	70	28	62	25	55	22	49	20	44	18	40	16	37	15	33		
62	137	59	132	57	127	55	122	52	117	50	111	47	105	45	99	41	92	39	86	36	80
68	152	67	149	65	145	64	142	62	138	61	135	59	131	57	127	55	123	54	119	52	115
78	173	76	169	74	165	72	160	70	156	68	151	66	147	64	142	62	137	59	132	57	127
72	161	69	154	66	147	63	140	59	132	56	124	52	115	48	107	44	98	40	89	34	75
72	160	68	151	63	141	59	130	54	119	49	108	44	97	39	87	36	80	32	72	30	67

(continued overleaf)

Table 25.2 (continued)

NOMINAL SIZE—METRIC	NOMINAL SIZE—IMPERIAL	WEIGHT		EFFECTIVE UNSUPPORTED LENGTH (KL) WITH RESPECT TO LEAST RADIUS OF GYRATION—												
				1.80M (6')		2.10M (7')		2.4M (8')		2.7M (9')		3.0M (10')		3.3M (11')		3.6M (12')	
		kg/m	lb/ft	kg (000)	lb (000)	kg (000)	lb (000)	kg (000)	lb (000)	kg (000)	lb (000)	kg (000)	lb (000)	kg (000)	lb (000)	kg (000)	lb (000)
254mm Pipe	10" Pipe	60.35	40.48	111	246	109	243	108	241	107	238	106	235	104	232	103	229
203mm Extra Strong Pipe	8" Extra Strong Pipe	64.68	43.39	117	259	115	255	113	251	111	247	109	243	108	239	105	234
203 × 203 × 9.5	8 × 8 × 3/8	56.05	37.60	129	286	126	281	125	277	122	272	120	267	118	262	115	256
152mm Double Extra Strong Pipe	6" Double Extra Strong Pipe	79.25	53.16	138	306	135	299	131	292	128	284	124	275	120	266	116	257
310mm Pipe	12" Pipe	73.88	49.56	136	303	135	301	135	299	133	296	132	293	131	291	130	288
254 × 254 × 7.9	10 × 10 × 5/16	60.15	40.35	140	311	139	308	137	305	135	301	134	297	132	293	130	289
254mm Extra Strong Pipe	10" Extra Strong Pipe	81.60	54.74	149	332	148	328	146	325	144	321	143	318	141	314	139	309
310mm Extra Strong Pipe	12" Extra Strong Pipe	97.53	65.42	180	400	179	397	177	394	176	390	174	387	172	383	171	379
203mm Double Extra Strong Pipe	8" Double Extra Strong Pipe	107.96	72.42	194	431	191	424	188	417	185	410	181	403	178	395	174	387
305 × 305 × 9.5	12 × 12 × 3/8	86.61	58.10	204	453	202	449	200	445	198	441	197	437	195	433	193	428
254 × 254 × 12.7	10 × 10 × 1/2	93.11	62.46	216	481	214	476	212	471	209	465	207	459	203	452	201	446
356 × 356 × 9.5	14 × 14 × 3/8	101.83	68.31	241	536	240	533	238	529	236	525	234	521	233	517	231	513
305 × 305 × 12.7	12 × 12 × 1/2	113.40	76.07	267	593	265	588	262	583	260	577	257	571	255	566	252	559
356 × 356 × 12.7	14 × 14 × 1/2	133.69	89.68	317	704	315	699	312	694	310	689	308	684	305	678	302	672
406 × 406 × 12.7	16 × 16 × 1/2	154.00	103.30	367	815	365	810	362	805	360	800	358	795	356	790	353	785
406 × 406 × 15.9	16 × 16 × 5/8	189.88	127.37	451	1003	449	998	446	992	444	986	441	979	438	973	435	966

Note: *ult AISC Steel Handbook for full range of structural shapes*
Structural Tubing (Square sections) are typically graded to 46 ksi (shown here) instead of 36 ksi

METRES (FEET) IN KIPS AND KG × 1000

3.9M (13')		4.2M (14')		4.5M (15')'		4.8M (16')		5.1M (17')		5.4M (18')		5.7M (19')		6.0M (20')		6.3M (21')		6.6M (22')		7.0M (23')	
kg (000)	lb (000)	kg (000)	lb (000)	kg (000)	lb (000)	kg (000)	lb (000)	kg (000)	lb (000)	kg (000)	lb (000)	kg (000)	lb (000)	kg (000)	lb (000)	kg (000)	lb (000)	kg (000)	lb (000)	kg (000)	lb (000)
102	226	100	223	99	220	97	216	96	213	94	209	92	205	90	201	89	197	87	193	85	189
103	229	101	224	99	219	96	214	94	209	91	203	89	197	86	191	83	185	81	179	78	173
113	251	110	245	107	238	104	232	101	225	99	219	95	212	92	205	89	197	86	190	82	182
111	247	107	237	102	227	97	216	92	205	87	193	81	181	76	168	70	155	64	142	59	131
128	285	127	282	125	278	124	275	122	272	121	268	119	265	117	261	116	257	114	254	113	250
128	285	126	280	124	276	122	271	120	266	117	261	115	256	113	251	110	245	108	240	105	234
137	305	135	301	133	296	131	291	129	286	126	281	124	276	122	271	119	265	117	260	114	254
169	375	167	371	165	367	163	363	161	358	159	353	157	349	155	344	152	337	150	334	148	329
170	378	166	369	162	360	158	351	153	341	149	331	144	321	140	310	135	299	130	288	124	276
190	423	188	418	186	413	184	408	181	403	179	397	176	391	174	386	171	380	168	373	165	367
198	439	194	432	191	424	188	417	184	409	180	401	176	392	173	384	169	375	165	366	161	357
229	508	227	504	225	499	222	494	220	489	218	484	215	478	213	473	210	467	208	462	205	456
249	553	246	546	243	540	240	533	237	526	233	518	230	511	226	503	223	495	219	487	215	478
300	666	297	660	294	654	291	647	288	641	285	634	282	627	279	619	275	612	272	604	269	597
351	779	348	773	345	767	342	761	340	755	337	748	333	741	331	735	328	728	324	721	321	713
432	959	428	951	425	944	421	936	418	928	414	920	410	912	406	903	403	895	399	886	395	877

Table 25.3 Allowable axial loading for selected Southern Pine/Douglas Fir column sizes.

Nominal size metric	Nominal size imperial	Effective unsupported length (KL) with respect to least radius of gyration—metres (feet) in kips and kg × 1000														
		1.80M (6')		2.4M (8')		3.0M (10')		3.6M (12')		4.2M (14')		4.8M (16')		5.4M (18')		6.0M (20')	
		kg (000)	lb (000)	kg (000)	lb (000)	kg (000)	lb (000)	kg (000)	lb (000)	kg (000)	lb (000)	kg (000)	lb (000)	kg (000)	lb (000)	kg (000)	lb (000)
100×100	4×4	5.0	11.1	3.3	7.3	2.2	4.9	1.6	3.5	1.2	2.6						
100×150	4×6	7.8	17.4	5.1	11.4	3.5	7.8	2.5	5.5	1.9	4.1						
100×200	4×8	10.3	22.9	6.8	15.1	4.6	10.2	3.3	7.3	2.9	6.5						
150×150	6×6	12.4	27.6	11.2	24.8	9.4	20.9	7.6	16.9	6.0	13.4						
150×200	6×8	16.9	37.6	15.3	33.9	12.8	28.5	10.4	23.1	8.2	18.3	6.6	14.6	5.4	11.9	4.4	9.8
150×250	6×10	21.4	47.6	19.4	43.0	16.2	36.1	13.1	29.2	10.4	23.1	8.3	18.5	6.8	15.0	6.0	13.4
200×200	8×8	24.3	54.0	23.2	51.5	21.6	48.1	19.6	43.5	17.1	38.0	14.5	32.3	12.3	27.4	10.4	23.1
200×250	8×10	30.8	68.4	29.4	65.3	27.5	61.0	24.8	55.1	21.6	48.1	18.5	41.0	15.6	34.7	13.2	29.3
200×300	8×12	37.3	82.8	35.6	79.0	33.2	73.8	30.0	66.7	26.2	58.2	22.3	49.6	18.9	42.0	15.9	35.4
250×300	10×10	39.8	88.4	38.7	85.9	37.4	83.0	35.6	79.0	33.1	73.6	30.2	67.0	27.0	60.0	23.8	52.9
250×300	10×12	48.2	107.0	46.8	104.0	45.0	100.0	43.0	95.6	40.1	89.1	36.5	81.2	32.7	72.6	28.8	64.0
250×350	10×14	56.7	126.0	54.9	122.0	53.1	118.0	50.4	112.0	47.3	105.0	42.9	95.3	38.4	85.3	33.8	75.1
300×300	12×12	58.5	130.0	57.6	128.0	56.3	125.0	54.9	122.0	52.7	117.0	50.0	111.0	46.8	104.0	43.0	95.6
350×350	14×14	81.0	180.0	80.1	178.0	79.2	176.0	77.4	172.0	75.6	168.0	73.4	163.0	70.2	156.0	66.6	148.0
400×400	16×16	107.1	238.0	106.2	236.0	105.3	234.0	103.5	230.0	101.7	226.0	99.9	222.0	97.2	216.0	93.6	208.0

this column (listed in the body of the chart) is only 14,600lb (6600kg) so it isn't acceptable. Moving down the chart, we find that the first column that can safely carry a load greater than 30,000lb (13,500kg) is an 8×8 (200×200), which can carry up to 32,300lb (14,500kg).

From Table 25.1, we read down the column under the 16ft (4.8m) heading and find—almost immediately—that a W5×16 (W130×24) will just do the job. Looking further down the chart, there are no smaller or lighter members, and thus this will be our best choice.

To check the wood for slenderness ratio we can use l/d because the 8×8 is a regular shape. The 8×8 is a nominal size which translates into 7.5″ actual dimension in each direction. There is no weak axis so this is the value for d. We find the slenderness ratio to be:

$$\text{slenderness} = (16\text{ft} \times 12\text{in/ft}) / 7.5\text{in} = 25.6$$

Checking this against the design standards for wood listed above, we find that this would be classified as an intermediate column length and is acceptable.

For the steel shape, we would have to use the l/r measurement for slenderness because we know a wide flange shape will have one strong and one weak axis. This is confirmed by consulting a Steel Construction Manual where we find the moment of inertia for resistance to bending around the x–x axis to be 21.3in⁴ and only 7.51in⁴ for bending around the y–y (or side to side direction). The Manual also tells us that the member's area is 4.68in². Using the lower value for I, and this area, A, we find the r value to be:

$$r = \sqrt{(I/A)} = \sqrt{(7.51\text{in}^4 / 4.68\text{in}^2)} = 1.27\text{in}$$

Using this to check for slenderness we find:

$$\text{slenderness} = (16\text{ft} \times 12\text{in/ft}) / 1.27\text{in} = 151$$

Checking against the design standards, we find that this is officially a long column, but the slenderness ratio is still below 200.

For multistory buildings, we must design based on the accumulated, or *tributary* load carried by each segment of the column. This is, of course, additive as we go down the building, as each column-story picks up additional load at each floor level. Columns at ground level are often, therefore, larger than those at the top level of high buildings. For smaller structures, however, we often find that it is more economical to design for the worst case, and to continue that column shape up the entire frame. This allows elevational consistency, standardization, and economies of scale at the price of weight.

Example: *Find acceptable A36 steel column sizes at the roof, top floor, and ground floor of a ten-story building. The tributary area for each floor is 625ft² (58m²). Floor loading is 100lb/ft² (488kg/m²), roof loading is 50lb/ft² (244kg/m²), and each story is 15ft (5m) high, except the ground floor which has a height of 25ft (7.6m). All columns to have fixed connections at top and bottom.*

Solution: Each column will have an effective length that is reduced by having fixed connections at both ends. From Figure 25.7 we find the K value modifier to be 0.65. In other words, these columns will effectively act as shorter columns; the effective length for each column will be:

Typical Floor:
$(0.65) \times 5m = 3.25m$
Ground Floor:
$(0.65) \times 7.6m = 4.94m$

Typical Floor:
$(0.65) \times 15ft = 9.75ft$
Ground Floor:
$(0.65) \times 25ft = 16.25ft$

The length of the column will need to be rounded up to match a column in the table, 10ft or 3.3m. The ground floor column will be rounded up to 17ft (5.1m).

Beginning at the roof, we find that the topmost column will carry a load of:

$$(58m^2) \times 244kg/m^2 = 14,152kg \qquad (625ft^2) \times 50lb/ft^2 = 31,250lb$$

Scanning across the table in Table 25.1, we find for our column length, 10ft (3m), that we are at the very low end of the spectrum. The smallest shape listed, a W4 × 13 (W100 × 19) wide flange, and it will carry a safe load of 39,000lb (17,550kg)—more than twice our anticipated load.

Just below the roof is the top floor, the first of nine typical floors. This column will need to carry the weight of its own tributary area of floor loading but also the vertical load from the column above that supports the roof. We will distinguish these load by calling the roof, P_R and the typical floor as all P_{TYP}:

$$P = P_R + P_{TYP}$$
$$P = 14,152kg + (488kg/m^2 \times 58m^2) \qquad P = 31,250lb + (100lb/ft^2 \times 625ft^2)$$
$$P = 42,456kg \qquad\qquad P = 93,750lb$$

Again looking at Table 25.1, we now find that we must jump to a W6 × 25 (W150 × 37).

In order to solve for the load in the ground floor column, P_G, we need to add up all the weights of all the floors from above *and* we need to adjust the column in the Table 25.1 because the column length has changed:

$$P_G = P_R + (9 \times P_{TYP})$$
$$P_G = 14,152kg + (9 \times 28,304kg) \qquad P_G = 31,250lb + (9 \times 62,500lb)$$
$$P_G = 268,888kg \qquad\qquad P_G = 593,750lb$$

Here, we go all the way to the bottom of the column for the 17ft (5.1m) column to find a W12 × 120 column (W310 × 179), safely carrying a safe load of 597,000lb (269,000kg). Before moving on, it is worth considering how much weight this is for one relatively modest column to safely carry (the equivalent weight of one the 100ft long Hoover Dam drum gates) over such a modest area (the Steel Manual lists the area for a W12 × 120 at 35.3in²).

In practice, significant reductions are often allowed in the assumed live load of a multistory structure, and codes assume that there will be a significant diversity factor—that floors will not be fully loaded all at the same time. In buildings over seven stories, for instance, columns are assumed to carry only half of the calculated live load.

MODIFICATION OF SHAPES AND CONNECTIONS

Nevertheless, we see that the accumulation of loading over a tall building creates a difference in the required sizes of columns at the top floor and the ground level. Having the largest columns in the building on the ground floor is inconvenient spatially and functionally if we wanted to open the floor up for a lobby. Skyscrapers will sometimes use transfer girders, or collecting piers, to reduce the size of, or eliminate columns to open up the ground floor, but these may become so deep because of the shear stresses involved that they themselves take up an entire story. Occasionally buildings will express this fact explicitly in the articulation of the building elements, while another approach simply allows the columns to line up and simply grow in size as needed. Allowing column sizes to vary makes sense in steel construction because steel is purchased by weight and assuming fabrication and erection cost would be comparable, a smaller member would save money. For concrete structures, however, the cost of concrete is relatively cheap and the amount of rebar could simply be varied from floor to floor as needed and the same formwork could be used throughout the building.

Columns also can potentially change their shape at the end conditions. The manner of connection between the column and the end conditions has been discussed in terms of the effect of column performance, but these connections also have specific construction strategies to make sure that the forces are effectively transferred without shearing—essentially this is accomplished by providing some sort of plate to help spread out the loading at each end. As was discussed in Chapter 24, when certain two-way cast slab systems intersect with columns, particularly columns that are modestly sized in diameter, punching shear can occur in which the column literally punches through the slab. To resolve this, either the column could get bigger (by sizing the column to be 2–2.5 times as long and wide in plan as the slab is deep) or by crafting a much larger column cap like the shear plate/drop panel and articulated mushroom capital. Essentially any strategy that expands the column perimeter at the point of connection, including the tree-like branches in Gaudi's Sagrada Família cathedral (Figure 25.9), is effective. Steel framed structures don't have the same issues

25.9
To avoid punching shear at the connections between columns and slabs, a broader column bearing perimeter was established by Antoni Gaudi at the Sagrada Família.

25.10
The cruciform shaped column from Mies van der Rohe's Barcelona Pavilion (1929) provides equal resistance to buckling in both directions with intentional aesthetic impact. At the Miller House (1957), Eero Saarinen uses the same shaped column but expands it at the column cap to reveal the skylight above.

with punching shear at the top (as typically it will be a steel to steel connection of framing members and the slab would also be a composite system above) but they do have a similar problem at the base. Typically steel columns will be welded to a relatively thick steel base plate that is larger in plan than the column itself (in order to spread out the load over a larger surface area). This base plate and column are secured to anchor bolts that go into the foundation and a leveling bed of grout is used. Although this conventional construction strategy is hardly meant to be visually interesting, it certainly could be, as it is clearly derived from the classical order of column design.

We have seen how a biaxially symmetrical column in plan, like a steel tube, is highly efficient in resisting buckling, but an efficient column design need not be limited to only this type of member. Mies van der Rohe often used a cruciform, x-shaped plan for his columns, including the iconic Barcelona Pavilion, and years later Eero Saarinen used a similar arrangement for columns in the Miller House, but in this case Saarinen also articulated a connection at the top the expanded the column support perimeter which allowed a skylight to be placed directly over the column (Figure 25.10).

Columns may change their longitudinal shape as well, to become efficient and visually interesting. Since long columns are essentially designed for both compression and bending loads, their behavior is somewhat like simply loaded beams, meaning that they have to resist maximum bending from the middle of their span. Therefore, columns can build up, or thicken, their shape in the middle and maintain quite narrow sections at the ends. These skylon shapes, or tapering columns, have often been used in classic high-tech design and more recently by Renzo Piano, Richard Rogers and Santiago Calatrava to spectacular effect.

CONCLUSION

The effective transfer or consolidated loading from horizontally spanning structural members to foundational support depends upon the structural integrity of the vertically oriented structural components, which are frequently designed as columns. Columns have unique behavioral considerations, that are at times unpredictable, so there are several critical design considerations that are necessary to ensure their stable performance, including a column's material, shape, end conditions, and slenderness ratio. All of these factors also present corresponding design opportunities to have a structural system's columns formally respond to the loading conditions.

FREQUENTLY ASKED QUESTIONS:

Why do architectural plans dimension everything back to the column center-lines?
Obviously structurally this is important to align columns from multiple floors at the same centroid and provides a consistent dimensional datum to allow column sizes to vary. If other elements are dimensioned to the centerlines, then variations in the column sizes can occur from floor to floor without confusing the overall dimensional strategy for the building. Often, establishing a structural grid occurs very early in the design process.

GLOSSARY

Column: Technically, any axially loaded member. Usually a vertical member carrying gravity loads and designed to resist both compression and buckling.

End conditions: How a column is connected to the beams or supports at its ends. Because these play a role in how much or little the column can move, they are important considerations in how well the column will resist buckling.

Radius of gyration: Basically, a measurement of a column shape's efficiency. Radius of gyration measures the average distance of a shape's area from its centroid, giving a usable measure of the column's "average width." Radius of gyration is defined by:

$$r = \sqrt{(I/A)}$$

where I is the shape's moment of inertia and A is the shape's area. Note that we must usually find r for the *weakest* axis.

Skylon: A column that is widest at the middle, tapering toward both ends. This is a "true" column shape that acknowledges the role of bending in determining column performance, and is often used to dramatic visual effect.

Slenderness ratio: A measure of a column's length divided by either its narrowest width or by its radius of gyration in the weakest axis. Generally we use the formula:

$$KL/r$$

where K is a multiplier based on the end conditions of the column, L is the column length in inches (or cm) and r is the shape's radius of gyration in inches or cm. This number then guides us through charts of allowable loads for a given material to select a shape.

Tributary area: The total area of floor plate that "flows" into a column. In multistory buildings, this will include the weight and loads of every floor plate above the column in question. Figured on each floor by assuming each column will carry an area defined by the centerlines of each surrounding bay.

FURTHER READING

Allen, E. and Iano, J. (2002). *The Architect's Studio Companion*, 3rd edition. New York: Wiley; Chapter 2, Designing the Structure, pp. 47–137.

Allen, E. and Zalewski, W. (2010). *Form and Forces, Designing Efficient, Expressive Structures*. New York: John Wiley & Sons; Chapter 19, Designing Columns, Frames, and Load-Bearing Walls, pp. 517–530.

Ambrose, J. and Parker, H. (2000). *Simplified Engineering for Architects and Builders*. New York: Wiley; Chapters 3.1–3.11, Investigation of Beams and Frames—Compression Members, pp. 122–135.

Mainstone, R. (2001). *Developments in Structural Form*, 2nd edition. Oxford: Architectural Press; Chapter 10, Supports, Walls, and Foundations, pp. 175–185.

Salvadoris, M. and Heller, R. (1963). *Structure in Architecture: The Building of Buildings*. New York: Prentice-Hall; Chapter 5, Basic States of Stress, pp. 83–87.

Sandaker, B. N. and Eggen, A. P. (1992). *The Structural Basis of Architecture*. New York: Whitney; Chapter 5, The Column, pp. 109–130.

26

FOUNDATIONS: SUBSTRUCTURES AND SOILS

Design considerations	Foundations and building loads Superstructures and substructures
Soils	Soil types and behaviour Boring, testing, and improvements
Foundation types	Shallow footings: strip, spread, and mat Deep foundations: piles
Retaining walls	Gravity, cantilever, and shear wall
Foundation failures	Settlements and heaving
Design process	Soil bearing capacity Footing area
Foundations and thrust	Alternate foundation orientations

FOUNDATIONAL CONSIDERATIONS

In previous sections we have investigated the design, arrangement, and resulting behavior of the major elements of building *superstructures*, that is, the portions of the structure that are above ground. The design for these elements (slabs, beams, columns, and walls) depends on a state of equilibrium created by both the external conditions of support and internal capacities of the material to resist stress. All of the loads are accumulated from the top down—growing dramatically in magnitude along the way—until they are eventually consolidated at the foundation and distributed into the ground. It is ultimately the *substructure*, or the collection of structural elements *below* ground level, that is responsible for ensuring a continued state of equilibrium for the building.

R. Buckminster Fuller frequently asked other designers, "How much does your building weigh?" For Fuller, a lightweight structure reflects an efficient combination of materials and forms that effectively resist and resolve structural forces. He felt that the amount of load that a building ultimately imparted into the ground through the foundations was the best way to assess the relative effectiveness of a building's design. But simply finding an efficient way transmit loads to the ground is no guarantee that equilibrium can be maintained. Hidden below the surface of the earth is a complex series of soil strata—each with a different capacity to resist and maintain resistance to the building loads.

Essentially, the design of substructures (e.g. foundation walls, footings, and retaining walls) has to mediate between these two important influences: the loads from the top acting down, and the resistance provided from the ground "pushing" up. The strategy for the design team (including the geotechnical and civil engineers that design and detail the foundations) is to study the potential impact these factors might have on the structure's behavior and find the right combination of solutions that keep the building, safe, stable, and responsive to the project's central goals.

This section will discuss the ways that information is gathered, assessed and implemented into a project's foundation design strategy. Basic design strategies for foundations and critical aspects of their structural behavior will be discussed, but first, as is the case in nearly all projects in practice, we have to know much more about the nature of the soil upon which we are proposing to build.

SOILS

Below the surface, soil materials with varying levels of color, consistency, and particle size are stacked in a series of layers, or soil horizons. The depth of these layers vary dramatically from location to location, as do the actual physical attributes of the soils found within each horizon—some soils are suitable for construction and some are not, and yet designers need to find strategies to transfer the building loads to the ground anyway. A fond myth about building science is that our structures are firmly rooted to solid earth, and that once fixed, they are stable. While this is true for a very limited number of structures—those that are anchored or screwed into bedrock—the vast majority of buildings are essentially floating in a state of relative equilibrium in a variety of soil types. In fact, all buildings move, or settle, over time—in most cases it can be controlled, minimized, or made imperceptible by the proper combination of matching a foundation design with the actual conditions of the soil. The Leaning Tower of Pisa is perhaps the most famous example of settlement gone awry. This tower's failure is not in the structure itself, but rather in the lack of understanding of the ground's diverse capacity to carry the intense load of the tower equally across its foundation. Thankfully, one rarely sees examples as dramatic or catastrophic as Pisa, perhaps thanks in a large part to the broader set of empirical knowledge gathered by scientists about soil behavior over the last few centuries, and the recent, regular, integration of geotechnical engineers as part of the design team.

The principles of soil mechanics are used to help study the physical, mechanical and chemical properties of soils, primarily as a means of assessing the potential risks associated with the building upon different soils. As with the design of other structural elements, in order to understand a material's behavior, we first have to know the types of stresses to which it will be subjected and what effect they have on potential structural performance.

Soils, for example, resist loading by a combination of compression and shear. Soil particles develop friction as they move past one another under loading, and

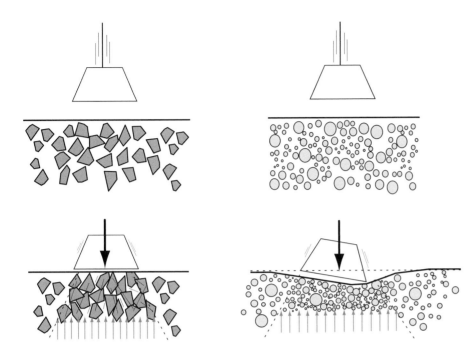

26.1
Simple soil physics. The geometric nature of soil particles helps determine their resistance to compaction. Some stiffen and compact in place while others "roll away" from the force.

the surface shapes and roughness of these particles determines their ability to resist loads. Specifically, as soils are compressed/compacted under loading, their particles physically engage with each other—in some cases, friction develops between the particles (a resistance to shear) and gives the material an improved resistance to further compression. Materials that are good for foundations have a higher internal capacity to resist compression, have a larger size of "grain," and a particle shape that facilitates friction between particles. This behavior can typically be found in the course, rough, and densely packed types of soils, like gravel (Figure 26.1).

Soils originate in either *residual* or *sedimentary* processes. Residual processes involve the gradual weathering of rock and tend to leave reliable, undisturbed soils. Sedimentary processes bring soil to a site from other sources through rivers, glaciers, etc., and while they often leave good tillable earth, they are often unreliable structural soils.

For the sake of assessing their behaviors under these stresses, soils are usually divided into five main classifications (in this case ranging from best to worst capacity for foundations). The first type, *rock* (or *bedrock*) is usually the ideal foundation material because it is basically a continuous, monolithic mass with a very high compressive capacity. Not all rock is the same; some types can be easily fractured (vulnerable to point loads) or porous.

Sands and gravels are coarse, granular materials that can be compacted and graded as needed to provide effective foundational support (gravel more so than sand). Both materials are quite stiff when compressed and have *non--plastic behavior*—that is, they do not "give" easily and therefore they tend to be good load-resistive soils.

Clays and *silts* are poor foundation materials because they are fine/small, granular materials that compress easily and offer little friction resistance under loading—their behavior is similar to a fluid so their resistance to settling is, at best, guesswork. Clays can also shrink and swell depending on changes to soil moisture so they are vulnerable to settlement, heaving, and liquefaction. As they become saturated, silts and clays act more like a liquid than a solid, meaning that buildings built on top of them will "float".

Finally, *organics* describe a range of topsoil-like materials that are composed of decaying vegetation. They offer little or no resistance to crushing and would need to be completely removed.

Rock, sand, and gravel are the best soil types to be located under foundations. Their non-plastic nature means that their resistance to crushing is reliable, and they will provide a generally geometrically stable base and can be compacted well into a relatively dense bed (this is why gravel is typically used underneath foundations). Hardpan is a general term for a layer of very dense soil that is largely impervious to water and has a high degree of compressive strength. It is usually found in locations just below the uppermost layer of organic topsoil.

BORING, TESTING, AND IMPROVEMENT

Structural designers need to anticipate and accommodate various loading conditions for their designs. As we've seen, soil materials have a diverse range of load-bearing capacities and structural behaviors that would factor in greatly in these design decisions. Without proper testing, there is no way of knowing with any certainty which soil types are below the ground (and at what depth they are located). Consequently, a structural designer wouldn't even be able to start planning for the size or arrangement of any of the loads coming from above without first knowing the potential resistance available from below.

Therefore, one of the first actions architects usually advise at the first stages of every project (often times even before a design team is fully assembled) is the collection and assessment of many soil test borings done under the supervision of a geotechnical/civil engineer. A cylindrical hollow drill is insert into the ground at various locations on the construction site—often in a grid pattern, but also in likely areas of structural necessity. These borings are looking for inconsistencies in the soil (pockets of clay), ecological liabilities (wetland soils), or contaminants. These sleeves of soil taken from the borings are then analyzed by the engineers. They provide tests to show the density, moisture content, and granularity of the recovered soils. The location, type, and strength of any bedrock reached will also be noted, as will the location of the water table on the site (Figure 26.2).

A final report is issued to the client, who then issues the report to the design team, in particular the structural engineer, to review the results. The report includes quantifiable information about soil types, depth, etc. but also a qualitative analysis, perhaps suggesting particular areas of the site to avoid, recommendations for how the soil conditions could be potentially improved, and a recommendation for which types of foundations might be most effective given those particular conditions.

For smaller construction, test pits or trenches may substitute for borings. In each of these cases, several holes are dug across the site to establish soil conditions at, and below, the bearing level of foundations. Digging several holes has the advantage of locating actual strata of soil, rather than just point locations.

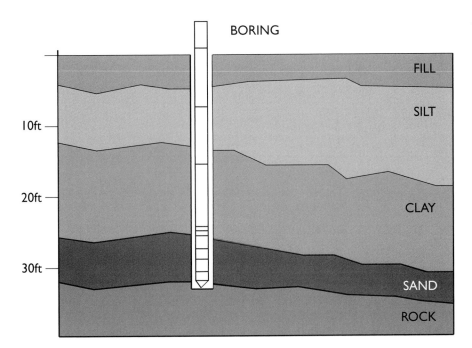

10ft —

20ft —

30ft —

BORING

FILL

SILT

CLAY

SAND

ROCK

26.2
Soil borings are taken from selected locations on the site. Depths, types, and configurations of soil strata vary widely across different sites (general example shown).

Very rarely do we build large projects on soils as we find them. More often, some simple measures taken at the beginning of construction can greatly improve the performance of a building's substructure:

Cutting and filling involves sculpting the site to allow placement of level structures. For large projects, loose organic soil is always removed from any location that will receive bearing pads or slabs. In general, we try to equalize the amount of cutting and filling of usable soil on a site to avoid expensive inhaul or outhaul. Thus, with a large enough site, we may add landscape elements using soil excavated from foundations. For large jobs (particularly midrise buildings with large footprints) we may cart off poor soil and replace it with a fairly large quantity of sand or gravel. Note, however, that this poor soil needs to go somewhere, and the fiscal and environmental penalties of this usually suggest working in some way with what we have to hand.

Densification and compaction are techniques for improving the performance of soils found on a site. At the very least, contractors would typically roll/compress the soil on which the slabs will sit in order to compact it and make it perform more monolithically. However, more involved techniques include the use of vibrating rollers, which can compact sand to a depth of 6ft (2m). For deeper compaction, vibrating piles and probes can compact sands to a depth of 40ft (12m). Occasionally these devices are coupled with saturation, so that the soil liquefies, permitting rapid consolidation, after which it is drained to form a tighter, denser underpinning. Perhaps the most radical form of compaction involves dropping multi-ton weights from heights of up to 120ft (30m). While extremely efficient, this technique is limited to areas without neighbors, whose structures might be damaged by the seismic force imparted to the soil. For clay soils, a similar technique known as *surcharging* works by piling weight on to the site equivalent to the estimated load of the final building. In this process, the clay is thus permanently deformed to (approximately) the level imparted by the structure. While effective, this process is time-consuming and requires "borrowing" loose fill for weight—often expensive. Surcharging is usually limited to relatively lightweight structures that cover a large footprint.

Grouting involves the injection of liquid cement into known underground cavities or fissures. It can also be used to solidify porous rock for either drainage or structural reasons, or to stabilize loose sand and gravel.

Drainage is the most common soil improvement. Removing water from existing soil—and keeping it out—allows the soil particles to achieve dry bonding, adding friction to their resisting capabilities. Providing permanent drainage and/or water exclusion at the site perimeter can prevent soil from liquefying, or from developing water films that reduce its strength.

Finally, soils can be reinforced using plastic rods or ribs that are threaded into the ground. Similarly, *geomembranes* can be placed under new soil to direct or control water infiltration.

FOUNDATION TYPES

Although there are many different specific tactical approaches to foundation design, they are all based essentially on the same strategy: disperse the consolidated heavy load points from the structure across a wide, stable area of ground—the same strategy as structural slab design, but reversed in direction. As with slab design, there are two major considerations in foundation design: sizing the depth of the "slab" to accommodate a certain amount of bending and accounting for *punching shear*. Foundations can be classified by either the type of load imparted upon it (point load versus distributed foundation) and/or by the range of depth to which they are embedded into the ground (shallow versus deep foundation). We will start with the simplest systems, shallow distributed foundations, like spread footing and trench footing.

The systems of support, including the foundations, for small-scale projects like a house are dramatically different from systems employed in the design of a large office building. In smaller-scale construction projects, the structural strategy typically involves the use of more affordable (i.e. smaller) structural components—this necessitates that, wherever possible, loads should be spread across larger areas, like bearing walls. Most frequently these loads are distributed continuously across a foundation, typically at the building perimeter—these can also be called *strip foundations*. A continuous trench footing is essentially poured around the perimeter to the point of frost depth resistance (to avoid heaving) and a continuous foundation wall is constructed vertically running in a strip, centered upon the spread footing below. The spread footing takes this vertically distributed load and spreads it out across the larger horizontal surface of its footing (Figure 26.3). For lightly loaded walls, the width of the footing need not be extended very far from the face of the wall above—(the load is already well distributed because it is continuously applied along the length of the foundation already). In addition to providing adequate resistance against the compressive forces from above, the footings have to be designed to resist the shear force that develops within a range of distance on either side of the wall. Because the footing isn't very wide, flexural, beam-like, bending isn't a design concern with the foundation.

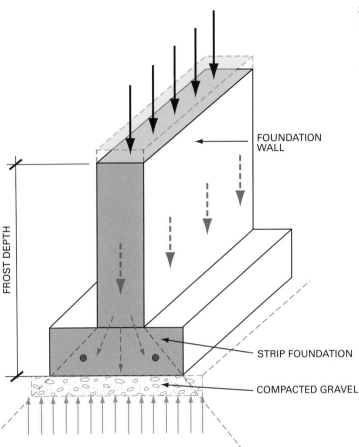

26.3
Strip foundation/trench footing.

FOUNDATION WALL

FROST DEPTH

STRIP FOUNDATION

COMPACTED GRAVEL

Shallow spread footings, or *pad foundations*, are commonly used in all types of construction methods as a way of supporting a point load, like a column. This is usually a square concrete pad of a uniform thickness with a column placed directly in the center, analogous to an upside-down two-way slab with a single point of support. The foundation wants to spread out the concentrated load across the area of the foundation without risking a reverse punching shear effect. Like a two-way slab, it makes sense to optimize the load distribution by maintaining a square footing shape if possible. The area of the pad is related to the bearing capacity of the soil pressure below and its depth is typically dictated by its ability to resist shear—one-way shear at the outer edges and two-way shear action at a concentric area around the column. Ultimately, the footing must be very rigid—by spreading its load out across a larger area, it is bending the pad in two directions, necessitating rebar running in two ways to resist flexural tension forces (Figure 26.4).

Depending on the soil conditions and spacing of supports, multiple columns may be resting upon the same combined footing pad to ensure that they all settle evenly. Spread footings work best on sands and gravels, where resistance can be accurately predicted and where plastic deformation does not occur.

Slab on grade, or structural slab foundations, are essentially the shallowest of all shallow foundations. This consists of a concrete slab poured directly onto the ground surface, typically with the outer edges turned downward to fix the slab in place. Structural elements resting upon the slab, either walls or

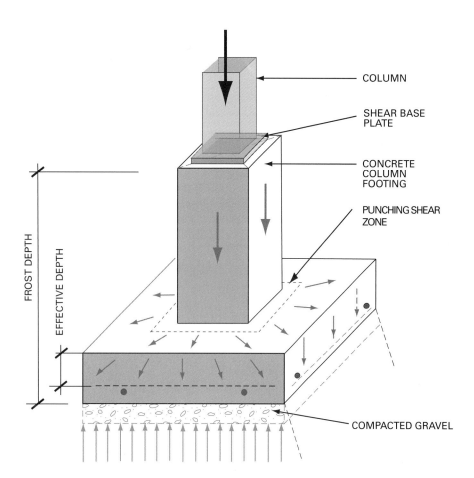

COLUMN

SHEAR BASE PLATE

CONCRETE COLUMN FOOTING

PUNCHING SHEAR ZONE

COMPACTED GRAVEL

FROST DEPTH

EFFECTIVE DEPTH

26.4
Column is placed in the center of footing and loads are distributed out in two directions.

columns, are tied into the reinforcing of the slab and the slab surface itself is typically thickened at the bottom to accommodate the larger load. It may be used where there is a threat of expansive soils because it essentially applies a constant pressure on the soil. As a foundation, it is cheap and strong but in climates where the ground freezes, or in locations where the subsoil has a tendency to settle, it isn't a good choice. Integration with other systems, such as plumbing and electrical, need to be coordinated and run before the slab is cast as there is no access to areas after the slab has been poured.

Another type of shallow footing is the *mat* foundation. The idea for this design is to provide a spread footing for the entire structure at once, connecting all columns and walls with a single concrete slab, often with deeper "beams" below the slab connecting the columns together. This has the advantage of equalizing pressure on the soil throughout the site, and it is thus good for sites with varying or locally unpredictable conditions. Mat foundations can be constructed at or near the ground surface or at the bottom of basement floors. Mat foundations are also quite good for silt or clay soils as they are supported not only by the soil's resistance to compression, but also by *displacement*—essentially the building can be made to "float" in viscous or liquid soil (Figure 26.5). This is usually called a *raft foundation* or, in extreme cases, a *tank*. Generally, careful calculation is needed to determine the final settlement of the finished building, and care needs to be taken when planning for utility interfaces in the foundation walls.

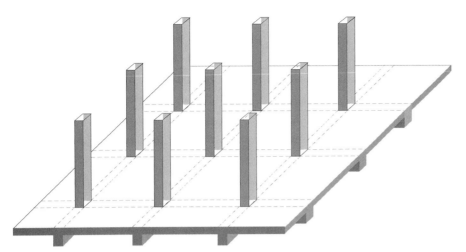

26.5
Mat foundations connect slab and multiple column points together to create a single large surface area designed to spread out load and avoid uneven settlement.

There are certain situations in which shallow foundations simply aren't possible. Typically where there are very large design loads, it is no longer efficient to try and spread the loads out across a horizontal surface—instead a deeper, more stable layer of strata is required. For these situations, deep foundations are used. Deep foundations are typically recommended for very large design loads, especially if only poor soil quality is available at a more shallow depth. Pile foundations and other larger-scale types are shown in Figure 26.6.

Pile foundations support loads either by carrying them deep into the ground to bedrock, or by friction with surrounding soil. In either case, they usually consist of wood piles or steel or concrete shafts that are inserted through the soil by excavation, drilling, or pounding. *Pile caps* are spread footings under columns or walls that sit atop a group of piles, rather than just on the ground. These are necessary, as placement of piles is inexact at best; the cap allows some tolerance

26.6
For larger buildings or for conditions with poor soil conditions, more complex foundation techniques may be required.

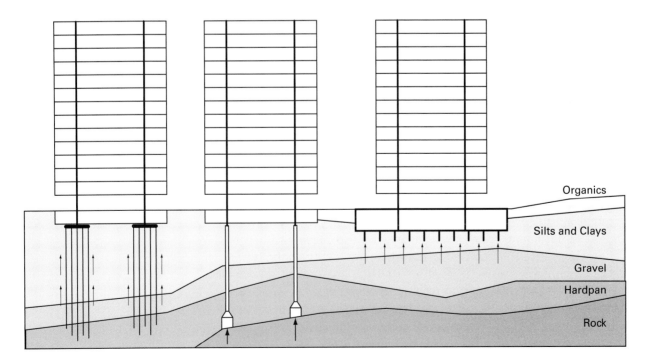

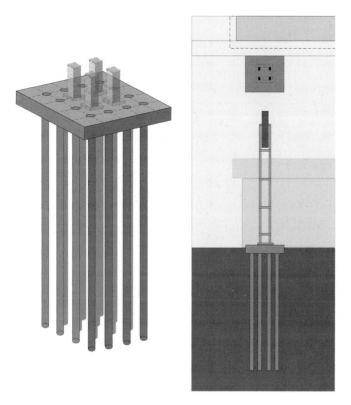

for the piles' final positions in relation to the column, Figure 26.7. *Bearing piles* are essentially long columns that carry loads past poor soil to rock. Occasionally these need to be supplemented by bell- or cone-shaped profiles to spread the load out across the surface of the rock. This is accomplished by remote excavating machinery that is sent down a drill shaft. More common are *friction piles*, which are simply driven into the ground until the friction between the soil and the pile itself becomes great enough to support building loads. Pile foundations present some problems, in that their end conditions can only be assumed—the pile might be sitting on bedrock, or it might have simply reached a particularly dense strata of hardpan. For tall buildings, bridges, and dams, holes are usually drilled for the pile's formwork, for a caisson to be lowered into the void. To ensure stability, an inspector (either mechanical or human) is lowered into the void to sample the base condition. The caisson is later filled with concrete.

26.7
Axonometric, plan and section example of pile cap and friction piles designed to support a scoreboard spanning over an adjacent building.

RETAINING WALLS

In many cases, these foundations have to accommodate occupied spaces below grade, like basements, so the foundations in these cases have to not only resist against the loading from above, they must also deal with the lateral pressure of soil and groundwater. If the superstructure above uses columns (i.e. consolidates the structural loads to point loads), then projects with foundational basements often have to modify their typical single width bearing wall to accommodate the added point loads with vertical pilasters cast integral with the foundation wall. The wall in this situation will need to be sized to resist

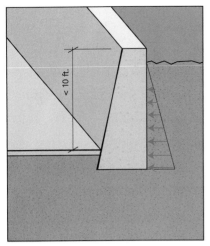

Gravity Wall

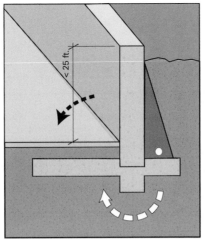

Cantilever Wall

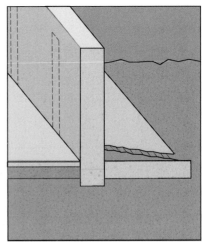

Counterfort Wall

against vertical and *lateral* loading. Typically, however, the term retaining wall generally refers to a cantilevered support condition—a foundation and wall with no means of supporting the top (Figure 26.8).

Retaining walls are often common site structures and are used when there is a need to have a change in ground elevation between two levels (past the point where grading the soil alone could handle the slope). Retaining walls are designed primarily to resist against the lateral pressure of the earth (and potentially) moisture from the back side—this load gradually increases as the wall gets deeper because of the weight of the soil (and potential pressure of moisture). Because it is a cantilever, it also has to resist against over-turning. They are usually non-load-bearing from above, and are supported by spread footings oriented in a manner to resist overturning moments. Often, the area around them must be cleared of unacceptable soil, and *backfilled* with sand or gravel that allows moisture to percolate and drain away from the building face.

There are three basic forms of resisting cantilever strategies. The sloped *gravity wall* resists overturning forces by its massive amount of counterweight. These low-tech walls are not very stable ultimately and they employ lots of mass, limiting the height to approximately 10′ (3m). The *cantilever wall* is the most common type of retaining wall and is used for applications up to 25′ (8m). It resists overturning by either placing the footing underneath the soil being retained (using this extra weight to resist overturning) or by moving the footing in the opposite direction in order to form an L-shape that resists over-turning by its shape. A shear key may need to be placed at the bottom of the footing to resist a sliding motion for the wall. For higher walls, a *counterfort system* is used. When the wall is too tall, the moment stress between the wall and footing becomes too great to overcome economically unless diagonal buttresses wall webs are cast between the elements on the back side, hidden below ground. For all retaining walls to better resist against overloading, they must be built with a porous material and have a drain tile in the back.

26.8
Three retaining wall design strategies.

FOUNDATION FAILURES

Most foundation failures occur because of *settlement*, or the inverse, *heaving*. Settlement occurs primarily when soils lack the bearing capacity needed to support the building loads (especially if the soils are untested or unaltered) or if the bearing strength of the soil is inadvertently altered, usually by water. Soft, wet soil offers much less resistance because of the lubricating effect of water, and foundations will often sink a significant amount after saturation from flooding, etc. The classic case is of subsidence occurring after a pipe leak, for example. If flooding occurs locally, for instance by saturation of the soil from a poorly placed gutter, the footing may bridge over a locally weak area. However, if the footing fails, the portion of the building above may sink while the remainder of the building remains in place, causing cracking of brickwork, interior finishes and structural members.

A notorious failure is the saturation—and dissolution—of limestone by newly introduced water. The discovery of limestone in a boring test may in itself disqualify a potential site.

Heaving occurs when a foundation is installed above the local frost line. As soil below freezes, it can displace the surface by an inch or more. The constant freeze-thaw motion will often cause buildings to settle differentially over time. Most commonly, porch foundations on old houses were often simple surface beams. When attached to a house on a basement foundation, the constant differential movement and settlement can lead to the porch's foundation settling further than the main one, causing the porch to slope away from the house.

Failure may also occur if a foundation's bearing capacity is altered due to certain construction circumstances. For example, in tightly confined spaces where new foundations are built adjacent to existing buildings, care must be taken to not undermine (or remove) underlying areas of foundational support or otherwise alter the stability (Figure 26.9). Likewise, the imposition of a new load in a tight urban site may compress soils beneath other buildings, also causing subsidence.

26.9
An unoccupied 13-story apartment building in Shanghai collapsed during construction. Extra dirt was erroneously piled up along one side creating a large lateral force against the foundations causing the collapse.

Table 26.1 Allowable bearing loads on various soil types.

Soil type	Allowable bearing	
	kg/m²	tons/ft²
Sound rock	585,900	60
Medium rock	390,600	40
Intermediate rock	195,300	20
Well-cemented hardpan	117,180	12
Compact, well-graded gravel	97,650	10
Poorly cemented hardpan	78,120	8
Compact gravel	78,120	8
Loose gravel	58,590	6
Weathered or porous rock	19,530 to 78,120	2 to 8
Coarse sand	29,295 to 58,690	3 to 6
Hard clay	48,825	5
Gravel/sand mix	39,060	4
Fine sand	19,530 to 39,060	2 to 4
Fill	19,530 to 39,060	2 to 4
Dense silt	29,295	3
Medium clay	19,530	2
Medium silt	14,647	1.5

BASIC FOUNDATION DESIGN

Foundations, particularly spread footings, can be quickly estimated if the total load of the building and the conditions of the soil below are known. Table 26.1 shows allowable bearing pressures for a variety of soil types. Note the range of performance between soft soils and sound rock—this explains why caissons and drilled piers are often economical. If the total weight on a column, wall, or floor is known, this figure can be divided by the allowable tons/ft² given in this chart to estimate the required area of a spread footing—a ton is assumed to be 2000lb (900kg). Further calculations to ensure the shear capacity of the slab/column connection are required.

There are circumstances where the weight of a building cannot be supported by the surrounding soil. In this case, a different system must be designed, taking the load of the building down to a point at which the soil material will suffice. For shallow strata, it is sometimes economical to excavate a deep basement, as hardpan material is often only a few yards beneath the surface. However for deep strata, this situation calls for piers or piles.

Example: *Develop foundation strategies for each soil strata for the building shown in Figure 26.10. Assume largest bay area is 900ft² (100m²) and the loading for each floor (and roof) is 100lb/ft² (488kg/m²).*

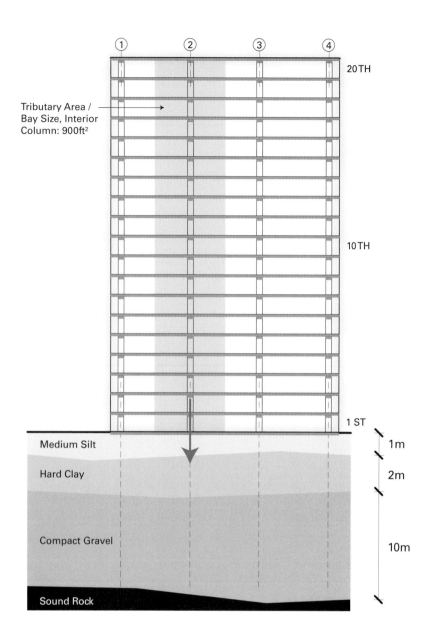

Tributary Area /
Bay Size, Interior
Column: 900ft²

26.10
Foundation depth design example
from text.

Solution: Although each edge column will hold less load because of the smaller bay size, it is often helpful to begin with the worst-case scenario. In this case, the foundations under the column in the two central bays will carry the most cumulative load. Given the bay size, this will be:

$P = $ (no. stories) × (bay area) × (loading per m²)
$= 20 \times 100\text{m}^2 \times 488\text{kg/m}^2$
$= 976,000\text{kg}$

$P = $ (no. stories) × (bay area) × (loading per ft²)
$= 20 \times 900\text{ft}^2 \times 100\text{lb/ft}^2$
$= 1,800,000\text{lb}$
$= 900 \text{ tons}$

Now we examine what area it would take to safely spread this load over each of the four strata. To do this, we can take a systematic approach, using a chart to list soil strata, safe bearing load, and the resulting area ($A = P/f_{all}$):

Table 26.2 Foundation depth design.

Strata	Total load, P tons(kg)	Allowable load, f_{all} tons/ft²(kg/m²)	A = P/f_{all} ft²(m²)
Medium silt	900 (976,000)	1.5 (14,647)	600 (83.8)
Hard clay	900 (976,000)	5 (48,825)	180 (20)
Compacted gravel	900 (976,000)	8 (78,120)	112.5 (12.5)
Sound rock	900 (976,000)	60 (585,900)	15 (1.7)

Think of these foundational areas as square-shaped pads. For Medium Silt, we can support the building on a large set of foundation pads 600ft² each (approx. 25′ × 25′). These are huge, nearly taking up the entire area between columns. Given the shallow nature of this layer, though, it might well be more economical to excavate to the layer of clay, where we could reduce the foundation size nearly in half, or to gravel, where the foundations could be reduced even further (approximately 10′6″ × 10′6″ for gravel). Excavating down to sound rock would allow for the smallest caissons but our decision would be affected by local concrete prices versus the cost of labor to excavate these strata.

EVOLUTIONS FOR EFFICIENCY

Foundation designs have developed into relatively efficient structural elements. Their different configurations are crafted to effectively respond to the loading conditions from above and the bearing capacity below. Although we typically think of foundations as flat pads sunken into the ground, foundation designs can also be formally configured in a manner that makes them more responsive to alternative methods of load distribution. For instance, form-active structures (e.g. cables and arches) and surface-resistant structures (e.g. shells), are highly efficient structural systems, but they inflect a certain amount of thrust outward at their foundations, at times highly concentrated—typically foundations aren't designed to handle any horizontally applied forces. In order to be truly effective, these structural systems rely upon the foundation design to effectively resolve these forces. Foundations can be oriented to accept the applied pressure at the idealized perpendicular angle, and then any angled force from the superstructure is typically split into horizontal and vertical load components (Figure 26.10). Resisting a sliding horizontal force either requires a large shear key at the bottom of the footing or a massive amount of surface area along the depth of the footing (spreading horizontal force out across a larger area). Depending on the amount of thrust, certain structures use underground tie-backs to other foundation pads on the opposite side.

CONCLUSION

Foundations are the point at which a building's load is ultimately consolidated and transferred to the ground. Although typically hidden in the final expression of

26.11
Foundations for columns at Madrid Barajas Airport by Richards Rogers (2006).

a building, the fundamental relationship between the load transferred from the superstructure above to the substructure below is of fundamental importance to the successful design of a structural system. Different variations in soil types and site conditions can greatly affect the potential options for the selection of different foundation systems and their particular arrangement and design.

FREQUENTLY ASKED QUESTIONS

How do engineers determine one type of foundation system over another? It seems as though there are always options to either modify the soil or change the foundation type to be responsive to nearly any condition, so how is the decision made?

The assumption is right, to a certain extent, that there are always multiple options available. The decision is typically made in regards to two factors: time and money. Structural engineers and geotechnical engineers rely upon years of practice experience to advise architects about the relative consequences of different approaches. For instance, if it was desired to use a slab on grade but you realized that you would need to haul away tons of bad soil and replace it with compacted gravel across the entire site, it wouldn't have a high cost-benefit ratio. Some solutions, like surcharging the soil, are incredibly effective but take time and, depending on the construction schedule, this may not be possible. Foundation design and placement takes up a great deal of time and requires careful consideration because of the potentially massive project-altering changes to cost and time that may result.

GLOSSARY

Boring: A test drilling that procures a long cylindrical sample of earth.

Caissons: Drilled or excavated voids in the ground that are later filled with concrete, creating a large, pile-like foundation.

Clay: Fine, granular soil that is subject to plastic behavior.

Cutting and filling: The process of, respectively, removing and adding earth to a site.

Densification: Compacting a site's soil to achieve better structural performance.

Geomembrane: A filter-like fabric used to control or direct water flow on a site.

Gravel: Coarse, granular soil composed of large grains.

Grouting: Adding cement or concrete to soil to increase its structural capacity, or to repair fissures or voids.

Heaving: Uplift in the ground caused by freezing or other soil expansion.

Mat foundation: A foundation type that uses the entire footprint of a building to spread its load over the soil below. Typically used for large volume, low-rise buildings where the foundation can be combined with the ground floor slab.

Organics: Decaying vegetation or peat with little capability of resisting loads.

Pile cap: A slab or mat that rests on a number of piles, spreading the load of a column or pier over them.

Pile foundation: A foundation type that uses long, usually cylindrical rods (piles) to either reach a firmer soil below, or develop bearing through friction with the surrounding soil.

Raft foundation: A foundation type that works by displacement, essentially "floating" the building in the soil.

Retaining walls: Foundation type that creates a vertical drop in the ground. Retaining walls must be designed as cantilevers to resist the overturning moment of the "held-back" soil.

Sand: Coarse, granular soil composed of small grains.

Settlement: The tendency of a structure to work its way down through the ground, often the result of a change in composition of the soil (from flooding, e.g.) or inadequately designed foundations.

Sheet piles: Planar elements that are driven into the ground to form an underground wall. Typically made of large-scale corrugated steel.

Silts: Fine soil that becomes suspended in water that flows rather than holding its shape (and is therefore structurally dangerous).

Spread footing: A foundation type that works like an inverted slab, taking the point load of a column or pier and distributing it over an area of foundation "pad" (usually concrete) so that the soil is not stressed past its capacity.

Substructure: The part of a building's structure below the ground floor.

FURTHER READING

Gupton, C. P. (1994). "Soil Mechanics and Foundations" in Frederick S. Merritt and Jonathan T. Ricketts, *Building Design and Construction Handbook*, 5th edition. New York: McGraw-Hill; Chapters 6.1–6.63.

Mainstone, R. (2001). *Developments in Structural Form*. Oxford: Architectural Press; Chapter 10, Supports, Walls, and Foundations, pp. 175–192.

Mario Salvadori, M. (1979). *The Art of Construction*. Chicago: Chicago Review Press; Chapter 7, The Part of the Building You Don't See, pp. 51–56.

27

FRAMES AND CONNECTIONS

Synergy in frame structures	Frame definition
	Historical frames
Connections	Pinned, roller and fixed
	Connections and resulting behavior
Multiple frames	Strategies for stabilization
	Determinate and indeterminate frames
	Hinged frames
Lateral stability	Large-scale building strategies

INTRODUCTION

In the previous sections we have covered most of the major structural elements in a typical multistory building—slabs, beams and girders, columns and foundations. In general, we have looked at the ways to design and size these structural components to resist gravitational loads and rotational instability within the component itself. But when all of these elements are placed together to make a structural *frame*, it is easier to more accurately assess how the overall structure will behave at a macro-scale, and through this analysis, new opportunities for tuning the performance of individual elements at the micro-scale become possible, simply by changing the types of connections between these elements.

Simply put, a *frame* is a system of horizontal and vertical structural members tied together in order to collectively resist both vertical and horizontal forces—the performance of the frame is determined by a larger structural strategy for how elements are connected to each other (generally either *fixed* and/or *hinged* connections). As high-performance steel and concrete frames have been developed and perfected in the last century, the frame has also become a primary element in the architectural expression of high-rise buildings (Figure 27.1).

Throughout most of history, column and beam structures were assembled by simply assembling the best available structural material, typically either wood or stone, into simple column and lintel frames that spanned across openings. Crucially, most of these structures did not provide for a fixed connection

27.1
The structural frame has been one of the defining architectural expressions of high-rise construction.

between column and lintel. While stone construction often included a key and channel connection between the two, and wood construction would tie or pin these members together, these connections were both quite flexible, and they allowed a great deal of movement—both rotational and translational—between beam and column (Figure 27.2).

For simple loading this does not present much of a problem. However, in extreme circumstances—large storms with high winds, for instance, or earthquakes—the lateral movement in such a system could easily cause the lintel to slide or rock off of its connection to the column. These frames, or more specifically the connections within the frame, translated gravitational force effectively, but had no mechanism for maintaining stability when subjected to lateral forces. This method of collapse is particularly dangerous, as it tends to crush anything inside the building footprint *and* a shadow area where the upper floor(s) rotate down.

Unfortunately, even contemporary construction methodologies are subject to these same failures if the structural frames aren't designed to resist lateral loading. For example, a 6.9 magnitude earthquake on the Loma Prieta Fault near San Francisco in 1989 caused 63 fatalities. The same scale earthquake

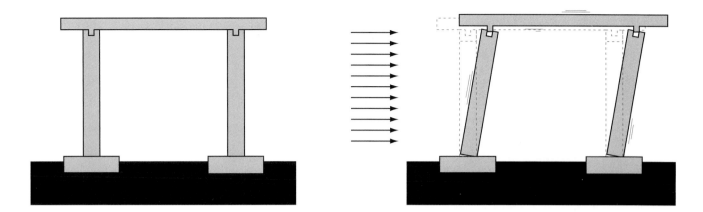

in Tajikistan in 1998 killed more than 5000, and a 7.0 magnitude earthquake in Haiti in 2010 left 2,000,000 people homeless. San Francisco's stringent seismic design codes mandate frames that resist the type of horizontal loading that occurs during the shaking of an earthquake. Buildings near the Tajikistan earthquake and in Haiti were built of brick and of concrete (often unreinforced) with inadequate connections to columns, and they tended to collapse in the manner that would be anticipated—quickly and tragically losing their geometric stability.

27.2
Lateral instability in a post-and–lintel structure.

CONNECTIONS

There are three ways that structural members can be connected to each other: pinned, fixed/moment, or roller connection (Figure 27.3). *Pinned joints* allow the connected members to rotate independent of each other. Rotation is a consequence of members under bending, and designers can choose to either have each element resist this bending moment independently (as with a pinned joint), or share this bending moment resistance (as with fixed connections). Pinned connections are quite commonly used in many different applications. Pinned joints can look like the small triangles used in our representations (e.g. an axle and bearing), they can literally be single pins connecting two elements

27.3
Three primary types of structural connections.

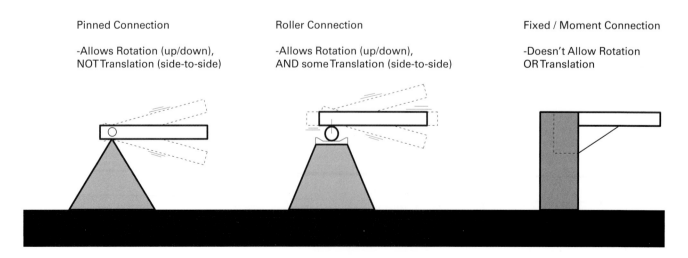

Pinned Connection

-Allows Rotation (up/down),
NOT Translation (side-to-side)

Roller Connection

-Allows Rotation (up/down),
AND some Translation (side-to-side)

Fixed / Moment Connection

-Doesn't Allow Rotation
OR Translation

27.4
Pinned connection at column base
connection at Heathrow Airport
Terminal 5 by Richard Rogers
(2012).

together (e.g. truss connection points or at the end of an X-bracing rod), or could look nothing like a pin at all (e.g. a connection between two steel beams with a multitude of bolts through a plate)—the types of joints can be crafted based on the amount of actual rotation desired/anticipated (Figure 27.4). With pinned connection (or simple supports) the behavior of each individual element can be analyzed accurately because the connections don't allow the elements to "recruit" other components to help resist loading.

Fixed or *moment* connections, are essentially the opposite of pinned connections. These connections literally fix different elements together, allowing neither translation nor rotation relative to one another (Figure 27.5). These types of connection can be quite beneficial from a structural perspective as they allow different elements to share in the resistance of loading—specifically, as we designed beams we had to assume that the end supports couldn't handle any moment capacity and so the member itself had to do all the work in resisting the load, but moment connections would allow this beam to actually transfer a moment through the connection at the supports and into the column below (which may be a problem if the column isn't sized for added bending). Moment connections are relatively easy to recognize. Typically it looks like a triangular bracket or plate connecting the beam and column together. In steel construction,

27.5
Roller connection commonly used on one end of a long bridge where thermal expansion and contraction are controlling concerns.

because it is assumed that only the flanges resist bending moments, in order to make a moment connection, the flanges between two members need to be fixed in place together (usually by welding). All cast in place concrete connections are fixed connections (the rebar is intended to connect everything together) but some precast connections are not (weld plates at the end supports would be considered pinned). Fixed joints are labor- and material-intensive connections to make because they must be fully affixed together.

Rollers are rarely used in buildings, but are typically found in long-span structures, like bridges, that are subjected to thermal expansion or shifting load locations. This connection allows *both* translation (side to side) and rotation (up and down) movement between the spanning member and support (Figure 27.6).

Frames behave in dramatically different ways depending on which of these connections are used and where. Not surprisingly, frames with fixed connections are generally stiffer than frames with hinges but the additional stiffness comes at a cost. Individual structural elements within fixed frames are all in bending and therefore must resist more complex stresses (by typically employing more material cross-sectionally). Because fixed frames are designed to transmit moment forces throughout the structure, they generally impart a bending moment and thrust into the foundations that make them more expensive and complicated to solve.

A frame with hinged connections between columns, beams, and foundations will be very loose under loading and will have no inherent ability to resist against geometric instability when subjected to any lateral loading, such as a

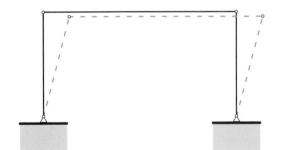

27.7
A simple hinged frame, like the unbraced post-and-lintel system, will easily collapse on itself if subjected to lateral loading.

stiff breeze (Figure 27.7). The beam will rotate with respect to the columns (it will *rack*), which will rotate with respect to the ground connections, and the frame will collapse.

Figure 27.8 shows more promising arrangements for options in which one or both of the end conditions can be made into a fixed connection. First, if the beam is fixed to the columns (but remains pinned to the ground), the fixed connections will maintain a 90-degree angle between beam and columns (no rotation is allowed). This connection transfers moment through the support, which causes the column to deflect. If the columns were not fixed against translation at the ground, they would tend to spread out, being twisted by the loading of the beam. However, since they are pinned, there must be a horizontal force at the ground that resists this *thrust*, or horizontal push. This thrust can be resisted by buttresses or a tie rod that essentially makes the frame work

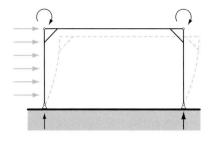

Single Braced Frames

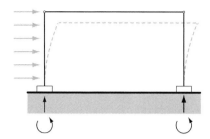

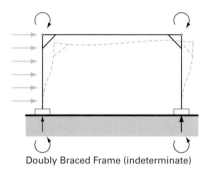

Doubly Braced Frame (indeterminate)

27.8
Basic frame theory considers the relative effects of stiffening connections between members, and between members and the substructure.

against itself, resolving the horizontal forces internally, or it can simply be taken up by the connections to the ground.

A doubly braced frame (one in which both end connections are fixed) offers even greater stiffness. Here, the columns are connected to the beam and ground by fixed connections. The columns maintain a 90-degree relationship with the beam and the ground connections, and as a result, it has to take on a great deal of bending. The columns don't start bending until a certain distance from the connections, called the *inflection point*—this occurs halfway up the column for the situation shown, which is why k for a column fixed at both ends discussed in Chapter 25 was theoretically listed as 0.5. Also note, however, that in addition to the thrust, the ground connection must resist a bending moment, keeping the column straight when the load is trying to force it to twist. This, again, requires extra foundation structure.

If fixed connections offer so much structural efficiency, why would we ever use pinned connections in a frame? For one thing, we often do not want to impart bending loads into foundations, as constant movement back and forth may weaken the soil under a footing, or compact it to a point where the footing is no longer fully bearing. This is particularly serious in bridge design, where constant live load changes can create significant movement.

Another reason that pins have been used historically is that, prior to sophisticated computer analysis, there has been no way to fully calculate the reactions in a beam fixed at more than one point. In this case, finding the reactions using simple methods is impossible, as there is no point at which we know the moment will be zero. These are called *indeterminate structures*, and while they are now easy to calculate using computer simulation, for centuries they presented an enormous problem, often leading to the use of pins simply to create a determinate structure.

MULTIPLE FRAMES

The synergy of two or more frames acting in concert with one another has some advantages. First, if we are able to add some reasonably stiff connections between columns and beams, the frames will begin to resist lateral loading through synergy. A load on one side of the multiple frames in Figure 27.9 will be resisted by each of the columns connected to the top beam, as shown. Note that the frame is rotating a little around each column, and thus the stiffness of the connections, the beam material, and the column material are all being recruited to help resist the deflection. Resisting deflection allows resistance to load, and the lateral load will end up being carried by the multiple columns to ensure that the frame remains in equilibrium. If the lateral force is large enough, the windward columns may resist the lateral load by going into tension. When this happens, the frame will rotate if the foundation isn't capable of sustaining the uplift load.

Note that the frame with pinned connections at the ground resists movement (*side-sway*) only by the stiffness of the ground joint, while the frame with fixed connections throughout resists by the stiffness of both. Also note that, for significant winds, there may be a fairly serious moment to resist that attempts to tip the entire frame over. In this case, the windward ground connection may go into tension, while the leeward connection may experience much greater compression. Adding multiple bays to the frame helps resist uplift and racking by spreading the lateral force out over several connections and by providing reactions with larger moment arms—a wind blowing against the multi-bay frames at the bottom of Figure 27.9 will have to overcome very large resisting

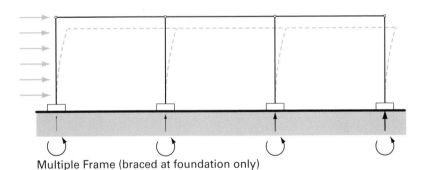

Multiple Frame (braced at foundation only)

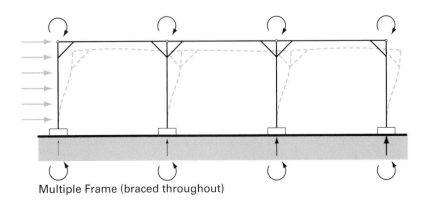

Multiple Frame (braced throughout)

27.9
Multiple frames provide the added benefit of the "table-leg" principle, with the column assisting in resisting the lateral load.

moments that can develop between the back columns and their relatively long distance from the front columns. This is known as the *table-leg* principle, and it allows relatively weak connections to work in synergy to resist wind forces along the length of a structure.

If we look inside the members of a fixed frame, we find a subtle variation on the standard shear and moment diagrams we've calculated previously. Note, for instance, that the column in Figure 27.9, while predominantly in axial compression, is also in bending. If we were to draw a diagram showing the compression loads in its cross section, we would essentially add a relatively small bending diagram (top) to a simple compression value (bottom). The result would be a diagram as shown, with a slight variation in compressive stress throughout the column's section. Likewise, the columns will resist bending in part through a compressive reaction at the beam. Thus, in addition to the primary bending action we expect from beams, we would add a small block of compression, leading to the diagram shown. Note that this moves the neutral axis slightly, and might require a bit of extra reinforcement along the top (compressed) edge.

DETERMINACY VERSUS INDETERMINACY AND FRAME SYNERGY

Thus far we have had a relatively simple method for calculating reactions on support members with pinned connections because the supports are not able to transmit any moment force. However, with the inclusion of stiff joints fixed joints, we are now in a mathematical realm that goes beyond the fairly straightforward algebra that has allowed us to quickly find reactions as noted above. We can, however develop a better understanding of the resulting structural behavior in order to approximate locations of maximum bending moments and ideally, as a consequence, responsive shapes/profiles of the structural elements. These modifications are all trying to reduce the maximum moment acting upon the beam in order to reduce the beam's size and/or increase the span. The scenarios start with the assumption that, by adding fixed connections, the total amount of moment that would typically have been resisted by the beam alone can now be distributed and resisted in the beam and columns together.

There are ways to calculate the resulting moment and shear diagrams in the frame, but these involve more complex engineering than the scope of this book. We can at least look at the effects of fixed connections on a relatively simple frame to give us some insight into how frames can "recruit" the stiffness of individual members to perform better than a simply supported beam.

The first frame in Figure 27.10, for example, shows a fixed connection between a stiff beam and stiff columns (approximately the same stiffness). Simplifying somewhat, the resulting moment diagram for the beam will have the highest moment value at the ends, with no moment in the middle of the span—this reverses the traditional moment diagram of a distributed load with simple supports which typically had the highest moment in the middle of the span. This phenomenon is called *moment attraction* because the bending moment will tend to "collect" around the stiffest connections or elements in a frame. In this case, the fixed corners of the frame are more capable of carrying moment than the center of the beam, and will experience the highest internal

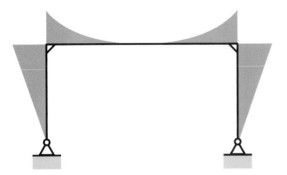

Stiff Beam, Stiff Columns

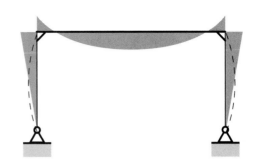

Stiff Beam, Weak Columns

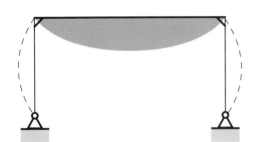

Stiff Beam, Very Weak Columns
(essentially pin supports)

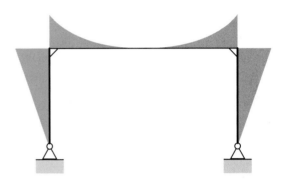

Weak Beam, Stiff Columns
(essentially a center pin)

bending. Note that the columns, too, participate in carrying the bending load by carrying some of the resisting moment. Here, we've hinged the "feet" of the frame, and the moment diagram decreases to zero at these points (as hinges cannot transmit moment force). Note, too, that the moment must be the same value in the beam and the column at the connection.

Using the logic of moment attraction, we can show what happens to the frame if we change the relative stiffness of one or more frame elements. For example, if we apply the same load as shown previously to a frame with significantly weaker columns (as shown in the second example), the columns will begin to bend, changing the shape of the moment diagram as they move away from the frame's ideal shape. Note how the moment transferred across the fixed connection is now much smaller because of the weakness of the columns. However, because the frame has to find somewhere to help resist the maximum internal moment and the columns have reached their capacity to do so, it essentially forces the beams to develop moment forces across the length. Note, too, that for an infinitely weak column, the moment diagram will have to start at zero at the connection, and we'll get a moment diagram on the beam that will be equal to the typical arch-like shape of a typical moment diagram for a distributed load condition (this is shown in the third diagram).

If, on the other hand, we weaken the beam and stiffen the columns, we get quite the opposite effect. Now, the columns are capable of taking quite a bit of bending load, and the need to equalize moment values across the fixed

27.10
Frame theory also considers the relative stiffness of columns and beams.

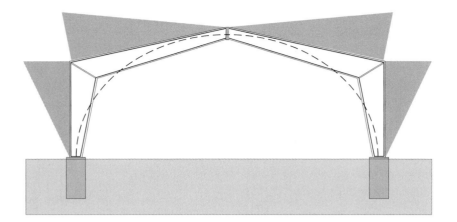

connection means that, as the columns get relatively stiffer in relation to the beam, we tend to *reduce* the maximum moment at the beam's center. In fact, if we add a hinge to the center of the beam, we get the final condition shown in Figure 27.11, in which the moment curve reverses, and the maximum internal bending stress now occurs at the two fixed connections.

This three-hinged arch system places an enormous amount of potential moment force at the connection points. To resist this, the columns and beams both get physically larger at this location, using their area and orientation to resist against this high amount of localized bending. As was demonstrated in Chapter 22, matching a structure's longitudinal shape to match the moment diagram profile is an effective strategy for ensuring that area under the most moment will have sufficient resistance while areas with low moments can be more judicious with material distribution. That, of course, is exactly the strategy found in the shaping, detailing, and construction of the extremely efficient, and highly economical, *rigid frame or hinged frame* structural frame systems. The deepest section of the frame occurs at the location of the highest moment and the frame narrows down to a small profile at the three hinges. Rigid frame buildings are the only type of purely section-active structural system that is an effective long-span strategy as typically very deep beams are simply too inefficient and too heavy to span long distances on their own. The base connections at the bottom of the columns must be pinned (or they can be called hinged) so they don't transmit a bending stress into the foundations. Because there is theoretically no moment force occurring in the middle of the beam area, another hinge can be located at that point as well—when this happens instead of having two columns holding up a beam, the structural system becomes more like two hybrid "column-beam" elements resting upon each other in the middle— essentially like two halves of an arch. In fact, the proper shape for locating the three hinges in the frame should be derived from the funicular shape of an arch.

LATERAL RESISTANCE—LARGE SCALE

Buildings obviously need to be able to respond to all loads that are applied to them. As we have seen in previous sections, this means sizing structural elements that are strong enough and stiff enough to resist loading *but* if the building isn't also stable then it is no longer safe and serviceable. Simply creating a building with geometrical fixed frames won't guarantee a stable building—the frames must be placed in a manner that develops a macro strategy of stability for the entire building. Many of the strategies for creating geometric stability within a frame as shown above can be applied to a more macro view of the building. Because we are never sure which way the wind may blow or the ground may shake, designs for the lateral resistance in large-scale buildings require many different locations (and orientations) for stabilizing systems throughout a building's design.

It is also worth noting that many of the structural elements employed to resist lateral instability are typically only sized and located for this purpose—they are not intended as resistance against gravitational loads. However, there are quite notable exceptions to be found in high-rise buildings as discussed in Chapter 29.

So far we've assumed that we can, in fact, develop a fixed frame between beam and column. In practice, there are essentially four methods to do this (Figure 27.12):

The first option is to build a *shear diaphragm wall* connecting one or more members with the ground. This wall needs to be a stiff plane, one that resists *racking* (conversion to a skewed parallelogram) and maintains its geometric stability. If a lateral force is applied to the side of the wall, the diaphragm wall will go into shear, carrying the lateral load into the ground via a shear-resistant foundation. Typical residential construction, for example, uses sheets of plywood on external walls to brace simple stud walls. Nailed connections, no matter how good, must be assumed to provide only pins, while plywood's quasi-isotropic nature means that it is excellent against racking. In larger-scale applications, this principle is applied in *shear walls*, often made of concrete. The effectiveness of these elements is entirely dependent on their length, along which shear resistance can develop. Note that shear walls can only provide stability to the frame for loading applied parallel to their planar surface—it cannot provide frame stability for loads applied perpendicularly, only a second shear wall with a rotated orientation can do that. Stairways and elevators are typically good candidates for shear walls as they already have two solid walls running perpendicularly to each other.

Structural slabs can provide a degree of stability against lateral forces by providing a way for laterally applied loads to be transferred across parallel frames until a resisting/bracing member can resolve the lateral force downward. When the slab is being used for this purpose it is called the horizontal diaphragm. Having a necessary architectural element which also provides helpful structural efficiency is nice—it is much more convenient to have slabs transfer loads horizontally to fewer braced frame locations as it allows for much more open interior spaces between column bays as a result.

The second type of laterally resistant member is a diagonal brace, essentially making a joint into a moment connection by triangulating the beam and column. The result, a *braced frame* offers the advantage of clear sectional area, though potentially limited head height in the corners. This is most common in timber construction.

The third type shown is triangulation via *cross bracing*, or physically connecting the pin between a beam and column with the pin at ground level. If

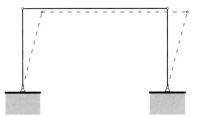

Unbraced Frame

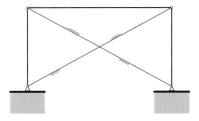

Diaphragm (Shear) Wall

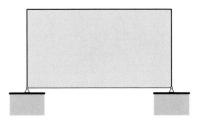

Braced Frame

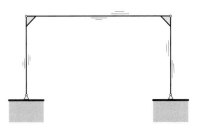

Cross-Braced Frame

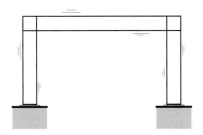

Moment Frame

27.12
Strategies for providing lateral resistance include stiff or braced joints (moment and braced) frames.

cross-braced in both directions, these members can be simple tension elements such as cables. A load from one direction will cause one cable to go into tension, while the other goes slack, and the tight cable will triangulate the frame, preventing movement. This is often the lightest solution, but presents conflicts with circulation through the frame.

Finally, we can provide adequate stiffness for most situations by simply oversizing the structural members involved and ensuring that they are able to connect with one another over a reasonably large sectional area. *Moment connections* are bulky, and often require oversized beams and columns, but they offer the advantage of open bays. In steel, these are often achieved by welding on additional plates that essentially extend one member's flanges across the perpendicular member's section, creating a *moment box* that offers considerably rigidity.

In general, multiple frames perform best when lateral resistance is evenly distributed throughout the footprint (Figure 27.13) and consistently applied in the same locations for multistory buildings. Uneven lateral resistance can cause the entire building to twist. Because this twisting is essentially a moment force about the center of the footprint, it follows that the most effective lateral bracing locations are at the extreme edges of the building. However, this is often where we want the greatest transparency; compromise is often inevitable, for instance, if exit stairs are placed along the perimeter.

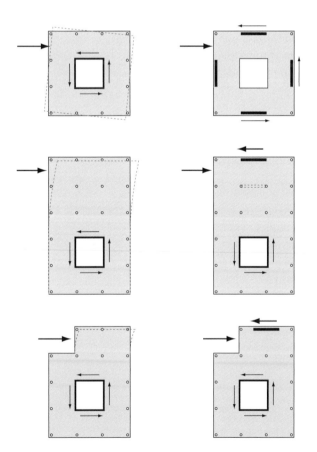

27.13
In addition to overall lateral stability, large buildings require consideration of torsional stability, or the resistance of a frame to twisting.

CONCLUSION

The structural components of a building must be sized to accommodate the different loading conditions through gravitational forces, but a structure is more than just a collection of appropriately sized components. A completed structure can be considered an amalgamation of frames and connections. The type of frame and arrangement of these connections dictates a great deal of the overall building's behavior. Basic structural design considerations of stability and stiffness are explicitly determined by a designer's choice of different combinations of frames and connection types.

FREQUENTLY ASKED QUESTIONS

Do designers really need to know, or decide, the manner of each joining method within a building?
Part of the answer depends upon the intentions of the designer to emphasize (or not) the importance of exposing each joint and, by extension, what the type of joint reveals about the overall structural strategy. For some designers, these types of considerations show a commitment to craft and consideration at multiple scales (imagine the Centre Pompedieu in Paris without beautifully articulated connections) or an aesthetic "celebration" of how a building works (typified by the high-tech movement). Designers can't determine the manner of connection for aesthetic reasons (some connections must be fixed or pinned) but it doesn't mean that the manner of connections need not be aesthetically interesting. In most cases, for traditional framing, especially where the structure isn't exposed, these decisions are determined in conjunction with the structural engineer and fabricator to determine efficient and effective methods of connections. Economics matters as well, so the manner of how elements are connected together needs to be evaluated in these terms also.

GLOSSARY

Braced frame: A method of providing lateral resistance to frames by triangulating the corners of a rectangular bay. This ensures that the corners themselves will remain rigid and that any lateral force will be absorbed by a combination of the vertical members bending and the horizontal member undergoing axial load.

Cross bracing: A method of providing lateral resistance to frames by triangulating a rectangular bay. Often this is done using steel cables, rods, or compact sections. When the frame undergoes lateral loading, the diagonal cross bracing will go into tension or compression and will transmit the lateral load directly to the frame's supports.

Determinate structure: A structure whose supporting conditions can be easily figured algebraically. For simple beams, this requires supports to be pinned, so that $\Sigma M = 0$ can be established.

Diaphragm walls: Planar, vertical panels designed to provide lateral stiffness to a structure. Essentially, shear walls work like cantilevers tipped up on their ends, absorbing lateral loads by bending and transmitting the loads to a foundation. Typically made of reinforced concrete in large-scale construction, or plywood in smaller-scale buildings.

Frame: A system of horizontal and vertical structural members that collectively resist gravity and lateral forces more effectively than they would on their own.

Indeterminate structure: A structure whose supporting conditions cannot be calculated algebraically, typically because fixed connections offer the capacity to take moment stresses.

Inflection point: The point in a bending structure at which the resulting curvature changes from one direction to the other.

Lateral stability: The second order of magnitude of structural design, after gravity resistance. Simply put, the ability of a structure to resist sideways forces.

Moment attraction: The phenomenon under which stiff members tend to develop the highest bending stresses in a frame. As weaker members shrug off bending forces by deforming, stiffer members are left carrying the bending load as they hold their geometry.

Moment connections: Another term for fixed connections, more accurately describing the fact that they can carry bending moment from one member to another due to their stiffness.

Racking: The tendency of a frame to change shape by skewing when undergoing lateral loading.

Thrust: Horizontal forces at the base of a frame (or any other structure) incurred due to the frame's stiffness. As loads deform a stiff frame, its "feet" will tend to spread out because of the joints' rotations.

FURTHER READING

MacDonald, A. (1994). *Structure and Architecture*. Oxford: Butterworth Heinemann Ltd; Chapter 2, Structural Requirements, pp. 9–15.

Salvadori, M. (1975). *Structure in Architecture: The Building of Buildings*. Englewood Cliffs: Prentice-Hall; Chapter 8, Frames and Arches, pp. 178–202.

Sandaker, B. N. and Eggen, A. P. (1992) *The Structural Basis of Architecture*. New York: Whitney Library of Design; Chapter 6, The Frame: Cooperation Between the Column and the Beam, pp. 131–148.

28

LONG-SPAN STRUCTURES: ASSEMBLIES AND BEHAVIOR

Long-span structures	Restrictions on scaling
	Qualitative differences and challenges
	Evolution in efficiencies
Vector-resisting systems	Truss behavior and arrangements
	Space frame trusses
	Geodesic domes
Surface-resisting systems	Rigid and non-rigid systems
	Cable and arch structures
	Cable membranes
	Air-filled structures
	Rigid system classifications
	Domes and vaults
	Shape and behavior

INTRODUCTION

Long-span systems are often considered a distinct and unique architectural problem for two main reasons. First, because they have spans with dimensions that exceed the spanning limits of standard beams and slabs, they require changes to their geometry, configuration, or shape to more effectively or safely carry loading. Second, because many long-span projects don't require a purely functionally driven form or volume, more contemporary long-span projects have been free to adapt to simpler, more effective structurally driven forms for the building design. Train stations, exhibition halls, airport hangars, assembly halls, industrial building and sporting arenas can all be enclosed in a number of ways, so the selection of a long-span system often depends on balancing desired structural performance with the aesthetics, materiality, constructability, and economic viability of each potential system.

There are several large, historically significant long-span structures that were built before the industrial revolution, but these structures were often very tall,

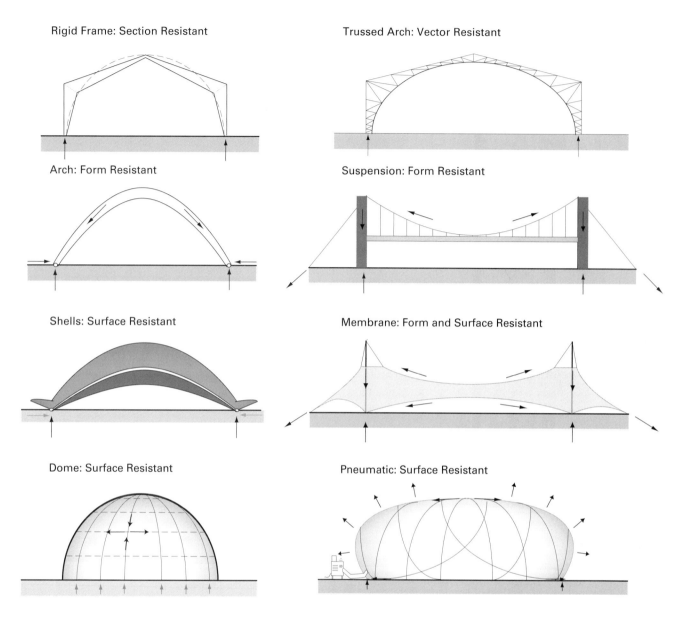

Rigid Frame: Section Resistant

Trussed Arch: Vector Resistant

Arch: Form Resistant

Suspension: Form Resistant

Shells: Surface Resistant

Membrane: Form and Surface Resistant

Dome: Surface Resistant

Pneumatic: Surface Resistant

very heavy, and very resource intensive. In the last two centuries, significant synergistic advances in material technology, fabrication methods, and analyses tools have continued to improve the performance of long-span structures and expand upon new opportunities for formal explorations. The development of viable long-span structures has focused on ways to make the structures lightweight, yet relatively strong and stiff (in other words efficient), with a clear strategy for affordable fabrication and erection. As a result, a diverse range of contemporary long-span structural options has emerged, each with a distinctive aesthetic identity related to its structural strategy. At first glance, many of the elements and materials in the different long-span systems look considerably different, but they all share a similar central design strategy: they all develop effective resistance through an intentional and artful formation of materials (Figure 28.1). As the Uruguayan designer Eladio Dieste explained, "The resistant virtues of the structure that we make depend on their form; it is through

28.1
Various classifications of long-span structures showing similar strategies of formal resistance to loading.

their form that they are stable and not because of an awkward accumulation of materials. There is nothing more noble and elegant from an intellectual viewpoint than this; resistance through form."

One of the most effective design principles with long-span structures is the ability to reduce the weight of the structure by increasing the efficiency of the way in which the load is resisted. As Buckminster Fuller said, "The sophistication of a building varies inversely with its weight." As we've seen in previous sections, there are many means by which traditional framing elements can be evolved to increase their efficiency: their lateral and longitudinal profiles can be altered by bending elements or redistributing area; they can be arrayed with other similar elements to form a more resistant system; they can incorporate advanced material technologies; or they can use innovative means of assembly. In long-span structures, frequently *all* of these methods are needed (Figure 28.2). We have also seen the distinct structural advantage found in eliminating the resource-laden sectional-resistant bending elements. There are a range of ways in which supporting elements and/or surfaces can be configured to avoid bending stresses altogether, opting instead for the axial stresses of tension and compression—two of these options, vector-resistant systems and surface-resistant systems will be discussed in this section.

Hypothetically, creating a long-span space can be achieved simply by modifying particular spanning elements; for instance, by making a beam deeper to allow it to span farther. But resisting bending stress purely through the manipulation of cross-sectional configuration has distinct and profound limitations related to the efficient distribution of weight in resistance of bending. The formulae in previous sections have shown us that doubling the span for objects under uniformly loaded bending conditions quadruples the maximum moment and increases the deflection by eight times the original amount (both calculations are also dependent on effective distribution of weight within the component). Therefore, in order to make a structural element span longer, it can't simply get bigger proportionately or else it will simply deflect too much or fail under its own weight. As Galileo demonstrated in 1638, the adequacy of a structure's proportions at one scale does not guarantee its success at another (Figure 28.3); past a certain point the weight of the structure itself will

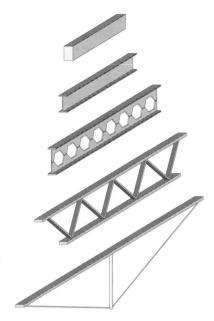

28.2
The formal evolution of a beam.

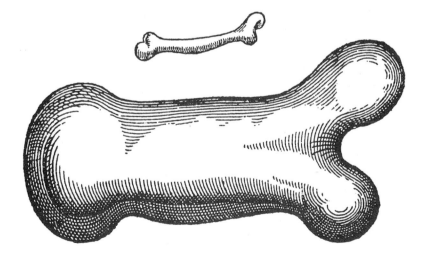

28.3
Galileo's classic demonstration of the relationship between shape and strength.

superimpose a dead load that begins to render the beam inefficient, and the beam will not be able to carry even its own weight.

The simplest way to do this is to remove portions of the spanning member that aren't structurally necessary, such as the statically inefficient web, leaving the outer edges of the beam's flanges intact. The structural idea is to maintain an effective section modulus without increasing the maximum spanning moment by including all of the spanning member's weight. This can be accomplished by cutting holes out of a steel beam, or casting voids in a concrete beam. In both cases, the resulting openings must be located on or near the beam's neutral axis. Steel beams lend themselves to a particular technique known as *castellation*, in which a zig-zag hexagonal cut is made in the web of a beam, which is then welded back together so that the resulting "tabs" attach to one another. This creates open voids in the beam, and increases the overall depth (and thus the section modulus) using the same weight of material (Figure 28.2).

TRUSS BEHAVIOR AND ARRANGEMENT

Another method of increasing section modulus while decreasing weight involves the elimination of the beam's web and replacing it with a series of one or more triangular panels that are linked together with short linear elements to create a highly effective and economical lightweight spanning member, known simply as a truss. Trusses are designed to resist bending stresses, but generate resistance quite differently than beams.

Unlike beams that rely upon effective distribution of cross-sectional area to resist the bending moment, trusses, by means of their triangular configuration and pinned connections, only transmit axial stress of tension and compression into the trussed web members—this allows all the components within the system to be relatively small because these axial loads (either tension or compression) can be resisted by the entire cross-sectional area of each one of the triangular web components.

As a result of this configuration, these truss systems have a high ratio of strength and stiffness, maintain an effective depth to span ratio, are economically simple in fabrication and erection, and generally are adaptable to many different loading conditions. Simply put, there is a reason trusses are used pervasively in construction, and these advantages become even more pronounced in long-span conditions.

For instance, a certain degree of flexibility in shaping an element's form is highly advantageous in long-span applications—especially if these adjustments can be made without harming the structure's effectiveness, affordability, or fabrication. Because trusses are made of a series of smaller, relatively lightweight, elements, different configurations for the profile and depth can be relatively easily accommodated to be more responsive to the loading scenario, using only the necessary depth in the determined locations. The top and bottom chords of the trusses can be configured in many different ways (parallel, pitched, curved, etc.) and help to create trusses that are often shaped in conjunction with architectural desires for aesthetics and spatial requirements. Many of the first long-span truss systems in the late nineteenth century used

28.4
The Galerie des Machines was the largest wide–spanning iron-framed structure ever built (spanning greater than 300ft (100m)).

trussed arch systems to cover rail stations and exhibition halls (Figure 28.4). These lightweight iron structures used trussed configurations for the vertical and horizontal components, developing the three-hinged arch profile now found in the modern rigid frame systems (Chapter 27).

With all long-span systems, there are unique challenges related to the final assemblage of the various parts, and trusses are no exception. While smaller trusses can be fully assembled off-site, long-span trusses require a certain amount of in-field assembly—typically the size of panels that can be fabricated off-site is limited in size by transportation limitations of truck sizes and bridge clearances. Fortunately, most of the in-field work can primarily be done on the ground before the trusses are lifted into place but these connection joints present distinct liabilities for failure so any modifications to panel points should be strictly avoided.

As pure spanning members, trusses are highly effective, but in most cases trusses need to be combined with other structural elements to form a complete structural system performance. For instance, most trusses, particularly deep and lighter configurations, need to be braced and stabilized against perpendicularly applied lateral forces, so diagonal bracing is often located between trusses to stabilize the lower chord (a strategy which also helps resist buckling in the member under loading). Additionally, because trusses in long-span systems are typically carrying large loads, they are typically secured directly into a vertical load-bearing member, like a column, leaving a particular distance between

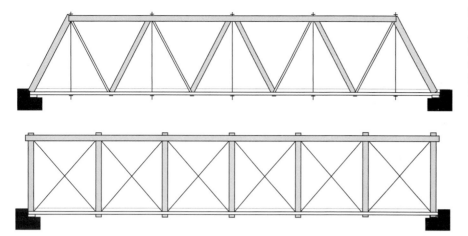

28.5
In bridge trusses there is often
a difference in the size of
the different web members.
Compressive members are
typically clearly larger in order to
resist against buckling.

trusses that need supporting systems as well. For these areas, another series of structural elements, like purlins and decking, run perpendicular to the trusses and are designed to collect and transfer their loads to the truss. Critically, in order to avoid having any bending stresses in any truss members, all of the loads must be transferred to the truss only at a *panel point* (where horizontal and vertical/diagonal members intersect) where it can be immediately split into different directions and stresses by the chord and web members.

Once the load is transferred to the panel points, web members are either tensed or compressed as needed to maintain equilibrium. Interestingly, truss components designed to resist compression stress are a specific concern in long-span truss designs because they act like columns and become highly susceptible to buckling, particularly in long-span arrangements where truss members are relatively long (Figure 28.5).

Depending on the spacing of the trusses, these perpendicularly running secondary structural members can become relatively significantly sized elements—they are bending members sized to span from truss to truss. This span can only be reduced if the trusses are placed more frequently (which is not cost effective) or by having the top chords of the truss split apart into two different top chords that form a V-shaped cross-sectional configuration of the truss. Because trusses are made from smaller, straight-line components, these types of modifications are somewhat easy to make and make for dramatic spatial composition as well (Figure 28.6).

The potential to consider the cross section of a truss as something more akin to a geometric solid configuration (e.g. tetrahedron) and less as a single plane also unlocks another evolutionary way of thinking about trusses. Instead of using parallel trusses with secondary framing systems, another set of trusses could be arranged perpendicularly to form a truss lattice. In this configuration, the load isn't distributed one way; both sets of trusses in the lattice convey loads to their supports, like a two-way slab system. In these structures, the load doesn't have to be transmitted along the line of a single truss, it can be transmitted diagonally across the span if needed, allowing for more flexibility in the placement of the support columns. This biaxial expansion of triangulated lattice girders is known by a simpler name, the *space frame* truss (Figure 28.7).

28.6
The triangular cross section used by the arched trusses at Portland International Airport.

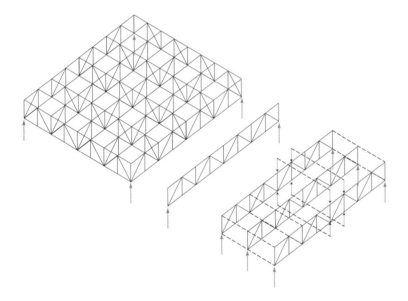

28.7
Single trusses running in parallel require column supports at each end of the span and secondary framing running perpendicularly at top and bottom chords.

SPACE FRAMES

Space frames are ostensibly full trusses that span in two dimensions, but they are more accurately described as repeating discrete modules, often tetrahedrons, with intersecting points that combine to form a continuous plane. This distinction is important because although one-way spanning trusses in long-span conditions are quite efficient, they are made from relatively heavy and large components that are somewhat difficult and expensive to fabricate and erect. For a long time it was widely understood that trusses could be configured like a two-way slab system, but because of well-founded concerns about the economic and structural ramifications of doubling the amount of connections

28.8
Konrad Wachsmann's proposal for
the U.S. Air Force space frame
(1959).

(and the structural integrity of the connections), space frames weren't considered a viable structural option for many years.

Crucially to the development of the system, the foci of the revived space frame experiments and prototypes weren't strictly structural or aesthetic—most knew the strategy would be strong and stiff enough—but instead they were focused upon ways to make the system more affordable to build and erect *while* creating dramatic and flexible architectural space. The first space frame experiments, prefabricated steel tetrahedrons, were patented by Alexander Graham Bell in1904, but there were limitations to the manner of fabrication and connections that remained somewhat unresolved until the middle of the twentieth century. Later, Max Mengeringhausen focused on creating the ideal joint connection, the Mero ball, which would allow up to 18 different bars to be screwed into a single spherical node. A reliable joint connection meant that smaller members could be used and fabricated somewhat more easily. Other major advancements in the spatial, technical, and functionally driven aspects of space frame design were developed by Konrad Wachsmann. He worked extensively on developing reliable joint-based modular construction techniques to make long-span spaces and famously proposed a space frame system, based on a 1×3×1m module, that would allow for a long-span hangar building with 150ft (50m) overhangs that could be quickly erected, demounted, and transported for military applications (Figure 28.8).

One of the concerns for long-span systems in general is the potential for sagging, but because the space frame is made from interlocking triangles (or more specifically triangular-based three-dimensional forms), it is very stiff. Because these modules are adjoined to each other, the system becomes completely stable from all directions (again owing to the geometric stability of the triangle), and this resistance to deflection obviously increases the potential length of the span. The performance of the components within the system, the chords and web struts and ties, still perform in the same manner (only tension or compression) so it is still highly efficient.

The smaller size of the modular pieces, coupled with their repeated geometric configuration, helps with fabrication, assembly, and economic concerns. There are variations in the configuration of different types of space frames, but most of these smaller modules are to be connected together at the joint itself. Because the joint is a simple pin (or Mero ball), it can make the method of assembly relatively easy, but depending on the span of the system, these joints can become enormous (typically each joint will need to adjoin between four and ten components). Due to the interlocking nature of the configuration, there is a bit of redundancy in the system as well—not every member is designed to take loading according to a particular path as we saw in typical trusses. Instead, load is transferred according to the shared stiffness of particular members. Space frames can be extremely efficient and can span up to 500ft (175m).

The strategy for locating vertical supports (e.g. columns) for a space frame system is analogous to the structural slab concerns for punching shear. The space frame is intentionally designed to distribute the bending loads relatively equitably across the span, but paradoxically, it must also consolidate these stresses at certain points to the columns below. If the number of columns is restricted and the point of transfer is consolidated, the space frame members around the support will need to be significantly larger. To avoid this, either more columns are added to the system (although this is expensive) and/or the columns themselves can be designed with a larger bearing perimeter that attaches to multiple points across the space frame across a larger area (a strategy discussed in Chapter 25, Column Design). By creating a larger column perimeter bearing area, spans are reduced and differences between localized stresses are minimized. Frequently, effective proposals typically mimicked the early arched truss frame configurations and simply brought the space frame system directly into the modified column forms.

In general, space frames have been configured in a typically planar arrangement, although the orientations of the planes could be tilted. However, no matter how efficiently designed the cross-section is, it pales in comparison to the increased efficiency available if the form could be curved upwards like an arch, or more specifically if the form could also provide enclosure, like a dome. This, Buckminster Fuller believed, would be the ultimate conjunction of design, engineering, construction, and a social/economic service, the *geodesic dome*.

GEODESIC DOMES

Fuller was not the first to experiment with lightweight dome frames. In 1922, Zeiss-Dywidag used bent and welded pieces of thin metal components to create a braced ribbed metal dome. This dome's form was based on the "revolution" method where the curved shape is revolved around an axis point to determine the three dimensional form (Figure 28.1). The typical *arch lines* (vertical longitudinal lines) and *hoop lines* (horizontal latitudinal lines) were articulated in the framing with diagonal bracing at each corner of the resulting smaller sections. The geodesic dome developed by Fuller in the late 1940s was based on a more complex spatial geometry of a sphere shape that was created by a set of small interlocking platonic solids (the icosahedron was frequently used). Geodesic domes are quite efficient in terms of *weight*; they use multiple nodes and connections to very effectively distribute both gravity and lateral loads across the dome's surface, eliminating a great deal of a classic dome's dead weight, and can be erected and demounted somewhat easily because of the small size of the components (Figure 28.9). Geodesic domes can be configured

28.9
Fuller's design for the U.S. Pavilion at the 1967 Exposition in Montreal.

to sit at, above, or below their equator line and still be stable structures. On the ground the forces acting with the dome will vary, but basically the top portion of the dome will all be in compression. The domes are so lightweight that often the concern with the foundation design isn't compression, but the uplift from wind! The configuration of the dome itself is strong and stiff thanks to the double curve of the spherical shape, but the spherical shape makes this type of long-span solution quite tall compared to other long-span options. Designers may also find it limiting (or beneficial) to have this geometrically contrived form serve as both interior and exterior spatial definition. There are several other limitations: the structure is designed only to be self-supporting (intermediate floors would need their own separate system), reliable enclosure systems around the dome are difficult to fabricate and secure (the acrylic panels in Fuller's Expo '67 dome burned), and the spherical form makes it hard to locate basic vertical surfaces, like a door, into the form.

Ultimately, Fuller believed the overall efficiency of the system's structural performance and the resulting economic affordability could be a solution for many different types of long-span conditions and, in fact, globally there are thousands of geodesic systems constructed.

In summary, one of the key aspects of truss behavior is the effective distribution of bending loads into pure compression and tension vectors. The truss becomes a deeper, more lightweight spanning element. It is easier to fabricate and erect than heavy beams (due in no small part to its lighter weight). Because trusses are made of relatively small components, truss shapes can be easily re-configured in cross section and/or profile to improve their structural advantage. The traditional one-way orientation of truss spans require a secondary system of framing to support the loads and provide stability so trusses evolved into more of a planar three-dimensional space framing. Advancement in fabrication and erection methods led to the increased viability of the system to span incredibly far distances, with an effective depth to span ratio, while maintaining a high degree of stiffness. The geodesic domes, which essentially curved the space frame into a geometrically stable configuration show a full evolution of various ways of solving the simple problem—how can we more effectively span farther? By simply breaking it apart, the solid beam has come a long way. Another strategy involves putting the beam back together and flattening it down to make a strong surface that can be twisted and folded to resist loads, in other words, to create surface-resisting systems.

SURFACE-RESISTING SYSTEMS

Like form-active cable and arch systems discussed in Chapter 21, surface-resistant systems are comprised of structures whose form (and ultimately aesthetic) is rationally defined by structural performance. Unlike those other systems, a surface form is developed to resist the loads, and this surface configuration creates profound formal and spatial consequences. Surface-resisting systems are not made of a collection of assembled structural elements; the surface itself *is* the structural system and it gives an identity to the architectural form indistinguishable from the structural strategy. Developing forms that are responsive to their principles of structural behavior and the manner of their construction enables designs to be responsive to larger architectural concerns, but conversely, if the selected shape doesn't enhance the desired service, the form can't be adjusted later to accommodate this.

There are two major classifications for surface systems, rigid and non-rigid (although both achieve adequate rigidity). Rigid systems may be considered more compressive-based surfaces designs (shells, domes, etc.) while non-rigid systems use tension cables to create a membrane surface. Both configurations share certain structural strategies and configurations with the form-active systems and so the following descriptions of these surface systems will assume this prior knowledge. We begin with non-rigid systems and a simple concept: form follows tension.

CABLE AND ARCH STRUCTURES

In an effort to lighten up the roof load from the heavier concrete compression shells, alternative configurations can be used that combine the logic of suspended cables and compressive arch funicular systems together to create suspended curved surfaces that are entirely in tension. In tension systems that rely upon cables, form doesn't follow function as much as it follows the forces.

When uniformly loaded cables are hung between two supports they will take an upwardly curving, catenary curve shape. These cables are quite efficient in supporting loads, but they are inherently unstable in dynamic load situations. Because these systems are subjected to lateral loads, uplifting forces, shifting load locations, and point loads they also require the use of a secondary set of non-load-bearing cables that run perpendicular to the bearing cables which are connected to the bearing cables and tightened down. Because the load-bearing cables have a naturally occurring sag, when the secondary cables are added, a double-curved surface emerges, creating an *anticlastic* shell, that can resemble a saddle. At any given point on the surface, the curvature bends in opposing directions—a mutually opposed bracing and support system. Even though some cables are convex, they are still in tension—in fact, the entire membrane surface is in tension in both directions.

The cables ultimately need to rely upon some type of structural compression member to carry the loads to the ground, like a column or wall. The configuration of these compression members is ultimately determined by how the system is designed to resist the thrust generated from the cables. Unless the load-bearing cables are extended downward from the supports, these vertically oriented compression elements must be designed to resist the overturning moments—most effectively done through formal manipulation and orientation of the compression member (e.g. by "leaning" a column backwards) or by creating a compression ring for circular structures. Fred Severud's engineering work for the Livestock Judging Pavilion (designed by William Nowicki) in Raleigh, North Carolina (1952) features two parabolic concrete compressive arches inclined in opposite directions from each other as the compressive elements and a suspended cable roof is draped between the arches. The arches carry compression and resist thrust while the two sets of cables create a double-curved membrane roof (Figure 28.10). Severud's structural design for the Yale University Hockey stadium (designed by Eero Saarinen) used a single central curving concrete arch spine that spanned across the length of the building while supporting draped cable roof systems on each side. The roof cables sag downward in a funicular form to the curving outer edges of the building's concrete walls—the curving roof and curving plan combine to create the necessary double-curved form. The thrust at the top is equalized by pressure from cables on both sides and the thrust at the lower supports is resisted by having

28.10
The saddle-shaped geometry of the roof is created by the orientation of the two concrete arches and the criss-crossed cables.

the perimeter concrete walls battered backwards with a deep horizontal compression ring running along the top exterior of the wall.

MEMBRANES

Tent membrane structures use a combination of suspended cables and compressive masts to create vast span of dynamically shaped space. As with other surface resisting structures, they rely upon continuous and equitable distribution of surface tension in all directions across the membrane which occurs when the membrane surface takes on the double-curved geometry defined by the bearing cables, stabilizing cables, and the systems of support (vertical masts and the ground plane).

Unlike the cable and arch suspended roof systems, tent structures have more possible free-form formal configurations—many of which can be quite complex. There is a geometric relationship that results from a designer's decisions about the desired height and span of the enclosed area under the membrane that determines the quantity and placement of supporting systems, which then has to be tested to ensure that the membrane and cables aren't subjected to excessive tension stress.

As with other membrane structures, the double-curved surface provides the resistance to loading while stabilizing the system—it is being pulled in two directions simultaneously. Ideally, then, the tension within the membrane must be the same everywhere in the surface to insure that no stresses are too high, which risks shearing, or too low, which would show slacking. These membranes are held up with collars at their mast supports (to avoid punching shear) and are draped downward to provide enclosure. This creates a particular geometric condition on the perimeter of the structure where funicular-shaped "arches" made from the large guy wires are anchored to the ground in certain locations and pulled tight (Figure 28.11).

28.11
The 1972 Munich Olympic Stadium, designed by Frei Otto (1972).

In order to be effective structurally, the membrane surface must be *pre–tensioned*, by being stretched in one direction while being held tightly in place. This is done by either pushing up the support rings at the masts or pulling the membrane tighter at the perimeter (shortening of the perimeter catenary edge cables and reducing its sag) until the desired level of tension is achieved. This strategy of stressing the membrane is quite similar to an umbrella, which is pre-tensioned against both uplift (wind) and loading (rain) by extending the metal frame beneath, which is attached to the fabric's extreme edges. Like an umbrella, total environmental enclosure from the elements isn't possible with this system alone which limits its viability in many climates.

The logic of the structure is quite simple, but the challenges related to the design, documentation, and fabrication of this type of system are profound. Again, these long-span structures were known theoretically to be capable of spanning long distances, but there were two critical impediments to implementation: the availability of adequate materials and the capacity to accurately design, document, and analyze the work. First, these structures required steel cable of a very high bearing capacity, so high strength steel needed to be used, but the major limitation was the options for the membrane itself. Until the 1970s fabrics didn't have enough reliable strength and, if left uncoated by PVC, the fabric would deteriorate over time. Securing the fabric to the supporting cables without damaging the structural or environmental performance of the membrane also required advancements in fabrication and erection techniques.

Because these geometries are so complicated and the resulting elements need to be so precisely analyzed and fabricated, tent membrane projects were some of the first types of structures that used purely mathematical procedures for determining the shape and behavior and this required the work of advancements in computer modeling software. Although the geometry of the membrane can initially be determined by running a model with the defined mast and boundary locations through patent soap solution to see the natural form of bubbles that occur upon the surface, this is more helpful visually than mathematically. The process of design and documentation had to evolve to allow these structures to be built.

AIR-FILLED STRUCTURES

A particular form of membrane structures, called *pneumatics*, utilizes a membrane enclosure that is pressurized to create a tensed membrane skin. The success of the structure demands that the space be continually pressurized—as a result, it is the only structural system that relies upon an active mechanical system for its performance. In the most common application, called an *air-supported* system, there is a single roof membrane sealed at the perimeter that can be inflated by air pressure. Air pumps blow up the interior space like a balloon, and keep the roof in tension by continuously running to maintain inflation (Figure 28.12). Alternatively, distinctly shaped smaller structural membrane tubes can be pressurized to create very unique *air-inflated* arches that can be combined together to create a span across an interior space that isn't pressurized. As one might expect, the pressure on the air-inflated arches must be very

28.12
The U.S. Pavilion at Osaka's Expo '70.

high to create enough rigidity and strength for a tension membrane to mimic the structural behavior of a compressive arch.

The architectural and structural strategic benefits for these pneumatic systems are clear—by pressurizing the interior air, it exerts an upward and evenly distributed force across the entire cable constrained membrane surface. Instead of relying upon very tall supporting elements to suspend the sagging cables (which may create unused space), pneumatic structures get the benefit of creating interior space with funicular arch shapes but without the liability of the heavy compressive structural arch elements. Further, like the cable/arch system, the membrane has a defined boundary along the edges and this boundary provides the necessary enclosure of the space. The membranes are pushed into tension in two different directions, constrained by cables to create the overall form of the membrane, and so shear becomes a concern, especially for lightweight fabric surfaces.

Shearing and deterioration of the fabric itself is a constant potential concern because without the integrity of the membrane, the system cannot stay inflated. Another particular concern with these systems, especially for long-span roofs in colder climates, is the capacity to handle the concentrated loads caused by the accumulation of snow and ice—these point loads can create low spots in the roof which collect more snow (exacerbating the problem) and at times leading to collapse. Sudden changes in roof loading, like large snow falls, require sudden changes in resisting air pressure which may not be quickly accomplished in large-volume spaces. Additionally, these structures can be vulnerable to collapse under asymmetrical loading (extreme wind) or impact (puncture). But because pneumatic structures are lightweight and the resisting pressure remains constant, they will fail slowly, allowing occupants time to evacuate. Ultimately, the structures are structurally efficient materially but they rely upon a continuous power source to maintain their proper form.

RIGID SURFACE SYSTEMS

As we have seen earlier in the section, in order to effectively span long distances, the structural assembly must be relatively lightweight and thin, but remain very stiff. Therefore, it may seem counter-intuitive to consider using a relatively heavy material, like reinforced concrete, for this task. Typically, if a material is thin, like a piece of paper, then it's not stiff; but because it is a cast material, concrete allows for different complex configurations that allow it to be both. Like a piece of paper, it has little capacity structurally as an unmodified plane, but if the paper (or concrete in this case) is simply folded or curved, it becomes incredibly strong and efficient. Essentially, this same strategy applies in the design of rigid surface-resisting structural systems. They are folded to make *folded plate* systems, singularly curved to make *vaults*, or doubly curved to make *domes, shells*, or other complex forms. When the surface material is reinforced, these structures can formally evolve beyond the funicular shapes found in many historic vault and arched structures discussed in Chapter 21.

Regardless of their shape, all surface-resistant systems essentially need to follow the three basic rules: the surface needs to be continuous, it needs to be correctly shaped to efficiently resist the forces, and it must maintain a stable shape under loading. Simply put, they are designed to equitably distribute small unit stresses across the entire surface, allowing for the entire structure to remain thin and to perform effectively. Achieving this depends primarily on selecting the correct structural form for the shell's geometry, but many of the basic concepts are rooted in the form of the funicular arch.

An arch can be turned into a three-dimensional structure by rotating it about a point to make a *synclastic* (dome) form, or by extruding its curve along a line to create *developable* shapes (vaults), (Figure 28.13). Synclastic dome shells have arch lines that run vertically around the dome (longitudes) that take compressive stresses downwards and horizontal hoop lines (latitudes) that are tensed near the bottom of the dome (as it resists splaying outwards)—these lines are typically articulated as the thickest parts of the dome. Some developable vault–like forms act essentially as a long extruded funicular arch so they carry loads only through compression and require a continuous support along the two long sides—without continuous supports on two sides, the vault would need to span longitudinally and act like a beam.

As a consequence of the arch shape, both domes and vaults will need something at the base to resist the outward thrust inherent in the system. Like the historic Gothic vaults, this may require buttresses or internal tension ties. Domes have the advantage that their outward thrust can be counteracted by circumferential tension members—one of the keys to Brunelleschi's dome over the Florence Cathedral is that it is literally wrapped with miles of iron chain to prevent it from splaying out.

Folded plates may look like flat-sided vaults, but they perform quite differently. Plates are essentially structural slabs that are tilted on their end so the forces can run parallel to the surface. Unlike the vault, plates act like beams, not arches, and are designed to resist compression, tension, and shear in the surface. These plates are essentially very tall beams, but they are typically laid out in a series with other tilted plates to create a stiff, V-shaped continuous surface, similar to some long-span truss configurations (Figure 28.14). The main

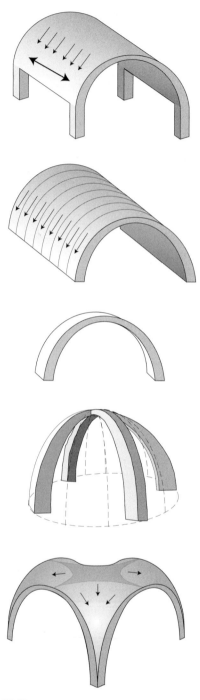

28.13
The generation of forms based upon funicular arch geometry.

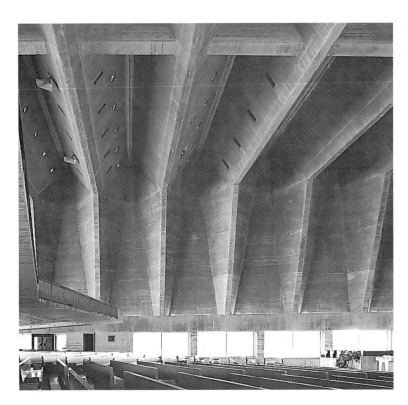

28.14
A cast-in-place concrete folded plate roof spanning across Marcel Breuer's St. John's Abbey Church (1961).

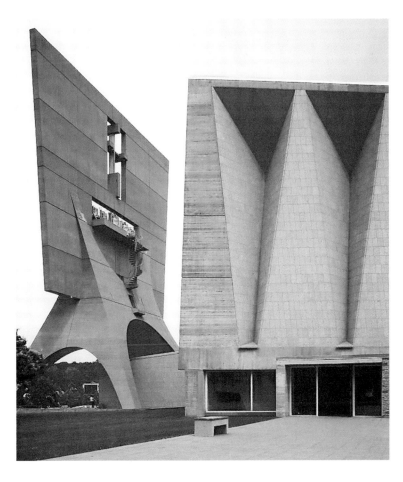

challenge with the structural performance of folded plates is the difficulty of keeping the entire configuration stable at the end bays. Typically, a smaller fold is placed at the outer edges, stiffening the shape against outward expansion. The behavior of folded plates can be applied to other cross-sectionally shaped structures as well. Most notably, perhaps, is the Kimbell Art Museum by Louis Kahn, where the curved shells can be easily mistaken for vaults but the roofs span long distances longitudinally and are designed to behave like thin, curved, folded plates. While folded plates are generally limited to about 55m (180') of span, note that they can serve as enclosure, thus saving the cost of a separate roof applied to a traditional beam or joist system.

The thinnest, most expressive, and effective rigid-surface systems are the double-curved structures generally known as shells. Heinz Isler, a Swiss engineer, and designer of hundreds of shells would often say, "Shells live and die with curvature." Double curvature, he argued, was the basis for every good modern structural shell because it allows the load to follow the shortest route to the foundation with very low stresses inside the surface (Figure 28.15). By inclining the surface towards the direction of the acting force (by folding or curving the structure to do so) it more effectively spans and encloses space and minimizes the inherent inefficiencies of slab mechanism resistance to bending. As a result, shells are typically much thinner than vaults or domes and can easily clear spans of more than 100ft (30m).

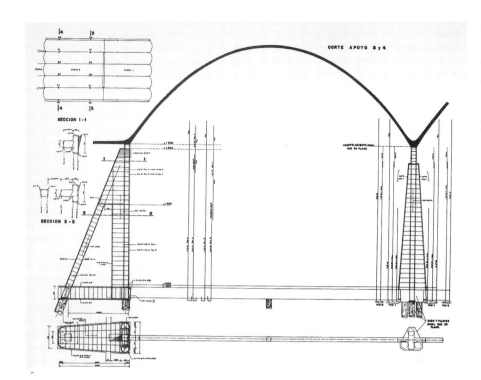

28.16
Surface structures are typically
stiffened by folding up or extending
the outer edges of the surface
on the perimeter. This drawing by
Eladio Dieste shows various means
by which the structure resisted
against the thrust generated by the
vault's thrust.

Like the tent and membrane structures, shells derive their load-bearing
capacity from pairs of in-plane stresses oriented in different perpendicular orientations. Because thin shells are essentially irregularly shaped domes, they
essentially compress downward while resisting an outward thrust. As a result,
tension, compression, and shear may be present in the membrane with varying
levels of each stress throughout the form. The double curve generates stiffness
but, like folded plates, double-curved shells typically need to be stiffened along
the outer edges to maintain their proper shape (Figure 28.16). Shells may have
a uniform thickness for ease of construction, but because the loads are cumulative the feet of the shell are frequently quite large and well articulated.

FINDING FORM

Finding, analyzing, and constructing the correct forms for double-curved thin
shells is quite difficult. The form of many shells looks like the static opposite
of many tent structures because they are both essentially funicularly informed
shapes. Isler argued that a properly configured scale model (in the form of an
upside-down hanging fabric or a pneumatically inflated bladder) would show
the idealized form that could then be scaled and analyzed. Other engineers,
like Eduardo Torroja and his student, Felix Candela, used complex geometric
formations to establish the correct shell forms. A particular favorite form of
Candela's was the saddle-shaped hyperbolic paraboloids, or hypars. Because
of their relatively tall height to span ratio, Candela would often group several
hypars together to form a contemporary version of the groin vault. However,
the choice of the hypar wasn't purely aesthetic or structural; it was also
intended to make construction easier. The form of a hypar can be gener-

28.17
The formwork for La Bolsa de Valores project by Candela. Note the straight boards used for the formwork throughout.

ated with rotating straight lines along an arched plane so Candela knew that the formwork could be made more efficient by using straight-lined framing members (Figure 28.17).

Typically, the greatest drawback in the use of thin shell systems, especially in long-span projects, is the inherent difficulty of developing accurate and affordable means for its construction. Pouring a shell is often done in the field, so an entire substructure of formwork (similar to the centering under an archway) needs to be designed and constructed first, often quite high above the ground. The placement of the reinforcing must be placed accurately and it ideally should also be pre-tensioned before the pour occurs. The concrete mixes must have a consistent strength, color, and consistency throughout the entire construction process and the ultimate integrity of the shell's behavior isn't known until after the formwork is removed—very high risks and rewards. While the form of the shells may seem complex, the construction process need not be overly cumbersome or expensive. Dieste created affordable (and beautiful) long-spanning thin shells for industrial applications by integrating re-useable formwork and the locally abundant material, brick, as the lower part of the shells—brick was laid over curving formwork, and bound together with prestressed reinforcing and finished with a topping slab of concrete (Figure 28.18). The earliest American vaults were built *without* centering, using Rafael Guastavino's patented Catalonian vaulting system in which interlocking terra cotta tiles, set in layers of mortar, are laid in closing concentric rings as the vault is constructed upward.

The traditional methods of forming and casting constructing shells have been labor-intensive and expensive, but several significant advancements suggest a greater potential viability for the structural type in the future. New, lighter materials, like glass fiber-reinforced concrete composites reduce the weight and cost without sacrificing strength. New options in formwork, such

28.18
The rolling brick Gaussian double-curved vaults and indirect lighting strategy for this wool warehouse storage facility by Eladio Dieste.

as lightweight fabric forms and pneumatics promise faster deployment and greater re-use of resources. Because thin shell structures can become very lightweight, portions of the shells can be precast off-site as well. Although they are difficult to design, analyze, and construct, ultimately, the benefits of concrete shells is clear. They efficiently span long distances using low-cost materials to create durable, somewhat energy-efficient, and self-finishing architectural space.

CONCLUSION

Long-span structures have to respond to a broader set of constraints than other types of structural systems, simply because of their increased span. Long-span systems can be highly efficient and effective solutions, which may result in a particular manner of expressiveness, but these benefits often come with consequences/liabilities inherently associated with their implementation and performance. Long-span structures must be lighter, stiffer, and relatively efficiently built, with materials that are responsive to these conditions. Their design must consider structural performance, the process of formal generation, constructability, and overall cost/economy/efficiencies of the system simultaneously. Not surprising, these are all relative considerations and the degree of their importance may vary depending on the type of system selected. A seemingly broad array of long-span options exists, but many of these systems share basic fundamental structural lessons about the potentially efficient relationship between form and forces.

GLOSSARY

Anticlastic: Referring to a surface that has curvatures in opposite senses (concave and convex) in different directions at all points.

Arch line: Also known as meridians. A series of vertical load paths in domes for compressive stresses. Under uniform loading, a dome is in compression along arch lines everywhere.

Cable-stayed: A structural system that uses linear cables to directly support a roof or beam.

Castellated beam: A beam, usually steel, that has been cut lengthwise near the neutral axis and reassembled so that it gains depth without gaining weight.

Developable curve: Referring to a surface that is singularly curved. They are straight in one direction, curved in the other, and can be formed by bending a flat sheet. Cones and barrels are developable.

Dome: A doubly curved shell in which both curves open in the same direction.

Double-curved: A surface that is curved in more than one plane. Such surfaces provide great resistance to deformation through their material strength. A dome is the simplest of these.

Folded plate: A surface whose sectional geometry has been modified to give it structural depth, allowing it to span as a beam.

Gable frame: A linear structural member that is angled or bent to transfer some of its load from bending into compression.

Geodesic dome: A name given to a type of a framed dome. Named after a word denoting the shortest possible line between two points on a surface.

Hoop lines: Also known as parallels. The horizontal sections of a dome; the largest parallel is the equator. In a shell dome outward thrust is resisted by tension along the hoop lines below about 45 degrees above the horizontal.

Membrane: A structural member that relies on surface stresses in tension and shear only to achieve its span. Compare with a *shell*, which uses tension, compression, and shear.

Panel point: Related to trusses. A panel point is an intersection of diagonal and/or vertical web members with the top and/or bottom chord.

Pneumatic: A structural system that relies on air pressure to keep a thin membrane in constant tension, enabling it to span considerable distances.

Prestressing: The use of tensioned steel in concrete beams to absorb much of the beam's tensile stress.

Shell: A three-dimensional compression structure whose geometry ensures that all loads are resolved through surface stresses, thus requiring little in the way of buttressing.

Space frame: A network of trusses arranged at an angle to one another and interconnected to span in two dimensions.

Synclastic: Surfaces are doubly curved with similar curvature in each direction; like revolved arch forms.

Suspension: A structural system that uses a main cable and smaller "hangars" to support a roof or beam. The main cable in suspension structures will take on a characteristic funicular shape, approximating a catenary shape as more hangars are added.

Thrust: An inevitable consequence of two-dimensional arched structures. The geometry of these systems creates a resultant force—outward in compression structures, inward in tension structures—that must be countered for the structure to stand.

Truss: A bending member that replaces the solid web of a beam with a network of axially loaded members, usually arranged in triangular panels.

Vault: A three-dimensional arch, with the arch's shape extruded perpendicular to its section. Like an arch, a vault implies a thrust that must be countered at its base.

FURTHER READING

Anderson, S. ed. (2004). *Eladio Dieste, Innovation in Structural Art*. New York: Princeton
   Architectural Press.

Bechthold, M. (2008). *Innovative Surface Structures Technology and Applications*. New
   York: Taylor & Francis.

Chilton, J. (2000). *Heinz Isler, The Engineers Contribution to Contemporary Architecture*.
   London: Thomas Telford.

Reid, E. (1998). *Understanding Buildings, A Multidisciplinary Approach*, 8th edition.
   Cambridge: MIT Press.

Robbin, T. (1996). *Engineering a New Architecture*. New Haven: Yale.

Wilkinson, C. (1996). *Supersheds: The Architecture of Long-Span, Large-Volume Buildings*.
   Oxford; Boston: Butterworth Architecture.

29

HIGH-RISES

Introduction	Economic, environmental, and socio-political issues in ultra–high-rises
Structural techniques	Tube and core
	Belted trusses
	Tubes and bundled tubes
	Diagrid tubes
	Buttressed cores
Other issues	Elevatoring
	Life safety
Conclusions	

INTRODUCTION

The construction of the 830m (2720ft) Burj Khalifa in Dubai between 2004 and 2009 highlighted the resurgence of ultra-tall skyscraper design. Not since the Eiffel Tower had a single structure so completely reset an existing height record, and while the Burj has several aspects that make it categorically different from former skyscraper record holders such as the Sears Tower in Chicago (1974, 442m, 1450ft to the top of its antenna) or Taipei 101 (2004, 509m, 1670ft), its successful completion has drawn attention back to the benefits and challenges of building ultra-tall buildings.

Skyscrapers represent extraordinary investments of labor, materials, and capital, and, as a result, their functional performance is paramount. Net to gross ratios must be extraordinarily refined, to the point where an additional inch or so in column thickness or curtain wall depth may have a substantial impact on the project's economic performance when multiplied over 80, 90, or 100 floors. Placing so many occupants in one tower also presents particularly difficult life safety issues, as was proven during the World Trade Center attacks in 2001. The impact on a city or region of such concentrated development can be profound, and the embodied energy and life cycle costs to build and run such large buildings are extraordinary.

Still, the benefits of such developments are important. If linked to adequate infrastructure, ultra-tall buildings can streamline traffic patterns, reducing cities' reliance on automobiles by encouraging huge numbers of occupants to use public transportation. Mixed-use projects combine commercial, retail, and residential functions, reducing travel for residents and workers. Large developments can also seed growth in downtown districts, placing a critical mass of people into commercial centers who will then naturally patronize other businesses while their employers may draw from collaborating or related businesses.

Large commercial developments inherently concentrate both wealth and resources, however, and can contribute to the decline of nearby commercial areas. The amenities provided by such projects are inevitably geared toward upper economic classes, and urban resources in the form of tax abatements, infrastructural improvements, and zoning variances can accrue value to developers while socializing costs. The politics of supertall development in developing countries have led to labor disputes and questions about resource equity as well.

On balance, the benefits of supertall construction are at best uncertain, and the sensitivity of these developments to economics suggests that they are often the product of overly optimistic financial forecasts, political will, and sometimes outright ego. However, the potential benefits in terms of ecological performance and traffic reduction may well be worth the technical and social challenges they represent.

STRUCTURAL TYPES

Past a height of about ten stories, skyscraper design becomes a balance between resisting gravity loads and wind loads. While the weight of a tall building produces onerous forces on lower story columns and foundations, these are relatively simple to deal with compared with the overturning and racking implications of wind loads. Column design is eased somewhat by structural codes and rules of thumb that permit some diversity in load factors—while a single office floor needs to be designed for the maximum possible load at any given time, often 50lb per square foot (250kg/m^2), it is unlikely that *every* office in a building will be loaded to this amount. Thus, codes permit significant reductions when calculating the total load borne by a column in a high-rise, leading to important reductions in overall column size. Because floor-to-floor heights are generally relatively small, especially compared to the size of a skyscraper column, gravity loads remain fairly straightforward—if daunting in scale. Wind, on the other hand, presents complicated design issues.

The classic mid- to late-twentieth-century commercial skyscrapers were built using a formula of rigid core and perimeter columns that maximized floor plan flexibility and left building skins open to maximum views (Figure 29.1). A basic core with a flexible perimeter frame can rise to no more than a dozen or so stories before wind loading produces noticeable deflections, however, and beyond this height it is necessary to use moment connections in the perimeter frame to make the building sufficiently rigid (Figure 29.2). While these connections increase the size of both beams and columns, limiting the size of openings, they are relatively easy to achieve, and rigid frame and core buildings can

29.1
For relatively low heights, a core composed of solid shear walls can be enough to brace a building against wind while also handling a significant portion of gravity loads.

29.2
Combining a rigid core with moment connections between girders and columns adds additional lateral stiffness.

29.3
Beyond about 600' (200m), drift becomes a critical issue. Rigid belt trusses resist this by enforcing a rectangular geometry between girders and columns at strategic points in the structure.

typically rise to somewhere around 30 stories before wind-borne deflection again becomes an issue.

Beyond 30 stories, the core takes on increasing importance in a wind-resistant system, and must be designed either as a shear wall or truss. The building at this height begins to act more like a vertical cantilever against lateral loads, and the core, coupled with the stiffness of the perimeter frame, resists these loads like a large beam turned on its end. Here, the conflict between the functional desire for an open perimeter and the structural requirement for as much material as possible on the extreme edges of a beam becomes apparent. Ideally, the structure would be concentrated on the *exterior* of a skyscraper, since that is where it can best resist the bending induced by wind. This is precisely where developers typically want the *least* interference with views out, however, and thus for intermediate heights of 30–60 stories the less efficient structural approach of stiffening the *interior* core and gaining as much stiffness as possible through relatively small moment connections.

Such systems can gain additional stiffness with belt, or outrigger, trusses that are firmly fixed to perimeter columns (Figure 29.3). These trusses are rigid enough to firmly resist sidesway by maintaining rigid 90-degree connections to the columns above and below—essentially very rigid moment connections. The result is that the building's drift is arrested at each truss and the structure is "reset" to vertical. A single-story height truss can provide stiff enough connections to effectively brace about 15–20 stories above before the tendency to drift needs to be stopped again, and these trusses are often integrated with mechanical floors, eliminating the inconvenience of blocked windows.

29.4
Tube structures make a skyscraper into a tall "super column" that uses the entire footprint of the building to achieve a hollow structural shape.

29.5
A braced frame employs very large cross-bracing to resist wind and to distribute gravity loads over multiple exterior columns.

Beyond 60 stories or so, the problems involved in lateral resistance become too great to be solved by internal shear walls, and the structure must be moved to the perimeter (Figure 29.4). The Chicago engineer Fazlur Khan was instrumental in developing so-called "tube" structures in the 1950s and 1960s that placed stiff moment frames around the perimeters of skyscrapers, taking the bracing function from the central core and relocating it to a structurally ideal location (Figure 29.5). This made a very large hollow column out of the

29.6
By bundling several tube structures together, a "bundled tube" gains strength by bracing each individual tube along its length.

entire building structure, and one can usefully compare the plans of a tube-framed building with a hollow box column to understand the parallel. Initially executed in concrete, Khan's tubes could also be built in steel, provided the connections between beams and columns were oversized and made very stiff through bolting or—even better—welding. The resulting facades were certainly less open, but the flexibility gained on the interior was considerable and a generation of skyscrapers with fairly large, closely spaced perimeter columns followed. (The World Trade Center towers were of this type of construction).

Since columns become stronger against buckling if they are braced along their heights, it makes sense to think of stronger tube structures made out of multiple tubes tied together at key points to prevent one another from bending, and this principle was employed by Khan and others as a "bundled tube" system. The Sears Tower in Chicago was the ultimate example of this: in plan, the Tower consists of nine steel tubes, each with all of their structure on their perimeter in the form of oversized beams and girders with very stiff moment connections (Figure 29.6). These nine super-columns are then tied together by belt trusses every 20 stories or so (these levels are, as suggested above, used for mechanical equipment), meaning that each tube is braced at regular intervals. The result is a heavy structure, but one that quite effectively resists the extreme wind loads that such a tall structure incurs while leaving reasonably sized openings for windows on the perimeter. Bundled tubes become less efficient after about 100 stories, as the amount of steel or concrete required becomes prohibitive.

Because of their weight, tube structures became less popular in the 1970s and 1980s as the price of steel doubled. Instead, engineers looked to more

29.7
Belt trusses can also be used with
concrete to form monolithic structures
that allow cores and perimeter columns
to work together.

efficient structures that combined the lighter weight of trusses with the efficient distribution of tube structures. The most visible model of this approach was Khan's Hancock Tower in Chicago (1969), which used large X-bracing on all four of its elevations to form a giant, 344-meter-tall vertical truss that (combined with the building's gently pyramidal massing) allowed it to resist wind forces with far less material than a moment-framed tube structure. I. M. Pei's Bank of China Tower in Hong Kong (1990, 367 meters) also used building-scale trussing to brace against wind and seismic forces (Figure 29.7).

Because of its triangular geometry, the external truss can be manipulated to make any three-dimensional shape, and the advent of sophisticated three-dimensional digital modeling and fabrication has allowed trussed tubes to produce a huge variety of skyscraper forms. These *diagrid* towers may wrap a trussed skin around a wind-shedding form such as a cone, a cylinder, or some combination. Norman Foster's proposed Millenium Tower for Tokyo (1989) was to have used a conical truss to enclose 180 floors of office, retail, and hotel space; eventually, the firm used the technique for the elliptical Swiss Re tower in London and the more rectilinear Hearst Tower in New York (Figure 29.8). More free-form structures employing diagrids include OMA's CCTV Headquarters in Beijing and their Seattle Central Library, and Wilkinson Eyre's 432-metre West Tower in Guanzhou, China (2010).

29.8
Diagrids take the principle of brace frames and wrap cross-bracing around shapes that may be based on program or (in this case) aerodynamics.

While diagrids offer extraordinary flexibility in form and efficiency in weight, their geometry is inevitably complex, requiring extensive fabrication and skilled placement on the job site. Diagrids are also almost necessarily steel, as the formwork for such complicated geometry in concrete would be prohibitively expensive. However, advances in mix design have revived concrete's application for supertall buildings, and currently the tallest projects rely on very strong concrete for their structures.

The Burj Khalifa in Dubai uses concrete shear walls and central "hub" to form a very tall, stem-like core structure with a triangular plan geometry, similar to the structure of the 553m (1800ft) CN Tower in Toronto. This so-called "buttressed core" provides a very stable footprint with a gradually tapering system of shear walls that brace a hexagonal core in the middle. The result is a very stable structural system that is analogous to a tall blade of grass—the folds of the triangular plan provide rigidity much as a folded plate allows a thin plane of concrete to perform as a deep cantilever. Toward the top, the structure switches to lightweight steel to support a very tall spire.

The Burj's buttressed core is undoubtedly a great achievement, but it is worth looking in some detail at the building's plans and functions to see how such a leap was possible. Unlike commercial skyscrapers like Sears, or Taipei 101, the Burj is almost entirely residential—and the offices that take

29.9
Burj Khalifa, currently the world's tallest skyscraper, relies on a system of shear walls and a dense core to achieve its 830m height.

up its upper floors are not the large, open plan spaces that form the bulk of tall construction in the U.S. and Europe. Instead, they are relatively small, boutique offices. What these have in common with the ninety or so floors of residences is that they do not require large, flexible floor areas. In fact, all of the Burj's floor plates are relatively shallow, one apartment or one office suite deep. Net to gross ratios here are far less important than access to the staggering views from the upper floors, and thus the economics of the typical skyscraper are somewhat backwards. As a result, the structure of the Burj, especially at the upper floors, takes up a far greater percentage of the overall floor plate, and it is necessarily much more extensive than in a more typical commercial skyscraper. The tower is closer in form and in configuration to a supertall concrete mast, as a comparison with Sears or Taipei 101 shows (Figure 29.9).

An important feature of the Burj's form is the tower's ability to actually shed wind in ways that reduce the lateral load on the main structure. The tower's Y-shaped form steps back at regular intervals, though these are staggered between the three lobes of its triangular plan. At each setback, wind that has built up pressure against the inner surfaces of the Y is shed at one edge, breaking up the overall force unevenly around the tower. This prevents large vortices from forming on the leeward side of the building, reducing the tendency of the building to sway back and forth (Figure 29.10).

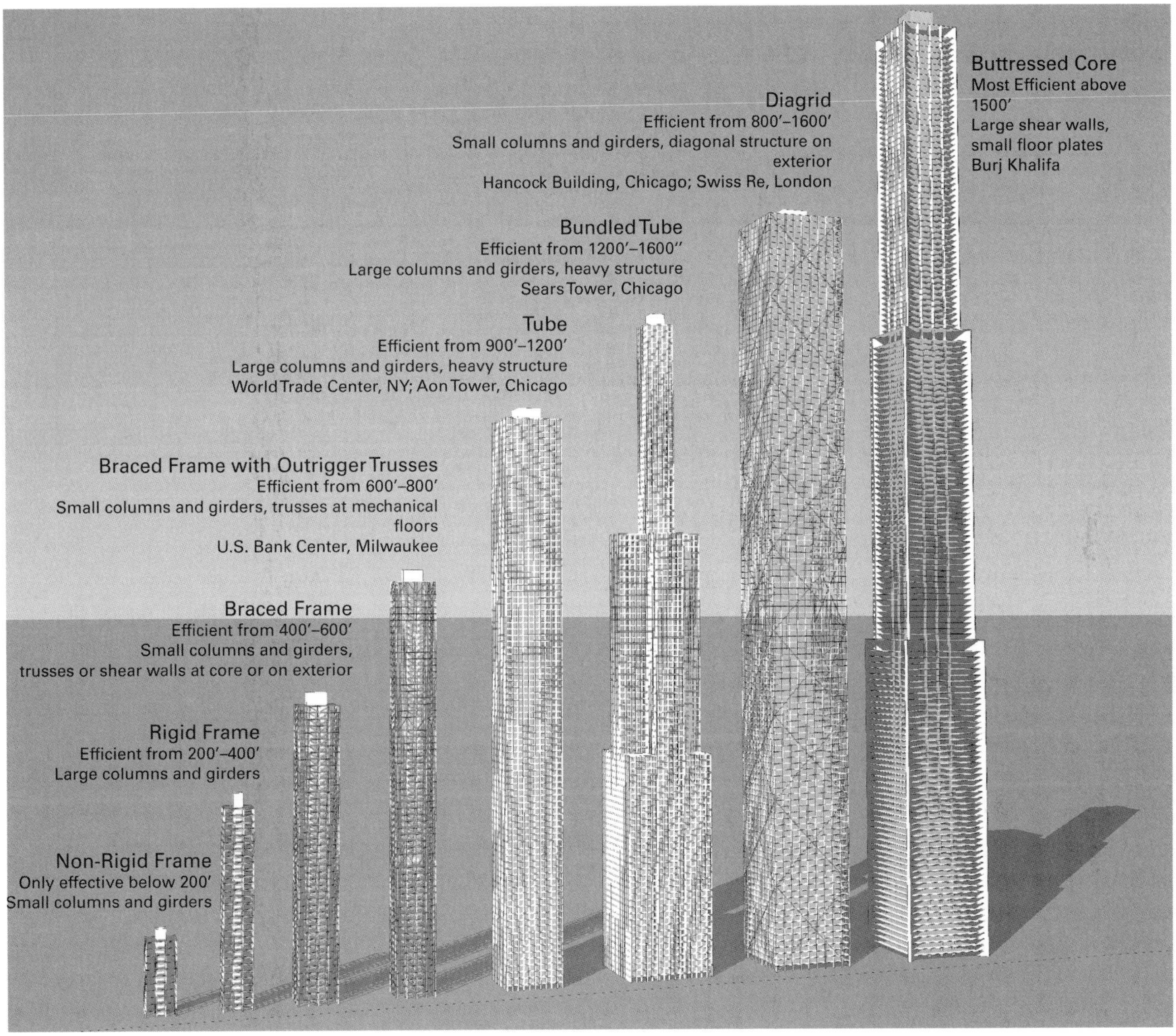

Buttressed Core
Most Efficient above 1500'
Large shear walls, small floor plates
Burj Khalifa

Diagrid
Efficient from 800'–1600'
Small columns and girders, diagonal structure on exterior
Hancock Building, Chicago; Swiss Re, London

Bundled Tube
Efficient from 1200'–1600''
Large columns and girders, heavy structure
Sears Tower, Chicago

Tube
Efficient from 900'–1200'
Large columns and girders, heavy structure
World Trade Center, NY; Aon Tower, Chicago

Braced Frame with Outrigger Trusses
Efficient from 600'–800'
Small columns and girders, trusses at mechanical floors
U.S. Bank Center, Milwaukee

Braced Frame
Efficient from 400'–600'
Small columns and girders, trusses or shear walls at core or on exterior

Rigid Frame
Efficient from 200'–400'
Large columns and girders

Non-Rigid Frame
Only effective below 200'
Small columns and girders

29.10
Supertall buildings require particularly efficient structural schemes, with economics often dictating which types are best for which heights.

SUPERTALL EFFECTS ON CIRCULATION AND ENVIRONMENT

The Burj was completed in the midst of the global recession of 2008–2010, and there were no similar towers constructed to which it can be compared. However, even though its structural system seems extensible to further heights, its record seems unlikely to be surpassed in the near future as it represents the furthest current extent of supporting technologies.

In particular, supertall buildings today are limited by the capacity of elevators to serve such remote floors. Cables as long as the Burj is tall will stretch to unacceptable lengths, leading to problems in leveling, while the time it takes for even a fast elevator to reach the upper floors of a supertall building mean unacceptable travel times for occupants, and inefficient round trip times for individual cabs. Instead, supertall buildings must employ shuttle and sky lobby elevatoring techniques, stacking local cab ranks on top of one another and providing access to and between express and local transfer sky lobbies with large, fast express elevators. Stacking elevators presents particular dangers in terms of overrun, and therefore every rank of local elevators has to be separated by two-story mechanical floors.

Life safety and evacuation also present particular problems of scale in supertall buildings. Firefighter access by designated high-speed elevators requires additional dedicated transfer floors and shafts. Occupant exiting is not physically possible by stairs to the ground from the upper levels of such tall buildings. Instead, the building is divided into vertical zones, usually corresponding with the elevatoring strategy, and areas of the mechanical/sky lobby floors are designated as areas of refuge, with increased requirements for fire separation and outdoor ventilation. In the event of an evacuation, occupants take stairs down to one of these refuge areas and wait for the building to be made safe by firefighters. The number of floors between any hazard and the refuge area, the absolute requirement for thorough sprinklering throughout, and the provision of speedy access for firefighters makes such a strategy possible. In the event of a non-fire emergency, elevators on standby power can be used as "lifeboats" to evacuate occupants, too.

CONCLUSION

The exceptional height of the Burj has inspired similar projects—all, as of this writing, unbuilt—that foresee incremental increases over its height to around a kilometer. All of these face the same limitations in elevatoring, life safety, and simple economics that determined the Burj's ultimate height, and the lengthy construction times for such large projects makes them particularly vulnerable to real estate cycles. The development of exceptional technologies for these towers, however, is likely to trickle down to smaller projects, and the structural, wind-resisting, and circulatory advances of the Burj may well become commonplace in towers far smaller than a kilometer.

FREQUENTLY ASKED QUESTIONS

How are building heights measured?
This is a particularly controversial topic because of the tendency for skyscraper design to include spires or antennae on their roofs. The Council on Tall Buildings and Urban Habitats stepped in after claims that the Petronas Towers in Malaysia had "beaten out" Chicago's Sears Tower for the title of "World's Tallest." There are now categories for height to "architectural top," which includes spires but excludes antennae; "highest occupied floor," which excludes any features that don't enclose actual space; and "height to tip," which includes any antennae, no matter how temporary. Burj Khalifa, for example, has heights of 828m, 585m, or 830m in these respective categories, while Sears has heights of 442m, 413m, and 527m. See the Council's website, www.ctbuh.org, for an exhaustive explanation.

How tall can skyscrapers go?

Right now, the limit appears to be about a kilometer, primarily based on the capacity of elevators and restrictions on their cables' lengths. At the time of writing, however, sluggish real estate isn't providing enough pressure to challenge these limits, and new records usually accompany explosive economic growth. If the skyscraper's history proves one thing, it is that "unsurpassable" records will eventually be shattered and, when economics again dictate, it is likely that research and development in elevator design will make kilometer–high buildings buildable and viable.

Are supertall buildings sustainable?

That depends entirely on how they are designed. Because they concentrate so much floor area into one project, small decisions about energy usage—in particular daylighting, passive cooling, and heat-island effects—are multiplied many times. Supertall buildings that ignore basic bioclimatic principles are likely to exacerbate consumption problems, while those that adopt these principles may enjoy large savings. There are important urban effects as well: if planned in conjunction with public transport, supertall buildings can drastically reduce a district's reliance on auto traffic. But if districts are planned without open space or green roofs, supertall buildings can contribute to heat island effects, which in turn increase cooling loads for all buildings in the area.

GLOSSARY

Belt truss: A truss located at an intermediate point in a skyscraper that is firmly fixed to columns above and below. These connections prevent the structure from racking, helping it to resist wind-related drift.

Bundled tube: Two or more tube structures attached at intervals by belt trusses so that they reinforce each other, reducing their unbraced lengths.

Buttressed core: A hybrid structure composed of a central "hub" and radiating shear walls that brace the hub over its height.

Diagrid: A three-dimensional truss wrapped around the perimeter of a skyscraper to channel gravity and lateral forces.

Tube structure: Structure where most of the bearing material is deployed at the building perimeter, creating a hollow "supercolumn" out of the building and placing the structural material where it can best resist wind forces.

FURTHER READING

Ali, M. (2001). *Art of the Skyscraper: The Genius of Fazlur Khan*. New York: Rizzoli.

Ascher, K. (2011). *The Heights: Anatomy of a Skyscraper*. New York: Penguin.

Baker, W. F. (2004). "The World's Tallest Building, Burj Dubai, U.A.E." *CTBUH Technical Paper*, CTBUH Conference, Seoul, October 10–13, 2004.

Nordenson, G. and Riley, T. (2003). *Tall Buildings*. New York: MOMA.

Weismantle, P., Smith, G. L., and Sheriff, M. (2007). "Burj Dubai: An Architectural Technical Design Case Study." *The Structural Design of Tall and Special Buildings*, 16, 2007, pp. 335–360.

APPENDIX TO PART 5

Structural Sizing Charts For Preliminary Design

INTRODUCTION

Part 5 gives a fairly thorough introduction to the physics of building structures, and in a few cases (beam, column, and foundation design) it provides a rough process for preliminary sizing of structural elements.

However, during the design process, architects and engineers often need to get a general idea about how large a structural member might be, or what material options are for particular situations. For about 50 years, there has been a tradition of handbook charts that provide vastly simplified, easy-to-use information on rough structural sizing based on experience and some analysis. While it's important to know the theory behind these elements, it's also important to be able to quickly assess what the consequences of certain spans or loading might be. In that spirit, the following charts compile information from several sources (including Henry J. Cowan's *Architectural Structures*, which used diagrams by Philip Corkill, Edward Allen and Joseph Iano's *Architect's Studio Companion*, and Odd Albert's charts in 1940s era *Architectural Graphic Standards*).

To allow for easier comparison, we've combined charts for various systems into more comprehensive diagrams based on typology—beams, columns, walls, short span floors, long-span floors, and long-span roofs. Elements can be roughly sized by reading the span across the horizontal axes, and finding required depth vertically. In all cases, the charts assume normal loads, standard connections and shapes, and standard specification materials.

These charts are intended for use as preliminary design aids only, and are—obviously—no substitute for proper consultation with engineering professionals.

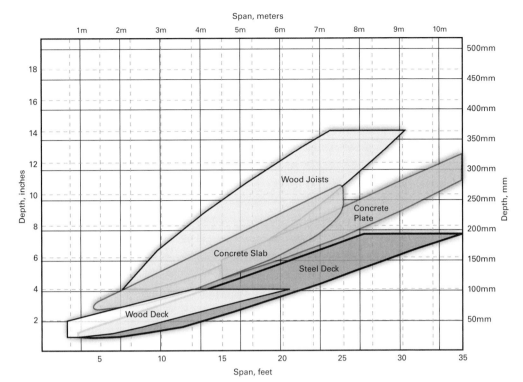

Figure A.1
Short span floor systems (less than 35 feet).

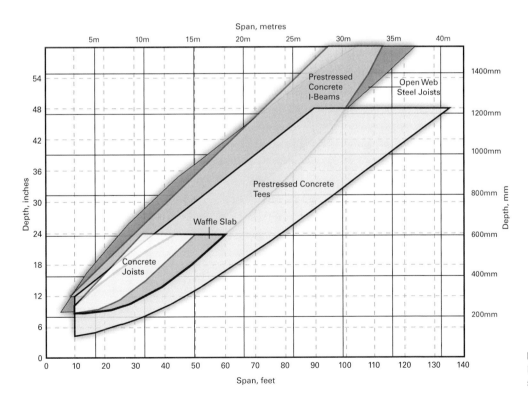

Figure A.2
Long-span floor systems.

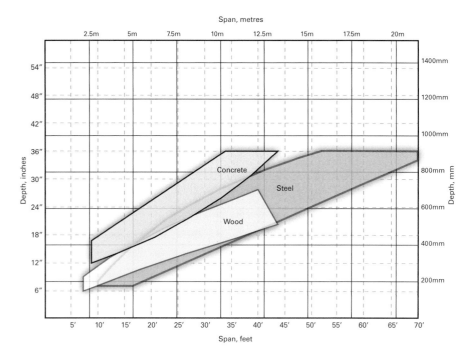

Figure A.3
Normal span beams.

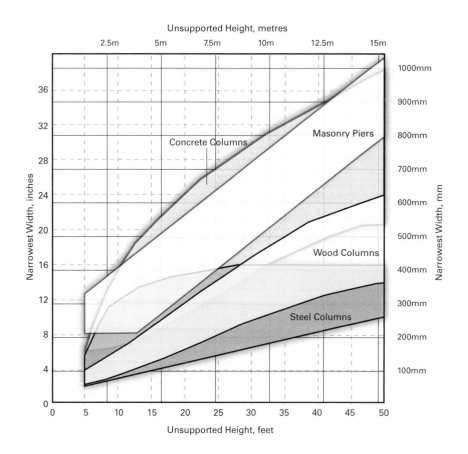

Figure A.4
Columns—single story, unbraced.

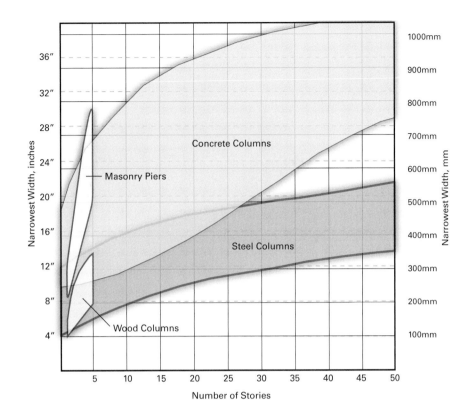

Figure A.5
Columns—multistory.

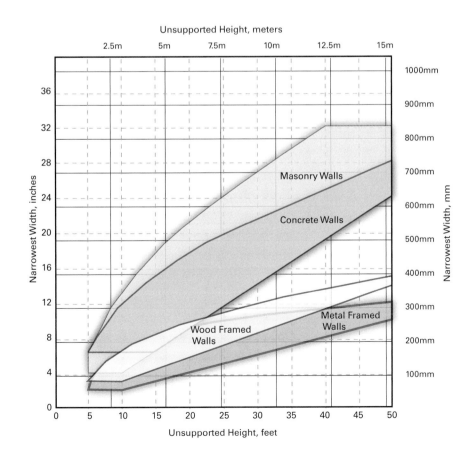

Figure A.6
Walls—single story, unbraced.

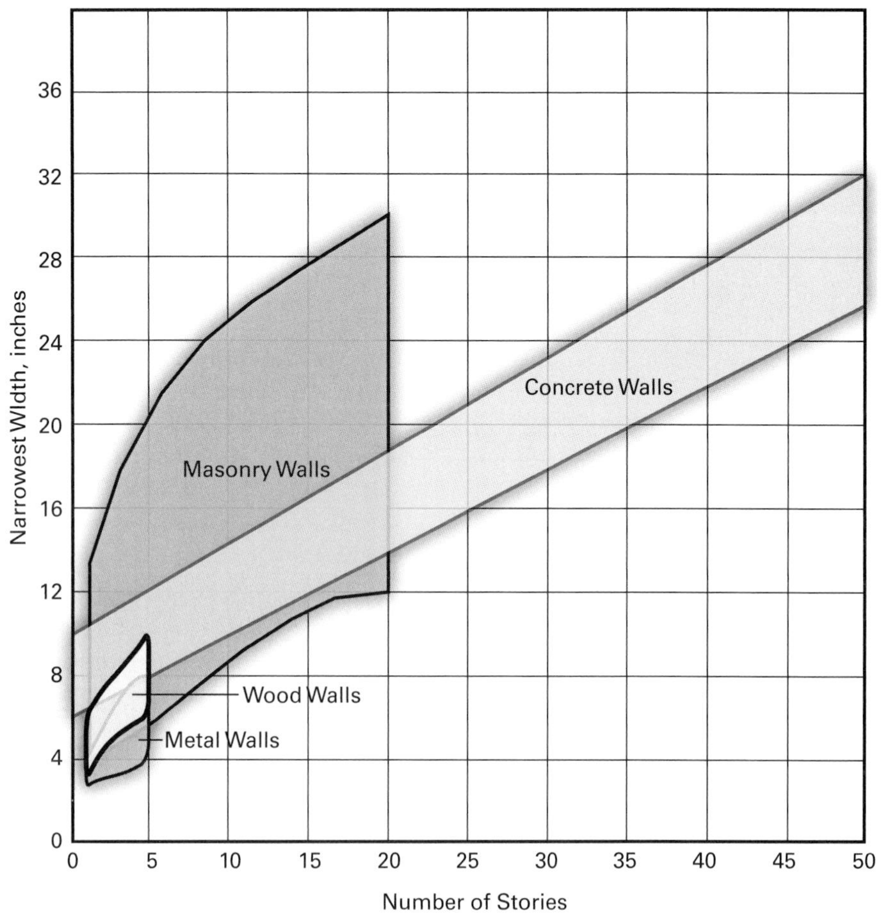

Figure A.7
Walls—multistory.

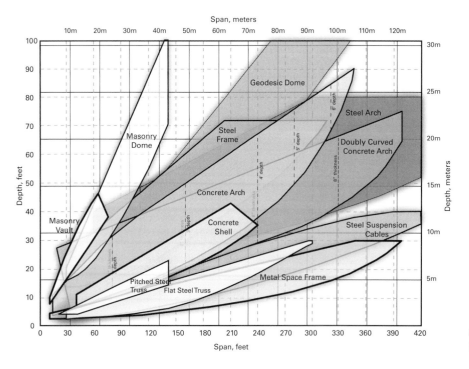

Figure A.8
Long-span roofs.

PART 6

BUILDING COMPONENTS

30

BUILDING ENVELOPES

Purpose of the building envelope	The elements and human comfort
	Regional differences
	Water, wind, heat, cold
	Ice and condensation
	Active and passive enclosures
Building enclosure components	Roofs
	Walls
	Foundations
Assembly/sequence	The general contractor
	Site, foundation, structure, roof, skin

INTRODUCTION

The building envelope is what we most commonly see as the image of architecture. This is the exterior enclosure, providing the form, material rendering and character of the building. Obviously there are innumerable factors involved in the creation of architecture, but the envelope or shell of any structure typically deals with more issues than any other part of a building. The primary issues being: structure (at times), warmth, dryness, ventilation, wind protection, daylight, view, entry, contextual relationship, scale, texture, color, etc.

One primary goal of understanding envelope is to promote a comprehensive and synthetic approach to design. Too frequently planning takes up the majority of design time, with the section and skin qualities of projects being ill considered and rushed. Much more time is spent during the development and documentation phases of a project figuring out the enclosure—and building envelopes poorly designed in schematics rarely get much better if they were not well conceived from the beginning. Also keep in mind that no one perceives a building in plan; they generally see the vertical surfaces.

Another goal of envelope design is durability, and the most destructive and stealthy enemy of enclosure is water. Most of your time designing the technical aspects of enclosure will be spent understanding how moisture can move through the system. All building shells are made of relatively small components—the largest of which are typically about 4′ × 8′ (1.2m × 2.4m) with the remainder being considerably smaller. Each joint between materials is a potential leak, and moisture has many ways to move through any gap in the system. There are six typical ways: gravity, capillary action, pressure differential, water vapor, thermal expansion, and percolation.

Finally, enclosure systems control thermal movement. Heat and cold move through the enclosure in many ways and different methods are required to deal with each type of thermal movement. A thorough understanding of the technical issues confronting building envelope design is necessary in order to achieve any aesthetic goals. In addition, the technical issues are inseparable from the aesthetic issues—each seems to feed the needs of the other, which is the goal of any sophisticated, elegantly conceived building design.

PURPOSE OF THE BUILDING ENVELOPE

The core purpose of the building envelope is to increase the comfort of its inhabitants over the conditions found in the exterior environment. This can mean many things but is mainly involved with moisture and temperature control. Sun, wind, air temperature, and precipitation are the primary weather elements to be controlled, along with security from intruders—animal, human, or insect. This seemingly simple task becomes more difficult due to the changing conditions of the exterior environment throughout the seasons; the same enclosure that works well trapping the heat in winter can become unbearably hot in the summer. Enclosures that transform themselves are much more difficult to build, tend to allow moisture in, and can vastly decrease durability. The task of creating increasingly complex enclosures to solve multiple problems is part of the evolving design process.

The severity and specific type of these problems has much to do with regional differences in climate; the same solutions do not work everywhere. Therefore it is not only necessary to know how to deal with varying seasonal conditions in one place, but to know the particular conditions of the place in which you are building.

While we may think the most critical element of human comfort is thermal control, the most difficult to deal with is water. As was stated earlier, moisture has six ways to move through any gap in the system (Figure 30.1).

Gravity simply moves water through horizontal openings and can be easily dealt with—the most effective way is to keep the surface sloped to keep water moving, rather than sitting and eventually eating its way through a surface.

Capillary action occurs when the space separating two open surfaces is small, so moisture is drawn into the gap. The best way to deal with this is to avoid small openings and create discontinuities or air gaps to give the water a pathway out of the system before it's drawn inside of the building. This is also related to surface tension, which allows water to cling to surfaces, creating flow on the underside of soffits and overhangs. These place water in positions where protection might not be covered—a drip edge condition at the outer edge of overhangs is a common solution to this problem.

Pressure differential is the most common leakage problem. If the pressure on the outside of the building is higher than on the inside, water will eventually flow in. This condition is combated by using a rain screen—an air space

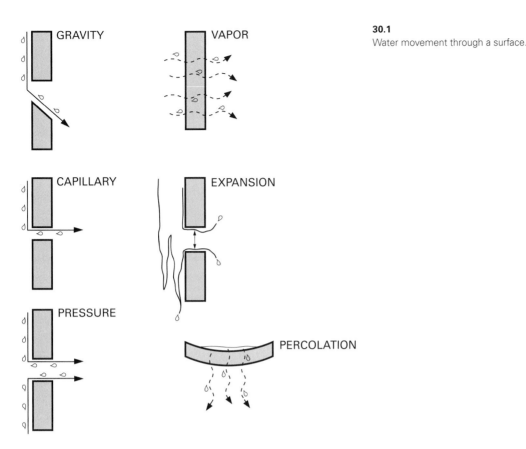

30.1
Water movement through a surface.

between the outer skin and inner enclosure that is kept pressure equalized by not tightly sealing the space between the outer wall and outdoors (Figures 30.2 and 30.3)—therefore the water will not be drawn through the outer wall and the inner wall does not need as much moisture protection. Wind pressure may also contribute to this; with water approaching a surface at high speed, the momentum carrying the water through any small opening. Covers or baffles can prevent this type of penetration.

Water vapor can move airborne moisture into spaces through any opening small enough for air to pass. Porous surfaces can also draw moisture in if they are below the relative humidity of the surrounding air. This type of moisture penetration tends to trap humidity inside of assemblies where it can condense into water or freeze and expand.

Thermal expansion occurs when water infiltrates a gap, then freezes and expands—forcing the gap wider and letting additional moisture inside. This is a particular problem of areas that experience frequent freeze/thaw cycles. Over time a very small opening can become quite large, or cracks can form that threaten the structural integrity of a building component.

Percolation is an issue of standing water that eventually finds its way through any porosity in the exterior cladding. Water eventually wins in this situation, as it tends to eat away at most materials through expanding and shrinking or freeze/thaw cycles. The goal is to always keep the water moving off of building surfaces.

Thermal protection in the enclosure comes from insulating against air temperature and mitigating solar radiation. Insulation is a simple process; the key is to keep the insulation continuous and consistent. It makes little sense to

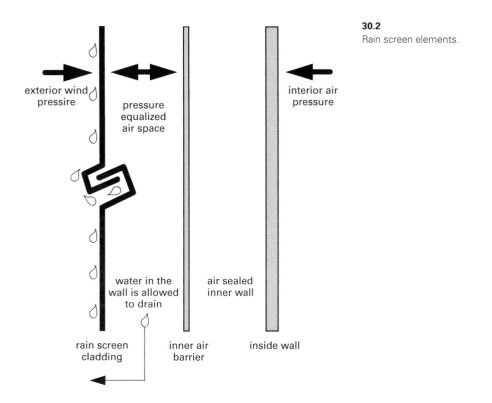

30.2
Rain screen elements.

exterior wind
pressire

pressure
equalized
air space

interior air
pressure

water in the
wall is allowed
to drain

air sealed
inner wall

rain screen
cladding

inner air
barrier

inside wall

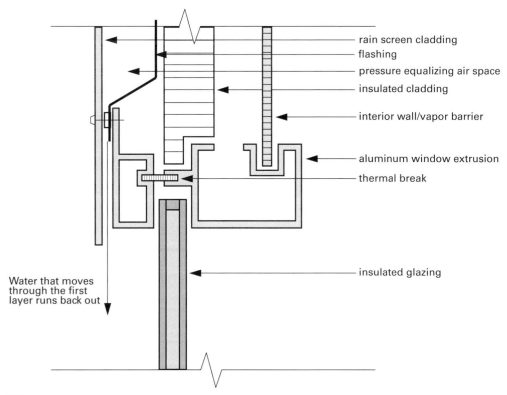

rain screen cladding
flashing
pressure equalizing air space
insulated cladding

interior wall/vapor barrier

aluminum window extrusion
thermal break

insulated glazing

Water that moves
through the first
layer runs back out

30.3
Rain screen detail.

insulate one part of the enclosure much more heavily than another, because the heat or cold will find its way through the weak point in the system. This gets more difficult when there are many different components to the exterior skin, creating the need to know how the varying pieces relate to one another's thermal performance. Most manufacturers publish their performance ratings and sources such as *Graphic Standards* and *Architects Data* list common thermal performances of building assemblies. Many municipalities now require a performance assessment of any new building's enclosure system to ensure minimum standards of energy efficiency. Another purpose of insulation is protection against condensation, or keeping the dew point off of the interior of wall surfaces, where moisture will collect. Proper use and understanding of vapor retarders will also assist in this regard—remember, the vapor retarder always goes on what will be the warm side of the wall in cold weather, and this is typically the inside of the building insulation. The inside of the building is where the humidity is coming from that will cause condensation; this is only untrue in tropical climates where the exterior heat and humidity are extreme and there are few situations where the interior needs to be heated. In colder climates, keeping condensation out of the building requires a "thermal break" at all places where metal passes from inside to outside, including all aluminum window assemblies (see Figure 30.3 again).

Mitigating solar radiation requires an understanding of where the sun is at different times of the day and year. Depending on the climate, location, and season, solar radiation can be very desirable or very undesirable. Because the sun's movement is completely predictable, it is possible to use shading and solar collection strategies to get the desirable sun and exclude the unwanted solar conditions. These strategies can be passive or active, and affect the building enclosure, siting, and landscaping.

BUILDING ENCLOSURE SYSTEMS

The components of a building's enclosure system are generally broken down into roofs, walls, and foundations—floors are not included in this, since they aren't normally exposed to the weather. These components each deal with the movement of water and thermal transmission in different ways.

Roofs
Since they are most exposed to falling rain, and since their vulnerability to gravity-caused flow is greatest, roofs are the most important area of concern regarding water infiltration. Historically, damp climates have developed surprisingly successful indigenous responses to heavy rainfall. Typically these include roofs with slopes proportional to the amount of rainfall received—steeper roofs in damper climates—and sophisticated devices for preventing water seepage, including bundled or layered grasses that wick water down the roof, and clay tiles designed to capture and direct water locally.

For residential applications, the gold standard of waterproofing is still the sloped roof, which relies on gravity to induce a flow down and away from habitable spaces and works naturally with triangular roof trusses. A typical sloped roof at this scale will include a deck of plywood, a layer of waterproofing, and

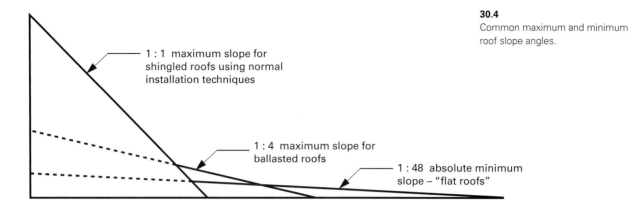

30.4
Common maximum and minimum roof slope angles.

1 : 1 maximum slope for shingled roofs using normal installation techniques

1 : 4 maximum slope for ballasted roofs

1 : 48 absolute minimum slope – "flat roofs"

overlapped shingles, which are positioned such that each shingle will cover the nail holes of the shingle beneath it. Shingles may be wood, asphalt, metal or clay, but in each case they will be impervious and fairly dense, to provide protection to the deck below and to resist being blown off by a heavy wind (which, of course, is often accompanied by heavy rains). Such roofs must be pitched to at least 1 in 6, or about 17 degrees. Steeper roofs will induce faster flowing water, and therefore shingles that are made of compositional material (asphalt in particular) will deteriorate more quickly on steep roofs. Generally, shingled roofs are no steeper than 45 degrees, and if over that require special installation techniques or a different cladding choice (Figure 30.4). The layer of waterproofing beneath is unlikely to get wet from water soaking through the shingles, but prevents wind-driven water that may get under the shingled layer from permeating into the roof structure. Current membranes include materials that self-heal around nail holes, preventing a common leak source, and are generally overlapped, like shingles, to ensure full coverage and watertight joints.

Flashing

Where sloped roofs intersect, their shapes will create valleys through which large quantities of water may be channeled. These areas are particularly vulnerable as the deck below will have a joint at the most vulnerable point, the waterproofing layer must either be cut or creased, and shingles will overlap in tight quarters where good workmanship may not be achievable. Therefore, roofs are typically *flashed* wherever their surface folds—at either a ridge or valley. Flashing normally consists of light-gauge metal sheeting that can easily be crimped or folded, although for residential applications this may just be an additional sheet of waterproofing membrane. At valleys flashing is tucked under both planes of shingles, which may then be mitered or overlapped on top of it. Flashing is also used where elements such as chimneys or vents penetrate the roof (Figure 30.5). Here, the lightweight metal is attached to the protruding object well above the roof level, and run underneath the shingle layer. While water may eventually flow down the flashing and under the shingles, it will still be on top of the waterproof membrane and in only small amounts that can evaporate before causing damage. For masonry penetrations, flashing may be set into a mortar joint—which must then itself be flashed to keep water from working its way into the brick. Where differential movement is anticipated, surfaces may have cap and valley flashing, where two sheets overlap one another.

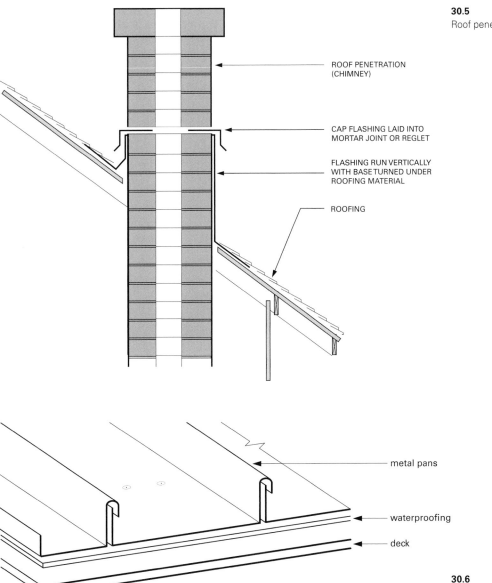

30.5
Roof penetration flashing.

ROOF PENETRATION
(CHIMNEY)

CAP FLASHING LAID INTO
MORTAR JOINT OR REGLET

FLASHING RUN VERTICALLY
WITH BASE TURNED UNDER
ROOFING MATERIAL

ROOFING

metal pans

waterproofing

deck

30.6
Standing seam metal roof.

Flashing is generally part of a two-stage strategy for water exclusion that relies on a generally watertight outer layer and a backup system that will capture whatever small amount of water may penetrate that layer. Typically flashing is composed of aluminum or stainless steel, although copper is occasionally used as well. Steel, because of its tendency to oxidize in water, is less often used. A variant on the standard shingled roof is a *standing seam metal roof*, which can be thought of as a roof system made entirely of flashing (Figure 30.6). Pans of light-gauge metal are laid over a roof and are seamed to one another by folding the edges of each pan up and into one another.

Eaves and gutters
Typical sloped roofs will extend past a building's exterior wall, providing a certain separation between the large flow of water off the edge and the vulnerable top

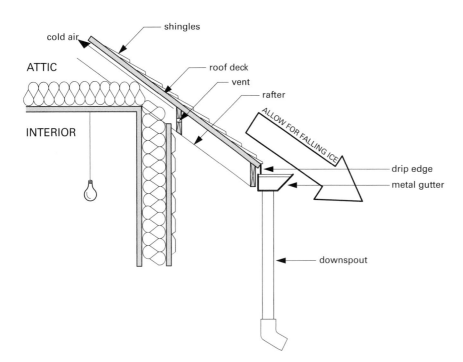

of the wall itself (Figure 30.7). This *eave* brings with it some problems that must be addressed. First, despite the guarantee of the overhang, the junction between eave and wall must still be made watertight, typically by taking the wall's waterproofing layer up past the junction several inches. Additional problems, however, occur in cold climates. In particular, snow on the upper portion of the roof, above heated, occupied spaces, will often melt, running down the roof's surface and hitting the roof above the overhanging eave, which is of course unheated. At this point it may freeze and water flowing down the roof may be trapped behind this ice dam (Figure 30.8). Eventually, this forces water up under the shingles, where it may sit until it works its way in to the roof through the waterproofing and decking causing leaks into the exterior wall. This *ice dam* condition can be quite destructive as freezing water can lift shingles, separate wall cladding, and push off fascia panels. To prevent this from occurring, the system should be designed as a *cold roof*, with the insulation held back to the ceiling or at least 25mm (1") away from the bottom of the roof deck. Outside air is then brought in through vents under the eave, or through wall vents in the attic, preventing snow from melting on the cold roof surface. Alternatively, there are products for heating eaves and creating channels for water to flow through, but these are less reliable than a well-designed and ventilated cold roof system. If a system is poorly designed or assembled it may require maintenance such as raking snow off of eaves to help prevent ice dams.

At the roof edge, it is important to quickly move water away from vulnerable edges to prevent water being driven under the waterproof layer by wind or capillary action. At its simplest, the edge of a pitched roof may have a *drip edge*, an angled piece of metal that moves water about 25mm (1") away from the roof edge, preventing it from running down the side of the fascia. However, this can still be a sizable quantity of water and it is often necessary to use gutters to move it away from the equally vulnerable foundation wall below.

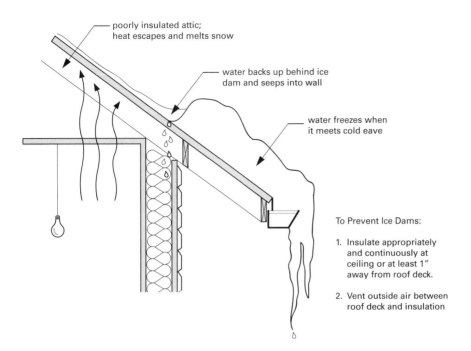

poorly insulated attic;
heat escapes and melts snow

water backs up behind ice
dam and seeps into wall

water freezes when
it meets cold eave

To Prevent Ice Dams:

1. Insulate appropriately
   and continuously at
   ceiling or at least 1″
   away from roof deck.

2. Vent outside air between
   roof deck and insulation

While sloped roofs have an inherent advantage, because they use gravity to move water toward the building edge, the majority of commercial and industrial structures have flat roofs. Aside from the disadvantages of slower water movement, there are well-tested methods of collecting, directing and eliminating rainwater for low-slope roofs. First, there is really no such thing as a "flat" roof. All roofs use slopes to move water toward building edges or drains. In general, flat roofs actually have slopes of 3 to 6.5mm (⅛–¼″) per foot. This can be achieved by using tapered rigid insulation, allowing the structural system to be flat, level, and standardized. Drains and outlets can be placed to minimize the total depth of the roof slope, giving the appearance of flatness. Codes will often limit the area of roof that can be directed to a single drain, ensuring that if one becomes clogged—a virtual guarantee over the lifetime of a building—the collected water will eventually spill over into adjacent drain tributaries and the total load of water and snow will not be too heavy for the structure below.

Like sloped roofs, the assembly of the roof structure itself is designed to keep water from percolating into the structure while it is moving toward a drain. However, in flat roof installations water may be moving much more slowly, and it is more likely that water will end up standing on the roof at some point. A waterproof layer is therefore applied that is both more durable and more reliably leak-proof than on sloped elements. This layer may be a felt and asphalt hybrid, in which layers of fabric are alternated with "mops" of hot tar, providing a monolithic but flexible layer that can, during hot weather, automatically self-heal. Most low-slope roof installations (in particular where the weather gets cold) have tended to use membrane roofing, in which a rubberized or plastic layer is rolled out onto the roof. Seams between sheets are then welded together, again providing a waterproof layer. The reliance on welding (in this case really gluing or bonding) and the potential for these membrane surfaces to be damaged, requires careful installation and maintenance. In some cases, a layer of ballast (usually small round gravel) will be placed on top of the

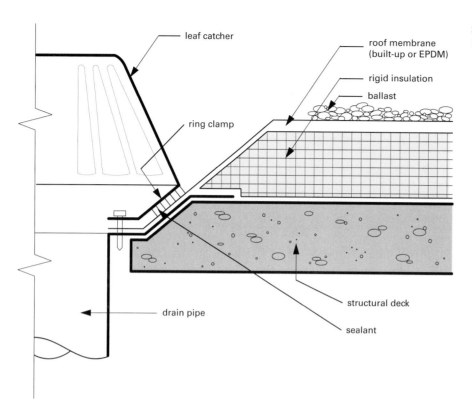

membrane for both protection and uplift resistance in a strong wind. EPDM (Ethylene Propylene Diene Monomer), a common roof membrane material, can also be mechanically fixed to the structure below, which eliminates the need for ballast but requires care in placing appropriate deck adhesion to the membrane.

Drains are installed at the low points of the roof slope. Their detailing is critical to roof performance, as they invariably involve a penetration through the waterproof layer (Figure 30.9). Typically, the waterproofing roof layer is laid over a drain base plate that sits on the roof opening and is sealed to it with mastic or adhesive. The drain cap is then bolted on top of the waterproofing, through the mastic, to the base plate below. The tight clamp of the drain cap and the sloped shape of the base plate ensure that the majority of water will flow, via gravity, into the drain itself, while the base plate will tend to "catch" any water that happens to get under the membrane and direct it to the drain. Drains must usually have a slotted collector to prevent leaves and debris from getting into the drainpipe itself, enabling someone to visually inspect and manually clear each drain from the rooftop. Most codes will require at least two drains from any rooftop surface, to allow drainage in the event that one becomes clogged. Once below the roof, stormwater is carried to the ground, into a storm sewer, or to retention on-site. Note that interior drain pipes must typically be insulated to prevent condensation in the winter, as their contents will often be runoff from snow and ice that has accumulated on the roof.

A simple solution for discharging rooftop stormwater is a *scupper*, or a channel off the edge of a rooftop into a downspout or simply away from the building surface. These are often unsightly, however, and run the risk of discharging water vertically down the face of a building, marring its appearance. The downspouts also should be on the south side of a building in cold climates, so the sun doesn't melt the snow causing water to run off of the roof in the shade, where it refreezes and explodes the downspout. Likewise, for large flat roofs, the necessary slope to the edge of a building places the greatest volume of water at a vulnerable point—where the roof and exterior wall intersect. At times, it's advisable on flat roofs to employ roof drains toward the center of the roof, with slopes arranged to keep the smallest volume of water at the building edges, and in fact to contain it slightly to prevent it from being blown down the sides of buildings. At its simplest, this may be a light metal gravel stop that lies on top of a sealed membrane edge and is only high enough to contain the necessary ballast for the roof. In larger installations, however, it is common to "tank" the rooftop by running the waterproofing up a *parapet*, or continuation of the exterior wall up past the roof surface (Figure 30.10). This prevents rooftop water from getting in to the exterior wall construction by raising the vulnerable top edge of the wall, and it provides a reliable side to the rooftop "tank" as the waterproofing layer runs vertically over it. Additional advantages to a parapet are aesthetic—a consistent line across the roofscape—and safety related, as workers on top of the roof are protected by the height of the parapet wall. The upper edge of the parapet must itself be waterproofed, usually by a layer of metal flashing that covers the wall's cross section completely and by a coping, which may be stone, masonry, or metal. The coping provides a firm connection between the flashing and the wall, while the flashing's base may be integrated with the rooftop flashing, forming a continuous liner for the rooftop volume (Figure 30.11).

30.10
Flashing and edge conditions.

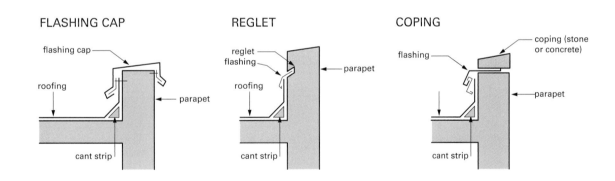

FLASHING CAP

flashing cap

roofing

parapet

cant strip

REGLET

reglet flashing

roofing

parapet

cant strip

COPING

coping (stone or concrete)

flashing

parapet

cant strip

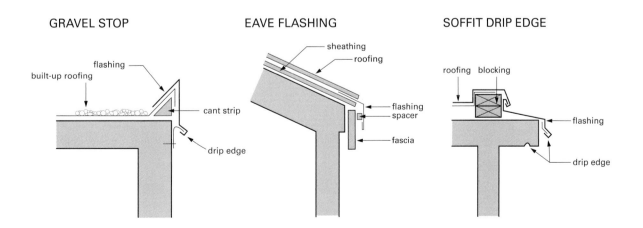

GRAVEL STOP

flashing

built-up roofing

cant strip

drip edge

EAVE FLASHING

sheathing

roofing

flashing spacer

fascia

SOFFIT DRIP EDGE

roofing   blocking

flashing

drip edge

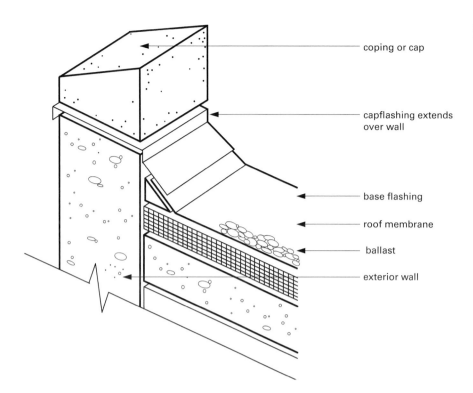

coping or cap

capflashing extends
over wall

base flashing

roof membrane

ballast

exterior wall

Walls

Because water is naturally shed off of vertical walls by gravity, they present somewhat less of a waterproofing problem than roofs. However, steps must still be taken to ensure that water does not penetrate wall assemblies by either wind pressure or capillary action. Porous materials such as wood or stone must normally be waterproofed, usually by a paint or liquid sealer, or else they must be backed up by a dedicated waterproof membrane. Typically, a "belt and braces" approach involves sealing the exterior as well as possible, and then providing a backup layer that both excludes and directs water down through the wall and out away from the building (Figure 30.12). Brick cavity walls, for example, provide a sloped flashing and *weep holes* at their base, permitting the moisture that inevitably penetrates through the porous outer brick layer to fall by gravity and be led out of the wall (Figure 30.13). Where exterior elements join, they are typically sealed with an elastomeric compound or sealant that flexibly adheres to both surfaces and excludes water. This is typically installed

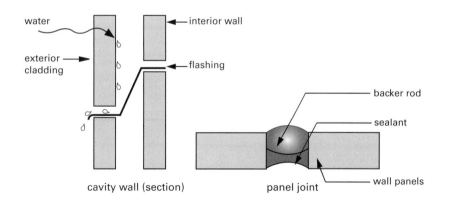

water

interior wall

exterior
cladding

flashing

backer rod

sealant

wall panels

cavity wall (section)

panel joint

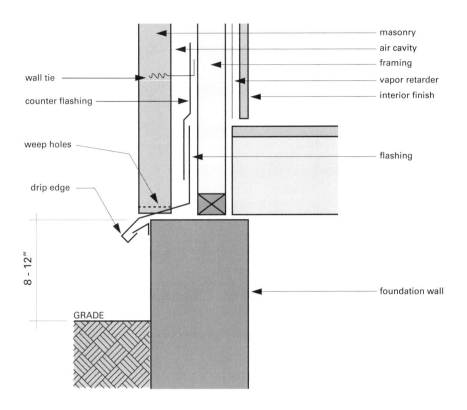

masonry

air cavity

framing

vapor retarder

interior finish

wall tie

counter flashing

flashing

weep holes

drip edge

8 - 12"

foundation wall

GRADE

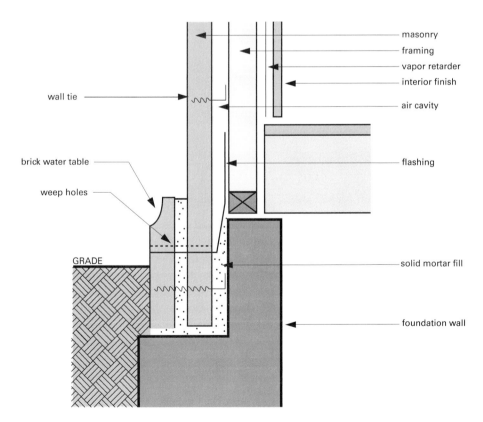

masonry

framing

vapor retarder

interior finish

wall tie

air cavity

brick water table

flashing

weep holes

GRADE

solid mortar fill

foundation wall

30.13
Masonry veneer flashing.

with a *backer rod* that is wedged into the joint providing resistance to the sealant, so it will compress and fill the joint properly.

Other areas of concern for exterior walls include projections, which may gather water and direct it into the wall assembly, and base conditions. On the top of a horizontal projection an inadvertent slope toward the building will direct water in by gravity. This can be corrected by designing in an outward slope on all projected or otherwise horizontal wall surfaces, or by flashing the top of the projection to make the water flow away from the wall. More difficult is water that flows across the bottom of a horizontal projection by capillary action. This can very easily continue flowing into the wall assembly if the underside joint is flawed. Providing a drip edge on any projection prevents water from traversing this surface. Finally, the point of contact between an exterior wall and the ground surface is a notorious area for water infiltration, as porous materials such as concrete, wood, or sedimentary stone can easily wick groundwater up into the wall, leaving unsightly stains or, worse, pulling moisture inside the wall assembly. Good detailing includes waterproofing at the ground level or a separation between the soil and porous building material.

Foundations

Foundations carry two major concerns—they are underground and therefore in constant contact with soil that may be wet, and they are covered by earth—which mean that problems are more difficult to find and can be quite costly. Generally, foundations are waterproofed in three ways—by treating the exterior of the basement walls and floors with an exclusionary membrane or coating, by modifying the surrounding soil to encourage drainage away from the building line, and by capturing water at the footing (Figure 30.14). The waterproof layer may be a simple "mop" of asphalt or a rubberized membrane—in either case it must extend down to and over the top of all footings, as well as rising up the exterior wall above the ground line to exclude water flowing across the surface. It is generally protected by a layer of rigid insulation or other protection board

30.14
Foundation waterproofing.

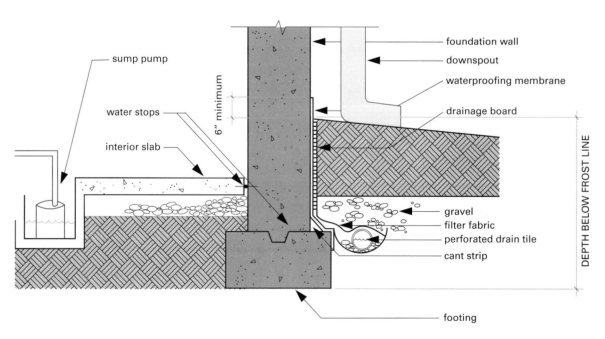

to prevent its being damaged by site work after installation. Waterproofing of slabs is usually accomplished by laying a gravel bed on top of the excavated surface, which allows water to drain away from the bottom of the slab by gravity, and then laying a vapor barrier above the gravel to prevent cold, moist air from seeping through the slab. An additional layer of cardboard impregnated with bentonite may also be used—bentonite expands when wet, forming a seal that is impervious to water. Penetrations through the foundation or slab must be protected in ways that allow for waterproofing the installation, usually by a combination of grout, sealant, and bentonite.

Just as the slab may be kept dry by a layer of gravel, the foundation itself can be protected by backfilling with gravel rather than soil, forcing any water that percolates through the ground to drain by gravity away from the foundation wall. To capture water moving through this gravel fill, a drainage tile is placed around the perimeter of the foundation, usually at the level of the footing's top surface. Drainage tile is basically a perforated pipe, which captures water and discharges it away from the building underground or into a storm sewer. It typically requires a filter fabric to be wrapped around it to keep sand and dirt that might cause a clog from entering, and it, like all drain and waste piping, must be sloped to fall between 3 and 6.5mm ($\frac{1}{8}$–$\frac{1}{4}$") minimum per foot of run.

In areas where the ground freezes a foundation system must be constructed that sits on earth that will not drop below 0C (32F), or is below the "frost line". This depth varies throughout the world, it is 1065mm (42") in the Upper Midwest of the U.S. and 450mm (18") in Southeast England, and must be a depth that the frost line will never reach. The reason a building foundation must set below this depth is due to the expansion of water when it turns to ice; if this expansion were to occur under the foundation the ground moisture would "heave" and cause the foundation to crack. This condition is seen in older buildings constructed incorrectly, and in conditions where the grade around an existing structure has been changed to expose a section of foundation wall previously covered (and therefore insulated) with earth. The freezing condition is very powerful and can "heave" and blow apart the heaviest of structures.

Finally, the best protection for foundations is to prevent water from reaching them in the first place. Proper roof drains, adequate drainpipe sizes, scuppers, and gutters that are sized properly and discharge away from the building line will prevent most water from ever reaching the foundation wall, particularly with an overhanging roof. Likewise, proper site grading to ensure that water flows away from, rather than toward, the building perimeter will prevent surface water from ever reaching the foundation wall. A final piece of insurance is a *sump pump*, located in a shallow well in the basement that automatically turns on when it detects water.

ASSEMBLY/SEQUENCE

When preparing documentation for a building, the architect, and their consultants, are responsible for describing all of the components of a building and their assembly. However, the means, methods, and sequence of construction are at the discretion of the contractor—this is not only because they are the most qualified to establish these, but also because it is their liability if things go wrong. The architect typically does not build the structures they design; the task of overseeing most construction falls to a general contractor. The general contractor determines the cost of the project and how to put it together; they hire all of the subcontractors, order all of the materials, coordinate the scheduling, obtain all of the permits, and take the risks involved with construction. This is not a liability most architects would want; we're responsible for our own errors and omissions insurance in case what we've drawn is built as we indicated, but doesn't perform acceptably. The general contractor is usually not contractually tied to the architect in any way; architects are simply the owner's representatives doing site "observation" (the term "inspection" is often avoided for fear of additional liability). The owner hires the architect and contractor separately and has the architect act as their expert in the field to see that the project is proceeding as drawn up.

This stated, the architect must know the construction sequence in order to prepare drawings that can be built correctly. Buildings are obviously assembled from the ground up, but there are some notable exceptions when dealing with building enclosure. Site clearing, underground drainage, and utilities are typically first, followed by foundation systems. Next is the basic framing structure, then the roof structure. Roof enclosure typically follows structural frame construction, due to the desire to get the interior dry as soon as possible for construction staging and material storage. The wall enclosure goes up next, again to get the inside dry enough to start the more weather-sensitive parts of interior construction. Lastly the glass and doors go in to seal up the interior and provide security for more valuable materials and tools. Once the building enclosure is done the interior work and remaining exterior details can be completed. Careful sequencing sometimes needs to take place so that large-scale assemblies are inside before final enclosure takes place, an example would be on a job site where the stair fabrications will not fit through the door. A debate would likely ensue about whether to tear down part of the wall or cut the stairs in half and re-weld them later. The architect would typically not direct which option to take, but could remind the contractor that the specifications on the stair welds would be difficult to meet in a site fabricated welding situation.

Regardless of what the construction documents state, if you have drawn something impossible to make there will be little sympathy from the contractor or the owner. The architect may end up redesigning it quickly and for free, along with losing some credibility with the client and the contractor. Additionally, the redesign may be less attractive than the original and cost more. This can make a simple mistake or oversight extremely costly. Think about how the process of assembly will work in the field as if you had to put it together yourself.

CONCLUSION

More lawsuits involve water penetration than any other single building failure. Often the problem can be traced back to an attempt to save construction costs (by, in some cases, eliminating flashing or sealant) or an attempt to retrofit waterproofing strategies to a design that failed to recognize potential infiltration at the start. Keeping in mind the six paths through which water can get into a building at all times is good practice, no matter what system is being considered.

FREQUENTLY ASKED QUESTIONS

What side of the wall does the vapor retarder go on?
The vapor retarder is intended to keep building moisture from migrating into the walls and ceilings of a structure that reaches the dew point. This moisture moves through permeable surfaces in the form of airborne humidity. In temperate, cold and hot/dry climates this humidity is greatest on the inside of the structure—so the retarder goes on the inside of the wall assembly. In very warm and humid climates the humidity can be greater on the outside of the building for the majority of the time, causing the vapor retarder to go on the outside of the structure so interior air conditioning doesn't draw humidity inside the wall. Occasionally it is recommended to eliminate the vapor retarder entirely in these situations so the wall can dry both inwards and outwards. Never install vapor retarders on both sides of a wall, as it will prevent drying of any moisture that finds its way into the assembly.

What is hydrostatic pressure?
Hydrostatic pressure occurs when the moisture in the surrounding soil presses against a building's foundation walls. Most soils retain some moisture, except coarse sands and gravel, causing foundations to be under some hydrostatic pressure constantly. This can cause foundation walls to leak or even buckle and fail over time. It is critical to give the water an alternate route, which is usually done by creating an air gap between the soil and wall that channels the moisture to a drain tile.

GLOSSARY

Backer rod: A flexible foam extrusion that is pushed into gaps to prevent sealant from passing through the opening. It also allows compression of the sealant to form a more reliable joint.

Bentonite: A clay material that expands when wet, forming a seal that is impervious to water.

Capillary action: water movement occurring when the space separating two open surfaces is small, so moisture is drawn into the gap.

EPDM: Ethylene Propylene Diene Monomer is a sheet rubber roofing material for use on flat roof installations.

Flashing: Used for waterproofing roof conditions, it normally consists of light-gauge metal sheeting that can easily be crimped or folded.

Freeze/thaw cycle: Temperature shifts that allow moisture to freeze and expand, then melt and flow into gaps. It is a particular difficulty of building in temperate climates where the temperature frequently drifts above and below freezing.

Frost line: The depth the ground in a location is subject to freezing. A building foundation must set below this line is due to the expansion of water when it turns to ice, if this expansion were to occur under the foundation it would "heave" and cause the foundation to crack.

Hydrostatic pressure: Pressure of moisture/water in the soil pushing against the foundation walls.

Ice dam: Melted snow that refreezes at the edge of a roof assembly, causing a dam that pushes subsequent ice freezing under the shingles. This ice will destroy the roofing components and potentially re-melt into the building assembly.

Parapet: A continuation of the exterior wall up past the roof surface.

Rain screen: An exterior enclosure system with an air space between the outer skin and inner enclosure that is kept pressure equalized to prevent moisture from being pulled into the interior.

Scupper: A channel off the edge of a rooftop or an opening in a wall to allow water to drain out.

Thermal break: A discontinuity inserted into a material assembly to prevent conductive materials from transferring temperature from outside to inside, creating a condensation problem. The inserted material, usually a plastic or polycarbonate, must not conduct temperature well.

Vapor retarder: A waterproof membrane that prevents humidity from passing into an exterior wall cavity.

FURTHER READING

Bassler, B. ed. (2000). *Architectural Graphic Standards Student Edition*, 9th edition. New York: Wiley; Chapter 7, Thermal and Moisture Protection, especially pp. 210, 214, 216–248.

Kwok, A. and Grondzik, W. (2011). *The Green Studio Handbook*, 2nd edition. Oxford: Elsevier.

Neufert, E. and Neufert, P. (2000). *Architects Data*, 3rd edition. London: Blackwell Science; pp. 51–61, 72–81, 111–116.

31

CURTAIN WALLS

History	The curtain wall from 1851 on
Principles	Structure Lateral support Modularity Connections Environmental enclosure
Solid systems	Precast concrete GRC/GFRP Metal
Glass systems	Glass material Capture techniques Subframe and wind support
Hybrid systems	Structural glazing Double skins

HISTORY

Until the 1890s, the idea of "cladding" a building structure would not have made much sense to builders or architects. The outer layer of any building was its environmental enclosure and its structure, as the vast majority of buildings relied on bearing exterior walls for support. This, of course, was due to the preponderance of masonry and timber as building materials.

However with the advent of steel construction in the late nineteenth century, architects and engineers had a new solution to problems of interior lighting. Since steel offered the potential for a lightweight, skeletal construction independent from the outer wall, that wall could thus also be lightweight, skinny, and composed of material that wasn't necessarily structural. To overcome the need for gas and electric arc lighting (expensive and dangerous) architects of early skyscrapers quickly recognized the potential for large plates of glass on the building's exterior, usually cantilevered off of an internal steel structure with only enough solid material on the skin to hold the glass in place and to give some sense of security to building occupants (Figure 31.1).

Throughout the early twentieth century, building skins underwent a complex

Bearing Wall

– Exterior Wall supports floors
– Thickest at base
– Punched windows
– Heavy

Curtain Wall

– Floors support Exterior Wall
– Thin throughout—allows open ground floor
– Skin can be transparent, translucent, or opaque
– Very light

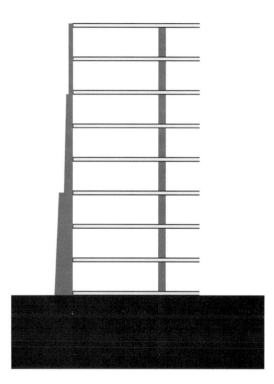 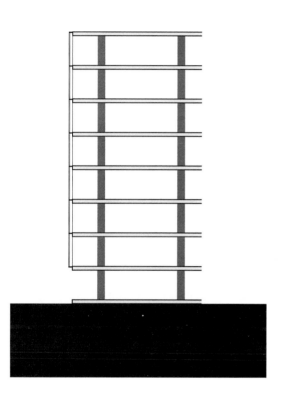

balancing act between the desire (partly aesthetic) for transparency and the simultaneous expense (both financial and environmental) of glass. After World War II the availability of insulated glass and the invention of the float glass process combined to make transparent, vitreous skins affordable in their construction and life cycle.

The "glass box" was one of modernism's greatest promises—and starkest failures. While the crisp aesthetics of such buildings as Mies van der Rohe's Lake Shore Drive Apartments (Figures 31.2 and 31.3) seemed to fulfill early experiments in transparency, the rapid industrialization of glass cladding meant that this was a default choice for cheap, speculative office towers the world over through the 1970s. Shoddy or poorly designed glass curtain walls doomed the all-glass skin for reasons both aesthetic and environmental, the latter in response to the 1973 energy crisis. Since then, there have been notable advances in building cladding—including a return of the solid (though not bearing) skin aligned with the postmodernist aesthetic of the late 1970s and early 1980s, and a re-engagement of the glass skin by architects and engineers keen to refine its aesthetics and fix its environmental shortcomings.

31.1
The fundamental difference between curtain walls and bearing walls.

31.2
A clear demonstration of the
curtain wall's configuration and
assembly.

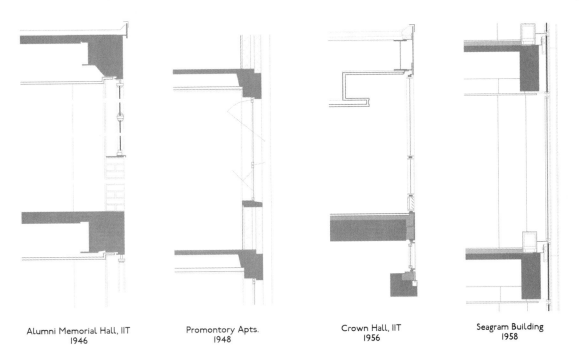

Alumni Memorial Hall, IIT
1946

Promontory Apts.
1948

Crown Hall, IIT
1956

Seagram Building
1958

31.3
Mies' buildings after World War II show the gradual development and standardization of the industrialized curtain wall.

PRINCIPLES

A "curtain wall" is any environmental separation that is hung from a building structure. While we tend to associate curtain walls with glass, it is also common to use solid paneling in much the same way. In all cases, there are issues that must be understood to design any successful cladding system—the cladding's gravity-resisting structure, its resistance to wind or lateral loads, its modularity and size, the connections between its components and its structure, and how it filters the outside environment.

Structurally, curtain walls depend on the building frame for their support. While lightweight, curtain walls still have a significant mass, and connections to the frame must be robust while allowing for installation and movement. Often, curtain walls will have a *subframe* of aluminum or lightweight steel that will mediate between the building structure and the panels of the wall itself. This subframe is usually tied to the structure using steel angle connections attached to a metal frame, or embedded in a concrete structure. This connection must be designed to accept a fair amount of thermal movement, particularly for aluminum systems since the exterior skin may be exposed to very different temperatures than the interior. Usually, a system of slotted connections allows for this while also permitting tolerance and adjustment during installation.

A second important structural consideration is the curtain wall's resistance to lateral—usually wind—loading. Because of its light weight and large vertical area, building cladding is vulnerable to wind pressure. Cladding systems must resist the "push" of a wind in toward the building, but as importantly they must resist negative wind pressure that can pull the cladding system off the building structure. Connections to the building frame must therefore be designed for tension, compression, and bending, while the system itself must have some depth to convert wind loading into a bending load—the subframe or panels must act like a vertical beam in these instances. For particularly tall or broad installations, cladding systems may have substantial trusses behind them, not so much to hold them up as to ensure their integrity in high winds.

In conjunction with the cladding system's structural performance, a key factor in the design of curtain walls is their modularity. Generally, the task of the cladding system is to cover broad areas of the building's exterior surface in as efficient a method as possible, so we typically seek materials that are produced in sheets (aluminum, or steel, or glass). Sizes of panels are limited by both manufacture (glass, for instance, which must fit into annealing ovens) and transport (panels are usually delivered by truck). Subframes, however, are generally composed of linear elements—like the building structure, but on a smaller scale. These elements are typically made of rolled or extruded materials, such as steel or aluminum. Aluminum in particular lends itself to curtain walls particularly well, as the tight tolerances of the extrusion process can form precise channels and fittings that can grip plates of glass or metal. When the subframe is expressed on the outside face of the curtain wall, its elements are called *mullions* (vertical) and *transoms* (horizontal). A typical aluminum mullion system is shown in Figure 31.4. Curtain walls built with individual mullion planar elements are called "stick-built" while those with panel and mullions assembled in the factory are called "panelized".

A good deal of effort often goes into the connections between the flat plate elements of a curtain wall and its linear supports. Here, we are concerned with structural connections and the ability of the joint to keep out intemperate air and all forms of water. For metal panels, we may rely on the precision of an aluminum mullion to accept a folded or crimped edge of an aluminum sheet. We almost always include some form of transitional material—usually neoprene—to allow for some movement, installation tolerance, and air and water exclusion. For glass panels, this neoprene serves the additional role of protecting the glass from bearing directly on the aluminum, which could cause cracking and breakage. With the addition of a *pressure plate*, the neoprene serves to hold the glass in place by friction, a more robust environmental attachment and a structurally more forgiving one. In some cases—so-called "slick skins"—glass may simply be adhered to the mullion's surface with silicone adhesive.

The curtain wall's primary function, of course, is environmental separation. We want to provide a system that keeps rain out, that keeps an environmental barrier between interior, conditioned air, and exterior air, and that admits only useful quantities of light. As noted below, this equation is changing as energy performance becomes a more important element of building design, and curtain walls have therefore increased in complexity. Advanced curtain walls may include provisions for allowing exterior air to filter in when its temperature and humidity are within acceptable ranges, may include insulating glass in addition to insulated solid panels, and may include solar shading, either within the system itself or as an outrigger structure.

SOLID CURTAIN WALLS

At its simplest, a curtain wall may consist of solid, precast concrete panels, attached at their top and base to a steel or concrete frame behind. This is inexpensive, and a certain measure of quality control is obtainable if the concrete is precast in environmentally controlled conditions. It is also speedy, as the panels can be formed independently of the construction process, trucked to the site as

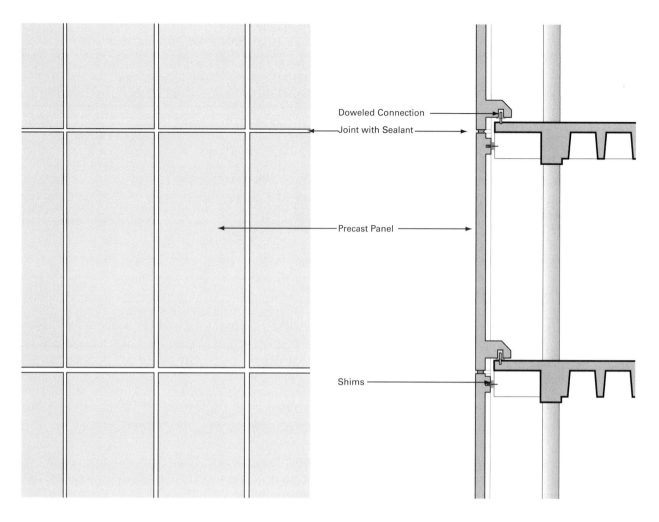

Doweled Connection

Joint with Sealant

Precast Panel

Shims

31.5
Anatomy of a typical precast concrete curtain wall.

needed and hoisted by crane quickly. However, it is usually not possible to obtain particularly fine detailing with concrete, as its aggregate size prohibits small elements from forming properly. Likewise, there is an economic tendency when using precast to eschew variety in favor of (often extreme) modularity. Precast can, however, be used as a substrate for other materials, notably stone, and designers can take advantage of its controlled production to ensure remarkable consistency and arrangement in cladding panels. Precast panels are typically bolted to plates embedded in concrete structures, or welded on to steel structures (Figure 31.5). Their attachments leave room for maneuvering once in place, with slotted connections for bolts and space for shims or packing (Figure 31.6).

Other solid materials that are often used as cladding include glass-reinforced plastic and glass-fiber-reinforced concrete (GRP and GFRC), and sheet metal, which can be superformed with ribs or brake-shaped with crimped edges to provide dimensional stability and rigidity. Small deformations in reflective metal may lead to "oil-canning," or large waves in the surface that are highlighted by reflection patterns. Metal panels are thus typically limited in size, which will be inversely proportional to its gauge, or thickness. Solid panels may be through-bolted to steel or aluminum subframes, or they may be "captured" mechanically with aluminum channels and neoprene seals. These panels must be insulated, often by incorporating rigid foam into the hollow space behind them.

31.6
Precast panels assembled on a concrete frame, showing joint detail and tolerance gap between panels and floor slab.

GLASS CURTAIN WALLS

The aesthetic and performance potential for lightweight, glass building skins has been an almost primal goal of modernist architecture. Throughout the 1920s, German modernism—Expressionism in particular—expressed an almost religious devotion to the ideal of a crystalline building. Until the 1910s, however, most glass was formed by the cylinder or crown method, both involving extensive hand production and labor. Commercial building glass used an energy-intensive casting and polishing process, which limited its use to only the highest-end installations. Beginning in 1914, progress in "drawing" glass from vats, and later in more efficient polishing processes, meant that glass's relative price dropped throughout the century. By 1960, with the development of float processes (in which glass is cast on top of a layer of molten tin, assuring a perfectly smooth finish) its price had dropped so precipitously that it became, by default, the cheapest way to clad large tower blocks.

However, the material development of glass was only part of the curtain wall story. Ways to physically attach the glass to the building structure also presented a variety of problems. Glass is both heavy and fragile, and it must thus be supported by a robust yet flexible system, able to hold large, weighty panes in place, yet with enough give to prevent the glass from bending and therefore breaking. In 1851, the Crystal Palace relied on wood frames and manually placed putty to adhere the glass to its structure. This was fine for a temporary exhibition structure that could (and did) leak ferociously. The Reliance Building, 40 years later, used timber and cast terra cotta, again with a clay-like putty, to hold its 36ft^2 panes in place, with better results. A major development in lightening the substructure for glass panes came about in 1919, when the Hallidie Building in San Francisco by Willis Polk used steel straps and rods to hold up its extensive (and, unfortunately, south-facing) seven-story glass facade. Steel continued as the framing material of choice for glass skins well past World War

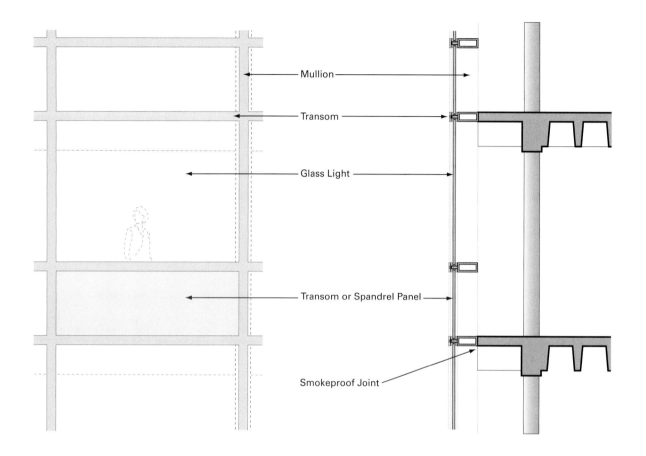

Mullion

Transom

Glass Light

Transom or Spandrel Panel

Smokeproof Joint

31.7
Typical glass curtain wall anatomy.

II, despite its relative weight, crude detailing and tendency to corrode unless carefully maintained. Likewise, putty remained the only available sealant until the fall in rubber prices after wartime. In fact, as late as 1951 the most technically advanced curtain walls (at for instance, Eero Saarinen's GM Technical Center) used steel and putty to hold single layers of glass in place and, where aesthetically necessary, covered this with bent aluminum plates.

Three developments after World War II revolutionized glass skins, creating the modern curtain wall as we know it. First, aluminum's price dropped dramatically, and extruding mills began producing standard (and thus cheap) sectional shapes for architectural production. Second, aircraft technology gave high-quality sealants to architecture, including neoprene, which has proven less vulnerable to weathering than rubber or putty. Third, after decades of failure, glass manufacturers began to produce reliable insulating glass, using two sheets of plate glass separated by metal spacers and filled with inert gases.

In its contemporary form, the standard glazed curtain wall consists of four main components: the glass itself, a system of metal (usually aluminum) mullions and transoms that keep the glass in place, sealants or gaskets that provide an environmental connection between glass and mullion, and a set of connections that transfer the weight of the entire cladding system to the building structure (Figure 31.7).

The glass itself will generally be tempered, that is, heated to near melting and then doused quickly with cold water. This post-tensions the outer layer of glass, adding strength and causing it to shatter into small, harmless grains if

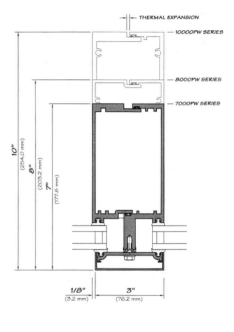

31.8
Detail of a typical stock aluminum mullion system.

WAUSAU
WINDOW AND WALL
SYSTEMS

CURTAINWALL

Architectural Windows

3" FACE - PRESSUREWALL Series

THERMAL EXPANSION
— 10000PW SERIES
— 8000PW SERIES
— 7000PW SERIES

10"
(254.0 mm)

8"
(203.2 mm)

7"
(177.8 mm)

1/8"
(3.2 mm)

3"
(76.2 mm)

③ MULLION STACKS
VARIABLE DEPTHS

Scale: 6"=1'0"   C3-6   Wausau 2000

broken. Glass may be tinted to reduce interior glare, or fritted. Frit is a baked-on ceramic coating that can be applied in a variety of densities, including a full, opaque coat or lighter, dotted or striped patterns to reduce the amount of light transmitted through a pane. Two sheets of glass may also be laminated together with a plastic interlayer. This adds a factor of safety in the event of breakage, and provides an acoustic separation. Plate glass is available in sizes up to a maximum of around 100ft^2 although widths are limited to around 12 feet in any one direction. This is due both to the size of available annealing ovens, and to the need to transport plates on commercially available trucks.

Transoms and mullions are typically made of aluminum, which can easily be extruded to very precise tolerances. Standard curtain wall elements will include a "box" and a set of grips. The box may vary in size from 2–6" wide, and from 3–12" in depth (Figure 31.8). Extrusions must be circumscribed by a circle no larger than 14" in diameter, the width of the largest commercially available extruding dies. The box may contain integral channels, usually on the inside, that allow precise connections between "sticks". The grips are typically formed on one side by the short end of the box, which is grooved to accept a sealer or gasket, and by a plate that is bolted on to a ridge that sticks out from the box's short side. Plates are then covered by a continuous cover strip, which

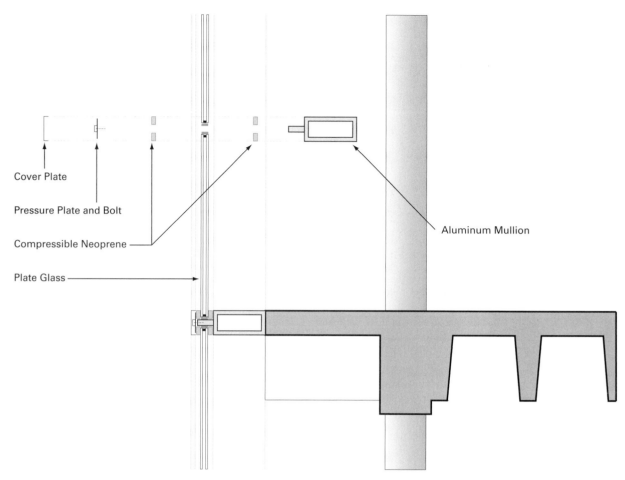

Cover Plate

Pressure Plate and Bolt

Compressible Neoprene

Plate Glass

Aluminum Mullion

31.9
Detailed anatomy of a glass and aluminum curtain wall.

provides a smooth finish on the exterior. Aesthetics may dictate that either vertical or horizontal elements be suppressed, and they can be composed of simply a box, with or without a ridge, siliconed to the back of the glass. To avoid thermal bridges, mullion sections may include neoprene gaskets that separate elements that come into contact with outside air from those that contact the interior.

Gaskets between the aluminum mullion system and the glass panels are usually neoprene, although silicone is also used. These provide a friction fit that supports the glass while allowing it to move a bit, preventing breakage caused by sudden shocks (Figures 31.9 and 31.10). The entire system must be supported both vertically and laterally by either the building structure, or (for large or tall spaces) a separate substructure designed to transmit these forces. Again, wind is the greatest concern, as large flat surfaces will act as sails, either driving the cladding wall into the building structure or (worse) sucking it away. At its simplest, these connections can be simple steel angles that bolt to the mullions and to concrete floor slabs; however, large systems may employ steel trusses, cable systems, or large freestanding columns to ensure stability.

RECENT DEVELOPMENTS

Among current standards in curtain wall practice are *rain screens*, or cladding systems that rely on a "loose fit" exterior layer to provide a pressurized zone that resists rain intrusion, and engineered shading systems that exclude direct sunlight during particularly warm periods of the year or working day. Rain screens are covered in Chapter 30, Building Envelopes.

Structural glazing eliminates mullions, using the inherent strength of glass in tension to support itself. The principle behind structural glazing is simple (Figure 31.11). Plates of glass are suspended from the roof slab of a structure and are connected to one another at the corners, either by patch plates (square pieces of metal with through bolts) or "spiders" (steel elements with four connections) (Figure 31.12). The glass literally hangs from the top of the building, relying on trusses or glass fins to keep it stable against lateral loading from the wind. Because each sheet is connected to three others at its top, a single pane breaking will simply force the redistribution of gravity loads, and will not cause the entire column to collapse. Sheets of glass are siliconed to one another at their edges to provide an environmental enclosure, and bolt connections use ball-in-socket joints to permit glass panels to rotate slightly, preventing breakage by "giving." A similar strategy must be adopted at the top, where sheets of glass are supported by a single axle, allowing the entire column to rotate very slightly, rather than gripping the glass and causing breakage. A base detail allows the wall to "ride" up and down from thermal expansion.

Double Skins. While glass cladding systems have become both affordable and constructionally efficient, their environmental performance, even when insulated glass is used, continues to be problematic. In climates where either extreme cold or extreme heat is prevalent for part of the year (i.e. about 75 percent of the U.S.), thin curtain walls incur, by their very nature, a substantial energy penalty. This, of course, is in addition to the embodied energy inherent in a system made of (energy-intensive) aluminum and (energy-intensive) glass.

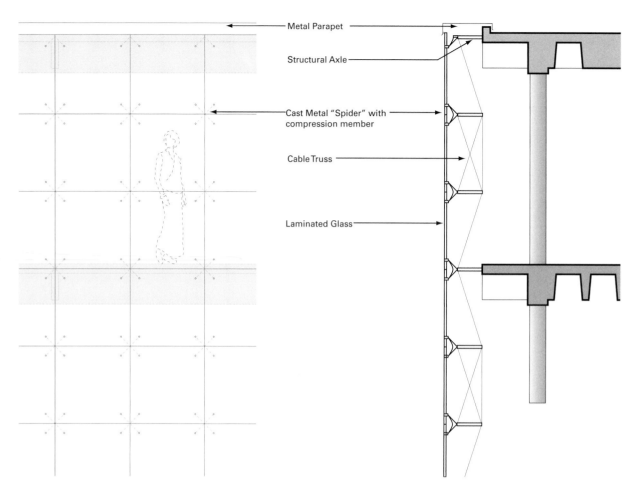

Metal Parapet

Structural Axle

Cast Metal "Spider" with
compression member

Cable Truss

Laminated Glass

31.11
Anatomy of a typical structural glass system.

Beginning in the late 1970s, in response to the growing impact of the energy crisis, environmental engineers began to investigate the potential for *thick curtain walls*, that is, with depth that would permit the introduction of cleverly deployed shading, air movement and/or encapsulation. The thinking was that these strategies could permit the aesthetic and lighting benefits that curtain walls offered while eliminating much of the life cycle performance penalty that they entailed. Integral *shading*, of course, adopted a standard climate response strategy, essentially bolting on metal fins, shelves, or louvers in response to solar geometry—vertical on east, west, and north sides to keep low sun and its attendant glare out, horizontal to keep low winter sun in and high summer sun out. In 1978, the Occidental Chemical Building in Niagara Falls took this strategy one step further.

Occidental's strategy was based on the failure of standard, venetian-blind responses to summer heat. The problem with internal blinds is that they block direct sunlight, but also absorb direct solar radiation, which is then discharged inside the building. Occidental's designers relocated a screen of fixed aluminum louvers, placing them between two glass skins—one a "storefront" system at the edge of the office floor plate, the other a glass curtain wall hung about 2'

31.12
A structurally glazed skin showing connection details.

beyond the slab, creating a vertical shaft between the two skins. Summer sun would hit the louvers and warm the air in the shaft, which would then rise and be ejected through a vent at roof level. Thus, the building got the full benefit of natural daylight with no appreciable heat gain, as the hot air around the louvers was exhausted directly to the outside. In the winter, the system could simply be closed up, and the hot air generated by the sun would serve as a super efficient insulator.

While effective, this system was expensive to build, and it provided only a limited environmental benefit. Double skins remained experimental until the 1990s, when energy prices in Germany encouraged engineers such as ARUP and Kaiser Bautechnik to look at the efficiency of their designs holistically. The double skin made a comeback in a slightly modified form. Instead of sealing the interior skin, these second generation systems included vents in the inner, office skin. With the advent of heavy computer use, heating offices became a non-issue—this happened naturally from CRT displays, high speed processors, etc. Cooling, however, became a year-round problem, and the vents in the inner skin allowed the rising air in the external shaft to pull exhaust air from the office, usually at the ceiling where hot air would tend to collect. Shafts within concrete cores provided naturally tempered supply air, which could be used to make up the volume extracted by the double skin wall (Figure 31.13).

This system has now become standard practice (Figure 31.14). Perhaps the most advanced double skin system is Renzo Piano's Debis Tower in Berlin, where east and west facades rely on a complex layering of operable glass panels, terra cotta shading bars, and interior vented window units. Digital con-

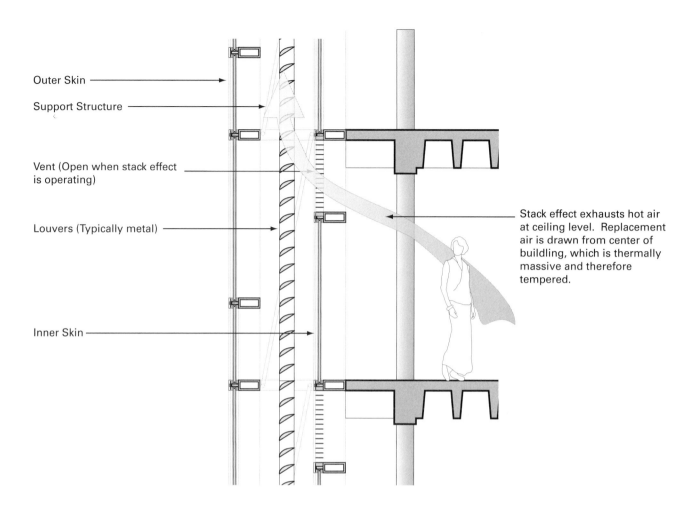

Outer Skin

Support Structure

Vent (Open when stack effect is operating)

Louvers (Typically metal)

Inner Skin

Stack effect exhausts hot air at ceiling level. Replacement air is drawn from center of buildling, which is thermally massive and therefore tempered.

31.13
Anatomy of a typical double (ventilated) skin.

trols permit the skin to tune itself to the exterior climate—on a moderate day, both layers can open to permit outside air into offices. On hot days, the outer skin closes, and the interior skin opens, sucking hot air out of offices and out the top of the building. On cold days, the skin can close up entirely, creating an insulating layer.

Double skins do present detailing problems, particularly around issues of maintenance and fire prevention. Contemporary designs typically include enough width for worker access, and may provide steel grates for cleaning personnel to stand on at each floor. Fire is a more pressing issue—most codes will not permit more than three consecutive floors to open on to a shaft without intensive fire protection. While the "solar engine" will work at this reduced scale, it loses a great deal of efficiency. European codes have changed to permit larger external shafts provided they are sprinklered and have fire shutters at every three to four floors.

FREQUENTLY ASKED QUESTIONS

Every so often a tall building is in the news for losing panes of glass. What causes this?
One of the most notorious building failures of all time was the loss of glass

31.14
Double skins offer visual depth and a refined texture.

from the John Hancock Tower in Boston, designed by I. M. Pei. Large panes of glass popped out of the building skin and crashed to the street below—ultimately, the skin had to be replaced while the building stood covered in plywood. Some speculated that the building was racking excessively due to unforeseen wind behavior, but the problem turned out to involve weakening in the glass panels themselves. Similarly, the shedding of large marble panels in the Standard Oil (now Amoco) building in Chicago turned out to be due to the unforeseen effects of that city's climatic extremes; as the panels expanded and contracted during winter and summer, the physical bonds within the marble deteriorated. Eventually, when it was noted that many panels were cracked and that some were bowing by as much as 1″ from true, the skin was replaced. In both of these cases, unanticipated stresses within the material proved to be disastrous, and the lessons from both involve knowing how a particular cladding system or material will work in a given situation. Cladding failures from basic principles are relatively rare—we know now how to waterproof building skins, how to make them stand up, and how to have them resist wind. Where failures occur, they are often the result of failing to properly anticipate the synergetic effects of climate, movement, and loading.

Isn't aluminum a good conductor of heat and an energy-intensive material? Why would you use it in an environmental enclosure—won't it drain heat in winter and transmit it in summer?

Yes, it will do both. Aluminum is an almost unavoidable material in precision curtain walls, however, due to its ease of formation (through extrusion) and its robust structural performance (nearly that of steel). Its considerable drawbacks include its grossly inefficient production and its ability to transmit heat (note that good cookware is made of aluminum for precisely this latter property). Curtain walls almost always include a thermal break within an aluminum section to provide better insulating performance. This usually occurs between the pressure plate and the "root" of the backup section. In terms of embodied energy, it is best to keep in mind the up-front ecological cost of aluminum, and to make sure that it is being used in the most efficient ways possible. A pound of aluminum can do the work of roughly 15 pounds of wood, if used properly. Shapes that eliminate "lazy" material and that maximize performance per pound are thus crucial to the design of aluminum components.

GLOSSARY

Curtain wall: Any lightweight building enclosure that is fully supported by the building's structure.

Double skin: A catch-all term for a number of curtain wall types that rely on an intermediate airspace between inside and outside for environmental performance—in some cases just insulation, in other cases solar-powered air movement.

Gasket: A soft material, usually rubber or neoprene, that is compressed into a gap between a cladding panel and its support, providing an environmental seal and, often, a friction-based structural connection.

Mullion: A linear element that provides support and environmental closure to a curtain wall's panels. Strictly speaking, the vertical members of a curtain wall's subframe are called mullions, while horizontal members are called *transoms*.

Pressure plate: In glass curtain walls, a metal plate attached opposite the main body of the mullion that compresses a neoprene or rubber gasket against the glass panels, providing a robust connection.

Structural glazing: A cladding technique that relies on the inherent tensile strength of glass, supporting a glass "curtain" from the top with only lateral bracing below.

Subframe: A structural system designed to transfer the gravity and lateral loads experienced by the cladding system to the building's structure.

FURTHER READING

Danz, E. (1967). *Sun Protection: An International Architectural Survey*. New York: Praeger.

Harris, J. and Wiggington, M. (2002). *Intelligent Skins*. Oxford: Architectural Press.

Hunt, W. D. (1958). *The Contemporary Curtain Wall: Its Design, Fabrication, and Erection*. New York: F. W. Dodge.

Rice, P. and Dutton, H. (1995). *Structural Glass*. 2nd edition. London: Spon.

Schittich, C. ed. (2001). *In Detail: Building Skins, Concepts, Layers, Materials*. Basel: Birkhauser.

32

INTERIOR FINISH MATERIALS

Interior finish materials	Walls
	Ceilings
	Floors
	Openings
Material assemblies	Plaster
	Gypsum board
	Wood panels
	Tile
	Terrazzo
	Wood flooring
	Resilient flooring
	Carpet
	Acoustical ceilings
Decision making	Ethics
	Design
	Quality

INTRODUCTION

Architectural space is defined by the elements of enclosure and structure. Beyond the definition of the shape, size, openings, and light is the consideration of inhabitation by *people*. Decisions about the interior finishes control the perceived quality and emphasis of the space. Regardless of the shape of a space, the finishes will almost always have more impact than the form. This will be amplified by the way in which those finish materials are detailed and assembled (Figure 32.1). Design does not stop once the configuration of the building is determined—far from it, the vast majority of the decisions will be made beyond this point. We often hear that "design" is only 10 percent of the architect's job, and that's true if your perception of design is only the schematic layout. However, almost every decision you make, and every contractor/client/ building official call or meeting is part of the design process. Operating in this mode of thinking is essential for architects, and is the only way to produce truly excellent work.

32.1
British Arts Center, 1970, Yale
University, New Haven, CT, Louis
Kahn.

INTERIOR FINISH MATERIALS

While any material you place inside a building may in some way be considered a finish material, the focus of this discussion will be on the primary interior surfaces—walls, floors, and ceilings. The finishes may be thought of as the interior cladding of the building, which is fundamentally different from the exterior. While the exterior is largely driven by environmental performance balanced with cost and aesthetic concerns, the interior is driven by aesthetics mixed with a variety of durability, cost, and performance concerns.

Walls generally consist of plaster, gypsum board, wood panels, glass, tile, and various metal or plastic coatings on a substrate. Other materials, such as concrete or masonry, can be used but are typically considered as exterior materials brought inside. Glass is usually installed as an interior partition or lighting assembly as opposed to exterior-style cladding brought indoors.

Ceilings can use many of the same finishes as walls, the most common being gypsum board. Acoustical ceilings are the other frequently used finish material and offer a wide range of options.

Floors run the range of hard to soft surfaces, with gradients in-between. Tile, stone, terrazzo, wood, resilient flooring, and carpet are the most common choices. Concrete is again used, but it is still primarily an exposed structural material and not specifically an interior finish.

Doors and windows have many varieties and trim options that need to be considered in terms of their impact on the interior environment.

MATERIAL ASSEMBLIES

Plaster is a cementitious material that is spread over metal lath, gypsum board lath, or wood strips. There are two types of plaster—gypsum plaster, which is lighter weight but only suitable for interior uses, and cement plaster or stucco,

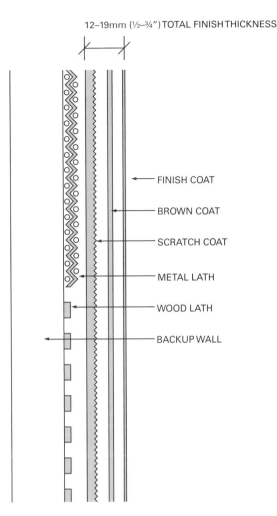

12–19mm (½–¾") TOTAL FINISH THICKNESS

32.2
Plaster assembly.

FINISH COAT

BROWN COAT

SCRATCH COAT

METAL LATH

WOOD LATH

BACKUP WALL

SECTION

which is made with Portland Cement and can be used on exterior surfaces (Figure 32.2). Plaster can be applied over wood, metal or block backup walls, but the weight of the material needs to be considered. Ceiling applications can be on direct applied furring or suspended on wires and tracks, similar to acoustic ceilings.

Plaster is applied typically in three coats—scratch coat, brown coat, and finish coat. The scratch coat is first, providing coverage and bonding to the lath. It is made rough on the surface or "scratched" to provide a bonding texture for subsequent layers. The brown coat levels the plaster out to the majority of its final thickness. Sometimes the brown coat is done before the scratch coat has set and is referred to as two-coat plaster. The finish coat is a thin surface that is troweled smooth and covers the metal trim that protects the edges. Typical thickness is between 12.5 and 19mm (½" and ¾").

The metal trim pieces protect edges and corners and provide a screed to finish the plaster to the correct thickness. Control joints also need to be installed into plaster because it acts like concrete in terms of movement and cracking. Aspect ratios closest to 1:1 are best, with longer runs possible, but the risk of cracking increases the thinner the material gets.

Gypsum board has a compressed gypsum powder core that is faced with a paper cover material that adds performance and allows for finishing. Boards come in modular sizes, typically 2.4m × 1.2m (4' × 8'), and are commonly applied over frame construction or on furring strips. Gypsum can be applied directly to block or concrete surfaces, but trapped moisture will damage the boards, it is difficult to get a perfectly level surface, and more difficult to fasten the board to concrete. Differential movement is also better accommodated with an intermediate furring piece that can allow for some flex. Ceiling applications also work on direct applied furring or suspended on wires and tracks, similar to acoustic ceilings.

Gypsum boards come in various types that can provide for additional water resistance (green board) or fire resistance (type X) if needed. Panels are typically screwed in place with tapered edges butting one another. Joint tape is applied to resist movement and cracking, and then joint compound is applied over the surface in multiple layers to provide a monolithic smooth surface (Figure 32.3). Metal trim pieces are used at the corners and edges to protect against damage and provide reveal joints where desired or needed for movement. For wet situations where tile will be installed, a cement board underlayment (such as Durock) is used that will not degrade under heavy moisture and has a rough finish to help mechanically bond with the tile mortar.

Wood panels are applied over frame construction or furring and are typically plywood or MDF (medium-density fiberboard) cores with wood veneer faces, or hardwood strips. Wood paneling is similar to gypsum board in installation, but the fasteners and joints cannot be hidden under joint compound. The edge conditions become critical with wood and the potential for differential movement needs to be carefully considered (Figure 32.4). Edges can be covered with a wood finish tape or hardwood edge banding; the thicker wood edging is preferable for both durability and aesthetics. Reveal joints or splines

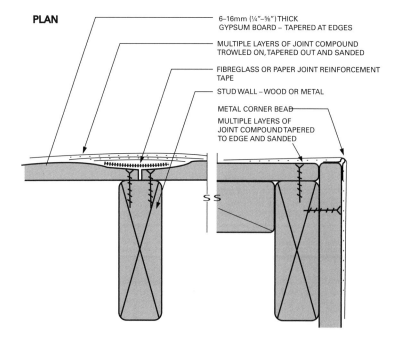

PLAN

6–16mm (¼"–⅝") THICK
GYPSUM BOARD – TAPERED AT EDGES

MULTIPLE LAYERS OF JOINT COMPOUND
TROWLED ON, TAPERED OUT AND SANDED

FIBREGLASS OR PAPER JOINT REINFORCEMENT
TAPE

STUD WALL – WOOD OR METAL

METAL CORNER BEAD
MULTIPLE LAYERS OF
JOINT COMPOUND TAPERED
TO EDGE AND SANDED

32.3
Gypsum board assembly.

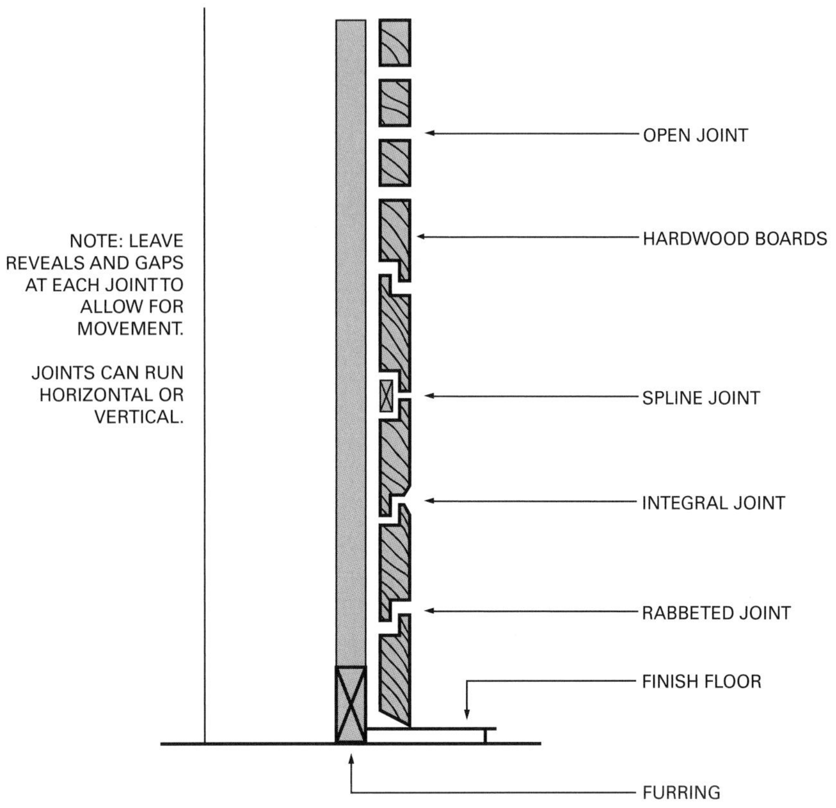

NOTE: LEAVE
REVEALS AND GAPS
AT EACH JOINT TO
ALLOW FOR
MOVEMENT.

JOINTS CAN RUN
HORIZONTAL OR
VERTICAL.

OPEN JOINT

HARDWOOD BOARDS

SPLINE JOINT

INTEGRAL JOINT

RABBETED JOINT

FINISH FLOOR

FURRING

32.4
Wood wall finish assembly.

are commonly used between panels to allow for movement and variations in grain patterns. Veneer patterns can be specified along with the desired layout. Remember that different species of wood have varying grain characteristics and the "figure" or pattern of the grain depends on the manner in which it was cut from the tree. There are also a great number of options for how veneers can be laid out that affect the look of the final product (Figure 32.5). Plastic and metal veneers on MDF can also be used and follow the same assembly logic as wood veneers.

Tile refers to small modular surfacing units typically made from fired ceramic materials or glass. They come in a wide variety of shapes and sizes, are very durable, waterproof, cleanable, and can be used on walls, floors, and ceilings (Figure 32.6). Tile comes in a few standard types based on use and look. Ceramic mosaic tiles are usually small units made from clay materials and can be glazed or unglazed. They are typically 3mm to 8mm (⅛" to ¼") thick and come in shapes from squares and rectangles to octagons and circles. Glazed wall tile is often larger in size and is normally closer to the 3mm (⅛") thickness. Glazed tiles have glossy or matte surfaces, various textures, and almost any color due to the glazes applied and bonded to the tile through firing. Unglazed tiles derive their color and finish from the base material and coloring agents mixed into the tile before firing. Tiles can also be pressed with patterns to create a textured surface. Quarry and paver tiles are unglazed, normally colored in more natural earth tones, and can be used in interior or exterior applications. Quarry and paver tiles are thicker than standard ceramic tiles, ranging from 12.5mm to 25mm (½" to 1") thick. Glass tiles have become much more popular recently, and come in various sizes and

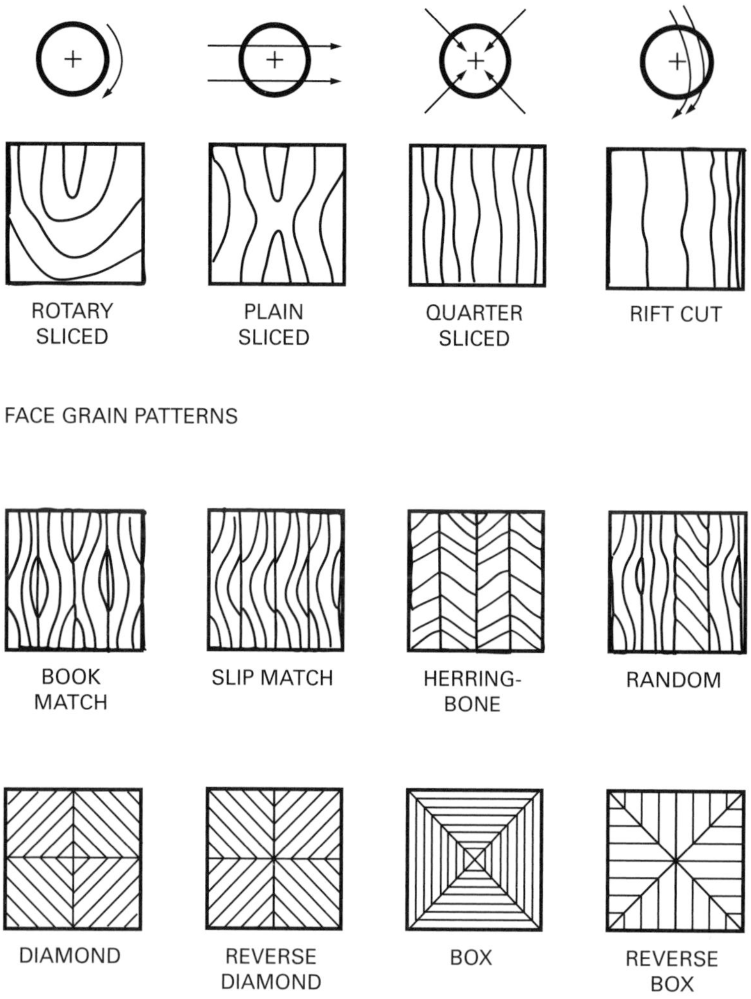

ROTARY SLICED

PLAIN SLICED

QUARTER SLICED

RIFT CUT

FACE GRAIN PATTERNS

BOOK MATCH

SLIP MATCH

HERRING- BONE

RANDOM

DIAMOND

REVERSE DIAMOND

BOX

REVERSE BOX

32.5
Wood grain and matching patterns.

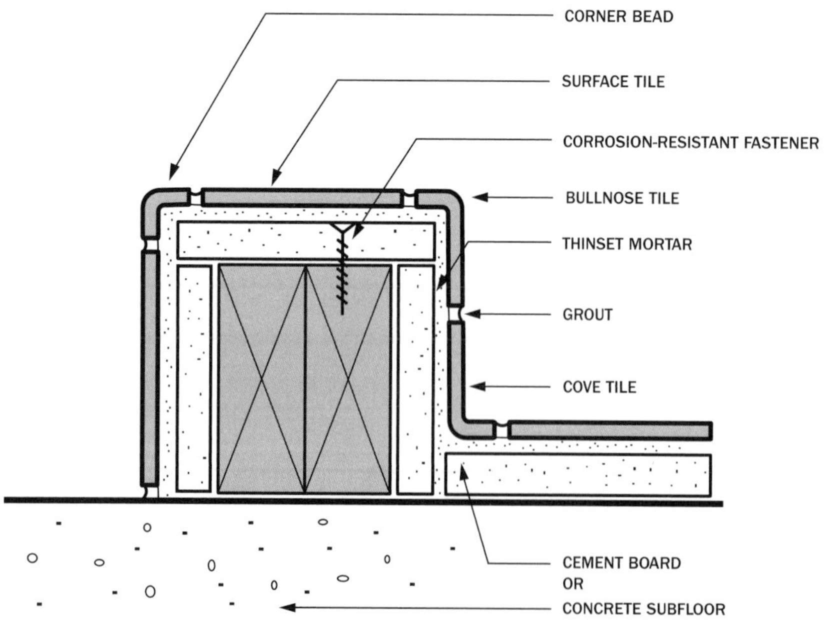

CORNER BEAD

SURFACE TILE

CORROSION-RESISTANT FASTENER

BULLNOSE TILE

THINSET MORTAR

GROUT

COVE TILE

CEMENT BOARD
OR
CONCRETE SUBFLOOR

32.6
Ceramic tile installation.

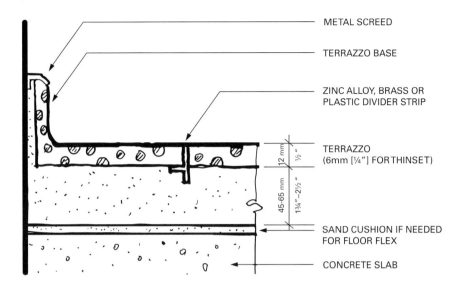

METAL SCREED

TERRAZZO BASE

ZINC ALLOY, BRASS OR PLASTIC DIVIDER STRIP

TERRAZZO (6mm [¼"] FOR THINSET)

12 mm ½"

45-65 mm 1¾"–2½"

SAND CUSHION IF NEEDED FOR FLOOR FLEX

CONCRETE SLAB

32.7
Terrazzo installation.

finishes. They are either cast in molds or cut from a cold sheet and polished. Glass tiles are very durable but can scratch over time in higher traffic areas and a sharp hit may crack a tile. Glass is non-porous, meaning moisture and mildew will not collect in the surface of tiles. They are installed in a similar fashion to ceramic tile, with particular care needed during grouting because you can often see through the edge or face of the tiles to the grout below.

Tile is applied over a waterproof base material with mortar or adhesives. Thin-set mortars, 3mm to 8mm (⅛" to ¼") thick, are most common in flat conditions, with thicker mortars used to create sloped surfaces. Once set in place, grout is troweled between the joints making the tile joints waterproof and is either smooth or with a sand finish.

Terrazzo is a hard continuous floor material made of stone chips in a cement matrix that is ground to a polished finish. The size and color of the stone chips affect the look of the floor, along with the color of the matrix—making a wide array of looks possible. The mixture is typically poured onto the sub-base of concrete then ground and polished smooth once set (Figure 32.7). Vertical surfaces can also be created, but the grinding process is more difficult. Terrazzo is extremely durable, yet has the cracking characteristics of concrete and needs to have carefully considered control joints. Joints are handled with divider strips, typically of zinc alloy, brass, or plastic. These allow for changes in color and pattern to be poured in and can have neoprene gaskets installed for movement. Older terrazzo is thick set with a 50mm (2") plus underbed of concrete material and a 12.5mm (½") topcoat of the terrazzo surface. Newer terrazzo is commonly thin-set as ¼" of finish material directly over a concrete base. Precast terrazzo shapes are available as wall bases and windowsills, along with stair treads, shower bases, and larger tiles.

Wood flooring is a strip or block flooring of durable wood species. They are manufactured carefully to avoid cracking and warping and are engineered to form a uniform surface. There are many species of wood used for flooring—the most common traditional types being oak, maple, beech, pecan, birch, southern pine and Douglas fir. Many newer floors use species such as cherry, recycled exotic woods, bamboo, and palm wood. Cork is also a wood floor

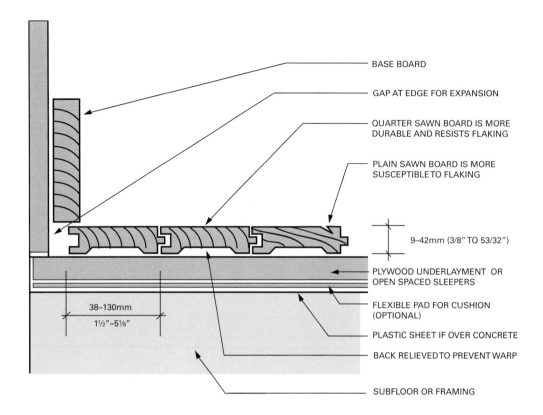

BASE BOARD

GAP AT EDGE FOR EXPANSION

QUARTER SAWN BOARD IS MORE
DURABLE AND RESISTS FLAKING

PLAIN SAWN BOARD IS MORE
SUSCEPTIBLE TO FLAKING

9–42mm (3/8" TO 53/32")

PLYWOOD UNDERLAYMENT OR
OPEN SPACED SLEEPERS

FLEXIBLE PAD FOR CUSHION
(OPTIONAL)

PLASTIC SHEET IF OVER CONCRETE

BACK RELIEVED TO PREVENT WARP

SUBFLOOR OR FRAMING

38–130mm

1½"–5⅛"

32.8
Wood tongue and groove flooring.

finish, but comes in fairly thin tiles that are considered resilient flooring, or in a composite panel bonded to a rigid substrate.

Strip or plank is the most common type of wood flooring in a tongue and groove configuration (Figure 32.8). The tongue and groove arrangement allows for the floor to fit tighter together and to be nailed down in a concealed manner with fasteners hidden by the groove of each adjacent board. Thicknesses range from 8mm up to 43.5mm ($^5/_{16}$" up to $^{53}/_{32}$"). The thicker the floor the more durable it is, which seems obvious, but this also has to do with how many times the floor can be refinished. The critical dimension in refinishing is the thickness from the top to the tongue; once this is too thin the floorboard will crack to the tongue and groove point and be ruined. Thin floors can be refinished once, where thicker floors have many more opportunities to be revived. Wood floors need to have room to expand at the edges, so the floors stop short of the wall and have base trim cover the gap. This can be a problem in situations where you want to change the base condition in an existing installation because often when you pull the old base a large gap is exposed. Finishes are done with a polyurethane sealer in a matte or glossy appearance and can be pre-finished or done on-site. Environmentally friendly finish choices, such as vegetable oils and waxes, are also available, but these require more frequent re-application.

Installation can take place directly over a concrete slab on plywood underlayment or on sleepers to provide some moisture ventilation. The underlayment must be firm when on open joists to prevent shifting and creaking. Sleepers can be cushioned with neoprene pads for comfort, but the sleepers should be rigid enough to not flex in small areas, again causing creaking problems.

Resilient flooring is a thin material that comes in tiles or sheets applied directly to slabs or an underlayment board. Thicknesses are typically about 3mm (⅛"). The resilience allows the material to not permanently dent and provides some comfort and warmth. It is often an inexpensive solution to utility areas, high traffic corridors, and classrooms, but there are higher- and lower-quality resilient floors depending on the application. The most common types are vinyl sheets, vinyl tiles, cork tiles, rubber tiles, and linoleum sheets and tiles. They are normally glued down and can be easily cut to fit. Other types of modular vinyl tiles can be mixed with harder materials, such as quartz, to produce durable flooring that is not as flexible, but can be easily cut and adhered to the subfloor.

Carpet can be made from a wide variety of fibers bonded or woven to continuous backings (Figure 32.9). Wool, acrylic, nylon, polyester, olefin, and cotton are used to achieve certain effects—aesthetic, performance, and cost. Carpet is generally divided into two categories, residential and commercial, with commercial typically being more dense and durable. Carpet comes in rolls and tiles, and can have a variety of backing pads for comfort. Beyond the fiber material, carpet is judged by the face finish and weight. Weight is simply the thickness and density; the higher the weight the better the quality and durability. Face finish is the loop or cut of the yarn. Loop carpets keep a continuous strand of yarn running through the weave and are very durable; cut carpet exposes the edge of the yarn and tends to be softer and a bit less durable. Berber is

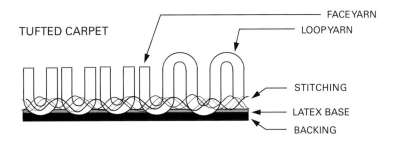

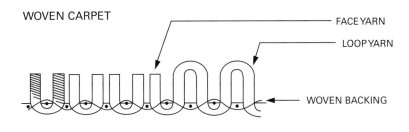

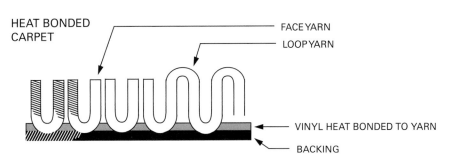

32.9
Carpet fabrication.

a commonly used term to describe loop pile carpet that is highly durable and inexpensive. Commercial manufacturers have become increasingly sophisticated and now produce multi-leveled loop and cut patterns with "tip sheared" finishes (cutting just a portion of the loop) as well. Carpet is colored and patterned in two primary ways—solution dyed or piece dyed, with combinations of the two happening on some patterned carpets. Solution dyed means the fibers are colored before the yarn is extruded; piece dyed is where the fibers are dyed after the final carpet is woven. Solution dye is far more durable, colorfast, and resistant to fading. Piece dyeing is currently the most popular method, with carpet sent through the dyeing process before the final backing is applied. Piece dying is sometimes done over a solution-dyed carpet to achieve an over-pattern rather than weaving it in. Carpet is unavoidable due to its inexpensive overall cost, comfort, and acoustical value. Flooring is a decision that affects approximately one-third of the entire interior surface area of your projects; use carpet and other flooring materials as an integral part of the design project, not as an afterthought or something to be handed off as unimportant.

Acoustical ceilings consist of fibrous material molded into modular tiles that are suspended in a metal grid (Figure 32.10). These systems are commonly used to provide acoustical control, flexibility, and access to mechanical systems and lighting. The ceiling plane can be easily suspended after installation of ducts, plumbing, electrical, communications, fire suppression, etc.—providing ample space to hide it all without the contractors needing to keep it clean and organized. Remember this when you decide to save money on a project by eliminating the acoustical ceiling and just trying to keep the "stuff" up there organized—by the time you're done it usually costs more. Tiles are typically 600mm×600mm or 600mm×1200mm (2'×2' or 2'×4') and the grids can be fully exposed, partly recessed (known as tegular edge tiles), or concealed (spline systems). The grids can also be regular or narrow profile. These are progressively more expensive. Tiles also differ in quality and finish, and have varying qualities of sound absorption and fire resistance. Keep in mind that if

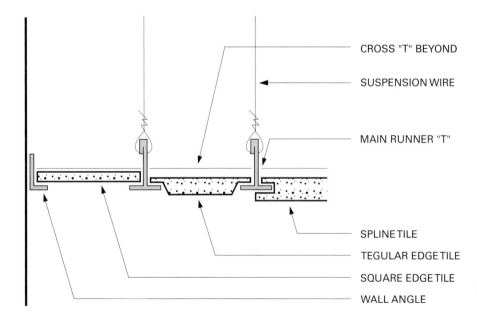

CROSS "T" BEYOND

SUSPENSION WIRE

MAIN RUNNER "T"

SPLINE TILE

TEGULAR EDGE TILE

SQUARE EDGE TILE

WALL ANGLE

32.10
Suspended acoustical ceiling types.

you paint a ceiling tile, the porous surface becomes sealed, reducing the acoustical performance and potentially voiding the warranty (something most clients will not support). The grid is hung from the ceiling deck or structural members above with thin metals wires that are twisted around the support channels and runners. Ceilings are leveled with a rotating laser that inscribes a path of light at the edges of a space. Other ceiling materials may be hung using the grid system, such as metal, wood, or gypsum board assemblies.

CONCLUSION

Every designer must be able to make decisions from an endless variety of choices of finish materials. How would one go about making these decisions when it is impossible to know all of the choices? The answer has to do with limiting the set of options and continually searching for better ways to achieve your goals. Limiting options means you will have preferences that you go to first because you have tested the results in projects. You will also learn these from the first offices you work in—a critical point. While you will continually broaden your lexicon of materials, it takes a vast amount of time learning how to specify, detail, and assemble. Determining what is good in a set of material choices is built on an ethic of sorts—designers must have opinions about what is better and worse in a subjective arena. Clients will constantly ask your opinion about aesthetic decisions and you must be able to deliver a confident assessment of your choices. You will also need to build up your knowledge base about what choices are both available and acceptable. The kinds of things you look at when visiting buildings will change over time to include specific materials and details. It's a process that never ends—you will pick apart your own and other's projects to constantly improve what you're doing. This is normal and is part of being a designer—be discreet while evaluating the work of others and be relentless in improving your own.

FREQUENTLY ASKED QUESTIONS

Why do so many buildings use bland patterned carpet as the floor finish?
There are a number of reasons why carpet is so popular, the primary one being cost. Carpet is one of the cheapest floor finishes available. It also assists in acoustical damping and is more effective than most ceiling options at absorbing sound. Carpet is comfortable to walk on because of its resilient quality and tends to show dirt less than many hard finish floors. Maintenance is relatively easy, with vacuuming being easier and less slippery than mopping, and if carpet tile is used a small area can be replaced easily if stained or damaged. The bland quality often comes from the desire to hide stains. It would obviously be a bad idea to use white or black carpet due to staining, so the medium tone colors and patterns extend this logic to mask the color and pattern of likely staining. If you install an essentially pre-stained floor finish it may look less dramatic on day one, but it will look about the same on day 500.

How do you decide when to use a suspended acoustical ceiling?
This is a common problem, because designers frequently want to leave every-thing exposed and have hard surface floors, ceilings, and walls. While this may meet aesthetic goals, it rarely meets acoustical or budgetary concerns. Often there is a question of choices; will the floor be absorptive (carpet) or the ceiling (acoustic tile), because something needs to absorb the sound and no one likes carpet on the walls anymore. This choice is sometimes solved by the need to conceal building systems, such as lights, ducts, conduit, etc. above a suspended ceiling. Hard surface ceilings like gypsum board look good until you install hinged access panels everywhere to get at mechanical systems. Acoustical ceilings allow for free access anywhere service is needed and solve the acoustical problem. Remember that ceiling grids typically come in modules of 600mm×600mm or 600mm×1200mm (2′×2′ or 2′×4′), and that these grids benefit from lining up with other parts of the space design rather than randomly blanketing a ceiling.

GLOSSARY

Acoustical ceilings: Consist of fibrous material molded into modular tiles that are suspended in a metal grid.

Carpet: Absorptive flooring material that can be made from a wide variety of fibers bonded or woven to continuous backings.

Gypsum board: Construction finish board that has a compressed gypsum powder core faced with a paper cover material that adds performance and allows for finishing.

Plaster: A cementitious material that is spread over metal lath, gypsum board lath, or wood lath strips.

Resilient flooring: A thin floor finish material that comes in tiles or sheets applied directly to slabs or an underlayment board.

Terrazzo: A hard cementitious floor material made of stone chips in a cement matrix that is ground to a polished finish.

Tile: Refers to small modular surfacing units typically made from fired ceramic materials or glass, although resilient flooring materials, carpet, and acoustical ceiling panels are also made in tile configurations.

Wood flooring: A strip or block finish flooring of durable wood species.

Wood panels: Wall or ceiling panels that are applied over frame construction or furring and are typically plywood or MDF cores with wood veneer faces.

FURTHER READING

Ching, F. D. K. (2008). *Building Construction Illustrated*. New York: Van Nostrand Reinhold; Chapter 10, Finishes.

Ramsey, C. G. and Sleeper, H. R. (2000). *Architectural Graphic Standards*, 10th edition. New York: John Wiley & Sons; Chapter 9, Finishes.

33

SITE DESIGN AND CONSTRUCTION

Heidi Hohmann

Associate Professor, Iowa State University Department of Landscape Architecture

Introduction	Site design
Exterior surfaces	"Hard" versus "soft" surfaces Slopes Types of hard surfaces
Plants and planting	Lawns and lawn alternatives Space-defining planting
Decision making	

INTRODUCTION

If site analysis is part of the design process, then site design should obviously be part of the design product. At the very least, a building's siting directs pedestrian access, controls storm water, and conveys a visitor's first impression of the building and interior spaces to come. On the other end of the spectrum, a landscape around a building can be designed as part of a holistic spatial experience. In other words, spatial design does not necessarily end at a building wall, but rather extends into the landscape around it, integrating interior and exterior design.

Exterior landscape design can be as simple as a sidewalk and a few street trees and as complex as a storm water catchment system that diverts water from building rooftops and parking lots into a constructed wetland designed for aquifer recharge and as wildlife habitat. Like building design, landscape design has its own set of opportunities and constraints, which primarily differ from architectural concerns in that they address issues of living species and ecological systems. As a result, in its most expanded sense, landscape design becomes an activity in its own right, performed by the allied profession of landscape architecture, and supported by specialists in other fields, such as horticulture, soil science, and conservation ecology. In general, however, landscape architecture includes the design of exterior space, such as plazas, terraces, sitting areas, parking lots, lawns, and parks surrounding buildings, as well as more extensive and programmed landscapes such as playing fields, gardens, forests, wetlands, and storm drainage systems.

This section provides some very basic guidelines and information about exterior landscape treatments, both "hardscape" and "plantscape," for the most common architectural applications. For larger, more complex issues of site design and management, especially those that address the requirements of plants and ecosystems, it may be necessary to consult other resources or other professionals. Though consultation with a landscape architect may seem like an "extra" expense, remember that a beautiful and ecologically sound landscape design can be a way to provide your client with value-added design.

EXTERIOR PLANTING AND PAVING MATERIALS

Landscape materials for building surrounds can be divided into two major types. "Hard" surfacing and paving is most often used for pedestrian and vehicular access and where durability for traffic is required, such as roads, sidewalks, paths, patios, and terraces. "Soft" surfacing, such as lawn and beds planted with groundcover or shrubs, are most often used in larger areas where pedestrian traffic is dispersed or recreational. In general, planted areas are also more pervious than most pavements, allowing water to better permeate their surfaces and percolate into the soil and groundwater below.

For both pavement and planted areas, the slope or gradient of surfaces is very important for access and drainage. In general, exterior grades generally range from 1 percent to 20 percent. Surfaces with a gradient of less than 1 percent are difficult to construct to drain properly and surfaces of more than 25 percent are difficult for pedestrians and vehicles to navigate and for lawn mowers to maintain. To provide ADA accessibility, paved surfaces should generally be 5 percent or less, though grades of 8.33 percent are permitted with appropriate handrails and landings (See Chapter 10, Accessibility). Table 33.1 shows recommended slopes and cross slopes for typical surface applications.

Table 33.1 Recommended slopes and cross slopes for typical surface applications.

	Recommended slope %	Maximum slope %	Minimum Slope %
Paved areas			
Sidewalk, longitudinal slope	1–5	10	0.5
Sidewalk, cross slope	2	4	1
Terraces, patios, etc.	1	2	0.5
Driveway, longitudinal slope	1–10	0.5	10
Parking lot, longitudinal slope	2–3	5	0.5
Parking lot, cross slope	2–3	10	0.5
Road, longitudinal slope	2–10	20	1
Road crown	2	3	1
Lawn/unpaved areas			
Lawns	5–10	30 (approx. 3:1)	1
Mowed slopes	20	30 (approx. 3:1)	—
Planted beds	3–5	10	1
Athletic fields, generally	1	2	0.5

HARDSCAPE AND PAVEMENT

In general, all pavements are layered constructions, consisting of a prepared subgrade, an aggregate base, and a wear or surface layer. *Subgrade* is the soil beneath the pavement, usually prepared through cutting, compaction or leveling to meet the designed slopes and elevations for proper surface drainage. *Aggregate base* is placed on the subgrade to transfer the pavement load to the subgrade, provide a level setting surface, and to create a well-drained base that reduces the heaving effects of the freeze-thaw cycles. Depth of aggregate therefore depends on frost depth and load requirements. In colder climates aggregate base depth may be 6″ to 8″ (15–20cm), with an extra layer of coarser sub-base gravel below it if heavy loads are anticipated. In warm climates, a light-duty pedestrian pavement might simply consist of a *wear layer* of flagstone pavers set in a few inches of sand that serves as both structural support and as setting bed. Pavements are further classified as rigid or flexible and may be either considered to be of monolithic construction (composed of a single, seamless construction) or unit construction (made of individual paving units).

Flexible pavements are so-called because they are able to move, expand, and contract in response to freeze-thaw cycles. They generally consist of thinner monolithic or unit surfaces applied over thicker aggregate bases. *Monolithic flexible pavements* (Figure 33.1) include bound aggregate and polymer pavements such as asphalt or rubberized athletic surfaces which are applied in smooth, extruded sheets 1½″ to 4″ (4–10cm) thick over a prepared base. Depth of surface pavement depends on load. Asphalt pavement for roads, for example, is thicker, often applied in two layers, a tack coat and a wear layer, over the aggregate base.

Flexible unit pavements include brick, concrete and stone pavers of various thicknesses (1½″ to 4″ (4–10cm), depending on the material structure of the paver itself) butt-jointed and set in a sand setting bed atop a prepared aggregate base (Figure 33.2). The wide variety of colors, sizes, textures, and patterns in which unit pavers can be placed make unit paving a popular way to show a designer's creativity, provided one guards against excess. Heavier loads require

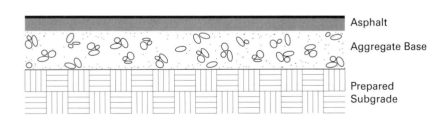

Asphalt

Aggregate Base

Prepared Subgrade

33.1
Flexible monolithic paving.

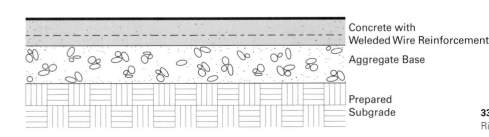

Concrete with Weleded Wire Reinforcement

Aggregate Base

Prepared Subgrade

33.2
Rigid monolithic paving.

thicker unit pavers, so that road applications utilizing brick, concrete, or granite pavers might use units anywhere from 3″ to 8″ (8–20cm) thick.

The butt joint construction and sand-swept joints of flexible unit pavement makes flexible unit pavements pervious to water. *Porous paving* is an increasingly important subclass of flexible paving designed to be even more permeable to storm water, and includes simple aggregate pavement such as stone dust or graded aggregate/fine mixtures that can be compacted into firm surfaces. Plant and polymer binders are now being added to these mixtures to make them more durable in public spaces. Other porous pavings include extremely coarse aggregate asphalt surfaces and specially shaped, gridded pavers, designed to be interspersed with gravel or turf. However, the efficacy of these different pavers varies widely based on different climatic zones, so it's wise to find and follow local methods in constructing porous pavings.

Rigid monolithic pavement usually means reinforced concrete pavement, cast in place on top of an aggregate base (Figure 33.3). Rigid concrete pavements, in contrast to flexible pavements, generally require a somewhat thinner aggregate base layer, at least in warmer climates, because it distributes loads more evenly; aggregate base here serves to provide a uniform and level subgrade. To allow its rigid nature to accommodate freeze-thaw cycle movement, concrete pavement is constructed with expansion joints (polymer-sealed and felt or Styrofoam-filled gaps between pours) approximately every 25 feet (8m). Control joints (scored cuts in the pavement surface) are also used every 5 to 10 feet (1.5–3m), depending on aesthetics and local construction practices, to prevent random cracking of the concrete pavement surfaces. *Rigid unit pavement* is simply individual stone, brick, or cast concrete paving units glued or mortared to a reinforced concrete base (Figure 33.4). Rigid unit pavement sometimes provides a more manicured or "finished" appearance than dry-laid flexible unit paving, and allows the use of larger, and thinner, almost veneer-like paving units, and is often used in urban plaza settings.

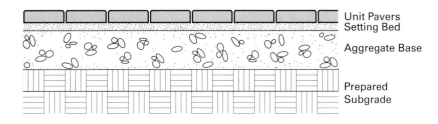

Unit Pavers
Setting Bed

Aggregate Base

Prepared
Subgrade

33.3
Flexible unit paving.

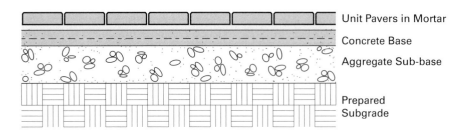

Unit Pavers in Mortar

Concrete Base

Aggregate Sub-base

Prepared
Subgrade

33.4
Rigid unit paving.

LANDSCAPE, PLANTS AND PLANTING

In contrast to pavement, planted surfaces or "natural" landscape can provide major benefits in exterior spaces, including, but not limited to, seasonal changes of color, form, and texture; microclimate modification; and, as noted earlier, an increased ability to manage storm water runoff on-site. Planting strategies range from simple plantings of turf or groundcover to more extensive designs such as groves, perennial borders, or rain gardens. Unlike paving, plants are living things, and as such have key requirements for their survival. These include an adequate healthy soil (non-compacted, pH-neutral, and rich in organic material); sun (a *minimum* of 4 hours per day for shade-tolerant species) and adequate water. In other words, plants cannot be planted right next to buildings, under building overhangs, in narrow courtyards that only receive light at high noon, or other inhospitable places.

In addition, it is important to choose plants that are suited for your site's climate, usually described as the site's USDA Plant Hardiness Zone (Figure 33.5). Using plants that are native to your site is also often a good idea, because these plants are adapted to local seasonal extremes and soil types, support local wildlife, and express the regional character of the building site. Native plants are best obtained from local nurseries and seed suppliers, to ensure the plants are truly indigenous to the area. Invasive, non-native species should be avoided at all costs.

33.5
Plant hardiness zones in North America.

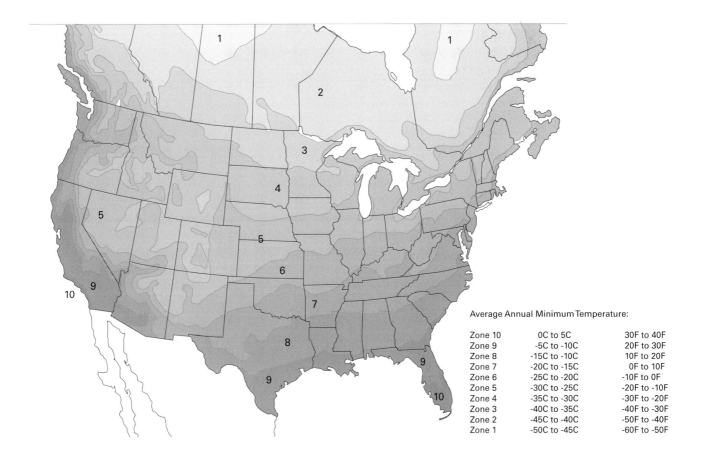

Average Annual Minimum Temperature:

Zone 10	0C to 5C	30F to 40F
Zone 9	-5C to -10C	20F to 30F
Zone 8	-15C to -10C	10F to 20F
Zone 7	-20C to -15C	0F to 10F
Zone 6	-25C to -20C	-10F to 0F
Zone 5	-30C to -25C	-20F to -10F
Zone 4	-35C to -30C	-30F to -20F
Zone 3	-40C to -35C	-40F to -30F
Zone 2	-45C to -40C	-50F to -40F
Zone 1	-50C to -45C	-60F to -50F

Since Le Corbusier, expanses of green turf have often been used as a foil for hard-edged contemporary building styles, or as a stand-in for "nature" in urban settings. As a result, today *lawn* is often a "default" landscape condition. Lawns are most commonly created by sodding or, more economically and conveniently in larger areas or on steep slopes, by seeding. Lawn is a poor choice, however, for high traffic areas; this is also the case in low maintenance situations, since it requires high inputs of mowing, irrigation, and herbicide and fertilizer to maintain a sufficiently lush appearance.

However, lawn alternatives do exist, especially for no traffic areas or for foundation plantings. The most common alternatives are a variety of *groundcovers*, which include low-growing plants and vines, such as English ivy (*Hedera helix*), periwinkle (*Vinca minor*); native prairie grasses; and prostrate shrubs such as juniper (*Juniperus* spp.) or fragrant sumac (*Rhus aromatica*). Groundcovers can be good choices on steeper slopes or where less maintenance over time is required or desired. The spacing of groundcover plants must be carefully worked out to both minimize the time to full area coverage and to avoid bare spots, and a mulch of shredded bark, wood chips, or compost over a weed barrier should be installed under plants to prevent weed growth until plants are well established and reach mature, ground-covering size. Mulch also provides other benefits for plants such as conserving soil moisture and moderating temperature.

Plants needn't just serve as surface treatments; *trees* and *shrubs* can be used architecturally to create spatial enclosure or separation, to provide shade for building facades or exterior spaces, to control circulation, and to provide visual screening. In other words, plants can be used spatially just as architectural materials can be—and often their purchase and installation costs are less than that for other built materials. Trees and shrubs are available from nurseries as dormant bareroot stock; in containers as young, growing plants; and when more mature and larger, as balled and burlapped plants. These three conditions require slightly different planting techniques as seen in Figures 33.6 and 33.7. Proper installation is important to plant survival and thriftiness. Key factors to consider are plant spacing to allow for full growth, especially for specimen trees, and digging adequately sized holes or trenches in appropriate, amended soils.

DECISION-MAKING

The designer's choice of exterior landscape materials is far more varied than the ubiquity of concrete, asphalt, and lawn would imply. While these three exterior materials are easily installed and relatively inexpensive, other materials—especially local stone and native plants—may, in fact, be less expensive and more visually interesting. And, of course, when dealing with plants, but also when dealing with pavement materials, climatic regions also influence a material's advantages and disadvantages. Some of these are summarized in Tables 33.2 and 33.3.

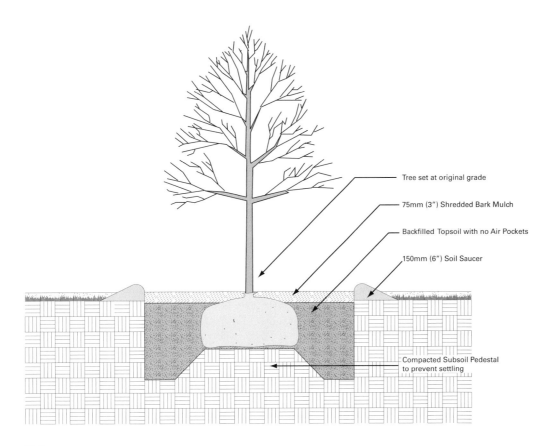

Tree set at original grade

75mm (3") Shredded Bark Mulch

Backfilled Topsoil with no Air Pockets

150mm (6") Soil Saucer

Compacted Subsoil Pedestal
to prevent settling

33.6
Typical "balled and burlap" tree planting.

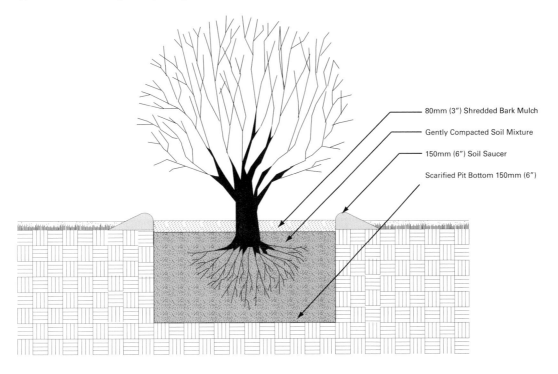

80mm (3") Shredded Bark Mulch

Gently Compacted Soil Mixture

150mm (6") Soil Saucer

Scarified Pit Bottom 150mm (6")

33.7
Typical bare root shrub planting.

Table 33.2 Typical landscape materials.

Landscape surface	Advantages	Disadvantages
Concrete	Easily installed, common material relatively inexpensive Multiple finishes, textures, colors Long lasting Hard, non-resilient surface Adaptable to curvilinear forms	Requires joints Can be ugly Difficult to color consistently Cracks easily
Asphalt	Easily installed, common material Relatively inexpensive Durable, low maintenance Adaptable to curvilinear forms Can be made porous Good for bike/walking paths	Edges will disintegrate if unsupported Can be ugly Can soften in warm weather Soluble by petroleum-based liquids
Brick pavers	Non-glare, non-skid surface Wide color range Good scale Easily repaired if dry-laid	Higher installation cost Susceptible to settlement if dry-laid Susceptible to spalling
Concrete pavers	Multiple types, sizes, forms available Wide color range Easily repaired if dry-laid	Higher installation cost Susceptible to settlement if dry-laid
Granite pavers	Hard and dense Very durable and permanent, supports heavy traffic Variety of color and finishes available	Hardness makes it difficult to work with Relatively expensive
Compacted aggregate	Relatively inexpensive/economical Local sources of aggregate help circulation routes blend into larger environment	Requires replenishment every few years Requires edging to hold material
Turfgrass/lawn	Easily installed, common material Relatively inexpensive, especially if seeded Well drained, pervious	Does not hold up under high traffic not drought or heat tolerant Expensive to maintain and irrigate
Organic mulch	Relatively inexpensive Quiet, cushioned walking or playing surface Compatible with natural surroundings	Does not hold up under high traffic Not permanent; degrades, requiring annual or bi-annual replenishment
Turf blocks/Gridded pavers	Similar to turf, but can withstand light vehicular traffic	Requires higher maintenance Less viable in northern climates

Table 33.3 Typical landscape plant materials.

Landscape surface	Advantages	Disadvantages
Container trees	Establish quickly Healthier over time	Take years to mature Roots can "circle" if contained too long
Balled and burlapped trees	Roots won't "circle" Hardier	Roots may be damaged by digging out Can be slow to recover from transplanting
Bare-root shrubs	Less expensive Establish faster than container plants Better long-term health	Sensitive to seasonal planting Flowers and leafs not apparent at planting
Container shrubs	Verifiable leaf and plant color Wider variety available Can be planted year-round	May be root-bound More expensive
Contained groundcover	Good for large areas Sturdier at planting	Bare patches must be avoided by careful design Slow to fill in
Flats	Economical, quick to plant	Small root balls may dry quickly

Table 33.3 (continued)

Landscape surface	Advantages	Disadvantages
Seeds	Cheapest Can be grown locally, thus adapted to local conditions Random patterns easily achievable	Pattern can be hard to control Long growing period
Hydroseeding	Large areas easy to plant Can be used on difficult slopes	Choice of seed may be limited Unattractive initially
Sod	Instant groundcover Even coverage	Must be installed quickly after delivery Can't be used on steep slopes or large areas

GLOSSARY

Aggregate base: Gravel or coarse rock placed between subgrade and pavement.

Flexible pavements: Pavements that can move, expand, and contract without damage or cracking.

Flexible unit pavements: Bricks, stones, or concrete units set on top of a sand setting bed and aggregate base.

Groundcovers: Lawn alternatives that offer leafy or flowering plants covering a broad area.

Lawn: Grass surface created by sodding or seeding.

Monolithic flexible pavements: Extruded pavement designed to accept minor movements.

Porous paving: Paving that allows water (storm water in particular) to percolate through to the soil below.

Rigid monolithic pavement: Solid hard surface, usually reinforced concrete, on top of an aggregate base.

Rigid unit pavement: Individual bricks, stones, or concrete units glued or mortared to a reinforced concrete base.

Subgrade: Soil beneath pavement.

Wear layer: A light duty pavement of pavers simply set in sand.

FURTHER READING

Harris, C. W. and Dines, N. T. eds. (1988). *Time-Saver Standards for Landscape Architecture: Design and Construction Data*. New York: McGraw-Hill.

Simonds, J. O. (1983). *Landscape Architecture: A Manual of Site Planning and Design*. New York: McGraw-Hill.

Walker, T. D. (1992). *Site Design and Construction Detailing*. New York: Van Nostrand Reinhold.

34

DETAILING

Six principles	Fit
	Organization
	Consistency
	Robustness
	Durability
	Finish
Balancing	Economics and quality

INTRODUCTION

Architects are faced with a vast myriad of component choices. While most of the buildings architects deal with are customized, they are largely assembled of mass-produced, pre-manufactured pieces. This is necessary in order to maintain both a consistency of performance and to keep costs under control; however, it can lead to a frustrating lack of choices when alternatives to the standard are desired. Further, it can create a bland similarity between buildings that use the same kit of parts for every situation. One of the first tasks for any designer is to learn the wide range of standards that are offered for building assembly; this takes years to begin and really never ends as new products are constantly introduced. Once the range of commercially produced options is known then it can be determined when something custom-made is desired. The process of custom design requires an understanding of the means of production and the materials available. This is time-consuming, but is the only way to produce results that extend beyond the range of mass-produced choices for building materials.

To some extent, nearly every architect-led design ends up being customized to some degree, and it is in this realm—in how we *render our designs in real materials*—that really good architects separate themselves from the pack. The jobsite and the world of users are our buildings' toughest hurdles. As designers, the more we understand how buildings are manufactured, put together, and then used and perceived, the more convincing our designs will often be. Most architects have the experience of traveling to see a recent building that's been in the magazines only to be sorely disappointed. Good photography can hide a multitude of sins, but buildings that stand up to experience are the real test. Our attention to how things are fabricated, put together, and perceived really comes home in two areas—*detailing*, or the art of figuring out how best to assemble building components for a visual and serviceable result, and *custom fabrication*, or knowing what tools and materials we have to hand to solve spatial, visual, and functional issues that aren't covered by typically available building components. We'll cover fabrication in the next chapter, but *detailing* itself is one of the great traditions and crafts of the profession and deserves its own discussion first.

DETAILING

Perhaps no one is more famous for their building details than Mies van der Rohe. But it's instructive to note that his famous quote—"God is in the details"—was actually borrowed from an old American Puritan saying—"The Devil is in the details". Both of these views are, in our view, absolutely true, in that the best and worst architectural experiences often occur at the level of tactility, where we recognize how parts come together, how they're finished, how our hands, feet, or eyes are invited to rest on them. If the architect has gotten it right, if he or she has understood fully the peculiarities of the material, how it will be put in place on the jobsite, how it will weather, settle, move, shrink, expand, etc. over time, the detail stands a chance of being a rich, expressive experience. If, however, the detail is less than well thought through, a misalignment or imperfect placement during construction—or an unanticipated movement or deterioration over time—may stick out and inflect people's perception of the building's durability. Humans are instinctively judgmental about structures and shelter, and the less we satisfy this sensibility the less appealing our buildings will be.

PRINCIPLES

When we sit down with a blank sheet of trace and begin thinking about how components of a building will come together, there are six basic considerations we should have to ensure that the detail will perform well, be reasonably efficient to construct, and maintain its appearance. In no particular order, these include *fit*, *organization*, *consistency*, *robustness*, *durability*, and *finish*.

To begin with, it is important to recognize the role of tolerance and *fit* on the job site (Figure 34.1). Precision is easy to achieve in an office, less so in the controlled chaos of construction. The straight lines we draw have to be put in place by machinery and human hands, often under intense schedule pressure and in hazardous conditions. Some of the materials we work with—concrete in particular—are sloppy and even crude, while others—aluminum or glass—come from fabrication shops or factories with much more control. Any material will have generally recognized *tolerances* that tell us how accurate we can expect it to be placed on the jobsite. These tolerances come in two forms—locational and dimensional. Location tolerances are based on the type of structure or subframe being used, and recognize that some degree of inaccuracy in

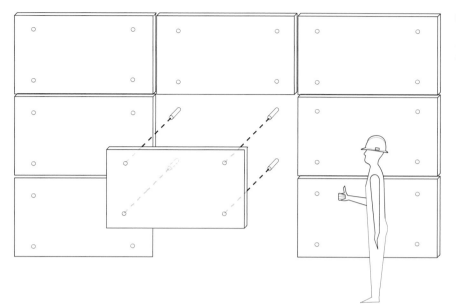

34.1
Fit in detailing relies on knowing
something about how elements
are assembled on-site.

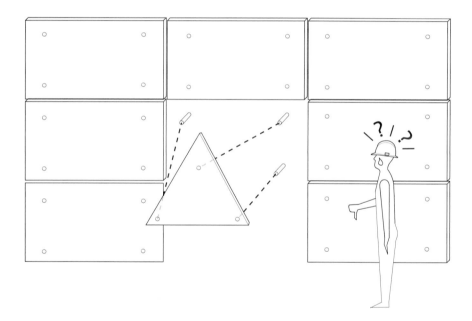

construction is inevitable. Dimensional tolerances tell us how accurately made
we can expect a material to be—how close a component will come to the drawings, essentially. Materials may sag, for example, while in transit, or may shrink
while curing. The more we're aware of these, the more we can design around
them. Concrete has notoriously low tolerances due to its liquid nature and the
difficulty of placing heavy formwork accurately. Trying to rely on a precise location or surface in a concrete element, therefore, isn't wise. Instead, we design
connections to concrete with plenty of adjustability, so that even if the concrete
isn't quite where we expect it, there will be ways for contractors to correct the
error later on, by *shimming* elements to their proper elevation or by adjusting

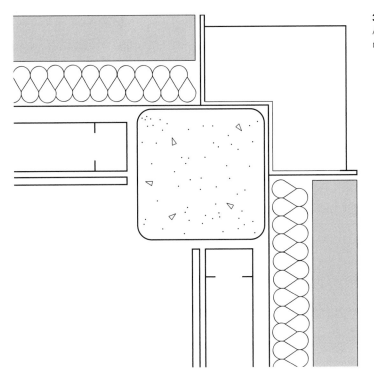

bolts in slotted connections. In aluminum, or steel, however, we can design to a fairly tight tolerance and expect the final product to be much closer in location and dimension to what we've assumed. If we're after a precise aesthetic in a concrete building, we may not express the concrete itself. It will be easier to attach steel or aluminum edges at any exposed slab edge to give the floor a reliably true "line" in the elevation. At the same time, there is inherent drama in the play of a slightly funky concrete structure against the precision of metal, and we may want to expose the imperfect concrete and set it against the more accurate systems. In this case, we want to make sure that we leave enough space between the two materials to prevent inaccuracy in the concrete from affecting the trueness of the metal.

This brings up the second key consideration: any exercise in detailing is essentially about *organization* (Figure 34.2). Tolerance and fit are important elements in this, but overall every detail we do is the result of absorbing and organizing information about finishes, supports, fixings, and assembly processes. A logical detail will almost always be a visually appealing one, since it will give the impression that the building has been carefully put together. This can also be thought of as bolstering the craft of the construction site with the craft of the drafting table. How can we think through the assembly process to give everything enough room, not only in the finished detail, but also as it is being put together? One way to do this is to think through each component, often working from the building structure out, considering each element and understanding how much space it will need to be cleanly placed and attached. We run into trouble when we try to do too much in too small a space—when we forget about the width of door frames, for example, or about the extension of a stair's handrail, or the clearance needed for a worker's wrench to tighten a bolt. When we have multiple materials, or multiple systems, a classic drafting aphorism is

34.3
Consistency is an important
aspect of materials selection and
placement.

to give each piece its own space, to separate pieces that do different things, and to remember that what we're drawing has to get built by machines or human hands. Drawing is actually a good tool for thinking this way—if we find it difficult to clearly draw through a detail it's probably complex enough to be trouble in the field. Accept that good details take a bit of space, figure out where that space can be had, and let the detail be what it needs to be. Think logically, get all the information on each piece, and draw through them sequentially, considering what the actual processes for fixing each component will be.

Consistency is something often taken for granted—when we draw a curtain wall, for instance, we often just assume that each panel will have the same color, or the same finish. Many building products, however, will vary in ways that can be visually jarring (Figure 34.3). Sometimes this is obvious; wood or marble, for example, have natural grains in them that are both unpredictable and part of the material's aesthetic appeal. Other materials have consistency issues that we might easily forget. Concrete is notoriously fickle, as its color and texture can change dramatically with small variations in temperature and humidity. Over a 21-day curing period, we can't absolutely know how a rainy day, a cold night, or a dry spell will affect the color of the pour. Even material that we use *because* of its consistency can be problematic—anodized aluminum can vary in color enough from the start of one dip to the end to be noticeable. There are two approaches to dealing with this. One is to fight the

34.4
Structural design on a small scale
is necessary to ensure that details
stand up to wear and tear.

nature of all materials to have some variation in their appearance or color, and to write tight specifications—often at a fiscal and environmental cost of rejecting material solely on a visual basis. A more productive method is to recognize that, like tolerance, variation in material is a given. Building in time during construction, for example, to shuffle stone tiling so that differently colored batches are intermixed (called "quilting") will spread the variation out, rather than turning it into a visible line in the floor. Likewise, understanding the veining patterns of stone or wood paneling leads us to think carefully about how we lay out an elevation—we can book match or randomly intermix rather than risking the unintentional patterning effects of a purely sequential layout.

Nothing gives away the illusion of a carefully crafted, solid building more than a detail that appears "flimsy" (Figure 34.4). *Robust* detailing involves thinking structurally at a small-scale, ensuring that elements are securely fastened to the building or to a subframe and that they themselves are sturdy enough to resist the inevitable bumps that will occur during construction and during the life of the building. Secure fastening involves finding a "path" for each piece of the detail that can take gravity and lateral loads—rarely on the scales we've discussed in Part 5, but just as important. Fastening only one end of a panel, for example, creates a small scale cantilever, with the relatively large bending moment at the root just as if it were a large beam. We can expect the panel, over its lifetime, to twist out of plumb over time if it's subjected to large enough loads. Often, the inclusion of an intermediate structure of light-gauge steel or wood will trade off some space in section for the security of widely available, reliable fixing points. Likewise, components themselves need to be designed to take loads, often from unanticipated sources. We may need to reinforce them around connection points to avoid shear failure, for example, and we may need to think through how the material will behave under high wind loading, or when a cart runs into it. Typical examples of this thinking include crimping or bending the edges of metal panels 90 degrees to give their edges some rigidity, installing heavier-duty plasterboard in areas likely to be impacted by traffic, including kick boards at wall bases to resist accidental shoe scuffs, and reinforcing corners with additional substructure or (better) metal guards.

This last suggestion touches on the *durability* of a detail or material—how will it hold up through weathering and/or constant use (Figure 34.5)? While there's no such thing as a "maintenance free" material or system, there are some materials that can take everyday punishment without losing their integrity more easily than others. Stone, for example, if detailed to the right thickness and anchored correctly, can shed rain, constant human touch, intense sunlight, and freeze/thaw cycles. But it's an expensive material, particularly if detailed correctly. Cement stucco might be a much cheaper alternative, but this material may not perform as well over time—if it's penetrated by water, for example, it may lose its adhesion, and it won't resist impacts as well. Over the building's lifetime, the initial cost of stone may easily repay itself by maintaining its appearance. Some materials do need more frequent maintenance—concrete, for example, should be water sealed regularly, while exterior wood will need painting every 8–12 years. Weathering is also a consideration when detailing around materials. Concrete, for instance, can easily be stained if it's exposed to regular flows of water. Draining a roof by using scuppers through a precast wall, therefore, needs to be done carefully to ensure that the water shoots well clear of the wall and isn't blown back by prevailing winds. Brick walls in contact with soil can wick water up into pores within the material, eventually leading to an integral water stain. Weathering can add to a building's appearance if handled correctly; oxidized copper, for instance, is invariably seen as a patina while oxidized steel is seen as "rusty". Knowing how well a material will hold up to the site's climate and its uses is important to making good decisions.

Finally, there are aspects to a material's finish that are important to its *finish and perception* (Figure 34.6). Some materials by their appearance connote strength (concrete, no matter how thin), others appear honed or polished

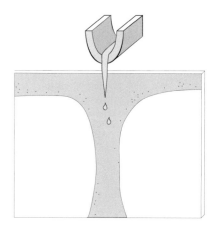

34.5
Durability has to do with the material itself.

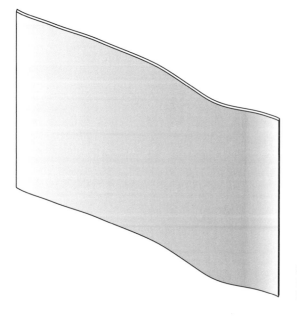

34.6
Finishes can amplify or suppress issues in detailing.

(stainless steel, for instance). The human eye interprets these in unforgiving ways—it tends to like a match between what it sees and how the mind behind it interprets how the building is held up. Shiny, polished materials can appear either refined or chintzy, depending on where and how they're used. Too much of one or the other can be visually boring or over-stimulating. Likewise, both ends of the spectrum have their own unique issues. Coarser materials, because they tend to absorb or diffuse light, tend to flatten visually and can often benefit from relief or patterning. More honed materials, because they tend to reflect light, must be very carefully placed as errors in positioning or orientation will be multiplied. Reflective glass walls, for example, can seem very flimsy if the reflections in them warp excessively, or don't match up from one pane to another. Worse, polished metal panels that "oil can" or warp even slightly will appear highly distorted due to the variation in reflected light that results. Here, in particular, a robust backup structure that allows for precise placement and offers robust support can reduce the problem. In general, bright or light finishes tend to amplify the quality of design and assembly—if either of these is questionable for reasons of cost or skill, a less reflective or darker palette is often advisable.

BALANCING

All of the above principles seem obvious—our details ought to be the robust, well-fit, visually appropriate, and durable details that are the hallmark of some of the most enduring buildings we study. Why, then, is shoddy detailing so prevalent?

The answer is, of course, that cost and time militate against perfect detail, and that the tradeoff for a building that's on time and on budget is often a compromise or the pressure-driven abandonment of one or more of these principles. This may be a straightforward zero-sum game—stone panels, for instance, are more robust, durable, and (arguably) visually engaging than cement stucco. But they cost a great deal more per unit of area, and they take more time to quarry, erect, and affix. Likewise, there is an almost one-to-one ratio between the time available to set concrete in its formwork and the quality of the finished product. No project has an infinite time frame or an infinite budget, and one of the profession's really valuable skills is the wisdom to know what can be redesigned, cut, refined, or changed to achieve savings in cost or schedule while minimizing the impact to the building's durability or its aesthetics. Ethically, we also need to balance the long-term health of the building with the short-term desires for something visually striking or, from our client's point of view, constructionally expedient.

As with many other aspects of design, some of this wisdom comes from a fluency in materials and methods—knowing how parts will be put together, how they will interact, and what their physical properties will allow. What we don't know, we can often glean from contractors or subcontractors, who will have an incentive to find solutions that will save them and their clients time and money without impacting the project's quality. Meetings in the midst of a budget crisis will produce some of the job's most innovative solutions, despite their inherent stress. It's also true that this pressure can, in fact, produce better solutions than those we might come up with otherwise; details that are refined under this pressure may well be cleaner, simpler, and less fussy than those drawn through only once.

The balance we usually seek in detailing is between economics (including cost and fabrication/construction time), performance (including functionality and durability), and aesthetics (how it looks on day one, and through the service life of the building).

CONCLUSION

Good detailing is the result of experience, logical, disciplined thought, and a firm grasp of the physics involved in joining materials together. Most architects only develop a really good sense of detail after a few projects, and in this sense detailing is very much like a language—vocabulary is good and relatively easy to learn, but fluency can only happen with repetition and practice. A fully educated architect is one who has taken the time to look at buildings with a mental microscope in addition to a wide-angled lens, and who has developed a sense of how the particulars of a building's assembly can have a dialogue with the generalities of form, rhythm, and style. Keeping in mind the six principles listed above—*fit*, *organization*, *consistency*, *robustness*, *durability*, and *finish*—is a good start toward developing a sense of how things go together best. Historically, details

34.7 and 34.8
Mies van der Rohe's Farnsworth House in Plano, IL, is a minimalist pair of planes with living spaces perched tenuously between.

34.9
In contrast to Mies' Farnsworth House, Louis Kahn's Kimbell Art Museum in Fort Worth, TX, adopted an intensive program of expression.

34.10
Renzo Piano's Menil Museum in Houston, TX, fit simple wood siding into a steel frame.

34.11
Detail can be structurally expressive.

34.12
Corbusier's Swiss Pavilion at the *Cite Universitaire* in Paris blends glass, concrete, stone, and metal into a rich pattern that has both regularity and variety.

have played a large role in expressing the aesthetic, functional, structural, and constructional "stories" of architecture (Figures 34.7–34.12).

FURTHER READING

Ford, E. R. (1990, 1996). *The Details of Modern Architecture*. Cambridge: MIT Press.

35

CUSTOM FABRICATION

Component design	Construction – standard vs. custom
	Innovation
	Responsibility
Production	Extrusions
	Metal castings
	Sheet metal forming
	Composites
	Glass
Prototypes and testing	Research design and development
	Performance and aesthetic criteria
	Types of testing
	Virtual and real prototyping

CUSTOM FABRICATION

Standardization in the construction industry has, by and large, been a good thing. It's possible to build buildings more efficiently, to have them operate more predictably, and to repair and maintain them more systematically as the industry has streamlined and coordinated its offerings. Much of our work today involves specification rather than design—selecting products and components with reliable sizes, interfaces, and performance and handing over at least some part of our building's appearance and operation to a well-catalogued, standard product.

There are times, however, when what's available on the shelf won't do, when there's a unique problem to solve, or when we just aren't satisfied with the standard offerings. In those instances, when we go off the chart and out of the catalogue, architectural design can be its most rewarding—and its most difficult. When we find ourselves having to come up with custom details, or to design custom components, we no longer have the safety of a manufacturer's testing or warranty behind us. Instead we have to rely on what we know about materials, about fabrication methods, and about the end use of the element. We're more exposed to liability here, but we're also able—if we know what we're doing—to really innovate and to solve problems in ways that are both creative and collaborative. There are also opportunities in custom component design to learn first hand how things are really made, always a valuable experience.

Often, the process of custom design will start with an existing product or system that, for whatever reason, doesn't meet the needs at hand. We may be able to work with a supplier or fabricator to make subtle alterations—at a cost—to existing products that will bring them in line with our needs. Some manufacturers are more open to this process than others; there are liabilities involved with any variation of a product that hasn't been thoroughly tested, and changing dimensions or components may not work with the way a factory line is set up. Still, there are manufacturers who appreciate the push that such projects provide, and many will be willing to at least meet to discuss what can be done if there's a large enough sale to be made (sometimes the results will improve the product's appeal—if one project needs a particular modification there may be similar opportunities for the manufacturer elsewhere). In these cases, setting up a work session with a company's product engineers, designers, or factory foremen can be a valuable way forward in finding out what would be involved with a "semi-custom" component. Often this is surprisingly easy; aluminum extrusion, for example, can be done to order with a custom extrusion using a unique die. Since the process chews up dies rapidly, the cost of a custom section can be easily amortized over the size of the project—in a large enough job, the extruder might go through a steel die anyway. In this case, the only excess costs involved are the design and tooling of the custom die.

In other instances, there won't be a product anything like the component we need, and we may need to look at custom designing a building element from scratch. This is riskier territory, as we won't necessarily have to hand the experience of a manufacturer that comes with "tweaking" an existing product. We may try to find a company that produces components made from a similar material—a steel fabricator, for instance, if we think the component might be best made from that—or that produces something with a similar function—a laboratory furniture manufacturer, perhaps, if we're designing a security station. In any case, it's advisable to agree on a fairly detailed program with the client, and to find expertise in fabrication, installation, and performance.

PRODUCTION

We've discussed typical building materials in Part 4, but it is worth summarizing a handful of production processes that we often rely on when designing custom components (Figures 35.1–35.4). These are drawn from Michael Stacey's 2001 book, *Component Design*, which is highly recommended as a more thorough introduction to the possibilities inherent in designing building elements from first principles.

All building materials are *cast*, *rolled*, *extruded*, *sawn*, or *carved*. At its most basic, component design includes working with a carpenter to design a simple set of cuts and joints in wood to build a cabinet, for example, or a door. At this level, all the aspects of component design are present, but in a relatively low-risk environment—we have a "program" for the component (to hold plates, for example, or to open and close), we have a material with definitive properties

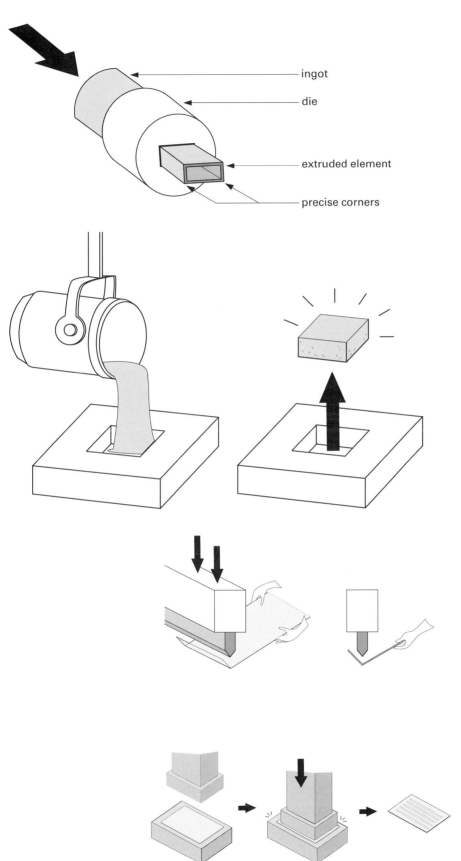

ingot

die

extruded element

precise corners

35.1
Extrusion processes produce constant sections, with sharp corners and very smooth surfaces.

35.2
Casting produces three--dimensional shapes, with options for smooth or rough surfaces depending on the molding process.

35.3
Sheet forming processes include brake-shaping, which involves crimping edges of sheet or plate metal in a brake-press.

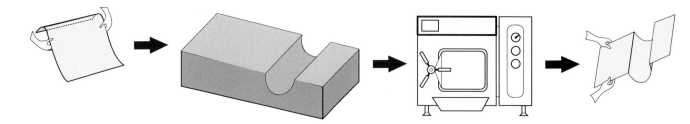

35.4
Composite materials are laid up as
sheets of fabric over a mold or jig.

and fabricational tendencies (wood is relatively weak but easy to carve, and it is readily available in both linear and planar forms), and we have expertise to hand in the carpenter, who can help guide us to a solution that balances what we want to achieve with what's possible to do in wood. We may, for instance, ask for advice in terms of cabinet door thickness, or proper hinges, or how best to finish a door opening. A really good carpenter may offer more opportunities than a journeyman.

In much the same way, materials such as steel, aluminum, and fiberglass all have distinct properties and fabricational tendencies based on how they're made and where they come from.

Organic materials are mined, quarried, or harvested. Hard materials such as stone and wood can be sawn to achieve planar or linear elements. Wood, additionally, can be laid up with resins to form strong plywood. Both stone and wood are subject to variations in color and pattern, which can either be visually rich or distracting, depending on how they're anticipated. Both can be hand-carved or sawn to achieve very fine tolerances and details. Wood, because it's softer, can be more easily worked by hand and it is thus an excellent material for ornamentation and small-scale structure—house framing, for example, is a uniquely suited use of wood's linear production processes and its ease of cutting and jointing. Both wood and stone are limited in size by the scale of cutting operations, and must therefore be assembled in panels for planar applications.

Some organic materials—in particular concrete and clay—can be *cast* or *molded* after their extraction. Both processes involve making a negative *form* into which the material can be pressed or poured and allowed to cure or dry. This can be a time-consuming process, but if forms can be mass-produced it can be a very economical one. Cost savings occur through production efficiency, and therefore these materials benefit from repetition. Terra cotta ornamentation in the early 1900s, for example, produced building skins that were highly repetitive, using a few patterns many times. Many architects (notably Daniel Burnham in Chicago) were able to exploit these properties to create highly unified, rhythmic building facades that were relatively economical because of their repetitive nature. Concrete offers particular opportunities and problems, as noted in Chapter 17.

Metals offer the most flexibility in terms of forming and shaping. Depending on their resistance to deformation, aluminum and steel alloys can be *rolled* into standard shapes, *extruded* through dies into standard or custom sections, *bent* or *brake-shaped* into forms based on sheets or plates, or *cast* using heat and molds into custom forms. Rolling is limited, because of the tooling involved, to standard shapes, but extrusion offers almost unlimited possibilities because of the relatively low cost of producing dies. While the initial cost for tooling is substantial (between US$10,000 and US$20,000 for a custom die), in a large job this can be spread over the total linear feet produced, which may make it quite affordable. Dies are usually limited to 36cm (14″) in diameter, and the section must allow for smooth, regular "flow" of the metal through the die. But the result can be a very precise section custom designed to meet the particular needs of the project. Bending (and stretch-forming) take metal sheet or plate and induce permanent (i.e. plastic) deformation around a shaped billet. This is an efficient process for curved plates or sheets. Steel tubes or structural sections may be bent using machinery that induces deformation around a mold, or by heating small sections of the steel and drawing the element along a gently radiused track. Brake-shaping uses a hydraulic or mechanical press with a long blade to force a bend into a metal sheet or plate. This is convenient for shallow box sections or lightweight framing. Sheets may be *stamped* using a positive mold, or they may be formed into molds by air pressure or vacuum, all of which can permanently deform patterns into the flat material. Finally, by melting metal and pouring it into robust, heat-proof molds, it can be cast into a permanent three-dimensional form. This can be time- and labor-intensive, but if the mold can survive multiple castings, or if molds can be mass-produced, casting can be reasonably affordable.

Another cast material is glass. While glass can be custom cast, the expense of re-tooling usually leaves us with standard sheets and blocks with which to design. Glass can be custom fabricated by cutting or by layering additional material such as ceramic frit. But plate glass can also be bent to very precise tolerances in bending ovens, where the glass is slowly heated to near its melting point and allowed to gradually drape over a heat-proof mold. This is limited by the size of heating ovens to about 4m (12′) in any direction.

PROTOTYPING, TESTING, AND MOCK-UPS

Depending on the complexity of the component that's being custom fabricated, we may need to go through a number of steps to design and test it that go well beyond the drawing board. Clients may be concerned about the functionality, appearance, or durability of the new piece, and as designers we'll want some assurance that the design we're contemplating will actually work in the situation we're designing for. Professional liability in this realm is also a concern—with standardized products and installations the manufacturer and contractor will bear most of the responsibility for the component, at least for a given warranty period; but in cases where we've designed something untried and untested, we bear a considerable responsibility for how it performs—and the component may well undergo more scrutiny than it would if it were a standard piece. Therefore, we'll often require a more rigorous program of research and testing for custom components.

This process begins with research and development. We may start with similar products, or with components that have parallel functions or manufacturing processes. Installers, fabricators and manufacturers may all serve as useful resources in laying out the new component's performance requirements, materials, and configuration. Brainstorming with engineers or designers who manufacture a similar product is often the most productive way of moving forward, and many companies will gladly take on such a project if it gives them an opportunity to expand their product line. This process will lead to a set of criteria for performance, cost, delivery, and aesthetics. As the design progresses, we'll often exchange information with a production team that consists of drawings, models, or CAD visualizations from the designers, and shop drawings from the manufacturer. Shop drawings show very clearly the intended dimensions, materials, and configuration of what the manufacturer understands they are to produce, and our role gradually shifts to reviewing these drawings and commenting on them.

For large or particularly critical components, designers will agree on a testing program to ensure that the final product appears, fits, and works as expected. The simplest tests involve *prototypes*, or single pieces that show clearly what the manufacturer intends to produce. Seeing a component in three dimensions brings up important issues of appearance, fit, and texture that can't be deduced from drawings, no matter how detailed. Prototypes may be made of the intended materials, or they may be carved from foam or wood, depending on the expense and workability of the material involved (aluminum or steel castings, for instance, need to be carved from wood first to make molds). A more involved test involves a *mockup*, which is a full-scale installation of the component into its intended surroundings. This may occur in a portion of the building that has been completed, or it may require a separate construction. Issues here include appearance, fit, and texture, but also compatibility with surrounding components and systems. How a prefabricated panel attaches to a building frame, and how much it can be adjusted, for instance, is a typical mockup issue. Mockups may also test on-site procedures, such as forming and curing times for concrete. Most concrete installations will require a mockup panel that includes typical formwork details, textures, and colors. These panels are usually required on-site, ensuring that the subcontractor works within the conditions that will exist during the actual placement of the project's concrete.

More involved tests may be required to ensure that a component performs under unusual or stressful conditions. In particular, custom designs for fire-rated walls, doors, or windows may need to be tested to ensure that they will remain intact if exposed to the extreme heat of a building fire. In this case, a testing agency will be contracted to assemble a test rig, place the component or assembly in the rig, and expose it to a standard temperature for a given period of time—usually one, two, or four hours. If the element passes, the agency gives it a rating, and it can then be used to meet containment or integrity requirements of a building code. While expensive, these tests are valuable for manufacturers, as they provide new details that can be reliably specified in future projects; testing agencies keep and publish libraries of fire tests that can be specified or copied. Other outside testing may include serviceability tests, in which a mechanical component may be actuated thousands of times to simulate a lifetime's use; water exclusion tests, in which cladding systems are subjected to torrents of wind-driven rain (often using aircraft engines to simulate hurricane forces); or structural tests, in which elements are loaded to an agreed upon multiple of their anticipated loading to check for deflection and integrity.

Developments in virtual simulation have made CAD modeling an important tool in assessing the appropriateness and performance of custom fabricated components and building elements. Structural design can be closely approximated for complex forms, and much of the required testing for static performance can be done digitally, saving the expense of multiple prototypes. Illumination, air flow, acoustics and heat transfer are among the other performance characteristics that can be reliably modeled in virtual environments. However, for many of these codes and clients will still insist, with some justification, that a physical test be carried out as well to ensure performance in the complex environment of the job site and the finished building. Virtual models are, in the end, only as accurate as the information that goes into them, and are thus subject to the potential human error that comes from failing to fully account for important—but perhaps not obvious—aspects of their surroundings. Rapid prototyping (see Chapter 36) is another area where digital technology has made this phase quicker and more efficient, as laser cutters and three-dimensional printers can very rapidly produce complex shapes and forms that allow us to assess components' spatial attributes.

CONCLUSIONS

For a certain breed of architect, custom fabrication is the best part of the job. Working directly with people who know materials and processes intimately is both challenging and productive, and it can be an unbeatable opportunity to better educate yourself about the ways and means with which we build. In an era where specification has taken over much of our design time, there is a unique reward in being able to point to a finished building element and tell the whole story—from "program" through design, fabrication, and installation. Likewise, digital tools that enable mass customization and extensive virtual testing have given us unprecedented opportunities to design elements that are uniquely suited to solving particular problems, and to get the design of these elements absolutely, incontrovertibly *correct*. Much of the work of leading contemporary architects—including Norman Foster, Renzo Piano and Nicholas Grimshaw, and more formally radical designers such as Frank Gehry, SHoP, and Zaha Hadid—owe their unique designs to their willingness to go "off track" and design key elements from scratch, rather than simply selecting them.

There are limits, however, to the effectiveness of custom design. It is invariably time-consuming, because of the additional days or weeks needed for design and tooling. Likewise, in most cases custom components will incur additional costs in both design and fabrication. The risks involved in an element that doesn't work because of an unforeseen condition can also discourage such innovation. Like detailing, then, custom fabrication of building components is very often a matter of knowing when the added attention, care, and risk of invention is warranted, and when more expedient, "off-the-shelf" solutions can be accepted or assimilated into a design.

FURTHER READING

Stacey, M. (2001). *Component Design*. Oxford: Architectural Press.

36

DIGITAL FABRICATION

New ways of making	Limits of mass production model
	Early efforts to translate digital technologies to real world
2-D techniques	Laser Cutters
	CNC routers
	Plasma and water jet cutters
3-D techniques	3-D printers
	Multi-axis CNC machines
Manufacturability and performance	What's possible
	New potential for efficiency

NEW WAYS OF MAKING

The twentieth century saw huge changes in the way buildings were assembled and fabricated. While hand labor still played an important role on almost all building sites, the impact of mass production technologies was profound. Rolled steel, extruded aluminum, and precast or molded elements took important elements of construction off of the job site and put it instead into factories, where production could be quicker, cheaper, and more accurate using these techniques. The fully "mass-produced building" never fully materialized, but prefabrication and manufacturing led to more and more *components* of buildings being made "off-line." Chapter 35 covers many of the processes by which we make such components today.

While mass production led to important economies in schedules and cost, it has always had drawbacks. Primarily, the *tooling* that enables multiple copies has generally been expensive and difficult to change or even to adjust. Steel production is a classic example of this: rolling plants invest heavily in hardened steel rollers and machines that can efficiently produce miles and miles of steel shapes with precisely the same section. But it is prohibitively expensive to change these rollers, or even to adjust their positions. While steel comes in a wide variety of shapes, there is little variation possible in these; custom fabrication in steel is thus based on doing something (cutting, welding, drilling, etc.) *after* the shape has come off the rollers. Aluminum offers a bit more flexibility, but the cost of extrusion dies must be amortized over a very large quantity of finished product. Mass production has thus added economic limitations to design. Even where we can customize shapes or components, there is almost always pressure to use these shapes as many times as possible, leading to repetitious design. In typical construction there is pressure to use existing shapes or components, making designers' jobs more about specification and less about *design* per se. While the techniques in Chapter 35 can all be used to address unique situations, we are more commonly faced with selecting from an existing array of possibilities.

Such constraints can be seen as a positive benefit; the discipline imposed by limitations can produce clarity, and the variety achievable even with standard steel construction is impressive. But it is irresistible to think of what might be possible if we could physically manufacture *any* steel or aluminum—or plastic or fiberglass—shape that we could think of, and this is where the revolutionary processes of digital fabrication have offered impressive new avenues for design and construction. In general, these offer ways to sculpt and form objects using CAD software, and to "export" these to the physical world through devices that cut, mold, drill, or aggregate materials. Just like more typical mass production, there are methods that are more applicable to different types of shape—some work with planar materials ranging from cardboard to plate steel while more complex tools can cut three-dimensional shapes out of blocks of wood, foam, or steel (among others), or add thin layers of material to a matrix, approximating smooth forms with two-dimensional shapes stacked atop one another (Figures 36.1 and 36.2).

36.1
Digital methods allow subtle alterations to standard shapes, making it possible to mass produce components with varying dimensions (Iwamoto Scott Architecture, 'Voussoir Cloud', 2008).

36.2
Three-dimensional printing can create models of structural members, which in turn can be used to mass-customize connections in steel (Antony Gormley, 'Quantum Cloud', 1999).

2-D TECHNIQUES

The simplest of these digital fabrication processes involve two-dimensional cutters that incise or score planar material using methods that are analogous to pen-based plotting. Sheets or plates of material are etched or cut to produce two-dimensional shapes using either a moving bed (*moving material* cutters), a moving cutting head (*flying head*), or a combination of both (*hybrid*). Finely tuned motors driven by Computer Numeric Control (CNC) software move the head and/or the material and control whether the cutter is on or off, and in some cases how strong the cutting action is. This allows very precise shapes and patterns to be cut or etched into the sheets, resulting in accurate components that can then be attached or assembled by hand or by robotic machines.

While the control technology is roughly the same, no matter what scale or material is being used—essentially similar to older, pen-based plotters that use two-axis mechanisms to move a head back and forth across the substrate—the cutter itself can be one of several types. The most basic tool, a drill bit, creates an automated machine tool that cuts a relatively thick path through a malleable material like plywood. For lighter material such as cardboard or paper the drill bit

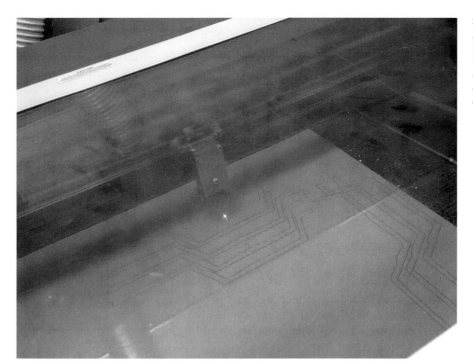

36.3
A laser cutter relies on a printer–like carriage system to move an intensely focused beam of light energy that can be tuned to cut or etch light materials such as wood or cardboard.

is substituted by a laser, though the most powerful laser cutters use a process similar to torch cutting that enables them to cut through up to ½" steel plate. Laser cutters are exceptionally precise, but they are inefficient and they produce a good deal of waste heat (Figure 36.3). They can also be relatively slow for thick materials—it can take up to a minute for a laser cutter to cut just a foot and a half of thick steel plate. Plasma jet cutters use high-temperature electric arcs to turn gas into superheated plasma, which melts a narrow line of metal. This technique can be faster for thicker plates. Water jets use high-pressure streams of water (sometimes with an abrasive) to cut. This eliminates problems with overheating or burning materials, and while it is still energy intensive, both the water and abrasive can be recovered and re-used (Figures 36.4 and 36.5).

With all of these techniques, software is available that will minimize the amount of waste by carefully positioning components on the material. Production times can also be reduced with software that finds the most efficient paths for the cutters. Additional benefits can come from automatically coding pieces with engraved numbers or titles, making them easy to sort and organize after cutting. 2-D fabrication, however, suffers from two inevitable limitations. First, of course, is the fact that everything that comes out of the machine is two-dimensional. Any depth in components must be created by layering flat elements, or by assembling them afterwards. This can, of course, become part of the process and the aesthetic—indeed a good deal of digital work in the past decade has focused on the idea of "folding" two-dimensional elements into spatial elements. But it can be labor- and time-consuming. Also, the use of two-dimensional processes for mass production is limited by the travel time involved in the cutting head traversing numerous elements. Still, because each piece is cut individually, these processes all allow significant customization at very little cost—no re-tooling is needed to make slight changes in configuration, and no labor is involved.

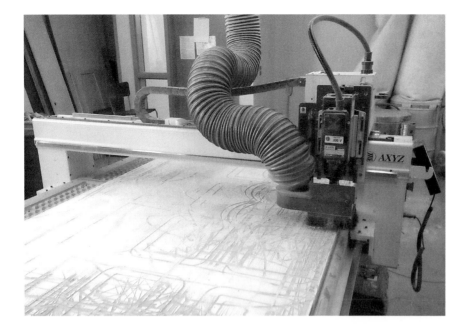

36.4
Other tools can be hooked up to carriage systems to perform two--dimensional cutting. This router can cut thick plywood using a range of bit sizes.

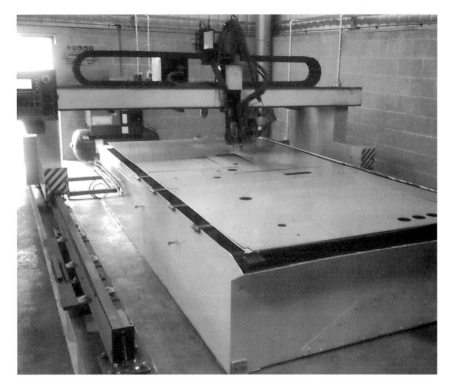

36.5
Carriage systems can work on much more robust materials, as well.

3-D TECHNIQUES

Full customization in all three dimensions is, however, possible with a number of slightly more sophisticated techniques. The quest for a fully digital, three--dimensional fabrication process has led to several advances, all of which are still costly and time-consuming compared to more traditional production techniques, but which offer vastly more opportunities for individual design and, as more efficient processes are developed, promise lower and lower costs.

Some of these are extensions of two-dimensional techniques. Water jets, laser cutters, and plasma cutters can all be mounted on multi-axial rigs instead of simple two-dimensional table matrices. Such rigs may have the appearance of robotic arms that enable precise positioning and rotation of the cutting head. The head here cuts or carves a block of material, leaving the desired component as a single piece and discarding the rest of the block. This is an inherently wasteful process, though this can be addressed by carefully considering the size of the initial block compared to the final component. It is also time-consuming, as the cutting head may need to excavate a considerable percentage of the block before reaching the desired dimension. The component must not only be designed for its final configuration, but must also be considered in terms of how the cutter will move and how much access it will have around various parts of the piece. There are, therefore, limitations on what can actually come out of the machine. Tolerance will depend on the method of cutting, but also on the resistance of the material, which can force mechanical cutters such as drill bits to slip and thus lose their positional certainty.

Three-dimensional printing is another technique that avoids the wastefulness of CNC cutting and routing. In this process, a print head produces a thin layer of powder or liquid in a shape that is a precise cross section of a digitally generated shape. Once laid down, a matrix may be sprayed over the layer to fix it. The printer then lays down another layer, representing the adjacent cross section, and this process is repeated until the component has been entirely built up layer by layer (Figure 36.6). Such an additive process eliminates the waste of cutting, but it can be immensely time-consuming, particularly if the resolution is quite fine (resolution in this case refers to the height of a typical layer, which can be thought of as a planar "pixel"). The process is also limited by materials, which must be sprayable and adherable. Plastics and some metals can be used for this, but these are

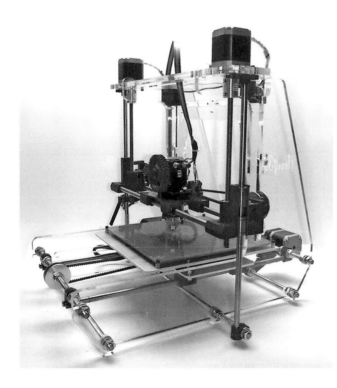

36.6
Three-dimensional printers work by laying up very thin sheets of powder and solidifying them with a spray-on matrix.

not often useful for architectural applications. Instead, the output from a three-dimensional printer may be used to form a mold, into which a more robust material can be cast. Three-dimensional printing has been one of the fastest-growing techniques in digital fabrication, and falling prices and improved technology have combined to make it available in desktop machines and in open-sourced software packages. It has thus been the preferred technique for *rapid prototyping*, in which study models or mockups are produced for review, testing, and discussion before actual components are manufactured using actual materials.

MANUFACTURABILITY AND PERFORMANCE

An issue that is coming to light as these technologies mature is *manufacturability*. Just as the ability to draw something does not guarantee the ability to build it, the translation of a digital model into a physical object does not guarantee either that it can be easily fabricated in real materials, or that it will perform as expected. Translating a three-dimensional form that can be readily produced by a three-dimensional printer, for example, may be far simpler than making that form out of a structural material such as steel or even aluminum. While two-dimensional processes have been successfully scaled up to produce large-scale building components, the widespread use of three-dimensional printing remains largely at the desktop scale, limited by processes and materials, but (in the case of multi-axial cutting) also by the sheer bulk of material necessary to carve out any full-scale shape. Other issues, such as the difficulty of routing out precise corners with CNC drilling, can be addressed by understanding on the part of designers—in the case of corners, substituting a simple radiused corner can save significant time and expense as it allows a larger bit that can, in turn, work more quickly (Figure 36.7). Software that can assess component

36.7
Multi-axis routing involves a robot-arm like appendage that maneuvers a cutting tool around a solid plate or block.

designs and identify potential problems in cutting or routing are making these processes more reliable, but the more sophisticated techniques available today are still used more for product and industrial design than architecture.

One area that offers great promise, however, is the ability to combine digital fabrication and analysis in chains of software that can continually test forms against a specified set of criteria, and use this feedback to continuously alter, re-test, and thus to evolve more efficient component designs. Software such as Grasshopper can be linked to design and production software to optimize geometry and production patterns through multiple iterations. At its most sophisticated, this design feedback process can intentionally introduce random "mutations" into iterations to find out whether approaches that may not have been apparent to the designer might offer additional benefits—this intentional mimicking of biological evolution can be particularly adept at tackling complex problems that require balancing a number of factors. Similarly, linking digital fabrication with building information modeling can allow very precise cost control and life cycle analysis. By making a broader array of forms economical, digital production techniques can allow designers to focus more closely on performance, leading to greater efficiencies in material use overall.

CONCLUSIONS

Just as mass production offered revolutionary new processes and, therefore, forms and materials to architects of the early twentieth century, the potential for digital production techniques to alter the designer's task in the twenty-first century seems limitless. Thus far, a great deal of experimentation in this area has been simple form-making—like any new tool, it has so far been irresistible to simply see what these processes can do. These experiments have been compelling, offering new visual and sculptural possibilities and translating the algorithms and patterns that come naturally from digital manipulation into engaging architectural objects. The real potential for these techniques, however, lies in their ability to help design and produce higher performance components—cladding elements, for instance, that use material more efficiently against combinations of wind, gravity, and environmental separation; or structures that eliminate more and more inefficient material to span further with lighter, less costly systems. These more efficient elements will very likely be just as engaging aesthetically as the early experiments in "digifab" have proven to be, but their ability to produce better functioning, more efficient buildings will be the primary reason for their application.

FURTHER READING

Beorkrem, C. (2012). *Material Strategies in Digital Fabrication*. London: Routledge.

Iwamoto, L. (2009). *Digital Fabrications: Architectural and Material Techniques*. New York: Princeton Architectural Press.

Kolarevic, B. (2005). *Architecture in the Digital Age: Design and Manufacturing*. London: Taylor and Francis.

37

CONSTRUCTION SPECIFICATIONS

Ann Sobiech-Munson, Architect, Specifier at substance architecture

Introduction	Construction specifications What do specifications do?
Forms of specifications	Preliminary Project Description (PPD) UniFormat™ Outline specification Project manual
Organization	MasterFormat® (50 divisions, 6-digit number) SectionFormat® (three parts) PageFormat®
Methods of specifying	Descriptive Reference standard Performance Proprietary "Open" versus "closed" Single-source
Writing specifications	Four Cs (clear, complete, concise, correct) Master or guide specifications

INTRODUCTION

If you have not heard the term yet, when you start to design buildings for construction, you'll hear people talk about "specifications." In this chapter, we'll explore the ways people use this term and provide an introduction to rules of thumb for producing construction specifications. Generally, *construction specifications* are written documents that describe the type, quality, and performance characteristics of the products and assemblies that go into a building project. They are often collected and organized into a book called a *project manual*, which complements the drawing sheets in a set of construction documents and becomes part of the contract for construction.

Some sources point to the Bible as a source for one of the very first examples of a construction specification. In the Book of Genesis, Chapter 6:14–16, God instructs Noah to build an ark:

14 *So make yourself an ark of cypress wood; make rooms in it and coat it with pitch inside and out.* **15** *This is how you are to build it: The ark is to be three hundred cubits long, fifty cubits wide and thirty cubits high.* **16** *Make a roof for it, leaving below the roof an opening one cubit high all around. Put a door in the side of the ark and make lower, middle and upper decks. (translation: New International Version)*

This example establishes a few key components to a construction specification. First, it uses verbal description to communicate aspects of construction, as opposed to visual instruction. This description establishes a specific type of wood to use: cypress. It also mandates a type of installation or fabrication: the ark shall be coated on both sides with pitch, a type of waterproofing. While dimensions in our contemporary construction documents are typically noted on drawings, the following verses establish at least one construction tolerance, still often found in construction specifications: leave an opening of one cubit below the entire perimeter of the roof. Finally, the entire excerpt is written as a command, in the imperative mood; you will see below that this is the most highly recommended form for writing construction specifications and is interpreted as a requirement for the contractor.

Our current understanding of construction specifications can be traced back to the point in history where the role of architect became distinct from that of master builder and documentation, in the form of both verbal and visual instructions from a designer to a builder, became a common part of the construction process. Most would date this from the Renaissance, around the time of Leon Battista Alberti, in the mid-fifteenth century. Letters from Alberti to builders provide evidence of written instruction with the specific intention of requiring the builder to carry out the architect's design intention. Construction specifications in the form we recognize today, however, date from a more recent era of architecture as a modern profession, after the Industrial Revolution.

Late-nineteenth- and early-twentieth-century journals in the U.S. and Britain illustrate discussions about construction specifications, their standardization, and their production. In the U.S., this coincides closely with the professionalization of architecture through the founding of the first architecture school and the establishment of professional organizations that would eventually form the American Institute of Architects. All of these discussions note the use of written documentation as part of construction documents and struggle with the best ways to make these documents clear and effective. Standardization began in earnest after World War II, during the ensuing building boom, replete with new technologies and materials for the post-war twentieth century. In 1948, an organization was founded to establish industry-wide standards for these written documents, which would become today's Construction Specification Institute (CSI). CSI develops and maintains the formats, standards, and organizational systems we use today, along with recommendations for best practices in specifications writing.

So what do specifications look like? Think about a simple plan drawing for a room. On the drawing, you can see the location of the wall and some notes about its assembly, such as minimum stud spacing. In a section cut and detail, you will understand wall thickness and dimension, along with some generic names of the materials included in the assembly: metal studs, wood blocking, gypsum board. But when you need to build the wall, lots of questions arise about each component. Take the gypsum board ("dry wall") alone. Does it need to be fire rated? Is it moisture resistant, abuse resistant, or impact resistant at all or some locations? Is any brand of gypsum board acceptable, or are there certain brands required by the project? Is any brand okay, as long as it meets a certain quality level? What kind of finish is required – level 1, 2, 3, or 4? And then imagine that you are an architect talking with the contractor on-site to determine whether the installation is acceptable. What types of construction tolerances are allowed? Are there the appropriate numbers and types of fasteners installed? Are the joints property taped and finished?

You get the idea. A few of these questions may be addressed through notes on the drawings, but the construction specification provides a place where most of these are answered. This example already illustrates a few key things that construction specifications *do*. The specification sections:

- establish quality standards, through reference standards or performance requirements;
- name products acceptable for the project and/or state criteria for acceptable products;
- list accessories and other items required for installation that may not appear on drawings;
- specify installation requirements and desired results.

Note that the specifications rely on the drawings to show locations, dimensions, arrangements, and other information more easily communicated visually. But the specifications work together with the drawings to create a set of requirements that become part of the construction contract.

FORMS OF SPECIFICATIONS

Specifications, or documents that work like specifications, come in a few different forms. In the very early stages of a project, such as schematic design, writing complete specification sections according to MasterFormat® section numbers (we'll get to this in a minute) may be difficult or impossible because there is simply not enough information, or because a number of options are being proposed and the design may change. In these cases, there is a form of written document called *preliminary project description*, or "PPD." These descriptions include information about the project organized according to systems and assemblies rather than products. The CSI format used for these documents is called UniFormat™ (Table 37.1). The *preliminary project description* allows the design team to keep track of information about types of systems without requiring the details of a complete specification. Cost estimators often use this type of format as well.

Another preliminary type of document is the *outline specification*. Unlike the preliminary project description, the outline specification does use CSI's MasterFormat® to organize information according to products rather than systems. However, it does so in an abbreviated format, which may take the

Table 37.1 MasterFormat® groups, subgroups and division titles (published by CSI)

PROCUREMENT AND CONTRACTING REQUIREMENTS GROUP

    Division 00 – Procurement and Contracting Requirements

SPECIFICATIONS GROUP

Division 01 – General Requirements	General Requirements Subgroup
Division 02 – Existing Conditions	Facility Construction Subgroup
Division 03 – Concrete	
Division 04 – Masonry	
Division 05 – Metals	
Division 06 – Wood, Plastics, and Composites	
Division 07 – Thermal and Moisture Protection	
Division 08 – Openings	
Division 09 – Finishes	
Division 10 – Specialties	
Division 11 – Equipment	
Division 12 – Furnishings	
Division 13 – Special Construction	
Division 14 – Conveying Equipment	
Division 15 – (Reserved for future expansion)	
Division 16 – (Reserved)	
Division 17 – (Reserved)	
Division 18 – (Reserved)	
Division 19 – (Reserved)	
Division 20 – (Reserved)	Facility Services Subgroup
Division 21 – Fire Suppression	
Division 22 – Plumbing	
Division 23 – Heating, Ventilating, and Air Conditioning (HVAC)	
Division 24 – (Reserved)	
Division 25 – Integrated Automation	
Division 26 – Electrical	
Division 27 – Communication	
Division 28 – Electronic Safety and Security	
Division 29 – (Reserved)	
Division 30 – (Reserved)	Site and Infrastructure Subgroup
Division 31 – Earthwork	
Division 32 – Exterior Improvements	
Division 33 – Utilities	
Division 34 – Transportation	
Division 35 – Waterway and Marine Construction	
Division 36 – (Reserved)	
Division 37 – (Reserved)	
Division 38 – (Reserved)	
Division 39 – (Reserved)	

(continued overleaf)

Table 37.1 (continued)

SPECIFICATIONS GROUP

Division 40 – Process Integration   Process Equipment Subgroup:

Division 41 – Material Processing and Handling Equipment

Division 42 – Process Heating, Cooling, and Drying Equipment

Division 43 – Process Gas and Liquid Handling, Purification and Storage
      Equipment

Division 44 – Pollution and Waste Control Equipment

Division 45 – Industry-Specific Manufacturing Equipment

Division 46 – Water and Wastewater Equipment

Division 47 – (Reserved)

Division 48 – Electrical Power Generation

Division 49 – (Reserved)

form of an annotated index or a series of half-page draft specification sections. Typically used during design development or early construction document stages, these types of specifications provide more product detail than the preliminary product description, but do not require complete specification sections. They often establish a working framework for developing a full set of specifications throughout the construction documentation phase in a design project.

Finally, there are short- and long-form full specification sections. The remainder of this chapter will focus on these types, which are the construction specifications found in a complete set of construction documents. In addition to being organized according to CSI MasterFormat® section numbers, these comply with CSI SectionFormat® and PageFormat® standards. Each section includes three parts, and each section has a standardized format. This means that once someone becomes familiar with the formats, finding information in the document becomes easier.

Before we continue to explore the full specification sections, let's zoom out to better understand how these appear in a set of documents. When a team issues a set of construction documents, the set consists of drawings bound together and a book, which may be more than one volume. The book is called a *project manual*, and that's where the construction specifications reside.

However, the project manual includes other documents as well; the specification writer often has a hand in reviewing or producing these documents along with the technical specifications for the project. (Table 37.2) A typical project manual may include the following categories of documents:

- bidding, or "procurement," documents: ad or invitation to bid; form of bid; other forms as required; instructions to bidders;
- contract conditions: may include sample contract form; general, supplemental, and/or special conditions; these may be standard or specially developed by the owner;
- reference documents: information provided by the owner for reference only; often these include soils reports or other information about project conditions.

Table 37.2 UniFormat Level 1 categories (published by CSI)

Project Description	
Introduction	
A	Substructure
B	Shell
C	Interiors
D	Services
E	Equipment and Furnishings
F	Special Construction and Demolition
G	Building Sitework
Z	General

These three categories of documents are often referred to as the "front ends" and require owner input in their preparation. Often the architect assists in coordinating them based on the owner's requirements for the project. Their official place in CSI's MasterFormat® is Division 00. In addition, the project manual includes:

- general requirements: specification sections that govern the entire project; Division 01.
- technical specifications: specification sections for each product or assembly in the project; sections in Divisions 02–49.

Together, these documents comprise the *project manual*. Contractors use the information to submit bids, and the requirements in the project manual become part of their contract with the Owner. During construction, the *project manual* acts as a handbook for the project.

ORGANIZATION

The first step to organizing the project manual is understanding CSI's MasterFormat® system of section numbering. Philosophically, it works like the Dewey Decimal or Library of Congress numbering systems in a library, or even like the aisles in your local supermarket: the system groups similar items together and establishes a commonly accepted standard for their location, making it easier to find information when you need it. MasterFormat® has evolved over the years, undergoing a major change in 2004 to a six-digit number format, in place of the old five-digit numbers, and an expansion from 16 to 50 divisions in response to changes in the way we design, construct, and maintain facilities. Many firms use the numbers to file information and to organize their product libraries, so even a basic familiarity with the system provides a leg up in navigating the huge amount of information about building materials that continues to proliferate.

A full and current list of the divisions and sections may be found here: http://www.csinet.org/masterformat. An abbreviated list of division numbers

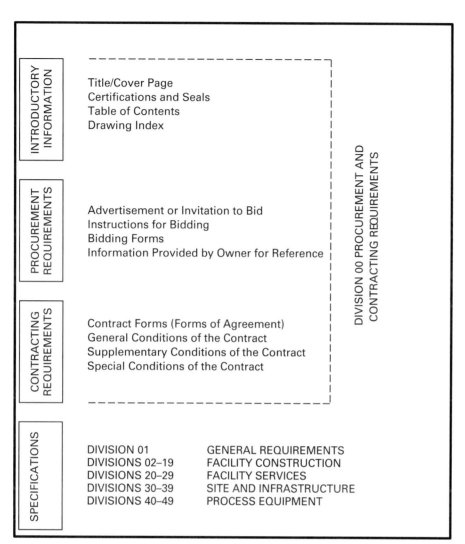

and titles is printed in Figure 37.1. But before you get too overwhelmed, let's start with the basics. You already know about Division 00 Procurement and Contracting Requirements; we discussed that one above. Ditto for Division 01 General Requirements, although a glance through the section headings included under the 01 sections will help you understand what types of activities must be considered as administrative and how procedural requirements are established. Another quick and easy tip: the first two digits of the six-digit section number always refer to the division. This means that whenever you see a section beginning in 00, you know that it relates to procurement (bidding) and contracting requirements. Or, for example, a section beginning in 08 relates to openings of some kind. While it is not necessary (or perhaps even feasible!) to memorize every section number, you should get a feel for the division titles, especially through Division 14.

From there, MasterFormat® organizes similar items together using the additional digits in the 6-digit number. We already know that any section beginning in 08 has something to do with openings. As you glance through the list, you'll see that this includes doors, windows, curtain walls, and related sections. Look at 08 11 00 Metal Doors and Frames. You can see that 08 = openings, 11 = metal doors and frames. You may need a section that gets even more specific than that, so there's a slot for 08 11 13 "Hollow Metal Doors and Frames." In this case, the last two digits provide a spot for a specific type of metal door and frame: 13 = hollow metal.

In the project manual, sections are assembled into order according to section number. For someone working in the design and construction industry, this standardized organization facilitates communication and information retrieval by always placing information about a category of product or assembly in the same place. Current practice extends this into building information modeling, using section numbers as part of data associated with model objects.

Now that you have an understanding of the overall organization of the project manual, let's look at the individual specification section. It also has a standardized format, CSI's three-part SectionFormat® mentioned above.

Part 1—GENERAL covers administrative and procedural requirements, such as submittals, warranties, project conditions, and meeting requirements.

Part 2—PRODUCTS lists all the products included in that section and includes requirements for manufacturers and fabrication.

Part 3—EXECUTION describes work at the project site, including installation and field-testing requirements.

PageFormat® standardizes the presentation of information on a page, including article and paragraph formatting. These interrelated formatting standards enable those preparing and using the specifications to access information in a clear and consistent manner.

METHODS OF SPECIFYING

There are four distinct types of specifications, or methods of specifying: descriptive, reference standard, performance, and proprietary. The specification writer must decide how to specify each product or assembly. At times, it makes sense to use a combination of these four types; a single section may also contain multiple categories, each of which uses a different method of specification.

Descriptive specifications provide salient characteristics of products and assemblies, without naming specific manufacturers or products. "Glazed porcelain tile" may be described in terms of finish texture, color, material composition, or other characteristics. Any product that meets the description could satisfy this specification.

Performance specifications describe how the materials, products, or assemblies have to function, focusing on expected results. These types of specifications may include required load requirements, for example, or requirements for thermal performance, and describe methods for measuring whether or not a product or assembly meets the performance goal. These performance requirements determine whether or not a product complies with the specification.

Reference standard specifications describe products by referring to commonly accepted and well-established standards in order to define quality.

These standards may be established by code-related organizations, such as UL or Warnock-Hersey; they may be testing organizations, such as ASTM or ANSI; or they may be groups associated with specific industries, such as the Architectural Woodwork Institute (AWI) or the American Concrete Institute (ACI). By referencing the procedures, standards and requirements of these organizations, these types of specifications define parameters for performance and quality.

Proprietary specifications list products by manufacturer and product name. Because this type includes an exact product, little else is required. When proprietary specifications do not allow substitutions or comparable products, they are referred to as "closed" specifications, since only the named product or products are allowed to be incorporated into the project. Proprietary specifications that list only one acceptable product are considered "single source" specifications. While these may be required by the client or determined by existing construction, "single source" specifications limit competition and thus may contribute to higher construction cost. In competitively bid projects, some clients may allow proprietary specifications but require a minimum of three products listed for each category of product or assembly, in order to encourage competition. In other cases, proprietary specifications can become "open" by allowing comparable products or substitution proposals.

In many cases, a specification includes a combination of these types. Even when one or more products is named in a specification section, the writer may include a description of the product's major characteristics, requirements for complying with testing or quality standards established by outside organizations, and/or performance requirements for the product or assembly. Including these characteristics can help an architect or contractor determine whether or not a proposed substitution complies with requirements; it may encourage competition by allowing multiple options for that particular specification section. When combining proprietary specifications with other methods of specifying, however, be careful not to incorporate information that creates a conflict between characteristics of the named product and the generic descriptions.

WRITING SPECIFICATIONS

The Construction Specifications Institute has developed a number of practice guides to help specifications writers in writing specifications. Perhaps the most important rule of thumb to remember is the "four Cs" of specification writing: all specifications shall be clear, complete, concise, and correct. In addition, CSI provides a number of tips to aid in the writing and editing of specifications:

- Say it once, and in the appropriate place. Specifications writing requires considerable coordination between drawings and technical specifications. Duplicating information in two or more locations increases potential for error or conflict in the documents. Drawings and specifications complement each other; one does not take precedence over the other. Locations and quantities, for instance, are typically shown on the drawings; the type of stainless steel required for a fastener is more appropriately described in a specification.

- Use the imperative mood to streamline the specifications. To be concise, the specification writer strives for balance between including all required information—being complete—and communicating that information in the most economical way possible. Since the specifications are instructions to the Contractor, simply changing a sentence from "Contractor shall submit. . ." to "Submit. . ." maintains the information but edits the text to its most concise form.
- Use "shall" instead of "should," "must", or "is to" when specifying requirements.
- Avoid the phrase "or equal." Instead, establish requirements so that comparable products can be reviewed and considered.
- Avoid phrases and requirements that cannot be enforced. When writing performance requirements, for instance, do not say "as smooth as possible." Instead, refer to ACI tolerances for the type of concrete construction the project requires, or write a measureable standard such as "no more than ⅛ inch in ten feet, as measured with a straight edge."

More tips and tricks of the trade can be found in the documents listed under Further Reading, at the end of this chapter.

Most specification writers do not prepare each section from scratch. Multiple programs exist to provide a starting point for each section. MasterSpec (Arcom) and SpecLink (BSD) are two common master guide specification programs that provide master specification sections that may be edited for each project. New offshoots of these programs integrate specifications with building information modeling programs, such as Revit. Other resources include guide specifications from manufacturers; government specification master sections, available online; specification sections used on previous projects; and office master specifications. Depending on the context, one or more of these resources may be used in the preparation of a specification section. The commercial specification programs require subscriptions and licenses; most firms will subscribe to one or more of these. Guide specifications from manufacturers require careful review; while they may provide much-needed information about a specific product or assembly, they usually cannot be used directly without significant editing for your project. Office master specifications may be a timesaver if your firm routinely does the same types of projects, but use caution when starting with sections used on previous projects; errors may result if the section is re-used with little or no editing.

CONCLUSION

Construction specifications play a significant role in the success of a project. They require coordination and attention to detail, along with knowledge of products and assemblies, research skills to explore and understand available options, and writing skills. The project manual will be well used during construction, and clarity of communication, consistency of language, and clearly defined and measureable or documentable requirements are essential to its effective-ness. Even those who may not be charged with preparing the specifications themselves will benefit from a basic understanding of formats, organization, and specification methods as projects move through the design and construc-tion process.

GLOSSARY

Descriptive: Method of specifying by listing product characteristics.

Four Cs: Overall rule of thumb established by the Construction Specifications Institute for preparing specifications; clear, complete, concise, correct.

Outline specification: Abbreviated list of products, typically used during schematic design or design development phases; similar to PPD except uses MasterFormat®.

Performance: Method of specifying by listing required results and methods for measuring those results.

Preliminary project description (PPD): Description of systems and assemblies used in early project phases; utilizes UniFormat™.

Project manual: Set of written documents included with the construction documents; includes procurement (bidding) forms and requirements, contracting forms and requirements, general requirements, and technical specifications.

Proprietary: Method of specifying by naming specific products and manufacturers; may be single source (one product named); closed (no substitutions allowed); or open (substitutions or comparable products allowed).

Reference standard: Method of specifying by listing established industry standards, published by third-party industry groups.

FURTHER READING

Construction Specifications Institute (CSI) (2011). *The CSI Construction Specifications Practice Guide*. Hoboken, NJ: John Wiley & Sons. Part of the CSI's Practice Guide Series this replaces the former *Manual of Practice* (MOP, first published 1967) and *The Project Resource Manual: CSI Manual of Practice*. (PRM, 5th edition of the MOP, 2004).

Construction Specifications Institute (CSI). *The Construction Specifier*. Available online at http://www.constructionspecifier.com/index.php

Emmitt, S. and Yeomans, D. T. (2008). *Specifying Buildings: A Design Management Perspective*, 2nd edition. Oxford: Butterworth-Heinemann/Elsevier.

Meier, H. W. and Wyatt, D. J. (2008). *Construction Specifications: Principles and Applications*. New York: Thomson Delmar Learning.

Rosen, H. J., Regener, J. R., Kalin, M. and Weygant, R. S. (2010). *Construction Specifications Writing: Principles and procedures*, 6th edition. Hoboken, NJ: John Wiley & Sons.

PART 7

BUILDING SERVICES

38

ENVIRONMENTAL CONTROL: PASSIVE VENTILATION

Wind movement	Exterior conditions
	Principles of air flow
	Pressure, eddies and direction
	General opening placement
	Air jets
Natural air flow in buildings	Ventilation—health/comfort/structure
Passive ventilation systems	Stack effect principles
	Bio-climatic chart review
	Cross ventilation
	Specific window opening locations and sizes
	Wind catchers
	Night cooled mass
	Mechanically assisted systems

INTRODUCTION

Most decisions affecting the energy use of a building happen during schematic design. The basic form and siting of a building determines most of its efficiency potential and trying to make changes to overall shape or location late in project development is difficult or impossible. Therefore a basic understanding of how to work with the environment should affect the earliest stages of design while other architectural issues are also being considered simultaneously.

Passive ventilation is one of the areas of building design most affected by siting and building configuration. It is also one of the areas that can be most beneficial to reducing energy consumption.

The mechanics of wind flow are relatively easy to understand, as are the way openings in buildings affect air movement and interior comfort. The rules of how to make buildings comfortable passively have been around since building began; there was simply no other choice until relatively recently. So why don't we always use these basic systems? The answer is curious—it's largely due to efficiency. When using mechanical cooling systems the goal is often to keep the building envelope as tightly sealed as possible to prevent inefficient losses of conditioned air. Once the sealed mechanical systems became the norm, the passive systems became less important.

We now better understand the need to reduce our dependence on active building systems and the energy they require. We've also created problems due to sealing buildings too tightly, recycling bad air and trapping harmful airborne illnesses. Passive ventilation systems are increasingly being used in lieu of, or as hybrids with, mechanical systems to create more efficient and healthier environments.

WIND MOVEMENT

Exterior conditions such as vegetation, adjacent buildings and landforms can greatly affect wind direction and speed. Most prevailing wind direction and speed information comes from airport locations, which may not accurately represent your local site conditions. Look at the land to analyze this like you would the other basic site conditions.

The difficulty in placing openings is determining what direction wind will be coming from and how fast it will be traveling. This is affected by everything from how you landscape the site to what buildings may be constructed around your project in the future—so you must be able to reasonably assess how your site will be developed and what surrounding building and landscape may take place. Openings may need to be oversized so that tree growth or neighboring buildings won't reduce the required air movement in your building in the future. Also keep in mind that insect screens can reduce airflow through a window by up to half.

Wind approaching a building slows and compresses as it hits the front face. This wind then diverts and flows around the sides of the building. As it flows around the sides it begins to separate from the surface and create negative pressure along these edges. Once it passes the building it creates eddies flowing in a circular pattern back toward the rear of the structure. The rear of the building is also in negative pressure, but not as much as the sides (Figure 38.1). The goal in placing openings is to take advantage of the natural tendency of wind to create these zones of positive and negative pressure to draw air into and through the space.

Openings placed on the front and back (or *windward* and *leeward*) sides of a building will allow air to cross ventilate and form small eddies back toward the direction of wind flow. Placing openings in the sidewalls instead of the back will utilize the greater negative pressure at the exterior sides to draw air through the building more efficiently. This also mixes the air through the interior better (Figures 38.2 and 38.3).

Winds that strike a building at an oblique angle will flow through better with openings on three sides rather than two (Figures 38.4 and 38.5). If the wind approaches from the side without windows, all openings are in negative pressure, eliminating good ventilation (Figure 38.6).

When only one side of a building can be opened, the windows should be as far apart as possible and the building should try to sit at an oblique angle to the wind. Short projections beside the windows can enhance the positive and negative pressures to improve airflow (Figure 38.7). The airflow in this situation

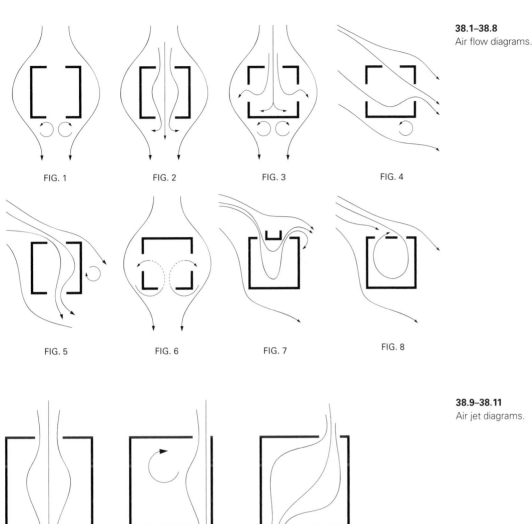

FIG. 1   FIG. 2   FIG. 3   FIG. 4

FIG. 5   FIG. 6   FIG. 7   FIG. 8

FIG. 9   FIG. 10   FIG. 11

38.1–38.8
Air flow diagrams.

38.9–38.11
Air jet diagrams.

needs to be kept from eddying back out of the first opening, therefore reducing air intake (Figure 38.8).

As a basic rule of thumb, the intake and exit sizes of windows should be equal to maximize airflow. To get lower airflow, but better air circulation, reduce the outlet size somewhat—but a greater than 60–40 ratio significantly reduces overall airflow.

Air passing through a room creates an *air jet*, an accelerated flow of wind traveling a set path—openings in the center of a space keep the jet free from clinging to a surface (Figure 38.9). Openings along walls or ceilings cling to the surface removing heat from that surface more rapidly than an open jet, which can be a valuable way to cool a radiant surface (Figure 38.10). Overall airflow mixing is maximized by offsetting intake and outlet locations; this promotes both surface cooling and room air changes (Figure 38.11).

AIR FLOW IN BUILDINGS

The three basic functions of passive ventilation are to promote health, increase comfort with air circulation, and remove heat from structural elements. *Health* requires enough fresh outdoor air be changed with the stale indoor air to resist airborne germs/bacteria/mold, etc. from building up. *Comfort* is achieved through evaporative and convective heat losses from adequate air movement. *Structural cooling* moves heat away from surfaces where it has built up before it radiates that heat into the space—this really qualifies as comfort also, but it's easier to explain it separately.

At times wind flow cannot be achieved through window openings or there is a desire to enhance flow through other passive means. The *stack effect* creates airflow by using the thermal principles of airflow. The density of air lessens as it warms, causing it to rise. Cooler air is drawn into the slight vacuum caused by the air displacement and tends to be drawn up after the warm air. Creating a chimney that separates lower cooler air from higher warmer air enhances stack effect—the top of the stack is allowed to heat, drawing warmer air up into it. Cool air flows into the lower space and up the chimney starting a natural convective loop of air movement. The bigger the stack, the more air movement; atriums can be used as the chimney to create this effect. Also, placing the openings at the top of the vent where prevailing winds will pass increases airflow. Houses in the Middle East traditionally use this system and it has been frequently been adapted for use in modern buildings as well (Figure 38.12).

The minimum rate of *air changes* per hour in a room is determined primarily by code and varies depending on the use of the space, but is typically a minimum of four. This means that every hour *all* of the air in that room has been renewed a minimum of four times (and can be up to 30–60 times in kitchens and industrial plants). This rate is based on very basic health requirements more than comfort—codes are mainly concerned with occupant health, safety and welfare—they're trying to prevent dangers like Legionnaires Disease (named after the first recognized outbreak of the sometimes fatal respiratory disease

38.12
Stack effect.

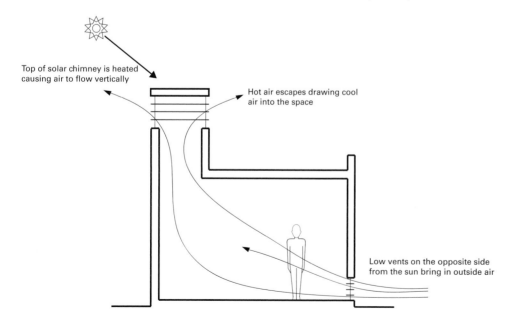

Top of solar chimney is heated causing air to flow vertically

Hot air escapes drawing cool air into the space

Low vents on the opposite side from the sun bring in outside air

at an American Legion Convention in Philadelphia in 1976). For comfort, the number of changes should take into account heat generation, the number of occupants, the level of activity, and potential airborne toxins. There are sources, such as *Graphic Standards and Architect's Data*, that have charts to assist in window sizing for varying air changes per hour.

PASSIVE VENTILATION SYSTEMS

The Bio-Climatic Chart is based on how to achieve comfort through the factors affecting the human body, or how to reach the "comfort zone" (see Chapter 2, Human factors: Basic human comfort). The comfort zone is a defined combination of factors—air movement, air temperature, relative humidity, and radiation where a human body with average clothing at rest in the shade will be comfortable. Passive ventilation can be figured into the wind speed area at the top of the bio-climatic chart and its effectiveness will depend on the climate zone of your building.

Cross ventilation is the most direct way to move air through a building for comfort. The effectiveness is largely dependent on the difference in temperature between the inside air and outside wind, plus the relative humidity. Structures tend to build up heat due to people, lights, equipment, solar radiation, and other factors—but if the wind outside is warmer than the air inside it's going to have difficulty cooling the space no matter how hard it blows through. Using basic charts of the building's heat load (the combination of factors heating the building) along with wind speed and temperature differential between inside and outside can determine the size of openings required (see *Sun, Wind and Light* by Brown and DeKay).

The design of window openings for passive ventilation should be based on a number of factors (Figure 38.13):

1 First the wind needs to be able to get to the opening. This means the area outside of the openings must be free of obstructions and have local climatic conditions that allow for airflow.
2 The air then needs to flow to where it's needed in the space—the velocity may be right based on the bioclimatic chart, but if it's on the ceiling or floor people are not being touched by the air. Think about where the inhabitants will be in a room and adjust openings to run air past the core and head of their body.
3 A variety of openings may be needed to both cool people and cool the wall/ceiling surfaces. The surfaces needing cooling jets are typically the ceiling and west walls—the areas heated by the sun the most during the warmest part of the year. The amount of cooling needed depends on the insulation value of those surfaces, but it makes little sense to primarily cool the floor if it's the coolest surface in the room already.
4 Air supply in a mechanical system usually follows the rule of supply high/return low when cooling is the primary concern, since the cool air naturally falls; the opposite is true when heating is the main factor, due to the warm air naturally rising into the space. Therefore you might think it best to place inlet windows high in order to let the cool air fall and place outlet windows low. However, with airflow through a building the opposite is usually true—

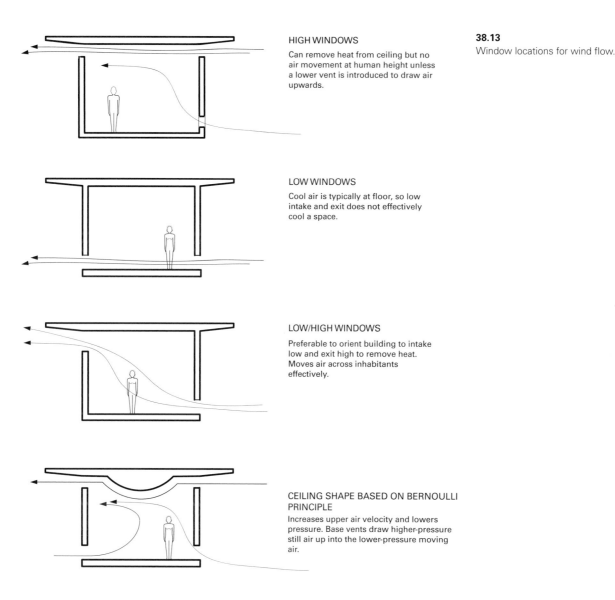

HIGH WINDOWS

Can remove heat from ceiling but no air movement at human height unless a lower vent is introduced to draw air upwards.

LOW WINDOWS

Cool air is typically at floor, so low intake and exit does not effectively cool a space.

LOW/HIGH WINDOWS

Preferable to orient building to intake low and exit high to remove heat. Moves air across inhabitants effectively.

CEILING SHAPE BASED ON BERNOULLI PRINCIPLE

Increases upper air velocity and lowers pressure. Base vents draw higher-pressure still air up into the lower-pressure moving air.

38.13
Window locations for wind flow.

you want to evacuate the warm air which is already on the ceiling, so you need to supply low and evacuate the warm air up high. This allows greater air mixing than if you supplied high and evacuated high—which would cause an air jet at the ceiling.

5 Bernoulli's Principle states that fast moving air has a lower pressure than still air (an airplane wing works in this way). By moving air quickly through a space and shaping surfaces to increase air velocity, this lower-pressure, moving air can draw the higher-pressure still air into the flow and increase air movement through a space.

Wind catchers allow buildings in densely built areas or where low winds are blocked to draw wind down from higher airflows (Figure 38.14). This has benefits and liabilities, the first liability being the need to evacuate warm air high. This is usually solved by creating a chimney to evacuate warm air and baffles to direct the air down into the space rather than straight to the chimney. The benefit of wind catchers is that wind is typically at a higher velocity farther from

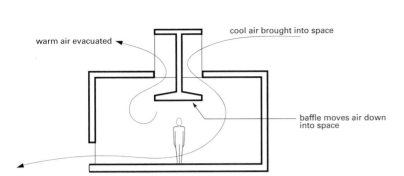

warm air evacuated

cool air brought into space

baffle moves air down into space

38.14
Wind catcher.

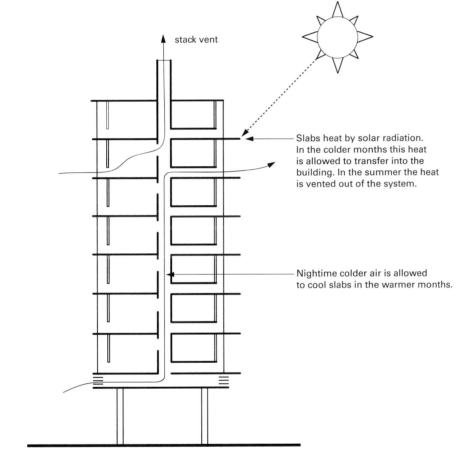

stack vent

Slabs heat by solar radiation. In the colder months this heat is allowed to transfer into the building. In the summer the heat is vented out of the system.

Nightime colder air is allowed to cool slabs in the warmer months.

38.15
Night cooled thermal mass system.

the drag of the ground, so it can be directed at higher velocities down into the space.

In other versions of passive ventilation cooling, systems like night cooled mass are possible. This operates on the principle of thermal mass temperature shift—like a thermal wall that stores heat during the day and radiates it back at night. In a night cooled mass, the building structure absorbs heat during the day as a closed system and at night vents are opened using airflow evacuate the stored heat. The mass is then cool for the next morning until it begins to store heat again. During cooler months the heat can be retained and used to warm the building. This system requires enough substantial diurnal temperature shifts to make it feasible (Figure 38.15).

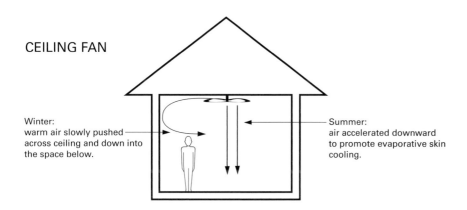

ATTIC FAN

evacuates warm air at top of spaces and circulates cooler air up into inhabited area of space

CEILING FAN

Winter:
warm air slowly pushed across ceiling and down into the space below.

Summer:
air accelerated downward to promote evaporative skin cooling.

Passive ventilation cooling systems are often hybridized with some components of a mechanical system to improve performance. The most common of these are fans that assist in air movement when wind is not adequate. A common and very useful type is the basic ceiling fan—creating downward airflow in the summer to promote evaporative cooling and reversing the flow to upward in the winter to push warm air gently sideways and back down the walls to get heat circulation off of the ceiling (Figure 38.16). Most people use fans in the summer direct downward mode but neglect the low-speed winter up mode, which is particularly effective in higher ceiling spaces. A long-established version of drawing the cool air up and evacuating warm air is the attic vent fan. The attic fan pulls the warm air up and out of the structure while drawing cooler air in from below. These are very effective systems that can mechanically enhance passive ventilation systems with low energy output. Other hybrid systems like evaporative coolers (swamp coolers) can work well in hot and dry climate zones by adding moisture and airflow to dry air (Figure 38.17). The system works by pumping water into absorptive pads that are being wetted with a pump, and blowing air across the pads with a fan. The system can lower the temperature in a space by 6.5C (20F) as the water

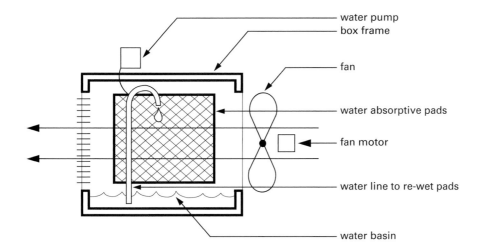

water pump
box frame
fan
water absorptive pads
fan motor
water line to re-wet pads
water basin

38.17
Evaporative cooler.

evaporates from the pads, and they use one quarter of the energy of refrigerated systems.

CONCLUSION

Passive ventilation acts as a logical, time-tested system of dealing with human comfort that has fallen out of favor for 50 of the last 10,000 or so years of making buildings. We happen to be arriving at the end of that period, with rising concerns over energy costs and the need to reduce the impact of building energy consumption, but there is still some lack of knowledge about how to make passive systems work effectively. There is also some resistance to the use of passive systems—this is due to the unpredictability of weather factors such as wind speed and air temperature. A mechanical system is known to be reliable in cooling a room, and trying a different approach that may cause an owner discomfort is difficult to propose. Architects are the primary decision makers that push forward the types of mechanical systems our designs will incorporate. There is considerable interest in sensibly considering passive building systems, and we're expected to be conversant with the design and implementation of these sustainable practices. This requires understanding of the capabilities of passive environmental control systems and educating our clients about the reliability and long-term benefits of lower impact approaches to building.

FREQUENTLY ASKED QUESTIONS

How do you determine how much wind a site will get and where it will come from?
The NOAA (National Oceanographic and Atmospheric Administration) in the U.S. and the Met Office in the U.K. provide national weather forecasting and meteorological history for most regions. This information includes prevailing wind speed and direction by month; however, it is typically taken from airports or other open areas. Local sites often have conditions that modify wind direc-

tion, such as hills, trees, buildings, etc. that must be taken into account. These conditions can speed or slow wind, along with changing the prevailing direction. Since it is normally impossible to survey a site for a year-long period to test these conditions there is a certain amount of research and weather modeling involved in determining wind speed and direction. Many environmental software tools now allow for proposals to be tested using historical weather data and airflow calculations.

Where should windows be placed to maximize cooling effects?
This is a complex problem that involves both local conditions and the form of the building; however, there are some fundamental rules. First you must know where the wind is coming from during the warm months of the year. Then you need to consider where inhabitants are in the spaces, so that the air can be moved across them and not just into the building. Lastly it is typically best to take cool air in low and exhaust it high, so warm air that is rising in a space will be moved out of the space. Consider the shape of the interior space and study the airflow diagrams to maximize air speed, mix, and location.

GLOSSARY

Air change: Indicates the number of times all of the air in a space has been renewed. It is typically measured by the number of changes per hour.

Air jet: An accelerated flow of wind traveling a set path through a space.

Bernoulli Principle: States that an increase in a fluid medium's speed (such as air) decreases its pressure.

Cross ventilation: Air moving into and through a space, rather than at the corners or edges. This is frequently enhanced by having narrower spaces with windows on opposite sides.

Leeward side: The back or opposite side of a building from the direction of the prevailing wind at that time.

Stack effect: Creates airflow by using the thermal principles of airflow. The density of air lessens as it warms, causing it to rise. Cooler air is drawn into the slight vacuum caused by the air displacement and tends to be drawn up after the warm air.

Wind catchers: Allow buildings in dense areas or where low winds are unavailable to draw wind down from higher areas. This is usually accomplished through a tower that directs wind down into the space.

Wind eddy: The tendency of a fluid medium such as wind to slow and swirl off of the main flow at the edges.

Windward side: The front or exposed side of a building facing the direction of the prevailing wind at that time.

FURTHER READING

Brown, G. Z. and DeKay, M. (2001). *Sun, Wind & Light: Architectural Design Strategies*, 2nd edition. New York: John Wiley and Sons.

Kwok, A. and Grondzik, W. (2011) *The Green Studio Handbook*, 2nd edition. Oxford: Elsevier.

39

ENVIRONMENTAL CONTROL: ACTIVE VENTILATION

HVAC systems	All-air systems
	All-water systems
	Direct expansion systems (refrigerant systems)
Mechanical air flow in buildings	Air distribution systems
Refrigeration and heat transfer	High vs. low supply and return
	Throw, spread and fall
	Ductwork and diffusers
	The refrigeration cycle
	Cooling
	Heat pump
	Chiller and cooling tower

INTRODUCTION

Active ventilation refers to HVAC (Heating, Ventilation, and Air Conditioning) systems that use energy to function. Most buildings use a combination of active and passive systems in practice. While passive systems can have a major comfort and cost impact on the interior environment, active systems are usually used to effectively maintain comfort beyond the capacity of the passive strategies. This, however, is the appropriate order to think about the problem of comfort—passive first with support from active, not the other way around. We're also moving closer to Net-Zero building systems that can allow the energy produced by the building to equal that used.

The purpose of HVAC systems is to adjust air temperature, radiant temperatures, relative humidity, and air motion to put human inhabitants into the "comfort zone". This can be done in numerous ways and must take into account several factors during system selection:

Initial cost, performance and long term expense of the system
Fuel and power sources required to run the system
Size and location of the equipment
Heating or cooling medium used

Distribution and return systems—particularly the size
Outlet size, type and locations
Humidity, fresh air, and filtering
Noise and vibration control

Keep in mind that by the time you're selecting mechanical systems you may already be past the point of making the major siting and formal decisions that will determine how efficient or inefficient your building will be.

HVAC SYSTEMS

There are three basic types of HVAC systems: all-air, all-water, and direct expansion or refrigerant systems. All systems follow the same issues listed above in system selection, but handle them in different ways.

All-air systems have the heating or refrigerating units control the quality of the air, from heat to cold and humidity to filtering. This air is then delivered through ducts to the final room destination. Common types are single and double duct systems.

Single duct systems force either warm or cold air at a constant temperature through low velocity ducts to the spaces. Variable airflow systems use dampers at the outlets to control airflow based on the needs of the space. Reheat systems can also heat air right at the point of delivery to avoid the loss of heat in the ducts.

Double duct systems deliver both warm and cold air simultaneously to mixing units that create the appropriate temperature to deliver to the space. This mixing takes place with dampers controlled by a thermostat. This is usually a high velocity system to reduce duct sizes. Mixing units or VAV (variable air volume) boxes may serve different individual spaces or zones of a building (Figure 39.1).

All-water systems deliver hot or chilled water to spaces, which runs in smaller piping than air ducts. This water runs into fan coil units that blow air over the hot or cold coils of fluid to heat or cool the space. Radiators are also used without the fans to heat spaces. Ventilation or air changes must be supplied separately from the system to get fresh air into the spaces.

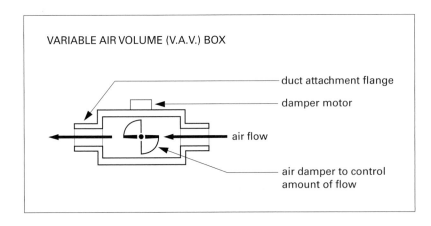

39.1
Variable air volume (VAV) box.

Two pipe systems circulate either hot or cold water into, then out, of the space.

Four pipe systems circulate both hot and cold water simultaneously in separate circuits to provide necessary heating and cooling to different parts of a building.

Direct expansion systems (refrigerant systems) are self-contained units used in rooftop or through wall applications. These systems can eliminate ductwork and can serve the individual needs of spaces without providing unnecessary capacity—in other words, you only run what you need. Small sections of ductwork can also be used to distribute air from a centrally located unit. Cooling is provided by air-cooled condensers or chiller units which require an indoor to outdoor loop. Heating is accomplished by gas or oil furnaces, electric heaters, or heat pumps.

A *heat pump* is an electrically powered heating and cooling unit. It uses an evaporative cooling cycle to absorb and transfer energy from a heat source to a heat sink. Heat pumps use a refrigerant and compression cycle to move thermal energy in the opposite direction of the natural flow. Heat flows from warm to cold according to the Second Law of Thermodynamics; a heat pump can reverse this flow (this will be covered in more detail below). Air source heat pumps (the most conventional type) work better in hot environments than cold because the increased temperature differential in winter (say from 0C to 22C) works against the efficiency of the heat transfer process. In these cases it's usually best to use ground source heat pumps or switch to gas or electric heat.

AIR FLOW IN BUILDINGS

Air distribution systems can be centralized or de-centralized which affects the method of distribution. De-centralized units often require minimal distribution runs or ductwork because they can blow air directly into the space. Centralized systems require a more extensive distribution system, which means equipment is all in one place but there are more duct runs (Figure 39.2).

Air duct systems require more space than water systems and must be thought of early in the design process in order to work with structural systems, lights, wall layouts, and other services. These various systems can take large amounts of space above a ceiling and need to be considered in terms of whether they go through or under the beams or joists—this mechanical system decision can determine whether you would use beams or joists in a structural system (Figure 39.3).

Ductwork distribution typically runs vertically in a chase to feed a floor and horizontally in the floor or ceiling space to feed areas within each floor. This system can be reversed with main feeds horizontally and individual feeds vertically, but it is less common as multiple vertical chases are required in the right locations to distribute air (Figure 39.4).

Horizontal distribution patterns are typically defined as radial, perimeter or lateral.

Radial patterns use minimal duct runs but rely on unobstructed space.

Perimeter loop systems work well to resist exterior heat/cold loads and are often fed from the floor.

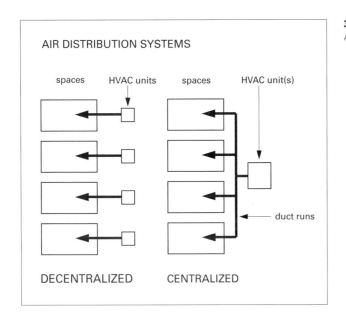

39.2
Air distribution systems.

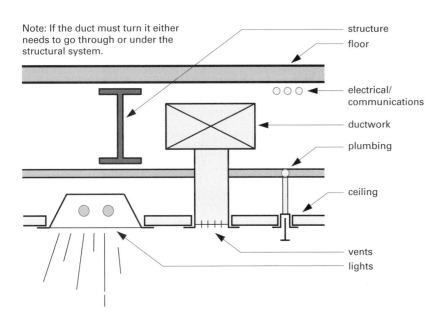

39.3
Ceiling space requirements.

Lateral systems use the most duct run, but accommodate flexible distribution patterns, structural obstructions and segmented spaces on a floor (Figure 39.5).

High v. low supply and return affects the efficiency of the system at different times of the year (Figure 39.6). The basic rule of thumb in cold climates is to supply low and return high; this puts warmth into the space at the bottom and as it naturally rises it returns into the system. The problem with this arrangement in warm weather is that you are trying to supply cold air low and it wants to stay low rather than mix into the space—making the system inefficient during this time of the year. The opposite is true in warm climates when supply is typically high to allow cool air to fall into the

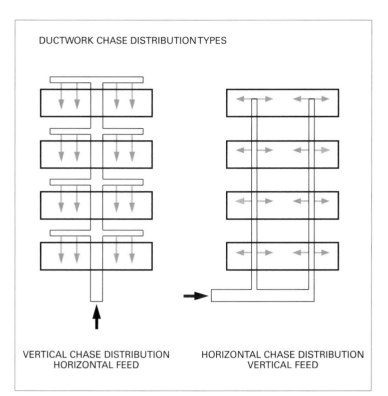

DUCTWORK CHASE DISTRIBUTION TYPES

VERTICAL CHASE DISTRIBUTION
HORIZONTAL FEED

HORIZONTAL CHASE DISTRIBUTION
VERTICAL FEED

39.4
Ductwork chase distribution types.

39.5
Horizontal ductwork patterns.

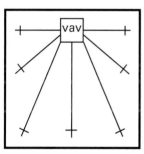

RADIAL DISTRIBUTION

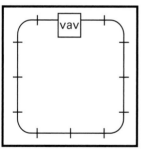

PERIMETER DISTRIBUTION

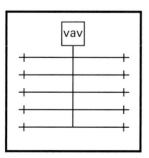

LATERAL DISTRIBUTION

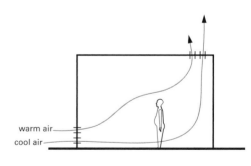

SUPPLY LOW/RETURN HIGH
Works well for heat, which naturally rises
Cooling is less efficient

warm air
cool air

warm air
cool air

SUPPLY LOW/RETURN HIGH
Works well for cooling, which naturally falls
Heating is less efficient

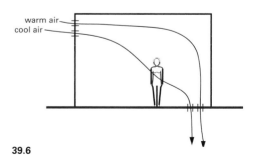

39.6
High vs. low supply and return.

space. In cool weather the high supply keeps the warm air at the ceiling. The typical way to deal with these problems is to increase the velocity of the air during the less effective cycle to blow past the natural tendency of the air temperature rise and fall, an inefficient means of solving this issue. This is certainly an area where you should be trying to use the most effective passive systems and use the mechanical systems to deal with conditions that the passive systems don't handle so well. Also, creating hybrid systems such as radiant heat at the base of cold window exterior surfaces with air systems elsewhere, and the use of ceiling fans, can improve performance and efficiency.

Throw, spread and fall are the actions of the air once it enters the space. Outlets should be located to distribute air comfortably, without drafts, and without stratification. Throw distance and spread must be considered along with avoiding obstructions to airflow. The standard throw of air into a room should be three-quarters of the total depth. At the three-quarter point the air should be at head height or approximately 1.8m (6') above the floor. Air is typically blown toward the exterior wall where the cooled or heated air can reduce the radiant temperature of the surface. Registers should be placed to supply air evenly into a space; therefore they are located away from sidewalls and far enough apart to mix with minimal overlap (Figure 39.7).

Registers and diffusers are arranged to create the desired effects of airflow. Diffusers typically supply air at the ceiling and have curved fins to run air away from directly blowing down on occupants. Registers are air supply grilles usually with operable damper fins to control air direction. Registers are normally wall or floor mounted (Figure 39.8). Return grilles are most often open grates or straight fins that simply pull air back into the system. The returns are placed away from the supply so as to not short-circuit the airflow through the space.

A common problem with ceiling and high wall diffusers are the dirt marks or smudging that occurs when small particles of dust are repeatedly blown across a surface. This can be prevented by not placing wall diffusers too close to ceilings and using materials adjacent to vents that will not collect or trap dust particles.

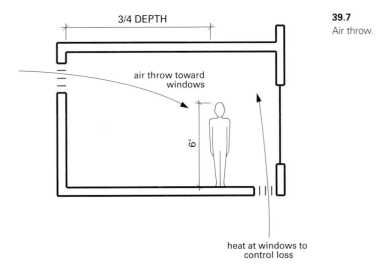

39.7
Air throw.

3/4 DEPTH

air throw toward
windows

6'

heat at windows to
control loss

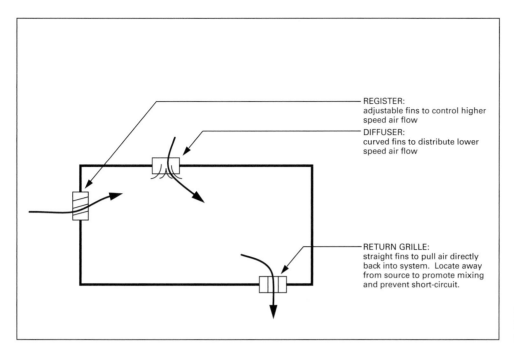

REGISTER:
adjustable fins to control higher speed air flow

DIFFUSER:
curved fins to distribute lower speed air flow

RETURN GRILLE:
straight fins to pull air directly back into system. Locate away from source to promote mixing and prevent short-circuit.

39.8
Registers, diffusers, and return grilles.

REFRIGERATION AND HEAT TRANSFER

The refrigeration cycle is a process that moves heat from one place to another. Kitchen refrigerators move heat from the inside cold storage area to the surrounding room. Air conditioners move heat from the interior rooms to the outdoors. As part of the cycle, heat is required to change the state of liquid to steam; this is referred to as latent heat. Latent heat is the key to moving large quantities of heat with small amounts of refrigerant. To move heat from an area of low temperature to an area of high temperature (for instance, 24C (75F) inside to 35C (95F) outside), refrigeration equipment needs to change the boiling temperature of the refrigerant. This is accomplished by changing the pressure of the refrigerant (which is why refrigerators go bad because the compressor fails).

During the *cooling* cycle an evaporator coil absorbs heat from its surroundings, as this occurs the refrigerant within the coils heats and changes state from liquid to steam. This refrigerant steam vapor is drawn into a compressor where pressure is increased, raising the temperature of the gas from cool to hot. This now very hot refrigerant vapor is discharged into a condenser coil, where it is cooled by blowing air across the coils, giving up the latent heat absorbed in the evaporator and returning it to a liquid state. Finally, the liquid refrigerant circulates through an expansion valve, where pressure is released which makes the warm refrigerant cold. Air is blown across these cold coils, air-conditioning the inside of the space, and changing the cold liquid refrigerant to a cool gas. The cycle is then repeated (Figure 39.9).

A *reversing heat pump* switches the cooling cycle to extract heat from a low temperature source, such as outside air, to heat a building. The basic equipment is unchanged, with the exception of a four-way reversing valve and controls that permit the condenser and evaporator to exchange functions so they can work in both heating and cooling modes.

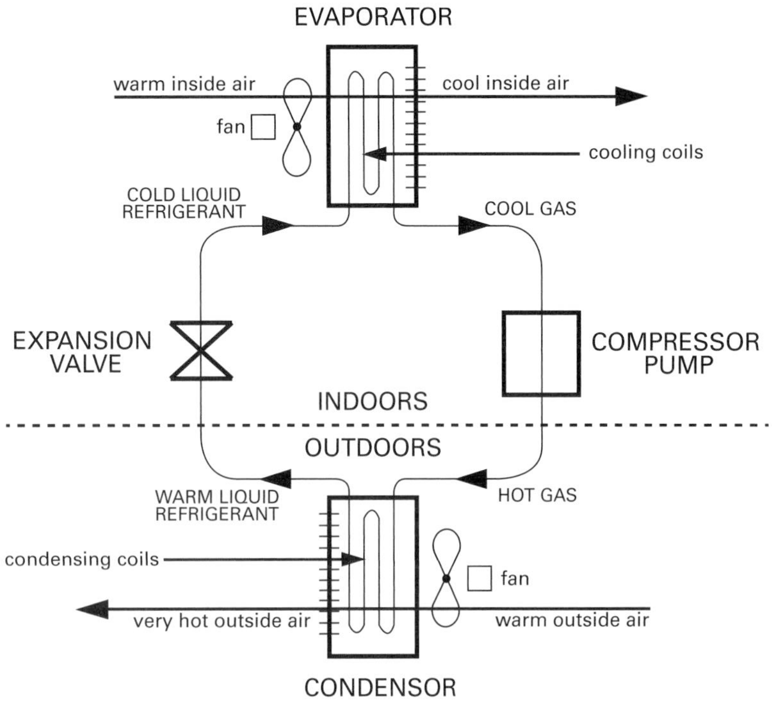

Chiller and cooling towers. In large buildings (or on campuses) it is impractical to move heat with air only because ducts would become too large. Therefore a chiller is added to the evaporator, and chilled water is circulated to air handling units throughout the building, or multiple buildings. Cooling towers increase efficiency by keeping the temperature of the outdoor exchange lower, by using at huge scale the evaporation of water to lower the exterior temperature that the refrigerant coil goes through (say 29C (85F) water rather than 35C (95F) air) (Figure 39.10).

A ground source heat pump works in a similar way by using the moderated temperature of the earth or a large body of water to run the refrigerant coils through in their "outside" mode. These require large coil layout areas or deep wells to get enough effective thermal transfer but can increase the efficiency of a system significantly.

CONCLUSION

Mechanical ventilation systems are unavoidable in most buildings, but much can be done to lessen their impact and expense. Don't automatically assume that buildings will be completely active; use the strategies of siting and form to improve performance long before you're selecting what system to use. Employ mechanical consultants who are skilled in the use of passive and active systems early in the design process to maximize the effects of passive and active strategies. Consider the specific conditions of the activities and locations of people in a building to provide comfort where it's most needed, rather than

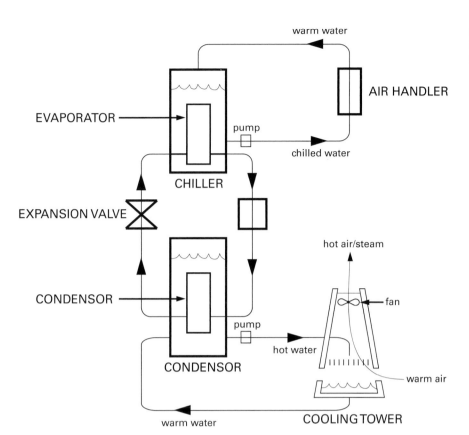

indiscriminately spreading the same HVAC conditions everywhere or, worse, where it's not needed at all. Finally, understand the strategies to maximize the performance of environmental control systems. Most buildings could be run with half the energy they currently consume if they had been designed with efficiency and energy conservation in mind (a common goal of LEED certification). This may cost more initially to construct, but the long term expense and impact on the environment can be vastly improved.

FREQUENTLY ASKED QUESTIONS

How do you determine the air distribution pattern in a building?
Air distribution tends to follow two sets of decisions: whether to supply high or low and what pattern to run the ductwork. Ideally you supply high and return low when the primary load on a building is cooling and the reverse when the primary load is heating. This is designed to work with the natural tendency of warm air to rise and cool air to fall. Sometimes there is no option, because the building configuration will only allow supply ducts to be run at the ceiling or floor. Determining how you want air distribution to work can influence early design decisions because you want to control where the supply ductwork goes. Duct patterns matter most when they are exposed. Sometimes the pattern you desire to see aesthetically will not be the best layout for the cost or to maximize efficiency of the system. When ducts are concealed, you typically run them in the shortest pattern to minimize thermal loss, reduce material cost, keep fan

velocities lower, and get supply to the exterior edges of a space where the heat gain/loss is the greatest.

How do you tell whether a vent is for supply or return in an existing space?
The obvious answer is to first check to see if air is blowing out or sucking into a vent if it is within reach. Often they are not easily accessible or the system is not running, but you can also usually tell just by looking at them. Supply vents tend to have baffles or fins that control the direction of airflow, while return vents are normally grilles that simply collect air at lower velocities. Any curved or adjustable louver will be for supply whether it is on the floor, wall, or ceiling. Long linear vents are also normally for supply, and any vent at the floor or ceiling next to a window opening is typically for supply also. Large square or rectangular grilles with egg crate fin patterns are for return, as they are designed to pull air in from all directions and generally limit debris being sucked into the system, along with not creating unnecessary resistance to the return air.

GLOSSARY

All-air systems: The heating or refrigerating units control the quality of the air, from heat to cold and humidity to filtering.

All-water systems: Deliver hot or chilled water to spaces, which runs in smaller piping than air ducts. Water is then run to radiators or fan coil units to distribute heating and cooling.

Diffuser: A louvered vent that distributes air into a space from the mechanical system. They typically supply air at the ceiling and have curved fins to run air away from the source.

Direct expansion systems (refrigerant systems): Self-contained units used in rooftop or through wall applications.

Heat pump: An electrically powered heating and cooling unit. It uses an evaporative cooling cycle to absorb and transfer indoor heat to the outdoors for cooling.

HVAC: Heating, Ventilation, and Air Conditioning. An active system of climate control.

Plenum: In construction this is a space that is used for air transfer in lieu of a duct. It typically occurs above the suspended ceiling or in a space below the floor.

Registers: Air supply vents with operable damper fins to control air direction.

Throw: The distance air is "thrown" into a room from a diffuser.

FURTHER READING

Bassler, B. ed. (2000). *Architectural Graphic Standards*, 10th edition. New York: Wiley; Chapter 15, Mechanical.

Kwok, A. and Grondzik, W. (2011). *The Green Studio Handbook*, 2nd edition. Oxford: Elsevier.

Neufert, E. and Neufert, P. (2000). *Architects Data*, 3rd edition. London: Blackwell Science; pp. 95–109.

40

ENVIRONMENTAL CONTROL: ILLUMINATION

Perception of light	Anatomy
	Color
	Contrast
History	The incandescent bulb
	Fluorescent bulb development
	High-performance lamps
Fixtures/lamps	Lamp sources
	Properties
	Fixture types
	Light Control

INTRODUCTION

Illumination, either natural or artificial, creates the conditions that allow us to use our sight to perceive and understand space. Traditionally, buildings were designed with minimal artificial light in mind (such as lanterns or fires) and needed to utilize daylight as the primary source of illumination. Since the invention of artificial lighting we have extended the ability of a building to function without sunlight but have often neglected providing adequate provisions for daylighting. This significantly impacts issues of health and well-being, along with energy consumption.

We covered the topic of daylighting during Solar Geometry (Chapter 4), and now concern ourselves with artificial lighting. As noted in the daylighting section, up to 50 percent of a building's energy consumption comes from artificial lighting—so this area offers some of the most significant impact on energy efficiency. Also critical is how lighting affects the way a structure is perceived. This is a concern that is often not fully considered during design, particularly in school, and is too often a last minute concern. It's troubling when the design consideration that affects the primary way an inhabitant perceives a space and impacts most of the energy consumption is frequently poorly executed. Why would that be the case? The answer is that it can be ignored in favor of the myriad of other concerns that are more tangible, such as bricks and mortar. This

40.1
Castelvecchio Museum, 1954–1967, Verona, Italy, Carlo Scarpa.

is certainly one of the complex issues that defines sophisticated practitioners (Figure 40.1).

PERCEPTION OF LIGHT

Light passes through the lens of the eye and focuses onto the retina at the back of the sphere. The retina is comprised of two types of light sensitive receptors, rods and cones, which transmit information for the brain to interpret. The rods gather around the edges of the retina and function to capture low light levels and movement, they do not gather information on color. The cones are closer to the center of the retina and function at higher light levels to perceive color

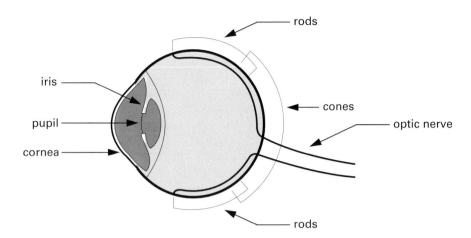

40.2
Eye diagram.

and detail (Figure 40.2). The level of light and contrast in an environment control the way the eye perceives an image. Too much contrast and the eye cannot focus on either the dark or light objects; too little contrast and objects cannot be discerned from one another. The iris of the eye adjusts to varying light levels rather quickly, but when presented with extremes will try to balance between the two—making both light and dark objects difficult to see.

When moving from very light to very dark spaces the eye also needs to change from one type of sight system to another. Cones work on the photopic or higher light level system, while rods work on the scotopic or lower light level range. Quick shifts between the two create problems because it can take as much as 40 minutes for the rods to fully adjust to low light levels.

Human eyes evolved in sunlight and therefore perceive that quality of light as "normal." Artificial lights vary in color temperature from sunlight and therefore affect the way color is seen. The color of the light that is reflected by an object establishes what color we see. When the light source varies in color (or wavelengths of color) from sunlight we see the same object differently because of the color of the light that is reflected. Visible light is actually in a small range of the electromagnetic spectrum and the wavelength of light rays determines the color perception of objects (Figure 40.3). Sunlight waves in the visible range run from violet to red as described by Newton and commonly portrayed by a rainbow as ROYGBIV (red, orange, yellow, green, blue, indigo, and violet)—all colors in equal proportion from the sun are seen as "white" light. Firelight is seen as more red because it is deficient in shorter wavelengths, and this is probably the reason we like incandescent bulbs better than fluorescent, because it is similar to fire or lamplight in color rendition.

HISTORY

Thomas Edison is frequently and incorrectly credited with the invention of the electric light in 1879, however it was commonly known that running electric current through a filament would produce light, and many previous inventors had produced lightbulbs. The problem was the filament would oxidize and burn out quickly, making the application not commercially viable. Edison perfected the use of carbon as a filament, which could burn up to 1200 hours. He also

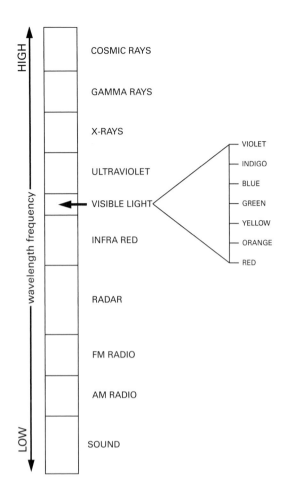

40.3
Electromagnetic spectrum.

created a vacuum in the bulb to resist oxidizing the filament. In 1913 Irving Langmuir used low-pressure gas instead of a vacuum to double the visible light in a bulb (Figure 40.4). These bulbs have remained virtually unchanged and last over 1000 hours, but are very inefficient with only 5 percent of the energy going to light and 95 percent to heat. By 1900 electric lights were common in American and British households. Due to the inefficiency of incandescent bulbs they are being phased out for use in general lighting in many parts of the world.

Fluorescent light experiments had occurred in the mid-1800s, but the first commercially viable lamps were not developed until 1934 by Arthur Compton. Fluorescent lamps work by passing an electric current through a gas; in this case electrons hit atoms of mercury vapor in the tube causing them to emit ultraviolet light (Figure 40.5). These invisible rays hit a phosphor coating on the inside of the tube, causing the atoms in the phosphor to emit white light. The conversion of light from ultra-violet to visible white is known as fluorescence. Fluorescent light is more efficient than incandescent (four to six times better) and does not produce as much heat, but the mercury vapor is considered a toxic material. Currently there is a common fee per bulb to dispose of fluorescent bulbs because of the mercury content. The light from fluorescent bulbs also tends to be more blue/green and to create odd color renditions, making people and food appear less appealing. Improvements have been made in the color rendition, but they are not perfect yet and have a higher initial cost than

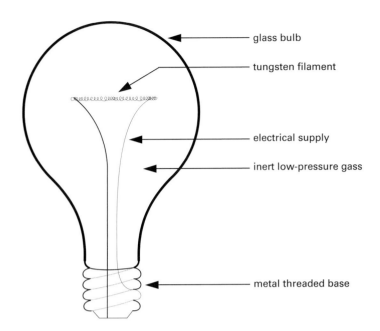

glass bulb

tungsten filament

electrical supply

inert low-pressure gass

metal threaded base

40.4
Typical tungsten lamp anatomy.

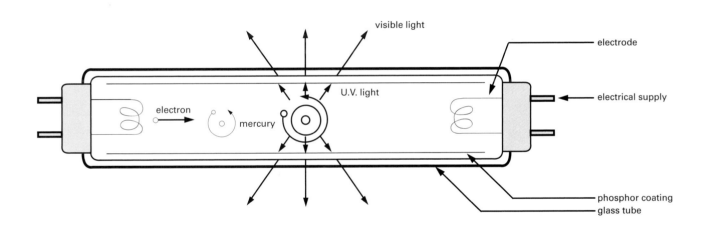

visible light

electrode

U.V. light

electrical supply

electron

mercury

phosphor coating

glass tube

traditional incandescent bulbs. Finally, the alternating current running through the gas can give a perceptible flicker to the lights, which can be made more troubling by an alternating vibration in older monitor screens—at times causing a type of motion sickness. This can be mitigated by using multiple light sources, including non-fluorescent lights, and using indirect lights to cover individuals in a space.

Other types of filament lights have been developed to improve the efficiency, size, and light output of lamps. Most innovations consist of the type and pressure of gas used in the lamp. Early examples of these were the tungsten halogen lamps developed for car headlights, which burn brighter due to different gases and pressure being used in the lamp. Metal halide, mercury vapor, and high-pressure sodium lamps are widely used commercially and can extend the life of filament bulbs considerably, but they have various color rendition qualities (and difficulties).

40.5
Typical fluorescent lamp anatomy.

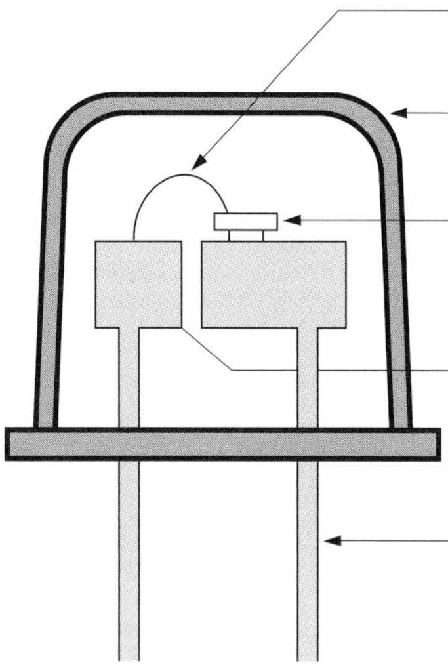

GOLD WIRE

EPOXY LENS

LED CHIP
SEMI CONDUCTOR DIODE

ANODE POST

LEAD FRAME

40.6
LED (light emitting diode) diagram.

LED (light emitting diode) lamps have recently become more common in the lighting industry (Figure 40.6). Practical LEDs of visible spectrum light were first developed by Nick Holonyak Jr. at the University of Illinois in 1962. They have taken over the task of most signage indicator illumination and are becoming more common in general lighting applications. A light emitting diode is a semiconductor diode that converts electric energy into electromagnetic radiation at visible wavelengths of light. They currently last twice as long as the best fluorescent bulbs (about ten years of normal use) and over ten times longer than the best incandescent lamps. The efficiency is better than that of incandescent lights, and about equivalent in lumens per watt to fluorescent bulbs. Efficiency is a problem constantly being worked on, and while the industry feels the compact fluorescent bulb is as efficient as it will probably get, the LED will probably become much brighter and more efficient in time—surpassing fluorescent lights in short order. They can be made in many colors, and the small scale and plastic lenses make then much more durable than other light sources using glass bulb or tubes.

FIXTURES/LAMPS

When choosing lighting there are a number of factors to be considered. Some primary issues are: the task being performed, the quality or mood of the space desired, where the focus is in a space, the efficiency of the solution, and what creates security.

The types of lighting can be categorized into six basic configurations (Figure 40.7):

1	Downlight	Virtually all down light
2	Partial downlight	Mostly downlight with some up or bounced light
3	Diffuse	Equal light distribution in all directions
4	Up/downlight	Roughly equal distribution both up and down
5	Partial uplight	Mostly up light with some downlight
6	Uplight	Virtually all up light

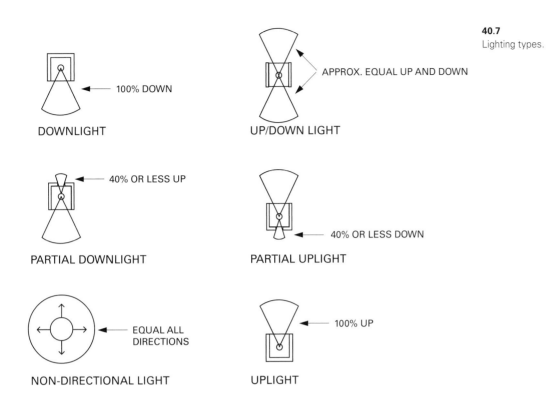

40.7
Lighting types.

Each lighting type has its benefits and liabilities; most lighting solutions use a combination of these along with natural light. A certain desired amount of uniformity is typically sought which tends to overlap lighting sources. This is in part because the intensity of light falls away in direct proportion to the distance from the source. Light directly under a source is brightest and dims quickly; overlapping keeps the light level more even and prevents too much contrast from developing (Figure 40.8). The idea is to get the right amount of light where you want it and not waste energy over-lighting areas that don't require it. In the 1970s many offices had light levels at consistently high levels of 100 footcandles or more. Studies had shown that this improved the ability to accomplish tasks, and it allowed flexible movement of furniture, but in practice the intensity fostered fatigue and became an immense energy consumer. Understanding the correct amount of light needed for the task and focusing that light where needed is more efficient and produces more comfortable environments. Remember that some variation is also helpful for productivity and stress relief.

Another common issue to deal with when selecting lights is glare. Glare is primarily a problem of excessive contrast that creates difficulty or discomfort focusing on an object or task. There are two main types of glare, direct and reflected (or veiling). Direct glare comes from a light source in the field of vision. This can be either from sightline directly to a lamp or bright window. Shielding or diffusing the light source typically prevents direct glare. The methods that limit glare also cut down on the amount of light given off and negatively impact efficiency, so a balance between putting enough light where desired while not directly viewing the source must be achieved (Figure 40.9).

Reflected or *veiling glare* is primarily a problem with computer screens or television monitors, due to the fact that they can have a glossy surface. Even

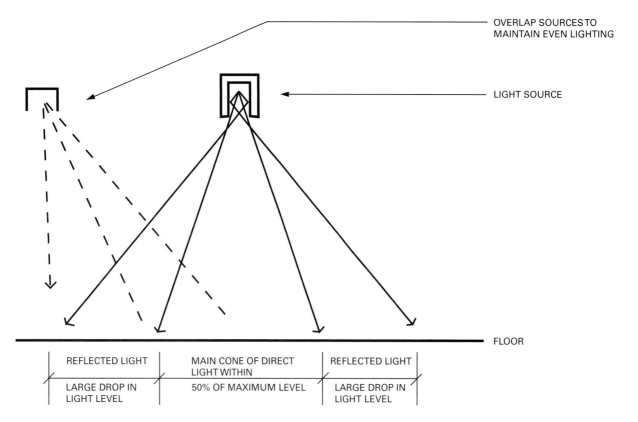

OVERLAP SOURCES TO MAINTAIN EVEN LIGHTING

LIGHT SOURCE

FLOOR

REFLECTED LIGHT	MAIN CONE OF DIRECT LIGHT WITHIN	REFLECTED LIGHT
LARGE DROP IN LIGHT LEVEL	50% OF MAXIMUM LEVEL	LARGE DROP IN LIGHT LEVEL

40.8
Lighting levels and overlap.

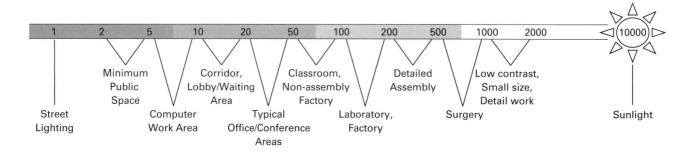

40.9
Typical footcandles for different activities.

matte finish flat or laptop screens have some difficulty with veiling glare, but to a lesser degree than older, glass curved screens. Reflected glare can be difficult to predict because computer or television locations are not always known in advance and can change; additionally the reflection that comes from a source behind the viewer can be a problem (Figure 40.10). Locating light sources so that the cutoff angle is greater than 45 degrees downward prevents most veiling glare from direct fixtures, while uplighting has also been used effectively to eliminate most artificially produced glare problems. The other difficulty comes from bright windows, which are desirable sources of natural light but can produce high levels of glare. Light shelves and louvers limit much of the direct sunlight into a space, but will not prevent a bright reflective light source from showing up on a computer screen. Proper orientation of the occu-

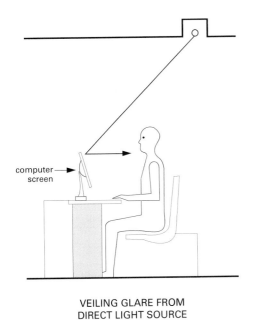

VEILING GLARE FROM
DIRECT LIGHT SOURCE

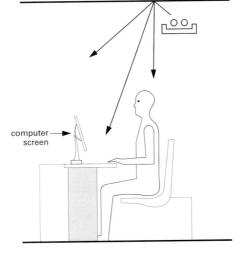

VEILING GLARE AVOIDED THROUGH
USE OF INDIRECT LIGHTING

40.10
Veiling glare.

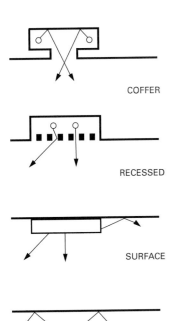

COFFER

RECESSED

SURFACE

SUSPENDED

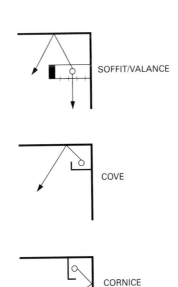

SOFFIT/VALANCE

COVE

CORNICE

40.11
Light locations.

pants relative to windows is necessary in order to utilize natural lighting. Some screening at the work surface can mitigate problems at the user instead of the source, but, as always, properly educating clients and managing expectations is critical when using large amounts of natural light in a work environment.

Light location can be recessed in the ceiling, flush, surface mounted, or suspended, along with combinations of systems. Edge or wall conditions can be handled with soffit, cove, cornice or valance lighting (Figure 40.11). Each of these locations affects the way the light is perceived and the quality of the space in a room. Consider multiple options beyond simply mounting standard grids of lights in the ceiling.

Switching lamps on and off can be done in a variety of ways. The simple one-way wall switch is the most common—being a direct connection between a toggle style switch and the fixtures connected to it. Three-way switches allow for a light source to be controlled from two locations, frequently found in residential applications at the top and bottom of stairs. In commercial applications, lights are often controlled from a central bank of switches or electrical box, preventing undesirable personal freedoms of the occupants. Switches can also be keyed for the operation of facilities personnel only. Digital switches and dimmers, along with computer-controlled timing systems, photocell zoning and motion sensors are becoming standard in commercial and institutional building applications.

CONCLUSION

Lighting considerations often have as much impact on the quality of space as form or assembly, yet are too frequently overlooked. Lighting also has one of the greatest impacts on building energy efficiency and is a primary concern of passive design strategies. Much of the information on lighting principles can be found in written or online sources, but nothing substitutes for experiential learning in this area. Pay specific attention to the quality of light in spaces you like and dislike and begin building a set of criteria for what makes light quality good or bad. These lessons will be used often and sometimes intuitively when designing projects. Use multiple types of lights for different purposes, provide adjustability, and get the light to where it's needed for activities, rather than generally illuminating spaces that don't need light everywhere.

FREQUENTLY ASKED QUESTIONS

How do I determine how much light is needed in the various parts of a building?
There are numerous references, such as *Architect's Data* and *Graphic Standards*, which have charts of typical footcandles for various activities. These give a starting point for where to focus the light for a specified activity; however, there are other factors that need to be weighed. One is the amount of natural light which is available during the times the building will be used; often the specified level may be attainable with minimal additional illumination. It's also important to understand the specific task being undertaken in the space; categories such as "office" do not make clear what is being done and can encourage general lighting levels which are too high everywhere. A rule of thumb is to keep general lighting lower to conserve energy and to light specific task areas more heavily, but also flexibly to allow for furniture movement. Also provide enough separate circuits and adjustability to allow lights to be lowered or turned off when an area is not in use.

GLOSSARY

Brightness: The density of light being reflected, transmitted, or emitted from a surface. It is measured in Footlamberts—which is footcandles × reflectance factor. This is a more comprehensive way of judging the intensity of the light, but is less frequently used due to the difficulty of measuring the reflectance factor. Footcandles can be measured more directly and objectively, if less accurately for perception.

Candela: A measure of a light source's intensity; often referred to as candlepower, it is originally based on the light of a wax candle.

Color temperature: Lamps are measured by color temperature, which is a rating of the frequency of light wavelengths. Different wavelengths reflect colors differently off of surfaces, so the color temperature of light affects the way your eye perceives colors in a space.

Footcandle: A unit of measure of the intensity of light falling on a surface, equal to one lumen per square foot. It was originally based on the intensity of a candle one foot from a surface. The metric version is called a Lux, which equals lumens per square meter. This is the most common measurement we use to determine how bright a space is. This can be an inexact science due to issues such as contrast, reflectivity of surfaces, whether you can see the light source, etc.

Glare: Primarily a problem of excessive contrast that creates difficulty or discomfort focusing on an object or task. Veiling glare refers to the reflected glare that can occur on a computer screen from light sources behind the user.

Lamp: The term used to indicate the bulb that actually emits the illumination. Therefore if you specify a "light" only, a fixture will arrive without the bulb.

LED: A light emitting diode is a semiconductor diode that converts electric energy into electromagnetic radiation at visible wavelengths of light.

Light: The term generally used for the fixture that houses the lamp (or bulb) that produces the actual illumination.

Lumen: A measure of luminous flux—or the rate of flow of light per unit of time. Light efficiency is measured in lumens per watt, a ratio of light output relative to energy input. For example, a 60 watt incandescent lamp produces 900 lumens, 900 lumens/60 watts = 15 lumens/watt. A 40 watt fluorescent lamp produces 3000 lumens, 3000 lumens/40 watts = 5 lumens/watt, much more efficient than the incandescent.

FURTHER READING

Ramsey, C. G. and Sleeper, H. R. (2000). *Architectural Graphic Standards*, 10th edition. New York: John Wiley & Sons; pp. 47–62.

Neufert, E. and Neufert, P. (2000). *Architects Data*, 3rd edition. London: Blackwell Science; pp. 24–26, 141–150.

41

PLUMBING

History		
Supply	Principles	
	Fixtures	
Waste	Drainage	
Design Standards	Fixture heights	
	Clearance	

INTRODUCTION AND HISTORY

While it is less glamorous than many other building systems, plumbing is a key factor in the design of any building of reasonable size, and the proper provision of fresh, clean water and safe disposal channels is among the most significant health and safety issues facing designers.

Anyone who has had their water service interrupted recognizes instantly the importance of fresh water for drinking and cleaning, and perhaps more importantly the vital need to quickly and efficiently dispose of human waste. Yet until the 1860s, deaths from diseases caused by poor sanitation from typhus and cholera were epidemic.

Sanitation is one of the few areas in which ancient builders actually exceeded the abilities of subsequent centuries, and the reform movements that arose in the late nineteenth century for the most part only demanded a return to standards of cleanliness and sanitation enjoyed by the Romans. Sewage disposal adopted the time-honored technique of throwing a chamber pot's contents into streets that were sloped toward a central channel, regularly flushed by water and engineered to flow into underground sewer lines. Fresh water from aqueducts was available throughout most large Roman cities, and the separation of spring-sourced drinking water from the effluent cast into rivers worked reasonably well.

However the aqueducts built by the Romans were still in use throughout the Middle Ages, while the sewers crumbled. The Middle Ages—and subsequent centuries—were horrifically unclean by modern standards, with human and animal waste piled in streets and only slowly oozing toward streams and rivers.

Roman principles of discharge and flow were largely forgotten, and formal disposal practices ranged from communal cesspits to residential gardens. In cities, the only formal requirements for sanitation were that citizens were usually required to warn passers-by before dumping chamber pots from upper stories.

Continual epidemics of waterborne diseases from cross-contamination of drinking water with human waste were exacerbated by the intense urban migrations of the Industrial Revolution. Chicago, built in a brackish swamp around a stagnant river, experienced devastating cholera epidemics, including one in 1854 that killed 6 percent of the city's population in a matter of days. Reform movements in the middle of the nineteenth century found deplorable conditions in working class housing, with underground cesspits commonly leaching into nearby wells, and similarly grave problems in cities such as London and New York. While common scientific opinion at the time focused on "miasmas," or foul air, as the cause of disease, there was a growing understanding that clean drinking water and proper waste disposal were essential to controlling disease.

The single most important innovation in urban sanitation was the water closet, which presented an efficient way to remove liquid and solid waste by relying on the flow of fast running, high-volume water through properly sized pipes. While rudimentary fixtures had been put into use as early as 1596 (Figure 41.1), the first patent on a water closet was issued in London to Alexander Cumming in 1775, using an iron bowl with a leather valve at its base covering a waste pipe and an overhead reservoir of water that emptied into the top of the bowl. By operating a lever, the user could simultaneously open the valve and start the flow of water, washing waste into the pipe below.

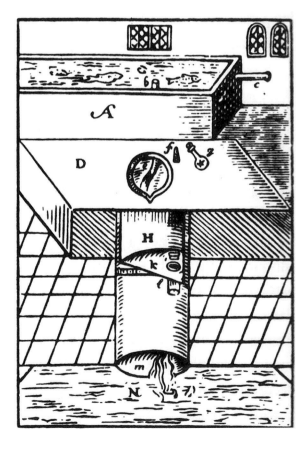

41.1
An early (c 1600) attempt at
sanitary removal of human waste.

Numerous improvements on this basic principle were paralleled by advances in piped supply water, purification using sand beds to filter out algae and organisms and rudimentary sewage disposal and treatment. Pipes which had been made of clay and wood were gradually replaced by cast iron, which offered less porous surfaces and more robust connections.

PRINCIPLES

Today, the provision and disposal of water both rely on the same basic principles as the Roman sewers, albeit with advances in supply, disposal and treatment that add efficiency and safety. All systems rely on tapping water from a natural source, and storing it in a way that adds pressure to the distribution system. Most buildings tap into a public source through a meter, which controls pressure within pipes inside. Supply fixtures rely on this built-up pressure, allowing water out through dedicated fixtures. Once out of the supply system, water is considered waste, and is taken out of the building through sanitary sewage systems, to be either disposed of or treated chemically and biologically.

While these basic principles are fairly simple, major health and safety issues require careful design and installation. Most importantly, fixtures are designed to avoid both cross-contamination of fresh water with waste, and to prevent noxious gases from public sewers backing up into occupied areas. Likewise, plumbing systems must be designed to avoid leaks and backups, and to encourage rapid flow into sewers—waste pipes don't benefit from the pressurization inherent in supply systems and must be designed as gravity systems to induce adequate speed and volume to prevent solids from settling. Finally, the intense forces involved with hydraulic and hydrostatic pressure must be taken into account when designing systems and fixtures.

Supply: potability, treatment, and distribution

Potable water is typically available from a municipal source, although in rural areas it may be necessary to drill a well if a public source is not convenient. Well water must be treated to remove bacteria and mineral deposits and it is vulnerable to plumes of ground-borne pollution. Of particular concern is the presence of calcium carbonate ($CaCO_3$), which causes "hardness." Hard water prevents other substances (soap, detergent and shampoo in particular) from dissolving, making washing difficult. It can also precipitate in boilers and water tanks. Softening by chemical treatment, sometimes done in municipal water facilities, may thus require significant mechanical space in a building fed by well water.

In addition to harmful biological or chemical substances, municipal treatment removes objectionable material that can cause turbidity (very fine powders suspended in water), colors, odors, or bad tastes. From this point forward, it is imperative that all pipes, fixtures, and tanks be sterile, to prevent bacteria breeding in the supply. Backflow and siphonage are two major concerns. Backflow involves contamination of the water supply from a foreign source (a gasoline tank that leeches into a buried pipe, for instance). Back siphonage occurs when a fixture backs up into the supply faucet, contaminating the sterile supply water with potentially foul water from a basin or tub. This can be prevented by a mandated air gap between an overflow drain and a faucet.

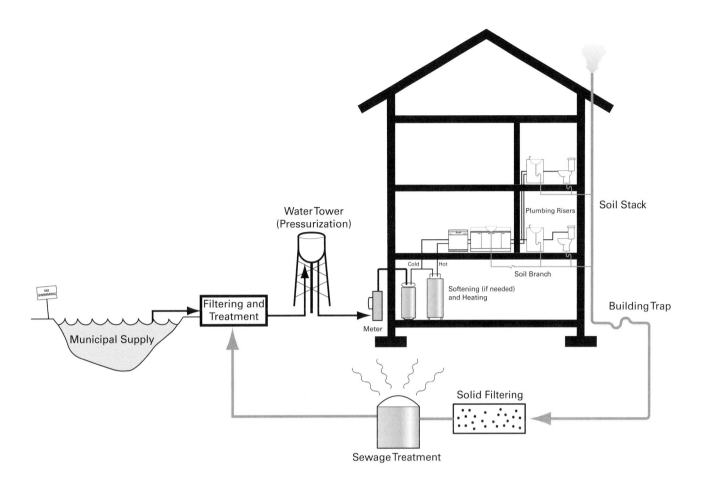

Water Tower
(Pressurization)

Soil Stack

Plumbing Risers

Cold   Hot

Soil Branch

Softening (if needed)
and Heating

Building Trap

Meter

Municipal Supply

Filtering and
Treatment

Solid Filtering

Sewage Treatment

NO
SWIMMING

41.2
Water supply and waste in a typical
small-scale installation.

Municipal water is typically pumped to a tower, whose height pressurizes the supply system. Systems must have enough pressure to overcome friction within pipes and at bends (which can significantly reduce flow) but must not be so highly pressured that caps or fixtures break. (Fire hydrants, for instance, are always put on a separate public line that is at a much higher pressure.)

Residential supply typically enters a building at a single meter, where its flow is recorded (Figure 41.2). Codes mandate a main shutoff valve near the supply's entrance so that the building's entire system can be shut down and purged in an emergency. Larger-scale buildings must typically have two separate systems, one for regular supply and the other for fire suppression, to ensure full sprinkler protection even if the regular supply is shut off. These may use a rooftop tank or pumps to ensure that both systems are pressurized. Supply water will typically be split into two systems, cold water that is supplied at the temperature at which it enters the house, and hot water that is heated. Buildings that use steam heat will have a third system that runs through a boiler. Heaters may be standard storage types, which use a gas or electric heating element to warm water in 30- to 400-liter insulated tanks, or on demand, which use heating elements to heat water as it enters the system. On-demand heaters are generally more efficient, as there is no heat loss during storage, and they are not limited in the quantity of hot water they provide.

PIPES

Depending on a building's age, intended use, and resources, supply pipe may be made of PVC, iron, steel, brass or copper. Pieces of metal pipe can be brazed (lightly welded), ensuring a more permanent connection, but this is much more expensive than plastic (PVC) pipe, which can be assembled using contact cement. Iron and steel pipe will corrode over time, particularly if the supply water is slightly acidic.

All pipe is manufactured in straight runs, with connecting elements and bends accomplished by pre-manufactured components. Flow through, into and out of piped systems is controlled by valves, also known as faucets or cocks. Long runs of pipe, particularly those carrying heated or chilled water, must have expansion joints at about every 15m (50'), while systems that experience rapid changes in water flow or direction will typically be supplied with air chambers that cushion water flow and prevent water "hammer."

Once inside a building, it is often necessary to maintain temperature within a pipe. Hot water pipes that travel a great distance are usually wrapped in fiberglass insulation, and any pipe in an exterior wall or chase must be insulated to prevent freezing. Water expands when frozen, which can burst pipes. Occasionally electric heating of pipes will ensure constant flow, but more typically pipe runs will be located well inside a building floor plate. All municipal pipes will be put below the frost line, meaning that supply water will rarely be much warmer or colder than 10C (55F) throughout the year.

FIXTURES

Plumbing codes require minimum numbers of fixtures, particularly water closets, urinals sinks, and drinking fountains (Table 41.1). In the past ten years, codes have been altered to include additional fixtures for women's bathrooms, recognizing the lopsided advantage of urinals in bathroom efficiency. For most occupancies, the requirement will work out to 1 toilet for every 20–30 male occupants, and 1 toilet for every 15–25 female occupants. This varies, however, with intensity of use. Assembly buildings have far more onerous fixture requirements per population, due to their heavily punctuated use at intermissions, end of performances, etc. Most codes require that any establishment that sells food must have restrooms for customer use.

Water closets are more complex, as they require significant pressure to remove solid waste (Figure 41.3). Generally, they come in two types—tanks, which rely on a reservoir to supply pressured water to the bowl, and valves, which rely on the pressure of the building's plumbing system (Figure 41.4). In both cases, the bowl's contents are flushed out by simultaneously supplying fresh water to the bowl and supercharging the waste line with high-pressure water, creating a siphon that literally pulls the contents of the bowl into the drain pipe. The siphon can be created either by siphon supercharging the drain with the pressured supply, or by vortex action, in which supply water is directed into the bowl to induce rotation as the bowl drains, creating a low-pressure jet in the middle of the waste stream. Tank fixtures include both a floating shutoff valve that stops incoming water when the tank reaches a certain level, and a

Table 41.1 Typical assumptions for fixtures in common building occupancies.

Water Closets			Urinals		Sinks	
Occupancy	Provide	Then	Provide	Then	Provide	Then
Assembly-male	3 for first 400 patrons	1 for every 500 patrons	3 for first 400 patrons	1 for every 300 patrons	3 for first 750 patrons	1 for each 500 patrons
Assembly-female	8 for first 400 patrons	2 for every 300 patrons				
Dwelling units	1–2 per dwelling				1 per W.C.	
Factories	3 for first 50 persons	1 for every 30 persons			1 for every 12 persons	
Institutional—male	1 for every 25 persons		1 for every 50 persons		1 for every 40 persons	
Institutional—female	1 for every 20 persons				1 for every 40 persons	
Office buildings	3 for first 55 employees	1 for every 40 employees	1 for every 50 males		1 for every 40 employees	
Restaurants	3 for first 300 patrons	1 for every 200 patrons	1 for every 150 males		3 for first 400 patrons	1 for every 400 patrons
Schools—nursery	2 for first 50 students	1 for every 50 students			2 for first 50 students	1 for every 50 students
Schools—male	1 for every 30 students		1 for every 75 students		1 for every 35 students	
Schools—female	1 for every 25 students				1 for every 35 students	
Secondary and university—male	1 for every 40 students		1 for every 35 students		1 for every 40 students	
Secondary and university—female	1 for every 30 students				1 for every 40 students	

flapper valve that uses the pressure of the tank water to seal the drain to the bowl.

Plumbing engineers are responsible for other piped services such as natural gas, laboratory gases, compressed air, and vacuum and sprinkler systems.

WASTE

Waste lines are more complicated than supply lines because they rely on gravity alone, not pressure, to work. There are additional considerations in their layout, as a leak in a waste line is a significant biological hazard. In designing for waste, it is advisable to keep the pipe system simple, with few bends or shifts, as clogs in a gravity system can lead to enormous head pressures and explosive failure.

Waste water systems have two features that prevent noxious sewer gases from entering a building. Drains are required to have traps, 50mm to 100mm (2″ to 4″) U-shaped bends that hold enough water to form an airtight seal. For this to contain gases, air pressure on both sides of the seal must be roughly equal, and therefore waste pipes must have vents to the outside that will

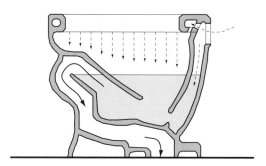

Washdown bowl relies on displacement to remove solids from bowl. Inexpensive but easily clogged.

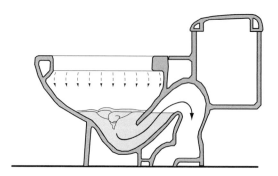

Siphon vortex uses shaped bowl to achieve low-pressure whirlpool to evacuate bowl. Moderate price, reasonably free from clogging.

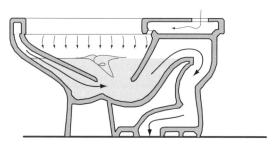

Siphon Jet uses directed flow of water to create siphonic action Expensive but less prone to clogs.

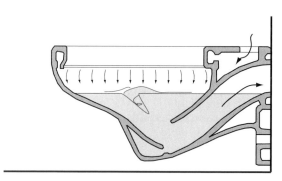

Blowout Flush uses pressure of building pipes to evacuate bowl. A flush valve is required meaning added expense, but spatially more efficient due to lack of tank.

prevent pressure from building up behind traps (Figure 41.5). In small buildings this can be accomplished simply by extending the main vertical drain (the *soil stack*) through the roof (the *stack vent*); however, larger buildings with multiple fixture washrooms are usually required to provide a separate pipe, called a *vent stack* that runs parallel to the soil stack. The two pipes can usually connect to one another above the highest fixture on a floor and below the lowest (Figure 41.6).

Horizontal runs of drain pipes must be placed at a slope that is neither so shallow that water won't run, nor so deep that the water filters away from

41.3
Types of toilet fixtures.

41.4
Tank and valve locations on typical toilet fixtures.

Floor-Mounted
Integral Tank

Least Expensive
Easy installation
Compact Section
No Support Needed in Wall

Floor-Mounted
Separate Tank

Less Expensive
Large Capacity
Easy Maintenance
Bulky Configuration
No Support Needed in Wall

Floor-Mounted
Flush Valve

Excellent Performance
More Expensive
Compact
Visible Flush Valve Hardware
No Support Needed in Wall

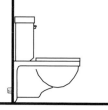

Wall-Mounted
Integral Tank

Less Expensive
Bulky
Support Needed in Wall
Easy to Clean Floor

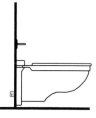

Wall-Mounted
Flush Valve

Most Expensive
Compact
Support Needed in Wall
Easy to Clean Floor
Concealed Hardware

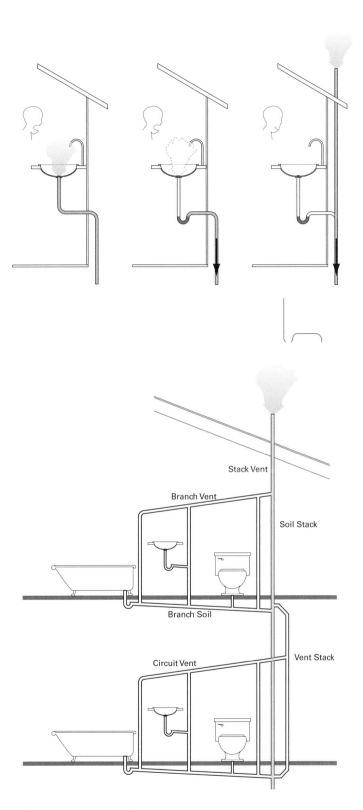

41.5
Fixture traps and vent pipes are important protections against the intrusion of sewer gases into occupied areas.

41.6
Multistory arrangement of vents and stacks.

Stack Vent

Branch Vent

Soil Stack

Branch Soil

Circuit Vent

Vent Stack

slower-moving particulates. Most codes require horizontal runs of between 1 and 4 percent. Cleanouts are required near any elbow and at each stack's connection to the main sewer. These allow a plumber to easily run a metal snake into drain pipes to remove blockages.

A main building sewer will collect all vertical stacks, and will flow at a 1 to 2 percent slope from the building to a public sewer. Again, straight runs are preferable, and codes require manholes or cleanouts at any bends in the pipe. A *building trap* is required immediately prior to the sewer's leaving the footprint of the building. Codes may also require a grease trap between the final stack and the main sewer, to intercept cooking grease and similar substances. Sewer pipes are usually cast iron, concrete, or tile, and they must generally be impervious to roots. Buildings in rural areas will often need to treat wastewater on-site using either a septic tank that allows solids to settle out of the effluent, which then leeches out into a tile field or sand filter. Bacteria in the tank itself gradually digest the remaining solid matter, which must eventually be removed manually.

A system for rainwater drainage (*storm sewer*) is required to be separate from the system described above (*sanitary sewer*). This is discussed in Chapter 33 under Site design and construction.

FIXTURE DESIGN AND LAYOUT

While architects rarely design or lay out plumbing themselves, the results are second only to structural design in their direct impact on the spaces of a building. Bathrooms are one of the few places where people will be guaranteed to physically interact with our designs, and therefore knowing a few parameters going in is likely to reinforce the resulting quality of a design—for better or worse.

From a space planning point of view, it is important to remember that plumbing is typically buried in walls, and these walls (plumbing or chase walls) must be designed to accommodate some rather large pipe (Figure 41.7). It is common to assume a 200mm (8") clear space in all plumbing walls for medium- to large-scale buildings, and to lay out toilet rooms so that this larger wall can serve more than one space. The cost of piping also suggests that toilet rooms, showers, kitchens, etc., should be clustered together, eliminating long supply runs, and long waste runs (Figure 41.8). Supply and waste pipes

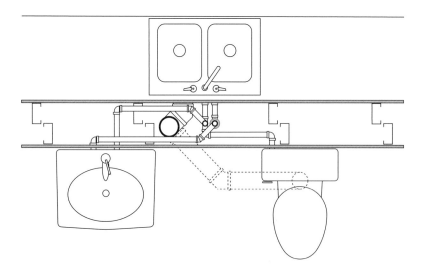

41.7
Typical plumbing chase, showing need for coordination and space for both pipes and access.

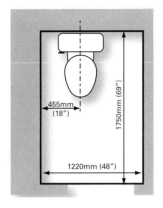

Accesible Toilet Stall—Minimum

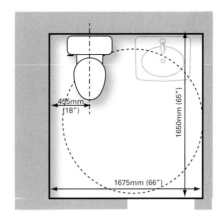

AccesibleToilet Stall—Preferred

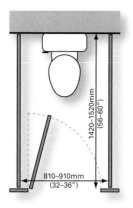

Non-accesibleToilet Stall

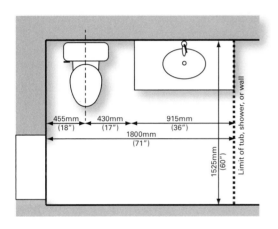

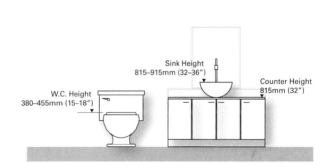

are run through ceilings only as a last resort, as they can be noisy and potentially leaky.

Aesthetics will often determine the selection of fixtures, however keep in mind that the ADA requires significant alterations to standard mounting heights and accessible areas (Table 41.2).

41.8
Standard arrangements of toilets and lavatories to ensure access.

Table 41.2 Recommended mounting heights and distances for typical plumbing fixings.

Fixture type	Mounting height mm (″)	Nearest distance to wall mm (″)
Toilet	450 (18)	450 (18) from centerline (for grab bars this is both max and min)
Urinals	430 (17) with elongated rim	450 (18) from centerline
Lavatory	810mm (32) (optimum) 860 (34) max 735 (29) for ADA-compliant fixture	450 (18) 430 (17) minimum—hot pipes must be insulated below fixture
Drinking fountain	900 (36) max to spout	760 × 1220 (30 × 48) clear approach
Shower	1010 (40) max for controls, no more than 505 (20) reach from bench	900 (36) minimum square floor plan

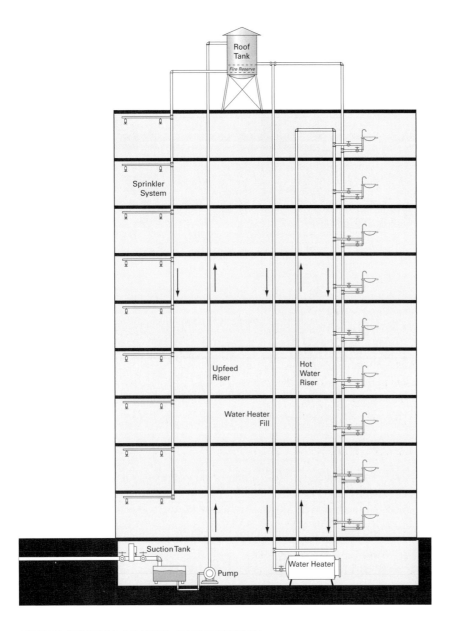

FREQUENTLY ASKED QUESTIONS

Do rest rooms need to stack in a multistory building?
Not necessarily, but there are maintenance and economic reasons why we stack rest rooms above one another whenever possible. First, plumbing is expensive in labor and materials costs. Adding enough pipes to take water and waste service to remote parts of a building will be costly. A more serious reason, however, has to do with head pressure in waste stacks. Shifting waste stacks requires a horizontal run of pipe, which must be sloped between 1:50 and 1:100. In long runs this will eat up ceiling space quickly. But consider what can happen if something gets stuck in the elbow between vertical and horizontal pipes. If the stack is tall enough, water and waste may back up. The head pressure that results may be enough to burst the pipe at the vulnerable elbow. Anything immediately below the break will be deluged with the contents of the

waste stack—not a pleasant thing for owner or architect. As a result, where possible we stack rest rooms and other plumbing fixtures, or at the very least make sure that waste stacks transition over unoccupied—and easily cleanable—spaces.

What's a waterless urinal?
Waterless urinals use an oil trap and rely on the relatively light weight of human waste to migrate through the trap and into the waste stack. They require occasional maintenance to ensure that the trap has a usable oil level, but they save very large amounts of water.

GLOSSARY

Backflow: Contamination of water supply from a foreign source.

Building trap: A U-shaped bend immediately downstream from a waste pipe's exit point from a building system. First line of defense against sewer gases migrating into occupied spaces.

Fixture: Any fixed equipment that offers users an interface with fresh water or a sewer. Includes *water closets*, *lavatories*, *urinals*, *mop sinks*, *showers and bathtubs*, and others such as *lab faucets*. Numbers of each type in public and commercial facilities are mandated by code.

Flush valve: Type of water closet that uses house supply pressure to evacuate its bowl. Mostly commercial and institutional uses.

Hard water: Water with high levels of calcium carbonate or similar minerals that prevent dissolution of soaps, etc.

Lavatory: In the Americas, a hand-washing sink. Elsewhere, a room containing washing facilities and, usually, a toilet.

Sanitary sewer: The opposite of what it says. Waste pipes that carry solid and liquid waste to municipal treatment facilities or on-site remediation (leach fields, septic tanks, etc.).

Siphonage: Contamination of a water supply through a faucet or fixture submerged in foul water. Broadly speaking, the tendency of water to "pull" itself uphill for short distances if its net effect is downhill.

Soil stack: The main vertical drain in a multistory building.

Stack vent: Extension of the *soil stack* through the roof, allowing pressure equalization in the stack and thus preventing water in *traps* from being siphoned out. Not to be confused with a *vent stack*, although this is a notorious exam question.

Storm sewer: A drainage system for rain water. Must typically be separated entirely from *sanitary sewer*.

Tank fixture: Type of water closet that relies on a reservoir of water to evacuate its bowl. Mostly residential uses due to low pressure.

Trap: A U-shaped bend immediately downstream from a fixture in the waste pipe. Water is left in this pipe after use, which prevents sewer gas from escaping through fixture.

Urinal: Plumbing fixture that allows sanitary evacuation of liquid human waste. While experiments in the 1970s proposed these for women, human anatomy makes these, for better or worse, male-only fixtures in most situations.

Vent stack: A separate, parallel pipe to the *soil stack* in large installations that provides pressure equalization to fixtures throughout a system, preventing traps from being siphoned out. Connected to the soil stack above the highest fixture on a floor.

Water closet: Internationally accepted term for toilet. Any device that allows sanitary evacuation of solid human waste.

FURTHER READING

Stein, B., Reynolds, J. S., Grondzik, W. T., and Kwok, A. G. (2005). *Mechanical and Electrical Equipment for Buildings*. New York: Wiley.

42

ENVIRONMENTAL CONTROL: ACOUSTICS

Sound	Physics
	Decibels
	Frequency
	Loudness
	"Airborne" v. "structure-borne" sound
	Reflectance
	Reverberation
Transmission/assembly	Tuning space
	Sight lines
	Paths of travel
	Echo—flutter
	Absorption
	Isolation
	Focus
	Diffusion
	Shadow
	Mass
	Insulation
	Stagger

INTRODUCTION

Sound affects the quality of all spaces we inhabit. Many sounds are desirable, such as listening to music or having a conversation—however once that becomes someone else's music or conversation it can move from being just sound to being noise. Proper acoustical design can contribute greatly to the architectural experience of a project, but bad decisions can easily damage the good qualities of a space. The experience of going to a restaurant and enjoying both the food and ambiance can be ruined by excessive noise and echoes from poor acoustical considerations. This is a problem that should be avoidable by any skilled designer. The quality of the sound is also important to the experience of place—a medieval church benefits from long echoes when an organ fugue is being played, but is a terrible place to hold multiple conversations. Architects control the quality of sound by the decisions we make during the design process, yet are often unaware of what the result will be. Understanding the way sound travels and can be controlled gives the designer not only the ability to avoid mistakes, but also another tool to use in improving the quality of our projects.

SOUND

Sound travels in waves from a vibrating source through an elastic medium. Air is the most common medium for transfer, commonly known as "air-borne sound", but any material that can vibrate will transmit sound. Therefore virtually any part of a building can transmit audible sound if it is set in motion within the frequency of human hearing. This type of sound transfer is known as "structure–borne sound". Both need to be considered in every project (Figure 42.1).

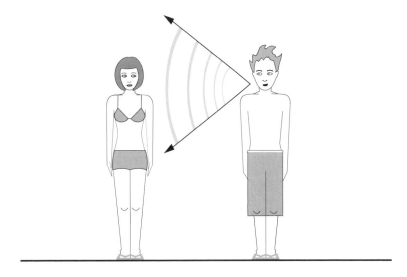

AIRBORNE SOUND

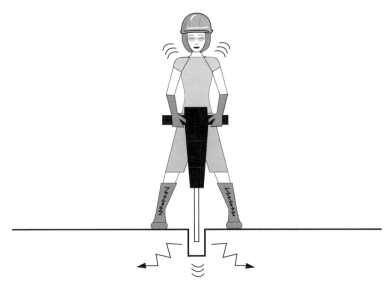

STRUCTURE-BORNE SOUND

42.1
Types of sound.

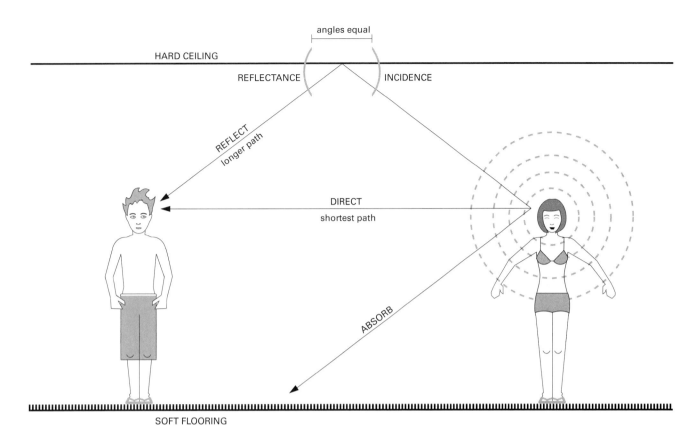

42.2
Basic sound path diagram.

Sound emanates equally outward from its source until reflected or absorbed by a surface material. We hear sounds directly from the source first, then reflections of the sound bouncing off surfaces (Figure 42.2). Sound that travels further requires a longer time to arrive, and the gap between the first and subsequent sounds is what determines how "live" or "dead" a space is. Live spaces have longer reverberations (echoing sounds) and dead spaces absorb most reflections (crisp sounding)—each is appropriate for different activities.

Decibel (dB) is a measurement of sound intensity from the lower limit of perception (0) to above the threshold of pain (140). It is based on a logarithmic sequence with differences in perception based on a subjective scale. The decibel levels of two noise sources happening at one time cannot be added directly, but there is a scale used to indicate the result of adding two sounds together. If the difference between two sound levels is between 0–1 decibels you add 3 to the higher decibel level. If the difference is between 2–3 decibels you add 2 decibels to the higher level; if it's between 4–9 decibels you add 1 decibel to the higher level. Anything above 10 decibels difference adds nothing to the higher level. So 50dB + 30dB = 50dB of perceived sound, and 50dB + 50dB = 53dB of perceived sound (Table 42.1).

The *frequency* of human hearing is measured on a hertz scale measuring pitch between about 16Hz and 16,000Hz (Figure 42.3). We hear and understand speech most clearly in the middle of that range, while sounds at the upper and lower ranges of the scale are less clear and eventually pass into inaudible. Human speech is a narrower band than what we hear but covers a broad range of the audible frequency range.

Table 42.1 Perception of changes in decibel level.

Decibel amount (dB)	Average perception of difference
3	Hard to notice difference
5	Clearly noticeable difference
10	2 times as loud
15	3 times as loud
20	4 times as loud

Note: For example 50dB to 53dB results in no noticeable difference.
50dB to 60dB results in a sound perceived as twice as loud.
50dB to 70dB results in a sound perceived as four times as loud.

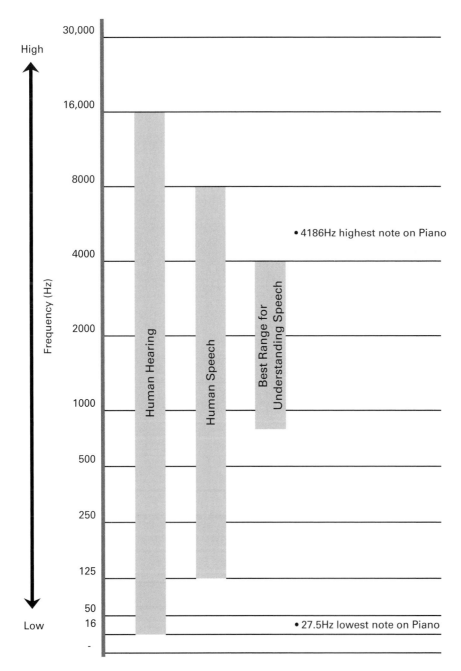

42.3
Sound frequency of human hearing and speech.

Table 42.2 Decibel levels and perception.

	Decibel level (dB)	Typical source	Perception
	140	Shotgun blast	Very painful
	130	Jet engine at 30m (100ft)	Threshold of pain
	120	Thunder	Sound can be felt
Hearing Damage	110	Jackhammer	
	100	Rock concert	Very loud
	90	Circular saw	
Hearing Risk	80	Shouting match	
	70	Vacuum cleaner	Loud
	60	Typical open office	Normal
	50	Face to face conversation	Quiet
	40	Quiet office	
	30	Library	Very quiet
	20	Whisper	
	10	Butterfly	Barely perceptible
	0		Not audible

Loudness is a relative scale of the perceived volume of sound. Sounds at the same decibel level but different frequencies do not always sound equally loud. We tend to perceive sounds at the middle range of frequencies as louder, while sounds of the same decibel level at the upper and lower ends of the frequency scale are perceived as much quieter. So hitting a key in the middle of a piano will sound louder than a key hit at the upper or lower end with the same force (Table 42.2).

Reverberation comes from multiple reflections of a sound—creating a lasting perceptible effect. This can be desirable at times, but tends to cause a lack of clarity in understanding speech. Broadcast studios tend to want no reverberation at all, as this makes speech much more crisp and articulate. Orchestral halls and churches benefit from the longest reverberations where music articulation desires a blending of sounds. Typically, spaces with some speech needs fall into the lower end of the reverberation times (Figure 42.4).

TRANSMISSION/ASSEMBLY

We acoustically design space to improve the sound we want and limit the sound we don't. Improving the sound we want comes from understanding what needs to be reflected, what needs to be absorbed and what needs to be blocked—and how much of each. This is tuning the space and can be thought of in terms of designing a musical instrument. It should be noted that different instruments are better for differing purposes and that is true of building acoustics as well—a space designed for an orchestra will be somewhat "live" or have longer reverberations, and not be well suited for recording speech, where you desire crisp annunciation without reverberation. It is possible to convert

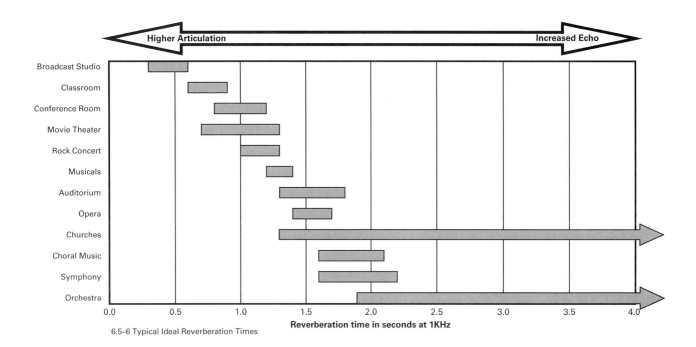

6.5–6 Typical Ideal Reverberation Times

spaces by modifying the reflective/absorptive surfaces, but this requires significant effort if the space is large. It is also important to consider dynamic systems as well as static ones—meaning people wear absorptive clothes that change the reflectance of interior surfaces. A full concert hall sounds different to an empty one, and a full one in the summer has a different sound to the same hall in the winter, due to the thickness and porosity of the inhabitants' clothing.

Limiting sound between spaces, or acoustic separation, is also a primary concern of building design and can be most easily accomplished during schematics rather than later. Simply considering the relationship between noisy spaces and the best ways to limit undesired sound transmission based on adjacency is better than trying to insulate a bad layout. This is very important in mixed-use spaces where you may have a concert practice room next to a classroom or office, but even the location of the mechanical room can have a major impact on sound transmission. For example, if you were laying out two music practice spaces with a bathroom and storage area, the preferred arrangement would put the bath and storage between the practice rooms. This allows the layout to limit sound transmission rather than having to heavily insulate walls between two directly adjacent practice rooms.

Material use for acoustical control falls into two types: lightweight sound absorbing materials for echo and reverberation control, and heavy impermeable materials for sound transmission control. Each serves a different purpose and both may be required to achieve the desired results. Lightweight materials generally trap air in an acoustical blanket, which captures sound waves within the open cells and prevents it from reflecting back into the space. Heavy materials deaden sound waves and limit transmission through and into an adjacent space.

The most direct path of sound travel is directly from the source to the listener and is related to the sightline of a viewer. Auditorium design is the easiest way

42.4
Typical ideal reverberation times.

POORLY CONSIDERED AUDITORIUM DESIGN

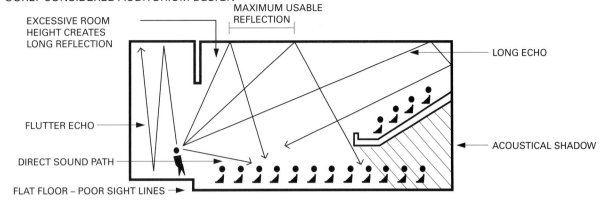

WELL CONSIDERED AUDITORIUM DESIGN

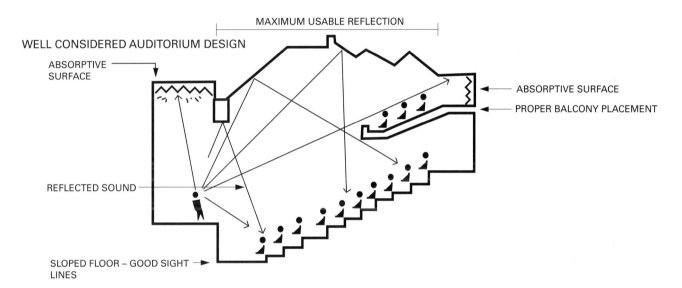

to describe tuning desirable sound transmission, as the principles are easily viewed and relate to every other condition of transmitting sound. In an auditorium people at the front are receiving mostly direct sound; however, in the back reflected sounds become more critical (Figure 42.5). In both cases there is direct sound and reflected sound, and the differential between the two needs to be controlled so the experience from front to back is similar. As sound travels at a constant speed in a space it is possible to calculate the distance from direct sound to reflectance, but there are so many reflections that calculating a single sound ray is not typically adequate to describe reverberance. Reverberation time is usually defined as the time it takes sound to drop 60 decibels below its original source level (described as RT60 in the reverberation formula). The most common way to determine reverberation time is the Sabine Formula. This is based on the volume of space and absorption of the interior surfaces.

42.5
Auditorium shapes.

$$RT60 = 0.049 \, V/A$$
RT60 = reverberation time
V = volume of space (ft3)
A = sabins (total room absorption at a given frequency)

Table 42.3 Common material sound absorption coefficients, for use in calculating the reverberation of a room using the Sabine Formula.

Material	Sound absorption coefficient (a)
Brick	0.03–0.07
Carpet (with backing)	0.08–0.7
Gypsum board	0.3–0.09
Marble/glazed tile	0.01–0.02
Medium velour curtain	0.07–0.6
Concrete (smooth)	0.01–0.02
Wood flooring	0.15–0.07
Window glass	0.35–0.04
Audience/upholstery (s.f.)	0.6–0.85

Note: Full absorption is 1.0 and full reflection is 0.0.

42.6
CY Stephens Auditorium. Iowa State University, Ames, Iowa.

This formula requires that you know and calculate all of the interior materials and areas of each. See Table 42.3 for common material reflectance values. Total room absorption, A, equals the area of each surface times the absorption coefficient. So A = S1a1 + S2a2 + S3a3 {. . .} (all areas added, with S1 being the area of surface 1 and a1 being the absorption value of material 1 and so on).

You can adjust the reflectances of materials in a space, and also the shaped configuration, to modify and improve reverberation times and the usable areas of reflectance (Figure 42.6). Problems such as acoustical shadow occur when balconies are too deep and stop reflectances from the ceiling reaching the seats below.

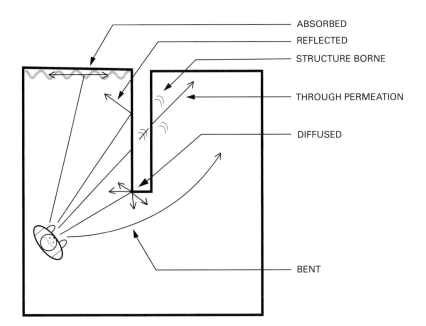

ABSORBED

REFLECTED

STRUCTURE BORNE

THROUGH PERMEATION

DIFFUSED

BENT

42.7
Sound behavior in a space.

Problems with tuning come from issues such as poor reverberation times, along with echo and flutter. Echo occurs in spaces beginning with parallel walls at 18m (60′) apart, where the direct sound and reverberations are heard as separate sounds. Flutter occurs in smaller spaces where sound reverberates back and forth off parallel hard surfaces causing a quick succession of short echoes. The shape of a surface can also cause undesirable focusing or diffusion of a sound.

The other area of concern is isolating sound between spaces, because sound can travel in two ways, through air or structure, and each must be considered in different ways (Figure 42.7). Airborne sound can travel through any opening between spaces, even if it's not a direct path. If an air duct serves two spaces, sound will travel into a vent then reflect off the metal and transmit into the adjacent space—or farther. Any gap is vulnerable and can allow sound to move easily through it. The mass of a material also factors into transmission—the more mass, the better it is able to limit overall transmission. Thin materials can often absorb sound, but can begin to vibrate themselves—turning airborne sound into structure-borne sound. A combination of absorptive materials and mass typically is required to limit transmission. STC, or the Sound Transmission Coefficient, is the measure of sound reduction through a membrane. The higher the coefficient, the better the sound reduction, as the number indicates the decibel level that the assembly will reduce a sound level by. For example, an 80dB source moving through an exterior wall with the STC of 45 will transmit 35dB to the interior (Figure 42.8).

Staggering construction components to prevent sound transmission is critical—this is mostly common sense, but requires some diligence to make the construction documents completely clear. If you don't draw or specify complete separation of components it will probably be constructed incorrectly, and a single breach in the system can transmit a large amount of sound. This includes items such as structural elements, outlets, cabinets and ductwork (Figure 42.9).

White noise or static frequencies refer to masking sounds introduced into a

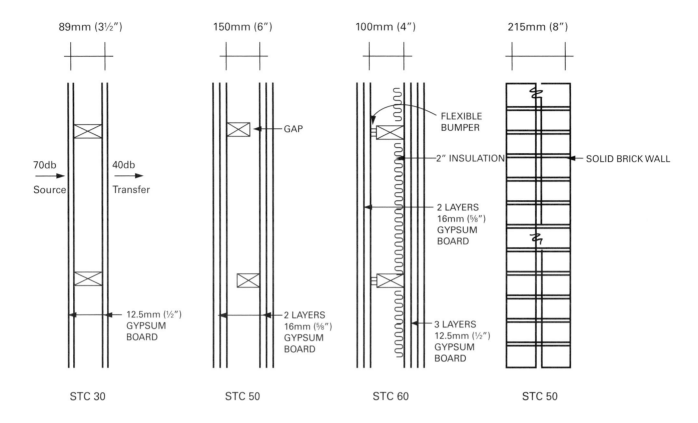

42.8
Typical sound transmission coefficients (STC).

space to limit the perception of background noise. This is achieved by creating a random signal at equal power within a fixed bandwidth and decibel level that interferes with the sounds you are trying to limit—the intention is that your introduced noise is less distracting than the original sound. It works quite effectively in most cases, as your ears tend to filter relatively high levels of sound as long as they are consistent; however, there are also studies that link white noise to cognitive function decreases. An acoustical consultant can assist in determining the best means of accomplishing this, as you need to be precise about the type and level of the white noise.

CONCLUSION

Sound quality is an important part and, as we frequently note, often overlooked part of building design. We've all had bad experiences with poor acoustics, and it is an area under the architect's control—no one else in the process is paying attention to this aspect of design unless a specific acoustical consultant has been hired. Different intended uses of a space can be enhanced or ruined depending on how the acoustics are considered, and while existing spaces can be modified to perform better acoustically it is always more difficult and less effective than planning ahead. Consider the user groups of a project, the shapes and arrangement of rooms, the materials being used on various surfaces, and the potential for structure-borne or outside environmental sounds. Acoustics are a powerful experiential tool that can enrich the quality of every project when properly considered.

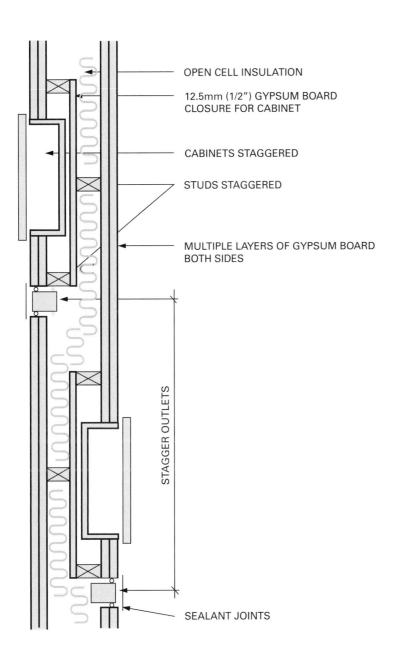

42.9
Proper sound partition
construction.

OPEN CELL INSULATION

12.5mm (1/2") GYPSUM BOARD
CLOSURE FOR CABINET

CABINETS STAGGERED

STUDS STAGGERED

MULTIPLE LAYERS OF GYPSUM BOARD
BOTH SIDES

STAGGER OUTLETS

SEALANT JOINTS

FREQUENTLY ASKED QUESTIONS

What makes some spaces sound lively while others sound dead?
Sound quality in a space is affected primarily by reflected sound waves. Direct sounds reach you regardless of the shape or reflectance of a space, but if there is no reflected sound the space will seem dead. The lively quality of a space is provided by the subsequent or reflected sounds. Very absorptive surfaces that prevent reflected sounds cause dead sounding spaces, which is often desirable where clarity of speech is important. Multiple reflections of sound make a space seem lively; however, this can also make a space seem noisy if there is too much reflected sound from many sources. Large historic churches are often the liveliest of spaces because there are many hard reflected surfaces that are far away from the listener, causing many long delayed reverberations.

GLOSSARY

Air-borne sound: Sound traveling in waves from a vibrating source through the elastic medium of air.

Decibel (dB): A measurement of sound intensity from the lower limit of perception (0) to above the threshold of pain (140).

Echo: Occurs in spaces where the direct sound and reverberations are heard as distinguishable separate sounds.

Flutter: Occurs in small spaces where sound reverberates back and forth off parallel hard surfaces causing a quick succession of short echoes.

Frequency: Human hearing is measured on a hertz scale measuring frequency of pitch between about 16Hz and 16,000Hz.

Loudness: A relative scale of the perceived volume of sound.

Reverberation: Comes from multiple reflections of a sound, creating a lasting perceptible effect.

Sightline: Both the direct view from the sound source to the intended audience, but also the direct path of sound travel. In other words, if you can see the source you can hear it directly, if you cannot see the source you are hearing reflected or indirect sounds only.

STC: Sound Transmission Coefficient is the measure of sound reduction through a membrane. The coefficient indicates the number of dB reduction through a material or assembly; the higher the number, the better the sound reduction.

Structure-borne sound: Sound traveling in waves from a vibrating source through the elastic medium of a building's structure or the ground.

FURTHER READING

Neufert, E. and Neufert, P. (2000). *Architects Data*, 3rd edition. London: Blackwell Science; pp. 117–124.

Ramsey, C. G. and Sleeper, H. R. (2000). *Architectural Graphic Standards*, 10th edition. New York: John Wiley & Sons; pp. 63–72.

Salter, C. M., Associates (1998). *Acoustics: Architecture, Engineering, the Environment*. San Francisco: William Stout; pp. 27–43.

ELECTRICAL AND DATA SERVICES

History	Influence of need for architectural lighting
	Supply and demand pricing
	Development of standardized, municipal utility services
Principles	Current, voltage and resistance (Ohm's Law)
	Municipal supply
	Switches and distribution
Devices and systems	Wiring
	Outlets
	Switches
	Safety

HISTORY

Of all building services, electricity is both the most recent and most hazardous. Prior to the 1880s, the only source of lighting and energy within buildings was fire, whether in the form of a hearth, a gas lamp, or a wood stove. One of the first buildings to be hardwired for electrical service was the Monadnock Block in Chicago in 1891, although municipal services had provided street lighting as early as 1881. While electrical service was often shoddy and nearly always operated by inexperienced (and thus often quite dangerous) companies in the 1890s, by the turn of the century Edison had established a monopoly in most cities, providing reasonably safe, often subsidized, electric current to commercial and residential customers.

Like water, electricity is brought to a building site from a municipal source, although on-site generation does occur, whether through integrated generators or solar panels. Generation is done at a power plant that uses steam from a boiler or head pressure from a dam to turn turbines. These in turn provide motive power to a generator, which generates current by rapidly rotating wire coils through a magnetic field. Even with a century of advancement, electrical generation is at its best only 40 percent efficient. Most of the energy that goes into a power plant, whether nuclear, coal, gas, or oil, ends up being wasted as heat.

Three terms describe the quantity and flow of electricity, and it is useful to think of these in terms of flowing water (Figure 43.1). The *voltage* in a system

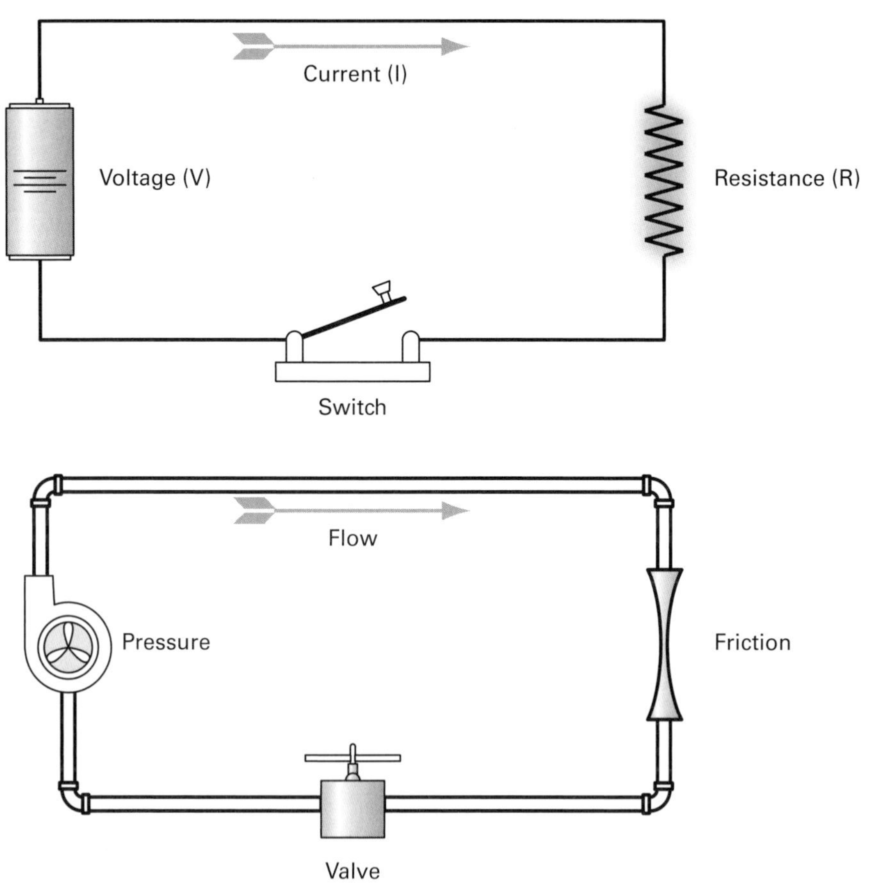

43.1
Electrical systems can be
compared to piped services, with
analogous measures and devices.

(V) is analogous to the pressure in a piped system, the *current* (I) is analogous to flow, and the *resistance* (R) is analogous to friction. For electricity, these are measured in volts, amps, and ohms, respectively, and are related by Ohm's Law, which states that the current flowing in a circuit will be proportional to the voltage (pressure), and inversely proportional to the resistance (friction):

$$I = V/R$$

Electric fixtures are rated by their capacity for voltage—the amount of "push" they can take—but they will also typically be rated for their resistance, that is, the amount of "friction" they offer to current passing through. Wiring is generally rated in terms of current—how much "flow" it can safely take. Appliances and fixtures use a differential in voltage between two sides of an electrical circuit to induce electrical flow, powering motors, illuminating filaments, etc. Current is additive, that is, every voltage drop on a circuit will "pull" more amperage. Thus, the current running through a given circuit will be:

$$I_{total} = (V_1 R_1 + V_2 R_2 + \ldots + V_n R_n)$$

More appliances, fixtures, or other elements that provide resistance and a voltage differential will pull more amperage through the system (Figure 43.2).

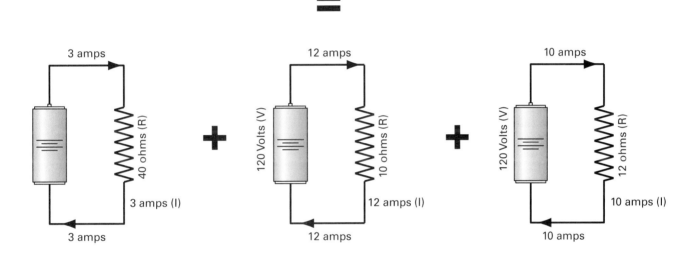

43.2
Basic current theory.

One of our greatest concerns is making sure that we don't add so many of these to a circuit that the amperage "pulled" through wiring is greater than that wiring's safe capacity.

The distribution of electricity relied on the development of alternating current, or AC. While direct current (DC) is relatively simple, its voltage cannot be changed. Alternating current, on the other hand, allows easy "stepping" up and down of voltage, so that a single generating plant can send out very high voltage current to substations, which can then send out moderate voltage to individual customers, where it can then be stepped down to relatively low voltage current for households. This development led to an implosion of electrical prices in the early twentieth century, permitting its wide spread throughout urban areas.

Appliances and systems within a building use the difference in voltage between wires to create a "voltage drop," or a difference in potential energy. Electricity will flow across this voltage drop. Some appliances will use high resistance elements to create heat or light, while others will use the flow of electrons to induce motion in magnetic motors, the opposite of the generation process. Solid state equipment will transform the incoming electricity much further, using micro-currents to manipulate relays, transistors, or microprocessors.

While practices and components have been developed to be generally safe, electricity poses some obvious and preventable hazards. First and foremost is the risk of electrocution, in which the body comes in contact with a voltage drop that can cause paralysis and death. This can occur through direct contact with electric wires, but it can also occur when a building element or appliance is accidentally charged. A more common hazard is fire. Resistance causes heat, and if electricity is pushed or pulled through a wire or appliance at a greater rate than anticipated, heat from resistance can build quickly, igniting nearby material. Likewise, a faulty connection can cause electricity to jump across an unintentional voltage drop, causing sparks that can start fires. Electrical codes are therefore geared toward isolating elements of electrical supply, limiting the flow of current, and guaranteeing standards of connection.

SUPPLY

Municipal power in the United States has been standardized, with three major supply elements to every building—two "hot," and one "neutral." The neutral line is grounded—no electric potential exists between it and the ground. The two hot cables carry alternating current in interlocking phases, so that at any given moment the potential between either one and the ground is 120 volts, but the potential between the two of them is 240 volts. This allows two different voltages within the building. Small appliances, lights, and other light-duty fixtures use 120 volts, while larger appliances such as ovens, water heaters, washers and dryers use 240 volts. Transformers are required to step down the voltage from municipal supply lines, and these may be provided either by the utility or within the building site itself.

The three wires enter a building either underground or through an exterior conduit—a metal pipe that protects the wires and serves as an automatic ground. At their entrance to the building, most codes require both a *meter* and a *shutoff*. The shutoff is located downstream from the meter, so that any faults, or "leakage," of electricity through a bad connection is registered. The meter itself reads the flow of current, recorded as current (sometimes peak) load, and total power delivered. This is measured in kilowatt-hours.

Electric power is metered at the entrance to a building, much like water. Because electricity must be used instantaneously, electric companies charge based not only on the total quantity of electricity provided (measured in kilowatt-hours, or kWh), but also on the *peak demand* of a given customer. Power is easy to supply at low levels, but times of maximum usage, particularly hot days when many customers may be using air conditioning, determine the required capacity of power plants. Therefore, utilities charge a higher rate for peak time usage, reflecting the overhead cost of maintaining a plant sized for this greater demand, along with the basic charge for the number of kilowatt hours. Large customers may therefore benefit from *demand control*, which monitors usage during peak times and adjusts electricity usage accordingly—water heaters, for example, may be set to a lower temperature during the day, and battery chargers may be programmed to operate only at night. At its most sophisticated, demand control may compare fuel costs with utility costs, and shift supply from a municipal source to an on-site generator.

Once inside a building, electricity flows through three elements—*control*, *wiring*, and *fixtures*. Control systems take power from either a utility or on-site source, transform its voltage, and direct it to various runs of cables and circuits.

To avoid transmission loss, electricity arrives at a building at a very high voltage—often 2400 to 13,200 volts. (Recall that Ohm's Law says that the amperage, or flow of current, is directly proportional to its voltage—so this represents a very big "push" through very thick, dedicated high-voltage lines.) Needless to say, this would quickly burn out household fixtures, which are rated for changes in potential of 120 or 240 volts. A *transformer* is therefore needed between the utility supply and the customer, usually one that drops to 240 volts for residential buildings, or 480 volts for larger commercial consumers. Upon entering a building, electricity is sent through a switchboard, which provides dedicated circuits at high and low voltage that can then be distributed appropriately throughout the building. For residential service, there will usually be a panel board composed of circuit breakers and switches that divides loads into 120 and 240 volt circuits. 120 volt power is provided by running a single hot wire and a neutral, while 240 volt power is provided by running two hot wires each charged with 120 volts—one positive, one negative, for a total voltage drop of 240 volts. Commercial service will use a similar technique to provide power up to 480 volts.

Circuit breakers are designed to allow the passage of current up to a given rating, usually 100, 150, 200, 400, and 600 amperes. Current flowing through a wire produces heat, and therefore circuits can overheat and catch fire if the amperage passing through them is too high. Wire is therefore rated according to the maximum amperage it can safely handle, and must be connected to a similarly rated *circuit breaker*. These devices sense when amperage goes above a given load, and mechanically "trip" to break the circuit. Adding too many appliances to a circuit will therefore trip a circuit breaker, shutting down the circuit and preventing a possible fire from overloaded and thus overheated wires (Figure 43.3). This arrangement also prevents a *short circuit*, where two wires with a voltage differential accidentally come in to contact (Figure 43.4). From Ohm's Law, it can be seen that this condition is quite dangerous—with little resistance offered by regular wires, the voltage will induce a very high amperage, quickly leading to overheating and fire. Because this amperage will exceed the rating of a circuit breaker, however, the circuit will be turned off quickly.

These conditions were handled in older houses by fuse boxes, using disposable, screw-in fuses that would fail at given amperages. However the reliance of these devices on untrained owners to replace fuses with the correct rating and type created an inherently dangerous situation. In particular, the common practice of replacing a blown fuse with a copper coin led, predictably, to disastrous consequences. Insurance companies have understandably led the move toward more foolproof circuit breakers to protect residential and smaller commercial and institutional systems or branches. Circuit breakers are contained in *panel boards*, which allow easy access in a central location (Figure 43.5).

Larger-scale installations use dedicated switchgear instead of circuit panel boards, based on similar principles but with much higher amperage to feed larger

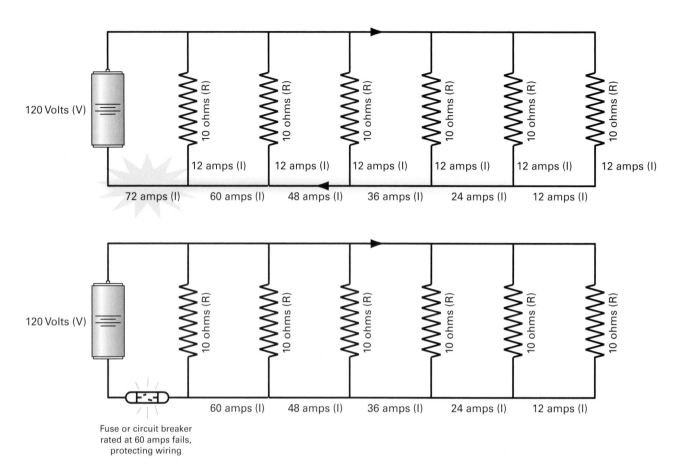

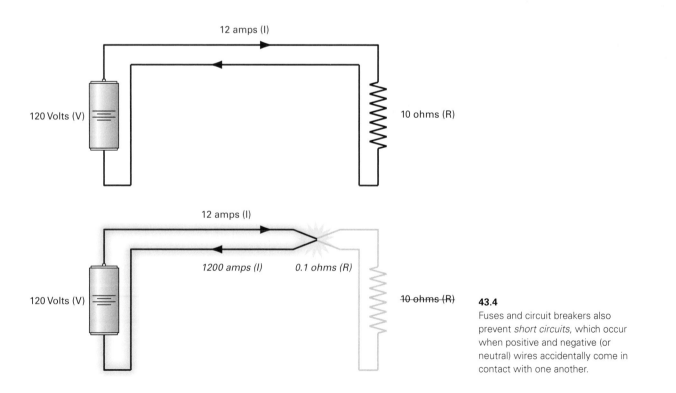

43.3
Overloading a circuit with multiple appliances can draw a dangerous current.

43.4
Fuses and circuit breakers also prevent *short circuits*, which occur when positive and negative (or neutral) wires accidentally come in contact with one another.

43.5
A typical panel board, which serves
as both a distribution panel and
a central point for disconnecting
individual circuits.

cables. These systems lead to smaller, more familiar panel boards in distributed electrical closets throughout a building. Switchgear will include dedicated circuits for high voltage equipment such as elevators. In all cases, electrical codes will require a large clear floor space in front of any panel board or switch to permit an electrician space to work and to ensure that they will not be trapped against a door or wall during accidental contact with a "hot" wire in the panel.

WIRING

Because even the largest typical electric wire in an architectural application is usually around 4″ in diameter, consideration of wiring paths and configuration is often left strictly up to electrical engineers or electricians themselves. Cable is inherently flexible, and it can be snaked in very tight spaces. Therefore, electrical supply tends to be easier to integrate than larger systems such as air handling and plumbing. A basic understanding of wiring principles, however, can often lead to more efficient and cheaper installations. All wiring is rated according to the maximum current it can safely carry, determined by its resulting temperature. High current cable must be thermally insulated to prevent possible ignition of surrounding materials, while low current cable may require little if any thermal protection.

Two factors influence all wiring design—insulation and grounding. "Hot" wires leading to typical interior appliances at 120 volts can kill a person in wet conditions, and therefore all charged cables must have a non-conducting insulating jacket. This may be as simple as a rubber or plastic sleeve for low voltage wire, but may also include glass tubing, fiberglass casings, or dedicated rubber insulators that separate charged cabling from a box-like enclosure. This ensures that any contact with the cable will not allow current to jump across the potential difference between circuit and ground through the person.

Grounding is a bit more complicated, but equally important. Most domestic electrical systems include a dedicated neutral wire for 120V supply, which is connected directly to a lead running into the surrounding earth, guaranteeing that the building will not develop a potential voltage drop with its surroundings. The supply charge, however, will always seek and find the easiest and most direct path to the neutral ground, whether it is the intended wire or not. If, for example, a wire within an appliance comes in contact with an external, conducting surface (a steel dishwasher, for example), that external surface becomes a potential hazard (Figure 43.6). A person touching that surface and another grounded piece of metal—a sink faucet, for instance—will instantly become part of a 120V circuit. Appliances are therefore required to connect potentially conducting surfaces to a dedicated ground wire, and such appliances must have a three-pronged plug. This third prong connects to a second dedicated ground circuit within the building, often tied to a copper water pipe, that will discharge any such unintentional circuit.

Wiring comes in a variety of sizes and configurations. (Note that the distinction between cable and wire is one of size—smaller than 6-gauge is called wire, larger is called cable.) In all cases, the resistance of wire or bus is inversely proportional to its cross sectional area—just as a wide pipe allows more water to flow through, a wide cable allows more amperage. Ratings are given based on the maximum amperage that can safely be carried at a given temperature, a combination of the cable's material, insulation, and location.

Large installations will often use a *busduct* to run from their main switchgear. This consists of flat copper or aluminum bars, stacked atop one another and insulated by rubber or plastic separators. While technically unlimited, ordinary busduct is often rated up to 4000 amperes, and can be configured to allow circuits to directly plug into its metal bars.

Most commercial and industrial installations are required by code to run wiring through rigid, metal *conduit* that provides protection to the flexible conductors inside. Conduit is rated in three categories based on its strength—rigid steel, intermediate metal conduit, and electric metal tubing. While the former

Ungrounded Appliance:

Fault between wiring and metal chassis provides path through user to grounded element. Shock is likely fatal.

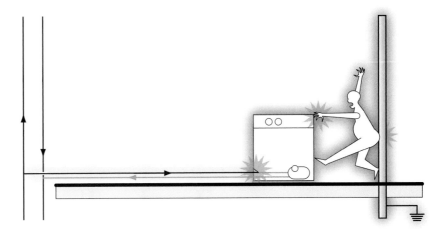

Grounded Appliance:

Fault between wiring and metal chassis is relieved by dedicated, grounded neutral (the third prong). User still receives a shock, but because the grounded neutral provides less resistance, most current will travel this path. Shock will be painful and annoying, but not fatal.

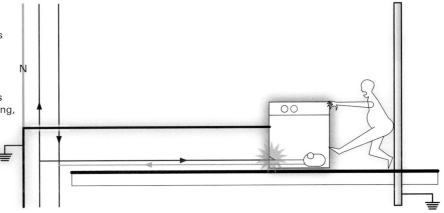

is more robust, the latter lends itself to easier bending. In addition to preventing damage to wiring, conduit provides a naturally fireproof environment, and it can be easily grounded, providing a quick, safe path for current from a damaged wire inside. Because of its smooth interior surface, conduit allows wire to be literally pulled through a building, meaning that cabling can be easily retrofitted. While available in up to 4" diameter, most installations will use 1 to 2" conduit to run from panel boards. Aluminum conduit is lighter, but more subject to corrosion and reaction with concrete.

Cable and wiring may also be run in *raceways*, metal trays that support flexible cables and wires and protect them from snagging. In addition to power, raceways often carry telecommunication and data cabling, though these are required to run in physically separate compartments from power cables, to prevent short circuiting that could energize telecommunications equipment. Raceways may be located within ceiling spaces, within rooms and corridors themselves, or under a floor. This last application is particularly useful for data- and power-intensive programs, such as trading floors, as access to the cabling can be easily accomplished without shutting down large areas to maneuver ladders for access to the ceiling. Raised floor systems have become common in the past 20 years, relying on a grid of floor tiles attached to vertical posts.

Another way to protect wiring and cable is by a dedicated metal sleeve, called *armor*, that is factory wrapped around the conductors. *Armored cable*

43.6
A final, serious danger is the possibility of wiring faults in metal appliances, which can charge its chassis or skin.

provides integral protection to individual wires by wrapping them in spiral metal shields. Both conduit and cable armor provide a convenient grounding strategy, in that they can both be easily attached to a grounded circuit. Being metal, they will carry any load induced by a fault safely to ground. However, both armor and conduit must be carefully cut and fitted to avoid damaging cable within, either from installation or from rubbing.

At its simplest, wiring will consist simply of a metal conductor wrapped by an insulator—typically strands of copper surrounded by rubber or plastic. Older installations may contain raw wiring, insulated by glass "knobs" connected to the building structure. Wiring that is to be pulled through conduit will have nylon sleeve surrounding the rubber insulation, to avoid friction or snagging within the conduit.

OUTLETS AND SWITCHES

Again, like plumbing, electrical services are only as useful as their interface with occupied spaces. Numerous standards exist for the installation of end-use attachments. In general, wire or cable will be attached at the point of use to a *junction box* that is firmly connected to the building structure. This is accomplished by metal arms or bridges that attach to adjacent studs and allow some horizontal adjustment, but boxes are also frequently cast into concrete slabs and fitted into brick walls. Electrical boxes are made of steel or aluminum, and include punched openings on all sides to allow cable entry from a convenient angle. The cable will be attached with some slack to the box, so that it does not get pulled or snagged if the box moves over time. Once inside the box, the cable will unwrap and connect directly to an outlet, a switch, or the wires inside of an electrical device.

Boxes, and thus switches and outlets, come in several standard sizes, referred to by the number of columns of available connections—a *one-gang* outlet contains a vertically arranged pair (or gang) of connections, a *two-gang* outlet contains two pairs, etc. Plugs (or *receptacles*) come in a variety of shapes and configurations, keyed to the power requirements of a given electrical appliance. Large motors, for example, may have plugs that can only be fit into outlets providing adequate voltage with proper phasing.

Two types of electrical receptacle and plug include important safety features for daily use. A *three-pronged* plug is used wherever a significant amount of conducting metal is used in the electrical device itself. As described above, the third prong is a dedicated ground circuit, connected directly to the metal structure or component of an electric device, which ensures that any "stray" current will have an easy connection to ground. While a user may still receive a shock, the majority of the current will flow through the third prong, eliminating any fatal amperage.

Similarly, a *ground-fault indicator, or ground-fault-circuit interrupt* (GFI or GFCI) includes a device that compares current flowing into an outlet versus current returning through an outlet. In the event that there is a significant difference, the device will automatically trip, stopping power flow through the circuit. This is also designed to protect users who contact an electrified device and a ground, in particular where water is present (Figure 43.7). Because water

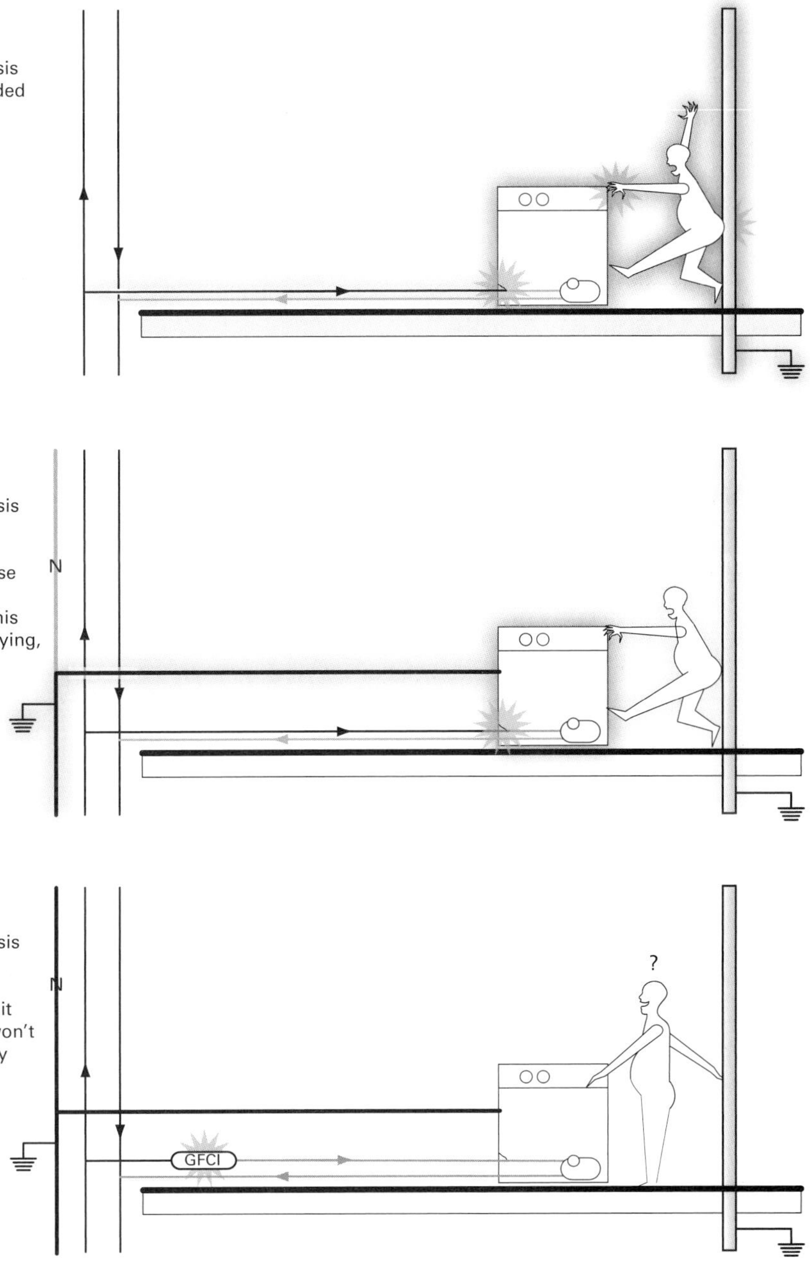

Ungrounded Appliance:

Fault between wiring and metal chassis provides path through user to grounded element. Shock is likely fatal.

Grounded Appliance:

Fault between wiring and metal chassis provides is relieved by dedicated, grounded neutral (the third prong). User still receives a shock, but because the grounded neutral provides less resistance, most current will travel this path. Shock will be painful and annoying, but not fatal.

N

Ground-Fault-Circuit Interrupt:

Fault between wiring and metal chassis is detected by GFCI as current flow between wires doesn't balance. The interrupt trips, breaking the circuit and protecting the user. Appliance won't work, but user will receive only a very brief, non-lethal shock.

N

?

GFCI

43.7
The danger of charged appliances and grounded occupants can also be eliminated with Ground-Fault-Circuit Interrupters.

conducts so well, a 120V shock through a bathtub, for instance, draws enough amperage to be fatal. A user who drops an electrified device in a bathtub will be protected, however, by a GFI, which will recognize the current "dump" outside the circuit and shut off within half a second.

Codes require that a GFI outlet be provided within 450mm (18") of any sink, guaranteeing safe electric power and discouraging users from stretching cords to other outlets without GFCI. Outlets and switches must be placed for convenient usage. A common household danger is the use of multiple extension cords and surge protectors to make up for a lack of easily accessible outlets,

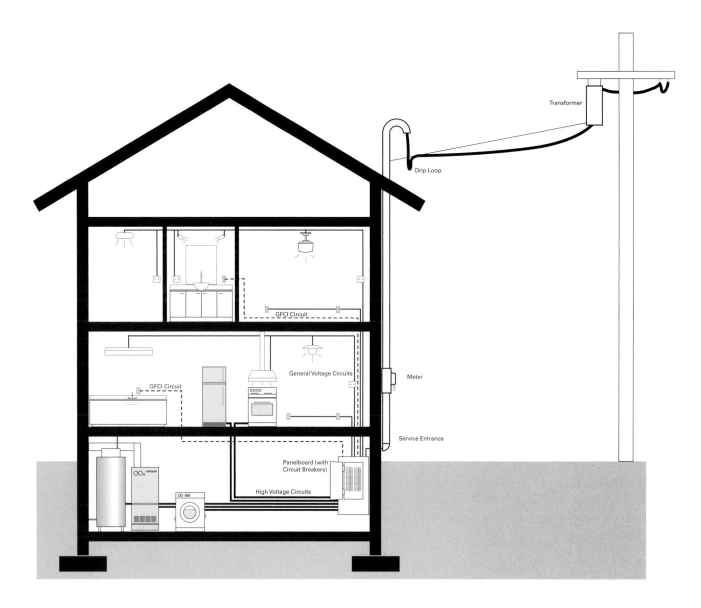

Transformer

Drip Loop

Meter

GFCI Circuit

General Voltage Circuits

GFCI Circuit

Service Entrance

Panelboard (with Circuit Breakers)

High Voltage Circuits

and proper provision in places that are likely to be available (i.e. not blocked by furniture) is by far the easiest way to prevent this. Likewise, switches must be properly located in intuitive places to allow easy use and access. While electricians or electrical engineers will typically lay out circuits and wiring paths, architects should consider locations of all elements for their functional and aesthetic implications (Figure 43.8). An electrical plan, as shown in Figure 43.9, will include general placement within rooms, and will show schematic representations of circuits, including paths from switches to lights and outlets. Both outlets and switches must be accessible to both standing occupants and wheelchair users. Common mounting heights and locations are shown in Figure 43.10.

43.8
Anatomy of a typical electrical installation.

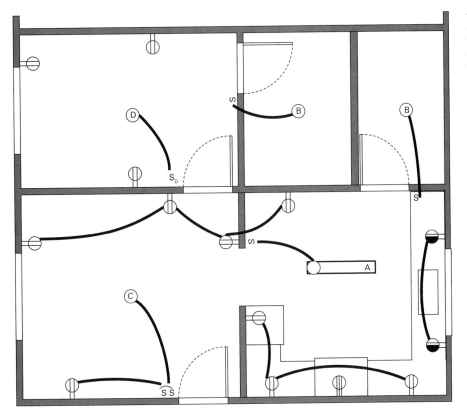

43.9
A typical electrical plan will show the basic locations of fixtures, switches, and outlets in addition to their types and their desired circuitry.

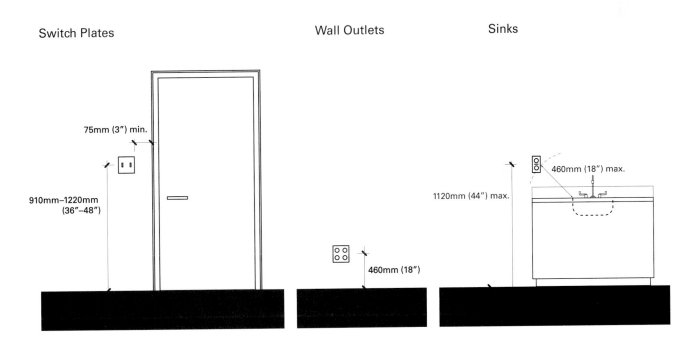

Switch Plates

Wall Outlets

Sinks

75mm (3") min.

910mm–1220mm
(36"–48")

460mm (18")

1120mm (44") max.

460mm (18") max.

43.10
Typical mounting heights and locations for common electrical interfaces.

FREQUENTLY ASKED QUESTIONS

I have a three-pronged plug but can only find a two-pronged outlet. Is it safe to just file off the third prong of the plug?
Not if there's a fault in the appliance you're plugging in. The third prong connects to the ground circuit in the building and will safely discharge any current that accidentally runs through the metal chassis or skin of the appliance or fixture. The third prong is there to ensure that the appliance is *only* plugged in to a grounded outlet.

How safe is old wiring? Does it need to be replaced if the building is being renovated?
Not necessarily. Old wiring may have several problems, which need to be investigated. Most importantly, insulation on cables or wires can deteriorate, particularly older rubber and plastic coatings. If this frays or cracks, the "hot" wire may come in contact with other wires, or with metal elements of the building structure. Likewise, constant tugging due to small building movements can pull wires out of place and lead to exposed ends. Wires themselves, being made of copper (or sometimes aluminum) are not prone to deterioration, but may corrode if exposed to water. Any of these can lead to a dangerous situation.

Given the proliferation of electronic office equipment in the last 15 years, isn't it dangerous to add so many computers, monitors, printers, etc. to electrical systems designed for previous generations?
The multiple surge protectors and extension cords that seem to define the office desktop today certainly don't look safe. But once these loads get back to the building system, they tend not to produce overloads. This is because electronic equipment (other than CRT monitors) tend to use very low voltages. Even a handful of CPUs on a circuit, for example, won't require nearly the voltage drop of an old electric typewriter. While the number of devices has grown, the power they use has dropped significantly.

GLOSSARY

Alternating current: Electrical supply that reverses polarity rapidly. This offers advantages in transmission and safety.

Armored cable: Insulated cable with an additional spiral-metal coating.

Busduct: High capacity power "cabling" consisting of flat, insulated metal plates.

Cable: Drawn metal larger than 6-gauge.

Circuit breaker: A mechanism designed to break a circuit if a certain level of current is exceeded. Circuit breakers are available in a range of current ratings.

Conduit: Metal tube through which insulated cable can be pulled, providing a protected path.

Current: A measure of the flow rate of electricity in a circuit, measured in amperes (or "amps").

Demand control: Building management systems that adjust electrical usage based on peak rate structures.

Direct current: Electrical supply that occurs at a constant positive/negative polarity (compare with alternating current).

Fuse: A small metal filament, usually encased in glass, designed to melt if a precise level of current is run through it. While still available, fuses have largely been replaced in new construction by circuit breakers.

Ground-fault-circuit interrupt: A special outlet that contains a mechanical device capable of recognizing a sudden "dump" of current and quickly breaking the circuit. This prevents a user from being electrocuted by accidentally completing a circuit, and is typically required in wet areas such as kitchens or bathrooms.

Grounding: Wiring designed to discharge any electrical potential from a building, appliance, or fixture into the earth, bypassing any users or objects that would be harmed by such a current.

Insulation: In electrical instances, non-conducting material designed to isolate wire, cable, or busduct from users and potentially conducting building elements.

Junction box: A metal box designed to provide a safe connection between a cable and its outlet. Contains attachments for a face plate, connections to the building substructure (e.g. often wall studs), and openings for cable access.

One- (or two-, three-, or four-) gang: A measure of the number of outlets in a face plate. One-gang contains two vertically stacked outlets; two-gang contains four, etc. These may be power outlets, or data, telecommunication, or indicator components.

Peak demand: Pricing policy often put in place by utilities that charges extra for use during particularly intensive periods.

Raceways: Flat trays in which insulated cable can be laid, providing easy access.

Resistance: A measure of a circuit's "friction" or impedance of current flow. Measured in ohms.

Three-pronged plug: A plug that contains a dedicated ground wire, designed to connect with a building's grounded circuit. This is capable of diverting any stray current in a faulty appliance to the ground, minimizing haza*rds for users.

Transformer: An electrical device that "steps down" supply voltage. Used to draw usable voltages from municipal supplies.

Voltage: A measure of the "pressure" within an electrical circuit, measured in Volts. Also a rating of the safe voltage for an appliance or fixture.

Wire: Drawn metal smaller than 6-gauge.

INDEX

Note: Page numbers followed by 'f' refer to figures and followed by 't' refer to tables.